# AMERICAN NURSING

GARLAND REFERENCE LIBRARY
OF SOCIAL SCIENCE
(Vol. 368)

# AMERICAN NURSING

## A BIOGRAPHICAL DICTIONARY

*Vern L. Bullough*
*Olga Maranjian Church*
*Alice P. Stein*

*GARLAND PUBLISHING, INC.*
*New York & London   1988*

**Library of Congress Cataloging-in-Publication Data**

American nursing.

(Garland reference library of social science ;
vol. 368)
Includes indexes.
1. Nurses—United States—Biography—Dictionaries.
I. Bullough, Vern L.   II. Church, Olga Maranjian.
III. Stein, Alice P.   IV. Series: Garland
reference library of social science ; v. 368.
[DNLM: 1. History of Nursing—United States.
2. Nurses—United States—biography.  WZ 112.5.N8 A512]
RT34.A44  1988     610.73'092'2  [B]     87-29076
ISBN 0-8240-8540-X (alk. paper)

Photo Credits

Nell Viola Beeby, by permission of the assistant librarian, Sophia Palmer Library, *American Journal of Nursing.* Florence Aby Blanchfield, U.S. Army Center of Military History, Washington, D.C.   Florence Dakin, NJSNA Archives.  Annie Damer, from *One Strong Voice: The Story of the American Nursing Association,* by Lyndia Flanagan, ANA, 1976.   Dorothy Deming, © Bachrach.  Sister Elisabeth Fedde, Ottaviano Studio, Brooklyn, N.Y.  Susan G. Francis, from *One Strong Voice: The Story of the American Nursing Association,* by Lyndia Flanagan, ANA, 1976. Martha Minerva Franklin, Connecticut Afro American Historical Society.  Alma E. Gault, ANA Publication G-123 8M 1984, "Nursing Hall of Fame."   Lydia Eloise Hall, Richard Saunders/Scope Associates, New York, N.Y. Esther Voorhees Hasson, from Editorial Comment, *American Journal of Nursing,* 8 (November 1908):  92. Mary Eugenie Hibbard, Archives of St. Catherine's General Hospital, St. Catherine's, Ontario.   Rose Hawthorne Lathrop (Mother Alphonsa), Frontispiece from *Mother Alphonsa: Rose Hawthorne Lathrop,* by James Joseph Walsh, New York: The Macmillan Co., 1930. Clara Louise Maass, Clara Maass Medical Center, Belleville, N.J. Mary Eliza Mahoney, Schomburg Library. Clara Noyes, American Red Cross. Amy Elizabeth Pope, from *Trained Nurse and Hospital Review,* July 1926. Sister Regina Purtell, West Central Province Archives.   Barbara Anna Thompson (Sharpless), University of Minnesota Archives.  Adah Belle Samuels Thoms, Schomburg Library.  Shirley Carew Titus, sketch by Lenny de Carlo.

*Printed on acid-free, 250-year-life paper*

MANUFACTURED IN THE UNITED STATES OF AMERICA

To those nurses
who went before us

# CONTENTS

# CONTRIBUTORS

## ADVISORY EDITORS

Bonnie Bullough
  R.N., Ph.D., F.A.A.N.

Elizabeth Carnegie
  R.N., D.P.A., F.A.A.N.

Signe S. Cooper
  R.N., M.Ed., F.A.A.N.

M. Patricia Donahue
  R.N., Ph.D.

Eleanor K. Herrmann
  R.N., Ed.D.

Rosemary McCarthy
  R.N., D.N.Sc., F.A.A.N.

Linda E. Sabin
  R.N., M.S.N.

Lilli Sentz
  M.L.S.

---

Patricia Baldwin
  R.N., D.N.Sc.

Nettie Birnbach
  R.N., Ed.D.

Lillian Brunner
  R.N., M.S.N., F.A.A.N.

Karen Buhler-Wilkerson
  R.N., Ph.D.

Vern L. Bullough
  R.N., Ph.D.

Brenda H. Canedy
  R.N., Ph.D

Olga Maranjian Church
  R.N., Ph.D., F.A.A.N.

Stephanie Cleveland
  R.N.

A. Lionne Conta
  R.N., M.S.

Signe S. Cooper
  R.N., M.Ed., F.A.A.N.

Eleanor L.M. Crowder
  R.N., Ph.D.

Eileen M. Danis
  R.N.

Althea T. Davis
  **R.N., M.A., Ed.M., Ph.D.**

Audrey Davis
  Ph.D.

Susan B. DelBene
  R.N., Ph.D.

Doris K. DeVincenzo
  R.N., Ph.D.

Geri L. Dickson
  R.N., M.S.N.

Theresa Dombrowski
  M.L.S.

M. Patricia Donahue
  R.N., Ph.D.

Joan L. Downer
  R.N., M.A., M.Ed.

Jerome O. Early
  M.L.S.

Susan Englander
R.N.

Ann Fabiszak
R.N.

Gerhard Falk
Ed.D.

Janet L. Fickeissen
R.N., M.S.N.

Shirley Fondiller
R.N., Ed.D.

Janice Fulton

Laurie K. Glass
R.N., Ph.D.

Enid Goldberg
R.N., Ph.D.

Cindy Gurney
R.N., Major, A.N.C.

Dolores Jean Haritos
R.N., Ed.D.

M. Isabel Harris
R.N., Ph.D.

Valerie Hart-Smith
R.N., M.S., C.S.

Judith C. Hays
R.N., M.S.N.

Phyllis Foster Healy
R.N., M.S.N.

Eleanor K. Herrmann
R.N., Ed.D.

Darlene Clark Hine
Ph.D.

Janet W. James
Ph.D.

Victory Jeffers
R.N., M.S.

Betty T. Johnson
R.N., B.S.N.

Mary Van Hulle Jones
R.N., M.A.

Marilyn Givens King
R.N.

Aurelie J. Knapik
R.N., M.S.N.

Joy T. Lawrence
R.N., Ph.D.

P.J. Ledbetter
R.N., Ed.D

Marilyn Thérèse Lieber
R.N., M.S.N.

Rosemary McCarthy
R.N., D.N.Sc., F.A.A.N.

A. Gretchen McNeeley
R.N., M.S.N.

Marguerite Lucy Manfreda
R.N., M.A.

Kenneth S. Mernitz
Ph.D.

Janet Milauskas
R.N., M.S.N.

Michaelene P. Mirr
R.N., M.S.

James Monahan
R.N.

Nancy L. Noel
R.N., Ed.D.

Thomas Obst
R.N., M.S.

Veronica O'Day
R.N., Ph.D.

Irene Palmer
R.N., Ph.D., F.A.A.N.

Susan Peterson
R.N., M.S.C.

Richard Redman
R.N., Ph.D.

Linda E. Sabin
R.N., M.S.W.

Sarah A. Sandefur
R.N., B.S.N.

Lilli Sentz
M.L.S.

Patricia E. Sloan
R.N., Ed.D., F.A.A.N.

Kathleen Smyth
R.N., Ed.D., F.A.A.N.

Claire M. Stackhouse
R.N., M.S.N.

Alice P. Stein
M.A.

Michael Stein
R.N.

Dorothy S. Tao
M.L.S.

Leslie M. Thom
R.N., Ed.D.

Grace Murabito Thomas
R.N., M.S.

Ruth Anne Vihenen
R.N., Major, A.N.C.

Margaret Wells
M.L.S.

Ruby L. Wilson
R.N., Ed.D., F.A.A.N.

# INTRODUCTION

The lives of women generally have received far less attention than those of men. The standard explanation of this neglect is that men have been the achievers and the doers while women have been the mothers and the housekeepers, and while housewifery is an important job, it does not get one into *Who's Who* or any of the standard biographical dictionaries. The answer, however, is far more complex than this. Women throughout history have done significant things but usually their accomplishments have either not been credited to them or dismissed as "something even a woman could do." Painting and sculpting, for example, in the past have been classed as male arts, while tapestry making, quilting, embroidery, and so forth have been female ones, and male arts receive attention and are collected but female arts, until recently, have been neglected.

There has also been a class difference present in recognition of achievement. Generally women who went into occupations and professions regarded as traditionally male have been recognized and honored if they were successful, but women in the "traditional" women's professions have not, if only because these professions have not been rated as high status by our society, perhaps on the assumption that if they were really worth doing, men would be doing them.

Some of this same sort of status consciousness crept over into the second wave of the feminist movement as it gained strength in the 1960s when the initial demand was for women to enter professions traditionally dominated by men. One wine company, which shall remain nameless, even ran a commercial about a father talking to his daughter and questioning why she should want to be a nurse when she could become a physician. Historians of women and the emerging women's studies groups tended to put down nurses and other traditional women's occupations that had developed in the first wave of the women's movement at the end of the nineteenth century. At that time professions and occupations such as nursing, social work, elementary school teaching, library work, bookkeeping, secretarial work, and retail sales were opened to, and soon dominated by, women, numerically if not politically. Fortunately such attitudes soon disappeared in the feminist movement and scholars in women's studies as well as historians of both sexes are increasingly paying attention to the lives and accomplishments of women in the past. This biographical dictionary of nursing leaders, the first of what I hope is to be a continuing series, is a part of this change.

Of the emerging professions, nursing is unique since it was one in which women were able to dominate not only numerically but also politically. Though men have always been in nursing, and there are two men included in this volume, they usually have played second fiddle to the women. This is different from social work or library work where women were often numerically dominant but the key leadership roles were usually held by men. Elementary school teaching was also dominated numerically by women while secondary education was male dominated, but even in elementary education, the major administrators were usually male. Few of the other women's occupations developed the internal power structure that nursing did in which women dominated and the "old girl" network was strong.

Yet, in spite of this, the accomplishments of many of the nursing leaders have been unknown outside of nursing. One of the surprising observations made while gathering the material for this biographical dictionary is the fact that so few of the subjects appeared in standard biographical indices. Though most of them were written up in the nursing literature, the biographers there were primarily interested in their contributions to nursing, and generally ignored the kind of biographical data so essential to a volume such as this, Thus, for many of them, key data are lacking.

Often missing was the mother's name, and sometimes even the date of birth of our subjects. Some of our biographees, perhaps following a feminine prerogative of earlier generations, had simply refused to list their birthdate on records since they did not feel their age was anyone's business. The more than 50 contributors to this dictionary, however, worked hard to ferret out all the information possible. Many traced down distant relatives to see if per chance they had kept a record of their great-aunt or their grandmother or their second cousin. Undoubtedly some remaining information might turn up about these individuals where data are somewhat incomplete. Most of them would prove an interesting special research project either for a seminar paper or for a doctoral dissertation.

To be included in this dictionary, the biographee had either to be deceased or born before 1890. One nurse, Staupers, who was born in 1890, is still alive as of this writing. Nurses or those who were in other ways identified with nursing and were technically not a "trained nurse," as

were many of those born before 1861, had to have made a significant achievement to nursing in some way or another. The largest number were best known for their contributions to nursing education. The second largest group were known for their writing and publications, although this was not always on nursing subjects, as in the case of Mary Roberts Rinehart. A number concentrated on public health or public health related areas while only a handful were best known for their innovations in other areas of clinical practice. The choice of whom to include or not to include was essentially made by the board of editors, who recognize that not all those who made significant contributions to American nursing and who are deceased are included. Additional figures will be included in a second volume. Space and time limitations worked against further expansion of this volume. Included in this edition are biographies of 175 women and two men for a total of 177.

When the biographies were surveyed for this introduction, it was apparent that the group is heavily weighted toward the East and Midwest, with a surprising number of Canadians, who made their reputation in American nursing. New York was the birthplace for 14 percent of the group and Massachusetts 9.6 percent. More attended Johns Hopkins Hospital School of Nursing than any other for their undergraduate work, and this was followed in order by the Illinois Training School in Chicago, and the New York Hospital School of Nursing. A few members of the group were originally educated in university schools with the largest number, three, from the University of Minnesota. Many, however, went on beyond their hospital training so that a total of 43 percent had college degrees in nursing, and many of them advanced degrees. Twenty-three earned master's degrees and sixteen earned doctorates. Fifteen of the nurses were members of religious orders; several of the secular ones served as missionaries. Only two persons included in this volume died before they were 40, one of them Clara Maass, a nurse heroine, and the second nurse killed while serving as a missionary in a third-world country. At least 126 (71 percent) lived to be 71 or older and at least 12 (6.3 percent) lived beyond the 91st year.

Though nursing in the past was usually a profession that one entered after high school, a significant number of the women in the study entered it somewhat later in life. A total of 33 (18 percent) of the group were elementary or secondary school teachers before turning to nursing. Only 18 percent were under 20 when they began their nursing education and eight percent were over 30. Most of the members of this group never married (57.6 percent), and probably another 29 (16.4 percent) where the records are unclear never married either. Clearly documented is the fact that 46 (26 percent) were married, four (2.3 percent) of them for less than five years, and 42 (23.8 percent) for more than five years.

Only one of those who married had more than four children while 14 had between two and four. At least three of the nurses had adopted children even though they were not married. Most of the women had not only active but in many cases glamorous lives since they did exciting things and met interesting people.

In sum, the biographees included in this collection present a picture of what it was like to be a nurse, the difficulties one encountered, and what it took to achieve eminence in nursing. It is hoped this volume will prove helpful to those who want to find out something about nursing in America, and about significant leaders in the field. We are today what we are because of what they did.

Vern L. Bullough

# THE DICTIONARY

# THE NURSES

## Charlotte Albina Aikens

### 1867–1949

Charlotte Albina Aikens is best remembered as the editor of *The Trained Nurse and Hospital Review* as well as the author of many basic nursing texts in the post-World War I period. Born in 1868 in Mitchell, Ontario, Canada, she graduated from Alma College in St. Thomas, Ontario, where her main interest seemed to be in writing.

It was not until she was 30 years old that Aikens turned to another early interest, nursing. She entered the Stratford Hospital School of Nursing in Stratford, Ontario, in 1897, in order to serve as a nurse in China. To better prepare herself for China, she enrolled in a postgraduate course in ward administration at the New York Polyclinic Hospital. Her plans were interrrupted by the Spanish-American War, in which she served on the American side. At the end of the war, she was appointed director of the Sibley Memorial Hospital, Washington, D.C.

It was at Sibley that Aikens became aware of the growing tensions between hospitals and their nurse-training schools. She felt the two had contradictory missions, with that of the hospital to provide care for the patients and that of the school to educate nurses. The result of this conflict was to shortchange the learning experience for nursing students. Hospitals, Aikens believed, usually tried to place students where cheap labor was needed and usually did not attempt to provide students with a variety of experiences. She calculated that only about 2 percent of the nursing student's education was devoted to learning nursing theory. Convinced that the key to effective nursing education was a standardized curriculum composed of both theory and practice, Aikens took on the task of trying to convince others of this. She wrote frequently on the subject for *The Trained Nurse and Hospital Review* and for the *Hospital Record.* She also became active in the Society of Superintendents of Training Schools (predecessor to the National League for Nursing, where she found widespread support for her ideas).

In 1902 Aikens became associate editor of the *Hospital Record* and shortly after superintendent of the Methodist Hospital in Des Moines, Iowa. She left this position for a similar position at Columbia Hospital in Pittsburgh. In both capacities, she continued to collect data for a report about training-school efficiency, which she gave at the 1908 convention of the American Hospital Association. The report resulted in an offer to join the staff of *The Trained Nurse and Hospital Review*, a position she accepted. In 1911 she retired from hospital administrative duties to become the journal's full-time associate editor in Detroit, Michigan. She also continued to write a variety of textbooks.

Her editorial activities, however, did not reduce Aiken's other nursing activities. In 1912 she served as chairman of the American Hospital Association's Committee on the Grading of Nurses, a study she hoped would bring the thinking of hospital administrators and nursing educators closer together. She also implemented a study of all hospital nursing services in an attempt to determine which nursing skills should be basic in all nurse training-school programs and which nursing activities could be delegated to less trained and educated hospital attendants. The conclusions of this study, reported in 1916, first introduced the idea of different levels of nursing according to types and depth of preparation and started a controversy that continues today.

Aikens was involved in many different projects. She organized the Detroit Nursing Home Association in 1913 and was active in the network agitating for a three-year nurse-training school curriculum, for an eight-hour work day for student nurses, and for a plan to register all nurses who received payment for care of patients. Much of her leadership came from being editor of *The Trained Nurse and Hospital Review*, a position to which she was appointed in 1916.

A strong believer in nurses teaching other nurses, Aikens also believed that nurses rather than physicians should be writing textbooks for nurses. She wrote six books to this end, one of which was translated into 14 languages.

Though she never became a missionary, Aikens retained her religious commitment. In 1920 she was chosen by the Methodist Church Mission Board to survey hospital administration in South America so that the Methodists could establish and maintain more effective medical missions.

This trip marked the end of her nursing activities. In 1922 she resigned her editorship, and at age 55 plunged into motherhood by adopting two older children, one boy and one girl. She spent her spare time writing for various religious publications and in revising her nursing texts. She did, however, serve as vice president of the American Hospital Association and as a member of several boards in which nursing played an indirect role.

During the last years of her life, arthritis and a broken hip restricted Aikens to her home in Detroit, where she maintained contact through letters and telephone. She died October 20, 1949, after having seen many of her ideas about nursing and nursing education come to fruition. She was survived by her daughter, Margaret Dryden, a physician, and her son Wayne Aikens, both in Detroit. She never married.

## PUBLICATIONS BY CHARLOTTE ALBINA AIKENS

### BOOKS

*Hospital Housekeeping.* Detroit: D.T. Sutton, 1906. The third and last edition was published in 1913.

*Hospital Training-School Methods and the Head-Nurse.* Philadelphia: W.B. Saunders, 1907.

*Clinical Studies for Nurses: A Textbook for Second and Third Year Pupil Nurses and a Handbook for All Who are Engaged in Caring for the Sick.* Philadelphia: W.B. Saunders, 1909. This text went through several editions, usually at approximately four year intervals. The seventh and last edition was published in 1933.

*Primary Studies for Nurses: A Textbook for First Year Pupil Nurses.* Philadelphia: W.B. Saunders, 1909. The sixth and final edition was published in 1927.

*Hospital Management: A Handbook for Hospital Trustees, Superintendents, Training School Principals, Physicians, and All Who Are Engaged in Promoting Hospital Work.* Philadelphia: W.B. Saunders, 1911.

*The Home Nurse's Handbook of Practical Nursing.* Philadelphia: W.B. Saunders, 1912. The fifth and last edition of this was published in 1931.

*Lessons from the Life of Florence Nightingale.* New York: Lakeside Publishing, 1915.

*Studies in Ethics for Nurses.* Philadelphia: W.B. Saunders, 1916. The fifth and last edition was published in 1943.

*Training School Methods for Institutional Nurses.* Philadelphia: W.B. Saunders, 1919.

### ARTICLES

See the *Trained Nurse and Hospital Review* for the years she was on the staff or editor.

### BIBLIOGRAPHY

"Charlotte A. Aikens." *American Journal of Nursing* 24 (August 1924): 914.

"Charlotte A. Aikens." *American Journal of Nursing* 49 (November 1949): 318.

"Charlotte A. Aikens." Obituary. *Detroit News,* 22 October 1949.

"Charlotte A. Aikens." *Trained Nurse and Hospital Review* 123 (December 1949): 279.

Kalisch, P.A., and B.J. Kalisch. *The Advance of American Nursing.* Boston: Little, Brown, 1978.

Janice Fulton and Vern L. Bullough

## Louisa May Alcott

### 1832–1888

Already a popular author when she became a Civil War nurse, Louisa May Alcott enhanced her fame substantially with *Hospital Sketches*, a book that dealt with her wartime nursing experiences. The six weeks she spent working in a Union army hospital profoundly affected both her later writing and her health, and *Hospital Sketches* increased public sensitivity to the suffering and sacrifice of the men who fought on both sides of the war.

Alcott was born in Germantown, Pennsylvania, on November 29, 1832, the second daughter of Amos Bronson and Abigail ("Abba") May Alcott. The date was her father's 33rd birthday, and later she was to die at the very hour of his funeral. Without much formal education, Alcott's father rose to become a leading transcendentalist and educator whose philosophy profoundly affected the course of American education. Her mother was of distinguished Boston stock, and Alcott had three sisters: Anna, who was older, and Elizabeth and Abba May, both younger. Although her father operated a number of schools, he tutored Alcott mostly at home. She also received instruction and guidance from his friends, Ralph Waldo Emerson, Henry David Thoreau, and Theodore Parker.

From early childhood, Alcott was encouraged to write by her mother. She first received recognition as a writer with the book *Flower Fables*, written when she was 16 as a tribute to Emerson's daughter and a token of her sentimental worship of Emerson.

Bronson Alcott's constant professional struggle kept his family on the move and usually poor. The only two constants in Alcott's life were her writing and her devotion to her family. She received her first serious experience with nursing when she performed night duty during the terminal illness of her sister, Elizabeth. She taught school, did domestic work, and, while she worked as a professional seamstress, plotted stories. Publication of her stories and poems brought her some income, but at age 26 she was yearning to write a great book.

In the first year of the Civil War, Alcott rolled bandages and feverishly wrote her first novel, *Moods*. However, she was restless and had before her the examples of Florence Nightingale, whose notes on nursing had just been published, and Clara Barton, a Boston native who was at the war front. Alcott volunteered her services as an army nurse, and soon her father was telling his friends that he was sending his "only son" to war.

Alcott was assigned to the Union Hotel Hospital in Georgetown. Though lacking in experience and inhibited in her relations with men, Alcott pitched in with good spirit. She called herself "Nurse Periwinkle" and the hospital "Hurly-burly House." In her writing she compared it unfavorably with other Washington area hospitals, such as the Armory Hospital. She nursed at least one Confederate soldier and noted that she was willing to take care of her enemies, although she could not love them.

The letters Alcott wrote home describing her experiences first appeared in the *Commonwealth* newspaper and then in *Hospital Sketches*. They were read widely because people were anxious to hear from the hospitals, where sons and brothers were nursed back to health.

> . . . as we quitted them, followed by grateful glances that lighted us to bed, where rest, the sweetest, made our pillows soft, while Night and Nature took our places, filling the great house of pain with the healing miracles of Sleep, and his diviner brother, Death. (Alcott, 39)

Soon Alcott had established routines, and she wrote at off moments during her night shift.

My ward was now divided into three rooms, and, under favor of the matron, I had managed to sort out the patients in such a way that I had what I called, "my duty room," my "pleasure room," and my "pathetic room," and worked for each in a different way. One, I visited, armed with a dressing tray, full of rollers, plasters, and pins; another with books, flowers, games, and gossip; a third with teapots, lullabies, consolation and, sometimes, a shroud.

Wherever the sickest or most helpless man chanced to be, there I held my watch. . . .    (Alcott, 41)

Six weeks of strenuous effort took their toll, and Alcott soon was bedded with symptoms of typhoid and pneumonia. She later wrote: "I was never ill before this time and never well afterward." (Cheney, 137) Dorothea Dix, then superintendent of army nurses, took a special interest in her author-nurse and visited her sickroom. Though Alcott was not always in agreement with Dix on many matters, she described her as tender in her care as any mother.

. . . and daily our Florence Nightingale climbed the steep stairs, stealing a moment from her busy life, to watch over the stranger, of whom she was as thoughtfully tender as any mother. Long may she wave! Whatever others may think or say, Nurse Periwinkle is forever grateful; and among her relics of that Washington defeat, none is more valued than the little book which appeared on her pillow, one dreary day, for the D.D. written in it means to her far more than Doctor of Divinity.    (Alcott, 71)

Alcott returned home to recover and pick up the strands of her life. The enlarged *Hospital Sketches and Camp and Fireside Stories* that appeared in 1869 included one of her most memorable short stories, "My Contraband." In it, she describes the compassion of a white nurse for a freedman (contraband) and evokes the spirit of the wartime nurse as she writes: "Feeling more satisfaction, as I assumed my big apron and turned up my cuffs, than if dressing for the President's levee, I fell to work in Hospital No. 10 in Beaufort." (Alcott, 192)

Late in 1865 Alcott was offered a chance to use her nursing experience in a different way and further her education at the same time. She accompanied a wealthy young invalid on a tour of Europe. On her return, she edited a juvenile magazine, and in 1868–69 her best-known novel, *Little Women*, appeared in two installments. With this book, she achieved the financial security she had sought for her family.

The remaining 19 years of Alcott's life were spent in writing, family activities, and bouts of illness. She wrote about 30 more books and hundreds of short stories. When inspired, she wrote 14–16 hours a day until a project was finished and then collapsed with nervous prostration. She went from doctor to doctor seeking relief. Some believed she suffered from shell shock from what she had seen in the Union Hotel Hospital and existed in a state of borderline hysteria thereafter.

Alcott retired in 1886 to the rest home of a doctor friend in the Roxbury section of Boston and spent her last years in depression and failing health. She died March 6, 1888, at the very hour of her father's funeral and was buried at his side in the Sleepy Hollow Cemetery.

Oh, lay her in a little pit,
With a marble stone to cover it;
And carve thereon a gruel spoon,
To show a "nuss" has died too soon.
(Alcott, *Hospital Sketches*, 79)

## PUBLICATIONS OF LOUISA MAY ALCOTT

*Hospital Sketches and Camp and Fireside Stories*. Boston: Roberts Brothers, 1869.

## BIBLIOGRAPHY

"Alcott, Louisa May." In *The Oxford Companion to American Literature*, edited by James D. Hart. New York: Oxford University Press, 1965.

Anthony, K.S. *Louisa May Alcott*. New York: Alfred A. Knopf, 1938.

Cheney, E.D. *Louisa May Alcott, Her Life, Letters, and Journals*. Cambridge: University Press, 1889.

Smith, D.E. "Alcott, Louisa May." In *Notable American Women*, edited by Edward T. James. 4 vols. Cambridge, Mass.: Belknap Press of Harvard University Press, 1971.

Alice P. Stein

## Anna Lowell Alline
### 1864–1934

A pioneer in nursing education, Anna Lowell Alline assumed the responsibility for the Hospital Economics Program at Teachers College, Columbia University, and became the first inspector of training schools in New York State. She helped secure an understanding of training school problems and inspired standardization in methods and practices of nursing education.

Born in 1864 in East Machias, Maine, Alline was educated in Iowa public and normal schools. She taught for six years before entering in 1891 the Homeopathic Hospital Training School for Nurses, Brooklyn, New York, against the wishes of her family.

After her graduation in 1893, Alline served in a number of positions at the training school, including that of assistant to Linda Richards, the superintendent. When she succeeded Richards, she kept in close contact with the Society of Superintendents of Training Schools, now the National League of Nursing, and was treasurer of the organization from 1900 to 1909. Through her efforts, the nursing course at Brooklyn Homeopathic Hospital was lengthened to three years, and an alumnae association was formed.

Alline was one of two pioneer students who enrolled in the beginning course in hospital economics at Teachers College, Columbia University, in 1900. She became so interested in the project that she consented to serve as secretary of the education committee and director of the course for a modest stipend. Associated with the beginnings of what is now the Department of Nursing Education, Columbia University, she did much to ensure the continuity of the department.

After her tenure at Teachers College, she served as the first inspector of nursing schools in New York State from 1906 to 1909. In 1910 she moved to Buffalo and was superintendent of the Buffalo Homeopathic Hospital until 1912. She retired from active work for a period of three years, then returned to the East for Red Cross work during the war.

Alline's last professional position was in Albany, New York, where she was in charge of laboratory work and of the outpatient department at the Albany Homeopathic Hospital from 1918 to 1923. After her marriage in 1923, she moved to Addison Ridge, Maine. She died on December 16, 1934, at her brother's home in Iowa.

### PUBLICATIONS BY ANNA LOWELL ALLINE

"The Supply and Demand of Students in the Nurse Training Schools." *American Journal of Nursing* 7 (1907): 758–64.

"Inspection of Nurse Training Schools. Its Aims and Results." In American Hospital Association. *Transactions of the Tenth Annual Conference.* Detroit: AHA, 1908, pp. 111–19.

"Report of Inspection of Nurse Training Schools, for the Year ending July 31, 1908." *American Journal of Nursing* 9 (1908): 175–79.

"State Supervision of Nursing Schools in New York State." *American Journal of Nursing* 9 (1909): 911–23.

### BIBLIOGRAPHY

Alline, A.L. Papers. Nutting Collection. Teachers College, Columbia University, New York.

"Alline, Anna Lowell." In *Leaders of American Nursing.* New York: National League of Nursing Education, 1923.

"Anna Lowell Alline." Obituary, *American Journal of Nursing* 35 (1935): 191.

Nutting, M.A. *A History of Nursing.* New York: G.P. Putnam's Sons, 1935.

Roberts, M. M. *American Nursing History and Interpretation.* New York: Macmillan, 1954.

Lilli Sentz

## Sister Bernadette Armiger
### 1915–1979

Sister Bernadette Armiger was a leader in nursing, teaching, and counseling. She was the first president of the American Association of Colleges of Nursing, founded in 1968, and led nursing programs at the Catholic University of America (Providence division) and Niagara University, Lewiston, New York. The latter won national acclaim and became a model for several schools built in the late 1960s and early 1970s. In these positions, she campaigned actively for the spread of baccalaureate curricula in nursing. In counseling, she established and directed the Consultation Center for Priests and Religious in Baltimore. In the 21 years between 1955 and 1976, she published 34 articles on clinical instruction, evaluation of students, and legal and ethical issues.

Mary Elsa Armiger was born in Baltimore, Maryland, on April 7, 1915. She was the middle of seven children of Joseph Griffith and Sallie Harcourt Armiger. Using the name Elsa, she was raised in a deeply religious home and had a happy childhood. Her sister Jane commented about her sister's talents in writing short stories for the other children to read.

Sister Armiger attended St. Martin's grade school in Baltimore until the family moved to the newly established parish Our Lady of Lourdes. She then attended Seton High School. Inspired by contacts with the Daughters of Charity of St. Vincent de Paul, she entered that order in September 1933, shortly after her graduation. For this organization, she taught in the primary grades at St. Francis, Staunton, Virginia, and later at Lourdes School, Utica, New York.

After 10 years Sister Armiger's interest shifted to nursing, and in 1944 she graduated from the Catholic University of America with a B.S. degree in nursing. In 1947 she was awarded a master's degree in nursing education with a major in nursing education administration and a minor in guidance. Interested in history, she wrote her thesis on "The History of the Hospital Work of the Daughters of Charity in the United States, 1823–1860."

An interest in guidance and counseling led her to further postgraduate work, this time in psychology, and in 1968 she was awarded a Ph.D. in psychology from St. John's University, Jamaica, New York. Her doctoral research was on the perception and response of clients to two drugs, carisoprodal and meprobamate.

Sister Armiger's earliest assignment was as a clinical instructor of nursing stu-

dents and director of the undergraduate division of the Providence division of the school of nursing at the Catholic University of America. Among her other academic administrative positions were director of nursing, De Paul Hospital, Norfolk, Virginia; coordinator of medical and surgical nursing at the Catherine Laboure School of Nursing, Dorchester, Massachusetts; and assistant professor of nursing at St. Joseph College, Emmitsburg, Maryland.

In Massachusetts she brought about the merger of three diploma programs in nursing: St. John's, Lowell; St. Margaret's, Dorchester; and Old Carney, South Boston. The combined program was named the Catherine Laboure School of Nursing and still exists in Boston today.

During the transition period between 1951 and 1955, Sister Armiger's philosophy of nursing education became incorporated into the curriculum. No longer were students of nursing to give service on the hospital floors nor was supervision by head nurses a part of the program. Faculty from the school were responsible for their clinical assignments. This concept of teaching nursing met with some resistance from head nurses who formerly had been responsible for student learning. However, Sister Armiger gained their cooperation.

In 1968 Sister Armiger became dean and professor of nursing at Niagara University, Lewiston, New York. During her seven-year tenure, she devoted much of her energy to fundraising. Capitation grant monies she secured provided scholarships for needy students.

In 1972 she secured $1.2 million in federal funds and helped design a nursing-school building at Niagara University. This building later was cited for excellence in architecture by the College and University Conference. The advanced technological features of the building included a circular demonstration room, a behavior laboratory with one-way observation windows, and several adaptations of multimedia technology that were pioneering firsts in nursing education.

At Niagara University, Sister Armiger also advocated the development of an inte grated curriculum that would prepare nurse practitioners at the baccalaureate level. In addition, she implemented a full-year course in health-status assessment skills that stressed the promotion of good health.

During this time she also served as a grant reviewer for the Bureau of Health Professions Education and Manpower Training in Washington, D.C. She not only reviewed grants, but also assisted in deciding which existing research needed to be expanded or curtailed.

In 1975 Sister Armiger received the President's Medal from Niagara University and resigned her post there. She returned to the Baltimore diocese after a 13-year absence to undertake the development and administration of the Consultation Center for Priests and Religious in Baltimore. As a certified professional counselor, she had found time in her previous positions for a limited amount of individual and group counseling. As the first director of the Center for Training and Consultation for Clergy and Religious of the Archdiocese of Baltimore, Inc., she was able to devote her full-time energies to this area. She conducted a mail survey of 26 counseling centers, gaining information on their organizational structure, staffing patterns, seminars, lectures, and workshops. Single-handedly, she procured a building and donated furniture, solicited funds from organizations, and elicited professionals to donate their services. She was successful in putting the center on a secure financial basis with psychiatrists, psychologists, and counselors available at the center or in their offices on a sliding-scale fee to accommodate priests and nuns who had limited funds for professional therapy.

Sister Armiger traveled to Puerto Rico as a guest speaker at Cencamex 72, a meeting of Catholic nurses from Central America, the Caribbean, and Mexico. She also traveled to Israel to take a course in health and health delivery systems at the University of Tel Aviv.

In 1969 Sister Armiger founded and became president of the American Association of Collegiate Schools of Nursing, which was composed of deans and direc-

tors of degree programs in nursing. The organization later honored her by establishing the Armiger Award, given to nurses who show outstanding leadership in collegiate nursing-education programs.

Her other positions and awards include membership on the boards of directors of the Counseling Center for Clergy and Religious of the Diocese of Buffalo, New York; the New York State division of the American Cancer Society; the Niagara chapter of the American Red Cross; and the Health Association of Niagara County, Inc. In addition to the American Nurses Association, she was a member of the American Psychological Association, Sigma Theta Tau, Psi Chi, and Delta Epsilon Sigma. She received a certificate of recognition from the U.S. Department of Health, Education and Welfare in 1973 for service on its nursing, research, and education advisory committee.

During the later years of her life, Sister Armiger was diagnosed as having leukemia. It was only in the last six weeks of her life that her illness became apparent to others, since she never complained about the fatigue that the disease was causing her. She died May 21, 1979, at the age of 64 at Roswell Park Memorial Institute in Buffalo. The burial mass was celebrated at the De Paul Provincial House, and burial was in the community's cemetery in Albany, New York. She was survived by three sisters, Jane Armiger, Ann Rector, and Sally Ringold, and one brother William Armiger.

## PUBLICATIONS BY SISTER BERNADETTE ARMIGER

### BOOKS

*Proceedings of the Mental Health Institute on Psychotherapy.* New York: St. John's University Press, 1965.

### ARTICLES ( SELECTED )

"Ethics in Nursing Responsibility." In *Should the Patient Know the Truth?* New York: Springer, 1955.

"Patient-Centered Clinical Instruction in Medical and Surgical Nursing." In *Proceedings of Workshop on the Dynamics of Clinical Instruction.* Washington, D.C.: Catholic University of America Press, 1955.

"Patient-Centered Clinical Instruction." In *Year Book of Modern Nursing 1956*. New York: G.P. Putnam's Sons, 1956.

"Planning and Carrying-Out a Clinical Teaching Program." *Hospital Progress* 38 (June 1957): 78–95.

"Objectives of Nursing Education." *Maryland State Medical Journal* 8 (April 1959): 152–54.

"Action Research Supervisory Development: Personnel Management." *Hospital Progress* 41 (September 1960): 94–98.

"Evaluation of Student Nurses: Concepts and Practices." *Hospital Progress* 43 (January 1962): 70–71, 162–63.

"Evaluation of Student Nurses: Tools and Techniques." *Hospital Progress* 43 (March 1962): 76–79, 134.

"Evaluation of Student Nurses: Appraisal Interview." *Hospital Progress* 43 (April 1962): 96–97, 162–63.

"Society's Need for Nursing: Challenge and Opportunity." *Catholic Nurse* 10 (June 1962): 32–35.

"Two Sister-Nurses Claimed by Cholera." *Nursing Outlook* 12 (September 1964): 54–56.

"Mutual Expectations of Layman and Religious." *Hospital Progress* 47 (April 1966): 75–78.

"Reprise and Dialogue: About Questioning the Right to Die." *Nursing Outlook* 16 (October 1968): 26–28.

"Unemployment—Is There a Nursing Shortage?" *Nursing Outlook* 21 (May 1973): 312–16.

"Scholarship in Nursing." *Nursing Outlook* 22 (March 1974): 160–62.

"Purposes, Roles and Relationships: American Association of Colleges of Nursing and Council of Baccalaureate and Higher Degree Programs." In *Response to Changing Needs*. New York: National League for Nursing, 1974.

"The Educational Crisis in the Preparation of Deans." *Nursing Outlook* (March 1976).

"Information—A Prescription Against Pain." *Nursing Research* 20 (September–October 1976).

## BIBLIOGRAPHY

Abbey, H. "N.U.'s New Nursing Building Is Growing as Landmark." *Courier Express*, 12 March 1972.

Cunane, O. "The Community How I Love It." In *The Lives of Deceased Sisters*, edited by O. Cunane. Albany: New York Daughters of Charity, 1979.

Kujawa, K. "Sister Bernadette Heads Center." *Catholic Review*, 12 March 1976.

Tunison, P. "Meet Nursing Department's Amazing Sister Bernadette." *The Torch* (St. John's University Press), 1 May 1964.

Wallace, W. "Counseling for Religious Set Up in Diocese." *The Sun*, 8 September 1976.

Kathleen Smyth

# Margaret Gene Arnstein

## 1904–1972

Margaret Gene Arnstein had a worldwide influence on public-health nursing, nursing education, and the application of systematic research in nursing and health care. Highlights of a career that spanned nearly a half century include 20 years with the U.S. Public Health Service (USPHS) and academic chairs at Yale University and the universities of Michigan and Minnesota.

Arnstein was born October 27, 1904, one of four children of Leo and Elsie (Nathan) Arnstein, on New York's upper East Side. She had one sister, Elizabeth, and two brothers, William and Robert. The parents were well-to-do, second-generation German-Jewish Americans and were active in public health and welfare concerns.

Arnstein knew with certainty during her high-school years at the Ethical Culture School that she wanted to be a nurse. However, her specific interest in public-health nursing had its genesis in the influence of Lillian Wald, whom she and her siblings visited at the Henry Street Settlement as children. Throughout his adult life, their father, a Yale graduate and prosperous businessman, served on the settlement's board of directors and executive committee.

Some years later, Arnstein recalled that Wald arranged for the firemen at the firehouse next door to the settlement to stage a drill for her. The incident left a marked impression on the young girl. According to Arnstein, the horses and the fire engines aroused her interest in public-health nursing.

When she was a teenager, a lack of support from family and friends temporarily deterred Arnstein from taking nurse's training. People had convinced her that she did not have the necessary skills because she was too awkward with her hands and too smart for nursing. Commenting some years later on what had appeared to be a commonly accepted attitude toward nursing, she noted that intelligence was not wasted in nursing, as she never had enough for every job she had done.

The Arnsteins believed their second daughter to be suited for the medical profession because she was an excellent student, making high points in the sciences. Also, her older sister Elizabeth, who attended Vassar, was studying to become a physician.

In the fall of 1921, Arnstein entered the premedical curriculum of Smith College, even though nursing remained her prime interest. She greatly admired Harrison Hawthorne Wilder, a professor of zoology, and her major areas of study were zoology, biology and physiology. Another influence was President William A. Neilson, a minister and teacher whose wisdom stayed with her throughout her life. Neilson's view that students should be exposed to many points of view was a precept that Arnstein found invaluable in the later 1960s, when she became dean of nursing at Yale.

The experiences that Arnstein acquired while at Smith were important parts of her personal and social development. Her classmate, Dorothy Smith, became a cherished friend whom Arnstein later joined in Paris, where Smith was studying music.

Arnstein graduated from Smith in 1925 and that fall enrolled in the New York Presbyterian Hospital School of Nursing's 27-month program designed for college graduates without previous preparation in nursing. Because of her strong undergraduate science background, Arnstein was able to tutor her eight classmates. She received her diploma in 1928 and left for a vacation in Europe. The next year she earned an M.A. degree from Teachers College, Columbia University.

Her first position in nursing was as a staff nurse in public health with the Westchester County Health Department in White Plains, New York. She later became a supervisor there and remained for the next five years. At that time, preventive care was primarily related to contagious diseases. However, many citizens did not understand the immunization process, and considerable persuasion was needed to induce them to accept the injections.

During Arnstein's second year of practice, immunization for diphtheria was instituted, but other conditions such as tuberculosis and venereal disease ran rampant. Public-health nurses were busy case-finding for tuberculosis patients, attempting to locate families and other contacts for early detection. Venereal disease was not discussed publicly until Thomas Parran, surgeon general of the U.S. Public Health Service, brought this health problem into the open on the radio in the 1930s.

In 1934 Arnstein received a master's degree in public health from Johns Hopkins University. By then, from her practice and study she had acquired a fuller understanding of the role of the nurse in the public-health arena. She later explained that because doctors were not always present, public health nurses often needed to make independent decisions. In addition, she cited the importance of work within the community.

After receiving her second master's degree, Arnstein joined the communicable-disease division of the New York State Department of Health as a consultant nurse. In 1937 she made her first venture into academia as a teacher of public health and nursing in the University of Minnesota's department of preventive medicine. She worked closely with Dr. Gaylord Anderson, who became another significant influence throughout her career.

In the early period of their association, Arnstein and Anderson collaborated on their first book, *Communicable Disease Control*, published in 1941. When it first appeared, it was hailed as a much-needed text as well as an important contribution and reference. It was geared not only to health officers and public-health nurses, but also to lay members on public-health boards, parents, nursing instructors, students, and others. Thirty years later, Anderson was still trying to persuade Arnstein to work on a fifth edition.

Arnstein spent three years at the University of Minnesota and then rejoined the New York State Health Department as a consultant nurse. She stimulated field studies in public-health nursing, designing research projects to analyze and systematize the observations of nurses. She also sought new ways to modernize the nursing profession and apply research techniques in the public-health field. She believed that because nurses were heavily preoccupied with patient care, they did not stop to analyze or assess health issues.

In the early 1940s, Arnstein went on leave for two years to serve in Cairo as chief nurse of the Balkan Mission of the United Nations Relief and Rehabilitation Administration, where she advised on nurse-training programs. In addition, she was assigned to the USPHS to establish the first program of federal grants to schools of nursing. For 20 years after the war, Arnstein held various staff positions with the USPHS.

As an employee of the federal government, Arnstein officially entered the service as the assistant to the chief of the division of nursing, who at that time was Lucile Petry. In 1949 she became chief of the division of nursing resources, and she remained in that post for eight years. Following her next appointment as chief of public-health nursing, she was promoted to chief of the entire division of nursing in 1960. She directed national field studies on nursing and assisted individual hospitals in carrying out their own clinical studies. She conducted international conferences on research, studied health issues and resources abroad, and worked with the World Health Organization.

In 1950 Arnstein went to Geneva to prepare *A Guide for National Studies of Nursing Resources* for the World Health Organization. The following year, that organization appointed her a consultant to Finland. At the organization's meeting held in New Delhi in 1961, she was a member of the United States delegation.

During the spring of 1958, Arnstein took leave from the USPHS to become a visiting professor at the Yale University School of Nursing, where she was the first person to hold the Annie W. Goodrich Chair of Nursing. At an interview on alumnae day, February 22, she explained some of the studies carried on by the Public Health Service. Research was an important part of nursing, she noted, adding that Florence Nightingale published several studies only after doing intensive research. She advocated studying how nurses could best work within the changing medical system.

Two years before her retirement from the service, Arnstein moved from the division of nursing to the office of international health. Involved in efforts supported by the Rockefeller Foundation and the Agency for International Development, she joined American and British physicians in studying health issues and needs in developing countries. Reflecting later on this experience, she pointed out the necessity to adapt nursing practices to the unique needs of developing nations.

In the 1960s Arnstein spent a brief period as full professor and head of the public-health nursing program at the University of Michigan. A long-time friend and colleague, Myron Wegman, then dean of the school of public health, influenced her decision.

Arnstein's tenure at Michigan was short lived because in the spring of 1967 she accepted an appointment as dean of the school of nursing at Yale University. She had warm ties there, not only because of her previous visiting professorship and numerous lectures, but because her father had graduated in the class of 1896 and her younger brother, Robert, was the psychiatrist-in-chief at the Yale Health Services.

In publicly announcing her appointment, President Kingman Brewster noted that Arnstein was succeeding Florence Wald, who had been dean since 1959 and was returning to full-time teaching, clinical practice, and research. He observed that with Arnstein as the new dean, Yale would have an opportunity to contribute to a national need for preparing professionals for health care of high quality.

The Yale years were stimulating ones for Arnstein in the many responsibilities that involved overseeing the nursing program and giving it leadership, stimulating faculty to grow and learn, meeting and socializing with students, and continuing with her numerous professional activities and contacts relating to national and international health care. She was consistent in her belief in the need for sound, valid research.

Over the years, Arnstein was recognized with honors and awards. In December 1966 she was the first woman to receive the $10,000 Rockefeller Public Service Award, given for distinguished service on the part of career employees in the upper levels of the federal government. While she was at Yale, the American Public Health Association (APHA) awarded her its highest honor, the Sedgewick Memorial Medal, which represented to her the culmination of her life's work. Although weakened by recent cancer surgery and subsequent radiation treatments, she was determined to attend the APHA convention in October 1971 to accept her award.

In September 1972 Arnstein announced her retirement from the school of nursing due to illness. On October 8 of that year, she died at her apartment in New Haven, Connecticut. Surviving were her brothers, William E., of New York City, and Robert L., of Hamden, Connecticut.

## PUBLICATIONS BY
## MARGARET GENE ARNSTEIN

### BOOKS

With G. Anderson, *Communicable Disease Control.* New York: Macmillan, 1941.

With E. Broe. *International Conference on the Planning of Nursing Studies.* London: International Council of Nurses, 1957.

Arnstein, M.G. *A Guide for National Studies of Nursing Resources.* Geneva: World Health Organization, 1953.

### ARTICLES

"Relationship of the Public Health Nurse to the Part-time Local Health Officer in Communicable Disease Work." *American Journal of Public Health* (May 1936): 512–16.

With G. Hanson and E. De Val. "The Recording of Home Visits." *Public Health Nursing* (June 1940): 385–86.

With M. Derryberry. "Nursing Visit Transcripts as Training Material." *Public Health Reports* (December 1940): 2351–55.

With E.S. Rogers and M. Robins. "Secondary Attack Rates in Pneumonia." *American Journal of Public Health* (February 1941): 135–42.

"New York Plans for Emergency Public Health Nursing." *Public Health Nursing* (March 1943): 125–26.

"Communicable Disease in Wartime." *Public Health Nursing* (April 1943): 194–96.

"Nursing in UNRRA Middle East Refugee Camps." *American Journal of Nursing.* 45. (May 1945): 378–81.

"Public Health Work in England: How It Is Like and Unlike Ours." *American Journal of Public Health* (January 1947): 83–90.

With L. Petry and R. Gillan. "Surveys Measure Nursing Resources." *American Journal of Nursing* 49 (December 1949): 770–72.

"Research in the Nursing Field." *American Journal of Public Health* (August 1950): 988–91.

"A World Guide for Studying Nursing." *Nursing World* (September 1951): 385–87.

With L. Petry and P. McIver. "Research for Improved Nursing Practices." *Public Health Reports* (February 1952): 183–87.

"Unity of Nursing Service." *Nursing Outlook* (April 1954): 201–02.

"Setting the Record Straight." *Nursing Outlook* (June 1954): 297–98.

With E. Levine, M. E. Odoroff, and John W. Cronin. "Sources of Nurse Supply for New Hospitals." *Public Health Reports* (April 1955): 356–61.

"Why Research in Nursing?" *Missouri Nurse* (May 1956): 10–11.

"Training of Nursing Aides and Auxiliary Helpers." *Journal of American Osteopathic Association, Hospital Supplement* (June 1956): 655–56.

"Florence Nightingale's Influence on Nursing." *Bulletin of the New York Academy of Medicine* (July 1956): 540–46.

"A Training Program for Nurses' Aides and Auxiliaries." *Hospital Management* (July 1956) 45 ff.

"Improving Nursing Service." *Canadian Nurse* (November 1956): 860–73.

"International Conference on the Planning of Nursing Studies." Editorial. *Nursing Research* (February 1957): 99.

"Balance in Nursing." *Quarterly Magazine* (Alumnae Association, Presbyterian Hospital School of Nursing, New York) (1958): 13–18. Also in *American Journal of Nursing* (December 1958): 1960–1961.

"Forward with Public Health Nursing." *Nursing Outlook* (May 1958): 261–63.

"Priorities in Public Health Nursing." *Public Health Reports* (July 1958): 577–81.

"Training Nurses for Research Work." *International Nursing Review* (October 1959): 38–42.

"A New Look at Community Nursing Service." *Public Health News* (New Jersey State Department of Health) (February 1961): 57–59 +ff.

### BIBLIOGRAPHY

News release. Yale University News Bureau, 14 March 1967.

Van Voris, J. Interview with Margaret G. Arnstein, 1971. Nursing Archives. Mugar Memorial Library, Boston University.

Wegman, M.E. "A Tribute to Margaret G. Arnstein (1904–1972)." *American Journal of Public Health*, 13 (1973): 97.

"Yale Nursing School Alumnae Meet New Visiting Professor." *New Haven Register*, 23 February 1958.

Shirley H. Fondiller

## Anne Lucippa Austin

### 1891–1986

Anne Lucippa Austin is remembered as the author of the *History of Nursing Source Book* and articles on historical research in nursing. As a professor at the Frances Payne Bolton School of Nursing, Western Reserve University in Cleveland, Ohio, her impact and influence on undergraduate and graduate students was intensified and personalized by her strong beliefs regarding meticulous and accurate documentation.

Austin was born on August 7, 1891, in Ischua, New York, the older of two daughters of William H. and Margaret MacLaren Austin. Her mother's sister Clara died while giving birth to a son, John, who was adopted by the Austins. Bertha, Anne's younger sister, had three children: George, Jr., Gordon, and Margaret. The latter child, Margaret, was a close family link

through the years and oversaw the well-being of Austin in her later years. Austin never married.

Austin's American-born parents were of English and Scottish descent. Her father, who lived to age 95, had little formal schooling but was intelligent and well read. He worked at cheese manufacturing and later in the laundry business. Her mother was a school teacher, and the family attended the Presbyterian church in Lockport, New York.

Austin spoke especially of a great aunt, Annie Tallent, the first white woman in the Black Hills of South Dakota, who subsequently became the superintendent of public instruction of Pennington County, South Dakota. Tallent wrote *The Black Hills* (or *The Last Hunting Grounds of the Dakotas*), a history.

Her cousin, Rev. Melvin Fraser, was a missionary to the Cameroons who, with colleagues, translated the New Testament into Bulu, the native language. Her great-grandparents were early pioneers in the Genessee Valley of New York State. Austin traced her first American ancestor (Austin) to 1638 when he came to Charlestown, Massachusetts. He later settled in Kingstown, Rhode Island, to be able to "worship God in his own way."

Austin attended High Street Grammar and High School in Lockport, New York, where she skipped seventh grade. The school was famous for having been the school where Belva Lockwood, the first woman admitted to practice law in the Supreme Court of the United States and to run for the presidency of the United States on a national ticket, taught in the late 1850s.

Austin's ambition was to be a nurse. She entered the Buffalo Homeopathic Hospital Training School for Nurses (later named the Millard Fillmore Hospital School of Nursing) in 1912 and received her diploma in 1915. There was no tuition, but each student received a monthly stipend of $8. The 100-bed hospital provided nurses' training in the areas of medicine, surgery, operating-room procedures, pediatrics, psychiatry, obstetrics, and communicable diseases. However, no outpatient experience was provided. The probationary period was three months; nurses worked 12 hours daily with one-half day off weekly and four hours free on Sunday for attending church.

Austin recalled that on her first clinical day she was assigned to make supplies in a room adjoining the delivery unit and as a result witnessed her first delivery. Her first head nurse, Mildred Coleman, was an excellent teacher and provided close supervision. Uniforms were blue and white striped gingham (plain blue for probationers) with long sleeves and long, white, starched cuffs; a skirt with an ample pocket; and a white, gored apron with a high white bib with straps that crossed and buttoned to the apron band in back. High-topped buttoned shoes were worn with black cotton stockings. The dress was worn to the top of the shoes.

Even though classrooms were in the building's basement, they were light and pleasant. Classes were held mostly in the late afternoon, with lectures on clinical subjects given by physicians and nursing classes given by the superintendent of nurses or a head nurse. Textbooks were purchased by the students. Practical nursing was taught in a laboratory. Clinical experience included private duty (caring for a single private patient) on 12-hour day or night shifts. On "capping day," each student received her cap individually in the office of the superintendent of nurses.

Following graduation Austin worked in private practice in Buffalo for two years before going to Vittel, France, with the Army Nurse Corps from 1917 to 1919. She later worked as a Red Cross nurse and as night supervisor and instructor at the Lockport City Hospital. At the Buffalo Homeopathic Hospital School of Nursing, she became assistant principal and taught for six years. Another seven years were spent as assistant principal of the Farrand Training School of Nurses, Harper Hospital, Detroit. Her major university teaching was at the Frances Payne Bolton School of Nursing, Western Reserve University, Cleveland, Ohio, where she progressed from assistant to full professor of nursing during her 14 years there.

As part of the university's basic baccalaureate program, Austin taught sociology, psychology, history of nursing, and trends of nursing. In the graduate nurse program, she was chairman of the committee on graduate nurse programs in teaching, supervision, and administration in hospitals and schools of nursing. Austin also taught at Teachers College, Columbia University, in 1934 and later at the University of California, Los Angeles, and the University of Pennsylvania School of Nursing in Philadelphia.

Three persons stand out in her professional life as being good friends. The first was Isabel M. Stewart, with whom she collaborated in writing. Austin revered Stewart, who was her mentor and role model.

A second life-long and close friend was Lura Eldridge, a professor who taught anatomy and physiology at the Frances Payne Bolton School of Nursing, Western Reserve University. Edell F. Little was a third friend for about 50 years, during part of which they shared a home. Little graduated from the School of Nursing at Woman's Hospital in Detroit, Michigan. Her major area of interest was the field of public health nursing, and she served as supervisor and director of the Visiting Nurse Association in Los Angeles, California, for more than 10 years. After short periods in Lincoln, Nebraska, and Cedar Rapids, Iowa, they moved to Philadelphia for a 10-year stay before settling in Salem, New Jersey. When Little died in 1980, Austin sold their home and moved to an apartment in the Riverside Towers, a Presbyterian Home in Philadelphia. She continued her lifelong hobby of writing letters to her many friends and completed an extensive search of her family tree which was documented and illustrated with family photographs. She had a strong attachment to animals and usually had a cat or a dog.

When asked about the future of nursing, Austin wrote in her unpublished papers in 1977:

> 1. The place for men nurses: Two questions: Is there a future for men from the standpoint of their own personal careers and lives? Is

there a major place for men from the standpoint of the patient? Now in 1977, I answer "Yes" to both questions.

2. There is need for more *personal* recruiting of students and more contact of *nurses* with patients.

3. There is a need to specify what a *nurse* is. The public is at present confused about terms and the functions of each of the personnel taking care of patients.

4. My advice to a prospective nursing student would be to get a liberal education either before or concurrently with nursing. The liberal aspects need more emphasis both before and during the nursing program.

5. The nurse should be prepared in a good college or university school with adequate experience in all the needed clinical fields and content in the liberal arts in order to be prepared for nursing service on a *professional* level. Neither one nor the other alone will produce the kind of nurse needed in our modern world.

6. The major responsibility of every graduate nurse is to promote by her own behavior the improved status of herself as a professional person, of her profession, and to improve her service in promoting health and caring for the sick.

7. The role of the nurse in the future is as a member and leader of a health team in society, and as a helpful professional colleague of other workers.

Austin's honors included honorary memberships in the alumni associations of the Frances Payne Bolton School and Millard Fillmore Hospital School of Nursing. She also received the Nursing Education Alumni Award (NEAA), Teachers College, Columbia University, for achievement in nursing research and scholarship and particularly for her contribution of her *History of Nursing Source Book*. Austin is also recognized for her collaboration with Isabel Stewart in writing *A History of Nursing From Ancient to Modern Times*. After retirement, Austin continued her activities in support of nursing research, particularly of historical research, through membership on the Historical Source Materials Committee of the National League for Nursing.

A fractured hip and dimming vision did not affect Austin's enthusiasm for life and sense of humor during her last few years. She died May 2, 1986, and was buried in Cold Springs Cemetery, Lockport, New York. She was survived by one niece and one nephew.

## PUBLICATIONS BY ANNE LUCIPPA AUSTIN

### BOOKS

With A.G. Deans. *The History of the Farrand Training School*. Detroit: Alumni Association, 1936.

*History of Nursing Source Book*. New York: G.P. Putnam's Sons, 1957.

With I.M. Stewart. *A History of Nursing from Ancient to Modern Times*. 5th ed. New York: G.P. Putnam's Sons, 1962.

*The Woolsey Sisters of New York. A Family's Involvement in the Civil War and a New Profession*. (1860–1900). Philadelphia: American Philosophical Society, 1971.

### ARTICLES

"Nursing in Its Community Relationships." In *Introduction to the Principles of Nursing Care*, edited by N.E. Smith. Philadelphia: J.B. Lippincott, 1937.

"Development of Nursing in Ohio." *Ohio State Archaeological and Historical Quarterly* 7 (October-December 1941): 551–65.

With H. Bunge and G.K. Bixler. "Research in Nursing Education." *American Journal of Nursing* 48 (January, 1948): 45–48.

"The Historical Method." In *Research in Nursing*, edited by A.F. Brown. Philadelphia: W.B. Saunders, 1958.

"The Historical Method in Nursing." *Nursing Research* 7 (February 1958): 4–9.

"Biography of Abby Howland Woolsey." In *Notable American Women 1607–1950*. Vol. 4, edited by E.T. James. Cambridge, Mass.: Belknap Press of Harvard University Press, 1971.

"Biography of Elizabeth Christophers Kimball Hobson." In *Notable American Women 1607–1950*. Vol. 2 edited by E.T. James. Cambridge, Mass.: Belknap Press of Harvard University Press, 1971.

"Wartime Volunteers, 1861–1865." *American Journal of Nursing* 75 (May 1975): 816–18.

"Biography of Isabel Maitland Stewart." In *Notable American Women 1607–1950*. Vol. 4, edited by B. Beckerman and C.H. Green. Cambridge, Mass.: Belknap Press of Harvard University Press, 1980.

### BIBLIOGRAPHY

Austin, A.L. Papers. Center for the Study of the History of Nursing. School of Nursing, University of Pennsylvania, Philadelphia.

Austin, A.L. Private papers, personal letters to, and conversations with, author, 1945–85.

Lillian Sholtis Brunner

# Harriet Bailey
## 1875–1953

Harriet Bailey has been referred to as one of the nation's best known nurses. Yet little is documented and much less known about her early years, personally or professionally. Bailey's efforts on behalf of mental-health nursing were instrumental in the emergence and shaping of this segment of nursing and nursing education.

Bailey graduated from the Johns Hopkins Hospital School of Nursing, and in 1908 along with Effie Taylor, Laura Logan, and other early pioneers in nursing education, she enrolled in Mary Adelaide Nutting's hospital economics class at Teachers College, Columbia University. Perhaps her first claim to fame is that she was the first nurse educator to write a textbook on psychiatric nursing. Published in 1920, *Nursing Mental Diseases* was highly praised and soon became the standard text on mental-health nursing; its use spanned two decades and four revisions and editions.

Having served as assistant superintendent of nurses at the Johns Hopkins Hospital School of Nursing with valuable experience at the Henry Phipps Psychiatric Clinic, Bailey was well versed in her subject. The Phipps, the site of the first nurse-organized psychiatric-nursing education program, with Effie Jane Taylor as its director, opened its doors in 1913. From 1917–20, Bailey was employed at the Manhattan State Hospital in New York as superintendent of nurses and at the same time was a special appointee to the League of Red Cross Societies in Geneva, Switzerland. She also served as secretary to the State Board of Nurse Examiners of New York from September 1927 through April 1930.

Bailey contributed to the nursing community her landmark study on what she referred to as the "unwelcome subject" of mental-health nursing. The Bailey Report, as it was later called, was sponsored under the joint auspices of the National League of Nursing Education (NLNE) mental hygiene section and the American Psychiatric Association (APA). This effort, supported by both the nursing and psychiatric communities, was pivotal in the emergence of psychiatric nursing in the United States.

The 1935 survey had four specific purposes: (1) to determine if state hospitals for mental disease should offer a basic nursing course, (2) to observe the nursing school, (3) to determine clinical resources of nursing education and practice needed in nursing schools, and (4) to offer recommendations to improve teaching programs and ward practice.

As an associate editor of the *International Journal of Public Health*, Bailey had access to a reading public for her ideas and concerns. She wrote on such diverse subjects as public-health nursing, child-welfare concerns, the nurse as a teacher of health, and the industrial nurse. In other journals, she emphasized the importance of mental-health nursing and why it should be included in nursing programs.

Bailey held that character building was also a responsibility of those who instructed nursing students. She was determined to change the state hospital educational facilities and persistently made suggestions for their improvement.

At the age of 65 Bailey was appointed one of eight members of the NLNE Accrediting Visitors Team. The team's work extended to all parts of the country.

On May 23, 1953, at the age of 78, Bailey died in Bangor, Maine, after a long illness.

## PUBLICATIONS BY HARRIET BAILEY

### BOOKS

*Nursing Mental Diseases.* New York: Macmillan, 1920, 2nd Ed., 1929; 3rd Ed., 1935; 4th Ed., 1939.

### ARTICLES

"A Plea for the Inclusion of Mental Nursing in the Training School Curriculum." *American Journal of Nursing* 22 (April 1922): 533.

"The Future of the Schools of Nursing in the State Hospitals." *Psychiatric Quarterly* 3 (October 1929): 491.

"Nursing Schools In Psychiatric Hospitals: Report of a Survey." *American Journal of Nursing* 36 (May 1936): 495.

### BIBLIOGRAPHY

Church, O.M., and K.C. Buckwalter. "Harriet Bailey: A Psychiatric Nurse Pioneer." *Perspectives in Psychiatric Care* 18 (1980): 62–66.

"Harriet Bailey." Obituary. *New York Times*, 24 May 1953.

Roberts, M.M. *American Nursing: History and Interpretation:* New York: Macmillan, 1954.

Olga Maranjian Church

## Clara (Clarissa Harlowe) Barton
### 1821–1912

Clara (Clarissa Harlowe) Barton was an outstanding philanthropist, activist, and woman of achievement in nineteenth-century American history. Her significant contribution to the nursing profession came in the field of disaster nursing and community assistance to large numbers of persons experiencing various catastrophies. Barton was a volunteer nurse during the American Civil War, and some biographers have highlighted this phase of her career. However, her major contributions to the development of community-oriented nursing came during the years following the war.

Barton was born on December 25, 1821, in Oxford, Mass. the third daughter and last of five children to Steven and Sarah Stone Barton, both members of old New England families. She was named Clarissa Harlowe after a fictional character, but she called herself Clara. As the youngest child in a large family, she received much guidance, teasing, and stimulation from her older siblings. Her parents' sense of humanitarianism and patriotism guided much of her adult life. Barton usually credited her mother for her quick temper and her father for her love of adventure.

Two experiences in her early years prepared Barton for the rigors of active adult life. First, when she was 11 years old she had the task of caring for an older brother during a prolonged illness, which taught her the significance of having patience with the healing process. Second, she seized the opportunity to acquire an advanced education in such broadly diverse subjects as Latin, mathematics, philosophy, chemistry, and history. She loved to identify problems and analyze issues, and these skills helped her greatly in later work organizing the Red Cross.

Barton grew from a shy, small girl who had few friends her own age to a lovely, outgoing woman. She began her teaching career at the age of 18 and found work with children stimulating. Her appetite for learning returned, and at the age of 30, she enrolled in additional courses at the Liberal Institute of Clinton, New York. After completing her studies, she moved to New Jersey to resume teaching. She convinced the civic leaders of Bordentown, New Jersey, to open their first public school in 1852. The school grew quickly and was popular with the students. After local officials hired a male teacher to direct the growing school and supervise its instructor, Barton resigned and moved to Washington, D.C.

A Massachusetts politician helped Barton obtain a position as a clerk in the patents office, which may have been the first type of civil-service appointment ever given to a woman. Barton experienced much discriminatory behavior from her male counterparts but continued in her job despite the difficult circumstances. Political changes in Washington propelled her out of her job in 1857, and she returned to Massachusetts to teach until called back to Washington in 1860.

When the Civil War broke out, Barton responded to the lack of organization among the relief groups in Washington and the absence of adequate first-aid supplies for battle victims by sending out independent requests for relief supplies and using her own home as a depot. She insisted on providing relief on her own with only a few supporters, refusing to cooperate with the army or the United States Sanitary Commission. Although this independent attitude risked confusion and possible duplication of assistance, her smaller organization proved more flexible and mobile during the early years of the war and by pushing relief through military lines, as she did near Charleston, S.C., and Fredericksburg, Va., she often arrived long before other groups. She proved capable of inspiring people to assist her, and her creativity and ability to handle crises smoothly increased her reputation as an efficient relief worker. Most of Barton's significant contributions to the war effort occurred in the early years, before the larger relief organizations became efficient and functional.

One of Barton's most outstanding humanitarian activities began in 1865, when she received permission from President Lincoln to open an office in Annapolis, Maryland, and begin what became a massive task of looking for missing soldiers. She composed lists of names for publication in newspapers all over the country and directed written reports to families of missing soldiers, based on responses to the newspaper appeals.

Shortly after this work began, news of the disaster in Andersonville, the Confederate prison camp, became a public scandal. A secret list of all Union prisoners who died in the Georgia camp had been kept during the war years, and the horror stories of death and deprivation raised much public indignation. Barton went to Georgia with a large work force of men, and the victims were reinterred with proper military burial. By the time the project was completed, almost 13,000 men who had perished had been identified

and burial markers placed in a memorial cemetery established at Andersonville.

Barton's work for the government in the effort to find lost soldiers lasted four years. Toward the end of this period, she traveled to many cities and spoke to audiences about her war and postwar work. This arduous project caused her to suffer the first of several periods of nervous prostration and led to her forced rest in Europe in 1869.

While in Switzerland, Barton learned of the activities of the International Red Cross, which had sought to relieve war victims since its founding in 1863. The international committee that had established the organization wrote a treaty aimed at neutral humanitarian aid of those in distress during times of armed conflict, and several countries in central Europe had already ratified this treaty. Barton discovered with dismay that the United States had refused to join this international group because it would not ratify the treaty.

Barton's rest trip ended abruptly with the outbreak of the Franco-Prussian War. She was able to observe the actions of the young Red Cross organizations in Europe during the disasters that followed the conflict. She volunteered to help in Strasbourg, France, working with women made destitute by the destruction from the fighting, and also worked with Red Cross groups in Lyons, Belfort, and Montpellier. These exertions led to another episode of nervous prostration. Barton left central Europe and spent much of 1872 in England before returning to a Dansville, New York, sanatorium for a prolonged rest.

During this period of semiretirement, she remained intensely interested in the International Red Cross and frustrated over the refusal of the United States to ratify the treaty. She wrote letters, approached public figures, and used all of her friends and contacts to spur interest in the issue. The outbreak of the Russo-Turkish War spurred Barton to greater action to lobby for the passage of the treaty. She wrote to the international committee and gained its support in her effort. Little did she know at this time, at the age of 56, that she had embarked on the most significant achievement of her career, a task that would demand the remainder of her active life to accomplish: the establishment of the American Red Cross.

Gaining ratification of the international treaty took Barton five long years of pamphlet writing and personal efforts to persuade influential people in Washington that membership would be beneficial to the country. Finally, in 1882 President Chester Arthur and Secretary of State James G. Blaine facilitated ratification of the treaty, and the National Society of the Red Cross received official status.

For the next 23 years, Barton led the Red Cross through major relief efforts following natural disasters, epidemics, and war. She instituted individualistic practices that she controlled, including special procedures for helping the needy. She insisted the Red Cross volunteers always be well prepared with supplies and daily necessities. She believed able victims should be put to work in order to help them feel useful and hopeful about the future. She used informal organizational methods and cared little for such details as careful bookkeeping. Barton's primary objective remained to provide assistance to the needy as quickly as possible and to organize volunteers to help. This leadership style worked during the early years of the organization, when efforts were limited and focused, but eventually proved unsuccessful when the organization and society grew to such an extent that more formal structures became necessary.

In one of Barton's last major efforts with the Red Cross, she travelled at the age of 76 to Cuba to direct relief efforts related to the victims of the Spanish-American War. Barton's insistence on doing her work independently of other relief groups slowed the progress of her own efforts, and as a result the Red Cross volunteers missed much of the direct service to the victims of this short conflict. She did manage to direct the establishment of an orphanage for children victimized by the disease and death of their parents.

Barton symbolized the caring humanitarianism of the Red Cross during the early vulnerable years of the organization. She used resources carefully and distributed materials with great skill. The organization gave over $2 million in relief during the first 20 years of its existence, with very little overhead going to the group itself. Barton's honesty, caring, and skill helped to make the Red Cross a significant force for good in the nineteenth century.

Unfortunately, the Spanish-American War experience began a new era for Barton and her leadership. Although the government charter for the Red Cross received approval in 1900, the much-needed reorganization of the group failed to take place. Barton, now approaching 80, could not recognize the need to change the format and structure of her ever-growing organization. For example, she never saw the need for strict accountability in the area of budgeting or reporting fund allocation. Her advancing age and other organizational problems led to a decline in public confidence in the American Red Cross, and donations dropped. Conflict within the organization led to her bitter resignation in 1904. This allowed a complete reorganization of the American Red Cross, bringing it up-to-date with other relief groups. Barton found this precipitate exit from her beloved organization and its subsequent redesign one of her life's greatest disappointments.

Barton could not see beyond the reorganization to the vital relief service that continued to reflect her strongest-held beliefs about care of disaster victims. Nevertheless, the changes would prove to be important when the Red Cross would need to carry heavy burdens during World War I. The solid foundation she had built would prove to be significant to this organization as it entered a new era.

After 1904 Barton retired to her home at Glen Echo, Maryland, outside Washington, D.C. She maintained many interests and activities throughout the remainder of her life, including Christian Science, spiritualism, diary writing, and an extensive correspondence. She strongly supported the women's suffrage movement and called for equal pay for women. She enjoyed several quiet years at Glen Echo and died on April 12, 1912, in her 91st year. She was buried in Oxford, Mass., the place of her birth.

Barton, only five-feet tall and a slender woman all her life, could maintain a calm composure regardless of the circumstances that surrounded her. She had boundless energy and strength to endure even the most rigorous conditions. Her zealous patriotism, sharp mind, and skill in public speaking enabled her to establish and maintain a prominent leadership role in nineteenth century society. While she never strongly urged the use of trained nurses in her work, the institution she created quickly recognized the valuable contribution of nurses in disaster relief. Much of her basic philosophy of helpfulness endures today, and much of what nurses offer in the Red Cross was originally envisioned by Clara Barton. She received international Red Cross honors from many countries and a place in the American Hall of Fame and is remembered as an outstanding woman leader of her time.

## PUBLICATIONS BY CLARA BARTON

### BOOKS AND PAMPHLETS

*Report of an Expedition to Andersonville, Ga., 1865 for the Purpose of Indentifying Graves.* New York: n.p., 1866.

*The Red Cross of the Geneva Convention.* Washington, D.C.: Darby, 1878, 1881.

*Official Report of the Red Cross Hospital at Camp George Washington May 23–30, 1887.* Washington: American Association of The Red Cross, 1887.

*The Red Cross; A History of This Remarkable International Movement.* Washington: American National Red Cross, 1895, 1898, 1899. Also published as *The Red Cross in Peace and War.* Washington, D.C.: American Historical Press, 1899, 1904, 1910, 1912.

*Story of the Red Cross.* New York: American National Red Cross, 1903; D. Appleton & Co., 1904, 1916, 1917, 1918.

*The Story of My Childhood.* New York: Baker and Taylor, 1907; New Haven: Atwater, 1924.

### BIBLIOGRAPHY

Barton, W. *Life of Clara Barton.* 2 vols. Boston: Houghton Mifflin, 1922.

Brockett, L.P., and M. Vaughn. *Woman's Work in the Civil War.* Philadelphia: Seigler and McCurdy, 1867.

Dulles, R.F. *The American Red Cross: A History.* New York: Harper and Brothers, 1950.

Epler, P. *Life of Clara Barton.* New York: Macmillan, 1915.

Henle, E. "Clara Barton, Soldier or Pacifist?" *Civil War History* 24 (June 1978): 152–60.

Linda E. Sabin

## Mary Beard

### 1876–1946

Mary Beard has been described as belonging to a generation of inspired pathfinders. She was a humanitarian whose special contributions were in the field of public-health nursing. The highlights of her career include her work at the Instructive District Nursing Association (IDNA) of Boston, the Rockefeller Foundation of New York City, and the American National Red Cross in Washington, D.C.

Beard was born November 4, 1876, in Dover, New Hampshire, to Ithamar Warren and Mary Foster Beard. Her father was a clergyman. Having chosen her profession by the age of four when she was sick with diphtheria, she began her nursing training without completing high school. She graduated from the New York Hospital School of Nursing in 1903.

Beard's nursing career began in 1904 in Westbury, Connecticut. Here she organized and for five years administered the Visiting Nurse Association. For the next two years she worked at the surgical pathology research laboratory of the College of Physicians and Surgeons, Columbia University, where she studied the origins and growth of cancer.

At the suggestion of Ella Crandall, who would become the first executive director of the National Organization for Public Health Nursing (NOPHN), she was recruited by the Board of Lady Managers of IDNA to become their new superintendent. After years of contemplation, the board had decided to reorganize the agency.

Beard began her new position in February 1912. She was confronted with 25 years of tradition as well as 27 "lady managers" whose expectations included elevation of their association to a new position in the country and 49 nurses caught in the middle. By April she had initiated a plan of reorganization that resulted in a complete institutional change.

Beard's plan called for combining the work being done by the various nurses. Each would no longer specialize in one type of problem. Instead, the nurses would become general practitioners—what Beard referred to as neighborhood or community nurses. She predicted that all the people of a neighborhood, regardless of income, would employ her nurses.

The outcome of her efforts was a success. The agency growth was sizable. The year before Beard became superintendent, the staff had made nearly 112,000 visits to 11,000 patients. Eleven years later, during her last year, nearly 440,000 visits were made to over 52,000 patients. As a result of her leadership, the IDNA had become the largest and most innovative visiting-nurse organization in the country.

The IDNA was not the only public-health nursing agency in Boston. Public-health nursing in that city was directed by five unrelated organizations. While they were cooperative, their work was not coordinated. Despite Beard's years of effort, these organizations were never brought under the control of a centralized health center. Although Beard achieved little success in her efforts to centralize public-health nursing in Boston, this experience would guide much of her career.

Beard's interest in nursing education also developed during her tenure in Boston. In 1907 the IDNA had established the country's first postgraduate course for public-health nurses. In 1913 this program joined with the School of Social Workers at Simmons College in establishing an eight-month course for nurses. By 1923 there were 205 students enrolled.

While director of the IDNA, Beard was also actively involved in the founding and early development of NOPHN. She was a member of the committee that studied the feasibility of creating this nursing organization; the committee reported its supportive findings at the June 1912 national nursing convention. Beard was elected to NOPHN's first board of directors, serving from 1912 to 1914. She was vice-president from 1915–16 and president from 1916–19. She was also a member of the board from 1918–20, 1926–30 and 1936–46.

As president of NOPHN, Beard obtained a three-year grant to the organization from the Rockefeller Foundation. This would be the first of the foundation's many appropriations to the nursing field.

At an invitational conference sponsored by the Rockefeller Foundation in December 1918, Beard was elected to serve on a committee to study the proper training of public-health nurses. By 1923 when the Goldmark Report, "Nursing and Nursing Education in the United States," was published, both the committee and the task had expanded considerably. The outcome was the first comprehensive study of the practice of nursing and the education of nurses.

In October 1924 Beard accepted an offer from the Rockefeller Foundation to conduct an extensive study of maternity care in England. The following year she was appointed a special assistant to the director of the foundation's division of studies to work on nursing education. She quickly rose to the position of associate director of the international health division of the Rockefeller Foundation. In this position she made numerous trips overseas to study European nursing. She studied in Europe, China, Japan, the Philippines, Siam, Burma, India, Egypt, Palestine, and Syria.

Beard's broad understanding of the special problems in the field of public-health nursing helped secure aid from the foundation for numerous progressive experiments in nursing education and service. Between the time of its first grant to NOPHN and 1937, the foundation spent over $5 million on nursing projects. Aid also was given to 7 nursing schools in the

United States, 2 in Canada, and schools in 11 European and Asian countries. Beard helped organize the foundation's fellowship program for teachers and nurses in the public-health field from 30 countries as well as its travel-grant program for nursing leaders to study at public-health centers abroad.

In 1938 Beard became the director of nursing services of the American National Red Cross in Washington, D.C. In addition to being in charge of enrollment for the organization's nurses reserve, she directed its 500 public-health nursing services, its disaster-nursing program, and its nationwide classes in home hygiene and care of the sick.

During World War II, Mary Beard was named the first chair of the subcommittee on nursing for the Federal Council of National Defense. This committee was solely responsible for the education, procurement, and distribution of nurses in both military and civilian defense services. She also assisted in the development of the Red Cross Nurses Aide Corp.

Beard was the recipient of several honorary degrees. She was awarded a doctor of humanities degree from the University of New Hampshire and a doctor of laws degree from Smith College.

In August 1944 poor health forced Beard to resign from the Red Cross. She first had become ill in September 1943 and was admitted to Massachusetts General Hospital with a gastric ulcer.

Beard died December 4, 1946, and was cremated the following day. Several hundred of her friends attended a memorial service in New York City. Her remains were returned to New Hampshire that spring. She was survived by her three sisters, Allison Colleen and Theodora Beard of Dover, New Hampshire, and Eliza Beard of Westport, Connecticut.

Those who knew Beard recalled her dauntless spirit, her strength and inspiration as a leader, and her vision and courage as a pioneer. In her memorial service, Alan Gregg, Director of Medical Sciences of the Rockefeller Foundation, described Beard as good-natured, dignified, and having a lucid mind. A witty conversationalist, he remembered her as inwardly serene, outwardly light hearted and always responsive. She was, as he suggested, a woman who lived a life of action.

## PUBLICATIONS BY MARY BEARD

### BOOKS

*The Nurse in Public Health.* New York: Harper and Brothers, 1929.

### ARTICLES

"How to Form a Visiting Nurse Association." *American Journal of Nursing* 8 (August 1908): 920–21.

"Generalization in Public Health Nursing." *Public Health Nurse Quarterly* 5 (October 1913): 42–47.

"Home Nursing." *Public Health Nurse Quarterly* 7 (January 1915): 44–51.

"Prenatal Nursing." *Public Health Nurse Quarterly* 7 (July 1915): 13–24.

"A Series of Talks on Public Health Nursing." *Public Health Nurse Quarterly* 8 (April 1916): 13–20; 8 (July 1916): 129–41; 8 (October 1916): 46–53; 9 (January 1917): 56–68; 9 (April 1917): 147–55; 9 (July 1917): 280–6.

"Midwifery in England." *Canadian Nurse* 23 (February 1917): 89–94; 23 (March 1927): 140–45.

"Public Health Nursing and Its Administration." *Public Health Nurse Quarterly* 9 (April 1917): 147.

"Presidential Address to the National Organization for Public Health Nursing." *Public Health Nurse Quarterly* 10 (July 1918): 246–48.

"Nursing As It Relates to the War: Sub-Committee on Public Health Nursing." *American Journal of Nursing* 18 (August 1918): 1082–83.

"The Health Center Idea in Cities." *Public Health Nurse* 12 (June 1920): 526–32.

"The Community Health Association of Boston." *Public Health Nurse* 15 (March 1923): 115–18.

"A Nurse Looks at the Future." *Public Health Nurse* 21 (May 1929): 257–59.

"Health Visiting in America." *British Medical Journal* 2 (August 1934): 229.

"Creative Nursing." *American Journal of Nursing* 36 (January 1936): 69–78.

"Fundamental Changes in Nursing Education." *Canadian Nurse* 32 (October 1936): 445–53.

"Wanted: 10,000 Nurses!" *American Journal of Nursing* 39 (March 1939): 227–32.

"American Red Cross Nursing Service." *Public Health Nursing* 31 (October 1939): 546–50.

"Home Nursing." *American Journal of Nursing* 42 (January 1942): 6–7.

"Expanded Program for American Red Cross Volunteer Nurse's Aides." *Hospitals* 17 (March 1943): 73–74.

### BIBLIOGRAPHY

Beard, M. Papers. American Red Cross, Washington, D.C.

Beard, M. Papers. Department of Manuscripts and University Archives. Cornell University, Ithaca, N.Y.

Beard, M. Papers. Nursing Records. Rockefeller Archive Center, North Tarrytown, N.Y.

Beard, M. Papers. Special Collections, Nursing Archives. Mugar Library, Boston University, Boston.

Buhler-Wilkerson, K. "False Dawn: The Rise and Decline of Public Health Nursing, 1900–1930." Ph.D diss., University of Pennsylvania, 1984.

Crandall, E.P. Letter to Mrs. Codman, 9 November 1911 and 20 November 1911. N34, box 1, folder 13, Nursing Archives. Mugar Library, Boston University.

Gregg, A. "Mary Beard—Humanist." *American Journal of Nursing* 47 (February 1947): 102–3.

Instructive District Nurse Association of Boston. *Annual Report.* 1911, 1917, 1921, 1923.

"Mary Beard." *Public Health Nursing* 39 (January 1947): 2.

"Mary Beard Dies; Leader of Nurses." *New York Times*, 5 December 1946.

"Miss Mary Beard, 1876–1946." *The Alumnae News* 21 (Spring 1947): 10.

Karen Buhler-Wilkerson

# Sister Mary Berenice Beck

## 1890–1960

Best known for her role in the development of the American Nurses' Association's Code of Ethics, Sister Mary Berenice Beck was one of the first nurses to hold a doctoral degree. She was instrumental in establishing the Marquette University College of Nursing and served as its first dean.

Born Annetta Beck on October 19, 1890, in St. Louis, Missouri, she was the daughter of James and Anna Mary Bauer Beck. A serious child, she was adept at her studies. Her father died when she was young, and after she finished eighth grade, she attended business school and took an office job to help support her family.

In 1910 when she was 20, she became a postulant in the Franciscan Sisters, Daughters of the Sacred Hearts of Jesus and Mary. The next year she took the name Sister Mary Berenice, and in 1913 she took her vows.

Sister Berenice was graduated from St. Anthony's Hospital School of Nursing in St. Louis in 1915 and was assigned to St. Joseph's Hospital in Milwaukee. The next year she became an instructor at St. Joseph's Hospital Training School for nurses. At this point, she completed her high-school education, became a registered pharmacist in the state of Missouri, and by 1927 had completed her bachelor of science degree from Marquette University. While studying for her degrees, she became assistant director of St. Joseph's School and served as director from 1929 to 1932. She received her master of science degree from Marquette in 1931.

Sister Berenice had taken several courses in nursing education at the Catholic University of America in Washington, D.C., and was invited to become one of the first three nursing instructors in its school of nursing in 1932. That year she also enrolled in the doctoral program, and in 1935 she was awarded a Ph.D. in nursing education by Catholic University. Records suggest that she was the first religious nurse and one of the first ten nurses in the nation to earn a doctorate.

After completing her doctorate, Sister Berenice returned to Milwaukee as director of St. Joseph's School of Nursing and began to urge the integration of the school into a university setting. She was able to complete the merger of the school with Marquette University, and the first collegiate students entered in the fall of 1936. Sister Berenice served as dean of the Marquette University College of Nursing from 1936 to 1942 and remained on the faculty, teaching graduate courses, for nearly another decade.

As a recognized educator, Sister Berenice was often invited as a visiting lecturer and summer-school instructor. She taught not only at Catholic University, but also at Mt. Mary College, Milwaukee; Maryville College, St. Louis; Incarnate Word College, San Antonio; Loras College, Dubuque, Iowa; Seattle College, Seattle; and Louisiana State University, New Orleans.

Sister Berenice was an active participant in a number of professional organizations at the national, state, and local levels. She served as a board member of the District of Columbia League of Nursing Education; as president, vice-president, and board member of the Wisconsin League of Nursing Education; and as a board member of the Wisconsin (State) Nurses Association (1935–42). She also served as a member of the Wisconsin State Board of Nurse Examiners.

At the national level, she served on the committee of nursing education of the Catholic Hospital Association from its inception in 1931 until 1938. She served on two committees of the National League of Nursing Education (NLNE), the sisters committee (1933–38), and the curriculum committee (1944–45). The latter committee sought to direct curriculum planning in nursing education toward broad social purposes and to improve the practice of nursing through better nursing education. When the NLNE began its school accreditation program in 1940, Sister Berenice was among the first eight nurses appointed field visitors, as the site visitors were then titled. She served on the American Nurses' Association (ANA) board of directors (1942–44) and on the board of directors of the American Journal of Nursing Company (1942–48).

Sister Berenice's greatest contribution to the ANA—and perhaps to nursing—was her role in the development of its Code of Ethics. Attempts at developing a code of ethics had been initiated as early as 1926 and again in 1940 but were never completed. The attempt was successful in 1949, accomplished by the ANA's Committee on Ethical Standards, chaired by Sister Berenice.

In writing about the code almost ten years later, Sister Berenice stated the following:

> When the Professional Code for Nurses was developed, it was recognized that practically every situation which faces the nurse (whether as nurse or person) contains more implications which need to be understood clearly and taken into consideration if the problem is to be grasped realistically, and sufficiently well to be solved correctly. Nurses are accordingly urged to keep the moral aspects of life, professional as well as personal, well in the forefront of their thinking, and to deal with problems, not from the viewpoint of shallow expediency, but with truth and justice ever before their minds as the goals most worthy of attainment.          (Paquette, 3)

A prolific writer, Sister Berenice was a frequent contributor to nursing and hospital journals, particularly to the *American Journal of Nursing and Hospital Progress*. She wrote on various aspects of education, and one handbook was designed primarily for nursing students, intended to help them meet the religious needs of Catholic patients.

From 1946 to 1948 Sister Berenice served as assistant administrator of St. Anthony's Hospital in St. Louis. By 1952 her health began to fail, and she went into semiretirement at St. Mary's Hospital in Racine, Wisconsin, where she died of a myocardial infarction on March 1, 1960. She was buried in Calvary Cemetery, Racine. She was survived by a sister, Mrs. Michael Burke, and a brother, Walter.

At the time of her death, the ANA board of directors paid a tribute to her, citing her leadership and her contributions. Her participation in the development of the code of ethics for professional nurses was lauded, as was her assistance to nurses in interpreting and utilizing the code in their daily practice. She was posthumously elected to the Nursing Hall of Fame in 1986.

## PUBLICATIONS BY SISTER MARY BERENICE BECK

### BOOKS

*The Nurse, Handmaiden of the Divine Physician.* Philadelphia: J.B. Lippincott, 1945.

## ARTICLES

"Training School Problems." *Hospital Progress* 4 (August 1923): 317–19.

"Preparation for State Board Examination." *Hospital Progress* 13 (April 1932): 137–44.

"The Administration of the School of Nursing." *Hospital Progress* 13 (September 1932): 330–44.

"Underlying Scientific Principles in Nursing Practice." *Annual Report of the National League for Nursing Education* (1934): 118.

"The Curriculum in the School of Nursing." *Hospital Progress* 15 (February 1934): 48–52.

"Coordinating the Teaching of Sciences and Nursing Practice." *American Journal of Nursing* 34 (June 1934): 579.

"Present Trends with Relation to the Catholic School of Nursing." *Hospital Progress* 15 (September 1934): 375–80.

"Staff Education Program." *American Journal of Nursing* 35 (September 1934): 901–7.

"Analysis of Nursing Service." *Hospital Progress* 16 (August 1935): 304–6.

"Hospital or Collegiate School of Nursing." *American Journal of Nursing* 36 (July 1936): 716–25.

"General Staff Nursing." *American Journal of Nursing* 37 (January 1937): 57–63.

"Survey of Private Duty Nursing." *American Journal of Nursing* 37 (July 1937): 860.

"Medical Staff Constitutions." *Hospital Progress* 18 (October 1937): 302–3.

"We're Going to be Accredited." *The Trained Nurse and Hospital Review* (April 1938): 459–62.

"What Part Should the Faculty Take in Curriculum Revision?" *Annual Report of the National League for Nursing Education* (April 1938): 181–87.

"Question of Catholic Ethics." *American Journal of Nursing* 38 (May 1938): 601.

"Extra-Professional Program in the School of Nursing—Its Relationship to the Professional Curriculum." *Annual Report and Proceedings of the Forty-Fifth Annual Convention of the National League for Nursing Education* (April 1939): 202–04.

"Educating Nurses for Specialties." *American Journal of Nursing* 43 (February 1943): 149–52.

"Financial Planning." *Workshop on Administration of College Programs in Nursing*, The Catholic University of America, Washington, D.C. (June 1944): 122–27.

"Is More Education Necessary?" *American Journal of Nursing* 51 (March 1951): 207–08.

"What's in Our Code?" *American Journal of Nursing* 56 (November 1956): 1406–7.

"Ethics of Nursing." In *The Yearbook of Modern Nursing 1957–1958*, edited by M. Cordelia Cowan. New York: G.P. Putnam's Sons.

"The Ethics of Nursing." In *The Yearbook of Modern Nursing—1959*, edited by M. Cordelia Cowan. New York: G.P. Putnam's Sons.

## BIBLIOGRAPHY

"A Tribute." *Annual Report to the House of Delegates*, Wisconsin Nurses' Association, 1960.

Beck, M.B. "A Study of Content and Achievement in the Materia Medica Course." Ph.D. diss., The Catholic University of America, 1935.

Cooper, S.S. "Sister Berenice Beck." In *Wisconsin Nursing Pioneers*. Madison: University Extension, University of Wisconsin, 1968.

"Former Dean of Nursing Dies." *Milwaukee Journal*, 2 March 1960.

Klein, Sister Rosalie. Letter to author, 19 September 1985.

"M. Berenice Beck, O.S.F., Ph.D., R.N." *Nursing Hall of Fame*. monograph. Kansas City, Mo.: American Nurses' Association, 1986.

Paquette, M. Unpublished speech, Sigma Theta Tau Founder's Day, 6 October 1983.

"Sister Berenice Beck, Nursing Leader, Dies." *Hospital Progress* 41 (April 1960):88.

Signe S. Cooper

# Nell Viola Beeby

## 1896–1957

Nell Viola Beeby was editor of the *American Journal of Nursing* from 1949 to 1956 and executive editor of the American Journal of Nursing Company from its founding in 1952 until her death in 1957. During this period, the publications *Nursing Research* and *Nursing Outlook* were inaugurated and the American Journal of Nursing Company founded. Beeby developed closer ties among nurses all over the world through her interests in missionary nursing, nursing journals of other countries, and the International Council of Nurses.

Born in Secunderabad, India, on August 1, 1896, Beeby was one of four daughters of Baptist missionary parents, William Henry and Clara Bridge Beeby. The other girls were Florence, Ruth, and Lois. Shortly after Nell's birth, Reverend Beeby retired from missionary work and returned to the United States. Beeby was proud of being a missionary's daughter, and her faithfulness to the Baptist church remained all her life.

Upon returning to the United States, the family settled in Urbana, Illinois, where Beeby attended the local schools. Directly after high-school graduation, she entered the nursing school of St. Luke's Hospital in Chicago.

As a student, Beeby discovered her special love for new mothers and their babies. She was described as practical and adaptable, a favorite nurse in family situations. After graduation from the nursing school, Beeby became a private-duty nurse at St. Luke's Hospital, specializing in obstetrics.

Beeby's missionary interest remained strong, but when she found in 1924 that the Baptist Board of Foreign Missions had no opening for a nurse, she turned to Yale-in-China, a nondenominational Christian organization that had established a college of nursing in China. Beeby's application was accepted by the personnel committee, and on May 27, 1924, she was appointed supervisor and instructor in surgical and obstetric nursing of the Yale-in-China nursing school for a term of four years.

Reginald Atwater, a public-health doctor who worked with Beeby in Changsha at that time, described her as a good nurse and a first-rate teacher. Beeby liked to tell funny stories about herself and was friendly with her fellow nurses and staff. Her visit cut short by the Chinese civil war, Beeby returned to the United States in the spring of 1927. The interests of Chinese nurses remained a lifelong concern.

Soon after her return, Beeby was made supervisor of the obstetrical department of St. Luke's Hospital in Chicago. Out of this experience came four articles pub-lished by the *American Journal of Nursing*. One of these articles discussed classes in child care for new mothers, while another addressed the need for private-duty nurses to educate their patients in health care.

In 1934 Beeby pursued her interest in furthering her education by enrolling full-time at the Teachers College of Columbia University. This brought her to New York City, where she resided for the remainder of her life. She received her B.S. degree from Columbia in 1936. In the spring of her senior year, she worked part-time as assistant news editor of the *American Journal of Nursing*. After graduation, Beeby became full-time assistant editor.

One of the journalistic assignments of which Beeby was most proud was her two-month assignment as a foreign correspondent for the war department in 1945. During this tour, she traveled extensively in Europe, reporting the activities of nurses serving in the armed forces.

In April 1949 Beeby succeeded Mary M. Roberts as editor-in-chief of the *American Journal of Nursing*. During her career at the journal, Beeby emphasized the educational and international aspects of nursing. Impatient with pretentious and over-written material, Beeby could be relentless about editing a manuscript. However, she was perceptive to the ideas of others, providing the facts were clearly stated. She never regarded herself as omniscient, and her office was a workroom where the occupant was seldom seen sitting still.

Beeby envisioned that the journal needed to serve the expanded scope of nursing activities after World War II, wanting the magazine to be in the vanguard of new developments in the profession. At the time, the Association of Collegiate Schools of Nursing was seeking to publicize the results of nursing research but had no funds to do so. In addition, the National League for Nursing wanted a new publication that would include public-health nursing. Although the journal was a wholly owned subsidiary of the American Nurses' Association, it had some freedom in deciding how to develop new publications. After considerable study and consultation, Beeby recommended the establishment of a new organization, the American Journal of Nursing Company. Founded in 1952, it began publishing *Nursing Research* and *Nursing Outlook*. Beeby became executive editor of the American Journal of Nursing Company as well as remaining editor-in-chief of the *American Journal of Nursing*.

The company expanded in other ways under Beeby's leadership. In 1954 the company appointed a special grants committee to allocate funds for research projects related to nursing. As a result, the Roberts Fellowship was established, and the Sophia Palmer Library was started on the premises of the journal office.

Beeby's close friends were almost exclusively women. She was so widely known in different nursing circles that her personal friends included most of the nursing leaders of her time.

Beeby was always a joiner and supporter of nursing organizations from the time she became a graduate nurse and joined the Illinois State Nurses's Association. Her international interests made her a valuable member of the International Council of Nurses. In 1956 at the height of her career, Beeby learned that she had terminal cancer. The board of the *Journal of Nursing* released her from editorial duties so that she could concentrate her energies on the Journal of Nursing Company. In February 1957 Beeby was awarded the M. Adelaide Nutting Award by the National League for Nursing for her adaptation of nursing practices to universal need.

Beeby died at her home in Jackson Heights, New York, on May 17, 1957. Her sister Ruth was with her. She was also survived by her two other sisters, Lois Stow of Nashville, Tennessee, and Florence Siebenthaler of LaSalle, Illinois. Obituaries and eulogies appeared in many journals and newspapers here and abroad, showering tributes on this missionary nurse who became an influential publisher and executive always striving to serve her profession.

## PUBLICATIONS BY NELL VIOLA BEEBY

"Mother's Classes." *American Journal of Nursing* 32 (July 1932): 727.

"Public Health Aspects of Obstetrical Nursing." *American Journal of Nursing* 33 (August 1933): 763–64.

"The Private Duty Nurse as a Teacher." *American Journal of Nursing* 36 (August 1936): 778–79.

"The World's Nursing Journals." *International Nursing Review* (October 1957): 57–59.

## BIBLIOGRAPHY

"Beeby, Nell Viola." In *National Cyclopedia of American Biography*. Vol. 45. Clifton, N.J.: James T. White, 1962.

Beeby, N.V. Papers. Yale-in-China Archives. Sterling Library, Yale University, New Haven, Conn.

Belote, M. Personal reminiscences. Retired news editor, *American Journal of Nursing*.

Brown, C. Personal reminiscences. Assistant librarian, Sophia Palmer Library, New York.

Hubbard, D.F. Personal reminiscences. Historian, First Baptist Church, Urbana, Ill.

Hubbard, L.O. Personal reminiscences. Student of Ruth Beeby, Oak Park, Ill.

"In Memoriam." *Canadian Nurse* 53 (July 1957): 628.

Kent, M.G. Personal reminiscences. Retired assistant editor, *American Journal of Nursing*.

Miller, L. Personal reminiscences. Retired librarian, *American Journal of Nursing*.

"Miss Beeby Receives the Nutting Award." *American Journal of Nursing* 57 (April 1957): 140.

"Nell V. Beeby." *Nursing Outlook* 5 (June 1957): 340–43.

"Nell V. Beeby, 1896–1957." *American Journal of Nursing* 57 (June 1957): 730–36.

"Nell V. Beeby." Obituary. *New York Times*, 18 May 1957.

"News About Nursing." *American Journal of Nursing* 36 (September 1936): 954.

Stephanie Cleveland

## Mary Ann Ball Bickerdyke

### 1817–1901

Mary Ann Ball Bickerdyke served as a nurse in the Civil War and for her services was commemorated with a statue in the public square of Galesburg, Illinois.

Though never officially trained as a nurse, she devoted much of her life to the nineteenth-century equivalent of public-health nursing, serving as a combination missionary, social worker, and nurse.

Born in Knox County, Ohio, on July 19, 1817, Bickerdyke was the daughter of Hiram and Annie Rodgers Ball. Her mother died when she was only 17 months old, and she was taken care of by her maternal grandparents in Ohio until her father remarried. She returned to her grandparents' house when she was 12 and lived with them until their deaths. She then moved in with other relatives and lived with them until, at the age of 30, she married Robert Bickerdyke in 1847, a widower with young children. In 1856, the Bickerdykes moved to Galesburg, Illinois, along with their two sons. His children by his previous marriage were left with relatives in Kentucky. Three years later her husband died, and Bickerdyke supported herself by practicing as a botanic physician, a position she apparently taught herself, much as she later taught herself nursing. In 1861 while attending a church service, Bickerdyke responded to a call from the preacher for a volunteer to help in the war effort by accompanying the delivery of medical supplies to the southern part of the state. Bickerdyke was facing a crisis in her own life, having not only recently lost her husband, but also her two-year old daughter, Martha.

When Bickerdyke left on her mission of mercy in 1861, she relied on trusted neighbors to care for her two remaining children, James, 13, and Hiram, 11. Believing she was engaged in the Lord's work and that she received her authority from God, she was not intimidated by the military milieu or by the medical officers who sought to curtail her efforts as a healing practitioner. Although her attitude undoubtedly helped her evade some of the military restrictions, she was also aided by her friendships with General Ulysses S. Grant and General William T. Sherman. Bickerdyke's successful intervention on behalf of the health and well-being of the soldiers was acknowledged by the name they gave her, "Mother Bickerdyke," and for which she became known.

The Northwestern Sanitary Commission, headquartered in Chicago, provided Bickerdyke with supplies, and to make her actions official, appointed her a field agent. She resigned from this position on March 21, 1866, the same day that the last soldier from Illinois received his discharge.

Bickerdyke sought for ways to continue work on behalf of the soldiers. Part of the post–Civil War governmental response to the service given by soldiers was to offer them the opportunity to settle on free land in sparsely populated areas such as Kansas. Bickerdyke borrowed money and managed to procure supplies for farming. In addition, she established a hotel so that the newcomers could be accommodated until they settled in. The Bickerdyke House in Salina, Kansas, was a rehabilitation and counseling center for veterans. Bickerdyke gave the soldiers free room and board, taught them about farming, and bought them equipment. Bickerdyke's travels and crusades were not limited to the Midwest. In 1870 at the age of 53, she arrived in New York City to accept a position with the Protestant Board of City Missions. For four years, she practiced her own special version of community welfare work. Although she did not clean out the slums as she thought she might, she took pride in her work.

Bickerdyke returned to Great Bend, Kansas, in 1874 to be with her sons who had settled in Kansas in 1867 when she did. She arrived just ahead of the devastating crop disaster, the result of a great plague of locusts. In the winter of 1874–75, Bickerdyke traveled extensively, working for grasshopper relief. As a result of her efforts, 200 loads of grain, food, and clothing were shipped to Kansas and distributed under her personal supervision. The citizens of Kansas thanked her by official resolution and by commissioning a portrait of her for the historical room of the state capitol building.

In 1876 after becoming ill, Bickerdyke traveled to California. Upon recovery, she set about trying to help the veterans and their families who, without pensions, were having difficulties in settling in the West. Armed with a sense of outrage and with power of attorney to represent 18 California veterans, she embarked on a cross-country trip to deal with the pension commission in Washington, D.C.

During her 11 years (1876–1887) in California, Bickerdyke helped organize the California branch of the Women's Relief Corp and auxiliary of the Grand Army of the Republic. In 1886, the U.S. Congress arranged for her to receive a pension.

Bickerdyke returned to Kansas in 1887 to live out her years with her son James. On November 8, 1901, at the age of 83, she died in the cottage she shared with her son in Bunker Hill, Kansas. She was buried in the Linwood Cemetery in Galesburg, Illinois. She was survived by her son. In 1904 in the Galesburg public square, a monument supported by public funds was erected commemorating Bickerdyke and her efforts on behalf of the soldiers.

### BIBLIOGRAPHY

Adams, G.W. "Mary Ann Ball Bickerdyke." In *Notable American Women*, edited by E.T. James, J.W. James, and P.S. Boyer. Cambridge, Mass.: Belknap Press of Harvard University Press, 1971.

Baker, N.B. *Cyclone in Calico: The Story of Mary Ann Bickerdyke.* Boston: Little, Brown, 1952.

Davis, M.B. *The Woman Who Battles for the Boys in Blue—Mother Bickerdyke.* San Francisco: Pacific Press, 1886.

DeLeeuw, A. *Civil War Nurse: Mary Ann Bickerdyke.* New York: Julian Messner, 1973.

Kellogg, F.S. *Mother Bickerdyke As I Knew Her.* Chicago: United Publishing, 1907.

Olga Maranjian Church

## Sister Kathleen Black

### 1908–1984

Sister Kathleen Black, the first director of the National League for Nursing's Psychiatric Nursing Advisory Service, was born December 19, 1908, in Kent, England. She was the third of four children, three daughters and a son, born to Alfred George and Gladys Keziak Bashford Black.

Two years later, in 1910, the family moved to Toronto, Ontario, Canada, where Kathleen attended elementary and high school. She graduated from the Ontario Hospital School of Nursing at Whitby and in 1936 received a certificate from the University of Toronto School of Nursing. In 1947 the University of Chicago awarded Kathleen a bachelor of science degree. She received a masters degree in 1950 from Teachers College, Columbia University.

Sister Kathleen's oldest sister, Gladys, had a strong influence on her. Gladys believed that courses in elocution and music appreciation should be part of every student's education. Sister Kathleen's love of and knowledge of classical music, literature, and drama stemmed from Gladys's philosophy. Vera, the second daughter, died when Sister Kathleen was well advanced in her nursing career. Sister Kathleen and her younger brother, Alfred Edward, were close companions. He later married one of Sister Kathleen's nursing-school classmates. Throughout their lives, the three often communicated and visited each other. Sister Kathleen's father, a self-educated laborer, was 21 years older than his wife. After his death, Sister Kathleen provided financial support for her mother.

Over the many years of her career, Sister Kathleen had first-hand experience in every role, ranging from that of beginning staff nurse to director of nursing and nursing education. She was appointed director of nursing education in the Sheppard and Enoch Pratt Hospital in Towson, Maryland, where Dr. Harry Stack Sullivan had conducted his early clinical research to test some of his theories. In the 1940's she also served as director of nursing education in the well-known Menninger Foundation in Topeka, Kansas. Sister Kathleen directed the graduate psychiatric nursing programs at the University of Minnesota (1950–1952), the University of Pittsburgh (1948–1950), and Teachers College at Columbia University (1947).

In 1952 when the National League for Nursing reorganized its structure, Sister Kathleen was appointed the first director of its new mental health and psychiatric nursing advisory service. With the help of her staff and associate colleagues, she initiated many projects that influenced positive changes in nursing education and the nursing of patients. The advisory service responded to requests for consultation from mental hospitals, allied facilities, and educational institutions. New programs and changes designed to upgrade nursing education and care were brought about through the foresight and assistance of the advisory service.

The Psychiatric and Mental Health Council, originally named the Interdivisional Council of Psychiatric and Mental Health Nursing, was organized under Sister Kathleen's direction. Theories and concepts of interpersonal nursing were promoted through national and state councils; thus, many nurses had the opportunity to learn and implement them in their practice. The councils also served as forums for nurses to come together to discuss problems and other matters of mutual interest.

Sister Kathleen was appointed as a member of the Joint Commission on Mental Illness and Health and of its board of trustees. (The group was made up of members of the American Psychiatric Association and the American Medical Association.) Its 1961 report, "Action for Mental Health," was a milestone and major force in bringing about subsequent changes in the hospitalization and care of the mentally ill.

During her career, Sister Kathleen conducted numerous institutes, workshops, and short courses throughout the country on various topics related to mental health, nursing, and nursing education. In 1955 she directed the National League for Nursing's conference project on graduate education in psychiatric nursing. In 1958 she initiated the organization's seminar project for teachers of psychiatric aides. The Association of Schools of Public Health sought her participation in its conference project devoted to teaching mental health in schools of public health. Because the league's membership was open to members of allied disciplines, Sister Kathleen's knowledge and experience had influential effects on persons of various backgrounds and interests. In turn, the interest of these people in matters of mental health and the mentally ill became additional sources of support.

Toward the end of her service with the league's psychiatric council Sister Kathleen underwent major surgery for cancer, from which she made a successful recovery. She became a convert to Catholicism, and following her departure from the league, she joined the religious community of the Sisters of Mercy and subsequently the faculty of the Catholic University of America from 1965 to 1969. Although she was required to follow a strict diet and to change to a less demanding lifestyle, she continued to organize education programs, teach, and write for the next 20 years. During her tenure, she was elected secretary of the executive board of the Catholic University of America assembly of the faculty and was a member of the faculty senate. In her last full-time position, she served as professor of nursing in the State University of New York at Binghamton. In 1977 this university conferred upon her the honor of professor emeritus.

Sister Kathleen was the author of numerous publications. One article "Appraising the Psychiatric Patient's Needs," is a classic on the subject of interviewing, observing, and assessing the patient's needs.

While visiting family members in Canada in the summer of 1982, Sister Kathleen suffered a cerebral aneurysm. Upon recovery she was taken by airplane ambulance to her small, hospital-connected apartment in Watertown, New York. Several months later she moved into the convent of Mercy of Mount Mercy in Dobbs Ferry, New York. While preparing to celebrate with friends and family her 25th anniversary in the Sisters of Mercy Order, she died suddenly of a cerebral hemorrhage on April 14, 1984. She was buried in the plot assigned to the Sisters of Mercy in Gate of Heaven Cemetery, Hartsdale, New York. She was survived by a brother, Alfred, of Brantford, Ontario, and a sister, Gladys, of Toronto.

## PUBLICATIONS BY SISTER KATHLEEN BLACK

### BOOKS

*Short-Term Counseling: A Humanistic Approach for the Helping Professions.* Menlo Park, Calif.: Addison-Wesley, 1983.

## ARTICLES

"Appraising the Psychiatric Patient's Needs." *American Journal of Nursing* 52 (June 1952): 718–21.

"Basic Principles of Nursing in Psychiatric Hospitals." *Hospital Management,* November 1952, 81–91.

"Are Our Basic Psychiatric Nursing Programs Adequate?" *Nursing Outlook* 1 (January 1953): 40–42.

With M. Shields. "Purposes of Programs Which Prepare Psychiatric Nursing Personnel." *Nursing Outlook* 2 (March 1954): 149–51.

With M. Shields. "Proficiency of Psychiatric Nursing Personnel." *Nursing Outlook* 3 (January 1955): 37–41.

"Nursing in Psychiatric Hospitals." *Mental Hygiene* 39 (October 1955): 533–44.

"Human Relations in the Basic Curriculum." *Nursing Research* 5 (June 1956): 4–17.

"The Five Year Look." *Nursing Outlook* 5 (March 1958): 170–72.

"Assessing Patients' Needs." *In Nursing Process,* edited by H. Yara and M. Walsh. Washington, D.C.: Catholic University of America Press, 1967, pp. 1–20.

"An Existential Model for Psychiatric Nursing." *Perspectives in Psychiatric Care.* (July-August 1968): 178–84.

"Teaching Family Process and Intervention." *Nursing Outlook* 18 (June 1970): 54–58.

"Social Isolation and the Nursing Process." *Nursing Clinics of North America* 8 (December 1973): 575–86.

## BIBLIOGRAPHY

Black, K. Personal visits, conversations, and correspondence with the author, 1979–1984.

Black, K. Curriculum vitae. Black family. Personal correspondence with members of Sister Black's family, 1986–1987.

Joint Commission on Mental Illness and Health. *Action for Mental Health.* New York: Basic Books, 1961.

Manfreda, Marguerite Lucy. "The Roots of Interpersonal Nursing." Privately published, 1982, pp. 54–57.

Marguerite Lucy Manfreda

## Elizabeth Blackwell

### 1821–1910

Elizabeth Blackwell was the first woman in the United States to graduate from medical school, practice as a physician, and establish a hospital to be conducted solely by women. With her sister Emily, she founded the first medical school for women in New York City that had clinical experiences comparable to those for men and initiated a short period of training for women aspiring to be nurses.

Blackwell was born on February 3, 1821, in Counterslip, England, near Bristol. She was the third daughter of Samuel and Hannah Lane Blackwell. There were two older sisters, Anna and Marian. A brother, Henry Brown Blackwell, was born in 1825 and married Lucy Stone, an anti-slavery and women's rights leader. Another brother, Samuel Charles Blackwell, married the first American woman minister, Antoinette Louisa Brown. Emily was born in 1826 and was also a physician. Another sister, Sarah Ellen, was born in 1828 and became an author and artist. She helped Elizabeth and Emily with their work at both the infirmary and the college. Three other Blackwell children died in infancy.

Blackwell's father was successful in the sugar-refinery business until a fire destroyed it in 1832. A religious man who was a dissenter against the Church of England, he decided to move his wife and children to the United States. Another child, George Washington Blackwell, was born in November of that year. In 1835 they moved to Jersey City, New Jersey, where they lived until May 1838, when Blackwell's father moved the family to Cincinnati, Ohio.

In August 1838 Blackwell's father died, and the family was left almost penniless. The oldest son, Henry, went to work but was unable to support the family alone. Therefore, the three oldest Blackwell girls and their mother opened a successful girls' school that existed until 1844. At that time, Blackwell accepted a position as the head of a girls' school in Henderson, Kentucky, where she stayed for only one year because of her views against slavery.

Upon Blackwell's return to Cincinnati, a friend who was dying of cancer suggested that she study medicine. Although no young women previously had attended medical school in the United States, Blackwell began thinking about the prospect. She next taught in Asheville, North Carolina, where she also privately studied medicine with a former physician, Reverend John Dickson. The following year, she continued her medical studies with his brother, Samuel H. Dickson, in Charleston, South Carolina, where she also taught music to support herself.

Blackwell went to Philadelphia in May 1847. There, Joseph Warrington and William Elder, both Quaker doctors, tried to help her get into medical school. She applied to all the medical schools in Philadelphia and in New York as well as Harvard, Yale, and Bowdoin. Twelve schools rejected her. Blackwell then applied to the Medical College at Geneva (later Hobart College) in New York State while working with Joseph M. Allan, another doctor. In October 1847 she was accepted by a unanimous vote of the class. Her formal medical education began in November 1847, and despite great harassment, she graduated in January 1849, receiving a doctor of medicine degree. She received the highest scores in her class on the final examinations.

Following her graduation, Blackwell returned to England in April 1849. There she received a congratulatory message from Florence Nightingale, among many other notables. She left England for further study in Paris at a school for midwives, the Hospital de la Maternité, in June 1849. Less than six months later, her eyes accidentally became infected while she was lavaging the eyes of an infant with a contagious opthalmia. The right eye eventually healed, but the sight of her left eye was lost as a result of the incident. Her hopes of becoming a surgeon ended.

In October 1850 following a long rest in Grafenberg, Germany, Blackwell returned to London again, this time for further study at St. Bartholomew's Hospital with James Paget, the noted physician. Ironically, she was restricted from the gynecology and pediatric wards. It was during this time that her friendship with Florence Nightingale was established. Blackwell encouraged her friend to pursue her interest in training to be a nurse.

Blackwell sailed from England to New York in July 1851, hoping to go into private practice there. However, the prejudice of male physicians prohibited her from doing so. She also was unable to open her own one-room, part-time, tenement-house dispensary to provide care for poor women on the lower East Side until 1853 because of local opposition to a woman physician. To fill the empty hours, she developed lectures on the principles of good hygiene, attended by the local Quaker women. These lectures were published in 1852 as "The Laws of Life, with Special Reference to the Physical Education of Girls."

By 1854 the dispensary had grown and was incorporated into an institution of women physicians for the poor. A 12-bed lying-in facility, it became known as the New York Dispensary for Poor Women and Children. Blackwell's sister Emily and a 26-year-old Polish woman physician joined her efforts in 1856, and eventually the New York Infirmary for Women and Children was opened in Greenwich Village on May 12, 1857. Over 3,000 patients were treated during the first year. This institution began a six-month training system for nurses with two students who received no compensation other than their keep. These planned nursing experiences included a weekly lesson on the different branches of nursing.

Blackwell had been following medical developments in England, and she returned to her homeland in August 1858 to take advantage of the Medical Act of 1858, which allowed her to be enrolled on the medical register of the United Kingdom. On January 1, 1859, she became the first recognized woman doctor in Great Britain as well as in the United States. In August 1859 she again returned to New York to work on plans to open a medical college for women.

However, the Civil War interrupted the project, and Blackwell involved herself with planning for the nursing care of soldiers. A meeting of about 60 women was held at Blackwell's New York Infirmary for Women and Children in April 1861 to suggest organizing the women of the country to serve as nurses to the sick and wounded of the army. Later the Women's Central Association of Relief was formally organized, and Blackwell chaired the registration committee for the selection and training of nurses. She arranged for 100 women to receive a four-week course of nurse training at Bellevue Hospital in New York, marking the first attempt for any large-scale nursing-education emphasis.

Blackwell's dream of opening a medical college for women was finally realized when the trustees of the New York Infirmary obtained a charter for the education of women physicians in 1865. Leaving the administration of the school in the able hands of her sister Emily, Blackwell returned to London in 1869 to establish her own private medical practice. She espoused the radical and popular cause of disease prevention and was instrumental in establishing the National Health Society, an organization committed to the prevention of illness. The Society for Repealing the Contagious Diseases Acts also was formed with Blackwell's participation. Because of her vivid memory about the difficulties she had experienced in entering a male-dominated field, she continued her supportive efforts of other women physicians in London. Suffering from poor health, she decided to retire in 1876 after a year as the chair of gynecology at the New Hospital and the London School of Medicine.

Blackwell spent the following 34 years in Hastings, England, at Rock House, which overlooked the sea. Her daughter, Katherine (Kitty) Barry, whom she had adopted as a seven-year-old orphan, lived with her and was her constant companion. Blackwell continued lecturing, writing, and publishing, especially on the moral and social aspects of medicine, throughout her retirement. During that time, Blackwell and her daughter also traveled to Europe and enjoyed visits from Blackwell family members. In 1906 Blackwell made a final visit to the United States. Summers were spent at the Kilmun Hotel in Argyllshire, Scotland, from 1902 until

Blackwell fell down the hotel stairs in 1907. She never recovered from the shock of the fall and died at her home in Hastings on May 31, 1910, at the age of 89. At her request, she was buried at the Kilmun Cemetery, Argyllshire, Scotland, and her grave is marked by a Celtic cross.

A visionary far ahead of her time, Blackwell was sensitive to the neglect suffered by women and advocated education of women about their own bodies and sex education. Her writings also addressed concerns regarding the social and moral issues of her day, especially those relating to medicine.

## PUBLICATIONS BY ELIZABETH BLACKWELL

### BOOKS

*The Laws of Life, in Reference to the Physical Education of Girls.* New York: Putnam, 1852. Reprint. In *Women and Children First,* New York: Garland, 1986.

*The Religion of Health.* London: publisher untraced, 1871, 1879, 1889.

*Counsel to Parents on the Moral Education of Their Children in Relation to Sex, under Medical and Social Aspects.* London: Hatchards, 1879; New York: Brentano, 1879; London: George Bell, 1913.

*The Human Element in Sex: Being a Medical Inquiry into the Relation of Sexual Physiology to Christian Morality.* London: Churchill, 1881, 1884, 1894.

*Rescue Work in Relation to Prostitution and Disease.* New York: Fowler and Wells, 1882.

*Wrong and Right Methods of Dealing with Social Evil.* London: Williams, 1883.

*The Purchase of Women: The Great Economic Blunder.* London: publisher untraced, 1887.

*The Influence of Women in the Profession of Medicine.* London: George Bell, 1889.

*Essays in Medical Sociology.* 2 vols. London: Ernest Bell, 1892, 1899, 1902; Salem, N.H.: Ayer, 1972.

*Pioneer Work in Opening the Medical Profession to Women.* Autobiography. London: Longmans, 1895; New York: Dutton, 1895. Reprint. In *Everyman's Library,* New York: Dutton, 1914.

*Scientific Method in Biology.* London: Elliot Stock, 1898.

### PAMPHLETS

*On the Decay of Municipal Representative Government: A Chapter of Personal Experience.* London: Moral Reform League, 1888.

*Christian Duty in Regard to Vice.* London: Moral Reform League, 1891.

*Christianity in Medicine.* London: Moral Reform League, 1891.

*Erroneous Method in Medical Education.* London: Women's Printing Society, 1891.

## ARTICLES

"Medicine and Morality." *Modern Review,* October 1881.

## LECTURES/ESSAYS

"A Cooperative Proposal," 1875.

"The Moral Education of the Young in Relation to Sex," 1879.

"Christian Socialism," London, 1882.

"Criticism of Grunland's Cooperative Commonwealth of Women," 1887.

"The Corruption Now Called Neo-Malthusianism," 1888.

"Prevention of Rabies," 1891.

"The Present Position on the State Regulation of Vice in British India."

## ADDRESSES

*Medical Education of Women.* Address to a meeting at the New York Infirmary with Dr. Emily Blackwell, December 19, 1863. New York: Baker and Taylor, 1864.

"An Era Begins." Address at the opening of the Women's Medical College of the New York Infirmary, November 2, 1868.

"Address to Working Women's College," 1869.

"How to Keep a Household in Health," 1870.

"Medical Responsibility in Relation to the Contagious Diseases Act." Address to the Medical Women, April 27, 1887.

"The Influence of Women in the Profession of Medicine." Address at the opening of the winter session of the London School of Medicine for Women, 1889.

"Christianity in Medicine." Address to the Christotheosophical Society, 1891.

"Why Hygienic Congresses Fail." Address to members of the International Congress at Brussels, September 1891.

## BIBLIOGRAPHY

Austin, A.L. *History of Nursing Source Book.* New York: G.P. Putnam's Sons, 1957.

Blackwell, E. "Pioneer Work for Women." In *Everyman's Library,* edited by E. Rhys. New York: E.P. Dutton, 1914.

Cook, E. *The Life of Florence Nightingale.* Vols. 1–2. New York: Macmillan, 1942.

"Editorial Comment: Death of Dr. Elizabeth Blackwell." *American Journal of Nursing,* 10, no. 10 (1910): 711–12.

Johnson, A., *Dictionary of American Biographies.* Vol. 2. New York: Scribner's, 1928.

Lee, S., *The Dictionary of National Biography: 1901–1911.* London: Oxford, 1912.

Marks, G., and W.K. Beatty. *Women in White.* New York: Scribner's, 1972.

*The National Cyclopedia of American Biography.* Vol. 9. New York: White, 1899.

Nutting, M.A., and L.L. Dock. *A History of Nursing.* Vol. 3. New York: G.P. Putnam's Sons, 1917.

Thomson, E.H. "Elizabeth Blackwell." In *Notable American Women: 1607–1950,* edited by E.T. James Vol. 1. Cambridge: Belknap Press of Harvard University Press, 1971.

*Who Was Who in America: 1897–1942.* Vol. 1, library ed. Chicago: Marquis, 1943.

Wilson, D.C. *Lone Woman.* Boston: Little, Brown, 1970.

Wilson, J.G., and J. Fiske, eds. *Appleton's Cyclopaedia of American Biography.* Vol. 1. New York: Appleton, 1886.

A. Gretchen McNeely
Irene S. Palmer

# Florence Guinness Blake

## 1907–1983

Florence Guinness Blake was respected nationally and internationally for her contributions to the nursing care of children. A scholar, teacher, author, and clinician, she initiated two graduate programs in pediatric nursing and pioneered the inclusion of clinical content in graduate programs at a time when this was not always done. She also was a frequent contributor to the nursing literature.

Blake was born November 30, 1907, in Stevens Point, Wisconsin, where her father, James Blake, was a Baptist minister. Her English-born father had been ordained an Episcopalian clergyman and had served as a missionary in the Belgian Congo before coming to the United States, where he attended the Moody Bible Institute in Chicago. Her mother, Thelma E.

Dunlap Blake, was born in Elroy, Wisconsin, and attended Wayland Academy, Beaver Dam, Wisconsin. She was an accomplished musician, gave piano lessons, and played the pipe organ in church. Florence was the younger of two daughters.

As a child, Blake frequently accompanied her father as he called upon his sick parishioners. She was influenced in her decision to become a nurse by an uncle, Victor Mason, a surgeon, who also encouraged her to attend Michael Reese Hospital School of Nursing in Chicago, where she would obtain a substantial amount of good clinical experience.

Blake received her diploma from the school of nursing in 1928. While she was there, the director of the school recognized her potential and arranged for her to spend three months of her clinical practice time at the University of Chicago, studying teaching and supervision. After she completed her nursing course, she was employed at her alma mater as instructor in nursing arts for six months. Following this she enrolled at Teachers College, Columbia University, for one year, then returned to Michael Reese Hospital, where she was appointed head nurse of a private pavilion, followed by an appointment as supervisor for the Sarah Morris Children's Hospital of Michael Reese. It was here that her ideas about the care of sick children began taking shape.

In 1932 Blake returned to Teachers College, and by this time, she knew she wanted to prepare herself for teaching pediatric nursing. She enrolled in all the available courses in pediatric nursing and supplemented them with nursery-school practice teaching, for she believed that nurses must understand normal growth and development if they are to provide effective care to children who are ill.

At Teachers College she elected to live in the campus international house, where she met several nurse faculty members from Peiping Union Medical College School of Nursing in Peiping, China. They encouraged her to apply to the Rockefeller Foundation for an appointment to their faculty.

Having completed her baccalaureate in 1936, Blake returned to Sarah Morris Hospital for a short time and then went to the Union Medical College in Peiping. She worked with a Chinese nurse to prepare her to assume the teaching position at the college, and by 1939 she considered her task accomplished. The threat of war in China also influenced her decision to return home.

Blake considered her experience in China important to her understanding the role of the nurse in the care of children. It was in China that she began the dual role of clinician and teacher, which provided the basis for her contribution to nursing knowledge and practice.

Before returning home, Blake spent one year of travel in various parts of the world. On this tour, she visited nurses she knew and arranged for short clinical experiences. She then enrolled in the graduate program in child development at the University of Michigan, Ann Arbor, and at the Merrill-Palmer School in Detroit, completing the requirements for her master's degree in 1941.

Blake served as instructor in pediatric nursing at the University of Michigan School of Nursing for one year. The next year she was appointed supervisor and assistant professor of pediatric nursing at the School of Nursing, Yale University. This school admitted only baccalaureate-prepared students. At Yale she worked with Edith Jackson, who developed the first rooming-in units for mothers and their newborn babies.

The year 1946 marked the publication of the fourth edition of *Essentials of Pediatrics*, a text extensively used in schools of nursing. That year its authors were Philip Jeans, Winifred Rand, and Florence Blake. As a contributor, Blake added a substantial amount of content on nursing care. In subsequent editions, she became senior author, and the amount and depth of child-development and child-care content increased, as well as the emphasis on the care of sick children.

In 1946 Blake was invited to establish a program of advanced nursing care of children at the University of Chicago. In Chicago she was invited to become a member of the first class in psychoanalytic child care at the Institute for Psychoanalysis, from which she received a diploma in 1951.

To communicate her concern that parents be assisted in supporting their children, Blake wrote *The Child, His Parents, and the Nurse*, published in 1954. The book is widely recognized as a classic, and has been translated into many languages.

The University of Chicago terminated its nursing program in 1959, and that year Blake began work under a Rockefeller grant at the university on a research project on the nursing care of acutely ill children. In implementing the objectives of this grant, Blake returned to the clinical arena, where she was actively involved in the study and provision of nursing care to acutely ill children undergoing open-heart surgery. Between 1961 and 1963 Blake worked part-time as a staff nurse for the Infant Welfare Association of Chicago while she was revising her pediatric nursing textbook.

In 1963 Blake was invited to the University of Wisconsin-Madison School of Nursing as professor of nursing and director of the graduate program in pediatric nursing. This was the first graduate program in nursing to be offered in the University of Wisconsin system. Its focus was on the development of advanced clinical nursing knowledge through the careful study of children and their response to hospitalization. The graduates of this program are now in positions of leadership in many parts of the world.

During much of her professional career, Blake frequently was invited to serve as a consultant in pediatric nursing to groups such as the U.S. Children's Bureau, the American Nurses' Association, the American Association for Child Care in Hospitals, and universities and hospitals throughout the country. She spoke at conventions of both the American Nurses' Association and the National League for Nursing.

Blake received a number of awards for her contribution to the nursing care of children. She was cited for special honors by Pi Lambda Theta at the University of Michigan in 1941. She also was presented awards from Teachers College, Columbia University (1968) and the American Nurses' Association (1974). Blake received the first annual award for distinguished contributions to parent-child nursing by the parent-child group of the University of Wisconsin-Madison School of Nursing in 1979.

Blake was a member of Pi Lambda Theta, the American Nurses' Association, and the National League for Nursing. She was elected an honorary member of the nurses' alumni organization of the University of Wisconsin-Madison School of Nursing. A charter member of the Friends of the Waisman Center on Mental Retardation and Human Development, she served on its board for several years.

Blake retired in Madison in 1970 and was awarded professor emeritus status by the university. In her retirement she was an active volunteer in the Older Adult Day Care Center of the Bethel Lutheran Church in Madison, a volunteer of the Madison Art Center, and a member of the Friends of the Madison Symphony. She died in Madison on September 12, 1983, and was buried in the family plot in Stevens Point. She was survived by two nieces.

Blake was an outstanding teacher, and her teaching influenced both nurses and physicians. She was among the first nurse educators to focus on the development of advanced clinical-nursing content and to advocate its inclusion in graduate programs at a time when the focus of advanced education tended to be on teaching and administration.

Blake developed a sophisticated case method for the systematic study of hospitalized children that was central to her teaching and her scholarly and clinical activities. She held high expectations of her students, consistently challenged them, and supported them without fail. She exemplified nursing care at its best to the many students who studied with her, her nurse colleagues, families, and the pediatricians who worked with her. The Florence Blake Nursing of Children Fund of the University of Wisconsin-Madison, a research and scholarship fund, was established under the provisions of her will.

## PUBLICATIONS BY
## FLORENCE GUINNESS BLAKE

### BOOKS

With P.C. Jeans and W. Rand. *Essentials of Pediatrics.* 4th ed. Philadelphia: J.B. Lippincott, 1946.

With E. Waechter. *Nursing Care of Children.* 9th ed. Philadelphia: J.B. Lippincott, 1946.

*The Child, His Parents, and the Nurse.* Philadelphia: J.B. Lippincott, 1954.

With P.C. Jeans and F.H. Wright. *Essentials of Pediatrics.* 5th and 6th ed. Philadelphia: J.B. Lippincott, 1954, 1958.

With F.H. Wright. *Essentials of Pediatric Nursing.* 7th ed. Philadelphia: J.B. Lippincott, 1963.

*Open Heart Surgery in Children: A Study in Nursing Care.* Washington, D.C.: U.S. Department of Health, Education, and Welfare, 1964.

With F.H. Wright and E. Waechter. *Nursing Care of Children.* 8th ed. Philadelphia: J.B. Lippincott, 1970.

### ARTICLES

"The Needs of a Student in a Pediatric Service." *American Journal of Nursing* 47 (October 1947): 692–95.

"Understanding Davy." *American Journal of Nursing* 54 (December 1954): 1495–98.

"The Supervisor's Task." *Nursing Outlook* 4 (November 1956): 641–43.

"In Quest of Hope and Autonomy." *Nursing Forum* 1 (Winter 1961–62): 8–32.

"A Search for Kathy's Problem." *International Journal of Nursing Studies* 2 (1965): 125–36.

"A Graduate Program in Pediatric Nursing." *International Journal of Nursing Studies* 5 (December 1968): 203.

"Immobilized Youth: A Rationale for Nursing Intervention." *American Journal of Nursing* 69 (November 1969): 2364–69.

### BIBLIOGRAPHY

Austin, D.W. "Children Help Faculty Teach Pediatric Nursing." *Milwaukee Journal,* 28 November 1964.

Blake, F.G. Curriculum vitae. School of Nursing files. University of Wisconsin-Madison.

Blake, F.G. Interview with author, 14 August 1975. Tape recording. School of Nursing, University of Wisconsin-Madison.

Blake, F.G. Papers. Archives. University of Wisconsin-Madison.

"Florence G. Blake." Obituary. *American Journal of Nursing* 84 (April 1984): 550.

"Florence G. Blake." Obituary. *Nursing Outlook* 31 November–December 1983): 342.

Memorial resolution of the faculty of the University of Wisconsin on the death of Emeritus Professor Florence G. Blake. Faculty document 540, 5 December 1983.

"Professor Emeritus Florence G. Blake," Obituary. *Wisconsin State Journal,* 13 September 1983.

Safier, G. "Florence G. Blake—Pediatric Nurse." In *Contemporary American Leaders in Nursing—An Oral History.* New York: McGraw-Hill, 1977.

Yost, E. "Florence G. Blake." In *American Women of Nursing.* Philadelphia: J.B. Lippincott, 1965.

Signe S. Cooper

## Florence Aby Blanchfield
### 1882–1971

As superintendent of the Army Nurse Corps (ANC), Florence Aby Blanchfield led the nation's largest military nursing organization through the tumult of global war. She was primarily responsible for building the Army Nurse Corps from an original strength of several hundred to the 57,000 nurses ultimately required to meet the tremendous demand for health care imposed by an army of nearly eight million soldiers and their families. Her tenacity and singleness of purpose were rewarded when members of the ANC became the first women to receive regular commissions in the United States Army.

Born in Shepherdstown, West Virginia, on April 1, 1882, Blanchfield was the second of three daughters and the fourth of eight children. Her father, Joseph Plunkett Blanchfield, was a stonemason and stonecutter of English and Irish descent. Her mother, Mary Louvenia Anderson Blanchfield, had a German and French background and was a practicing nurse. The healing professions were well ingrained in the family. Blanchfield's maternal grandfather and an uncle were both physicians, and all three daughters of Mary and Joseph Blanchfield became nurses. The youngest, Ruth, studied under her older sister Florence.

As a young girl, Blanchfield attended public schools in Walnut Springs, Virginia, from 1889 to 1898 and the Oranda Institute, a private high school in Oranda, Virginia, in 1898 and 1899. Her abiding interest in nursing further developed during her early adulthood while she nursed her younger brother Lloyd during his illness. Despite all efforts, Lloyd died of yellow fever at age 17, but Blanchfield's resolve to enter nursing strengthened.

Blanchfield studied nursing at Southside Hospital Training School for Nurses in Pittsburgh, Pennsylvania, and graduated in 1906. Her classmates described her as a tireless, precise student and a kind person.

After graduation Blanchfield continued her studies, attending Dr. Howard Kelly's Sanitarium and Johns Hopkins University while working as a private-duty nurse in Baltimore to defray her expenses. Her postgraduate course in operating-room supervision and technique prepared her to return to Pittsburgh in 1907 to assume a position as operating room supervisor at Southside Hospital and in 1908 a similar position at Montefiore Hospital.

Blanchfield established her executive talents in 1909 during her position as superintendent and director of the nursing school at Suburban General Hospital, Bellevue, Pennsylvania. She remained there until 1913, when she accepted a civil service appointment to the Panama Canal Zone. For six months she served in the Canal Zone as a surgical nurse and anesthetist for the Ancon Hospital. The high point of her tour, however, was her return as a passenger on one of the first ships to sail through the newly completed locks of the Panama Canal.

Upon returning to Pennsylvania, Blanchfield decided to continue her studies while working as an emergency nurse for the United States Steel Corporation in Bessemer. This allowed her to study full-time at nearby Martin Business College, graduating in 1915.

In 1916 Blanchfield returned as superintendent of nurses at Suburban General Hospital in Bellevue. The school prospered under her leadership, becoming an approved school of nursing.

The United States entered World War I in April 1917, and the U. S. Army quickened its pace to find qualified nurses to meet the urgent requirements of wartime. At the urging of several of her friends, Blanchfield obtained a military leave of absence from her position at Suburban General Hospital and joined the United States Army Nurse Corps in August 1917 as a reserve nurse. Less than a month later, she sailed for France with Base Hospital No. 27, based in Angers, France. Its staff was taken from the University of Pittsburgh Medical School. From December 1917 to January 1919, Blanchfield served as acting chief nurse at Camp Hospital No. 15, located at Camp Coetquidan, France, an artillery training area. Her leadership potential in the ANC was evident early in her service.

After the Armistice, Base Hospital No. 27 remained in France. In March 1919 the unit returned to the United States, and the reserve nurses' commitment terminated. Blanchfield left the army and resumed her position at Suburban General Hospital. Although she had enjoyed her brief term in military service, she felt obligated to return to the institution that had generously granted her a military leave of absence. Her stay at Suburban General, however, was short lived. Just eight months later, she reentered the ANC for a career in military nursing.

When Blanchfield commenced her second tour of duty in the army in January 1920, nurses had no military rank, but rather received titles such as nurse, chief nurse, or assistant superintendent. Early in her career, Blanchfield changed assignments frequently, serving first as a general duty nurse at Letterman General Hospital for four months and later as chief nurse at the camp hospital at Camp Custer, Michigan. In June 1920 ANC officers achieved "relative" rank, and Blanchfield became a first lieutenant. The honor was cosmetic, however, because the nurses did not receive pay, privileges, or authority equal to those of male officers of equal rank.

In October 1920 Blanchfield became chief nurse at the station hospital at Ft. Benjamin Harrison, Indiana, but returned to Letterman General Hospital in San

Francisco one year later. While an instructor and recreation director for the Army School of Nursing at Letterman, she found time to study dressmaking, public speaking, commercial law, and auto shop for women at the University of California. Later in her career she studied English composition via extension courses from Columbia University.

An overseas tour took Blanchfield to the Philippines in 1922, where she served as assistant chief nurse at Sternberg General Hospital and later as chief nurse at Camp John Hay. On her return to the United States, she reported to Walter Reed General Hospital in Washington, D.C. Her assignment placed her at the home of ailing Secretary of War John Wingate Weeks for special duty from April to October 1925. She returned to Walter Reed when he resigned due to poor health.

Frequent transfers had became a way of life for Blanchfield. Her assignment as chief nurse at Fort McPherson, Georgia, in 1925 provided her a rare opportunity for continuity. She remained at Fort McPherson for four years, departing in June 1929 to become chief nurse at Jefferson Barracks, Missouri. Enroute she stopped at Walter Reed for five months' duty.

Blanchfield's second tour in the Philippines began in February 1932. She served until October 1934 as chief nurse at Fort William McKinley, near Manila. She then received the unusual opportunity to serve in China, and from October 1934 to March 1935 she served as chief nurse for the army garrison on duty at Tientsin.

Blanchfield's nomadic life ended when she assumed new duties in the United States upon her return from China. She spent the next 12 years in key positions on the central staff of the ANC in Washington, D.C. Assigned first to the personnel section of the ANC, Office of the Surgeon General, from July 1935 to February 1939, she was responsible for nurse officer assignments, transfers, discharges, and other personnel aspects of officer records. This was a first step to positions of even greater responsibility.

Army Nurse Corps promotions through this time were limited. A nurse could expect to enter military service as a second lieutenant and serve her entire career in that rank unless she were allowed to test for a chief nurse position. If she passed the test, she could be promoted to first lieutenant, but only when a chief nurse's position became available. In all cases ranks remained relative ranks, denying nurses the full rights and privileges of commissioned officers in the U.S. Army.

Blanchfield received her cherished promotion to captain in 1939, when she was appointed assistant to the superintendent. At that time Superintendent Julia O. Flikke's overriding concern was the pressing need to expand the ANC. The European war that erupted in September 1939 forced President Franklin D. Roosevelt to declare a state of limited emergency. With only 625 army nurses on active duty, the superintendent of the ANC understood that thousands more would be required if the United States entered the war.

While Flikke and Blanchfield prepared to expand the ANC, Blanchfield also endeavored to gain the corps its proper place as a permanent corps within the army by winning commissioned status for nurses in the Regular Army. It was a difficult struggle. In March 1942, however, Flikke received a temporary commission in the Army of the United States (AUS) in the grade of colonel. Blanchfield rose to the rank of lieutenant colonel (AUS), although neither officer received commensurate pay for their rank. Ten years later in 1952, a special Congressional bill corrected that injustice and gave Flikke and Blanchfield their rightful back pay.

Blanchfield served temporarily as acting superintendent of the ANC beginning in March 1942. On July 1, 1943, after Flikke's official retirement due to poor health, the secretary of war appointed Blanchfield seventh superintendent of the ANC. Now a colonel, Blanchfield led the largest military nursing organization in U.S. history.

Monumental problems faced the new superintendent. In addition to the massive buildup in ANC officer strength, she had to provide the army with the necessary mixture of clinical specialties needed in wartime and orient a massive number of nurses to military life. Blanchfield insured the establishment of basic training centers to provide military orientation to new army nurses before their first duty assignments. Units receiving nurses noticed and commented on the positive influence this orientation had on the nurses' adaptability and attitudes.

To enhance the already vigorous recruitment effort, Blanchfield established the Army Nurse Branch of the Technical Information Service in the Office of the Surgeon General. This office dedicated its efforts to disseminating information about the ANC to civilian organizations. *The Army Nurse*, a monthly publication sharing information and serving as a forum for discussion, also resulted from the efforts of this office, as did the "Army Nurse Corps Song," ANC song book and ring. Information officers stationed in Europe and the Pacific provided many of the best, and occasionally the only, accounts of nursing activities in the field. Blanchfield had adopted this approach for recruiting nurses because she strongly opposed a draft of nurses.

One of Blanchfield's major achievements was to ensure that the wounded combat soldier received immediate surgical and postoperative nursing care. She deployed nurses in field and evacuation hospitals, thus moving them closer to the front lines than ever before. She also realized her efforts to modernize the archaic nurse uniform, and when nurses landed on the Anzio Beachhead in Italy in February 1944, they landed in fatigue uniforms, which were eminently more practical in a field hospital than the standard white hospital uniforms.

The drive for full military rank for nurses continued throughout World War II. Blanchfield enlisted the support of Congresswoman Frances Payne Bolton, and in 1944 they won temporary commissions for army nurses for the duration of the war plus six months. This fell short of their goal, but they realized it was the best they could achieve under wartime conditions. The Army-Navy Nurse Act of 1947 achieved their ultimate goal. In this act, Congress authorized creation of the ANC within the Regular Army and provided that nurses commissioned in the ANC should enjoy the same pay and promotion privileges as officers of similar rank in other branches of the service. This achievement, 46 years after the establishment of the corps, would have been impossible without Blanchfield's tireless effort and superior executive ability. On July 18, 1947, General Dwight D. Eisenhower, the Army Chief of Staff, commissioned Blanchfield a lieutenant colonel in the Regular Army. She thus became the first woman to receive a Regular Army commission.

Blanchfield faced formidable problems in administering a nursing service that reached a peak of 57,000 members by 1945, yet she never lost her abiding concern for the individual officer. Her correspondence is replete with personal letters exchanged with army nurses stationed worldwide. She frequently visited army facilities throughout the United States and overseas to inspect and visit her nurses and made three extended trips to Europe, the Antilles, and the Far East. A talented leader, she remained alert to nurses' problems and listened to identify their needs in the field. She molded the shape of ANC activities in the immediate postwar years based on her direct observations during these trips.

In particular, specialty training of nurses was a critical concern during the war years and immediately after. Blanchfield insisted that the inculcation of the standards required to render proper and safe care to patients lay in permanently established schools founded on a sound curriculum and expert instruction. Under Blanchfield's guidance in the postwar era, the ANC established specialized schools for training in anesthesia, neuropsychiatric nursing, air-evacuation nursing, pediatrics, obstetrics, and operating-room administration. Based on her suggestion, the Army Medical Department established a school of administration for all medical department officers. This has evolved into a two-year master's degree program in health care administration.

The war in Europe ended in May 1945 and in the Pacific four months later. Soon thereafter the army demobilized nearly 50,000 of the 57,000 nurses on active duty, even though requirements still existed to offer a full range of treatment capabilities for soldiers and their families in the United States and occupied countries. The problems of relocation, reassignment, and retraining created tremendous turmoil in the corps, felt nowhere more keenly than in the superintendent's office. Blanchfield was determined that neither nursing care nor her dream of an education system for specialty nurses would be sacrificed to achieve demobilization goals. Her efforts ensured that they were not. By the first anniversary of V-J Day, ANC rolls had dropped to 8,500. Nevertheless, in June 1946 a psychiatric nursing course opened, and in July 1947 a 56-week anesthesia program commenced at four army medical facilities around the country. Furthermore, two 24-week operating-room technique and management courses also began.

Blanchfield met each challenge presented to the ANC with characteristic vigor and exceptional executive ability. In 1945 the army officially recognized her contributions and awarded her the Distinguished Service Medal, its highest award for meritorious service. It was the first such award made to an army nurse in World War II. Her other military service awards include the World War I Victory Medal, the American Campaign Medal, the World War II Victory Medal, and the European, African, Middle East Campaign Medal.

In September 1947 Blanchfield retired from active duty after more than 29 years of devoted service to the ANC and her country. During her professional career she also served as secretary of the Philippine Islands Committee on Red Cross Nursing Service and for five years as a member of the District of Columbia Committee on Red Cross Nursing Service. She was also a member of the National Committee of the American Red Cross for three years. Other affiliations included the Southside Hospital Nursing Alumnae Association, the American Nurses' Association, the National League of Nursing Education, the National Nursing Council for War Service, and the Joint Committee on Women Reserves. In 1951 she received the highest award possible for a nurse, The

Florence Nightingale Medal of the International Red Cross, presented by the American National Red Cross for exceptional service on behalf of humanity. In recognition of her lifelong interest in sports, a perpetual trophy for the all-army women's tennis singles championship was named in her honor, and she presented the first winner's trophy in 1956. The state of West Virginia presented its native daughter its Distinguished Service Medal in 1963.

Following her army retirement, Blanchfield coauthored a manuscript history of the ANC. She also pursued her many other interests in reading, writing, travel, and spectator sports. She took special delight in watching the educational field in nursing expand and in seeing collegiate education in nursing grow. As early as 1916, she had voiced the conviction that every superintendent of a school of nursing needed a college education.

In her later years, Blanchfield lived with her sister Ruth and brother-in-law in Arlington, Virginia. On May 12, 1971, she died at Walter Reed Army Medical Center of atherosclerotic cardiac disease and was buried with full honors at Arlington National Cemetery. On September 17, 1982, the Army Medical Department again honored her memory when it dedicated the Colonel Florence A. Blanchfield Army Community Hospital at Fort Campbell, Kentucky. Perhaps the most enduring monument to "the little Colonel," as she was fondly called, it symbolizes her life of proud leadership and untiring service to the United States soldier.

### PUBLICATIONS BY
### FLORENCE ABY BLANCHFIELD

#### ARTICLES

"The Needs of the Army Nurse Corps." *American Journal of Nursing* 43 (November 1943): 991–92.

"New Status in Military Nursing." *American Journal of Nursing* 47 (September 1947): 603–05.

#### BIBLIOGRAPHY

Aynes, E.A. "Colonel Florence A. Blanchfield." *Nursing Outlook* 7 (February 1959): 78–81.

Blanchfield, F.A. "The Army Nurse Corps in World War II." Washington, D.C.: U.S. Army Center of Military History. Unpublished.

Blanchfield, F.A. Interview by E. Dent, *Washington Star*, 23 February 1964.

Blanchfield, F.A. Interview by K. Jump and C. Ferebee, Army Nurse Corps, U.S. Army Center of Military History, March–April 1968.

Blanchfield, F.A. "Organized Nursing and the Army in Three Wars." Washington, D.C.: U.S. Army Center of Military History. Unpublished.

Blanchfield, F.A. Papers. Colonel Florence A. Blanchfield Collection, Nursing Archives. Mugar Library, Boston University, Boston.

Blanchfield, F.A. Papers. U.S. Army Center of Military History, Washington, D.C.

"Blanchfield, Florence A." *Current Biography*. Bronx, N.Y.: H.W. Wilson, 1943.

"Blanchfield, Florence A." *Who Was Who in America, Vol. 7, 1977*–1981. Chicago: Marquis Who's Who, 1982.

Egge, D.W. *A Concise Biography of Colonel Florence Aby Blanchfield, ANC.* Washington, D.C.: U.S. Army Center of Military History, 1974.

"Florence A. Blanchfield." Obituary. *New York Times*, 14 May 1971.

"Florence A. Blanchfield." Obituary. *Washington Post*, 14 May 1971.

Henry, L.J. "Blanchfield, Florence Aby." In *Notable American Women, The Modern Period*, edited by B. Sicherman, and C.H. Green. Cambridge, Mass.: Belknap Press of Harvard University Press, 1980.

National Archives. Records of the Army Nurse Corps. Surgeon General's Office, Record Group 112.

Cindy Gurney

# Mabel Thorp Boardman

## 1860–1946

Mabel Thorp Boardman never studied nursing, nor did she ever practice as a volunteer nurse, yet she has earned a place in the records of American nursing because of her ceaseless efforts to organize and stabilize the American Red Cross. She directly influenced the role of nurses in the critical pre–World War I period, and in the immediate postwar period she was influential in the Town and Country program.

Boardman was born in Cleveland, Ohio, October 10, 1860, the first of three daughters and three sons of William and Florence Sheffield Boardman. Both of her parents came from prominent New England families, and her father was a well-established lawyer. Boardman grew up in a wealthy environment and received her education in private schools in New York and Ohio. Like many of her social class, she became interested in social welfare projects through serving as a volunteer with various groups in Cleveland in the 1880s. She left this to live and travel abroad with her uncle, William Walter Phelps, United States Minister to Germany from 1889 to 1893.

In 1893 she again joined her parents, then living in Washington D.C., and threw herself into volunteer work, particularly the Children's Hospital. It was through this connection that she made her first contact with professional nurses. Her interest in nursing increased when she became part of a campaign to recruit nurses to serve in the Spanish-American War. In 1900 she became part of an effort to regularize the workings of the Red Cross, founded and still headed by Clara Barton, then in her 80's. Boardman soon found herself at odds with Barton, and when Barton was removed from the executive committee, the result was a split in the organization. After Barton retired, Boardman was elected president of the American Red Cross. She used her knowledge of foreign Red Cross societies to redesign the national charter of the Red Cross here, which received congressional approval and was signed by President Theodore Roosevelt in 1905.

From 1905 until 1915, Boardman worked tirelessly to increase support for the American Red Cross, financially, politically, and professionally. She traveled, raised funds, and persuaded professional organizations, such as the American Nurses' Association, to support the organization. Boardman envisioned a multifaceted volunteer organization which would have disaster relief as only one of its activities.

Boardman proved a staunch ally of nurses and felt they should have their own division within the American Red Cross, and that this division should be directed by nurses. This reorganization which seems quite simple was difficult to implement since the Red Cross was not a unified body but a diverse collection of small and large chapters. The reorganization took numerous visits, countless speeches, and much correspondence.

Jane Delano was appointed by Boardman to organize and direct the newly established nurses department in 1909. Boardman gave Delano and her committee, mainly recruited from the American Nurses' Association, all the support possible from the national staff. The organizational efforts of both women received a boost with the outbreak of the World War I, when the nurses bureau managed to recruit and place over 20,000 nurses during the war. Even before the war the nurses had served with distinction in the Serbian typhus epidemic of 1914.

After the war, Boardman continued to support new roles for nurses in the Red Cross, most notably through the Red Cross Town and Country nursing service. In addition to her interest in organizational work, Boardman was an energetic fund raiser and a key figure in raising the money for the national headquarters of the Red Cross as well as other activities of the Red Cross. Though she strongly believed in volunteerism, she also wanted a strong nursing profession in which the nurses were well clothed, fed, and provided for in order to meet the human ills that they encountered.

Boardman spent almost all of her life serving the Red Cross in various capacities and although the world and her organization changed through the years, she remained firm in her belief in the importance and value of volunteerism. Her most effective period, was from 1910 to 1925, which was so crucial to the emergence of nursing. She received many medals from many countries as well as honorary degrees from Yale, Western Reserve, and George Washington universities and Smith College. She died in Washington, D.C., March 17, 1946, and was buried in the National Cathedral there.

## PUBLICATIONS BY MABEL THORP BOARDMAN

### BOOKS

*Under the Red Cross Flag at Home and Abroad.* Philadelphia: Lippincott, 1915, 2d ed., 1917.

### SPEECHES AND PAMPHLETS

*Miss Boardman's Answer to the Letter of the Red Cross Executive Committee Notifying Her of Her Suspension.* Washington, D.C.: N.p., 1903.

*Conservation, the Principle of the Red Cross.* An address before the National Conservation Congress. St. Paul, Minn.: National Conservation Council, 1910.

*Report of War Relief Activities 1917–1919.* Washington, D.C.: Red Cross. District of Columbia Chapter, 1919.

### BIBLIOGRAPHY

Boardman, Mabel T. Personal Papers. Library of Congress, Washington, D.C.

Boardman, Mabel T. Clippings et al. Archives of the American Red Cross, Washington D.C.

Dock, Lavinia L., et al. *History of American Red Cross Nursing.* New York: Macmillan, 1922.

Dulles, Rhea Foster. *The American Red Cross: A History.* New York: Harper, 1950.

Elsey, George. "Mabel Thorp Boardman." In *Notable American Women,* edited by E.T. James. Vol. 1. Cambridge, Mass.: Harvard University Press, 1971, 183–85.

Linda Sabin

# Frances Payne Bingham Bolton

## 1885–1977

Frances Payne Bingham Bolton was known for her continued support of nursing, although she was a nurses' aide only temporarily. She championed nursing and nursing education in both world wars, and she gave generously to establish a nursing school and other social-service institutions.

Bolton was born Frances Payne Bingham on March 29, 1885, in Cleveland, Ohio. The fourth of five children of

Charles William and Mary Perry Payne Bingham, she came from a successful and wealthy family. Both her father and mother traced their families back to early English colonists, and her ancestors included such notables as Robert Treat Paine, signer of the Declaration of Independence, and John Howard Payne, author of "Home Sweet Home." Her maternal grandfather, Henry B. Payne, was a U.S. senator from Ohio, and her paternal great-grandfather and grandfather served in the Ohio legislature.

As a descendent of two of the wealthiest families in Cleveland, Bolton was heavily influenced by the money and social obligations she inherited. Her father distinguished himself at Yale and was later successful in steel, coal, copper, and banking. Her uncle and later benefactor began his fortune with John D. Rockefeller before entering other financial and industrial activity.

Bolton's early education was neither consistent nor rigorous. The family traveled between their country house in Ohio and Palm Beach, Florida, because her brother benefited from the southern climate. With the aid of her tutor, she learned of the sea, the stars, and scattered bits of languages but otherwise received little formal education. At the death of her mother when Bolton was 14, she was sent to an exclusive school outside Paris, where she studied French and Spanish for two years. She then traveled to New York City to enter Miss Spence's School for Girls and to study briefly at the Mannes Music School. Although she did not graduate or develop her promising soprano voice, she returned to Cleveland in 1904 ready to adopt her role as debutante.

The next several years were crucial to Bolton's appreciation of nurses and their profession. Debutantes in Cleveland at the turn of the century traditionally adopted a social cause, and Bolton's group became the Visiting Nurse Supply Corps. They accompanied visiting nurses, carried their heavy supply bags, and helped the nurses in their ministrations to the sick and the poor. Coming in contact with people and conditions that she never would have encountered otherwise, Bolton later reminisced that the opportunity broadened

her life. So extraordinary were the group's duties that her father, upon learning of his daughter's activities for the first time, told her he would not have approved initially but encouraged her to continue her activities. The work gave her an enthusiasm for nursing and an appreciation of nurses' training.

In 1907 Bolton married a long-time acquaintance, Chester Castle Bolton. A Harvard graduate and rising steel industrialist, his fortune later gave him the title of "richest man in Congress." From 1909 to 1917 Bolton gave birth to three sons: Charles, Kenyon, and Oliver.

With the outbreak of World War I, Bolton moved with her husband to Washington, D.C., where he served on the Munitions Standard Board and with the army. She became chair of a special war program committee of the National Organization for Public Health Nursing. She was instrumental in winning from a long-time neighbor, Secretary of War Newton D. Baker, approval of Miss Annie Goodrich's Army School of Nursing after the plan had been rejected initially by the army's general staff.

Bolton filled the two decades after the war with philanthropic activity that benefited nursing and education. Inheriting a fortune from her uncle in 1917 and returning to Cleveland in 1918, she soon became a member of the board of trustees of Lakeside Hospital and served on its nursing committee. She and her sister and brother furnished the old Perry homestead for the creation of a nursing center, Perry House.

Increasingly enthusiastic about nursing education, Bolton proposed to endow a school of nursing at the Western Reserve University; from 1923 to 1928 she contributed $1.5 million as part of a program to encourage other donations. She remained active in the administration of the Frances Payne Bolton School of Nursing. In the 1920s Bolton also served on the Committee on the Grading of Nursing Schools and gave the organization $93,000, which along with donations from thousands of nurses funded the first systematic survey of nursing schools in the United States. She also created and supplied the Possum Bend Center of the

Frontier Nursing Service in the Kentucky Mountains. Committed to education in general, Bolton established two research institutions: the Payne Fund, which studied literature and films and their affect on juveniles, and a research fund for parapsychology at Duke University.

The sudden death of her husband in October 1939 and her election to his congressional seat in 1940 marked the beginning of Bolton's political career and her efforts to benefit nursing through governmental means. Her husband had been a member of the Ohio legislature from 1922 and a representative from Ohio in Washington, D.C., since 1929. Bolton had helped in her husband's election campaign of 1932 and had become active as vice-chair of the National Republican Program Committee from 1937 to 1940 and a member of the Republican State Central Committee of Ohio in 1938–40. After successfully standing for election to the House as a Republican in February 1940, Bolton became concerned about nursing education should the United States enter World War II. In the summer of 1941, she was instrumental in the congressional appropriation of $1.25 million for nursing education; this program was so successful that in 1942 the amount was raised to $3.5 million. These funds aimed to increase enrollment in nursing schools, to prepare additional teachers and personnel in the nursing field, and to provide refresher courses for inactive nurses willing to return to active positions.

This legislation laid the foundation for the Bolton Act of 1943 and further nursing legislation. In 1942 Bolton sponsored the Nurse Training Act, more commonly known as the Bolton Act, that created the U.S. Cadet Nurse Corps. Passed by Congress in 1943, this massive governmental program offered prospective nursing students free schooling, uniforms, and a small stipend for a 30-month period in return for their pledge to enter the armed forces upon their graduation or to participate in critical civilian nursing. The government was obligated to give participating universities both short-term payments and long-term assistance to expand nursing facilities. The act alone was responsible for

training 125,000 nurses in two years and enjoyed the cooperation of 1,125 nursing schools. Although the act had the disadvantage of solving the nursing shortage through student services, its more positive attributes—in addition to the nurses educated—were a streamlined training period, the improvement of educational facilities, and the prohibition of any discrimination on the basis of race or marital status.

Bolton followed the U.S. Cadet Nurse Corps legislation with many other efforts to improve the position of nurses. In 1943 and 1944 she worked to equalize the pay of nurses with that of male officers of similar rank and to raise the rank of the Army Nurse Corps by giving its members regular officers' commissions. Also in 1944 she traveled to England and France to see firsthand the care of wounded American soldiers; she therefore became the first woman in Congress to enter a war theater.

After the war, Bolton sponsored another bill in 1951 to provide $47 million for long-range nursing education. But the American Medical Association opposed the bill, and it died in committee. In 1954 she authored the congressional resolution that resulted in the presidential proclamation of National Nurse Week. In 1955 she successfully shepherded through Congress an act encouraging the military to commission male nurses as reserve officers, and she later introduced legislation to give them regular commissioned rank.

Bolton distinguished herself not only with nursing legislation, but also with other social-service concerns. Although she followed the Republican party's fiscal policy and voted against rent subsidies to the poor and in favor of using the Taft-Hartley Act to halt a steel strike in 1952, she also voted for the Civil Rights Act of 1964 and for poverty programs in 1967. She urged the nation's support for the United Nations International Children's Emergency Fund in 1953, and she was instrumental in the creation of Piscataway Park to preserve the view across the Potomac River from Mount Vernon.

Bolton's other love while in Congress was foreign affairs, and by the time of her retirement she was the ranking minority member of that House committee. She arranged for extensive trips to the Soviet Union immediately following the war in 1945 and to Africa in 1955. After each journey, she published reports, the more famous being the committee's *The Strategy and Tactics of World Communism* in 1948. After her extensive African tour she adopted a benevolent attitude toward the continent but was criticized by many experts for her superficial knowledge of the land and for doing nothing legislatively to support the Africans. She helped shape Republican foreign policy platforms, was appointed to the United Nations as a delegate in 1953, and held many assignments outside Congress related to foreign policy.

Throughout her long life as benefactor and legislator, Bolton displayed poise, warmth, and an instinct for personal relations. By the time she lost her House seat in 1968 when she was 83 years of age, she had received numerous awards and honorary degrees. Among those were the William Freeman Snow Award of the American Social Hygiene Association, the M. Adelaide Nutting Award of the National League of Nursing Education, and the wings and the award of honorary flight nurse of the U.S. Air Force. She also belonged to many organizations, among them the Daughters of the American Revolution, the League of Women Voters in Cleveland, and the Pen and Brush club of New York City. After her defeat in the election of 1968, she became trustee of several colleges and the Central School of Practical Nursing in Cleveland. After several months of ill health, she died in Lyndhurst, Ohio, on March 9, 1977.

## PUBLICATIONS BY FRANCES PAYNE BINGHAM BOLTON

### BOOKS

*Letters from Africa.* Washington, D.C.: N.p., 1955.

*This and That from Washington.* Washington, D.C.: N.p., 1955.

### ARTICLES

"Bolton Act—Implications for the Present and Future." *Modern Hospital* 61 (September 1943): 59–60.

"Report to Congress on the Nursing Shortage: Crisis in Health Care." *Hospitals* 28 (April 1954): 83–85.

## PUBLIC DOCUMENTS

U.S. Congress. House. Committee on Foreign Affairs. *Report on the Strategy and Tactics of World Communism.* Washington, D.C.: U.S. Government Printing Office, 1948.

———. *Report of the Special Study Mission to Africa, South and East of the Sahara.* Washington, D.C.: U.S. Government Printing Office, 1956.

## BIBLIOGRAPHY

*American Journal of Nursing* 42 (February 1942): 180.

*American Journal of Nursing* 44 (December 1944): 1178.

"Bolton, Frances P." *Current Biography.* 1940, 1954.

"Bolton, Frances P." *The National Cyclopaedia of American Biography.* Vol. K. New York: James T. White, 1967.

"Bolton, Frances P." *Who's Who in America.* 38th ed. Vol. 1. 1974–75.

Bullough, V.L., and B. Bullough. *The Care of the Sick: The Emergence of Modern Nursing.* New York: Prodist, 1978.

Chamberlin, H. *A Minority of Members: Women in the U.S. Congress.* New York: Praeger, 1973.

Dolan, J.A. *Goodnow's History of Nursing.* 11th ed. Philadelphia: W.B. Saunders Co., 1963.

"Frances P. Bolton." Obituary. *Current Biography Yearbook, 1977.* New York: H.W. Wilson Co., 1977.

"Frances P. Bolton." Obituary. *New York Times,* 10 March 1977.

Kalisch, P.A., and B.J. Kalisch. *The Advance of American Nursing.* Boston: Little, Brown, 1978.

Lamson, P. *Few Are Chosen. American Women in Political Life Today.* Boston: Houghton Mifflin, 1968.

Loth, D. *A Long Way Forward: The Biography of Congresswoman Frances P. Bolton.* New York: Longmans, 1957.

"Mrs. Chester Bolton." *American Journal of Nursing* 32 (May 1932): 549–50.

Paxton, A. *Women in Congress.* Richmond, Va.: Dietz Press, 1945.

Pennock, M.R. *Makers of Nursing History: Portraits and Pen Sketches of Fifty-Nine Prominent Women.* New York: Lakeside, 1928.

"Presentation of the 1949 Award of the Snow

Medal." *Journal of Social Hygiene* 35 (March 1949): 115–16.

Roberts, M.M. *American Nursing: History and Interpretation.* New York: Macmillan, 1954.

Roosevelt, E., and L.A. Hickok. *Ladies of Courage.* New York: G.P. Putnam's Sons, 1954.

"William Freeman Snow Award for Distinguished Service to Humanity Presented to Frances Payne Bolton." *Journal of Social Hygiene* 35 (February 1949): 97–100.

Kenneth S. Mernitz

# Mary Breckinridge

## 1881–1965

Mary Breckinridge introduced the first modern rural comprehensive health-care system in the United States. To provide professional service to neglected residents of a 1,000-square-mile area in southeastern Kentucky, she created a decentralized system for primary nursing-care services comprising nurse midwives, district nursing centers, and hospital facilities. She also was a key factor in the growth of nurse midwives in the United States.

Breckinridge was born in Memphis, Tennessee, on February 17, 1881, the eldest daughter and second of four children of Clifton Rhodes and Katherine Carson Breckinridge. Her father was the son of John C. Breckinridge, vice-president of the United States in the Administration of President James Buchanan and later a major general in the Confederacy as well as secretary of war. Breckinridge's father was a U.S. Representative from Arkansas and in 1890 he was appointed as minister to Russia during President Grover Cleveland's second administration. He also held other important political appointments.

Breckinridge was educated by private tutors during her early years. Between 1896–98 she attended the Rosemont-Dézaley School in Lausanne, Switzerland, and from 1898–99 she was sent to the Low and Heywood School in Stamford, Connecticut. Though she wanted to attend college, her family did not think college was suitable for a woman of her standing and class. She then lived in the Indian territories (now part of Oklahoma) when her father was appointed a commissioner to the Five Civilized Tribes. She also spent several summers in the Muskosa Lakes area in Ontario, where her family had a summer home.

Breckinridge was married twice. Her first marriage to Henry Ruffner Morrison in 1904 ended with his death from appendicitis in 1906. On October 8, 1912, she married Richard Ryan Thompson, president of Crescent College and Conservatory for Young Women in Eureka Springs, Arkansas. She taught French and hygiene at the school during the first years of marriage. She had two children from this marriage, a son, Breckenridge, born in 1914, and a daughter, Mary, born in 1916. Her daughter died a few hours after birth, and her son died January 23, 1918. Breckinridge left her husband in June 1918 and divorced him in 1920, resuming her maiden name.

It was after she was first widowed that Breckinridge decided to become a nurse, motivated in part by the illness of the child of a friend. She entered St. Luke's Hospital School of Nursing in New York in 1907 and graduated in 1910. However, she did not immediately work as a nurse but again became a wife and later a mother. Following the death of her son, she volunteered to serve as a nurse in World War I, but because she already had a brother in the service, she had to wait for special permission. Breckinridge was in Washington, D.C., when the influenza epidemic of 1918 struck, and she was put in charge of one of the five medical areas, where she supervised five other nurses and a number of hastily trained aides. Encouraged by this test of her abilities, she volunteered to travel to France after the war on behalf of the American Committee for Devastated France. She attended a special course in Boston, sponsored by the Visiting Nursing Association, while awaiting her sailing papers. During her two-year stay in France, she organized a child-hygiene and visiting-nurse association, and for this she received the Medaille Reconnaissance Française.

By the time of her return to the United States from France in 1921, Breckinridge had decided to work among the poor children in her ancestral state of Kentucky. To prepare herself, she attended Teachers College, Columbia University, from 1923–24 to learn the latest developments in public health. She spent her summers riding about the Kentucky mountains and found neither physician nor nurse in the mountainous and roadless areas, only unskilled midwives.

Breckinridge soon realized she needed to become qualified as a midwife, which she did at the British Hospital for Mothers and Babies in the Woolwich area of London in 1923. After she received her certificate, she toured the nursing stations of the Scottish Highlands and the Inner and Outer Hebrides to gain further ideas about rural nursing before returning to Kentucky.

In 1925 at Wendover, Kentucky, Breckinridge organized the Kentucky Committee for Mothers and Babies, which in 1928 became the Frontier Nursing Service (FNS), financed in large part through a legacy she had received from her mother. By 1930 she had established six outpost nursing centers covering an area of 700 square miles and nearly 10,000 people. She also established medical, surgical, and dental clinics and provided nursing and midwifery services 24 hours a day, aided in large part by gifts she received from committees of supporters she had established.

Staff members of the FNS in 1929 formed the incipient American College of Nurse Midwives, and the first school of nurse midwives was started at the Maternity Center in New York in 1932 by a FNS member. The center of the FNS was in Hyden, Kentucky, where a hospital and health center was developed beginning in 1928, and where in 1939 a graduate school of midwifery was formed. If a husband could get a message through to a nurse midwife, the FNS promised that the midwife would travel to the expectant wife, usually on horseback. As the nursing service became organized, Breckinridge spent more of her time raising funds, but she usually returned quickly to Hyden.

The depression years in the 1930s cut into the funds available to the FNS, and both staff and salaries were cut although the service continued to function. It also survived the traumas of World War II, when many of its British nurses returned home. By 1951 the nurse midwives had delivered 8,596 babies, 6,533 of them in the homes of the mothers. In only 50 cases had it been necessary to use forceps, and of the 40 cesareans, 19 of them were due to a contracted pelvis. These figures were very low for the time. In fact, her success in lowering the death rate in childbirth and of infants substantially below the national average has been frequently cited as proof of the benefits of nurse midwives.

In the last years of Breckinridge's life, she received many honors, including an honorary doctor of laws degree from the University of Kentucky, the Eleanor Van Rensselaer Fairfax Medal from the National Society of Colonial Dames, the Distinguished Service Medal from the National Federation of Business and Professional Women's Clubs, and the Mary Adelaide Nutting Award of the National League of Nursing. Breckinridge died May 16, 1965, in Hyden, Kentucky.

## PUBLICATIONS BY MARY BRECKINRIDGE

### BOOKS

*Wide Neighborhoods: A Story of the Frontier Nursing Service.* New York: Harper and Brothers, 1952.

### PAMPHLETS

*The Nurse-Midwife—A Pioneer. American Journal of Public Health* (November 1927).

*Matins and Evensong.* Lexington, 1935.

### ARTICLES

Many articles, both signed and unsigned, appear in *Frontier Nursing Service Quarterly Bulletin.*

## BIBLIOGRAPHY

Crowe-Carraco, C. "Mary Breckinridge and the Frontier Nursing Service." *Register*, Kentucky Historical Society, July 1978.

Dodge, B.S. *The Story of Nursing.* Boston: Little, Brown, 1954.

Faust, D.G. "Mary Breckinridge." *Notable American Women.* Vol. 4. Cambridge. Belnap

Press of Harvard University Press, 1980. pp. 103–105.

Obituary. *New York Times*, 17 May 1965.

Poole, E. *Nurses on Horseback.* New York: Macmillan, 1933.

Wilkie, K.E., and E.R. Mosely. *Frontier Nurse: Mary Breckinridge.* New York: Julian Messner, 1969.

Vern L. Bullough

# Frances V. Brink

## 1889–1978

Rural nursing, public-health nursing, and hospital nursing were all areas of Frances V. Brink's experience. As superintendent of nurses of the Minnesota State Board of Health, she was responsible for the supervision and growth of rural and state nursing in Minnesota. She brought the wealth of these state experiences to her position as the assistant director of the National Organization for Public Health Nursing. Her employment in administrative and educational positions in institutions such as Bellevue Hospital, New York; Milwaukee County Hospital, Wisconsin; and the Children's Memorial Hospital in Chicago added to the impact of her leadership in hospital nursing and nursing education.

Brink was born February 14, 1889, in the small town of Goodwin, South Dakota. Her father, Andrew Christian Brink, was active in state government and public affairs, having served as a state senator during Brink's childhood. Her mother was Albertina Johnstone Brink. Frances had one brother and one sister.

While her origins were in a small town, Brink received her nursing education in the Philadelphia Hospital Training School for Nurses. The philosophy of this school exerted an influence on Brink that surfaced in her later years as an administrator and teacher of nursing. She later was described by her students at Milwaukee County Hospital School of Nursing as a disciplinarian with high expectations

who was devoted and committed to her students.

After graduation and staff-nurse work at Philadelphia General Hospital, Brink became active in the advancement of public-health nursing. As superintendent of nurses of the Minnesota State Board of Health, Brink conducted a survey of state board of health executives and supervising nurses to determine the practices of various states in regard to governmental or nongovernmental supervision of field public-health nursing. The results of that survey were published in *The Public Health Nurse* in 1920. While holding this supervisory position in Minnesota, Brink also acted as a representative of the department of nursing of the northern division of the Red Cross and was responsible for Red Cross public-health nursing in Minnesota.

Following economic cutbacks by Minnesota legislators that resulted in the abolition of the superintendent's position, Brink accepted a staff position in the National Organization for Public Health Nursing in 1921. This organization, founded in 1912, concentrated on the establishment of public-health nursing as a nursing speciality. In her assignment as field secretary to the organization, Brink traveled throughout the United States to assist individual public-health nurses and public-health organizations in identifying and solving problems. In addition, the field secretary acted as liaison between the national headquarters and the field. Brink continued in this position until a lessened need for the field service, coupled with decreased funding, forced her resignation in 1926.

After her public-health experiences, Brink's attention turned toward hospital and nursing education. She filled the position of assistant director of nursing at Bellevue Hospital, New York, from 1927 to 1931. She then served as superintendent of nursing and principal of the school of nursing at Milwaukee County Hospital from 1931–1944.

In 1931, Milwaukee County Hospital was in the process of completing a large, new hospital. While the Milwaukee County Hospital School of Nursing had been in operation since 1888, the building of a larger hospital necessitated an expansion of the school of nursing. In a recollection of her experiences, Brink aptly described the situation that prompted the previous superintendent to accept 57 applications from young women, the largest class ever to enter the school in September 1931. Brink wrote that at that time, student nurses were still regarded as necessary economical labor.

Brink recognized the difficulty of nurses seeking employment during the depression years of 1931 through 1933. As a result of her efforts, the number of student admissions was decreased, and the available graduate nurse positions in the hospital increased.

During this same period, Brink wrote in her memoirs that there had been a general move in the city and state to consider an eight-hour shift for private-duty nurses and for graduate nurses employed in hospitals. Brink chaired a citywide committee of nurses and doctors in Milwaukee who met to adopt this proposal. The eight-hour day for nurses at Milwaukee County Hospital became a reality, thereby shortening their work week to 48 hours from 58 hours. Brink noted that at the same time the salaries for the supervisors, head nurses, and floor nurses also improved.

While superintendent of nursing at Milwaukee County Hospital, Brink put her creative talents to use in devising a new, more humane form of restraints to be used with restless patients. Her invention was named the "Brinksides" and was a device consisting of a canvas strip laced with holes that replaced the wooden bars formerly used on the beds of such patients.

Accreditation of nursing schools was implemented by the National League for Nursing Education during this period. It was during Brink's tenure as superintendent that Milwaukee County Hospital School of Nursing became one of the first schools in the nation to receive national accreditation.

In 1944 Brink left Milwaukee County Hospital to take the position of director of nursing and principal of the school of nursing at Children's Memorial Hospital, Chicago. This hospital was a forerunner in its mission to supplement medical care with social work and in its role as a hospital founded and managed by women. Until 1951 all paid administrators were women. Brink later described how she cherished her recollections of her experiences there.

Numerous positions in a consulting role followed. Brink held a three-year position with the Florida State Tuberculosis Department, during which she dispensed nursing scholarships to those who intended to work in the state's four tuberculosis hospitals. In addition she acted as consultant to these hospitals. Brink considered this a great experience, and it offered her the opportunity to travel to Cuba.

An offer to consult in the reorganization of the Morris Memorial Polio Hospital in Milton, West Virginia, was the next highlight of her career. The hospital cared for polio cases and with the advent of the polio vaccine was eased out of existence in the late 1950s. However, it was this consulting position that brought Brink to Huntington, West Virginia, which became her home for the remainder of her life.

Instruction and administration at St. Mary's School of Nursing and at the West Virginia State Mental Hospital in Huntington were her final accomplishments in her nursing career. According to Brink's writings to a former student, while in her 70s she also wrote a procedure book for a nursing home and provided some consulting services regarding nursing-home establishment.

Brink lived to the age of 89 and enjoyed reasonably good health, although she suffered fractures of her hip, leg, and foot. The last few years of her life were spent in the Morris Memorial Nursing Home in Milton, West Virginia. Though she lived alone, Brink was never lonely, due to her pleasant memories, good friends, books, and beautiful scenery.

Brink died on June 20, 1978 in Milton, West Virginia. Her siblings had preceded her in death, and her survivors included two nieces, two nephews, and one great-niece. No visitation or service was held at the time of her death. However, contributions were suggested to a medical education fund at the Marshall University Medical School, West Virginia.

## PUBLICATIONS BY FRANCES V. BRINK

### ARTICLES

"An Analysis of Present State Recognition of Public Health Nursing." *Public Health Nurse* 12 (1920): 849–58.

"Suggestions for the County Nurse." *Public Health Nurse* 13 (1921): 172–75.

"Activities of the National Organization for Public Health Nursing: The Field Service." *Public Health Nurse* 15 (1923): 205–6.

### BIBLIOGRAPHY

Braver, C. Interview with author. Milwaukee County Hospital, Milwaukee, June 2, 1986.

Brink, F.V. *Personal Memoirs.* Manuscript. Historical Room, School of Nursing. Milwaukee County Medical Complex, Milwaukee, 1963.

Brink, F.V. Letter to Mrs. Lawrence Fry, former student. Historical Room, School of Nursing. Milwaukee County Medical Complex, Milwaukee, 1969.

"County Nurse Chief Resigns." *Milwaukee Journal,* 20 April 1944.

Fitzpatrick, M.L. *The National Organization for Public Health Nursing, 1912–1952: Development of a Practice Field.* New York: National League for Nursing, 1975.

"Francis V. Brink." Obituary. *Huntington Herald-Dispatch,* 22 June 1978.

Hinding, A., A.S. Bower, & C.A. Chamber, eds. *Women's History Sources: A Guide to Archives and Manuscript Collections in the United States.* New York & London: R.R. Bowker, 1979.

West, R.M. *History of Nursing in Pennsylvania.* Philadelphia: Pennsylvania State Nurses' Association, 1926.

Geri L. Dickson

## Elizabeth Chamberlain Burgess
### 1877–1949

Elizabeth Chamberlain Burgess taught nursing at Teachers College, Columbia University, for 27 years, retiring with the rank of professor emeritus. During a long and varied career, she worked to improve the working conditions and educational standards of nursing schools and was an authority on legal questions related to nursing.

Burgess was the daughter of George and Marcia Hill Woodbury Burgess. She was born in Bath, Maine, on November 2, 1877, and had one brother, Louis, who became an artist. The family was of English descent, was well off, and moved early in Elizabeth Burgess's life to New Haven, Connecticut.

She graduated in 1895 from a five-year program at the Misses Orton and Nichols Private School. She wanted to enter college, but had to remain at home because of parental illness. Her mother died in 1898, and her father the year after.

Burgess entered the Roosevelt Hospital School of Nursing in New York and received her diploma in 1904. Mary L. Samuel, her superintendent there, recognized her potential and gave her added responsibilities during her training.

After graduation, Burgess was recommended by Samuel for a challenging position at the French Hospital in New York. For a year she organized a modern operating-room service and prepared a staff of sisters to direct it.

She then returned to Roosevelt, where she was assistant superintendent of nurses for four years. After Roosevelt trustees reduced the nursing course to two years from three, both Samuels and Burgess left.

On the advice of Annie W. Goodrich, Burgess became a student in the nursing and health department at Teachers College, where Adelaide Nutting nurtured her professional growth. She supported herself by teaching part-time at Bellevue Hospital from 1910–11 and St. Luke's Hospital from 1911–12. She completed a two-year program in nursing-school administration and for the next four years was superintendent of nurses at Michael Reese Hospital in Chicago.

At Michael Reese, Burgess worked intensely to improve the lot of her nurses. She secured the first full-time nursing instructor, the allocation and equipment of the first classroom, the reorganization and enrichment of the educational program, the change of classes to days from evenings, and the shortening of the nurses' hours of duty. Sensitive to the role that even small comforts can play in morale, she got rid of an outdated outdoor uniform and put pie on the nurses' menu.

When Goodrich resigned as inspector of nurses' training schools for the New York State Department of Education in 1916, Burgess succeeded her. However, the entry of the United States into World War I soon brought them together. Burgess was asked to assist Goodrich in making a national survey of nursing in military hospitals for the committee on nursing of the general medical board of the Council on National Defense. After that, the two organized the new Army School of Nursing. The committee in which the school and several other World War I nursing projects originated was headed by Nutting, who later described Burgess as steadfast, tireless, and tenacious.

Burgess was secretary of the New York State Board of Nurse Examiners from 1920–22, taught a course for nurse supervisors at Teachers College, Columbia University. She also finished her B.S. degree there in 1923.

Burgess began teaching full-time at Teachers College that year as an instructor. When she received her master's degree in 1925, she was promoted to assistant professor. In 1927 she became an associate professor and head of the division of nursing-school and hospital administration and supervision. She was a full professor from 1935–47. Among many contributions, she helped to develop courses on legislation, accreditation in nursing, and administration of nursing services.

During these years, she shared an apartment in New York with her friend, Abby Porter Leland, a public-school principal. They also maintained a home on the Housatonic River in Connecticut, which provided a respite not only for themselves, but for many troubled students and co-workers.

When Burgess retired, she was awarded the rank of professor emeritus. The alumnae association of the college established a lectureship in her honor.

Burgess held several offices in national, state, and local nursing organizations. In the National League of Nursing Education she was president from 1929–33 and a director from 1933–41, chairman of the Committee on the Grading of Nursing Schools from 1939–48, and a member of several other committees. She was a member of the national committee of the American Red Cross Nursing Service, and she wrote many articles on nursing education and other nursing subjects for professional journals.

Burgess died July 22, 1949, of cancer at age 72 at Roosevelt Hospital, where she had commenced her training more than 40 years earlier. The funeral was at St. Paul's Chapel of Columbia University, and burial was in New Haven, Connecticut. She was survived at her death by a brother, Louis W. Burgess of Chicago; a nephew, Colonel Woodbury Burgess of Norfolk, Virginia; and a niece, Mrs. W.B. Worden of Shreveport, Louisiana.

## PUBLICATIONS BY ELIZABETH CHAMBERLAIN BURGESS

"Eight Years of the Grading Committee." *American Journal of Nursing* 34 (October 1934): 937–45.

"What Are Nurses Going to Do About It?" *American Journal of Nursing* 32 (May 1932): 553–56.

## BIBLIOGRAPHY

"Burgess, Elizabeth Chamberlain." *Who's Who in America.* Chicago: A.N. Marquis Co., 1948, 346.

"Elisabeth Chamberlain Burgess." Obituary. *American Journal of Nursing* 9 (September 1949): 25.

"National League of Nursing Education Biographies of Candidates." *American Journal of Nursing* 40 (March 1940): 348.

"Prof. E.C. Burgess, Nursing Educator." *New York Times*, 23 July 1949.

"The State and Nursing Education, Elizabeth C. Burgess, R.N., M.A.." *American Jour-*

nal of Nursing* 34 (December 1934): 1183–84.

Stewart, I.M. "Elizabeth Chamberlain Burgess." *American Journal of Nursing* 58 (August 1958): 1101–5.

"Who's Who in the Nursing World." *American Journal of Nursing* 28 (July 1928): 714.

Alice P. Stein

# May Ayres Burgess

## 1888–1953

May Ayres Burgess was appointed director of the Committee on the Grading of Nursing Schools in 1926. The Committee's in-depth study was completed eight years later and confirmed the recommendations of the Goldmark Report of 1923. Burgess, an educator and statistician, was a staunch advocate for the nursing profession although she was not a nurse.

May Ayres Burgess was born on May 17, 1888, in Newton Highlands, Massachusetts, the daughter of Reverend Milan Church and Georgiana Gall Ayres. Her father was the editor of the *Boston Daily Advertiser* in the 1890s. She had a brother, Leonard, with whom she co-authored a book, and two sisters, Delanis and Lucy.

In 1905 Burgess graduated from the normal department of the University of Puerto Rico, and in 1911 she received her B.S. degree from Simmons College in Boston. She worked in the Department of Education at the Russell Sage Foundation from 1913 to 1915. She left to pursue her doctoral studies at Columbia University, where she met Warren Randolph Burgess, who was studying for a doctorate in education. The couple married on May 17, 1917. During World War I Burgess's husband was in charge of a team of statisticians in the office of the secretary of war in Washington, D.C. Burgess herself worked in the Food Administration in 1917 and then in the statistics branch of the War Department later in 1917 to 1918.

After the war, the couple returned to New York City, and Burgess earned her Ph.D. from Columbia in 1920. From 1923 to 1926 she served as director of the Joint Statistics Bureau of the Commission on Dispensary Development in New York City.

In 1926 the Committee on the Grading of Nursing Schools was organized, and Burgess was appointed director. This 21-member committee represented the American Nurses' Association, National League of Nursing Education, National Organization for Public Health Nursing, American Medical Association (which later withdrew), American College of Surgeons, American Hospital Association, American Public Health Association, and nine members at large, who included prestigious educators from various institutions. The committee was commissioned to conduct an eight-year study in three separate areas: the supply and demand for nursing services, job analysis of nursing and nurse-teaching, and the grading of nursing schools. Burgess previously had participated in a study of private-duty nursing in New York State. She also had served as the director of the joint statistics bureau of the Commission on Dispensary Development in New York City from 1923–26 and was noted for her expertise with statistics.

The first phase of the grading committee's work explored nursing economics. In 1928 this investigation resulted in the publication of *Nurses, Patients and Pocketbooks*, which presented proof that there were both too many and too few nurses to meet the health needs of the nation. Unemployment problems existed for nurses, but the nursing shortage was in quality, not quantity.

At the 1928 American Nurses' Association Convention, Burgess addressed the delegates and made pertinent suggestions based on the data in *Nurses, Patients and Pocketbooks*. She explained that four main aspects were the responsibility of the nursing profession to address the proliferation of graduate nurses who were not receiving sound educational preparation. The first aspect, reducing and improving the supply of nurses, should be implemented by demanding specific standards for nursing education programs. The second aspect, replacing nursing students with graduate nurses, referred to the staffing of hospitals predominantly with student nurses. In 1927 it was reported that 73 percent of all hospitals with schools of nursing had no graduate nurses employed for general duty. The third aspect, helping hospitals meet the cost of graduate-nursing services, addressed the need for hospitals to assign funds to hire salaried graduate nurses. Finally, the fourth aspect, securing public support for nursing education, focused on the need for society to become aware that funds for nursing education must become a public responsibility if the public was to receive good nursing care. Burgess advocated that nursing education should no longer be an apprentice-type of learning experience; instead, a sound education program should be provided.

Additional publications from the Committee on the Grading of Nursing Schools included other results of studies of nursing schools. Stella Goostray, who worked closely with the committee on grading from 1926 to 1934, described Burgess as someone who always was forthright and willing to tackle controversial matters.

Burgess traveled throughout the country campaigning for better nursing schools. She was made an honorary member of the National League of Nursing Education in 1943. Her studies were used as a model, and similar studies on nursing were made in Canada and Great Britain.

At the time of her death on July 15, 1953, Burgess maintained a hotel residence in Washington, D.C. At that time her husband was the special deputy to the secretary of the treasury, George M. Humphrey. She was survived by her husband and two sons, Leonard R. and Julian Burgess, and two sisters, Delanis A. Drake and Lucy Ayres. Her brother, General Leonard Ayres, predeceased her. Burgess was buried in Mt. Hope Cemetery, Hastings-on-Hudson, New York. Ruth Sleeper, president of the National League for Nursing in 1953, in a special tribute to Burgess described her as tireless in her efforts to expand the usefulness of the studies conducted by the grading committee.

## PUBLICATIONS BY MAY AYRES BURGESS

### BOOKS

With L.P. Ayres. *Health Work in the Public Schools.* Cleveland: Survey Committee of the Cleveland Foundation, 1915.

With L.P. Ayres. *School Buildings and Equipment.* Cleveland: Survey Committee of the Cleveland Foundation, 1915.

With J.F. Williams and T.D. Wood. *Healthful Schools—How to Build, Equip, and Maintain Them.* Boston: Houghton Mifflin, 1918.

*The Measurement of Silent Reading.* New York: Department of Education, Russell Sage Foundation, 1918.

*Nurses, Patients and Pocketbooks: Report of a Study of the Economics of Nursing.* New York: Committee on the Grading of Nursing Schools, 1928.

*Results of the First Grading Study of Nursing Schools.* New York: Committee on the Grading of Nursing Schools, 1930–1931.

*Results of Second Grading of Nursing Schools in the U.S.* New York: Committee on the Grading of Nursing Schools, 1933.

*Nursing Schools Today and Tomorrow.* New York: Committee on the Grading of Nursing Schools, 1934.

### ARTICLES

"High Points of the Supply and Demand Study." *Proceedings of the Twenty-sixth Convention (June 4–8. 1928) of the American Nurses' Association.* New York: The American Nurses' Association, 1928.

"Which Schools Survive." *American Journal of Nursing* 31 (February 1931): 209–13.

### BIBLIOGRAPHY

"Burgess, May Ayres." Obituary. *American Journal of Nursing* 53 (September 1953): 1046.

"Burgess, May Ayres." Obituary. *New York Times,* 16 July 1953.

"Burgess, May Ayres." *Who Was Who In America.* Vol. 3. Chicago: Marquis Company, 1963.

Dolan, J. *Nursing in Society.* Philadelphia: W.B. Saunders, 1978.

Flanagan, L. *One Strong Voice. The Story of the American Nurses' Association.* Kansas City: Lowell Press, 1976.

Goostray, S. *Memoirs: Half a Century in Nursing.* Boston: Nursing Archives, Boston University Mugar Memorial Library, 1969.

Kalisch, P., and B. Kalisch. *The Advance of American Nursing.* Boston: Little, Brown, 1978.

Kelly, L.Y. *Dimensions of Professional Nursing,* 4th ed. New York: Macmillan, 1981.

"Mrs. W.R. Burgess, A Nursing Expert." *New York Times,* 16 July 1953.

Roberts, N. *American Nursing History and Interpretation.* New York: Macmillan, 1964.

Sleeper, R. "Tribute to Mrs. Burgess." *New York Times,* 31 July 1953.

Veronica O'Day

# Ida de Fatio Butler

1868–1949

Ida de Fatio Butler made outstanding contributions to nursing, first as a Red Cross nurse in France during World War I. Later, she served as assistant director and director of the American Red Cross Nursing Service during the crucial years of its existence.

Butler was born in Watertown, New York, on March 18, 1868, daughter of Major John Hartwell and Ida de M. Fatio Butler. Butler's father, an easterner of New England heritage, had lost a foot in the Civil War. He was an invalid for 15 years, eventually confined to his home for several years before his death. Her mother, a southerner of Castilian heritage, had been a volunteer nurse in the Civil War and had met her husband in the hospital where he was taken when injured. Butler's grandfather was John S. Butler, a pioneer psychiatrist and founder of the Hartford Retreat. He strongly influenced Butler's early life and also that of her cousin, nursing leader Annie N. Goodrich.

Butler attended private and boarding schools in Hartford and Berlin, Connecticut. In 1901 at age 33, she received a diploma from the Hartford School of Nursing.

Following her graduation and a short time at the University of Pennsylvania Hospital, Butler served at the Hartford

Hospital in several posts, most notably as supervisor of the maternity and obstetric department. She then became director of probationers. While at Hartford Hospital, Butler taught classes, on her afternoons off, in home hygiene and care of the sick to mill operatives and homemakers in South Manchester, Connecticut.

In 1906 Butler joined the American Red Cross, becoming one of its earlier members and holding pin number 248. With the outbreak of World War I, she was appointed chairman of the Hartford area nursing service committee to recruit women for war service. In 1918, although 47 years old and two years past the age for active overseas service, Butler was sent to Lyons, France, where she organized and directed Red Cross nursing services at two hospitals that served refugee children and French children repatriated from Germany. Her brother had interceded on her behalf to urge that the overseas-service age requirement be waived because of Butler's recognized capabilities.

Butler first was chief nurse at Hospital Violet, where there were many nose, throat, and dental cases. Later she was sent as chief nurse to Hospital Holtzman to organize it for care of acute diseases of children. For a period at Holtzman, Butler, one other Red Cross nurse, a French nurse, and ten nurses' aides provided all the nursing care.

For her service at Lyons, Butler was decorated by the French government with the French Reconnaissance Medal for her outstanding work with children during World War I. When she revisited Lyons 20 years later, Butler was gratified to find that on the basis of the Red Cross service the city had founded a permanent child-welfare program.

Back in Washington after World War I and under the auspices of the District of Columbia chapter of the American Red Cross, Butler organized and directed convalescent homes for government employees who were victims of the infamous influenza epidemic. Later that year, pursuing her interest in public-health nursing, she became an itinerant nurse-lecturer and instructor on the Chautauqua lecture circuit. She traveled from May to

September to 95 small towns and gave 190 speeches. On her travels, she became aware of the primitive health conditions in much of rural America. This strengthened her interest in the Delano and other public-health nursing services in the American Red Cross. In her Chautauqua lectures, Butler advocated the use of community nurses, the need for more public-health nurses, and the need for more young women entering nursing schools.

In 1919 Butler was made director of the nursing service of the Foreign and Insular Division of the Red Cross, and six months later she became assistant director of the Red Cross Nursing Service under Clara D. Noyes. She held the post of assistant director from 1920 until 1936. Her main charge was to manage and develop the enrollment records of the nursing service, a task that she executed with the attention to detail for which she became noted. In times of disaster, the enrollment records she so meticulously maintained enabled the Red Cross to quickly call up reserves for the army and navy nurse corps. This work earned her the admiration of the chiefs of those services.

Butler also spoke about the Red Cross at state association meetings and to school groups. She was a good public speaker and a gifted organizer. She dealt warmly and diplomatically with the relationships with professional groups, always using the right word of praise or comment. According to reports, Butler was unselfish, unassuming, and thoroughly competent, an ideal second-in-command.

Although she had planned to retire June 30, 1936, on the sudden death of Noyes on June 4 Butler was appointed director of the Nursing Service of the Red Cross. Her appointment automatically made her a member of the board of directors of the American Nurses' Association. During the short time she was director of the Nursing Service, though still loyal to Noyes and knowing that her tenure would be short, the 67-year-old Butler proved herself to be more open to change and more flexible professionally than Noyes. These qualities were exhibited in her willingness to listen to arguments in favor of the development of nurses'-aide programs, to which Noyes had been opposed, and also in her recognition of the need for changes in the organization of the nursing service and its advisory committees.

In 1937 Ida Butler was awarded the Florence Nightingale Medal, the highest honor of the International Red Cross Committee in Geneva, Switzerland, for her national and international nursing service. On her retirement from the Red Cross on November 15, 1938, she returned to Hartford, where she had already selected an apartment near family and friends. In 1940 and 1942, Butler devoted her organizational talents as manager of the biennial nursing conventions sponsored jointly by the American Nurses' Association, the National Organization for Public Health Nursing, and the National League for Nursing Education, each conference attended by more than 10,000 nurses. She was also a member of the Connecticut State Council for War Services. At the end of World War II, Governor McConaughy awarded her the Connecticut Distinguished Service Medal. Additionally she was named chairman of the Red Cross Nursing Committee of Greater Hartford. Butler's hobby was needlepoint, and her favorite pastimes were theater and reading. She was an Episcopalian and a Republican.

Butler died at Hartford Hospital on March 11, 1949, at the age of 80. She was the sister of the late Louis F. Butler, former president of the Travelers Insurance Company. She left three nephews and a niece, three grand-nieces and four grand-nephews. As was characteristic of her, Butler had overseen every detail of her funeral, including a postfuneral luncheon in her own apartment.

Butler's verve and droll sense of humor were revealed in the detailed reports and letters, many written to Noyes, that describe her war work and later Chautauqua endeavors. Butler devoted her life to service of others, both in public-health nursing and in Red Cross administration. It is for her selfless and meticulous service, her vibrant character, and her exceptional organizational talent that she is most remembered.

## PUBLICATIONS BY
## IDA DE FATIO BUTLER

"Lyons Revisited." *American Journal of Nursing* 37 (November 1937): 1219.

### BIBLIOGRAPHY

Adams, E. "End of a Pioneer Era." *Red Cross Courier* 28 (April 1949): 22–23.

Butler, I. Papers. Archives, National Red Cross, Washington, D.C.

Dock, L.L., et al. *History of American Red Cross Nursing.* New York: Macmillan, 1922.

Howes, Durward, ed. "Butler, Ida Fatio." *American Women.* Vol. 3. Los Angeles: American, 1939.

"Ida de Fatio Butler." Obituary. *American Journal of Nursing* 49 (May 1949): 34, 36.

"Ida de Fatio Butler." Obituary. *New York Times*, 12 March 1949.

Kernodle, P. *Red Cross Nurse in Action 1882–1948.* New York: Harper, 1949.

"News About Nursing." *American Journal of Nursing* 38 (November 1938): 1278–1279.

Stimson, Julia C. "Ida F. Butler." *Biographic Sketches 1937–1940* New York: National League of Nursing Education, 1940.

Dorothy S. Tao

# Ida Maud Cannon

## 1877–1960

Ida Maud Cannon was a nurse and social worker who was a founder and guiding hand of medical social work in the United States. Though this field started with nurse social workers, it was soon dominated by professionals trained primarily as social workers, due in large part to Cannon and the Massachusetts experience.

Cannon was born June 29, 1877, in Milwaukee, Wisconsin, the third of four children and the second of three daughters of Colbert Hanchet and Sarah Wilma Denio Cannon. Her father was an official of the Great Northern Railroad. Her mother was a former schoolteacher who died when Cannon was four years old, and her father eventually married a woman who was devoted to his young children.

The family moved to Minnesota, where Cannon graduated from St. Paul High School in 1896, after which she entered the nurses' training school at City and County Hospital in St. Paul, Minnesota. Her first position was at the Minnesota State School for the Feeble Minded in Faribault, Minnesota. She returned to St. Paul in 1900 after being temporarily blinded while fumigating a room with formaldehyde and began taking classes at the University of Minnesota. While there, she attended a lecture by Jane Addams, who described tenement and factory conditions in such a moving fashion that Cannon immediately committed herself to social improvement. This commitment lasted throughout her life.

Shortly after (1903–06), Cannon became a visiting nurse for the Associated Charities of St. Paul, and this experience served to verify for her the relationship between social conditions and poor health. This was followed by summer employment as director of a tuberculosis camp for Minneapolis children.

Determined to do more, Cannon moved to Cambridge, Massachusetts, where she lived with the family of her brother, Walter Bradford Cannon, a well-known physiologist, and attended the Boston (Simmons) School of Social Work during 1906 and 1907. Cannon remained a member of her brother's household for most of the rest of her life, and his family became her own.

In 1907 Cannon began working in the social-service program at Massachusetts General Hospital, probably the first in the nation, which had been started by her brother's friend Richard Clarke Cabot in 1905. Prior to her employment at the hospital, she had worked briefly as a volunteer in the program, and in 1908 she became head of the program, a position she held until her retirement in 1945.

It was from the collaboration of Cabot and Cannon that the field of hospital social work developed. Basic to the program was the assumption that the social worker could provide the physician with information about the whole person, which would enable the physician to do a better diagnostic work-up and give more effective treatment. The hospital social worker was also to see that the regime prescribed by the physician was carried out. Though Cannon was a nurse, increasingly the program relied on non-nurses and emphasized the casework method.

In 1912 Cannon toured most of the hospital social service departments then in operation under the sponsorship of the Russell Sage Foundation and helped solidify the field of hospital social work. Her book *Social Work in Hospitals*, first published in 1913 and revised in 1923, added to her influence, as it was the formative force in the field. Cannon remained very much interested in social diagnosis, and although psychiatric social work was also initiated at the Massachusetts General Hospital in 1918, this remained outside her own area of interest and expertise. One reason for this might have been because Cannon, perhaps as a result of her early training in nursing, insisted that therapy be left to the physicians, and psychiatric social workers increasingly were entering into therapy.

The reputation of the program at Massachusetts General brought a stream of foreign and domestic visitors, and its success led to the establishment of a specialized medical social-work curriculum offered jointly by the hospital and the Boston School of Social Work, with Cannon as one of the teachers. She also was a leader in the founding of the American Association of Hospital Social Workers in 1918. She served as vice-president in 1918–19 and was the organization's president in 1920–21, and she was a major spokesperson on issues of medical social work.

During World War I Cannon was assistant director of the New England division of the American Red Cross. She was a delegate to the White House Conference on Child Health and Protection in 1930–31 and chaired the committee on medical social service. In 1938–39 she served as vice-president of the National Conference of Social Work. By that time, 11 schools of social work had established special postgraduate training courses in medical social work.

Cannon retired in 1945. After suffering a stroke in 1957, she lived in a nursing home in Watertown, Massachusetts, where she died July 8, 1960. She was survived by her nieces, including Linda Burgess and Marian Schlessinger, and several nephews. Among other honors she received was the Lemuel Shattuck Award of the Massachusetts Public Health Association and honorary degrees from the University of New Hampshire and Boston University.

## PUBLICATIONS BY IDA MAUD CANNON

### BOOKS

*Social Work in Hospitals.* New York: Survey Associates, 1913. Revised. New York: Russell Sage Foundation, 1923.

*On the Social Frontier of Medicine: Pioneering in Medical Social Service.* Cambridge, Mass.: Harvard University Press, 1952.

### ARTICLES

"The Function of the Social Service Department in Relation to the Administration of Hospitals and Dispensaries." *Hospital Social Service* (February 1921): 17–26.

"Changes in Hospital Care Through Social Service." *Trained Nurse and Hospital Review* (April 1938):

"Medicine as a Social Instrument." *New England Journal of Medicine* (May 10, 1951): 717–24.

## BIBLIOGRAPHY

Benison, S., A.C. Barger, and E. Wolfe. *Walter B. Cannon: The Life and Times of a Young Scientist.* Cambridge: Belknap Press of Harvard University Press, 1987. This biography of her brother gives a great deal of information about her family.

Cannon, I.M. Papers. Social Service Department Archives. Massachusetts General Hospital, Boston.

Lubove, R. "Ida Maud Cannon." *Notable American Women.* Vol. 4. Cambridge: Belknap/Harvard University Press, 1980, pp. 133–135.

Vern L. Bullough

## Alice Griffith Carr

### 1887–1968

Active in international nursing in the 1920s and 1930s, Alice Griffith Carr was director of public health for the Near East Foundation in Greece from 1930 to 1941. Internationally known for her public-health work, she was decorated by the Greek government three times for her successful elimination of malaria from Corinth and for organizing health care in Greece. With her determination and excellent leadership, she greatly improved the health conditions of the Greek and Armenian refugees who fled to Greece from Smyrna, Turkey, after the massacres by the Turks in the 1920s.

Carr was born January 7, 1887, in Yellow Springs, Ohio. Her ancestors had received land grants in Ohio for services rendered in the Revolutionary War, and she traced her roots to George Carr, who sailed from England on the Mayflower in 1620. Her parents were William Wallace Carr, owner of Carr's Nursery in Yellow Springs, Ohio, and Mary Ladley Carr. There were five children in the family: three boys (George, Oscar Edwin, and Charles) and two girls (Katherine and Alice). Carr's maternal grandfather was Reverend D.F. Ladley, one of the founders in 1852 of Antioch College in Yellow Springs.

Carr grew up in Yellow Springs and attended the local schools. When she was 13 years old, her mother died. Carr then was raised by an older cousin, Bessie Totten, a librarian and archivist at Antioch College.

At age 17, Carr received a B.A. degree from Antioch College in 1904. She then taught high-school mathematics in West Mansfield, Ohio. However, she soon realized that teaching was not for her and enrolled in a Cincinnati beauty college.

In 1908 Carr became a beautician and was employed in a beauty shop in Montgomery, Alabama. Later she worked for Florence Crumpton in her beauty shop in Montgomery until 1911. Crumpton was significant in her support and encouragement of Carr during her early nursing career.

Eventually, the necessity of being self-supporting for the remainder of her life became clear to Carr. Believing that she did not have sufficient business ability to manage her own beauty shop, she wrote to her parents in February 1911 of her plans to enter Johns Hopkins Training School for Nurses in Baltimore.

In August 1911, at age 24, she entered Johns Hopkins Training School for Nurses, a three-year program, on money borrowed from Crumpton, her former employer. During her training, Carr received supportive and encouraging letters from Crumpton, from Totten in Yellow Springs, and from her sister Katherine and brother George.

Carr described her early days at Johns Hopkins with happiness. She wrote of working hard while she was on duty and of enjoying herself during her free time. She also described being on duty day and night in a contagious isolation ward, nursing a doctor and a baby who had diphtheria.

In November 1914 Carr received her certificate from the Maryland State Board of Examiners of Nurses after having graduated from Johns Hopkins. She worked as a private-duty nurse and later became a Red Cross nurse. In June 1917 she sailed as an army nurse with the Johns Hopkins unit to France. She was stationed at Base 18 Hospital, one of the first American hospitals established in France, at Bazoiles-sur-Meuse, amid the heavy fighting in the Argonne Meuse region.

In February 1919 after nearly two years overseas, Carr and the Johns Hopkins unit returned to the United States. She immediately requested a foreign-service assignment with the Red Cross, and in 1920 she was with the Red Cross in Poland at the front line of the war between the Bolsheviks and Poles. She was appointed chief nurse of the hospital in Vilno, Poland, near the Lithuanian border. Traveling in boxcars of a freight train, she and the Red Cross nurses brought thousands of orphans to the safety of Leskos, in southern Poland, from the Russian border during the Bolshevik invasion of Poland.

Assigned to Serbia in January 1921, Carr spent six months in child-welfare work and established health centers.

From there she traveled to Susice, Czecho-slovakia, to establish much-needed child health centers.

After several months of difficult service under severe hardship conditions, Carr returned to the United States via Europe and Egypt, stating that she was through with relief work forever. She and another nurse toured Europe and Egypt for three months on their savings.

By December 1922 Carr was in Greece with the Red Cross, working with the refu-gees from Smyrna, Turkey. Earlier that year the Turks had entered Smyrna, mas-sacred a large proportion of the Greek population, and deported thousands of Greek civilians. Armenians living in Smyrna also went to Greece as refugees. When the Red Cross withdrew its emer-gency work there, Carr joined the Near East Relief. Carr was decorated by King George of Greece for her health work and care of the refugees.

In Corinth in 1924 the Near East Relief placed 3,000 orphans from Smyrna in old army barracks. The staff and the orphans immediately became ill with malaria, and an epidemic began. Carr rounded up a group of older orphan boys and took on the formidable task of ridding the city of malaria, which had plagued Corinth since ancient times. They drained swamps and searched out and applied crude oil to mos-quito breeding locations. Carr did the same thing in the Marathon plains, al-though she could not drain the huge swamp there. As a result of the decrease in malaria, people were able to work and fam-ily incomes rose substantially.

Carr believed that relief work was not enough, that people needed knowledge to improve their conditions. She also be-lieved in the power of women as the guardians of the health of their families. She organized health classes for the Greek women, teaching them sanitation, nutri-tion, and child care. She taught the women that flies carried germs and that the slovenly merchant who did not cover his food was the enemy of every person who wanted to remain healthy, demon-strating how food should be protected.

Carr was responsible for the health and welfare of 3,000 refugee children in Greece. The fame of her successful work in Corinth spread to the Near East, and in 1927 she was loaned by the Near East Relief to Turkey to establish a model baby home and children's clinic in Izmir (Smyrna), where she was able to reduce the infant mortality rate significantly. In 1928 she was loaned by the Near East Relief to Syria and Iraq for relief work with the Assyrian refugees. She established a mobile medical unit in Mosul and a phar-macy in the border mountains of Kurdis-tan for the refugees.

Carr escaped a near tragic end in the desert when she traveled alone in her car from Baghdad, Iraq, to Izmir, carrying with her $10,000 for Assyrian relief work. Her car broke down, and she wandered helplessly in the desert for three days. Fears arose that she had been attacked by bandits, but a British officer and Assyrian soldiers found her and brought her to safety. She received honors for her work in Mesopotamia from the British govern-ment.

In 1929 Carr returned to Greece to work with tuberculosis patients at the Kaisariani Refugee Camp. In 1930 she be-came director of public health for the Near East Foundation, which was the succes-sor to the Near East Relief. In a letter from 1931, she wrote that she had organized a large public-health effort. She had formed health classes for women, established a large tuberculosis clinic, worked in pre-ventive medicine with refugees, provided lunches for refugee children, began a children's day nursery, and done case work among the poor. She stated that she saved 2,000 children from tuberculosis with sunbaths and nutrition. In 1934 she received the highest honor from the Greek government, the Order of the Phoenix.

In 1937 Carr returned to the United States to receive honorary LL.B. degrees from Antioch College and Ohio State Uni-versity. The American Red Cross and the Veterans of Foreign Wars also honored her during this visit.

From September 1937 to 1941, Carr was again in Greece active in educational health work and also assisted refugee women to develop their own businesses, embroidery and weaving, and to send their goods to market. The additional income improved the welfare of their families, and the women were able to work at home while caring for their children. Before this the women had placed their children in a corner of a field, where they would be bitten by insects, while the women tended the crops with their husbands to provide income for their families.

When Italy invaded Greece at the beginning of World War II, Carr and members of the Near East Foundation staff offered their services to the Greek government. Soon after, the Germans invaded Greece, and Carr, assisted by the U.S. State Department in her departure, was one of the last Americans to leave Greece. A woman who had helped refugees for many years suddenly became one herself, leaving behind the cherished home that she had helped build.

From 1941 to 1943 Carr's public-speaking tour of the United States for the Near East Foundation raised funds for aid to the Greeks. During this period she lived in Yellow Springs, Ohio, in a near-poverty state, although she would not admit this until much later. Attempts to gain compensation for her army-nurse experience from the United States government proved futile.

Carr dreamed of building a small home for herself because she had lost her home in the suburbs of Athens, where she had lived for many years. Instead, she moved into one of her family's houses in Yellow Springs. To earn income, she rented rooms to soldiers from a nearby military base.

In 1944 Carr did volunteer work in the canteen at Wright Field, Dayton, Ohio. She retired in 1948 and the following year moved to Melbourne, Florida, to a home that she had built with her niece's assistance. She was known in Melbourne for her horticultural abilities; she grew vegetables and giant chrysanthemums.

On July 8, 1968, Carr died alone in her Florida home at age 81. Her body was cremated. Known survivors were her grandniece and an elderly niece and nephew. Carr had never married. Her two most faithful companions while she was in Greece had been her dogs, Sappho and Brie, and later in the United States the Afghan hounds she raised.

Carr's work on disease prevention helped the people of Greece and the Near East reach a level of wellness that was unknown to them as refugees. She exemplified the independence and autonomy of public-health nurses of her time.

## PUBLICATIONS BY ALICE GRIFFITH CARR

### BOOKS

*Public Health, Medicine and Sanitation in Greece (Before the Axis Occupation)*. Monograph. New York: Near East Foundation, 1942.

### ARTICLES

"Working in Depths of Suffering Unspeakable." *Red Cross Courier*, 1 March 1928.

"Home Sweet Home." *Near Eastern News*. (Fall 1933): 1–2.

"Nursing in Pre-War Greece." *American Journal of Nursing* 42 (April 1942): 370–72.

### BIBLIOGRAPHY

Alice Carr Collections, Wright University Archives and Special Collections, Dayton, Ohio.

Archer, L. *Balkan Journal*. New York: W.W. Norton, 1944.

Barton, J.L. *Administration of Relief Abroad: The Near East Relief (1915–1930)*. New York: Russell Sage Foundation, 1934.

Beatty, J. *Americans All Over*. New York: John Day, 1938.

Beatty, J. "The Woman Who Wouldn't Come Home." *Reader's Digest*, November 1938, 65–68.

"Belief Relief Is Evil." *Cleveland Plain Dealer*, 9 February 1934.

Bernheim, B.M. *The Story of the Johns Hopkins*. New York: McGraw-Hill, 1948.

"Famed Ohio Nurse Retires After 20 Years in Europe." *Dayton Daily News*, 8 August 1941.

"In Memoriam, Alice Carr." *Daily Times* (Melbourne, Fla.), 24 July 1968.

"In Memoriam Alice Carr—1914." *Alumnae Magazine*, Johns Hopkins Nursing School 67: (December 1968): 103–4.

Morgenthau, H. *I Was Sent to Athens*. Garden City, N.Y.: Doubleday, Doran and Co., 1929.

"Yellow Springs Girl Wins Fame Fighting Epidemics." *Dayton Journal Herald*, 20 January 1929.

"Yellow Springs Nurse Rescued from Wolves on Desert in Asia." *Springfield Daily News*, 29 January 1928.

"Yellow Springs Woman Is Angel of Mercy." *Springfield Daily News*, 22 December 1940.

"Yellow Springs Woman Wages 'Second Battle of Marathon' to Check Malaria in Greece." *Springfield Daily News*, 1 May 1936.

Grace Murabito Thomas

# Teresa Elizabeth Christy

## 1927–1982

Advocate, pathfinder, risk-taker, and America's foremost nursing historian are labels that have been used to describe Teresa Elizabeth Christy. Throughout her lifetime, she fought for the establishment of historical research as a legitimate method of inquiry in the discipline of nursing. It was her strong belief that accurate knowledge of the past would not only lead to better understanding of current problems, but would also prevent the repetition of mistakes. She strongly ascribed to the philosophy that those with no knowledge of the past are doomed to repeat it.

Christy was born March 31, 1927, in Brooklyn, New York. She was the third of four children (three girls and one boy) of James P. and Charlotte Pardy Christy. Her father, a lieutenant in the New York City Fire Department, was a traditional head of a family that functioned in an environment of strict discipline. The Christy family's devotion to Roman Catholicism stemmed from their ancestral Irish roots and the fact that several relatives were members of Catholic orders. The family home was eventually moved to Queens (Cambria Heights, New York), where the children attended elementary school and graduated from Andrew Jackson High School.

"Terry" Christy constantly struggled to achieve in order to gain recognition from her father. She believed that he had been disappointed when she was born, as he had expected her to be the second boy in the family. She consequently engaged in "boys'" activities such as sports and became particularly proficient in tennis. She emerged as a leader in both elementary school and high school and received honors and awards during those years. In addition she excelled in scholastic work. Her drive for achievement and recognition continued to be a vital part of her character throughout her life.

Christy began her involvement in the nursing world at Manhattanville College of the Sacred Heart in Purchase, New York. She entered nursing as part of the Cadet Nurse Corps and obtained a B.S.N. degree in 1949. During 1947–48 she was an operating-room staff nurse at Halloran Veterans Administration Hospital, Staten Island, and in 1949–50 she was a labor and delivery-room staff nurse at French Hospital, New York.

It was at this time that Christy decided to enter the order of the Nursing Sisters of the Sick Poor of the Child Jesus. The convent was located in Rockville Centre, New York, and Christy's aunt was the mother superior. After three months of attempting to adjust to the prescribed life of the order, she asked permission to leave and began her first teaching position as an instructor of nursing arts at St. Joseph's Hospital in Joliet, Illinois. She remained there for the next ten years (1950–1960). This was the longest period of time that she spent in any one position. In addition to her teaching responsibilities, she commuted weekly to Chicago to attend De Paul University, from which she graduated in 1957 with an M.S.N. degree. It was at St. Joseph's School of Nursing that Christy first demonstrated her excellence in teaching.

Christy returned to New York in 1960 as an assistant professor of medical-surgical nursing at Molloy College, Rockville Centre. She held this position until 1963, when she was named chairman of the department of nursing. In 1964 she entered Teachers College, Columbia University, to begin work toward a doctoral degree. In a 1965 national competition by Nurses Educational Funds, she was awarded the $6000 Clara Hardin Fellowship for doctoral study in nursing. While pursuing her studies, Christy worked in various capacities, including research assistant to Professor Mildred Montag on the second evaluation of the Community College Project and instructor (1966–67) and lecturer (1967–68) in the department of nursing education.

It was during her time at Teachers College that Christy became interested in history and historical research. In order to be able to write her dissertation in that field, she extended her program of study for one year and took courses that prepared her in historical methodology. The end result was the publication of her dissertation, *Cornerstone for Nursing Education: A History of the Division of Nursing Education of Teachers College, Columbia University, 1899–1947* (1969). This book was cited by a reviewing service for libraries as a well-written, carefully-documented history. Christy's other historical publications also demonstrated careful documentation and the thoroughness of a scientist.

On graduation with an Ed.D. in 1968, Christy became an assistant professor of nursing education at Teachers College for two years. This position was followed by that of associate professor of nursing (1970–74) in the graduate program in medical-surgical nursing at Adelphi University, Garden City, New York. For the first two years, she was also the director of the program. In 1974 she moved to The University of Iowa College of Nursing, where she remained until her death. During her first year there, she was an associate professor in the graduate program in medical-surgical nursing. She was promoted to full professor in 1975 and taught the undergraduate course in historical, philosophical, and social foundations of nursing and a graduate course in nursing issues. From 1977 to 1979 she also commuted weekly to Chicago to teach a doctoral-level course in nursing history at the University of Illinois as a visiting professor.

Christy's career demonstrated her active involvement in all aspects of nursing. She continually participated in college and university life, in professional organizations, in nursing research, and in historical associations. She held member-

ship in numerous organizations that included the American Nurses' Association (ANA), the National League for Nursing (NLN), the American Association of University Professors, the American Public Health Association, the American Historical Association, and the National Organization for Women. She held a variety of positions in both professional and civic organizations, including the following: member of the state committee on functions, standards, and qualifications of the Illinois State Nurses Association (1954–55); member of the Nassau County Civil Defense Committee (1963–64); member of the ANA-NLN National Historical Source Committee (1968–70); member of the ANA National Bicentennial Celebration Committee (1973–76); chairperson of the ANA National Hall of Fame Committee (1977–78); member of the board of directors of the Iowa Citizens' League for Nursing (1977–82); member of the legislative committee of the Iowa Nurses' Association (1977–78); second vice-president of the Iowa Nurses' Association (1978–82); and member of the national commission on nursing research of the ANA (1980–82).

Christy was particularly proud of serving on the commission on nursing research. She believed that as an elected member of this prestigious national group she would be able to increase exposure and help generate support for historical nursing research. Through her continual efforts, the commission's prior position to support only clinical studies was revised to include support for historical and philosophical studies in nursing.

Christy was one of nursing's strongest advocates for historical research. She was constantly forced to defend her position that the rigors of historical methodology would satisfy criteria for the nursing thesis requirement. She struggled to obtain financial support for historical research and engaged in any activity that she believed would help foster the acceptances of historical research. She was a charter member and first president of the International History of Nursing Society (renamed the American Association for the History of Nursing in 1980), which evolved as part of a federally funded project for the development of nursing research in the Midwest. Most importantly, however, she served as a role model through her own research, writing, and teaching.

Christy's enthusiasm for history was evident as she presented numerous speeches, keynote addresses, and workshops for major functions in nursing in addition to her regular teaching responsibilities. Her teaching style was often described as charismatic, dynamic, exciting, intriguing, interesting, and provocative. Her particular style was similar to the Socratic method through which she always labored to develop critical thinking skills in her students. In 1976 and 1978 students at The University of Iowa College of Nursing elected her recipient of the Outstanding Teacher Award.

Christy's writings appear in numerous professional journals and cover a variety of subjects. The "Portrait of a Leader Series," however, which was published in *Nursing Outlook*, is probably the best remembered of her publications. In this series, Christy made some of the greatest leaders in nursing become alive and visible to thousands of nurses. Each of her publications attests to the "hope of history" and provides an historical perspective to the issues being discussed.

Christy was recognized for her achievements and scholarship by various professional and academic groups. She was a member of Pi Lambda Theta, Kappa Delta Pi, and Sigma Theta Tau. In recognition of distinguished participation in the Johns Hopkins University Centennial Scholars Symposia, she received the Johns Hopkins University Centennial Scholar Award (1976). Other awards include Distinguished Achievement Award for outstanding contributions to research and scholarship presented by the Nursing Education Alumni Association, Teachers College, Columbia University (1976); the Elizabeth McWilliams Miller Award for Distinguished Research, Sigma Theta Tau (1977); and the Distinguished Achievement Award from the De Paul University Alumni Association (1978). In September 1978 Christy was admitted as a fellow of the American Academy of Nursing.

Of all her prestigious awards, Christy was particularly proud of the honorary doctor of public service degree that she received from McKendree College in Lebanon, Illinois (1978). This award was presented in recognition of her scholarship, dedication to the profession of nursing, and service to all those who requested it. Christy was also listed in *Leaders in Education* (1971), *Who's Who in the Mid-West* (1977–78), and *Contemporary Authors* (1977–78).

In 1981 Christy was scheduled for a sabbatical from The University of Iowa to begin research for an illustrated history of nursing. However, in June of that year she became seriously ill and began the last struggle of her lifetime. In November 1981 she was diagnosed as having cancer of the pancreas. After much reading about the disease and discussions with colleagues, Christy asked that she be allowed to die at home. When she was released from the hospital in December 1981, she was cared for by a team of colleagues and friends in the comfort and familiarity of her home. She died April 3, 1982, at age 55. Survivors included her father, a brother, and sisters. Her body was cremated, and her ashes were buried beside her mother's grave in Thorn Rose Cemetery in Staunton, Virginia.

## PUBLICATIONS BY TERESA ELIZABETH CHRISTY

### BOOKS

*Cornerstone for Nursing Education: A History of the Division of Nursing Education of Teachers College, Columbia University, 1899–1947.* New York: Teachers College Press, 1969.

### ARTICLES

With D. Silva. "A Process of Instruction—An Application of Jerome Brunner's Notion of Structure to Teaching in Nursing." *Nursing Forum* 6 (Fall 1967): 419.

"Nursing Education and the Johns Hopkins: The Ideas of M. Adelaide Nutting." *Alumnae Magazine.* 66, (December 1967).

"Critique of Historical Research." American Nurses' Association Fourth Annual Research Conference, New York, March 5, 1968.

"Portrait of a Leader: M. Adelaide Nutting." *Nursing Outlook* 17 (January 1969): 20.

"Portrait of a Leader: Isabel Hampton Robb." *Nursing Outlook* 17 (March 1969): 26.

"Portrait of a Leader: Lavinia Lloyd Dock." *Nursing Outlook* 17 (June 1969): 72.

"Portrait of a Leader: Isabel Maitland Stewart." *Nursing Outlook* 17 (October 1969): 44.

"Portrait of a Leader: Lillian D. Wald." *Nursing Outlook* 18 (March 1970): 50.

"Equal Rights for Women: Voices from the Past." *American Journal of Nursing* 71 (February 1971): 288.

With M.A. Poulin and J. Hover. "An Appraisal of an Abstract for Action." *American Journal of Nursing* 71 (August 1971): 1574.

"ANA—The First 50 Years." *American Journal of Nursing* 71 (September 1971): 1778.

"Liberation Movement: Impact on Nursing." *AORN Journal* 15 (April 1972): 67.

"Privileges, Challenges, Responsibilities of Nurses in the 70's." *Nursing '73* 3 (November 1973): 6.

"The Methodology of Historical Research: A Brief Introduction." *Nursing Research* 24 (May–June 1975): 189.

"The Fateful Decade, 1890–1900." *American Journal of Nursing* 75 (July 1975): 1163.

"Nursing History neither Dead nor Dull." *American Nurse* 7 (July 1975): 10.

"Portrait of a Leader: Sophia F. Palmer." *Nursing Outlook* 23 (December 1975): 746.

"Historical Perspectives on Accountability." In *Current Perspectives in Nursing Education: The Changing Scene,* edited by Janet A. Williamson. St. Louis: C.V. Mosby, 1976, pp. 1–7.

"To Honor Our Past . . . To Herald Our Future." *Virginia Nurse,* Spring 1976, 7–17.

"Hopkins Pioneers in Nursing: Isabel Hampton Robb and M. Adelaide Nutting." *Alumni Magazine* (The Johns Hopkins Hospital School of Nursing), 75 (July 1976): 37.

"The Hope of History." In *Historical Studies in Nursing,* edited by M. Louise Fitzpatrick. New York: Teachers College Press, 1978, pp. 3–11.

"Entry into Practice: A Recurring Issue in Nursing History." *American Journal of Nursing* 80 (March 1980): 485.

"Clinical Practice as a Function of Nursing Education: An Historical Analysis." *Nursing Outlook* 28 (August 1980): 493.

"The Need for Historical Research." Editorial. *Research in Nursing and Health* 4 (June 1981): 227.

"Can We Learn from History?" In *Current Issues in Nursing,* edited by Joanne Comi McCloskey and Helen K. Grace. Boston: Blackwell Scientific Publications, 1981, pp. 122–128.

### BIBLIOGRAPHY

Christy, T.E. Papers. Special Collections. Main Library, University of Iowa, Iowa City.

King, I.M.: "Dedication." In *Nursing: The Finest Art.* by M.P. Donahue. St. Louis: C.V. Mosby, 1985.

*Leaders in Education,* 4th ed. New York and London: Jacques Cattrell Press/R.R. Bowker, 1971

Locher, F.C., ed *Contemporary Authors.* Vols. 73–76. Detroit: Gale Research, 1977–78.

"Noted UI Nursing Historian Dies." Iowa City Press-Citizen, 5 April 1982.

Schweer, K. D. "Lessons from Nursing's Historian: A Tribute to Teresa E. Christy, Ed.D, F.A.A.N. (1927–1982)." *Image* 14 (October 1982): 66.

*Who's Who in the Midwest, 1977-78.* Chicago: Marquis Who's Who.

M. Patricia Donahue

## S. Lillian Clayton

### 1876–1930

S. Lillian Clayton served as superintendent and director of several training schools, on the Pennsylvania Board of Nurse Examiners, as president of the National League for Nursing Education, and as president of the American Journal of Nursing Company. At the time of her death, she was president of the American Nurses' Association (ANA).

Clayton was born in Kent County, Maryland, in 1876. Her mother died when she was very young, and she was raised by a deeply religious relative who was very strict. She decided early to be a nurse and a missionary, and at the age of 16, she began working at the Children's Hospital in Philadelphia.

In 1894 Clayton entered the Philadelphia General Hospital (Blockley) School of Nursing, from which she received her diploma in 1896. She had been appointed night supervisor before she completed her training, and she remained in that post for a short time thereafter. Determined to be a missionary, she prepared for this work by attending the Baptist Institute for Christian Workers for two years.

The outbreak of the Boxer Rebellion in China thwarted Clayton's plans to travel to China as a missionary. Instead, she went to Dayton, Ohio, to become assistant superintendent of the Miami Valley Hospital. Her friend Ella Phillips Crandall, who had been in the class after her in Philadelphia, was superintendent there. She remained in Dayton until 1910. Though she apparently decided against a missionary career at this point, Clayton lived an ascetic and austere life while in Dayton.

To better prepare herself for teaching, Clayton in 1910 enrolled in Teachers College, Columbia University, and remained there for most of the year. From 1911 to 1914 she served as a teacher and administrator at the Minneapolis City Hospital. She then spent a year as educational director of the Illinois Training School for Nurses in Chicago, after which she returned to Philadelphia General Hospital School of Nursing to become director of the training school.

While at Philadelphia, Clayton upgraded the nursing school. She organized a prenursing course, established three residences for nurses, and used the reputation of the school and of the city to offer postgraduate courses. Under the sponsorship of the Rockefeller Foundation, she and Annie Goodrich visited nursing centers in Europe, and from these contacts and with support of the Rockefeller Foundation, a growing number of nurses came to Philadelphia.

Although in her early years Clayton was not particularly interested in the work of nursing organizations, she later changed her mind and became a dedicated supporter of these organizations. The American Nurses' Association Code of Ethics was formulated while she was chair of the committee on ethical standards, a position she resigned to become president of the ANA. Earlier, she served as president of the National League of Nursing Education as well as of the board of directors of the American Journal of Nursing Company. For five years she was president of the Pennsylvania State Board of Nurse Examiners.

Clayton died after a brief illness on May 2, 1930, in Philadelphia. She was given a posthumous honorary master of nursing science degree by Temple University, which had planned the award before her death.

## PUBLICATIONS BY S. LILLIAN CLAYTON

*How Shall Philadelphia Receive Health? Through the Nurse.* All Philadelphia Conference on Social Work, 1926.

## BIBLIOGRAPHY

Goodrich, A.W. "S. Lillian Clayton." *American Journal of Nursing* 30 (June 1930): 871–72.

Roberts, M.M. "S. Lillian Clayton, 1876–1930." *American Journal of Nursing* 54 (November 1954): 1360–63.

"S. Lillian Clayton." *American Journal of Nursing* 30 (June 1930): 679–88.

Vern L. Bullough

# Genevieve Cooke
## 1869–1928

Genevieve Cooke, founder of the *Pacific Coast Journal of Nursing* and seventh president of the American Nurses' Association, was born February 26, 1869, to William F. and Lucy Rutledge Cooke in Dutch Flat, California, a mining town in El Dorado County. Her parents had immigrated to the United States from England and had joined the thousands who crossed the country in covered wagons during the gold rush years. They arrived in California in June 1852 with their first child. Cooke was the eighth child in the family, which would eventually consist of five sons and four daughters.

After attending public school, Cooke came to San Francisco and enrolled at the California Woman's Hospital nursing school in 1887. She graduated in 1888 and practiced private-duty nursing for 13 years before specializing in massage and corrective exercises. After completing a course of study in anatomy and dissection at the Cooper Union Medical College in San Francisco, Cooke traveled to Boston, where she continued her education at the Harvard Summer School of Physical Training and at several private Boston clinics in 1901–3.

Cooke returned to San Francisco and opened an office in 1903. She was also a visiting instructor in massage at several San Francisco hospitals and was a charter member of the Women's Athletic Club. Cooke continued to practice nursing throughout her years of involvement in professional-nurse organizations and nursing journals.

Several concerns became dominant themes in Cooke's life. The first was her commitment to nursing journals as tools for education and communication among nurses. Shortly after the California State Nurses' Association (CSNA) was founded in 1904 with Cooke as one of 96 charter members, she urged that the organization issue a regular publication. CSNA president Sophia L. Rutley believed that the association was too new to take on the task and that none of its members was capable of directing such an effort. Cooke, however, was assigned the job of heading up the committee that would prepare the first CSNA annual report.

Shortly afterward, Rutley went abroad. In her absence, Cooke enlisted the help of vice-president S. Gotea Dozier, and in August 1904 she produced the annual report in magazine form, entitled "Journal of the California State Nurses' Association." The response to the report must have been positive, because in December 1904 the *Nurses' Journal of the Pacific Coast* was launched.

Cooke edited the *Nurses' Journal* in her apartment with the assistance of CSNA secretary Theresa Earles McCarthy and Lucy B. Fisher. It appeared quarterly and in August 1905 became one of the benefits of CSNA membership. Association dues were raised by $1 to cover the cost of the subscription. By 1907 it was published on a monthly basis. Cooke was directly responsible for these advances.

McCarthy and Dozier recalled that although her house and belongings were destroyed in the 1906 earthquake and fire, Cooke saved the *Nurses' Journal*'s financial records, subscription list, and advertising contracts. Following the disaster, Cooke searched for and located the *Nurses' Journal*'s printer, who had taken refuge across San Francisco Bay in Oakland. She produced the June issue only six weeks behind schedule. Following the earthquake, she served on the relief committee of the San Francisco County Nurses' Association.

Cooke served as editor of the *Nurses' Journal* until 1909, when illness and an undisclosed disagreement caused her to resign. She returned to the post in 1912 and convinced the CSNA board of directors to change the name to the *Pacific Coast Journal of Nursing.* Cooke also made other format changes at this time, including doubling the size of the journal. She remained in the position until 1915. During her tenure, the *Nurses' Journal* presented articles on professional issues (i.e., the status of nurse training and nurse registration), nursing care, nursing history, nutrition, hygiene, cross-cultural experiences, book reviews, and personal information on individual nurses.

During this period, Cooke also committed her energy to the advancement of nurse registration and professional-nurse organizations. She helped found the San Francisco County Nurses' Association in July 1905 and was elected to the CSNA Committee on Legislation, formed to promote nurse registration. She advocated registration in the *Nurses' Journal* and, after the registration bill passed, chastised the University of California's board of regents for dragging its feet on the sections of the bill delegated to it by the state legislature.

Cooke was the first CSNA delegate to an American Nurses' Association (ANA) convention, attending the one held in Detroit in 1906. She not only reported details of earthquake devastation, but also reassured those assembled that San Francisco was ready to host the 1908 ANA convention. Cooke was elected ANA first vice-president in 1907–09, attended the International Council of Nurses in Paris in 1907, and was twice elected San Francisco County Nurses' Association president.

The ANA elected Cooke to the American Journal of Nursing Company board of directors in 1910–12. Cooke believed that like the *Nurses' Journal*, the *American Journal of Nursing* (*AJN*) stimulated membership growth for the ANA, educated its readership, nurtured an atmosphere of professionalism, and unified nurses on their own behalf as a cooperative force in the advancement of nursing. Cooke also saw the *AJN* as a public-relations tool, communicating nursing values and concerns to the public and promoting a greater understanding of nursing outside the profession.

Cooke also served as the corresponding secretary of the College Equal Suffrage League in 1911. Based in Berkeley, the league organized college-educated women in the fight for woman suffrage in California and was a vital part of the victorious campaign of 1911.

Cooke was elected ANA president at the 1913 convention in Atlantic City and reelected to the office at the St. Louis convention in 1914. In St. Louis Cooke advocated the creation of a house of delegates as the governing body of the ANA. This concept was a move toward a more democratic organization oriented toward the state nursing associations rather than hospital alumnae chapters, and it became a reality through an ANA bylaws change in 1917.

This same address also contained a strong endorsement of the eight-hour work day for women in general and nursing students in particular. At this time, nursing students were considered employees, as they formed the bulk of hospital staff nurses. Cooke's forthright support of the eight-hour day and of nurse registration in the pages of the *Nurses' Journal* antagonized hospital administrators, causing them to withdraw advertising income from the *Journal*. However, Cooke continued to express these sentiments on behalf of nursing students and the profession. The Eight-Hour Day Law for Student Nurses passed the California legislature in 1913.

Cooke also recognized that financial survival was the chief concern of many nurses and that these women would join the ANA if they felt that the association was willing to act on their behalf as wage earners. She called on the ANA to investigate ways to respond to this need and to address economic as well as professional issues.

After Cooke stepped down from the national presidency in 1915, there is little information about any further activity. It is known that she lived with her niece, Viola M. Priest, and her dear friend, Mrs. Dyer, in Berkeley, California, for the last four years of her life. During that time, she suffered from an unknown nervous disorder. Cooke died January 28, 1928, at age 59 of brain disease and was buried beside her mother in Mountain View Cemetery in Oakland, California. She was survived by two sisters, Sara Lane of Reno, Nevada, and Lucy C. Hatch of Oakland, and a brother, Joseph Cooke.

## PUBLICATIONS OF GENEVIEVE COOKE

"Address of the President of the American Nurses' Association." *American Journal of Nursing* 15 (August 1915): 919–21.

## BIBLIOGRAPHY

College Equal Suffrage League. Folder. Sutro Library, San Francisco, Calif.

"The Committee on Legislation." *Nurses' Journal of the Pacific Coast* 2 (December 1905): 5–6.

"Deaths." *American Journal of Nursing* 28 (March 1928): 307.

Downing, F.B. "Third Meeting of the C.S.N.A. . . ." *Nurses' Journal of the Pacific Coast* 2 (September 1905): 224–26.

"Excerpts from the First San Francisco County Nurses' Association Meeting." July 18, 1905. Golden Gate Nursing Association Archives, San Francisco, Calif.

Flanagan, L., ed. *One Strong Voice*. Kansas City, Mo.: American Nurses' Association, 1976.

"Genevieve Cooke." Obituary. *San Francisco Examiner*, 29 January 1928.

"Greetings from the Original Editor." *Nurses' Journal of the Pacific Coast* 8 (August 1912): 351–52.

McCarthy, T.E. "History of the Association." *Nurses' Journal of the Pacific Coast* 1 (December 1905): 7–13.

McCarthy, T.E. "Minutes of the Second Annual Meeting C.S.N.A." *Nurses' Journal of the Pacific Coast* 1 (September 1905): 247–50.

McCarthy, T.E., and S.G. Dozier. "Genevieve Cooke." *Pacific Coast Journal of Nursing* 24 (March 1928): 146–47.

*Polk's Directory of Oakland.* Oakland: R.L. Polk & Co., 1926.

"Proceedings of the Twentieth Annual Convention of the American Nurses' Association." *American Journal of Nursing* 17 (July 1917): 1007.

Santa Clara County Vital Statistics Office. Death Certificate, Recorder's No. 19A. San Jose, Calif., January 28, 1928.

"Who's Who in the Nursing World." *American Journal of Nursing* 23 (July 1923): 852.

Susan Englander

# Ella Phillips Crandall

## 1871–1938

Ella Phillips Crandall was one of the chief leaders in public-health nursing during its embryonic state. She dominated the commission from which grew the National Organization for Public Health Nursing and helped guide the organization through its formative years.

Born in Wellsville, New York, on September 16, 1871, Crandall was the first of two daughters of Herbert A. and Alice Phillips Crandall. The Crandall family had lived in upstate New York for two generations and were descendants of Elder John Crandall of England, who migrated to Rhode Island in the late seventeenth century. In 1872 Crandall's parents moved to Dayton, Ohio, where her father found a position with a railroad and then quickly went into manufacturing. Her mother had been a seamstress before her marriage. Crandall's father was active in the Presbyterian church and in the 1890s served on school and health boards in Dayton. Crandall attended public school in Dayton and graduated from high school in 1890.

After several years, Crandall became interested in nursing and traveled to Philadelphia to complete the two-year course at the General Hospital School in 1897. Her first professional challenge came in 1899, when she returned to Dayton to become the assistant superintendent of the Miami Valley Hospital and the first director of its new school of nursing. Along with the new superintendent, S. Lillian Clayton, Crandall transformed the hospital from an old-style institution to a modern hospital and nursing school. Crandall and Clayton worked closely together, and later the hospital placed a fountain and a plaque in the building to their memory. Crandall remained in Dayton until 1909, the last year of her tenure on the executive council of the Society of Superintendents of Training Schools for Nurses.

Crandall confronted her second and most notable professional challenge in 1909, when she entered the new field of public-health nursing. She began as a supervisor in Lillian Wald's Henry Street Visiting Nurse Service in New York City, while enrolling at the same time in the New York School of Philanthropy. In 1910 she joined Mary Adelaide Nutting at the Teachers College, Columbia University, in the first university department for the education of nurses. The college offered a graduate nurses' program, and Crandall developed courses in the evolving specialty of public-health nursing. Fearing the dilution of the new field because of the growing demand for visiting nurses, Crandall advocated the establishment of courses in sociology, economics, and psychology.

She thus quickly emerged as a key leader in public-health nursing. Advised by Lillian Wald and Mary Nutting, Crandall soon became the main force of the group that formed the National Organization for Public Health Nursing. Visiting nursing had evolved over the preceding three decades to address growing problems of disease, sanitation, and poverty in American urban areas. A variety of agencies, such as churches, hospitals, settlement houses, tuberculosis associations, the Red Cross, and municipal health departments, had recruited nurses with hospital training to attend to the needs of the slums. But standards, rules, and experiences remained different. In the face of this general lack of standardization came an immediate threat to the growing field from the Metropolitan Life Insurance Company, which planned to lower requirements for the nurses it supplied to visit chronically ill workers with company policies.

In 1911 Crandall launched a writing campaign through which she enlisted the support and opinion of leading public-health nurses concerning the need for a national organization of their specialty. When a joint committee of the American Nurses' Association and the Society of Superintendents of Training Schools for Nurses was established in January 1912, Crandall was made a member, and she soon dominated the organization. Following this commission's recommendations, the National Organization for Public Health Nursing (NOPHN) was founded in June 1912 with Crandall as executive secretary.

Crandall seemed particularly well suited to lead the fledgling organization in its duties of professional standardization, stimulation, and education of public-health nurses. She worked long hours and traveled extensively to mold the new association. Through her many letters and her personal contacts, she became a guide to countless nurses in the field. She counseled not only nurses, but also nurse executives, lay managers, and business and civic leaders. In one year during this second decade of the twentieth century, she traveled over 82,000 miles and gave 83 public addresses. The Ford Model T automobile encouraged rural nursing, and Crandall added forays with rural nurses to her agenda.

At home in the office as well as in the field, Crandall proved to be an expert administrator. Not only did she work hard and long with details and grand designs, but she also coaxed extra efforts from her subordinates. Her efforts gained for NOPHN a growing membership and national acclaim.

Using the considerable financial resources of private donations to the organization, Crandall established in New York City the first national headquarters of any nursing group, and quickly enlarged the staff from 1 to 20. She converted the quarterly magazine of the Cleveland Visiting Nurse Association into the respected professional journal, *Public Health Nurse*

(later *Public Health Nursing*). And by employing the journal to mobilize readers, she convinced Metropolitan Life to end its plans to use attendants or practical nurses for visits to the chronically ill, even though this resulted in the company's cessation of the sending of any nurses to such patients.

NOPHN developed certain professional standards, including graduation from a two-year course in nursing in a hospital of 50 beds or more. Crandall and NOPHN banned nurses without the proper credentials, although she recognized that sometimes those women were just as qualified as duly admitted members.

In addition to these successes at establishing status and autonomy for public-health nurses, Crandall also helped draw the nursing profession into a larger and expanding public-health movement and encouraged others to think of nursing as a form of social service. An indication of the immediate success of NOPHN was its receipt of a Rockefeller Foundation grant of $30,000 in 1917, which was an unprecedented gift to any nurses' group at this time.

Crandall continued her commitment to nursing during World War I by moving to Washington, D.C., and serving as executive secretary of the three committees on nursing of the Council of National Defense, two of them connected with the Council's General medical board. Through her efforts with these committees and her membership on the nursing committee of the American Red Cross (1916–18), she helped coordinate nursing activities for the war effort and aided in the compilation of a national census of nurses. She also served on the board of directors of the American Nurses' Association (1918–20).

Resigning from the National Organization for Public Health Nursing in 1920, Crandall remained interested in the profession while turning her energies directly to programs for poor women and for children. She became executive secretary of the Committee to Study Community Organization for Self Support for Health Work for Women and Young Children (1921) and explored the establishment of nursing on a low-cost, contributory basis.

One year later she became director of the Bureau of Educational Nursing of the Association for Improving the Condition of the Poor, and from 1922 to 1925 served as associate director of the American Child Health Association.

In 1927 Frances Payne Bolton established the Payne Fund to promote the education of youth for peace, and she appointed her friend, Crandall, as executive secretary. Bolton, a Cleveland philanthropist and later a congresswoman, had met Crandall while serving as a director of the National Organization for Public Health Nursing during World War I. Crandall focused especially on a study of reading habits of youth, and this and other work filled the rest of her life.

At the age of 67, Crandall became ill suddenly from pneumonia and died on October 24, 1938, in Roosevelt Hospital, New York City. Her remains were cremated at her request.

### PUBLICATIONS BY ELLA PHILLIPS CRANDALL

#### BOOKS

*Organization and Administration of Public Health Nursing.* New York City: The State Charities Aid Association, Committee for the Prevention of Tuberculosis, 1914.

#### ARTICLES

"The Nurses' Part in the Promotion of Public Health." *Canadian Nurse* 9 (July 1913): 442–57.

"The Relation of Public Health Nursing to the Public Health Campaign." *American Journal of Public Health* 5 (March 1915): 225–35; (July 1915): 626–30.

"New Allies in Public Health." *Public Health Nurse* 11 (November 1919): 859–61.

"An Historical Sketch of Public Health Nursing." *American Journal of Nursing* 22 (May 1922): 641–45.

#### BIBLIOGRAPHY

Armeny, S. "Resolute Enthusiasts: The Effort to Professionalize American Nursing, 1880–1915." Ph.D. diss., University of Missouri-Columbia, 1983.

Crandall, E.P. Manuscript material. U.S. National Archives. Army and Old Navy Division. Record Group 112. Army Nurse Corps Historical Files.

"Ella Phillips Crandall." Obituary. *American Journal of Nursing* 38 (December 1938): 1406–9.

"Ella Phillips Crandall." Obituary. *Public Health Nursing* 30 (December 1938): 726–27.

Farnham, E. *Pioneering in Public Health Nursing Education.* Cleveland: Press of Western Reserve University, 1964.

Gardner, M.S. *Public Health Nursing.* New York: Macmillan, 1952.

Martin, F.H. *The Joy of Living: An Autobiography.* Vol. 2. Garden City, N.J.: Doubleday, Doran, and Co., 1933.

Mumford, E.W. "A Chat with the First Director of the N.O.P.H.N." *Public Health Nursing* 29 (April 1937): 208–11.

Roberts, M.M. *American Nursing: History and Interpretation.* New York: Macmillan, 1954.

Kenneth S. Mernitz

## Frances Elisabeth Crowell

### 1875–1950

Frances Elisabeth Crowell, as a member of the Commission for the Prevention of Tuberculosis of the Rockefeller Foundation in 1917–22, directed the organizing of clinics and training of health visitors. This contributed to the remarkable recovery of France from a devastating tuberculosis epidemic. Recognition of her administrative ability and nursing experience led the Rockefeller Foundation in 1922 to appoint her to implement her recommendations for nurse training in Europe. In 1931, the *American Journal of Nursing* described her as:

> one of the most influential persons in European nursing . . . her advice has led to the establishment of some of Europe's most progressive schools of nursing.

Born in Pittsfield, Massachusetts, in 1875, Elisabeth Crowell attended St. Mary's of the Springs boarding school in Columbus, Ohio, following the death of both of her parents. She entered the first class of St. Joseph's Hospital Training School for Nurses in Chicago in 1893 and graduated in 1895. In 1906 after graduating from the New York School of Philanthropy (now the Columbia University School of Social Work), she became a special investigator for the Association of Neighborhood Workers in New York City.

Crowell spent the first ten years of her professional life in Florida as half owner and superintendent of the Pensacola Infirmary. In 1901 she founded a training school for nurses at St. Anthony's Hospital in response to the need for trained nurses and the demand for private duty in the homes of Pensacola.

Having left Pensacola in 1905, Crowell began the work in New York City that led to her illustrious career in public health and nursing administration in Europe. Two of her studies of midwives in New York and Chicago led to state legislation for upgrading and regulating the practice of midwifery. During her tenure as executive secretary of the Association of Tuberculosis Clinics in New York City in 1910–17, Crowell wrote and published educational materials on tuberculosis and its control. This highly acclaimed work brought her to the attention of the Rockefeller Foundation.

Crowell's subsequent work with the Rockefeller Foundation, published in 1922 was titled "Sick Nursing and Public Health Visiting." This survey of European nursing became the basis for the founding of nursing schools partially funded by the Rockefeller Foundation.

For her contribution to the prevention of tuberculosis in France, Crowell was awarded the Legion of Honor. In addition, the International Council of Nurses made her an honorary member in 1941 for her contribution to the advancement of nursing throughout the world. On her retirement in 1941, she became an advisor on refugees for the American Red Cross. She lived in Italy until 1950, when she died there following a stroke.

The acclaimed work of F. Elisabeth Crowell led to the upgrading of nursing education and improved nursing care, and promoted the ideals of American nursing education. Said to have been endowed with a dynamic personality and the intellectual qualities of the true states-

man, Crowell's value to the Rockefeller Foundation was assessed in these words from their 1917 personnel files:

> She is keen and intelligent in her analysis of situations, sympathetic in her appreciation of individuals and institutions and effective in her work. We have in her a leader in whom we may place great confidence.

## PUBLICATIONS BY FRANCES ELISABETH CROWELL

### BOOKS

*The Work of New York's Tuberculosis Clinics; A Critical Study of Its Own Work.* New York: B.H. Tyrell, 1910.

*Adequate Clinic Control.* Philadelphia: National Association for Study and Prevention of Tuberculosis, 1912. Also printed in the *Transactions* of their eighth meeting.

*Tuberculosis Dispensary Methods.* New York: Vail-Ballou, 1916.

### MONOGRAPH

*Sick Nursing and Public Health Visiting in Europe 1922–1924.* New York: Rockefeller Foundation, 1924.

### ARTICLES

"The Midwives of New York." *Charities and Commons* 17 (12 January 1907): 667–77.

"The Midwives of Chicago." *Journal of the American Medical Association* 50 (25 April 1908): 1306–50.

"A Life Income at Age Sixty." *American Journal of Nursing* 18 (18 October 1917): 31–33.

### BIBLIOGRAPHY

Crowell, F.E. Personnel Files. Rockefeller Foundation, 1917.

"News About Nursing." *American Journal of Nursing* 40 (July 1940): 826–27.

*Rockefeller Foundation History.* Vol. 9. The Rockefeller Archive Center, Tarrytown, N.Y.: p. 2223.

"Specialists in Internationalism." *American Journal of Nursing* 31 (December 1931): pp. 1411–1412.

Stewart, Isabel M., & Anne Austin. *A History of Nursing.* New York: G.P. Putnam's, 1962, p. 198.

Vickers, Elizabeth D. "Crowell in Pensacola." *Journal of the Florida Medical Association* 70 (August 1983).

Aurelie J. Knapik

## Kate Cumming

### 1838–1909

Kate Cumming provided future nurses with one of the few detailed accounts of actual nursing experiences in Confederate military hospitals. She practiced nursing in these hospitals from 1862 until the end of the Civil War in 1865. This tenure in actual service provided extensive background information for her diary, which she maintained faithfully.

Cumming was born in Edinburgh, Scotland, to David and Jessie Cumming. She was one of four children, having two sisters and a brother. While she was still a young child, her family emigrated to Mobile, Alabama. Her father prospered as a clerk in banking and insurance businesses. She grew up in a middle-class environment and developed a strong sentiment for the southern cause.

As a southern woman in her 20s when the Civil War broke out, Cumming felt moved by the accomplishments of Florence Nightingale to help injured soldiers. She received inspiration from the Reverend Benjamin M. Miller, an Episcopal minister who urged women to serve the Confederacy.

In April 1862 she left for northern Mississippi along with a party of other women from Mobile. They arrived just as the victims of the battle of Shiloh swarmed into the hospital. The nursing duties, filth, hardships, sickness, and death overwhelmed most of these volunteers, but Cumming remained on duty. Although she had received no formal nursing training, she soon proved capable in nursing the wounded soldiers. By October 1862 legislation had passed the Confederate Congress, providing funds for the employment of women by the Confederate medical department. Cumming received formal recognition for her services by being appointed a matron in the medical department.

For the remainder of the war, Cumming served as a matron in various Confederate hospitals in Tennessee, Mississippi, and Georgia. Her role as matron included superintending the domestic economy of the hospital, the cooking, the cleaning, and the laundry. Physical nursing duties required for the care of soldiers remained the duty of male nurses who were recuperating patients.

Cumming faced many problems shared by her contemporaries in her efforts to fulfill her duties. Her family disapproved of her doing such unladylike work. Her efforts to recruit other women to help never fully succeeded due to opposition to women nurses from Confederate doctors and officers. Her efforts to recruit help also suffered setbacks when volunteers only stayed long enough to care for relatives. In spite of these problems, Cumming made many lifelong friends during the rigors of her war service.

Because her role as defined by law limited her activities to domestic duties, her diary gives little data about physical nursing tasks or techniques. Cumming saw herself as a small contributor to a great cause. What remains unique in her contributions is the honest, detailed diary of her life with the Confederate army from 1862 to its collapse in 1864. It was first published in 1866.

After the war, Cumming prepared her diary for publication. She never married, moving with her father to Birmingham, Alabama, in 1874. After her move, she taught school and music. She actively participated in the Episcopal church and the United Daughters of the Confederacy. She died June 5, 1909 of acute gastritis and senility at her home in Rosedale, Alabama, and was buried in the graveyard of St. John's Episcopal Church in Mobile, Alabama.

### PUBLICATIONS BY KATE CUMMING

*A Journal of Hospital Life in the Confederate Army of Tennessee, from the Battle of Shiloh to the End of the War: With Sketches of Life and Character, and Brief Notices of Current Events during That Period.* Louisville: J.P. Morton, 1866; New Orleans: W. Evelyn, 1866.

*Gleanings from Southland; Sketches of Life and Manners of the People of the South before, during, and after the War of Secession, with Extracts from the Author's Journal.* Birmingham, Ala.: Roberts & Son, 1895.

### BIBLIOGRAPHY

Harwell, R., ed., *Kate: The Journal of a Confederate Nurse.* Baton Rouge: Louisiana State University Press, 1959.

Harwell, R. "Kate Cumming." *Notable American Women*. Vol. 1. Cambridge Mass.: Belknap Press of Harvard University Press, 1971, pp. 414–15.

Herringshaw, T. *Herringshaw's Encyclopedia of American Biography*. 1898.

"Kate Cumming." Obituary. *Birmingham News*, 7 June 1909.

"Kate Cumming." Obituary. *Daily Item*, Mobile, 7 June 1909.

Linda E. Sabin

# Florence Dakin

## 1868–1958

Florence Dakin was a force for the improvement of nursing education in New Jersey during the second and third decades of the 1900s. As educational adviser for the New Jersey State Board of Nurse Examiners from 1923 until 1938, she guided nursing schools from the apprenticeship model into a more professional basis for nursing education.

Dakin was a descendant of several preeminent New England families, including John and Priscilla Alden and Massachusetts governors John Winthrop and William Bradford. She was born in Brooklyn, May 29, 1868, to George W. and Anna Olcott Dakin, but little is known about her parents.

Dakin attended the Brooklyn Seminary and Hollins College in Virginia prior to receiving her nursing education from the New York Hospital School of Nursing. She graduated with a diploma in 1902.

Following completion of the program at New York Hospital, Dakin served there for five years as assistant of the commissary department. As a graduate nurse, she held a number of supervisory positions around the country. She served as superintendent of nurses at Fannie Paddock Hospital (now Tacoma General) in Tacoma, Washington, was the operating-room supervisor at City and County Hospital in San Francisco, and later became the super-intendent of the Middletown Hospital in Middletown, Ohio.

In 1912 Dakin was an instructor of nursing at Paterson General Hospital School of Nursing in New Jersey when Governor Woodrow Wilson appointed her to New Jersey's first board of nurse examiners. This board appointment was the beginning of her long-term commitment to nursing education in New Jersey.

During her term on the board (1912–15), Dakin developed a standardized curriculum for use in New Jersey's nursing schools. Developed at the request of the New Jersey Board of Nurse Examiners, it was one of the first statewide standardized curricula in the country and emphasized the principles and practice of nursing. The board received requests for copies of the curriculum's *Illustrations of Modern Methods of Class Instructions* from Finland, Australia, and South America. The curriculum was adopted as a model by some nursing schools in Germany. In addition 216 copies were sent to Annie Goodrich for use in classes at Teachers College, Columbia University.

In 1923 Dakin was appointed by the New Jersey Board of Nurse Examiners to serve as the first educational director for schools of nursing in New Jersey. At that time there were 43 hospital schools of nursing in New Jersey. Her title was later changed to adviser, emphasizing her role in persuading schools to voluntarily upgrade their programs. A high-school diploma for entrance into a nursing school was not required by New Jersey law until 1936, but with her coaxing, nursing schools were persuaded to increase their entrance requirements to include four years of high school. By 1927 three-fourths of entering nursing students had high-school diplomas.

Dakin worked to have schools enhance their programs by offering specialty affiliations such as public health, communicable diseases, and psychiatry. She also pushed the schools to hire nursing instructors instead of relying solely on physician lectures and to outfit dietetic and chemistry laboratories for the nursing students.

Another advance in New Jersey nursing education credited to Dakin was the move to eliminate 12-hour night shifts for students and the institution of eight-hour work shifts. Along with this change came an important reform for patients: nurses were no longer to awaken patients before seven o'clock for morning care.

Dakin discouraged the practice of nursing students transferring from one school to another with credit allowed for time served in previous programs. She also stimulated interest and assisted in the development of courses that led to college credits for diploma-school students. The extracurricular life and living conditions for nursing students also were enhanced by her recommendations.

Dakin also conducted periodic surveys of the 47 hospital schools of nursing in New Jersey. These surveys were in addition to the mandatory yearly reports filed by each school.

Originally hired for an annual salary of $1,200 plus expenses, Dakin received $2,500 plus expenses after 15 years in her position of educational advisor. She was an active member of both the New Jersey State Nurses' Association and the New Jersey League for Nursing Education.

In addition to her work for the Board of Nurse Examiners, Dakin was the author of *Simplified Nursing*, which was written for home, or untrained, nurses. It was originally published by J.B. Lippincott in 1925. Dakin was sole author of the first five editions, and in 1956 she and Ella M. Thompson coauthored the sixth edition. The seventh edition was published in 1961 with Ella M. Thompson and Margaret LeBaron as coauthors.

Citing poor health, Dakin resigned in 1938 at the age of 70 from her position as advisor to schools. She was credited with moving the schools of nursing in New Jersey toward a professional basis.

Dakin spent her last years of her life in a nursing home. In December 1958 she fell and broke her hip at the age of 90 and succumbed three days later on December 24, 1958, in Paterson, New Jersey. She was buried at Forest Hill Cemetery in Utica, New York.

## PUBLICATIONS BY FLORENCE DAKIN

*Simplified Nursing.* Philadelphia: J.B. Lippincott, 1925.

With Ella M. Thompson. *Simplified Nursing.* 5th ed. Philadelphia: J.B. Lippincott, 1956.

## BIBLIOGRAPHY

Archives. New Jersey State Board of Nursing. Newark, N.J.

Murdoch, J. M. "Florence Dakin, R.N." *American Journal of Nursing* 34 (June 1934): 575–76.

*New Jersey Nurse 60th Anniversary Issue.* Montclair, N.J.: New Jersey State Nurses' Association, 1962.

New Jersey State Board of Nursing. Letter to Florence Dakin, 30 March 1938.

New Jersey State Department of Health, Vital Statistics. Florence Dakin. Death certificate. 24 December 1958.

*Who's Who of American Women.* Chicago: Marquis, 1958.

Janet L. Fickeissen

# Annie Damer

## 1858–1915

Annie Damer served in nursing associations on the local, state, national, and international levels. As president of the American Nurses' Association (ANA) for five years, she significantly advanced the state of the nursing profession during the early twentieth century.

Born in Stratford, Ontario, on November 30, 1858, Damer's early years were spent in Guelph, Ontario, and in Manitoba. She had one sister. In October 1883 she wrote to the New York City Training School, connected with Bellevue Hospital, and applied for admission. After graduation from the school in 1885, she went into private-duty nursing. For eight years she cared for a young girl at the request of the child's dying mother.

The following ten-year period marks the time that Damer made significant contributions to the nursing profession before an accident curtailed her activity. In 1899 she took the position of investigator for the Buffalo Charity Organization Society. She also began her work in the Nurses' Associated Alumnae, serving as chairman of the educational committee. In September 1901 the International Congress of Nurses held their meeting in Buffalo, New York, and Damer was in charge of securing accommodations for the members as well as arranging an exhibit that depicted the work being done by nurses around the world. Books, magazines, and papers written by nurses, bylaws, constitutions, and reports of nurses' societies were included in the exhibit.

Damer's zeal for public-health nursing resulted in the provision of a social-service department for tuberculosis patients at Bellevue Hospital in New York. She was elected president of the New York State Nurses' Association and the Bellevue Nurses' Alumnae, serving for several terms in both societies. Later her position in national nursing organizations allowed her to promote public health through temperance. She worked with Isabel Hampton Robb and Lavinia Dock to secure a resolution that the members of nursing societies would do all they could to teach the effects of alcohol and narcotic drugs and to discourage their use.

Damer was the only woman to hold the office of president of the American Nurses' Association for two nonconsecutive terms. She served in this capacity in 1901–2 and 1905–9. During these early days, the ANA was being reorganized and the bylaws revised. Damer's knowledge of parliamentary procedure was invaluable in this effort.

While continuing to work for efficiency and success in nursing, Damer viewed these as only a means to an end. In her presidential address at the ANA's 9th annual convention in Detroit in 1906, she advised her fellow nurses that their aim was to use their knowledge and service to prevent disease and to provide efficient nursing care. She worked hard and long to secure legal recognition of nursing as a profession, impressing upon the members of the ANA that increased privileges bring with them an increase in their responsibility to the public. Regarding the need for a representative association for nurses, Damer stated her strong feelings on the matter.

Because of her feelings that one of the marks of a profession was the publication of its own journal in which members of the profession could share advances taking place, Damer worked on a committee to acquire the *American Journal of Nursing* for the ANA (then known as the Nurses' Associated Alumnae of the United States). She later became president of the American Journal of Nursing Company.

Aware of the efficacy of people working together for a common goal, Damer was also instrumental in bringing together the members of the American Nurses' Association and the American Red Cross. She was never to realize the great work the American Red Cross Nursing Service provided during World War I, but this service would not have been possible without her early work. In addition to her presidential addresses, Damer also published articles comparing the nursing profession in the United States and Great Britain.

Damer's efforts for the promotion of nursing and public health were cut short when she was thrown from a carriage in 1910, causing her to be an invalid for the remaining five years of her life. Her interest in nursing continued, but she was no longer able to participate actively in the affairs of the profession. In July 1914 it was unanimously decided by the members of the ANA to make Damer an honorary member in recognition of her pioneering efforts as president of the association. She died in New York City on August 9, 1915. After brief services in her apartment, her body was taken to Toronto, where her married sister arranged for her burial.

## PUBLICATIONS BY ANNIE DAMER

"Presidential Address [Nurses' Associated Alumnae of the United States]." *American Journal of Nursing* 2 (July 1902): 750–53.

"Presidential Address [Nurses' Associated Alumnae of the United States]." *American Journal of Nursing* 7 (August 1907): 815–22.

"Presidential Address [Nurses' Associated Alumnae of the United States]." *American*

*Journal of Nursing* 9 (September 1909): 901–04.

"Nursing Organization and Public Good in the United States of America." *British Journal of Nursing* 47 (August 19, 1911): 149–51.

"The Quinton Polyclinic in London [Eng]." *American Journal of Nursing* 12 (November 1911): 136–37.

"Among the District Nurses in England and Ireland." *Visiting Nurse Quarterly* 4 (April 1912): 14–23.

## BIBLIOGRAPHY

Archives. New York State Nurses' Association. Guilderland, New York.

Flanagan, L. *One Strong Voice: The Story of the American Nurses' Association.* Kansas City, Mo.: American Nurses' Association, 1976.

Theresa Dombrowski

## Frances Elliot Davis

### 1882–1965

Frances Elliot Davis broke barriers for black nurses. Her story is indicative of the obstacles that many early nurses had to overcome.

Davis was born April 28, 1882, either in or near the town of Shelby, North Carolina, to Emma Elliot, the daughter of a plantation owner and Methodist minister, and Darryl Elliot, a part black, part Cherokee sharecropper. Darryl Elliot's mother had assumed the Elliot name while a slave on the family's plantation in Asheville, North Carolina. Because interracial marriage and cohabitation was illegal in North Carolina, Darryl Elliot fled from North Carolina and died a few years later. Emma Elliot was ostracized because white women impregnated by black men were considered prostitutes. She moved to Tennessee where she lived in poverty, was ill with tuberculosis, and died in 1887.

Young Frances Elliot Davis was passed from one black neighbor to another. Although her grandfather left her a small inheritance when he died, she did not receive it. Eventually she ended up in Pitts-

burgh, in the home of the Reverend Vickers. Vickers lived in Pittsburgh's Hill District, the home for thousands of blacks who had moved into the area looking for employment. Though Davis, then 12 years of age, believed Vickers had received her inheritance, she was little more than a maid in his household. She scrubbed floors, cooked the family meals, and cared for the baby. Although she was allowed to attend school for brief periods, the minister usually took her out of school after a few weeks so she could help at home. However, she did learn to read and continued to read even when not attending school.

After two years, Davis sought relief through outside employment and went to work for the Joseph Allison Reed family, well-to-do Pittsburgh residents. Vickers consented to this but required her to give him any money she earned. Two years later, Vickers demanded she leave her position and return to his household. Davis turned to the Reeds for help, and they agreed to assist her.

Davis was sent to a boarding school in Knoxville, Tennessee, run by the United Presbyterian Church. The Reeds agreed to pay her expenses until she finished normal school. Though Davis had talked about being a nurse, the Reeds felt she lacked the required physical strength, and it was on their advice that she attended the normal school. Although she arrived in Knoxville in 1899, it was not until 1905 that she had enough education to enter the normal school. She graduated in 1907 at age 25.

During her last years at what was then known as Knoxville College, a hospital was built to provide services for blacks. Following graduation, Davis worked there for one year as a practical nurse. Illness forced her to leave, and she then took a job in Henderson, North Carolina, teaching third and fourth grades at the Henderson Normal Institute. By now determined to be a nurse, she saved most of her wages in order to attend a professional nursing school. In 1910 she applied for admission to the school of nursing at the Freedman's Hospital in Washington, D.C. Concerned that she would be considered too old for nursing at 27, she changed her birth year from 1882 to 1889.

At the time Davis graduated from the nursing school, in June 1913, black and white nurses were given different exams by the District of Columbia, with the exam for white nurses regarded as more difficult. Davis insisted on taking the exam with the white nurses, the first black to do so and pass.

Davis worked as a private-duty nurse in the Washington area for three years before applying to the American Red Cross to serve in the Town and Country Nursing Service. She was the first black nurse accepted to take the approved course for this at Teachers College, Columbia University. Her field work at Columbia was at the Henry Street Settlement with Lillian Wald. In 1917 she was assigned to work in rural areas near Jackson, Tennessee.

When World War I broke out, Davis requested assignment to the Army Nurse Corps, but the Red Cross authorities indicated that she would not be accepted because there were no provisions for black nurses. In 1918 while working with soldiers near Chickamunga, Tennessee, she contracted a severe case of influenza, which left her heart permanently damaged. It was during the influenza epidemic in the army camps that black nurses were assigned for the first time to care for white soldiers.

In 1919 Davis became director of nurses' training at John A. Andrew Memorial Hospital in Tuskeegee, Alabama. She left this position to take a similar one at Dunbar Hospital in Detroit. It was here on December 24, 1921, that she married William A. Davis, a musician who played professionally in a band and taught music privately. She temporarily left nursing to take on the role of housewife, but after her only child was stillborn in 1922, she returned to Dunbar to take up her former position.

The nursing school at Dunbar was underfunded. Davis managed to secure funds from James Couzens, then a senator from Michigan and a significant figure in the development of General Motors. The physicians at Dunbar refused to accept the money for nursing and instead tried to divert it for their own use. As a result, Davis resigned and in March 1927 began working with the child welfare division of the Detroit Health Department.

In 1929 Davis returned to Teachers College under a Rosenwald Fellowship to work on a B.S. degree in nursing, but illness prevented her from completing her degree.

Davis returned to Detroit and the health department, and she worked primarily among the blacks in Inkster, Michigan, just outside of Detroit. During the height of the depression she ran a commissary for the unemployed at a Ford plant, and to this she devoted her full-time efforts. Henry Ford was one of her sponsors, and for many of her clients, Ford paid utility bills and helped financially with other problems.

As conditions improved, Davis joined the Visiting Nurse Association. She also started a nursery for Inkster residents, which attracted the attention of Eleanor Roosevelt, who helped solicit funds for it. From 1945 to 1951 she worked at Eloise Hospital in Detroit. The illness of her husband forced her to retire from most of her active projects in order to care for him, and she stayed in retirement after he died in 1959. She died May 2, 1965, in Mount Clement, Michigan, shortly before she was to be honored at the American Red Cross national convention.

## BIBLIOGRAPHY

Elmore, J.A. "Frances Elliot Davis," *Dictionary of Notable American Women.* Vol. 4. Cambridge, Mass.: Belknap Press of Harvard University Press, 1959, pp. 180–82.

Pitrone, J.M. *Trailblazer.* New York: Harcourt, Brace, and World, 1969.

Thoms, A. *Pathfinders: A History of the Progress of Colored Graduate Nurses,* (1929). Reprint. New York: Garland, 1984.

Susan B. DelBene
Vern L. Bullough

## Jane Arminda Delano

1858 (1862 ?)–1919

Jane Arminda Delano played a unique role in the history of nursing from the turn of the century through World War I. Throughout the war years, she directed the American Red Cross Nurses Bureau, which had the responsibility of recruiting and assigning over 20,000 nurses working in the war effort for the Red Cross, army, navy, and Public Health Service nursing programs. This unusual relationship between the American Red Cross and other services helped to integrate nursing services in order to meet the needs of our society during crises. Delano, like other Red Cross workers in her time, worked as a volunteer throughout her years of service. Her efficient, diligent leadership during this period made her a beloved superintendent of American nurses, regardless of their assignments.

Delano was born March 26, 1858 (according to records at Bellevue Hospital), in Townsend, New York, to George and Mary Ann Wright Delano. Most sources, however, report her birth as March 12, 1862. She was the second daughter born to the family, and she developed a strong relationship with her older sister. Her father died of yellow fever in 1864 while serving in the Union army in Louisiana.

Delano completed her basic education at Cook Academy, Montour Falls, New York. She tried teaching in school as a young woman, but it did not satisfy her. In 1883 she lost her only sister through an illness, and within a year she entered the Bellevue Hospital Training School for Nurses. She graduated in the class of 1886 and soon became a head nurse in one of the hospital's large units.

While at Bellevue, Delano worked with Sollace Mitchell, a young doctor from Jacksonville, Florida, who developed a deep respect for this dignified, capable head nurse. When a disastrous yellow-fever epidemic broke out in Jacksonville in 1888, Mitchell requested that Delano come to the city and superintend nursing care of patients at the Sand Hills Hospital. Upon her arrival in the city, she insisted that screens be installed over the beds in the barracks-type hospital, and soon her yellow fever cases began to improve. None of her volunteers ever contracted the disease, which can probably be attributed to the installation of the screens, thanks to Delano's dislike of Florida mosquitoes. During this time, the primary approaches to controlling yellow fever consisted of shooting cannons in the evening and burning large quantities of sulfur to purify the air.

The following year, Delano served as superintendent of nurses at a copper mining company hospital in Bisbee, Arizona. She then practiced privately for two years before assuming the position of superintendent of nurses at University Hospital, Philadelphia, for five years. From 1900 to 1902 Delano was the superintendent of the girl's department of the House of Refuge, Randall's Island, New York. Her next position, director at Bellevue's school of nursing, proved arduous, as it involved reorganization and management changes. After four years at Bellevue, Delano left to nurse her mother through a terminal illness. She returned to nursing soon after her mother's death.

Delano had joined the American Red Cross in 1899 during the Spanish-American War, but along with other nurses, she was concerned over the disorganization and poor allocation of nursing services during the crisis. After the reorganization of the American Red Cross under Mabel Boardman's direction in 1905, nurses secured a direct affiliation with the Red Cross through their professional organization, the Nurses Associated Alumnae. It was hoped that this direct relationship would encourage the enrollment of nurses before disasters or war conditions arose. Preparation for these sudden needs for skilled nurses seemed imperative, and Boardman worked hard with nurses like Delano to encourage a nurse-directed recruiting program.

In 1909 Delano assumed three major tasks. First, she became the superintendent of the newly reorganized Army Nurse Corps (ANC). She also became the chairman of the national committee of the Red Cross Nursing Service. Finally, she assumed the presidency of the American

Nurses' Association (ANA, formerly the Nurses Associated Alumnae), which required extensive traveling and writing for the organization. She managed many important changes in the ANC and completed her term as ANA president by 1911, but the tasks had taken their toll. She decided to limit her future activities to what she believed to be her most important calling, the organization of the Red Cross Nursing Service.

Delano applied to Boardman for a position as director of this fledgling organization, citing an annuity from her mother as adequate support for herself while she served the Red Cross. Boardman accepted her application, and Delano immediately began extensive travels to recruit nurses from all sections of the country. She envisioned a large body of well-trained nurses ready to serve in any crisis, and she wanted Red Cross nurses to come from the professional ranks only. To this end, she designed requirements to exclude all but well-educated nurses from the Red Cross service.

With Boardman and others on her committee, Delano helped to organize the first group of Red Cross nurses who sailed on the Red Cross mercy ship in 1914, just weeks after the outbreak of the World War I. This initial relief group taught Delano and her organization many important lessons about survival in Europe under war conditions. Every aspect of sending nurses abroad, from their attire to their training, received scrutiny during this first year of service. These lessons saved time, energy, and lives when the larger groups of nurses left for Europe in 1917 after the United States entered the war. Delano thrived on the work and made many friends during the great efforts required to meet war demands. Friends commented often in recollections of Delano about her genuine concern for the details that could mean so much to the nurse in the war zone.

Many of Delano's attributes helped her to win the respect and admiration of peers. A tall, reserved, graceful woman, she was stern and authoritative when necessary, especially if the welfare of her nurses was at issue. It was just as characteristic of her,

however, to display a warm compassion for those in need and to deal with problems with a gentleness of spirit. A modest person, Delano was equally comfortable addressing a convention session of the American Nurses' Association as sitting on the floor of her Red Cross office, sorting application folders on a Sunday morning.

The influenza epidemic of 1918 came as a new challenge to Delano to make progress in nursing assistance in public-health problems. Public health had always been of major interest to her, and thus she worked long hours throughout the epidemic to recruit and supply nurses wherever they were needed. One of the ways Delano maintained her high standards was through her ability to recruit capable assistants and then give them adequate autonomy to achieve their goals. She selected Clara Noyes to be her assistant in the American Red Cross nursing service and then allowed her to use her extensive administrative ability to coordinate many nursing assignments during the war and the flu epidemic.

In addition to her administrative duties, Delano wrote extensively throughout her ten-year career at the Red Cross. The book she wrote with Isabel McIsaac, *American Red Cross Textbook on Elementary Hygiene and Home Care of the Sick*, quickly became a classic for volunteers. She also wrote a monthly column called "Red Cross Nursing" activities for the *American Journal of Nursing* for almost ten years.

The last year of the war took its toll on Delano's health, and in January 1919 she sailed for postwar France to rest and inspect Red Cross facilities. Once her inspection tour began, she became overtired and exposed to severe weather. She developed mastoiditis and failed to survive repeated surgical procedures designed to relieve her infection. She died April 15, 1919, in Savenay, France, and was buried in Arlington National Cemetery under a large memorial marker. In the garden of the Washington headquarters of the American Red Cross stands a sculptured memorial dedicated to Delano and the 296 nurses who died during service in World War I. She left an estate of over $500,000, most of which was bequeathed to the Bellevue Alumnae association.

Delano had a broad vision of the many roles nurses could play in meeting society's needs and found herself in a position to create opportunities available to willing and interested nurses. Her directorship allowed nurses to manage nurses during the first massive appeal for professional nursing care of war victims. With her help, nursing took a step forward in the search for identity, autonomy, and a positive public image.

## PUBLICATIONS BY
## JANE ARMINDA DELANO

With I. McIsaac. *American Red Cross Textbook on Elementary Hygiene and Home Care of the Sick*. Philadelphia: P. Blakiston's Son, 1913.

## BIBLIOGRAPHY

Boardman, M. "Relation of Jane A. Delano to the American Red Cross, the Army and the Nursing Profession." *Proceedings*. New York: 29th Convention, American Nurses Association, 1934.

Clarke, M.A. *Memories of Jane A. Delano*. New York: Lakeside, 1934.

Delano, J. American Nurses Association Archives. Mugar Memorial Library, Boston University, Boston.

Delano, J. Papers. American Red Cross. National Archives, Washington, D.C.

Delano, J. Records and Newsletter Collection. Bellevue Hospital Archives, New York.

Delano, J. Records and Archives. Surgeon General's Office and the U.S. Army, World War I. National Library of Medicine, Bethesda, Md., and Army War College, Carlisle, Pa.

Dock, L.L., et al. *History of American Red Cross Nursing*. New York: Macmillan, 1922.

Gladwin, M.E. *The Red Cross and Jane Arminda Delano*. Philadelphia: W.B. Saunders, 1931.

Kernodle, P. *The Red Cross Nurse in Action, 1882–1948*. New York: Harper, 1949.

Nichols, J. *Notable American Women*. Vol 1. Cambridge, Mass.: Belknap Press of Harvard University Press, 1971.

Roberts, M. *American Nursing: History and Interpretation*. New York: Macmillan, 1954.

Linda Sabin

# Dorothy Deming
1893–1972

The professional achievements of Dorothy Deming reflect her talents as a scholar and an author. She was a public-health nurse who directed the activities of the National Organization for Public Health Nursing and served as a public health nursing consultant to the American Public Health Association. She gathered data on health and nursing and disseminated her findings in professional books and journals. Her avocation was writing juvenile fiction with nursing as the theme, and her novels enjoyed wide readership and encouraged many teen-age girls to consider entering nursing.

Deming was born June 8, 1893, in New Haven, Connecticut. Her parents were Clarence and Mary Bryan Whiting Deming. She was the youngest of three children, with one brother and one sister. Deming's family was privileged—as a child, Deming summered in Litchfield, Connecticut, attended private schools, and anticipated a debut after college graduation.

Deming graduated from Vassar College in 1914. The death of her mother prevented her debut that year, and Deming became involved with volunteer work at the New Haven Visiting Nurse Association. She intended to follow the family tradition of matriculating at Yale University and was enrolled there as a doctoral student in American colonial history. Although a portion of her dissertation was published in a monograph by Yale in 1935, Deming did not graduate. Her volunteer work and the entry of the United States into World War I combined to direct her interest to nursing.

Deming left Yale toward the end of World War I, and entered nursing school at Presbyterian Hospital in New York City. She graduated with the class of 1920; as a college graduate she had entered a shortened program of 30 months of study. She had affiliated with the Henry Street Visiting Nurse Association as a senior student, and after a brief period of private-duty nursing, she focused on public-health nursing for the remainder of her professional life.

Deming's first public-health position was with the New Haven Visiting Nurse Association. She later returned to the Henry Street agency and worked as a supervisor and field director under Annie Goodrich. She also served for one month as acting director when Goodrich left Henry Street. Deming then became the director of the Holyoke Visiting Nurse Association.

Deming's first affiliation in 1927 with the National Organization for Public Health Nursing (NOPHN) was related to her writing skills; she served as assistant to the editor (Ada Carr) of *Public Health Nursing*, the organization's journal. She was also the assistant to the director of NOPHN. In 1935 Deming was named the director general of NOPHN and also served as editor of *Public Health Nursing*. She served as general director until 1942. In that same year, her book *Home Nursing* was published by Little, Brown, and Company.

Under Miss Deming's leadership, NOPHN served as a primary source of knowledge in this field. Data on the health status and needs of the public were made available to individuals and volunteer and government groups. The organization also provided practice guidelines and criteria for the preparation of public-health nurses. NOPHN became increasingly involved in joint efforts with other nursing groups to study trends and problems of nursing and health care, and this cooperation was particularly important as wartime shortages of nurses developed.

In 1942 Deming was hired as a subject consultant by the American Public Health Association. She served in that capacity for ten years, and her responsibilities included participating in a merit-system study to prepare questions for civil service/merit examinations for employees of official public-health agencies. She also served as the public-health nursing consultant for the National Health Council's study on voluntary health agencies.

Deming's observations and studies were frequently published as scenarios that demonstrated the health needs and status of populations in settings affected by the social changes of a society at war.

She was able to articulate current and project future health-care needs.

As a public-health nurse, Deming was concerned that public welfare be served with a focus on both quality and cost effectiveness. Study and observations of auxiliary nursing personnel led her to conclude that there was a place for such vocations in the health-care field. Her study of practical nursing, *The Practical Nurse*, was published by the Commonwealth Fund in 1947. She also addressed the issue of practical nursing in the *American Journal of Nursing*. Her conclusions in 1944 were similar to the American Nurses' Association's position paper of 1965; she identified a need for two levels of nursing practice with differing educational preparation. One of her concerns with practical nursing was the proper utilization of each type of practitioner. Deming believed that practical nurses should be appropriately educated and licensed to protect both the public and the nurses themselves from exploitation. She also envisioned that nursing aides would become a means of increasing the professional activities of registered nurses.

Deming's articles on nursing careers in various settings provide today's social historian with a fascinating picture of the past. At the time, however, they served to inform nurses themselves of various employment opportunities. For example, in September 1944 her account of nursing in a railroad terminal documented the necessary qualifications for the position, the benefits of the job, and the types of patients and services that could be expected. This and similar articles provided registered nurses with a perspective on the many opportunities in nursing. Deming also wrote a book to be used in guidance counseling of student nurses and those considering nursing, *Careers for Nursing*.

Perhaps the most interesting perspective on Deming's views comes from her juvenile fiction. She wrote a number of nursing novels as part of a career book series written by practitioners of various occupations. Deming's books were so popular that "Penny Marsh Clubs," named for the heroine in Deming's first juvenile novel, were started in some high schools for future nurses. The books all presented nursing as a challenging career and incorporated facts on employment in many areas of nursing. One book described the need for nurses in wartime and for postwar nurses; others emphasized the need for college education for nurses. The use of guidance counseling in choosing a specialty and obtaining postgraduate education for the best nursing jobs was another theme. Male-female relationships in the books were also indicative of future social changes. Penny Marsh delayed her marriage to take advantage of a supervisory position offered her, continued to work as a nurse after her marriage and the birth of her children, and retained the use of her maiden name for professional use. Throughout all of her books, Deming presented heroines who were intelligent and committed to providing an essential health service.

Deming, a Republican and a Congregationalist, never married. Her summer vacations were spent in a farmhouse in New Hampshire, where she enjoyed her cat, dog, garden, and reading detective stories. Physically vigorous, she was also fond of swimming and hiking.

Deming died in Winter Park, Florida, on January 27, 1972. She was survived by three nieces and her sister-in-law.

## PUBLICATIONS BY DOROTHY DEMING

### BOOKS

*Penny Marsh, Public Health Nurse.* New York: Dodd Mead, 1938.

*Ginger Lee: War Nurse.* New York: Dodd Mead, 1942.

*Home Nursing.* Boston: Little, Brown, 1942.

*Penny and Pam: Nurse and Cadet.* New York: Dodd Mead, 1945.

*Careers for Nursing.* New York: McGraw-Hill, 1947.

*The Practical Nurse.* New York: Commonwealth Fund, 1947.

*Sharon's Nursing Diary.* New York: Dodd Mead, 1949.

*Linda Kent, Student Nurse.* New York: Dodd Mead, 1953.

*Nursing Assignment in El Salvador.* New York: Dodd Mead, 1954.

*Trudy Wells, R.N., Pediatric Nurse.* New York: Dodd Mead, 1957.

*Hilda Baker, School Nurse.* New York: Dodd Mead, 1960.

### ARTICLES

"Trailer Town." *American Journal of Nursing* 43 (June 1943): 524–28.

"S.O.S. from Norfolk, Virginia." *American Journal of Nursing* 43 (July 1943): 619–23.

"We Couldn't Do without Aides." *American Journal of Nursing* 43 (October 1943): 889–94.

"Mental Hospitals in Wartime." *American Journal of Nursing* 43 (November 1943): 1013–17.

"Practical Nurses—A Professional Responsibility." *American Journal of Nursing* 44 (January 1944): 36–43.

"Serving the Traveling Public." *American Journal of Nursing* 44 (September 1944): 869–71.

### BIBLIOGRAPHY

Block, M., ed. *Current Biography: Who's News and Why.* New York: H.W. Wilson, 1943.

"Dorothy Deming." Obituary. *New York Times,* 30 January 1972.

Fitzpatrick, M.L. *The National Organization for Public Health Nursing, 1912–1952: Development of a Practice Field.* New York: National League for Nursing, 1975.

"The National Headquarters Staffs." *American Journal of Nursing* 43 (1943): 101.

Ross, G. *Dorothy Deming.* Biographical sketch, copyright *National League for Nursing.* Special Collection. Milbank Memorial Library, Teachers College, Columbia University, New York. Photocopy.

Leslie M. Thom

## Sister Mary Joseph Dempsey
### 1856–1939

Sister Mary Joseph Dempsey was superintendent of St. Mary's Hospital in Rochester, Minnesota, from 1892–1939. During her tenure and under the leadership of physicians Charles and William Mayo, who later founded the Mayo Clinic, the hospital grew from an unknown, 27-bed country hospital to a world-renowned 600-bed hospital serving about 13,000 patients annually. A Catholic nun of the Third Order Regular of Saint Francis of the Congregation of Our Lady of Lourdes, she also served William Mayo for more than 21 years as surgical nurse assistant. In addition she took part in the organization of the Catholic Hospital Association of the United States and Canada in 1915 and served as its first vice-president.

Sister Dempsey was born May 14, 1856, in Salamanca, a small town on the Erie railroad in southwestern New York. She was the daughter of Patrick and Mary Sullivan Dempsey. She was christened Julia and had two brothers and four sisters, all younger. Two of the sisters later joined the same religious community she did. Prior to the Civil War, her Irish immigrant parents moved to Haverhill, Minnesota. Sister Dempsey spent her childhood in Olmstead County, near Rochester, and attended public schools in Haverhill.

At the age of 22, in 1878, she joined a branch of the Sisters of Saint Francis known as the Congregation of Our Lady of Lourdes, which was newly founded the previous year by Mother Alfred. Sister Dempsey became the director of the Holy Family School in Ashland, Kentucky, 11 years later when her career took a new turn.

A disastrous tornado in 1883 brought together the Sisters of St. Francis and the Mayos in what was to become a lifetime mission in the care of the sick. As a result of the damage and injuries caused by the tornado, Bishop John Ireland suggested to Mother Alfred that the sisters build a hospital in Rochester, Minnesota. Because her sisters were trained for teaching rather than nursing, Mother Alfred paid a visit to William W. Mayo, a physician and father of the Mayo brothers, to seek his advice about opening a hospital in the area. Although he presented arguments against it, she convinced him to undertake the hospital's administration as the sisters would finance the building. To engage in a project of this magnitude took courage and frugal living on the part of the community of nuns. When the hospital was completed, Mother

Alfred selected four of her nuns to staff it, and Sister Dempsey was one of them.

Sister Dempsey was taught the essentials of nursing care by Edith Graham, who had graduated from Women's Hospital School of Nursing in Chicago and was the first trained nurse in town. Employed to assist the Mayos in their office practice, Graham was loaned to the sisters to get the hospital work started. In six weeks Sister Dempsey was made head nurse, and three years after being assigned to St. Mary's, the new hospital, she was appointed superintendent, a position she held until her death 47 years later.

As it became impractical for the Mayos to assist each other, Sister Dempsey became the regular first assistant to William Mayo. She developed a quick understanding of surgical procedures. She was able to anticipate the surgeon's intentions, and her hands were so tiny she could reach into parts of the body he could not reach.

Sister Dempsey was the first person to call attention to an umbilical nodule that often is the only physical indication of a particular intraabdominal malignancy. Hamilton Bailey named this nodule after her in the 11th–13th editions of his textbook, *Physical Signs in Clinical Surgery.*

Although her own nursing preparation was minimal, in 1892 Sister Dempsey began working to establish a training school for nurses. In 1906 a program was begun at St. Mary's Hospital under the leadership of a graduate of the Johns Hopkins School of Nursing. The program offered a two-year course of instruction and a six-month postgraduate course in surgical nursing.

Aware of the impact of the Flexner Report which evaluated medical education in 1910, Sister Dempsey was convinced of the need for the nursing profession to keep pace with professional standards. In 1914 the Mayo Clinic was affiliated with the graduate school at the University of Minnesota. Sister Dempsey supported the curriculum changes that lengthened the nursing program to three years. In 1915 St. Mary's Hospital Training School received accreditation from the Minnesota State Nurses' Association. Sister Dempsey was determined to have a school that would be comparable in quality to the famous hospital with which it was associated.

In 1919 Sister Dempsey was the first hospital executive to develop a plan whereby nuns in religious orders could undertake studies at universities to prepare themselves for hospital and nursing-school administration. She recognized the rich pool of talents within the various orders, and in her officership role within the Catholic Hospital Association she looked ahead to preparation of future nursing leaders. Before Sister Dempsey died, members of her order had obtained advanced degrees from Columbia University and the University of Minnesota in dietetics, hospital administration, and nursing education, had taken back from nonprofessionals the management of the hospital and the school of nursing, and were recognized as national leaders in their profession.

Acclaimed as an executive with vision, Sister Dempsey spearheaded the building of five additions to St. Mary's Hospital, a nurses' residence, and a hospital chapel. In 1922 a new surgical pavilion was opened, and the first floor was reserved for classrooms and laboratories for the school of nursing. In 1927 cooperative agreements with the department of nursing education at the College of St. Theresa, Winona, and St. Mary's Hospital were made, which enabled graduate nurses to pursue a bachelor of science degree in nursing.

Encouraging her fellow nuns to participate in professional and public activities and to seek educational preparation in universities, Sister Dempsey confined her own activities to St. Mary's. Nevertheless, she became known to people involved in medical and hospital work throughout the world for her kindness, charity, sympathy, sense of humor, religious fervor, and sound judgment, especially in administrative matters. Twice selected as a recipient of an honorary degree of doctor of science by the trustees of Creighton University, she declined this honor.

Comments on her achievements and ideals include one that accompanied the bust that was a gift of the Mayo Clinic to the Sisters of St. Francis honoring her

memory on the occasion of the golden jubilee of St. Mary's in 1928. The inscription cited her high ideals in ministering to the sick.

Delegating much of the responsibility to younger assistants, Sister Dempsey remained the hospital superintendent until her death on March 29, 1939, at age 82, of bronchopneumonia. The archbishop of St. Paul and three bishops were among the many people who came to the small chapel for her funeral service. Activities in the operating rooms were suspended during the hours of the funeral service. She was buried in St. John's Cemetery in Rochester. Within six months, both William and Charles Mayo, with whom she had worked so closely in life, followed her in death.

## BIBLIOGRAPHY

Archives. St. Mary's Hospital, Rochester, Minn.

Brigh, M. Interview with author.

Callahan, B. "The Doctors Mayo and the Sisters." *Hospital Progress*, July 1965, 65–73.

Cassidy, M.B. "In Memoriam Sister Mary Joseph." *St. Mary's Alumnae Quarterly* 23 (May 1939): 6.

Clapesattle, H. *The Doctors Mayo*. Minneapolis: University of Minnesota Press, 1940.

Horton, B. Interview with author.

Key, J.D., D. Shephard, and W. Walters. "Sister Mary Joseph's Nodule and Its Relationship to Diagnosis of Carcinoma of the Umbilicus." *Minnesota Medicine* 59 (August 1976: 56–64.

Richardson, J.P. *Mother Alfred and the Doctors Mayo*. New York: Benzeger Brothers, Inc., 1959.

Steller, R.E. "Sister Mary Joseph Dempsey." In *Notable American Women*, Vol. 1. Cambridge, Mass.: Belknap Press of Harvard University Press, 1971.

"The Golden Jubilee of St. Mary's Hospital, Rochester, Minnesota 1889–1939." *Hospital Progress* 20, (1939): 402–412.

Theodora, M. Interview with author.

Kathleen Smyth

## Mary Elizabeth Brown Dewey

### 1853–1936

Mary Elizabeth Brown Dewey was the first superintendent of the Illinois Training School. She left that position to serve as assistant superintendent at Bellevue Hospital, then returned to Illinois Training School for a second term as superintendent. She also earned an M.D. degree. Although she remained active in providing nursing instruction to the staff at the Illinois State Institution for the Insane at Kankakee, after her marriage she devoted most of her time to her role as wife and mother.

Dewey was born in Manchester, New York, on January 18, 1853, the second daughter and third child of Thomas Anthony and Emily Ayer Brown. Her father was a physician. There were six children in the Brown family, four boys and two girls. Dewey attended the local elementary school in Manchester and later attended high school in Newark, New Jersey, where she lived with relatives. She completed two years of finishing school in Trenton, New Jersey, in February 1873.

Returning to upstate New York, Dewey briefly taught summer school before enrolling in the Women's Medical College of New York City. After completing one year's work, economic concerns led her to attend the nurses' training program at Bellevue Hospital, anticipating that she could complete her medical education at a later date.

Just before completing her nurses' training at Bellevue, Dewey was asked by the superintendent to serve as her assistant. Her duties included holding classes for the student nurses. While she served as assistant, she completed her studies and received her diploma in 1878.

Within two years, Dewey was interviewing with the Illinois Training School (ITS) Board for the position of its first superintendent. On February 22, 1881, her formal acceptance of the position as superintendent for a period of six months was received by the board, and she became their first "lady" superintendent. By May of the following year, she tendered her resignation in response to an invitation to return to Bellevue Hospital to her former position of assistant superintendent. On leaving ITS, she was commended by the school and hospital officials for her outstanding contributions in establishing the school.

After two years, the ITS board managed to persuade Dewey to return to her former post. In April 1885 she again served as superintendent of the Illinois Training School for one year.

During this period, Dewey was living with her brother, Charles, first in New York and then, upon her return to ITS, in Chicago. While in Chicago and before her second term as superintendent of the Illinois Training School, she attended the Women's Hospital Medical College and received her MD degree in April 1885.

During her second term as superintendent at ITS, she was introduced to Richard Dewey, a physician and the superintendent of the State Institution for the insane at Kankakee. Richard Dewey was in search of a trained nurse for his institution. Trained nursing staff for insane asylums was a relatively new concept, as the first training program for nurses for working with the insane had only been established a few years earlier in 1882.

The couple was married on June 22, 1886. At 33, Dewey became mother to her husband's two children, Richard and Ethel, as well as a dutiful daughter-in-law to her husband's mother, who lived with them. The family lived in a home on the Kankakee institution's grounds. Eventually two children were born to the couple. In addition to her family activities, Dewey arranged to provide instruction to the nursing staff at the institution.

It is not clear how long the family lived in Kankakee, but they moved to Chicago for a few years and then further north to a sanatorium in Wauwatosa, Wisconsin, where Richard Dewey was in charge for the next 25 years.

Over the years, there were many family trips to Europe and Mexico, and finally the couple settled in La Canada, California, to retire. After suffering a debilitating stroke in June, Richard Dewey died on August 4, 1933. Not long after in 1935, Mary Elizabeth Brown Dewey also died.

**BIBLIOGRAPHY**

Dewey, M.E.B. *My Life*. Manuscript, c.1935.

Schryrer, G.F. *A History of the Illinois Training School for Nurses*. Chicago: Illinois Training School, 1930.

Olga Maranjian Church

## Katherine De Witt

### 1867–1963

A leader in the fields of private-duty nursing and nursing journalism, Katherine De Witt devoted the early years of her career to private-duty practice. Specializing in maternal and infant care, she wrote numerous articles on those topics. Hired by Sophia F. Palmer to join the editorial staff of the *American Journal of Nursing*, she contributed extensively to the success of that publication for 25 years.

Born in Troy, New York, on June 11, 1867, Katherine De Witt was one of five children in the family of the Reverend Abner and Mary Hastings De Witt. Katherine's father, a graduate of Williams College, was a Presbyterian minister originally from New England; her mother was a graduate of Mt. Holyoke Seminary, which later achieved status as a college for women. Little is known about De Witt's early childhood years, but it is evident that education was valued by the family.

De Witt attended Troy Seminary and in 1887 graduated from Mt. Holyoke Seminary, intending to embark on a teaching career. Subsequent teaching experience convinced her that she was unsuited for that occupation, and she enrolled in the nursing program at the Illinois Training School in Chicago.

Published segments of the diary De Witt maintained as a student provide insights into the life of a nurse trainee in a large metropolitan hospital during the latter part of the nineteenth century. Stressful conditions combined with long work hours and insufficient staff are vividly detailed in her "Hospital Sketches," published in the *American Journal of Nursing*.

Following graduation in 1891, De Witt remained in Chicago, signed with the registry of private-duty nurses affiliated with the Illinois Training School, and acquired the majority of her cases through that agency. On occasion she accepted cases in other states such as Ohio, North Carolina, and Massachusetts. Considered a trailblazer in the private-duty practice field, De Witt's book *Private Duty Nursing*, published in 1913, was at that time the definitive textbook on the subject. The book describes qualifications for private-duty nursing, needed technical skills, and problems confronting the private-duty nurse of that era. A prolific writer on a variety of nursing topics, De Witt had an article accepted for publication in the first issue of the *American Journal of Nursing* in 1900 and became a frequent contributor to the nursing literature.

In 1907, De Witt joined the staff of the *American Journal of Nursing* as assistant editor, a career change that came about through an earlier chance encounter with Sophia F. Palmer, editor-in-chief of the journal. During a visit to Chicago, Palmer required assistance with her correspondence. Isabel McIsaac, superintendent of the Illinois Training School, recommended De Witt for the task, and her appointment to the journal followed soon after.

De Witt and Palmer worked together for the following five years. Between 1912 and 1913, the office was relocated and the staff enlarged. Following Palmer's death in 1920, De Witt became acting editor until 1921, when Mary Roberts was appointed coeditor. In 1923 Roberts was named editor and De Witt managing editor.

During eight of the years she spent as assistant editor, De Witt also served as secretary of the American Nurses' Association (ANA). She held that position at a particularly critical time in the ANA's development, its reorganization as a federation of state associations. At the same time, the ANA was involved in recruiting prospective nurses into the profession for service in World War I. Annie Goodrich, president of the ANA during part of De Witt's tenure as secretary, later praised De Witt for her consistent commitment to her professional responsibilities throughout a significant and difficult period.

At various times, De Witt served as president of the alumnae association of the Illinois Training School and as president of district 2 of the New York State Nurses' Association. In addition she helped establish and subsequently held the position of secretary for the Isabel Hampton Robb Scholarship Fund and the Isabel McIsaac Loan Fund. Both funds were combined in 1954 to become part of Nurses' Educational Funds, Inc., which continues to provide scholarship monies for the education of nurses.

In 1932 De Witt retired from the *American Journal of Nursing*. The New York State Nurses Association at its 31st annual convention in 1932 presented her with a book listing more than 4,300 subscriptions to the journal that were purchased in her honor by nurses across the country. Annie Goodrich, then dean of the Yale School of Nursing, spoke in tribute to De Witt and highlighted her many contributions to nursing.

Following her retirement, De Witt traveled abroad and in 1934 settled in Poughkeepsie, New York, where she resided until her death. She shared her home with a cousin and friend, Ruth E. Conklin, who was professor of physiology at Vassar College. She held membership in the New York State Nurses' Association, served on its board of directors and on numerous district committees, and for a brief period, was acting president. She also was a member of the board of the Poughkeepsie Visiting Nurse Association. In addition to her involvement in nursing, De Witt was a member of the First Congregational Church in Poughkeepsie, president of its women's fellowship group, and leader of another religious affiliate, the MacLeod Circle.

On October 10, 1950, at the *American Journal of Nursing*'s 50th anniversary dinner, De Witt greeted the guest of honor, Eleanor Roosevelt, who received the Distinction in Humanitarian Service Award from the journal. In 1954 at its 39th convention in Chicago, the American Nurses' Association gave De Witt its first Honorary Recognition Award.

De Witt died at her home in Poughkeepsie on December 3, 1963 at the age of 96 and was buried in the family burial lot at Mt. Ida Cemetery in Troy, New York.

## PUBLICATIONS BY KATHERINE DE WITT

### BOOKS

*Private Duty Nursing.* Philadelphia: J.B. Lippincott Co., 1913.

### ARTICLES

"Practical Points on Private Nursing." *American Journal of Nursing* 1 (October 1900): 14–17.

"The Opportunity and Responsibility of the Graduate Nurse of Today." *American Journal of Nursing* 2 (November 1901): 75–77.

"The Training of Babies." *American Journal of Nursing* 4 (May 1904): 588–89 and 4 (June 1900): 691–92.

"Hospital Sketches." *American Journal of Nursing* 6 (April 1906): 455–59 and 6 (June 1906): 610–13.

"The Babies Dispensary and Hospital of Cleveland." *American Journal of Nursing* 8 (September 1908): 961–63.

"The County Association and Its Relation to the State." *American Journal of Nursing* 9 (August 1909): 809–15.

"How to Select Applicants for Scholarships and Loans." *American Journal of Nursing* 35 (April 1935): 319–21.

"The Journal's First Fifty Years." *American Journal of Nursing* 50 (October 1950): 590–91.

### BIBLIOGRAPHY

*The American Journal of Nursing and Its Company.* New York: American Journal of Nursing Co., 1975.

De Lee, J. "Katherine De Witt—Student Nurse and Private Duty Nurse." *American Journal of Nursing* 32 (September 1932): 963–66.

"Honor to Miss De Witt." *American Journal of Nursing* 54 (June 1954): 702.

"Katherine De Witt." *American Journal of Nursing* 32 (December 1932): 1233–37.

"Katherine De Witt." Obituary. *Poughkeepsie Journal*, 3 December 1963.

"A National Tribute to Miss De Witt." *American Journal of Nursing* 32 (November 1932): 1147.

"News." *American Journal of Nursing* 32 (November 1932): 1215.

New York State Nurses Association. Transcript of convention proceedings, 4 October 1932, Lake Placid, N.Y.

"Report of the Thirteenth Annual Convention of Nurses' Associated Alumnae of the United States." *American Journal of Nursing* 10 (July 1910): 827–28.

"The Robb and McIsaac Funds." *American Journal of Nursing* 34 (March 1934): 254.

Roberts, M. *American Nursing: History and Interpretation.* New York: Macmillan, 1954.

Roberts, M. "The Private Duty Nurse Who Became a Recording Angel." *American Journal of Nursing* 55 (March 1955): 306–08.

Nettie Birnbach

# A. Louise Dietrich

## 1878–1962

A. Louise Dietrich's most notable contributions were those made to the Texas Graduate Nurses Association (TGNA) as general secretary from 1929–55. She also served in several elected offices of the organization.

Dietrich was born in Ossining, New York, one of 11 children of Valentine and Mary Dietrich. Her birth date, as reported by her closest friend, was November 17, 1878. She obtained her early education in Ossining before continuing to St. John's Riverside Hospital in Yonkers, New York, for her nursing training. She graduated from nursing school in 1899.

Dietrich launched her nursing career by working for three years as a private-duty nurse in New York City. However, from 1902 until her retirement in 1955, Dietrich's nursing activities were conducted from El Paso, Texas. She served as "directress" of nursing at Providence Hospital for seven months before being promoted to superintendent. In 1907 she assumed the position of superintendent for the St. Louis Skin and Cancer Hospital in El Paso.

In February 1907 the TGNA was organized. In 1908 Dietrich was sent to its second annual convention in San Antonio as a delegate from El Paso. At that meeting, she responded to the welcome address delivered by a mayoral representative, presented a paper entitled "The Use and Abuse of the Uniform," was appointed to the nominating committee, and was elected as the representative to the upcoming Associated Alumnae meeting in San Francisco.

Two weeks later she departed for San Francisco to present TGNA's application for membership and act as its delegate if admitted. She was successful in her endeavor and acted as the Texas delegate to the Associated Alumnae that year.

After 1908 Dietrich's TGNA activities are widely reported in the minutes of the state association, although her nursing activities between 1908 and 1924 are somewhat less known. She is reported to have undertaken further education in New York on two different occasions, first after leaving the St. Louis Skin and Cancer Hospital to do postgraduate work and in 1916 to attend the public-health course at Teachers College, Columbia University. Earlier, however, Dietrich and Emily Greene, another nurse, had opened St. Mark's Hospital in El Paso. When Greene left in 1916, the hospital was closed, and the building was converted to apartments that Dietrich used as source of revenue for many years. After the hospital's closing, Dietrich traveled to the public-health course at Teachers College, Columbia University. In 1920 Dietrich took charge of the El Paso Public Health Center and ran the center for several years.

In 1923 the Texas legislature enacted a Nurse Practice Act, which included a provision for an educational secretary for the board of nurse examiners for the state. Dietrich assumed the job in 1924 as the first secretary. The minutes of the board and her reports to the board reflect many of her activities in that position. A major responsibility was writing and evaluating schools of nursing throughout the state. In one six-month period, she traveled 13,254 miles and wrote 783 letters, all without the benefit of a secretary. She resigned from her position in May 1928.

Within the TGNA, Dietrich held numerous offices. She was secretary treasurer in

1909–11 and 1920–31, first vice-president 1911–12, president 1912–14, and council member 1914–15. In 1929 she assumed the role of full-time general secretary to the association, a position she had held on a part-time basis since 1909. She continued in that position until her retirement in 1955. While she served as general secretary, the association office was located in her home and Homoisella Moss served as her secretary. Acting in the capacity of general secretary of the TGNA, Dietrich was involved in many activities, including initiating a public-health course at the University of Texas and conducting institutes throughout the state as a form of continuing education.

In 1948 TGNA members honored Dietrich for her many contributions to the association by establishing a fellowship in her name. Numerous nurses from Texas were helped to further their careers with financial help from this fellowship. In 1951 she was further honored by the TGNA for her contributions to the organization and at its annual convention, she was awarded the Jenny Cottle Award for her distinguished service.

In April 1955 Dietrich attended her last TGNA convention as general secretary. At the end of that meeting, a resolution was passed thanking her for her leadership of the organization and her many contributions to it.

In addition to her nursing activities, Dietrich had been involved in many organizations, including St. Albans (Episcopal) parish, the Texas League of Women Voters, and the Parent Teachers Association. Dietrich died January 22, 1962, at age 82, and was buried in Restlawn Cemetery in El Paso. Commemorating her contributions, the Texas Legislature passed a resolution in tribute to her.

Dietrich never married, but she developed a deep and lasting friendship with Moss, with whom she shared her home in El Paso for many years. As a lasting memorial to Dietrich, Moss designed and had manufactured a stained-glass window, incorporating likenesses of Deitrich's nursing cap and training-school pin into the design. Called the Resurrection Window, it is installed inside St. Alban's Church in El Paso.

## BIBLIOGRAPHY

Archives. Texas League for Nurses and Texas Nurses' Association, Southwest Center for Nursing History. Austin School of Nursing, University of Texas, Austin.

Board of Nurse Examiners. Educational secretary's report, 1 May to 30 November 1924.

Brown, S. Telephone interview with author. 10 April 1986.

"News Highlights." *American Journal of Nursing* 51 (May 1951): 14.

Texas Federation of Woman's Clubs. *Who's Who of the Womanhood of Texas*. Fort Worth, Tex.: Stafford Lowdon Company, 1924.

Texas Graduate Nurses Association. Minutes, February 1907–1934.

Eleanor L.M. Crowder

## Dorothea Lynde Dix
### 1802–1887

In a tireless one-woman campaign, Dorothea Lynde Dix spearheaded nationwide reforms in the treatment of the mentally disabled. During the Civil War, she served as superintendent of nurses for the Union army.

Dix was born April 4, 1802, in the village of Hampden, Maine (at the time part of Massachusetts). She was the eldest child and only daughter of Joseph and Mary Bigelow Dix. She had two younger brothers. Her father had dropped out of Harvard to marry and worked unsuccessfully at farming and land management. Later, however, he achieved some fame as an itinerant Methodist preacher and partially supported his family by selling printed copies of his sermons and tracts. His wife was uneducated and became a semi-invalid when Dorothea was a child. Paternal grandparents were Elijah Dix, a prosperous Boston physician, chemical manufacturer, and land promoter, and Dorothy Lynde Dix, who came from a leading Worcester family.

Dix acquired a taste for education

when she went to Boston at age 12 to live with her widowed grandmother and later to Worcester to live with a great-aunt. In 1816 when she was only 14, she opened a school for small children in Worcester. In 1819 she returned to Boston to be with her aging grandmother and used the public library, public lectures, and other means to advance her education. In 1821 she opened a "dame school" for young girls in Boston and also taught at another school. Her elementary science text, *Conversations on Common Things* (1824), was a success. Another book, *Hymns for Children*, was published the next year.

In 1824 exhaustion and incipient tuberculosis forced Dix to lighten her schedule. However, she continued to write children's books and teach periodically. She opened a new school in Boston in 1831, and her reputation as a teacher and author enhanced its success. However, in 1836 she collapsed, and for about five years she traveled, living on an inheritance.

Dix's interest in the welfare of mental patients was sparked in March 1841, when she was invited by a Harvard divinity student to teach a Sunday-school class for women prisoners in the East Cambridge house of correction. She found that the only "crime" of many of these women was insanity.

The insensitive treatment of the women so angered Dix that she went directly to a local court. Samuel Gridley Howe, a philanthropist, backed her with an article in the *Daily Advertiser* newspaper, and improvements were made. Dix began to feel that she had found her calling. She surveyed existing mental institutions in the United States and Europe and found a few positive models, such as York Retreat in England, Bicêtre mental hospital in Paris, McLean Hospital and the Boston Lunatic Asylum in Boston, and the Hartford (Connecticut) Retreat.

Armed with this background information, Dix set out on an 18-month survey of the prisons, poorhouses, and asylums of Massachusetts. Howe lent her further encouragement, and Unitarian leader William Ellery Channing added his blessing. Her grim findings were summarized in her "Memorial to the Legislature of Massachusetts," which she presented in 1843 with an introduction by Howe. In the ensuing debate, Howe, Charles Sumner, and Horace Mann spoke out in her support. The legislature approved funds to expand and improve the state asylum at Worcester, and Dix, triumphant, eventually carried her crusade to every state east of the Rockies. At her first stops in Rhode Island and New York, she secured funds for additional facilities in both states.

In New Jersey Dix saw the establishment of the state's first mental hospital, which she called her first-born child, at Trenton. Establishing a routine, she surveyed and prepared "Memorials" in Pennsylvania, Kentucky, Maryland, Ohio, Illinois, Mississippi, Alabama, Tennessee, and other states. Though ill much of the time, she traveled 30,000 miles and often stayed in a state until the funds she sought were appropriated.

While these endeavors were enjoying success, another of her proposals was heading toward failure. Dix wanted the federal government to set aside some public land in a perpetual trust and to use the income for the care of the insane. For six years she commuted between her state campaigns and Washington, D.C., working toward this goal. Finally, in 1854 a bill was approved by both houses of Congress—and then President Franklin Pierce vetoed it. Frustrated, Dix carried her mission abroad and even secured the cooperation of Pope Pius IX in improving hospitals near the Vatican.

When the Civil War broke out, Dix's career entered a new and frustrating phase. Toward the end of her life, she told prospective biographers to downplay her Civil War experience because she did not want to be judged by it.

Dix volunteered her services, and although she had no hospital-management experience, she was appointed superintendent of army nurses on June 10, 1861. This was the highest office attained by a woman during the Civil War, and she was responsible for appointing and supervising all women army nurses. The stern, arbitrary, and often erratic manner she had shown in her earlier careers ill suited her for her new position. At one point, she accepted only applicants who were over 30 and plain looking, and she arbitrarily refused nuns and members of other religious sisterhoods.

Dix created friction by constantly criticizing hospital administrators who did not meet her rigid standards. Matters came to a head in October 1863, when the secretary of war gave the surgeon general a share in appointing nurses and made them responsible to the medical officers of the individual hospitals.

After the war, Dix never regained her old momentum. Tired and aging, she visited some hospitals and prisons, many of them damaged in the war. She also engaged in other useful projects, such as assisting in the campaign to finish the Washington Monument. Finally, in October 1881 she returned to the hospital in Trenton, New Jersey, that she had founded, in Dix's words her "first born," and lived there for the remaining six years of her life. In her mind her hospitals were her family and her life. Suffering from arteriosclerosis and failing faculties, she died July 18, 1887, with a copy of John Greenleaf Whittier's "At Last" under her pillow. She was buried under a plain marker in Mt. Auburn Cemetery, Cambridge, Massachusetts.

Throughout her life, Dix showed a shy but wholly committed character. She laid the groundwork, did the writing and let others give the speeches. She rarely spoke to large groups, and wrote her "memorials" and other tracts with eloquence and power. Her dedication was to the service of the common good.

## PUBLICATIONS BY DOROTHEA LYNDE DIX

*Conversations on Common Things.* Boston: Munroe & Francis, 1824.

*Hymns for Children.* Boston: Munroe & Francis, 1825.

"Memorial on Behalf of the Pauper Insane and Idiots in Jails and Poorhouses throughout the Commonwealth to the Legislature of Massachusetts." Boston: Munroe & Francis, 1843, and 20 similar memorials for other states.

## BIBLIOGRAPHY

Marshall, H.E. "Dix, Dorothea." *Notable American Women,* edited by E.T. James. 4 vols. Cambridge, Mass.: Belknap Press of Harvard University Press, 1971.

Marshall, H.E. *Dorothea Dix: Forgotten Samaritan.* Chapel Hill, N.C.: University of North Carolina Press, 1937.

Warren, J.F. "Dix, Dorothea." *The Encyclopedia Americana International Edition,* B.S. Cayne, Editorial Director; A.H. Smith, Editor-in-Chief. 30 vols. Danbury, Conn.: Grolier, 1985.

Alice P. Stein

# Lavinia Lloyd Dock
## 1858–1956

Lavinia Lloyd Dock was a leader in both the nursing profession and the women's suffrage movement. As an editor of the *American Journal of Nursing* and cofounder and officer of the International Council of Nurses, she established lines of communication among nurses worldwide. By helping document its history, she gave nursing new respect as a profession. As a labor leader, she encouraged nurses to organize and fought to improve the lot of women in other vocations. In the early 1900s, Dock became the only nurse to join the physicians' crusade against venereal disease. For many years she served the needs of the sick and poor at the Henry Street Settlement in New York City.

Dock was born February 26, 1858, in Harrisburg, Pennsylvania. She was the second of six children of Gilliard and Lavinia Lloyd Bombaugh Dock. Her parents were Pennsylvania Germans, well educated, deeply religious, and liberal in their views. The family was well off financially and owned a large amount of valuable land.

George, the only boy in the family, became a medical-school professor. One sister became a prominent horticulturist, and the others were gifted artists and musicians. One grandfather had been a friend of Dorothea Dix and helped her work toward the establishment of a state hospital in Harrisburg.

Dock attended a girls' academy in Harrisburg and became an expert piano and organ player. When she was 18, her mother died after a short illness, and she and her older sister, Mira, took over the care of the younger siblings. She still had not set any particular career goals for herself. It was not until some years later that a magazine article on nursing motivated her to enter nursing, a career not yet approved by society as suitable for "ladies."

In 1884 Dock began studies at the school for nurses of Bellevue Hospital in New York and graduated two years later. The school followed the principles of Florence Nightingale. The students worked 12 hours each day among the poor and sick on the wards and then gleaned what they could from scant formal instruction in the evenings.

Having an income from inherited property, Dock did not need to consider money in making her vocational choices. She worked after graduation as a visiting nurse with the Woman's Mission of the New York City Mission and Tract Society and later for three months with a charitable society for women in Norwich, Connecticut. She also was a night supervisor at Bellevue.

In 1888 Dock took supervision of a ward in a temporary hospital for yellow-fever victims under her old Bellevue classmate, Jane Delano. In the spring of the following year, she went to Johnstown, Pennyslvania, to help flood victims.

During this time, she wrote *Materia Medica for Nurses*, aided by her brother. Published in 1890 with financing from her father, it was the first nurses' manual on drugs and was the standard nursing-school text in the subject for a generation. More than 100,000 copies were sold.

In November 1890 Dock joined the staff of the new Johns Hopkins Hospital, serving as assistant superintendent of nurses under Isabel Hampton Robb. M. Adelaide Nutting was a student in that first Hopkins class, and these women were to become three of the greatest American nursing leaders of the time.

At Hopkins Dock taught first-year classes and most of the ward instruction. Three years after she had come to Hopkins, she and Robb were featured speakers at an international conference on hospital organization organized by Johns Hopkins doctors in conjunction with the Chicago World's Fair. Together they pleaded for the separation of the medical and nursing spheres of authority.

Dock stayed on in Chicago, spending two years as superintendent of the Illinois Training School. She then returned to the family home in Harrisburg. Her father died, and she took over the care of the family for one year, enabling her sister Mira to study horticulture at the university level.

In 1896 Dock went to New York City and established residence at the Nurses Settlement, which had been organized by Lillian Wald. She remained there for 20 years, caring for the sick among the immigrant poor, doing preventive care, health education, and school nursing.

At this time, she began to focus her energies on social concerns and the professional organization of nurses. One influence was the philosophical anarchist, Prince Peter Alekseevitch Kropotkin, who argued for a society built on custom and voluntary agreement rather than on formal law. She became active in the labor-union movement and helped organize a women's local of the United Garment Workers of America.

Dock helped Robb guide the American Society of Superintendents of Training Schools through its early years and was its secretary from 1896–1901. She researched the structure of various women's organizations, which paved the way for the founding in 1896 of the Nurses Associated Alumnae (later the American Nurses' Association), a general-membership group. At Teachers College, Columbia University, she was a volunteer faculty member in a postgraduate course for nurses established by Robb and Nutting.

In London in 1899 with her sister Mira, Dock attended meetings of the International Council of Women. Then, together with Ethel Gordon Fenwick, organizer of British nursing, she founded the International Council of Nurses (ICN). She served as its secretary and urged European nurses to challenge medical authority.

When the *American Journal of Nursing* was established in October 1900 by Sophia Palmer, Dock joined as a contributing editor. Her highly influential article, "What We May Expect from the Law," appeared in the first issue and gave strong backing to proposed legislation for control of nursing practice. In articles and the monthly "Foreign Department," she promoted international understanding of nursing issues. Through her writing for the journal, Dock urged nurses to band together and stand as an independent unit while keeping in mind their strong obligation to be socially useful. She also contributed to a sister publication, the *British Journal of Nursing.*

Dock believed that nursing would not be fully accepted as a profession until its history was soundly documented. After her research and with Nutting as coauthor, *A History of Nursing* was published in two volumes in 1907. Dock updated it and added two more volumes in 1912.

As she approached age 50, Dock stopped practicing nursing. She helped Adah Thoms and other black nurses establish a national organization for their group. However, her main concern was the economic, sexual, and political inequities that women faced in society. In 1905 she became the lone nurse to join a physicians' crusade against venereal disease. In that same year, she started to publish news of the fight against venereal disease in the foreign department of the *American Journal of Nursing.* She was one of the earliest members and one of the few women in the American Society of Sanitary and Moral Prophylaxis. A member of the New York Women's Trade Union League, she also walked with picketers at the shirtwaist strike of 1909.

In 1910 Dock helped lead demonstrations against a state law that sought to regulate, rather than suppress, prostitution. Her book, *Hygiene and Morality,* published in 1910, called for more self-control by men and suffrage for women. It came out at a time when venereal disease still was not a socially acceptable topic and showed Dock's keen social insight and willingness to promote her convictions.

Another influential book in which Dock had a hand was *The History of the Red Cross Nursing Service,* published in 1922. She was one of several contributing authors, and the book had a strong positive effect on the development of American nursing at the time.

Dock pressed tirelessly for women's suffrage, and was jailed three times for her militant demonstrations. She participated in poll watching and was active in the National Women's Party. These activities caused friction with her companions at Henry Street, and she moved out in 1915 and resigned from the board. After writing a controversial *American Journal of Nursing* column promoting birth control, she resigned from her post there in 1922, and in the following year she also resigned as secretary of the ICN.

Dock returned to Pennsylvania to live in 1922. None of the five Dock sisters had married, and they took up residence together at the family farm in the countryside near Fayetteville. Dock gradually lost her hearing and seldom left home. Though her arguments on behalf of the Equal Rights Amendment widened the breach between herself and her old colleagues, she kept in touch with Wald and renewed ties with Nutting. She also continued to work with Isabel Stewart on an abridged version of *A History of Nursing.* In 1947 at age 89, she was a guest of honor with Annie Goodrich at the ICN convention in Atlantic City.

After breaking a hip in a fall in March 1956, she died April 17 in the hospital in Chambersburg, Pennsylvania, of bronchopneumonia at age 99.

## PUBLICATIONS BY LAVINIA LLOYD DOCK

### BOOKS

*Materia Medica for Nurses.* New York: G.P. Putnam's Sons, 1890.

*Short Papers on Nursing Subjects.* New York: M.L. Longeway, 1900.

With M.A. Nutting. *A History of Nursing.* New York & London: G.P. Putnam's Sons, 1907.

*Hygiene and Morality.* New York: G.P. Putnam's, 1910.

With Sarah Elizabeth Pickett, Clara D. Noyes, Fannie F. Clement, Elizabeth G. Fox, and

Anna R. Van Meter. *The History of the Red Cross Nursing Service*. New York: Macmillan, 1922.

## *ARTICLES*

"What We May Expect from the Law." *American Journal of Nursing* 1 (October 1900): 8–12.

"Self-Portrait." *Nursing Outlook* 25 (January 1977): 23–26.

## **BIBLIOGRAPHY**

American Journal of Nursing. Files. New York.

American Journal of Nursing Collection. Nursing History Archives. Boston University, Boston.

American Society of Superintendents of Training Schools. *Proceedings, 1894–1900*. Harrisburg, Pa.: Harrisburg Publishing Company, 1894–1900.

Bland, S.H. "Techniques of Persuasion: The National Women's Party and Woman Suffrage, 1913–1919." Ph.D. diss., George Washington University, 1972.

Blatch, H.S., and A. Lutz. *Challenging Years*. New York: G.P. Putnam's Sons, 1940.

Breay, M., and E.G. Fenwick. *The History of the International Council of Nurses, 1899–1925*. Geneva: International Council of Nurses, 1931.

Cook, B.W. "Female Support Networks and Political Activism: Lillian Wald, Crystal Eastman, Emma Goldman." *Chrysalis* 1 (1977).

Daniels, D. "Building a Winning Coalition: The Suffrage Fight in New York State." *New York History* 60 (January 1979): 59–80.

Dock, L.L. Papers. Library of Congress, Washington, D.C.

Dock, L.L. Papers. Pennsylvania State Archives. Harrisburg, Pa.

Duffus, R.L. *Lillian Wald*. New York: Macmillan, 1938.

Gardner, J.F., Jr. "Microbes and Morality: The Social Hygiene Crusade in New York City 1892–1917." Ph.D. diss., Indiana University, 1974.

Harper, I.H., ed. *History of Woman Suffrage*. Vol. 6. New York: Fowler & Wells, 1922.

Irwin, I.H. *The Story of the Woman's Party*. New York: Harcourt Brace, 1921.

James, J.W. "Isabel Hampton and the Professionalization of Nursing in the 1890s." In *The Therapeutic Revolution*, ed. M.J. Vogel and C.E. Rosenberg. Philadelphia: The University of Pennsylvania Press, 1979.

"Lavinia Lloyd Dock." Obituary. *American Journal of Nursing* 56 (June 1956): 712.

"Lavinia L. Dock, Nursing Leader" Obituary. *New York Times*, 18 April 1956.

Nutting, A. Papers. Teachers College, Columbia University, New York.

O'Reilly, L. Papers. Schlesinger Library, Radcliffe College, Cambridge, Mass.

Paul, A. Interview. Bancroft Library, University of California, Berkeley.

Pennsylvania Department of Health. Death Certificate.

Roberts, M.M. *American Nursing: History and Interpretation*. New York: Macmillan, 1954.

Roberts, M.M. "Lavinia Lloyd Dock—Nurse, Feminist, Internationalist." *American Journal of Nursing* 56 (February 1956): 176–79.

Robinson, V. *White Caps*. Philadelphia: Lippincott, 1946.

Staupers, M.K. *No Time for Prejudice: A Story of the Integration of Negros in Nursing in the U.S.* New York: Macmillan, 1961.

Stevens, D. *Jailed for Freedom*. New York: Boni and Liveright, 1920.

Stewart, I.M. Interview. Oral History Collection. Columbia University, New York.

Wald, L. Papers. Columbia University, N.Y., and New York Public Library, New York.

Wald, L. *The House on Henry Street*. New York: Henry Holt, 1938.

Janet Wilson James
Alice P. Stein

# **Margaret Baggett Dolan**

## 1914–1974

Margaret Baggett Dolan was a nursing executive and educator who served as president of the American Nurses' Association, the American Journal of Nursing Company, the American Public Health Association, and the National Health Council. She campaigned for health legislation at both the state and national levels and was a strong advocate of the creative use of nursing skills in primary care.

Dolan was born in Lillington, North Carolina, on March 17, 1914, to John Robert and Allene Keeter Baggett. She received an A.A. degree from Anderson College in 1932; a nursing diploma from Georgetown University in 1935; a B.S. degree in public-health nursing from the

University of North Carolina at Chapel Hill in 1944; and an M.A. degree from Teachers College, Columbia University, in 1953. She was awarded an honorary LL.D. degree from Duke University in 1970 and an honorary D.Sc. degree from the University of Illinois in 1973.

Dolan's first position was that of staff nurse with the Instructive Visiting Nurse Society of Washington, D.C., from 1935–36. She was an epidemiological nurse and tuberculosis nursing consultant for the United States Public Health Service (USPHS) from 1936–41. On June 3, 1941, she married Charles E. Dolan.

From 1941–43, Dolan was a staff nursing supervisor for the Greensboro (North Carolina) city health department. She returned to the USPHS as a tuberculosis nursing consultant in 1945–46 before becoming a supervisor and special consultant in the generalized public-health program of the Baltimore County Health Department in Towson, Maryland, from 1947–50.

She joined the staff of the University of North Carolina School of Public Health in 1950 as an associate professor and became professor and head of the department of public-health nursing in 1959. She retired as professor emeritus in 1973.

In the American Nurses' Association (ANA), Dolan was president from 1962–64 and also served as second vice-president, a member of the board of directors, and chairman of its public-health nurses section. She was president of the American Journal of Nursing Company from 1960–62. In 1969 she was honorary chairman of the "BE-INvolved" campaign to encourage nurses to participate more in solving the social problems of their communities.

Dolan was elected to a one-year term as president of the American Public Health Association (APHA) in 1972 after a quarter-century of activity with that organization. She also was a member of its executive board, governing council, and numerous committees.

She was president of the National Health Council from 1969–70 and also chaired its executive board. Her other offices included the vice-presidency of the American Nurses' Foundation.

Dolan was a member of many organizations, including the following: Department of Defense Nursing Advisory Committee (1966); President's Advisory Committee on Health Resources (1962–68); committee on social insurance and taxes of the President's Commission on the Status of Women (1962–64); National Advisory Council for Nurse Training (1964–68); National Commission to Study Nursing Education; health insurance benefits advisory council, Social Security Administration (1968–72); board of directors, National Assembly of Social Policy and Development (1968–72); national and North Carolina tuberculosis associations; board of directors, North Carolina Nurses' Association; North Carolina Medical Care Committee; National League of Nursing; and American Association of University Professors. Her fraternal affiliations included Sigma Theta Tau, which she served as national treasurer; Phi Theta Kappa; Kappa Delta Pi; and Delta Omega.

Dolan was an active spokesperson for health-care legislation. For more than 20 years, she gave testimony to Congress on behalf of the ANA. She took part in the White House Conference on Health in 1965 and was a nursing consultant to the Army Surgeon General from 1969–71. She represented the ANA at the International Councils of Nurses held in Melbourne, Australia, and Frankfurt, Germany, and was a consultant to the governments of Ghana and Thailand. She also wrote many articles for professional journals and government publications.

Throughout her career, Dolan sought new ways to use education and legislation to effect improvements in public health programs. She saw the nurse as playing a key role in raising the quality of life in the community, and promoted advances in nursing education that would equip nurses to serve the public need more fully.

Dolan was given the John Carroll award of the Georgetown University Alumni Association in 1962. She received an honorary membership award from the ANA, and in 1968 she was further honored with its Pearl McIver Award. The APHA gave her its Public Health Nursing Section Centennial Award in 1972 and later established a memorial lectureship in her name. Her portrait was hung in the Health Science Library of the University of North Carolina, and the Margaret B. Dolan Memorial Library Fund was established there.

Dolan died of cancer on February 27, 1974, at Cherry Hill, North Carolina. Funeral services were held in Chapel Hill on March 3. At the time of her death, she was survived by her husband, four sisters— Miriam Baggett Rigby and Edna B. Crook of Lillington, Winifred B. Fuller of Leonia, New Jersey, and Lucy B. Davidson of Indianapolis, Indiana—and a brother, Dr. Joseph W. Baggett of Fayetteville.

## PUBLICATIONS BY MARGARET BAGGETT DOLAN

"Employment Opportunities for Nurses." *Nursing Outlook* 9 (April 1961): 225–26.

"Putting Our House in Order, What Changes Are Needed in ANA?" *American Journal of Nursing* 62 (December 1962): 76–79.

"Nurse and Public Health Official." *American Journal of Public Health* 64 (May 1974): 578.

## BIBLIOGRAPHY

"About People You Know: Mrs. Margaret B. Dolan." *American Journal of Nursing* 51 (January 1951): 19–20.

"Association News: A Tribute to Margaret Dolan." *American Journal of Public Health* 64 (May 1974): 518–21.

"Dolan, Margaret Baggett (Mrs. Charles E. Dolan)." In *Who's Who in America, 1974–75.* Chicago: A.N. Marquis, 1974.

"Dolan, Margaret Baggett (Mrs. Charles E. Dolan)." In *Who's Who of American Women, 1974–75.* Chicago: A.N. Marquis, 1974.

Flanagan, L. "Margaret B. Dolan." In *One Strong Voice.* Kansas City, Mo.: American Nurses' Association, 1976.

"Margaret B. Dolan 1914–74." In *ANA Publication G-123: Nursing Hall of Fame.* Kansas City, Mo.: American Nurses' Association, 1984.

Alice P. Stein

# Sister Mary Domitilla
## 1889-1955

Administrator of St. Mary's Hospital, Rochester, Minnesota, Sister Mary Domitilla was nationally known for her work in nursing education and hospital administration.

Lillian DuRocher was born in Monroe, Michigan, on September 11, 1889, to La-Combe and Josephine LaFontaine DuRocher as the second oldest of ten children. She decided to forego her final year of high school because teachers were needed in the rural schools in her home community, and in opposition to her family's wishes, she began teaching. On August 13, 1910, she was admitted as a postulant at the Motherhouse of the Sisters of Saint Francis in Rochester, Minnesota, and completed high school and began college during her novitiate. She received the habit of the sisters the following August, and was given the name of Sister Mary Domitilla. Her first vows were pronounced in August 1912, her final vows in June 1918. From 1912 to 1915 she taught at Sacred Heart School in Waseca.

In 1915 Sister Domitilla returned to Rochester and became a student at St. Mary's School of Nursing. Because of her outstanding academic ability, she was sent to study further at Teachers College, Columbia University, where she was one of the first nuns to undertake advanced work in the department of nursing and health. She received a bachelor of science degree from Teachers College in 1920 and returned to St. Mary's, where she became educational director and science instructor of the school of nursing, a position she held until 1931, when she was appointed director of the school. In 1934 she returned to Columbia and the following year was awarded a master's degree from Teachers College. From 1935 until 1937 she was assistant superintendent of St. Mary's Hospital and later, in 1939, its superintendent.

Sister Mary Domitilla had the difficult and often unappreciated task of reorganizing a hospital that had grown to a size that made it impossible for it to function effectively on an informal basis. She assisted in the organization of the home-nursing service and the section for the care of the mentally ill patients, and she organized the Rochester School of Vocational Nursing. Her responsibilities as administrator required that she give up most of her teaching, but she continued her interest in the school of nursing, improving the curriculum and promoting the inauguration of a four-year degree program for professional students and a one-year program for vocational students.

Sister Domitilla was a member of the general council of the Sisters of St. Francis of Rochester from 1933 to 1946 and again from 1952 to 1954. She served as chair of the congregation's building committee, an assignment that gave her the opportunity to use her unusual appreciation of architecture. In 1956 her memory was honored by St. Mary's when a seven-story addition was dedicated as the Domitilla Unit.

In November 1949 Sister Domitilla was relieved, at her own request, of the position as superintendent and received a special citation of honor from the board of governors of the Mayo Clinic as a testimonial to her long association with this group. She was appointed hospital consultant for four hospitals operated by the Sisters of Saint Francis. She was a speaker of note, and her many publications included two textbooks: *Outline of Materia Medica and Special Therapeutics* (1927 and 1933) and *Outline of Chemistry* (1931). From 1923 until her resignation in 1940, she was a member of the Minnesota State Board of Examiners and Nurses, and she served on many committees formed by the National League of Nursing Education.

Sister Domitilla was a woman of varied skills and interests, which included music, art, handicrafts, gardening, and fine cooking. She died on February 17, 1955, at the age of 65, after seven months of critical illness at St. Mary's Hospital, and was survived by her mother, five brothers, and four sisters.

## PUBLICATIONS BY
## SISTER MARY DOMITILLA

### BOOKS

*Outline of Materia Medica and Special Therapeutics.* Philadelphia: W.B. Saunders, 1927; 2nd ed. 1933.

*Outline of Chemistry.* Philadelphia: W.B. Saunders, 1931.

### ARTICLES

"An Experiment in the Project Method of Teaching." *American Journal of Nursing* 21 (1920): 30–37.

"Improved Method of Applying Hot Surgical Dressing." *American Journal of Nursing* 24 (1923): 12–14.

"An Experiment Suggesting a Teaching Method for the Head Nurse." *American Journal of Nursing* 24 (1924): 537–41.

"The Examination of Student Nurses in Dietetics." *Journal of the American Dietetic Association* 2 (1927): 209–15.

"State Board Examinations." *American Journal of Nursing* 34 (1934): 587–91.

### BIBLIOGRAPHY

Motherhouse Archives. St. Mary's Hospital, Rochester, Minn.
Dusbabek, C. "Sister Mary Domitilla." (Unpublished Ph.D. Dissertation.)
"Sister Mary Domitilla, O.S.F." *The Minnesota Registered Nurse* 23 (1950): 83.
"Sister Mary Domitilla." *New Bulletin,* St. Mary's Hospital 14 (1955): unpaged.
"Sister M. Domitilla." *American Journal of Nursing* 39 (June 1939): 690.
"Sister Mary Domitilla." Obituary. *American Journal of Nursing* 55 (1955): 538.
"Sister Mary Domitilla." Obituary. *Rochester Post Bulletin,* 18 February 1955.

Lilli Sentz

## Edith Augusta Draper
d. 1941

Edith Augusta Draper, a Canadian nurse, served as superintendent of the Illinois Training School for Nurses from 1890–1893. She was also on the school's faculty and previously served as assistant superintendent. Little is known of Draper's early years. In 1884 she graduated from the Bellevue Hospital Training School for Nurses, and prior to joining the Illinois Training School, she spent one and one-half years as a nurse in Rome. On her return, she became assistant superintendent of nurses at St. Luke's Hospital in Chicago. Her experience in Rome had been at the same institution where Isabel Hampton Robb had previously worked, St. Paul's House, an Episcopalian institution that furnished English-speaking nurses to travelers.

During her tenure as superintendent at the Illinois Training School, Draper oversaw the involvement of the school with the special exhibit of a model emergency ward in the Women's Building at the Columbian World's Exposition in 1893. This was an important event for nursing because it gave nurses visibility in demonstrating their effectiveness. Not only did the exposition show what trained nurses could do, but it also was the first occasion on which nurses came together publicly at a national/international gathering.

Important papers were presented in the nurses' section of the International Congress of Charities and Corrections, which was part of the exposition. One of the most significant was Draper's presentation, "Necessity of an American Nurses' Association," in which she advocated a national organization of nurses. According to Draper, such an organization would provide its members with their own association and the benefit of being recognized as belonging to a profession in its own right. As a direct result of Draper's presentation, a society called the American Society of Superintendents of Training Schools for Nurses in the U.S. and Canada, was formed.

In July 1893 shortly after this development, Draper resigned as superintendent of the Illinois Training School to return to her native Canada for a supervisory position at the Royal Victoria Hospital in Montreal. In 1896 she resigned from this position and retired from active nursing, making her home in Toronto.

On April 5, 1941, after a long illness, Draper died in Oakville, Canada.

## PUBLICATIONS BY
## EDITH AUGUSTA DRAPER

"Necessity of An American Nurses' Association." In *Nursing of the Sick*, edited by Isabel Hampton et al. 1893. Reprint. New York: McGraw-Hill, 1949.

"Congratulations from Miss Draper." *The Quarterly: A Journal Devoted to Nursing and Philanthropy Among the Sick of the State of Illinois* 3 (May 1906): 22.

## BIBLIOGRAPHY

*Announcement*, School of Nursing, St. Luke's Hospital, Chicago, 1940.

"Edith Augusta Draper." Obituary. *American Journal of Nursing* 41 (May 1941): 632–33.

"Edith Augusta Draper." Obituary. *Canadian Nurse* 37 (June 1941): 412.

Schryver, G.F. *A History of the Illinois Training School for Nurses, 1880–1929.* Chicago: Illinois Training School, 1930.

Olga Maranjian Church

## Katharine Jane Densford Dreves
### 1890–1978

Katharine Jane Densford Dreves served as the director of the University of Minnesota School of Nursing for 29 years. In addition, she led the profession through the years of World War II as the president of the American Nurses' Association and served in numerous other leadership positions during her career.

Dreves was born on December 7, 1890, in Crothersville, Indiana, to Loving Garriott Densford and Mary Belle Carr Densford. While actually the fourth child in the family, she grew up as the third and youngest child due to the death of her sister, Nora. William Leonard Densford was seven years older than Katharine, and Cora Mabel Densford was five years older. Of English and American ancestry, the Densford family lived on a farm in southern Indiana. Mary Densford was a teacher prior to her marriage to Loving in 1882. She continued to give music lessons and to be active in church and community affairs after the birth of her children.

In the family, great emphasis was placed on education and maintaining a cultured outlook. The girls were given the same opportunities as brother William, including attendance at boarding school and college. Dreves attended school in the Crothersville area until she was 16. In the fall of 1906, she left the family farm for Ohio to attend the preparatory department of Oxford College for Women. At the age of 18, she transferred to the college department for one year before transferring to Miami University in Oxford, Ohio. Dreves's college education was interrupted by the need to return home to care for her father after her mother's death and her sister's marriage. During this period, she completed professional teaching courses at Indiana University in Bloomington and taught fourth and sixth grades and manual training at the Indiana Girls School for two years.

Dreves returned to Miami University in 1913, completed her senior year, and graduated magna cum laude in 1914 with a B.A. degree in history and Latin. Having received a scholarship for graduate school, she entered the University of Chicago. In June 1915 she received an M.A. degree in history.

As a child, Dreves described herself as feeling there was something she must do, something that was needed and worthwhile. When the family frowned upon her choice of medicine as a career, she decided to go into teaching. During the 1915–16 school year, she taught Latin and German and coached girls' basketball and tennis at Harbor Springs High School in Harbor Springs, Michigan. During the next two school years, she taught history at the high school in Bismarck, North Dakota. In the spring of 1918, because of World War I she decided to change occupations and become a nurse.

Dreves's nursing education began at Vassar Training Camp during the summer of 1918. She then entered the University of Cincinnati School of Nursing and Health, which was under the direction of Laura R. Logan. What began as a mentor relationship eventually became a lifelong friendship. Dreves graduated from the University of Cincinnati with a graduate nurse diploma in October 1920. The only additional formal nursing education

that she had was some course work at Teachers College, Columbia University, in 1937. Early in her career, she also enrolled in short courses in public-health nursing and tuberculosis nursing.

After graduating, Dreves spent a year as a head nurse at Cincinnati General Hospital. This job was followed by one as a public-health nurse in Hamilton County, Ohio. In 1922 she became supervisor of nurses at the Cincinnati Tuberculosis Sanatorium and instructor of tuberculosis nursing and public-health nursing at the University of Cincinnati School of Nursing and Health. In February 1925 she accepted the position of assistant dean of the Illinois Training School and assistant director of nursing service at Cook County Hospital. In September 1930 Dreves moved to Minneapolis to assume the directorship of the University of Minnesota School of Nursing. She stayed at Minnesota until June 1959, when she retired.

In August 1959, two months after her retirement and at the age of 69, she married Carl A. Dreves. Carl was a lawyer from St. Paul who managed a family food-import business. The couple enjoyed 16 years together before Carl died of a stroke in December 1975 at age 89.

During her years at Minnesota, Dreves also had served the nursing profession by publishing books and articles, being elected to leadership positions, and suggesting innovations in nursing education. In her lifetime she had more than 97 publications (including two books), which span 53 years, 1922–75. Her books, *Counseling in Schools of Nursing*, co-authored with H. Phoebe Gordon and E.G. Williamson, and *Ethics for Modern Nurses*, coauthored with Millard S. Everett, were significant. The counseling book presented the innovative idea that a university counselor be employed solely to deal with problems specific to nursing students. The ethics book was the first such book to discuss nursing ethics as philosophical, moral, and ethical issues that extend beyond etiquette and behavioral standards.

Dreves served in 42 offices and committee seats from 1927 to 1959. She served on the American Nurses' Association (ANA) board of directors from 1934 until 1948, including two terms as president (1944–48). Her ANA presidency was noteworthy in that the demands of World War II amplified the nation's need for quality nursing care, and she traveled extensively to represent nursing. Other important issues during her presidency were economic welfare and collective bargaining for nurses, the restructuring of the nursing associations, the integration of minority groups, and international postwar recovery for nurses.

Other important offices include president of Alpha Tau Delta (1936–38); president of Sigma Theta Tau (1941–45); second vice-president of the International Council of Nurses (1947–57); member of the special medical advisory group of the Veterans Administration (1946–53); member of the steering and executive committee of the National Health Assembly (1948–49); consultant for the Army Nurse Corps, Surgeon General's Office (1948–52); and member of the national advisory committee of the American Red Cross (1956–62). During her retirement years, she served in many additional positions, and some major involvements were chair of the committee to raise $1 million for the American Nurses' Foundation (1960–64); member of the Minnesota Board of Health (1961–67); and member of the Governor's Commission on the Status of Women (1963–67).

Dreves also was an expert in parliamentary procedure and was recognized by the National Association of Parliamentarians. She was known worldwide. Her love of travel and interest in nurses in other countries were encouraged by at least 14 international trips during her working years.

The University of Minnesota School of Nursing under Dreves's leadership was known for its variety of curricula for generic-nursing and registered-nursing students, its ability to accommodate large numbers of students when necessary, its innovative ideas for nursing education and research, and the growth and development of a competent faculty with members who became leaders in nursing.

Dreves's retirement years (1959–78) were filled with activities related to nursing, women, and aging issues. For four years (1960–64) she and her husband traveled around the country, encouraging nurses to donate or help raise the funds for the American Nurses' Foundation. They were successful in raising about $750,000.

Dreves died in St. Paul, Minnesota, on September 28, 1978, as the result of a brain tumor. She was buried beside her husband in Acacia Park Cemetery in Mendota Heights, Minnesota. At the time of her death, her family included her five nieces and her husband's nieces and nephews.

## PUBLICATIONS BY KATHARINE JANE DENSFORD DREVES

### BOOKS

With M.S. Everett. *Ethics for Modern Nurses.* Philadelphia: W.B. Saunders, 1946.

With H.P. Gordon and E.G. Williamson. *Counseling in Schools of Nursing.* New York: McGraw-Hill, 1947.

### ARTICLES

"Staff Education, In Service." *American Journal of Nursing* 29 (October 1929): 1239–46.

"How Shall We Select and Prepare the Undergraduate Nurse?" *American Journal of Nursing* 32 (May 1932): 557–66.

"Student Health; Studies of Illness." *American Journal of Nursing* 35 (April 1935): 333–36.

"Nursing 1941—For All the People." *Hospital Management* 51 (February 1941): 49–54.

With Ruth Johnston. "Guiding Practical and Professional Nursing Students." *Nursing Outlook* 1 (October 1953): 580–82.

"This I Believe about Nursing in a Changing World." *Nursing Outlook* 12 (February 1964): 50–51.

"Nurses in American History: Vassar Training Camp." *American Journal of Nursing* 75 (November 1975): 2000–02.

### BIBLIOGRAPHY

Dreves, K. Papers. The Katharine Densford Dreves Papers. University of Minnesota Archives. University of Minnesota, Minneapolis.

Glass, L.K. "Katharine Densford Dreves: Marching at the Head of the Parade." Ph.D. diss., University of Illinois, 1983.

Laurie K. Glass

# Lucy Lincoln Drown

## 1848–1934

Lucy Lincoln Drown was an early leader in nursing education in the United States. She was the superintendent of nurses and the training school at Boston City Hospital for a quarter of a century, from 1885 until 1910.

Drown was born on August 4, 1848, in Providence, Rhode Island, the older daughter of Leonard and Mary Lincoln Drowne. (The final *e* was later dropped.) Her sister, Mary Leonard Drown, was 13 years younger, and a brother, Israel, died of consumption in 1879. During the Civil War, Drown's father fought as a captain with the Union army and was mortally wounded in Williamsburg, Virginia, on May 4, 1862. Her mother moved the children to New Hampshire to be close to her own family, which was descended from Mordecai Lincoln, just as President Abraham Lincoln was. Drown's middle name, Lincoln, reflects this heritage.

Drown's childhood was spent in Rhode Island and New Hampshire, where she attended both public and private schools. She enrolled in a course of study at the Salem, Massachusetts, normal school in February 1869. She then became a public school teacher in New England for the next 12 years, and her first teaching position was in the Newton, Massachusetts, school system from 1872–74. Later she taught in the Fisherville, New Hampshire, school system.

Boston City Hospital was the institution in which both Drown and her sister, Mary, chose to train for nursing. Mary was accepted into the program first and graduated in 1883; Drown began as a probationer on December 5, 1881. Though frail and delicate, she epitomized a stalwart New England ancestry. She was hardworking and never complained of hardships.

By the time Drown was graduated on February 11, 1884, she had a reputation as an enthusiastic pupil who had demonstrated an ability for organization and administration. These capabilities led to her appointment as the assistant to Linda Richards, the superintendent of nurses

who also was responsible for the training school. When Richards resigned to go to Japan, Drown succeeded her as the superintendent in 1885. She brought to the position a sharp mind, a keen intelligence, and an unswerving sense of duty.

Drown never married. She maintained close personal relationships with the many friends she cultivated through the years as well as with her numerous colleagues and students, and she received letters and visits from many nurses over the world. Her compassion and concern for nurses and students are illustrated in one incident. One student nurse in particular need of recuperation in order to recover from an illness was sent by Drown to her mother's seaside cottage in Cohasset, Massachusetts, until she was well enough to return to work.

The subordination of the superintendent of nurses to the medical superintendent of the hospital is evident in correspondence with the latter about students to be dropped and the discontinuation of stipends and pay on certain affiliations that required either the approval or decision of the medical superintendent. Drown's concern for people is revealed in those aspects of her correspondence that included many responses to inquiries about patients' conditions, explanations to applicants to the nursing school regarding the fate of their applications, and requests from other hospitals for agencies for nurses to fill positions.

At the time Drown became the superintendent of the Boston City Hospital Training School for Nurses, alumni associations were being established. Drown assumed the initiative of forming the nurses' club at the training school for the graduates of the hospital program. This nurses' club was the predecessor of the hospital's nurses' alumni association. Drown joined Henry H. Sprague, chairman of the training school committee, and G.H.M. Rowe, superintendent of the hospital, in sending a circular in November 1891 to the school's graduates inquiring about their interest in forming a nurses' club. A preorganizational meeting subsequently was held in January 1892. This meeting resulted in the establishment of the nurses' club and the acceptance of its constitution. So well loved and respected was Drown that the alumni installed her as the first president of the alumni association, a position she retained for many years.

When the alumni association voted to send a representative to the Third International Congress of Nurses which met in Buffalo, New York, during September 1901, Drown was its elected representative. She also was elected as the vice-president of the Suffolk County Nurses' Association at its meeting in Boston in May 1905. Drown was active also at the state level as the historian of the Massachusetts State Nurses' Association, which was founded February 26, 1903, when the alumni associations of Boston City Hospital and Massachusetts General Hospital joined efforts on the issue of nursing registration.

As the superintendent of nurses and the training school for nurses at Boston City Hospital, Drown was a charter member of the American Society of Superintendents of Training Schools for Nurses (ASSTSN), which held its preorganizational meeting in Chicago in June 1893. She participated on many committees of the ASSTSN and chaired some of them as well. Though she did not attend the preliminary meeting, she was elected as the first treasurer of that organization and served on the executive committee on organization until the first annual convention on January 10, 1894. At that time, the name of the executive committee was changed to executive council and she was reelected as treasurer, an office that she held until 1900. Also at that first convention, Drown was chosen to serve on the committee on eligibility. She was appointed as the chair of the committee on protection of training schools at the second annual convention in February 1895. At that same meeting, she also was selected as a member of the committee on a uniform curriculum. In February 1898 at the fifth annual convention, she was appointed to the committee to recommend a parliamentary law manual. In 1901 upon the expiration of her term as treasurer, she was elected to the office of vice-presi-

dent. In this capacity as an officer and a member of the council, Drown exerted influential leadership in the early years of the ASSTSN.

Drown's wide interest in social, cultural, and professional issues is illustrated through her responsibility for the monthly column "Progressive Movements" in the *American Journal of Nursing* from October 1900 to September 1901. This regular feature included a variety of topics by several authors, including "Work for Nurses in Play Schools," "School Nursing in London," "The Boston City Hospital Nurses' Club," and "The Committee of the General Federation of Women's Clubs on the Industrial Problem as It Affects Women and Children."

"Journal clubs" had been formed in both Baltimore and Boston during the years prior to the turn of the century. Both Drown and Isabel Hampton Robb reported on the progress of their clubs at the ASSTSN meeting in January 1894. These clubs were considered important educational experiences in the life of the pupil nurses. As the name implies, the nurses involved in these clubs were interested in engaging in discussions of the professional literature available to them.

Drown's professional career reflected a continued concern for the enhancement of educational standards. This concern was illustrated in her presentation of a paper entitled "A Consideration of Methods for the Protection of Training Schools for Nurses, from Applicants Who Have Been Discharged for Cause from Other Schools" at the second annual convention of the ASSTSN and in her article "Discussion on the Subject of Nurses' Homes and School Buildings," published in the *American Journal of Nursing*.

It was through Drown's proposal that graduation exercises were instituted in the training school at Boston City Hospital prior to her retirement. In 1912, two years after her retirement from the superintendent's position, a residence building that housed 80 students was purchased by Boston City Hospital and named Drown House in her honor.

On June 20, 1923, Drown made her last formal professional appearance when she addressed the National League of Nursing Education at a banquet in Swampscott, Massachusetts, given in honor of Linda Richards and Mary E.P. Davis. In this speech, Drown recalled the early years of the ASSTSN, both the work of the organization and its key participants. Drown applauded the contributions of her distinguished colleagues, Isabel Hampton Robb, Louise Darche, Diana C. Kimber, Lavinia L. Dock, Isabel McIsaac, and Sophia F. Palmer.

Following her retirement in 1910, Drown went to live with her sister, Mary Leonard Drown Drake, in Lakeport, New Hampshire. Here she was nursed back to health and able to once again take an interest in her friends, nursing, and world affairs. When Drake died in 1932, Drown maintained the home and continued to reside there until she died due to chronic myocarditis after a short illness on June 21, 1934, at the age of 85. It was not generally known that she was in poor health or ill, although she had suffered from chronic myocarditis. Funeral services were held at her home, and she was buried with her family in a cemetery near Concord, New Hampshire.

Committed and dedicated to the establishment of nursing in a large city hospital, Drown was instrumental in the advancement of educational standards and the protection of the public. Her 25-year tenure was characterized by a sense of humanity, thoughtfulness, and sensitivity to students and graduates.

## PUBLICATIONS BY LUCY LINCOLN DROWN

"A Consideration of Methods for the Protection of Training Schools for Nurses, from Applicants Who Have Been Discharged for Cause from Other Schools." *Trained Nurse* 14(1895): 198–200.

"Discussion on the Subject of Nurses' Homes and School Buildings." *American Journal of Nursing* 5(1904): 568–69.

"An Address." *American Journal of Nursing* 23(1923): 923.

## BIBLIOGRAPHY

Boswall, E.O. "The Boston City Hospital Nurses' Club." *American Journal of Nursing* 1(1901): 351–54.

Dock, L.L. *A History of Nursing.* Vol. 3. New York: G.P. Putnam's Sons, 1912.

Doona, M.E. "Nursing Revisited: Lucy Lincoln Drown (August 4, 1847—June 21, 1934)." *Massachusetts Nurse*, no. 6(1985): 6–7.

Drown, L.L. Early Leaders of American Nursing. *National League of Nursing Education*, 1922. Nursing Archives. Boston University. Sophia Palmer's Historical Collection.

Drown, L.L. Response to correspondence from physicians to trustees of Boston City Hospitals, 1 August 1910. Boston City Hospital School of Nursing Collection, Nursing Archives. Boston University, Boston.

"Editor's Miscellany: A Literary Club." *American Journal of Nursing* l(1900): 161.

Letter from physicians to Board of Trustees of Boston City Hospital, 22 July 1910. Boston City Hospital School of Nursing Collection, Nursing Archives. Boston University, Boston.

"News of Organizations: Boston City Hospital Alumni Association." *American Journal of Nursing* 1(1901): 892.

Nutting, M.A. Letter to Isabel Maitland Stewart, 25 November 1940. Nutting Historical Collection. James S. Copley Library, University of San Diego.

Nutting, M.A., and L.L. Dock. *A History of Nursing.* Vol. 3. New York: Putnam's, 1917.

"Official Reports: ASSTSN." *American Journal of Nursing.* 2(1901): 218.

"Official Reports: Suffolk County Nurses' Association." *American Journal of Nursing* 5(1905): 898–99.

"A Pioneer Passes: Lucy Lincoln Drown." *American Journal of Nursing* 34(1934): 841–42.

Reverby, S., ed., *The History of American Nursing: Annual Conventions of the American Society of Superintendents of Training Schools for Nurses (1893–1899).* New York: Garland, 1985.

Riddle, M.M. *Boston City Hospital Training School for Nurses: Historical Sketch.* Boston: Alumni Association, 1928.

"Who's Who in the Nursing World." *American Journal of Nursing* 22(1921): 92.

A. Gretchen McNeely
Irene S. Palmer

## Adda Eldredge

### 1864–1955

Adda Eldredge is best known for her efforts in promoting state registration of nurses through the enactment of state nurse practice acts. She served as the American Nurses' Association's president from 1922 to 1926.

Eldredge was born November 27, 1864, in Fond du Lac, Wisconsin, the youngest of five children of Charles and Ann Marie Bishop Eldredge. She is said to have displayed signs of leadership early in life. Her father, a native of Vermont, settled in Wisconsin in 1847 to practice law and served as a state senator. Later as a U.S. congressman, he voted against the impeachment of President Andrew Johnson. Her mother, a graduate of Russell Sage College, gave her children a love for history, fiction, and poetry.

Eldredge was educated in private schools in Fond du Lac and then enrolled in the St. Luke's Hospital Training School in Chicago, Illinois, believing that it offered the best technical advantages then available of any school in the Midwest. She received her diploma in 1899. From 1915–17 she took a public-health nursing course at Teachers College, Columbia University.

As was typical of nurses of her time, she began her nursing career as a private-duty nurse, often caring for patients in their own homes. She did this for eight years, then was appointed supervisor of instruction at St. Luke's Hospital School of Nursing in Chicago (1908–15).

While she was in Illinois, Eldredge toured the state to interest nurses and the public in the passage of a nurse practice act and developed a lifelong interest in nursing legislation. Her contributions to nursing in Illinois were recognized by the state's according her the honor of holding the first nurse-registration certificate. She served as president of the Illinois State Association for Graduate Nurses (now the Illinois Nurses' Association) from 1911 to 1912 and the next year as chairman of the legislative committee to defend the nurse practice act.

After one year's study at Teachers College, she spent a year with the Association for Improving the Conditions of the Poor in New York City. Then for three years (1917–20), Eldredge served as interstate secretary for the American Nurses' Association (ANA), National League of Nursing Education (NLNE), and *American Journal of Nursing* (AJN). She traveled extensively to promote the interests of the three organizations and to interpret their purposes to members and potential members. Her work in this position was frequently noted in the section titled "Editorial Comment" in the *American Journal of Nursing*.

It was a time of reorganization for the ANA, so Eldredge discussed reorganization with the groups she met with and encouraged the development of local leagues. During the early years of this appointment, she also assisted and advised directors of schools of nursing to increase their facilities to meet the war demands for nursing services.

For several months, Eldredge was on loan to the nursing committee of the Council on National Defense in Washington, D.C., to assist the members in assigning student nurses to schools. As her term came to an end, she concluded her report at the 22d ANA convention (April 1920) with a number of recommendations, including the establishment of a national headquarters for the association. Another recommendation urged the legislative section to encourage states to work for compulsory laws for the registration of nurses. Her own state, Wisconsin, did not enact such legislation until 1955, the year she died.

Eldredge's work as interstate secretary entailed visits to many states and talks to many groups. With her keen mind and observant nature, she learned a great deal from this experience, knowledge she used throughout the rest of her professional career.

Following this period, Eldredge served one year as a temporary member of the New York State Board of Nurse Examiners to help process applicants wishing to be licensed under the waiver of the New York Nurse Practice Act. In 1921 she was invited to return to her home state of Wisconsin to serve as the first director of the

Bureau of Nursing Education, established under revisions of the state's nurse practice act. The bureau was placed under the state board of health. In organizing and building the Bureau of Nursing Education, she established a precedent for maintaining high educational standards for schools of nursing. Her efforts were recognized by the Rockefeller Foundation, and during her tenure, Wisconsin became a study site in nursing education for other states and countries.

Eldredge is credited with strengthening the Wisconsin Nursing Practice Act. When she came to Wisconsin, there were few requirements for schools of nursing; any hospital could establish one. The entire curriculum was taught by the hospital's superintendent of nurses, supplemented by a few lectures by doctors. Student nurses were exploited in the name of education.

Eldredge inaugurated a program of inspection, evaluation, and accreditation of the state's schools of nursing. Always concerned about the welfare of students, she took a personal interest in their well-being and promoted plans for better housing, shorter working hours, and longer vacations. In 1933 she was able to secure high-school graduation as a prerequisite for entering any school of nursing in the state. She supported the employment of a well-prepared faculty and encouraged better education of nursing students through programs of affiliation to hospitals with more adequate clinical experience. Not limiting her interest to student nurses alone, she encouraged staff education programs for practicing nurses, as well as participation in postgraduate courses.

Eldredge was considered by many to be one of the nursing profession's "first citizens" during the 1920s and 1930s. She was recognized by Mary Roberts in her book *American Nursing* as one of the country's outstanding personalities in the movement for state registration for nurses. She was one of three persons who studied private-duty nursing for the 1923 Goldmark Report. A fluent speaker, she addressed many professional and lay groups in Wisconsin and elsewhere. As a frequent contributor to the nursing litera-ture, Eldredge wrote about legislation and various aspects of nursing education.

Throughout her career, Eldredge was active in the American Nurses' Association, serving as first vice-president (1913–18), board member (1919–22, 1926–34), and two terms as president (1922–26). In her capacity as president, she also served on the board of directors of the International Council of Nurses (ICN) and was an official delegate to three ICN congresses: Helsinki (1925), Montreal (1929), and Paris and Brussels (1931). In 1928 she was appointed chair of the Jane Delano Committee, responsible for selecting a suitable memorial to Jane Delano and the 296 nurses who died in World War I.

Eldredge resigned from her position in Wisconsin in 1934. Among the various budget cuts of state employees, she received the highest percentage, inspired, some believe, by the fact that she had instigated the closing of many of the state's poor schools of nursing. The state nurses' association protested the budget cuts to no avail.

Although she was 70 years old, Eldredge continued to work for the next three years as director of the Nurse Placement Service in Chicago. After her retirement, she remained in Chicago to teach courses on nursing legislation at the University of Chicago. In 1939 she taught a course in nursing jurisprudence at the University of Minnesota.

In the fall of 1941, Eldredge went to Pittsburgh to live with her niece, Dorothy Rood. She was given an honorary appointment as professor in the school of nursing at the University of Pittsburgh and served in an advisory capacity on the school's executive committee.

Although a number of honors came to Eldredge during her lifetime, one of the most outstanding was the Walter Burns Saunders Medal presented to her in 1935 for distinguished service in the cause of nursing. Eldredge was the sixth nurse to receive this award. Membership in Sigma Theta Tau, conferred by election and only to those with recognized achievements in nursing, was awarded to Eldredge in May 1940.

A scholarship fund that bears Eldredge's name was established by the Wisconsin (State) Nurses Association at its annual meeting in 1935. Known originally as the Adda Eldredge Postgraduate Scholarship Fund, for many years it provided scholarships to registered nurses to continue their educations and eventually was absorbed by the Nurses' Foundation of Wisconsin.

Eldredge was recognized for her contributions to her native state by inclusion in one of the series on *Famous Wisconsin Women*, published by the State Historical Society of Wisconsin. In 1986 she was elected to the Nursing Hall of Fame.

Eldredge died of cerebral thrombosis on October 24, 1955, at a nursing home in Oconomowoc, Wisconsin, where she had lived for three years. She was buried in Rienzi Cemetery at Fond du Lac. Her survivors included nieces and nephews—Dorothy Rood, Malcolme Rood, Adda Eldredge, May Eldredge, Elsie Blackwell, and Ralph Eldredge—and three grandnephews and one grandniece.

Eldredge was a person with strong convictions who worked to achieve professional goals. Her special contributions to nursing were the promotion of constructive legislation in nursing and the establishment of high standards for schools of nursing.

## PUBLICATIONS BY ADDA ELDREDGE

### ARTICLES

"The Common Things of Nursing." *American Journal of Nursing* 7 (December 1906): 173–74.

"How to Organize for Registration." *American Journal of Nursing* 7 (August 1907): 839–44.

"The Progress of the Past Year in Nursing Legislation and Some Lines of Future Effort." *Twentieth Annual Report of the National League for Nursing Education.* Baltimore: Williams and Wilkins, 1914.

"Mrs. Murphy." *American Journal of Nursing* 17 (December 1916): 213.

"The Responsibility of the Hospital to the Training School." *American Journal of Nursing* 19 (February 1919): 350–54.

"The Unwritten Curriculum." *American Journal of Nursing* 25 (April 1925): 273–77.

"The American Nurses' Association, A Review of

Its Work Since 1922." *American Journal of Nursing* 26 (1926): 533–37.

"State Standards." *American Journal of Nursing* 28 (January 1928): 66–70.

"Nursing Legislation and Its Effect on Professional Education." *The ICN* 3 (July 1928): 177–81.

"Future of Schools of Nursing." *American Journal of Nursing* 29 (January 1929): 71–78.

"Effective Standardization Programs." *American Journal of Nursing* 31 (April 1931): 471–80.

"What Is Quality in Nursing?" *American Journal of Nursing* 32 (November 1932): 1189–96.

"Legislation and the Future of Nursing." In *Proceedings, Twenty-Ninth Biennial Convention.* New York: American Nurses' Association, 1934.

"Nursing Bureaus and Professional Counseling." *American Journal of Nursing* 36 (1936): 807–08.

"Some Vocational Problems." *American Journal of Nursing* 37 (July 1937): 725–28.

"Current Challenges" and "Years of Progress." In *One Strong Voice: The Story of the American Nurses' Association,* edited by L. Flanagan. Kansas City, Mo: Lowell Press, 1976.

## BIBLIOGRAPHY

"Adda Eldredge," In *American Women.* Vol. 2, 1939–40. New York: Zephyrus Press, 1974.

"Adda Eldredge." *Bulletin of the Wisconsin State Nurses Association* 1 (June/July 1933): 6–7.

"Adda Eldredge." Obituary. *American Journal of Nursing* 55 (December 1955): 1456–58.

Brink, F.V. "Adda Eldredge." In *Biographical Sketches.* New York: National League of Nursing Education, 1940.

Cooper, S.S. "Adda Eldredge—Progressive Educator." In *Wisconsin Nursing Pioneers.* Madison: University Extension, University of Wisconsin, 1968.

Cooper, S.S. "Adda Eldredge." In *Famous Wisconsin Women.* Vol. 2. Madison: State Historical Society of Wisconsin, 1972.

Eldredge, A. "Current Challenges" and "Years of Progress." In *One Strong Voice: The Story of the American Nurses' Association,* edited by L. Flanagan. Kansas City, Mo.: Lowell Press, 1976.

"Former Leader in Nursing Dies." *Milwaukee Journal,* 25 October 1955.

Knight, G. "Adda Eldredge, R.N." *American Journal of Nursing* 34 (February 1934): 165–66.

Roberts, M.M. *American Nursing: History and Interpretation.* New York: Macmillan, 1954.

"Sigma Theta Tau to Confer Honorary Membership." *American Journal of Nursing* 40 (May 1940): 587.

Stimson, J. "The History of the Delano Memorial." *American Journal of Nursing* 33 (July 1933): 671–74.

"The Saunders Medal Award." *American Journal of Nursing* 35 (July 1955): 649.

Wisconsin Bureau of Nursing Education. Reports by Adda Eldredge. Archives, State Historical Society of Wisconsin. Madison, Wis.

"Who's Who in the Nursing World: Adda Eldredge." *American Journal of Nursing* 21 (July 1921): 735.

Signe S. Cooper

# Betty Louise Evans

## 1930–1982

Betty Louise Evans was recognized nationally and internationally for her work in psychiatric and mental-health nursing. In 1974 she was elected as a fellow to the American Academy of Nursing.

Evans was born in Chester, West Virginia, on September 13, 1930. She was the only child of Orville and Velma Miller Evans and the half sister of Patricia Shreve, David Evans, and Barbara Evans. She attended public school in Chester and was graduated from high school in 1948.

Evans was graduated from the Ohio Valley Hospital School of Nursing, Steubenville, Ohio, in 1951. She received a B.S. degree in nursing education (1954) and an M.Litt. degree (1957) and a Ph.D. degree in nursing administration (1968) from the University of Pittsburgh.

Evans had extensive experience in psychiatric and mental-health nursing. From 1951–54 she was employed as a staff nurse, charge nurse, and then night supervisor in the psychiatric department at St. Francis Hospital, Pittsburgh. In 1954 she became an instructor at the University of Pittsburgh School of Nursing.

During 1955–56 Evans attended the Kennedy School of Missions at Hartford Seminary Foundation. From 1957–59 she was director of nursing and nursing education at the Nur-Manzil Psychiatric Center, Lucknow, India, and for the following three years she was director of all India extension programs in psychiatric nursing and mental health for the Methodist Church in Southern Asia in India.

In 1964 Evans was appointed an associate professor and head of the department of psychiatric nursing at Emory University, Atlanta, Georgia. Three years later, she became a visiting professor of psychiatric nursing at the University of Pittsburgh, and the following year she assumed responsibility of chairing the department of psychiatric and mental-health nursing and was director of nursing services at Western Psychiatric Institute and Clinic, Pittsburgh. She held this dual position until 1973. She had been awarded tenure at the University of Pittsburgh in 1969.

From 1974–76 Evans was associate dean for graduate studies and professor of psychiatric and mental-health nursing at the University of Rochester, New York, and held a secondary appointment as professor of psychiatry at the University of Rochester School of Medicine and Dentistry. In 1976 she returned to the University of Pittsburgh as professor and director of the graduate programs in psychiatric and mental-health nursing. She held this position until the time of her death.

Evans was the recipient of many awards. She was a member of Sigma Theta Tau and Pi Lamba Theta. She had received the Evelyn Riley Nicholson Scholarship for outstanding work in India in 1962 and 1963. She was selected as an outstanding educator in America in 1974 and was the recipient of the Distinguished Alumni Award at the University of Pittsburgh School of Nursing in 1979 for outstanding achievement in the nursing profession. She was also a charter member of the Council of Advanced Practitioners in Psychiatric-Mental Health Nursing of the American Nurses' Association.

Evans began the Ph.D. program with specialization in psychiatric and mental-health nursing at the University of Pittsburgh. This was the first such program to be approved for funding by the National

Institute for Mental Health (NIMH). She was an advanced candidate in the program for research and special training in the Pittsburgh Psychoanalytic Institute and a member of the American Psychoanalytic Association.

Evans's work with the American Nurses' Association was extensive. It included being chair and member of the executive committee of the Division of Psychiatric-Mental Health Nursing, member of the Congress on Nursing Practice, and chair of the subcommittee on clinical doctoral programs for ethnic and racial minorities. She was a consultant on nursing education, on the unification of nursing education and nursing practice, and on psychiatric and mental-health nursing with a variety of educational institutions.

Evans was the author of many publications and director of numerous grants. She was director of three five-year psychiatric and mental-health nursing training grants from the National Institute of Mental Health: one for baccalaureate education, a second one for master's degree programs, and a third for doctoral study. She was director of a conference grant award from NIMH for the third national conference on graduate education in psychiatric and mental-health nursing, which was held in Pittsburgh. In 1978 she again wrote the grant and chaired the planning committee for the fourth national conference, which also was held in Pittsburgh.

Evans was coauthor of the grant for the psychiatric and mental-health nursing clinical doctoral fellowship program for nurses from ethnic and racial minorities that was awarded to the American Nurses' Association from the National Institute for Alcohol, Drug Abuse, and Mental Health Administration. At the time of her death, her research involved: (1) the development of a scale to assess levels of helplessness and hopelessness; (2) a study of the impact of federal funding in determining directions for graduate psychiatric and mental-health nursing education; (3) a study of the effects of nursing intervention on depression and autonomy in dieting obese patients; and (4) a study of the relationship of autonomy and "burn out" in church-related professionals.

Evans died July 8, 1982, at St. Francis Hospital, Pittsburgh, after a brief illness. Funeral services were held in Pittsburgh and in Chester, West Virginia, and burial was in Chester's Locust Hills Cemetery. A memorial service was held at Heinz Memorial Chapel, University of Pittsburgh, on October 1, 1982, to honor the memory of Evans, who served the University of Pittsburgh and the Pittsburgh community for many years. An annual lectureship in her name on psychiatric and mental-health nursing was established. Evans will be remembered for her outstanding contribution to the field of psychiatric and mental-health nursing education and for her service to the academic community and to the nursing profession.

## PUBLICATIONS BY BETTY LOUISE EVANS

"Report from Group 1, Summary of Discussions April 25–27, 1967." *Report of Work Conference Psychiatric-Mental Health Graduate Education in Nursing April 24–28, 1967* (1967): 23–29.

"Introduction." *Report of Work Conference Graduate Education in Psychiatric-Mental Health Nursing. October 7, 8, 9, 1970* (1970): 7–9.

"Unification—A Challenge to Nursing." *Challenge to Nursing Education . . . Preparation of the Professional Nurse for Future Roles* (1971): 51–56.

"Should We Educate for Service Priorities." *Fourth National Conference on Graduate Education in Psychiatric and Mental Health Nursing* (1979): 17–19.

## BIBLIOGRAPHY

Finneran, M. Interview with author, April 14, 1983, Pittsburgh, Pa.

Knox, J. Interview with author, February 18, 1986, Pittsburgh, Pa.

Martin, E.J. Interview with author, February 18, 1986, Pittsburgh, Pa.

Shreve, P. Interview with author, July 29, 1982, Pittsburgh, Pa.

Enid Goldberg

Margaret Gene Arnstein

Anne Lucippa Austin

Clara (Clarissa Harlow) Barton

Mary Beard

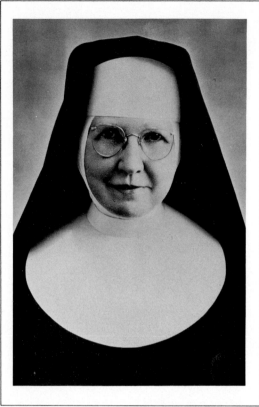

Sister Mary Berenice Beck

Nell Viola Beeby

Sister Kathleen Black

Florence Guinness Blake

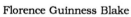

Florence Aby Blanchfield

Frances Payne Bingham Bolton

Frances V. Brink

Alice Griffith Carr

Genevieve Cooke

Florence Dakin

Annie Damer

Jane Arminda Delano

Dorothy Deming

Sister Mary Joseph Dempsey

Katharine Jane Densford Dreves

Lucy Lincoln Drown

Adda Eldredge

Sister Elisabeth Fedde

Susan C. Francis

Martha Minerva Franklin

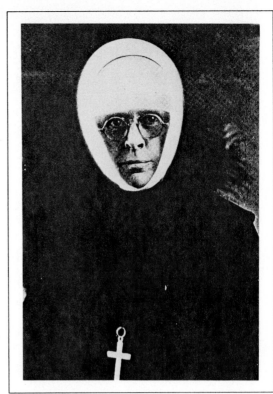

Ruth Benson Freeman (Fisher)    Sister John Gabriel

Alma Elizabeth Gault    Leila Ione Given

Annie Warburton Goodrich

Stella Goostray    Hazel Avis Goff

# Irene Taylor Fallon

### 1866–1952

Irene Taylor Fallon left a legacy for nursing historians in handwritten letters that detail her efforts to have New Jersey's nurse registration bill passed in 1903. She indicates the ability of nurses to do what is necessary in an important situation, and then go back to what they ordinarily do.

Very little is known about Fallon. She was born in New Jersey November 25, 1866. Her father was Edward Fallon; her mother's name is unknown. Nothing is known of her family background, her childhood, or her education, until at the age of 26 she entered the two-year nurse training program at Cooper Hospital in Camden, New Jersey. She completed the program in February 1894 and, immediately following graduation, became the night supervisor at the Chestnut Hill Home for Consumptives in Philadelphia. She remained at Chestnut Hill until early 1896, when she returned to Cooper Hospital to work, first as a head nurse, and later as the night supervisor. According to hospital annual reports she remained at Cooper for 10 years.

In June 1901 Fallon was one of the organizers of Cooper Hospital's School of Nursing Alumni Association. She wrote the constitution and by-laws and served on the soliciting committee. In the fall of 1901 an organizational meeting for the New Jersey State Nurses' Association was announced at an Alumni Association meeting. Fallon spoke to the nurses about the goals and objectives of such an organization. Though two alumni members were elected to attend the state nurses' association meeting as delegates of Cooper Hospital, Fallon was not one of them.

Nonetheless, she attended the first meeting of the New Jersey State Nurses' Association in December 1901 in Newark as an individual and was elected president of the organization. She served as its leader during its formative years when the goal was to gain the passage of a registration bill to license nurses.

During the time the bill was being lobbied, Fallon wrote a series of letters chronicling the effort to pass the bill and these give a unique insight into legislators' ettitudes both toward women and toward nursing. She also effectively countered the attacks of newspapers, hospitals, and some physicians, and kept a tally of the vote commitments of legislators, allowing readers to reconstruct the New Jersey campaign effectively.

Fallon emphasized the importance of grassroots support from other nurses in New Jersey, exhorting them to be actively engaged in the struggle. On one occasion she recruited fifty nurses to travel to Trenton in order to have a visible force present in the Senate gallery during a vote on the bill.

The New Jersey law was passed in April 1903 and was the second state nurse registration bill in the country. Her colleagues gave Fallon credit for getting the bill through. Her letters reveal an astute awareness of political maneuvering to defeat the bill, and her actions counteracted the opposition.

Following the completion of her two-year term as president of the New Jersey State Nurses' Association, she shared her lobbying expertise with other states. She was present at the organizational meeting of the Pennsylvania Nurses' Association in April 1903, sharing with them New Jersey's experiences of obtaining a registration bill.

Fallon continued to be active in the New Jersey State Nurses' Association, contributing her invaluable political experience. She chaired the legislation committee from 1905 through 1907 when nurses were attempting to amend the registration law to enact a board of nursing.

In 1907 Fallon left Cooper Hospital and became the district nurse in Millburn, New Jersey. In 1909 she became the infirmary nurse at St. Mary's Convent in Peekskill, New York, where she remained until 1918. Then she returned to Camden, working as an "hourly" or private-duty nurse. The following year she went back to work at the Chestnut Hill Home for Consumptives as night supervisor, and remained in this post for the rest of her life.

Fallon died September 1, 1952, at the age of 86 from a cerebrovascular accident.

She is buried at the Mount Moriah Cemetery in Philadelphia. Her passing received only a death notice; there was no obituary for this forgotten pioneer of nursing and politics.

### BIBLIOGRAPHY

Archives, New Jersey State Nurses' Association, Trenton, New Jersey.

Cooper Hospital Annual Reports 1894–1919. Cooper Medical Center Archives, Camden, N.J.

Death Certificate, Vital Statistics, Pennsylvania Department of Health, New Castle, Pa.

Minutes, Cooper Hospital School of Nursing Alumni Association. Cooper Medical Center Archives, Camden. N.J.

Janet L. Fickeissen

## Sister Elisabeth Fedde

### 1850–1921

Sister Elisabeth Fedde, a Lutheran deaconess and nurse, left her native Norway to serve the health and nursing needs of the Norwegian seamen and immigrants in the United States from 1883 to 1896. Her nursing endeavors resulted in the organization and establishment of the Lutheran Medical Center of Brooklyn, New York. Sister Fedde also started and guided the formation of two Lutheran deaconess institutes, one in New York, the other in Minneapolis, Minnesota.

Sister Fedde, the third of seven children born to Andreas Willumsen and Anne Marie Knudsen Fedde, was born December 25, 1850. Flekkefjord, the place of her birth and early life, is a small town located in the southwestern section of Norway close to the North Sea. Like most Norwegians of the 19th century, Sister Fedde's father was a farmer and former sailor. In her memoirs, Sister Fedde described him as her greatest support throughout her childhood and early youth. Her mother died while she was still very young. According to family records,

Sister Fedde was listed as Tonette Elisabeth, the fourth of eight children, one of whom must have died in infancy since the same name was given later to another son.

The compulsory education of children 7 to 14 years of age became effective in Norway in 1860 when Sister Fedde was 10 years old. Despite the isolation of many Norwegian communities, illiteracy was practically unknown. Families with several daughters placed as many as could be spared with neighborhood housewives for whatever learning they could acquire. Sister Fedde attended the local public school and remained at home with her father until, at the age of 19, she went to live with the Siqueland family in Stavanger. The Siqueland household provided her with an opportunity to expand her reading about Christianity.

Norwegians have been described as a people with a deep concern for the spirit of the individual; their political, social, and economic thrusts were a combination of both private and public concerns. The literature of Sister Fedde's time focused on the social issues of the day and the need for social reform. The Norwegian Association for Women's Rights was in the formative stages while Sister Fedde was a young, active deaconess striving to upgrade nursing and health care.

It was during her time with the Siquelands that Sister Fedde's father died. His death had a profound effect on her, and the separation from him caused a great change in her life. Her faith deepened, and at the age of 23, she joined the Deaconess Institute at Kristiania (now Oslo) in December 1873. Her natural kindness and compassion for others were fostered during her years at the Deaconess Institute, where she was under the direct inspiration and instruction of Mother Catherine Guldberg.

Mother Guldberg, the first nursing nun in Norway, motivated the Deaconess Institute to undertake the first steps to implement modern nursing according to the Kaiserswerth Training Center in Germany. In 1868 the Florence Nightingale influence began to impact on Norway, and the deaconesses strove to raise the moral and technical standard of hospital workers.

Sister Fedde profited from the nursing practices and ideals she learned at Kristiania. In fact, her approach to the care of the sick in the various assignments given her by Mother Guldberg mirrored Florence Nightingale's own activities. Her first endeavor was always to establish a clean, comfortable environment, demanding from directors and governing boards the necessary mattresses, blankets, linens, and supplies for patients. Public-health nursing had long been a fact among Norwegians. By the late 1800s, the Norwegian Women's Public Health Association was active not only in the care of the wounded and sick, but also in fostering an intensely social and patriotic spirit.

Mother Guldberg identified Sister Fedde's alertness to patients' experience, nursing competence, and organizational ability. She assigned her to organize a dispensary at the state hospital where the new nursing methods finally were being accepted. Later, Sister Fedde replaced Mother Guldberg and was in charge of the Deaconess Institute during her absence. In 1878, Mother Guldberg assigned Sister Fedde to extend advanced nursing knowledge and techniques to the town of Tromsö, located within the Arctic Circle.

Sister Fedde previously had proven her ability to take risks and confront fearful situations. In 1887 without the advantage of antitoxins, she went forth to care for a young child with typhoid fever, realizing that she might be facing her own death. She drew upon all her nursing knowledge and skill to care for the child and was assertive in her refusal to comply with demands for services that were beyond the sphere of nursing care.

These personal and professional strengths came to her aid again during the four years she worked in the Arctic. It was during her experience in Tromsö that Sister Fedde performed an autopsy when there was no one else available to do so. She afterwards contracted blood poisoning, an illness that terminated her services in the Arctic Circle in the spring of 1882.

Because of widespread unemployment in Norway during the period from 1860–1925, more than 850,000 Norwegians emigrated, chiefly to the United States. In late 1882, Sister Fedde received a letter inviting her to come to the aid of Norwegian immigrants in the waterfront community of Brooklyn. The dean of the Lutheran pastors in New York had asked Sister Fedde's brother-in-law to write the letter calling her to serve in Brooklyn. Since the invitation was extended to Sister Fedde personally rather than to the Deaconess Institute, she could not be sent as a representative of the institute. Nevertheless, Mother Guldberg encouraged her, and Sister Fedde accepted the challenge. Because of her past credibility as a deaconess, she was permitted to wear the Norwegian deaconesses' garb.

On April 8, 1883, at the age of 33, Sister Fedde arrived in Brooklyn, where she was met by her brother-in-law. With a commitment of $150 for the first year from Anna Børs, wife of the Norwegian consul general, Sister Fedde was successful in gaining additional support for her work among the ill and poor from the pastors of the Norwegian Seamen's Mission and the Norwegian Lutheran Church in Brooklyn. The plight of the sick immigrants was difficult, especially among those who needed hospital care, since few institutions accepted charity patients. Each week Sister Fedde visited her sick countrymen at Ward Island Immigrant Hospital, where conditions were deplorable, and as a result, she became increasingly determined to build a hospital to serve them.

Sister Fedde gathered a group of women, or ladies' aid society, to assist her in her work. One of the first tasks she set before them was sewing bed linens for the new hospital. When a building site for the desired new hospital was found on the corner of 46th Street and Fourth Avenue, the price of the lot was $3,000. Although the ladies' aid society had in its treasury only $4,000, the women decided to begin building at once. An intensive building campaign was launched, and such names as Consul Børs, Cornelius Vanderbilt, and John D. Rockefeller were listed as early contributors. On May 29, 1889, the cornerstone of the new Brooklyn Deaconess Hospital, the predecessor of today's Lutheran Medical Center, was laid.

In 1884 Sister Fedde attended a legislative session in Albany, New York, where she witnessed the organization of the boroughs of New York into the greater New York area. On this occasion, she addressed a committee of legislators and convinced them of the need for state aid for the Norwegian hospital. Subsequently, a bill was passed allotting financial assistance to the hospital.

In the course of her professional career, Sister Fedde established especially close relationships with two women. Her friendship with Mrs. Hilmbo began when she was caring for the sick in Tromsö. Hilmbo was the wife of the physician with whom Sister Fedde worked, and her death was a great loss for Sister Fedde. Her other good friend and associate was Anna Børs; many times Sister Fedde noted in her diary how grateful she was for Børs's loyal support and friendship. Sister Fedde also often spent time with her sister Marie, who lived in New York, and she enjoyed these family encounters, especially those with her three young nephews. It was Marie's husband who extended the invitation to Sister Fedde to come to New York.

In the summer of 1888, Sister Fedde attended the convention of the Lutheran general council in Minneapolis. The Lutheran community convinced her that there was need for a Norwegian Lutheran home and hospital there. Sister Fedde was later granted a leave of absence from her work in Brooklyn and devoted two years in establishing the deaconess hospital in Minneapolis.

On returning to Brooklyn, Sister Fedde continued her nursing endeavors until 1896, when she returned to Norway because of declining health. In 1898 at age 46, Sister Fedde married Ole Andreas Slettebo and lived with him on a farm near Egersund, a southern seaport on the North Sea. According to the Lutheran Deaconess Institute, a deaconess is free to marry, but must leave the institute because the two responsibilities are considered incompatible. During her married life, she witnessed Norway's national independence from Sweden in 1905, its neutrality during World War I, and its membership in the League of Nations in 1920. She also saw the formation of the Norwegian Nurses Association in 1912. Like other professionals, the Norwegian nurses united to protect their rights and to safeguard the discipline from unauthorized practitioners.

In 1904 Sister Fedde returned to Brooklyn as the guest of honor when the new hospital building replacing the original Norwegian Lutheran Home and Hospital was dedicated, and she was later made an honorary member of the Norwegian Lutheran Deaconesses Home and Hospital Corporation. She died in Norway on February 25, 1921, at the age of 71. Her husband died in 1924. Sister Fedde's surviving relatives in the United States included Alva Fedde Calvin of Wilmington, Delaware; Helen Fedde of Monroeville, Pennsylvania; G. Bernhard Fedde of Portland, Oregon; Norman A. Fedde of Guilford, Connecticut; and Gretog Nordbo and Anita Sutliffe, both of Brooklyn, New York.

In 1941 Johnson and Johnson Company published a calendar honoring 12 outstanding nurses. Sister Fedde's family in the United States felt proud and privileged that she was included in the group. The Sister Elisabeth Memorial Hospital, a baby clinic building at the Brooklyn deaconess institution, was dedicated in her honor in 1943.

## PUBLICATIONS BY SISTER ELISABETH FEDDE

*The Diary of Sister Elisabeth Fedde 1883–1888*. Translated by P.J. Hertsgaard. Typescript, 1952.

"Elizabeth Fedde's Diary, 1883–88." Translated by B. Folkedahl. *Norwegian American Studies and Records* 20 (1959).

*Memoirs*. Translated by P.J. Hertsgaard. Typescript, 1959.

## BIBLIOGRAPHY

Bjork, K.O. "Fedde, Sister Elisabeth." In *Notable American Women 1607–1950. A Biographical Dictionary*, Vol. 1, ed. by E.T. James. Cambridge, Mass.: Belknap Press of Harvard University Press, 1971.

de Mello Vianna, F., ed. *The International Geographic Encyclopedia and Atlas*. London: Macmillan Press, 1979.

Frontispiece. "Sister Elisabeth Fedde, A Norwegian Pioneer in America." *The Trained Nurse and Hospital Review* 86 (January 1931): 64.

Gindlesperger, N.L. *Sister Elisabeth Fedde (1850–1920) Founder of Lutheran Medical Center.* Brooklyn, N.Y.: Lutheran Medical Center, 1982.

Hintz, M. *Enchantment of the World. Norway.* Chicago: Children's Press, 1982.

Larsen, K. *A History of Norway.* Princeton, N.J.: Princeton University Press, 1970.

Naess, H.S. In *Merit Students Encyclopedia,* edited by W.D. Halsey and L. Shores. New York: Macmillan Educational, 1978.

Pei, M.A. In *Merit Students Encyclopedia,* edited by W.D. Halsey and L. Shores. New York: Macmillan Educational, 1978.

Rolfsrud, Erling Nicolai. *The Borrowed Sister.* Minneapolis: Augsburg Publishing House, 1953.

Stewart, I.M., and A.L. Austin. *A History of Nursing from Ancient to Modern Times. A World View.* 5th ed. New York: G.P. Putnam's Sons, 1962.

Marilyn Thérèse Lieber

# Alice Louise Fitzgerald

## 1874–1962

Alice Louise Fitzgerald was one of nursing's most interesting pioneers because she held a variety of international positions during the dynamic World War I era. Few nurses have had the colorful opportunities that captured Fitzgerald's attention and professional commitment.

Born in Florence, Italy, on March 13, 1874, to American parents, Mr. and Mrs. Charles Fitzgerald, she was the first of three children. Richard, her brother, arrived two years later and was followed in 1880 by Margherita. Since her father was a scholar, Fitzgerald received a carefully planned education in France, Switzerland, and Germany. During this period, she developed fluency in four languages: French, German, Italian, and English. This versatility in communicating enhanced what she would bring to her positions in later years.

Fitzgerald moved to Baltimore in 1894 in order to make her debut. While in the city, she learned of Johns Hopkins, a new hospital with a medical school and a nurses' training program. She inquired about the nurses' training program and discovered that she would have to wait at least five years to gain admission, for students were required to have good educational backgrounds and be at least 25 years old. She held on to her goal, but once she reached the required age, family problems interfered with her departure to enter school.

At the age of 28, Fitzgerald finally entered Johns Hopkins Hospital Training School after stringent screening by its director, Adelaide Nutting. She graduated with the class of 1906. Her studies at Johns Hopkins took place during an exciting era of development for the institution. Physicians William Osler and Howard Kelly participated in her training, as physicians played a major educational role in training nurses during this period.

During the final months of her program and for a year following graduation, Fitzgerald served as head nurse on a unit at Johns Hopkins. This role included teaching responsibilities for student nurses as well as clinical responsibilities for her patients. In 1908 she returned to her family home in Italy for a rest and vacation, but after a massive earthquake, she served in a disaster area. Her nursing skills, combined with her ability to communicate with the victims, made her a valuable relief worker. She proved able to assist patients and served as translator for French and English volunteer relief doctors. The Italian Red Cross awarded her a medal for her services to the victims of this disaster.

Fitzgerald's career progressed rapidly as she served as supervisor of the operating rooms at Bellevue Hospital and then as superintendent of nurses at Wilkes-Barre General Hospital in Pennsylvania. Bellevue, a massive public institution, forced her to use skill and tact in her reorganization efforts; these skills would be crucial in later years. Wilkes-Barre, though a much more rural environment, helped her to see the problems of general hospitals not affiliated with schools and the plight of miners who frequently fell victim to mining disasters.

A new challenge came with the superintendency of nurses at Robert W. Long Hospital in Indianapolis, Indiana. In addition to the traditional duties of her job, Fitzgerald had the task of introducing public-health nursing, which was a new concept at that time in Indiana. There was much ignorance regarding the role and possibilities for help in a community from the modern public-health nurse. This position demanded much perseverence from her in promoting such a radically new idea.

By 1915 Fitzgerald was 41 years old and working as a head nurse of a student medical service at Wellesley College in Massachusetts. Thousands of miles away in Belgium, Edith Cavell, an English nurse and internationally known educator, was killed by a German firing squad after being found guilty of participating in an underground railroad for Allied soldiers seeking to escape from German-occupied Belgium. A committee formed in Boston shortly after the execution decided to fund an Edith Cavell Memorial Nurse who would serve in Europe under the British Red Cross. Fitzgerald received the appointment to this important position and began her international career.

Fitzgerald sailed for France in February 1916. For the next year she was involved in field-hospital nursing, working to the point of exhaustion when troops needing medical care poured into the tent hospital after major battles. She encountered wounds, infectious diseases, and death, and her personal suffering included severe frostbite, weight loss, and fatigue. In spite of her heavy clinical load, she corresponded with her sponsoring committee and wrote articles for the American nursing community.

When the United States entered the war in 1917, Fitzgerald transferred to the American Red Cross and served war victims in France and Italy. She provided valuable leadership for American nurses in the closing months of the war. During this period, she educated health workers from varied cultures in how to understand each other. This proved critical in units trying to serve medical needs of soldiers under stressful conditions.

After the war ended in 1918, Fitzgerald remained in Europe as the chief nurse of the American Red Cross. Her two goals for nursing in postwar Europe included providing direct care and relief to war victims through public-health nursing and developing nursing-education programs in war-torn countries so that nursing could evolve as an honorable career for women. Her work became more administrative as she traveled to assist her nurses in each affected country. In this capacity, she filled some of the gap left in the American nursing ranks when Jane Delano, the director of American Red Cross nursing, died in France in early 1919.

In late 1919 Fitzgerald assumed the position of director of nursing of the League of Red Cross Societies in Geneva, Switzerland. She hoped to fulfill her dream of establishing model nursing schools in each country receiving recovery assistance. A school was established in England, and a serious public-health nursing movement began in Europe.

Returning to America in 1922, Fitzgerald served the Red Cross by speaking to groups throughout the country on the need for nurses to join the Red Cross. She tired of this task quickly, however, and accepted a new position with the Rockefeller Foundation as an advisor on public-health nursing to the governor of the Philippines. At the age of 48, she sailed to the Philippines to assess and correct public-health nursing problems. She quickly identified the need for nursing programs to educate Filipino nurses in the management of rural public-health problems and helped to establish a program to provide the type of nurse that the country desperately needed. However, political problems and conflicts with the appointed governor in the region made it impossible for Fitzgerald to continue her plans for the area.

In 1925 while fulfilling a short-term position with the International Red Cross in Paris, Fitzgerald recieved a second appointment to serve the Rockefeller Foundation as an advisor to the king and queen of Siam. During the next four years, she organized the first government-sponsored training school for nurses in Siam.

She learned how to use her diplomatic skill and the support of the royal family to introduce a westernized nursing school into a culture with many restrictive practices regarding women. Fitzgerald successfully planted the seeds of a modern nursing educational system in the country.

When she returned to America in 1929, Fitzgerald served on the Maryland State Board of Nurse Examiners for two years, then moved to New York City to assume her last professional nursing position as director of nursing at the Polyclinic Hospital. She remained there for six years, establishing several significant friendships and putting down the deepest roots of her career. Her last job as a housemother to nursing students at the Sheppard Pratt Institute in Baltimore ended with her retirement in 1948 at the age of 74. She returned to New York and entered the Peabody Home in the Bronx where she lived as a semi-invalid until her death at age 89 on November 10, 1962. She was buried in the Bronx.

During her lifetime, Fitzgerald received many national and international awards for her work, including the British Red Cross Medal, Campaign Medal and Victory Medal; the French Campaign Medal and Victory Medal, and the special French Medaille d'Honneur with Rosette; and the Red Cross medals of Poland, Serbia, Hungary, Russia, and the United States. In 1927 she received the International Florence Nightingale Medal.

Fitzgerald epitomized the spirit of adventure and the pioneering attitude of her generation of nurses. She loved animals, art, and having fun with friends. She had high ideals, but she approached life with a realistic, no-nonsense attitude.

## PUBLICATIONS BY ALICE LOUISE FITZGERALD

### BOOKS

*Mademoiselle Miss.* Boston: W.A. Butterfield, 1916.

*The Edith Cavell Nurse.* Boston: W.A. Butterfield, 1917.

### ARTICLES

"My Experience in Naples after the Messina Disaster." *American Journal of Nursing* 9 (1909): 482–92.

"To Nurses Preparing for Active Service." *American Journal of Nursing* 18 (1918): 188–91.

"Congratulations to Italian Nurses." *American Journal of Nursing* 26 (1926): 30.

"The Nursing Situation in Italy." *American Journal of Nursing* 30 (1930): 292–98.

"Joyful News from Florence." *American Journal of Nursing* 30 (1930): 467–68.

"Italian Nurses Launch Magazine." *American Journal of Nursing* 35 (1935): 290–92.

## BIBLIOGRAPHY

"Alice Louise Fitzgerald." *American Journal of Nursing* 41 (1941): 849–50.

"Alice Louise Fitzgerald." Obituary. *New York Times*, 11 November 1962.

Noble, I. *Nurse Around the World: Alice Fitzgerald.* New York: Julian Messner, 1964.

Linda E. Sabin

## Edna Lois Foley
### 1879–1943

Edna Lois Foley lead the Chicago Visiting Nurse Association to a position of national prominence during a quarter-century of leadership in the early 1900s. She advocated the rights of black nurses and made her organization one of the first visiting nurse associations to help black nurses. She was a president of the National Organization of Public Health Nurses and also campaigned for the improvement of nursing in Europe.

Foley was born in Hartford, Connecticut, in 1879 and graduated from Smith College with a baccalaureate degree in 1901. Inspired by her mother and grandmother to become a nurse, she received her R.N. from the Hartford Hospital School of Nursing in 1904.

Foley served as head nurse at Hartford Hospital in 1904–05; Albany Children's Hospital, 1905–06; Boston Children's Hospital, 1906–07; and Consumptive Hospital, 1907–09. She increased her awareness of the social dimensions of nursing by doing postgraduate work at the Boston School of Social Work between 1908–09. Upon concluding her studies in Boston, she accepted a position in Chicago, supervising field nurses of the Chicago Tuberculosis Institute for three years. In 1911 she was appointed a member of the Red Cross committee of the Chicago Board of Charities. Foley's leadership qualities were recognized, and when the second superintendent of nurses of the Chicago Visiting Nurse Association, Harriet Fulmer, resigned in 1911, Foley was hired to replace her and held the position until her retirement in 1937.

Building on its strong foundation, Foley lead the Chicago Visiting Nurse Association (VNA) to a premier position among VNAs in the United States. Constantly studying the methods of other VNAs in the United States and Europe, Foley introduced the best of their programs and procedures to Chicago. Her early model was the Providence VNA under the leadership of Mary Gardner.

Foley's advice and recommendations were sought on all aspects of visiting nursing, and she assisted those who called upon her expertise throughout her career. She prepared a manual for visiting nurses in 1914, which the board of directors of the Chicago VNA published and republished in revised editions in 1919 and thereafter. The manual served as a textbook for other visiting nurse associations, young nurses entering the field, and social-welfare agencies.

The National Organization of Public Health Nurses (NOPHN) grew from an initial meeting of visiting-nurse leaders held in Chicago in 1912. Foley served for one year of a two-year term as president of the NOPHN from 1920–21, leaving office early due to the pressure of her responsibilities in Chicago. Through NOPHN, which she supported throughout her life, and her role as superintendent of the Chicago VNA, she promoted and defended all VNAs. In 1916 when the Metropolitan Life Insurance Company, a major provider of home health care to VNA patients who were its policyholders, suggested changes in the payment to nurses that would adversely affect the budgets of small VNAs, Foley became a spokesperson for opposing the new system.

Foley was a gifted speaker and lectured to nursing and other organizations, including VNAs, schools at all levels, tuberculosis institutes, social-welfare groups, and fund-raising events. She carried on a voluminous correspondence with colleagues in VNAs throughout the United States and with health-department staff and community leaders seeking to establish home health programs.

Through Foley's guidance, the Chicago VNA became a clearinghouse for staff nurses who could not be employed in Chicago or whose special skills enabled them to become superintendents of other organizations. Through the placement of nurses trained at the Chicago VNA and Foley's firm commitment to home care, VNAs were launched and strengthened in Omaha, Clinton, Cleveland, Milwaukee, Madison, South Bend, Indianapolis, Peoria, Springfield, Rockford, Louisville, Dayton, Portland, Seattle, Washington, Denver, Youngstown, Pittsburgh and Worcester. Visitors from these and other community organizations were welcomed by the Chicago VNA. The annual report of the Chicago VNA was distributed to all who requested it, including the New York Academy of Medicine Library, John Crerar Library, Public Welfare Board of Houston, and the New York Public Library.

Foley championed the role of women in many endeavors and was appointed to several committees and boards of directors previously restricted to men. She became a director of the National Society for the Study and Prevention of Tuberculosis in 1916, a member of the executive committee of the National Tuberculosis Association in 1920, and a director of the Chicago Tuberculosis Institute in 1931.

She also encouraged her staff to be innovative and to accept new challenges. Responding to a myriad of local demands for visiting nursing services resulted in some unusual careers for VNA nurses. For example, a staff nurse was assigned in 1913 to the Court of Domestic Relations at the judge's request. Her position was legalized when she was appointed bailiff of the court, among the first women to be appointed to this office in the United States.

In 1919 Foley served as chief nurse of the American Red Cross Tuberculosis Commission in Italy. Upon her return to the VNA, she continued to support the improvement of nursing in Europe and welcomed European nurses to Chicago.

Foley's response to racial discrimination was forthright in a period before civil rights had become a public issue. Among the staff changes Foley encouraged was increasing the number of black nurses to work with black people in Chicago. The Chicago VNA was among the first to hire black nurses and advance their careers.

Education remained a cornerstone of Foley's supervision of the VNA nursing staff and her advisory relationship with the board of directors. She read, collected, and recommended the best books on all aspects of public-health nursing. She introduced new titles to the board of directors and advised them to give these books as gifts to the staff. She invited lecturers, designed special courses given on VNA premises, and encouraged nurses to take courses and do postgraduate work in New York and other medical centers.

Foley was a keen student of statistics related to visiting nursing. She understood the value of the large volume of data gathered by the nursing staff and organized the large number of volunteers needed to file data cards. By 1931 volunteers were no longer capable of handling the vast amount of data turned in to the central office, and Foley instituted a department of statistics. Pertinent facts concerning the budget, donations, number of patients, and types of diseases suffered were published in the annual report, along with pictures of nurses serving patients in their homes, schools, and infant-welfare centers.

Foley's many honors included an honorary doctorate of science degree from her alma mater, Smith College, in 1928. The citation described her as "a skilled nurse and teacher of nurses, a wise and rigorous administrator, an authority on public health and social welfare, a large-hearted and keen-sighted student of human welfare." In 1934 the city of Chicago recog-

nized her efforts on their behalf when she was made a Citizen Fellow of the Institute of Medicine for her service to the people. Among her highest awards was the Florence Nightingale Medal, which she received in 1937. In that year, she retired from the Chicago VNA, and a substation of the VNA was given her name.

Foley died suddenly of a stroke on August 4, 1943, at age 64 at the home of her sister, Mrs. Joseph B. Crane, in New York City.

## PUBLICATIONS BY EDNA LOUISE FOLEY

### PAMPHLETS

*Visiting Nurse Material Prepared for the Visiting Nurse Association of Chicago and Other Public Health Nurses.* Chicago: National Organization of Public Health Nurses, 1914.

*Visiting Nurse Manual Prepared for the Visiting Nurse Association of Chicago.* 2nd ed. Chicago: National Organization of Public Health Nurses, 1919.

### ARTICLES

"The Place of the School Nurse in the Public School System." *Transactions of International Congress on School Hygiene, Buffalo 1913* (1914): 475–77.

## BIBLIOGRAPHY

"Edna Lois Foley." *American Journal of Nursing* (September 1943).

"Edna Lois Foley." Obituary. *Chicago Tribune,* 5 August 1943.

Minutes of the Board of Directors and Superintendent's Reports of the Chicago Visiting Nurse Association, 1912–1937.

Smith College Archives, Northampton, Mass.

*Trained Nurse and Hospital Review* (September 1943).

Audrey Davis

# Elizabeth Gordon Fox

## 1884–1958

Elizabeth Gordon Fox is best remembered for her progressive insights into the growth of nursing, particularly public-health nursing, and for her ability to translate her ideas into nursing practice. Her creative vision, constructive planning, and broad concept of the role of public-health nursing won her recognition as an outstanding leader in nursing, not only in her local community and state, but also nationwide.

Fox began her career in nursing at the University of Wisconsin, graduating with academic honors in 1907 and then enrolling for three years of nursing at Johns Hopkins Hospital. Her clear thinking and organizational abilities won her a senior scholarship for postgraduate study at Johns Hopkins School of Nursing, where she began to develop a keen interest in the field of public-health nursing.

After completing her studies, Fox chose to serve as superintendent of the Dayton, Ohio, Visiting Nurses Association from 1913 to 1915 and then as superintendent of the Washington, D.C., Visiting Nurses Association from 1915 to 1918. In 1918 she became national director of the Public Health Nursing Service (PHNS) of the American Red Cross in Washington, D.C.

Fox used her newly gained influence to develop and expand the organization of hundreds of nursing services in rural communities nationwide. Under her leadership, rural public-health nursing grew from a small service in a few communities to approximately 2,000 nurses in nearly half the counties of the United States. In recognition of her remarkable achievements, Fox was the first civilian nurse ever chosen to receive the Florence Nightingale Medal of the International Red Cross. Considered the highest honor that can be paid to a nurse by an international organization, the medal was awarded to her in 1931.

Although devoted to her work as national director of PHNS, Fox also found time to become active in national nursing politics. She became involved with numerous organizations and committees, and in 1921 she became president of the National Organization of Public Health Nursing (NOPHN), an office she held until 1926. Later, she served as president of the Connecticut State Nurses Association.

While president of NOPHN, Fox became an outspoken advocate of the concept of holistic patient care. Although this idea is widely accepted today, it was revolutionary at the time. She believed in visualizing the individual as a whole, the family as a biological and social entity, and the community as a base of service operations.

Motivated by her concern for the future quality of nursing, Fox also joined the faculty at Yale School of Nursing in 1929. She taught there for the next 19 years.

Ready for new challenges, Fox left the Red Cross in 1930 to become executive director of the Visiting Nurses Association (VNA) in New Haven, Connecticut. Her work in New Haven was outstanding, and soon the New Haven VNA had gained a reputation as a service distinguished for high quality as well as for pioneering to improve nursing care. New Haven became a model VNA, and visitors came to observe the program and exchange ideas. In 1948 alone, visitors came from eight foreign countries and from over half of the United States to observe the New Haven VNA.

While director of the VNA, Fox began writing extensively about a new path she envisioned for nursing's future, that of the nurse as an equal partner in a balanced health-care team. This idea is well-known today, but in her time the concept created tremendous controversy, even among nurses. The New Haven VNA became a working model for this concept and encouraged nurses nationwide to strive for this goal.

On November 13, 1958, Fox collapsed and died at a ceremony arranged in her honor by the Connecticut Public Health Association in tribute to her work in the field of nursing. She was 74 years old. Fox was to receive the 1985 Winslow Award for distinguished service in the field of public-health nursing. This award is the highest honor that the Connecticut Public Health Association gives to an individual, group, or organization for contributions to public health in Connecticut. Fox would have been the first nurse to have received it.

## PUBLICATIONS BY ELIZABETH GORDON FOX

"New Sources of Nursing Power." *Public Health Nursing* 34 (May 1942): 246–80.

"Analysis of Defense Needs." *American Journal of Nursing* 41 (1941): 637.

## BIBLIOGRAPHY

"Elizabeth Gordon Fox." Obituary. *American Journal of Nursing* 59 (January 1959): 38.

"Elizabeth Gordon Fox." Obituary. *New York Times*, 15 November 1958.

"The Florence Nightingale Medal." *American Journal of Nursing* 49 (September 1949): 579–80.

Fox, E.G. Remarks at a dinner in her honor, 19 October 1949, New Haven, Conn.

Hiscock, I.V. "Individual and Family Health." *Public Health Nursing* 42 (February 1950): 84–88.

"Our Contributors." *American Journal of Nursing* 41 (June 1941): 690–91.

Janice Fulton

## Susan C. Francis

### 1873–1962

Susan C. Francis served as an administrator of Children's Hospital in Philadelphia and as director of the nursing service of the Pennsylvania–Delaware Division of the American Red Cross during World War I. From 1934–38 she was president of the American Nurses' Association.

Born on August 16, 1873, in Bridgeport, Pennsylvania, a town near Philadelphia, Francis had ancestors who were Pennsylvania Dutch and Swedish. Her school-teacher father and her mother were cousins.

After her father's death, Francis entered the training school of the Reading Hospital. Her early upbringing had not allowed music and dancing, and her entrance into the training school marked a change in her life. Her classmates remembered her as a social person who did well in her studies.

Francis spent two years as a private-duty nurse after graduation in 1894. For seven years, she served as superintendent of nurses at City Hospital in Washington, D.C. (now Gallinger Memorial Hospital). Her next position, as superintendent of the Touro Infirmary in New Orleans, was cut short after only nine months because of poor health.

Returning to her native state, Francis began a long career of service to the nursing profession in Pennsylvania. For the next eight years (1909–17), she was the superintendent of nurses at the Jewish Hospital in Philadelphia. When World War I started, she was called upon to become the director of the Pennsylvania–Delaware division of the American Red Cross, where she was able to use her considerable talents as an organizer.

In 1921 Francis was made superintendent of Children's Hospital in Philadelphia, a position she held until 1942. During this time, the hospital grew from a small unit in an inadequate building to a 134-bed institution that made great strides in providing preventative care to children. It was also at this time that Francis made known to the hospital board the educational needs of both the medical and nursing staff so that improvements could be made in these areas.

Although Francis continued to work at Children's Hospital until 1942, her many duties as hospital administrator and head of the nursing school did not prevent her from remaining an active participant in nursing-association activities. She first became involved on the national level when she was in Washington, D.C., as the first secretary of the Philadelphia League of Nursing Education. She also became interested in the activities of the American Nurses' Association (ANA), another national association for nurses, and was elected president of the Pennsylvania State Nurses' Association from 1914–16.

Her colleagues soon recognized her sound judgment and asked for her help in other areas. She was appointed chair of the headquarters committee for the American Nurses' Association when they were establishing their office following World War I. When the secretary for the ANA, Agnes Deans, resigned, Francis was asked to fill the unexpired term. She continued as secretary until 1934, when she was nominated as president of the American Nurses' Association, a position she held from 1934–38.

During her presidency, Francis worked hard to achieve unity and strength for the nursing profession. She corrected rules in the state and local chapters that were inconsistent with the national policy, thus making it easier for nurses to transfer their memberships when they were assigned to different states. She also tried to make membership in the nursing associations as attractive as possible. Her goal was to make each nurse realize that the good of the community and the good of the nursing profession depended upon the individual efforts of each nurse.

As her second term as president of the ANA ended, Francis asked that her name not be placed on the ballot for the board of directors because she believed that a person should be found who would be more representative of the present, rather than the past, generation. Despite her protests, the delegates of the Kansas City convention believed that during her administration, Francis had demonstrated sound judgment. Her name was placed on the ballot, and she was overwhelmingly voted a member of the board of directors.

In addition, Francis served as secretary of the board of directors of the *American Journal of Nursing* and was a representative of the ANA on the Committee on the Grading of Nursing Schools. Stella Goostray, another leader in the nursing profession, praised Francis's steadfastness of purpose, sense of justice, tolerance, objectivity, and loyalty.

Francis died on October 18, 1962, at the age of 89 in the Ephrata Community Hospital, Ephrata, Pennsylvania. She was buried in St. Paul's Cemetery, Amityville, Pennsylvania.

### PUBLICATIONS BY SUSAN C. FRANCIS

"A Practical Crib." *American Journal of Nursing* 24 (April 1924): 545–47.

"The Value of Affiliations." *American Journal of Nursing* 24 (May 1924): 645–51.

"The Milk Laboratory, Children's Hospital of Philadelphia [Pa]." *American Journal of Nursing* 24 (September 1924): 949–55.

"Nursing [in] Small Hospitals." *American Journal of Nursing* 24 (December 1924): 1190–97.

"The Committee on the Grading of Nursing Schools, U.S.A." In *International Council of Nurses: [Seventh] Congress Reports.* Paris-Brussels, 1933. London: The Council, 1933.

"American Nurses Association 1934–36." *American Journal of Nursing* 36 (July 1936): 655–59.

"The Private Duty Nurse in a New Era." *American Journal of Nursing* 36 (August 1936): 773–77.

### BIBLIOGRAPHY

Archives. American Red Cross, Washington, D.C.

Flanagan, L. *One Strong Voice: The Story of the American Nurses' Association.* Kansas City, Mo.: American Nurses' Association, 1976.

"Francis, Susan C." In *National League of Nursing Education: Biographic Sketches, 1937–1940,* edited by S. Groostray. New York: National League of Nursing Education, 1940.

Theresa Dombrowski

## Martha Minerva Franklin
### 1870–1968

Martha Minerva Franklin was one of the first nurses to campaign actively for racial equality for black nurses. She worked for collective action by black nurses in the early twentieth century. Through her pioneering interest to improve the status of the black nurse, she was the founder and organizer of the National Association of Colored Graduate Nurses (NACGN).

Franklin was born on October 29, 1870, in New Milford, Connecticut. Her parents were Henry J. and Mary E. Gauson Franklin. Three children were born to them. The eldest was Florence, Martha was the middle child, and the youngest was William. Franklin's father was a laborer, and during the Civil War, he served as a private of the Connecticut volunteer division.

The Franklin family resided in Meriden, Connecticut, and Franklin attended Meriden Public High School, where she graduated in 1890. Her father died in 1892, and her mother encountered much difficulty in collecting his Civil War pension. Franklin aided her mother by writing numerous letters to the government to collect the full pension.

In 1895, at age 25, Franklin entered the Woman's Hospital Training School for Nurses of Philadelphia. The Women's Hospital of Philadelphia had been incorporated in 1861 by a group of 24 women to counter the discrimination affecting women in medicine, to provide medical care to women and children by female physicians, and to train nurses. Strict rules and regulations governed the nursing student from entry to graduation. Student nurses were required to sign a written agreement to remain under instruction for one year and to give one additional year in the service of the school. After the initial first month of probation and five months of instruction, a small compensation was considered a fair equivalent of their services. During the last six months of training, students received an increase in pay and an additional increase during the following year of service.

Franklin graduated with the full recommendation of the hospital in December 1897. She was the only black graduate in her class. After graduation she returned to her home in Meriden, where she did private-duty nursing for a few years, later pursuing the same type of work in New Haven, where she relocated.

Franklin's specific experiences as a black nurse that prompted her to become a pioneer for civil rights have not been recorded. However, during the era between 1879, when Mary Mahoney graduated as the first black professional nurse, and 1908, when the NACGN was organized, the United States had developed rigid patterns of racial discrimination and segregation. Nursing was no exception. Exclusion of black students forced the establishment of hospitals and nursing schools for black patients and student nurses.

In addition, in many states black nurses were prohibited from membership in the state nurses' associations, the only avenue to membership in the American Nurses' Association. Therefore, they were precluded from joining the American Nurses' Association although they qualified for membership in every other aspect. This discrimination in part urged Franklin to begin her quest to organize the NACGN.

In the fall of 1906, Franklin began to study the status of the black graduate nurses in the United States. She discovered that many black nurses shared her concerns. As a result of her two-year survey, Franklin recognized that black nurses needed effective help that they must initiate themselves. She believed that only through collective action could their problems be identified, analyzed, and thus eliminated. She further believed that the organization of a national association of black nurses would gain them recognition and would in time make it possible for them to serve the American public without racial bias. Thus, she sent out 1500 letters asking nurses to consider the advisability of a meeting in the near future.

Adah Belle Samuels Thoms, president of Lincoln Hospital School of Nursing Alumnae Association, responded, inviting Franklin and interested nurses to meet in New York City as guests of the association. Fifty-two nurses attended the August 1908 meeting, and Franklin set forth its purpose. She suggested that a permanent national organization of black graduate registered nurses be formed, to bring the nurses together to share and understand their problems. Her interests were to eradicate discrimination, develop leadership among the nurses, and to promote higher standards in administration and education. In addition, Franklin believed that collective action would secure cooperation and more professional contact with nursing leaders. She convinced the group that this was the only way to stimulate nurses toward a higher standard of nursing and to raise the requirements for admission to schools of nursing.

The group decided to attempt to improve any inadequate schools, and if these efforts were not successful, to encourage their closing. It also decided to accept nurses from these schools, although future members would need to meet the prevailing standards for all nurses. State registration would be a qualification for membership. Franklin was unanimously elected the first president of the new organization.

After three days of discussion, the NACGN became a reality, with 26 charter members. Nurses in a few communities had organized local associations prior to the foundation of the NACGN. Norfolk, Virginia, had a local group in 1901, and in New York, Chicago, and Washington, graduates of established black schools had organized alumnae associations by 1908.

Black physicians also had experienced discrimination in their profession and had organized the National Medical Association (NMA). Their annual meeting was in New York City in 1908, the same time the nurses were having their first meeting. Many black doctors from the NMA came to the nurses' meeting to give encouragement and to pledge their support for the new endeavor. John B. Hall of Boston invited the nurses to meet in Boston the next year.

In 1909 Franklin again was unanimously elected president, thus serving the first two years of this organization as its president. She was nominated and urged to serve a third term as president, but refused. However, she was designated honorary president for life. She remained involved with the organization and was permanently elected its historian.

One of the first nursing leaders to recognize the NACGN was Lillian Wald of the Henry Street Settlement. Another leader and early friend was Lavinia Dock, who gave the officers of the NACGN advice on organization. The recognition by these two leaders was a valuable asset to the NACGN. Dock, as secretary of the International Council of Nurses (ICN), invited the NACGN to send a representative to the 1912 ICN meeting in Cologne, Germany. This was the first opportunity black nurses had to meet with other nurses at an international convention. The NACGN became internationally recognized, and this was the beginning for black nurses to join and participate in the ICN.

From its small beginnings, the NACGN grew to a membership of 2,000 during World War I and over 12,000 by 1940, with members from nearly every state. As membership increased, a national registry was established to aid black nurses in securing positions. The NACGN developed community and national support systems by establishing a local citizen's committee in New York State and an advisory council on the national level. In 1951 the NACGN voluntarily merged with the ANA, with a special program set up for intergroup relations.

During the 1920s Franklin relocated to New York City. She enrolled in a six-month postgraduate course at Lincoln Hospital, became an R.N. in New York State, and was employed as a school nurse in the New York City public school system. At the age of 58, still interested in continuing her education, she became a student at Teachers College, Columbia University. She was enrolled in the department of practical arts, today known as the department of nursing education, from 1928 to 1930.

Through Franklin's position as founder and organizer of the NACGN, she came to know Thoms and Mahoney. These women had a special friendship and an alliance of support and respect for each other, with common goals that would improve the status of the black nurse in American society. These three pioneer nurses, who were posthumously admitted to the Nursing Hall of Fame in 1976, were the early cornerstones of the NACGN.

Franklin had a close friend in Maude Carter, who resided in New York City. She also had many friends in Connecticut, in particular Ernest Saunders, his wife, Georgie, and Franklin's minister, Edwin Edmonds. Franklin did not marry; however, Saunders was like a grandson to her.

After living and working in New York for many years, Franklin returned to New Haven and resided with her sister, Florence. Florence also had never married. Franklin lived to age 98, and died on September 26, 1968. The cause of death was listed as senility; the major contributing factors were the physiological aging process and anorexia. She was buried in the family plot with her brother William, who died in 1905, and her mother, who died in 1934. There appear to have been no surviving relatives. The gravesite is at Walnut Grove Cemetery in Meriden, Connecticut.

## BIBLIOGRAPHY

American Nurses' Association. *Nursing Hall of Fame.* Kansas City, Mo.: American Nurses' Association, 1976.

Carnegie, E. Interview with author. New Haven, Conn., 13 June 1986.

"Colored Nurses in Public Health Work." Rockefeller Archive Center Project Report, 1924–25.

Davis, A.T. "Architects for Integration and Equality: Early Black American Leaders in Nursing." Ed.D. diss., Teachers College, Columbia University, 1987.

Edmonds, E. Interview with author. New Haven, Conn., 13 June 1986.

Fiftieth Annual Report, Board of Managers, Woman's Hospital of Philadelphia, January 1911. Nutting Collection. Teachers College, Columbia University, New York.

Franklin Family Folder. Connecticut Afro-American Historical Society, New Haven, Conn.

Franklin, M. Minutes of the NACGN, August 25–27, 1908. Schomburg Public Library for Research in Black Culture, New York.

"History of the Nurses Training School of the Woman's Hospital of Philadelphia 1865–1925." Nutting Collection. Teachers College, Columbia University, New York.

Johns, E. "Study of Present Status of the Negro Woman in Nursing." Rockefeller Archive Center Project Report, 1925. Pocantico Hills, Tarrytown, New York.

Kalisch, P., and B. Kalisch. *The Advance of American Nursing.* Boston: Little, Brown, 1978.

"Martha Minerva Franklin." Death Certificate. Connecticut Department of Health, Public Health Statistics Section. #18466.

Massie, W.J. Interview with author. New Haven, Conn., 12 October 1985.

"Negro Nursing Education Survey, 1924–1927." Rockefeller Archive Center Project Report. Pocantico Hills, Tarrytown, New York.

Pierce, L. Interview with author. Wallingford, Conn., 27 March 1986.

Rinsland, R., Registrar, Teachers College, Columbia University, Interview with author. New York, 10 October 1985.

Saunders, G. Interview with author. New Haven, Conn., 14 October 1985.

Sloan, P. "A Commitment to Equality: Early Afro-American Schools of Nursing." Ed.D. diss., Teachers College, Columbia University, 1978.

Staupers, M. *No Time for Prejudice.* New York: Macmillan Co., 1961.

Staupers, M. Telephone interview with author. March, July, August, 1984; February, 1985; April, 1986.

Stewart, I., and A. Austin. *A History of Nursing.* New York: G.P. Putnam's Sons, 1962.

Thoms, A.B. *Pathfinders.* New York: Kay Printing, 1929.

Williams, I., and D. Williams. Interview with author. New Haven, Conn., 13–14 October 1985.

Althea T. Davis

# Ruth Benson Freeman (Fisher)
## 1906–1982

Ruth Benson Freeman was known in the field of public health for her early and consistent advocacy of cooperation among all health professionals and her insistence on the importance of health administration. She is remembered for the inspirational quality of her teaching, whether the students were nurses, physicians, or other health professionals. Her writings on public-health nursing have become classics in both nursing and administration.

The oldest of three children, Ruth Freeman was born in Methuen, Massachusetts, on December 6, 1906, to Wilbur Milton and Elsie Lawson Freeman. Her mother died when she was young, and her father remarried and had three more children. Freeman graduated from Methuen High School in 1923, and her grandmother, Anaret Freeman, encouraged her to leave Methuen and obtain higher education. Although she had not been a particularly good student in high school, she entered Lowell Normal School. When she proved she was capable of doing the work, her grandmother gave her the money to further her education in New York.

Freeman entered Mt. Sinai Hospital School of Nursing in 1924. She had never felt a particular interest in taking care of people, but chose nursing because her grandmother thought she would be safer living in a dormitory and her aunt worked at Mt. Sinai hospital as a secretary. In later years, Freeman described her nursing career as accidental.

In nursing school Miss Freeman was somewhat of a maverick. She talked to social workers and to physicians in a time when nursing students were supposed to know their place. Refused permission to attend a postmortem, she disguised herself as a man and was smuggled in by medical students. Nursing students who got into trouble were given extra hours to work off after graduation. Freeman was the last of her class to leave the school.

In 1927, shortly after graduation, she married Anselm Fisher. Freeman later credited her accomplishments to her husband's support and enthusiasm about her career. They had one daughter, Nancy Ruth. She continued to use her maiden name in her professional career.

After a short time as a private-duty nurse, Freeman accepted a staff-nurse position at the Henry Street Visiting Nurse Service in New York City. It was there while working with Lillian Wald, Helene Buker, Elizabeth Mackenzie, Marguerite Wales, and Elizabeth Phillips that Freeman formulated her concept of nursing and her commitment to nursing as a career.

One of Freeman's reasons for joining Henry Street was to have regular working hours so she could attend Columbia University's part-time program for nurses pursuing a degree. She entered Columbia in 1929 and for the next 22 years worked and went to school intermittently, receiving a B.S. degree in 1934 from Columbia University and an M.A. degree in 1939. In 1951 she received her Ed.D degree from New York University after writing her doctoral dissertation on supervision in public-health nursing.

Just as Freeman had been persuaded by Buker that accepting a position as a supervisor at Henry Street would not separate her from nursing practice, she was again persuaded in 1937 by Helen Mauzer, director of the nursing program at New York University, that teaching was also a part of nursing service. She taught at the university for four years.

Freeman was professor of public health nursing at the University of Minnesota School of Public Health from 1941 to 1946. The dean of the school Gaylor Anderson was unusually supportive of nurses and nursing and Freeman wanted to experience public health nursing outside of New York City. At the University of Minnesota, she had the opportunity to work with students in remote areas of Minnesota and Manitoba, Canada. She later described the years spent in Minnesota as one of the most satisfying periods of her life. While there, she served as a special consultant to the Minnesota State Board of Health.

In 1946 Freeman went to the American National Red Cross as administrator of its nursing services, a complex job involving coordination among the voluntary group, the paid staff, and the local communities. She stayed there until 1950 with time out to act as a consultant for the National Security Resources Board, which was planning for the utilization of nurses in civil defense programs and in cases of national emergency.

In 1950 Freeman went to the Johns Hopkins School of Hygiene and Public Health as associate professor of public-health administration and coordinator of nursing programs. In 1962 she was promoted to full professor, and in 1971 she became professor emeritus.

At Johns Hopkins, Freeman turned down the opportunity to establish a separate department of public-health nursing. She saw nurses as managers of public-health enterprises and did not want them to become compartmentalized. Instead of a department, she created what she called a nursing presence in the school, directly responsible to the dean with free access to talk with people in other disciplines about nursing. Nursing students were enrolled in the existing departments of their choice, and there were no specialty courses for nurses. As the number of nursing faculty members increased, Freeman formed a nurse faculty council to share ideas and coordinate the nursing effort.

It was during her tenure at Johns Hopkins that Freeman's professional activities flourished. She was the president and a member of the board of directors of both the National League for Nursing and the National Health Council. She served on the governing council and executive board of the American Public Health Association and as chair of the American Nurses' Association Committee on Functions, Standards, and Qualifications of Public Health Nurses. She was the chair of the nursing research study section of the United States Public Health Service, and she was a consultant to the Veterans Administration, the Air Force, the Pan American Health Organization, and the World Health Organization.

Freeman was a prolific author. Over 50 of her articles were published in nursing and public health journals, and there are many remaining unpublished manuscripts.

In recognition of her contributions to nursing, public health and health care, Freeman was honored by various organizations. She received the Pearl McIver Public Health Nurse Award from the American Nurses' Association, the Florence Nightingale Medal from the International Red Cross, the Mary Adelaide Nutting Award from the National League for Nursing, and the Bronfman Prize from the American Public Health Association. She was named an honorary fellow of the American Academy of Nursing in 1981 and was elected to the Nursing Hall of Fame in 1984.

Freeman's greatest honor was the way in which she was remembered. She was praised for her integrity, her advocacy for nurses, and her insight. Anna Scholl, a friend and colleague, remembered her as a woman with a warm personality who was sensitive to those around her and to whom people responded easily. She died December 2, 1982, in Cockeysville, Maryland, of Alzheimer's Disease. She was survived by her husband, her daughter, Mrs. Nancy Smith, and four grandchildren.

## PUBLICATIONS BY RUTH BENSON FREEMAN

### BOOKS

*Techniques of Supervision in Public Health Nursing.* Philadelphia: Saunders, 1945.

*Public Health Nursing Practice.* Philadelphia: Saunders, 1950.

*Administration in Public Health Services.* Philadelphia: Saunders, 1960.

*Community Health Nursing Practice.* Philadelphia: Saunders, 1970. This was translated into Spanish and French.

### ARTICLES (SELECTED)

"Meeting Nursing Needs through Citizen Participation." *Nursing Outlook* 5 (January 1957): 43–44.

"Nurses, Patients and Progress." *Nursing Outlook* 7 (January 1959): 16–18.

"Measuring the Effectiveness of Public Health Nursing Service." *Nursing Outlook* 9 (October 1961): 605–07.

"Organization for a Purpose in an Organization with a Purpose." *Nursing Outlook* 14 (August 1966): 35+.

"NLN at Twenty: Challenge and Change." *Nursing Outlook* 20 (June 1972): 376–84.

### BIBLIOGRAPHY

American Nurses' Association. *Nursing Hall of Fame.* Kansas City, Mo.: American Nurses' Association, 1984.

Bushel, A. Interview with author. Baltimore, Md., 17 April 1986.

————. Letter to Maryland Nurses' Association, 3 November 1983.

Freeman, R.B. Curriculum vitae, 1971.

Heinrich, J. "In Memoriam." *Public Health Nursing* 1(1984): 60.

"Hopkins professor posthumously elected to Nursing Hall of Fame." Press release, Johns Hopkins School of Hygiene and Public Health, 15 June 1984.

Kinsman, C., ed. *Contemporary Authors.* Vol. 41–44. Detroit: Gale Research Company, 1974.

Obituary. "Ruth B. Freeman." *New York Times,* 8 December 1984.

Safier, G. *Contemporary American Leaders in Nursing.* New York: McGraw-Hill, 1977.

Scholl, A. Telephone conversation with author, 24 April 1986.

Smith, N. Telephone conversation with author, 24 April 1986.

Joy T. Lawrence

## Sister John Gabriel
### 1874–1951

Sister John Gabriel, a member of the Sisters of Charity of Providence, gave 40 years of service as a nurse, educator, and hospital administrator in the Pacific Northwest during the early twentieth century. She was a resourceful, innovative woman who brought the nursing profession to new frontiers.

Born Mary Ann Ryan on August 30, 1874, in Manville, Rhode Island, she was the youngest of three children of Thomas and Mary Dwyer Ryan. Her mother died in childbirth, so she was raised by her blind father and a stepmother. She had little formal education beyond the little red schoolhouse, St. James School, but she increased her fluency in reading and speaking by reading aloud to her father the English and American classics.

She accepted a teaching position at St. James School, but the desire to consecrate her life to God in a teaching order soon changed her plans. When at age 19 she asked her father for permission to enter religious life, he refused and arranged for her to marry a young man in their town. On the night of her engagement party, she ran away to Canada to join the Sisters of St. Anne in Montreal. However, before completing her novitiate training, she contracted tuberculosis and was sent home. Her father welcomed her back and hoped she would think no more about becoming a nun.

As her health improved, she worked in her father's general store. When she asked again to enter the convent, her father forbade it, saying that she was needed to care for him in his old age. Her brother Simon generously offered to stay with their father, and Ryan was free to begin religious life. In 1899 she entered the novitiate of the Sisters of Charity of Providence in Montreal. On August 7, 1901, she made her profession of first vows and was given the name Sister John Gabriel.

Her first assignment was in the pharmacy at Columbus Hospital in Great Falls, Montana. In 1904 she passed the examination for the Montana State Board of Pharmacy. Although she had no training in nursing, she was often called upon to assist with patients in the hospital. Her first experience with a woman coming out of anesthesia turned her life in a new direction. The woman was moaning, and Sister John Gabriel did not know what was the proper thing to do. Determining that action was better than inaction, she took a moist cloth and bathed the patient's face. The woman expressed how wonderful it was to be cared for by such a capable nurse at a time like this. Sister John Gabriel realized that nursing was action on behalf of the sick, and she decided to dedicate the rest of her life to nursing.

Sister John Gabriel began her nursing studies and in 1906 graduated from the Columbus Hospital School of Nursing. At that time, the hospital had a teaching staff of four physicians. As there were few trained public-health nurses at the time, Sister John Gabriel often cared for the American Indians in the region as well as the members of the lumber camps, mining towns, and railroad crews in the Pacific Northwest.

To gain as much knowledge as she could, Sister John Gabriel entered the St. Vincent Hospital School of Nursing in Portland, Oregon, which was reputed to be one of the best schools in the Northwest. In 1913 she and a colleague were the first two sisters to take the Oregon state board exams and become registered nurses. Until this time, sisters had urged their nursing students to take these exams but had not felt it necessary to take the exams themselves.

For the next 15 years, Sister John Gabriel traveled from nursing school to nursing school in the three western provinces of the Sisters of Charity of Providence, teaching dietetics and psychology to nursing students. In 1924 she was named director of schools of nursing for these provinces. She constantly strove to improve the curriculum, and her classes were far from dull. In addition to teaching the basic skills, Sister John Gabriel imparted to her students enthusiasm to become excellent, caring nurses.

Her goal was to improve the quality of nursing education, and the next step she took was to raise the educational level of the sister-supervisors in the nursing schools. She worked to allow these supervisors time off from their duties so they could attend a university and earn a degree. Sister John Gabriel took these courses herself so that she could check the course content and the professor's attitude. Since it wasn't possible for all the sisters to receive a university education, Sister John Gabriel taught many of them herself, using correspondence courses that she had developed. On December 20, 1927, she obtained a five-year normal diploma in food and nutrition and a B.A. in education from the University of Washington in Seattle.

Under Sister John Gabriel's guidance, the hospitals and nursing schools of the Sisters of Providence went through a period of rapid development as she strove to raise the quality of care to meet the standards of the accreditation committees. She worked with Malcolm T. Mac-Eachern, director of the American College of Surgeons, to bring about the necessary improvements. In the early 1930s, the American College of Hospital Administrators was organized with the purpose of raising the educational standards of all hospital supervisory personnel. Realizing that few of the sisters had adequate preparation for administrative positions and that the time had come when this was necessary, Sister John Gabriel worked quickly. She directed her energy to developing and teaching short courses in administration. Because textbooks were not readily available, she compiled her own reference library from hospital magazines. The articles were bound into booklets and were required reading in her courses.

Sisters from other religious communities also attended her courses and considered Sister John Gabriel as a benefactor. From 1932 to 1938 she taught courses at Loyola University in Chicago; Holy Name College in Oakland, California; Holy Cross Hospital in Salt Lake City; Creighton University in Omaha; St. John of God Hospital in Montreal; and Seattle University. In 1935 the American College of Hospital Administrators conferred upon her an hon-orary fellowship in recognition of her contribution to the hospital field.

Sister John Gabriel took an active part in local, state, and national nursing and hospital associations. From 1930–34 she was chair of the national ethical standards committee of the American Nurses' Association. She was a member of the board of directors for the *American Journal of Nursing* and the Washington State Nurses' Association. Sister John Gabriel also served as a collaborator in the revision of the national curriculum of schools of nursing. She was a forceful speaker and won a victory over the state legislators in Olympia, Washington, when they tried to introduce a law that she thought would be detrimental to nursing schools.

In 1937 she received her master's degree from Seattle College after presenting a thesis on nursing education. Throughout this time, she was responsible for the general supervision of 16 nursing schools in the Northwest. In addition to her numerous publications in nursing journals, she found time to write five books on nursing education. One of them, *Through the Patient's Eyes: Hospitals, Doctors, Nurses*, which discussed nurse-patient and physician-patient relations, won Sister John Gabriel an honorary membership in the Eugene Field Society, a national association of authors and journalists.

In 1938 her health failed, and Sister John Gabriel retired from active work. Although she retired, she did not give up her concern for the needs of the sick. When she was convalescing at Sacred Heart Hospital in Spokane, Washington, she saw the need for a patient library. She organized the library and distributed books to the patients. As she visited the patients, many of them confided their problems to her, and she gave them spiritual advice that comforted them.

In 1950 her rapidly declining health forced her to be transferred to Mount St. Vincent's Hospital in Seattle, Washington. She died there on December 25, 1951, at the age of 77 and was buried in Calvary, Seattle, Washington. She was survived by a brother and niece.

## PUBLICATIONS BY
## SISTER JOHN GABRIEL

### BOOKS

*Principles of Teaching in Schools of Nursing.* New York: Macmillan, 1928.

*Practical Methods of Study.* New York: Macmillan, 1930.

*Teacher's Work Organization Book.* Philadelphia: Saunders, 1931.

*Professional Problems: A Text-book for Nurses.* Philadelphia: Saunders, 1932; 2nd ed., 1937.

*Through the Patient's Eyes: Hospitals, Doctors, Nurses.* Philadelphia: Lippincott, 1935.

### ARTICLES

"The Relative Value of Various Types of Teaching in Schools of Nursing." *American Journal of Nursing* 28 (March 1928): 271–76.

"Dietetics, an Important Subject in the Education of the Nurse." *Pacific Coast Journal of Nursing* 24 (May 1928): 269–70.

"Development of Nursing Education by the Sisters of Charity of Providence." *Trained Nurse* 80 (June 1928): 707–08.

"St Elizabeth's School of Nursing." *American Journal of Nursing* 30 (April 1930): 447–50.

"Community Health in Relation to the N.R.A. [National Recovery Act]." *Hospital Progress* 15 (August 1934): 352–54.

"The Higher Aspirations of the Nurse." *Pacific Coast Journal of Nursing* 31 (April 1935): 169–72.

### BIBLIOGRAPHY

Charboneau, J.F. "Sister John Gabriel and Her Contribution to Nursing from 1912–1939." Master's thesis, Catholic University of America, 1959.

"Gabriel, Sister John. "In *National League of Nursing Education: Biographic Sketches, 1937–40*, edited by M. Felton. New York: National League of Nursing Education, 1940. Sisters of Providence Archives. Seattle, Wash.

Theresa Dombrowski

## Nina Diadamia Gage
### 1883–1946

As dean of the Hunan-Yale School of Nursing and as president of the Nurses' Association of China, Nina Diadamia Gage raised the level of nursing and nursing education in China. She developed a standard curriculum and provided for national examinations as well as accreditation of schools of nursing.

Gage was born June 9, 1883, in New York City, the daughter of Charles and Sarah Ann Perrin Tyler. She received her secondary education at the Training Department, Normal College, New York City, and graduated with a bachelor's degree from Wellesley College in 1905. At Wellesley she studied German, French, and history, served as dormitory vice-president, and did volunteer committee work with the YWCA. Although Gage's surname was different from that of her parents, there is no record in the available sources of her marrying.

Gage's choice of profession and location was influenced by a brother who traveled to Ya-li, China, in 1904. She entered the Roosevelt Hospital School of Nursing in New York City, graduating in 1908, and received her R.N. certification at the University of the State of New York that same year. After holding the position of night supervisor at the Roosevelt Hospital for several months, she went to China.

In January 1909 Gage arrived at Ya-li, Changsha, Hunan. Ya-li served as a preparatory department for the local college and hospital, and the College of Yale in China was planning a medical school and a school of nursing there in cooperation with a group of Chinese educators. Gage spent her first year at Ya-li studying Chinese for six hours each day and closely observing the operations at the hospital. At the time, nursing was provided by coolies and treatment provided by students of Edward H. Hume, a physician who described his experiences in China in the book *Doctors East, Doctors West.* Patients brought their own linen, but by the fall of 1909 Gage was helping to order linen from England, and soon she supervised tailors transforming the cloth into sheets, binders, pillow cases, and mattresses acceptable to the Chinese patients.

On April 14, 1910, riots erupted in Changsha and all foreigners withdrew from that area. In Hankow Gage came down with typhoid fever and traveled to Japan to convalesce. She returned in September and began inaugurating new methods of hospital administration and directing her first class of student nurses.

When the Hunan-Yale School of Nursing opened in 1911, the concept of a trained person caring for the sick was new. Tending to the sick was done most commonly in the home by female relatives or a hired woman. A new Chinese term had to be coined for the word *nurse*, and Gage selected *scholars to watch and guard*, or *guard scholars*, as the equivalent of nurse. The Chinese belief that there is something degrading in manual service, under which nursing was classified, made the opening of the school a difficult enterprise, but on the appointed day 12 girls and 40 boys applied, and 12 (5 girls and 7 boys) were finally accepted.

In October 1911 the Chinese revolution broke out, and Gage again had to interrupt her work, this time going to Shanghai. She returned in March 1912 and served as superintendent of nurses at the hospital for 13 years until her appointment as dean of the school.

During a year of absence in 1917–18, Gage took courses in administrative work at Teachers College, Columbia University, and was professor of nursing education at Vassar Training Camp for Nurses, Vassar College. This camp was opened to provide three months of intensive course work in preliminary nursing to college graduates only. In 1924 she again returned to the United States. She completed her master's degree and obtained a diploma in hospital and school of nursing administration from Teachers College.

On Gage's return to China, she became dean of the Hunan-Yale school. She also helped organize the Nurses' Association of China and was president of that organization for two years. As dean and as president she was able to influence the development of a standard curriculum, providing for national examinations and accreditation of schools of nursing, and to arrange for conventions of nurses in China. When Gage left Hunan in 1927, 65 graduates of the Hunan-Yale School of Nursing were serving throughout China.

In 1925 Gage was nominated for president of the International Council of Nurses (ICN). She offered to withdraw her name, since China was far removed from most ICN activities, but was dissuaded from doing so by the argument that it would mean much to 450 million Chinese to have a president of the ICN from that country. Gage was elected and served as president from 1925 to 1929.

After returning permanently to the United States in 1927, Gage held posts as educational director and later director of nursing service at Willard Park, New York (1927–28); executive secretary of the National League of Nursing Education (1928–31); director of the School of Nursing at Hampton Institute (1931–34); instructor of Jersey City Medical Center School of Nursing (1934–35); director of nursing service and of the school at Newport Hospital in Rhode Island (1935–43); and at the Protestant Hospital at Nashville, Tennessee (1943–45). In addition to the ICN, she was active in a number of professional organizations, including the American Nurses' Association, the National League of Nursing Education, the National Organization for Public Health Nursing, and the American Association of University Women.

The author of numerous articles on nursing education and leadership as well as missionary nursing, Gage published two books. She also revised Lucy R. Seymer's *A General History of Nursing* for American publication and translated a number of English and American texts into Chinese.

Noted for her humor and steadfast courage, Gage was a quiet person who saw her work as a means of living out Christian principles. She died on October 18, 1946, after a long illness in Syracuse, New York, at the age of 63.

## PUBLICATIONS BY
## NINA DIADAMIA GAGE

### BOOKS

*Mathematics for Nurses.* New York: Teachers College, Columbia University, 1918.

*Communicable Diseases.* Philadelphia: Davis, 1939, 1940, 1942, 1944, 1948.

### ARTICLES

"The Recent Riots in Changsha (China)." *American Journal of Nursing* 11 (October 1910): 39–40.

"Nursing in Mission Stations. Nursing in China." *American Journal of Nursing* 18 (June 1918): 797–99.

"The War in China." *American Journal of Nursing* 19 (February 1919): 347–50.

"Some Problems in Nursing Education." *Quarterly Journal of Chinese Nurses* 4 (July 1923): 14–20.

"Leadership in Nursing." *Quarterly Journal of Chinese Nurses* 4 (October 1923): 3–9.

"Nursing Magazines." *Quarterly Journal of Chinese Nurses* 11 (April 1930): 24–26.

"Some Observations on Negro Nursing in the South." *Public Health Nursing* 24 (December 1932): 674–80.

### BIBLIOGRAPHY

Bridges, D.C. *A History of the International Council of Nurses.* London: Pitman, 1967.

Hume, E. *Doctors East, Doctors West.* New York: W.W. Norton, 1946.

"Nina D. Gage." Obituary. *American Journal of Nursing* 46 (1946): 892.

"Nina Gage." Obituary. *New York Times,* 19 October 1946.

"The New President of the International Council of Nurses." *British Journal of Nursing* 73 (August 1925): 157–58.

Nutting Collection. Teachers College, Columbia University.

Pennock, M.R. *Makers of Nursing History.* New York: Lakeside, 1928.

Roberts, M.M. *American Nursing History and Interpretation.* New York: Macmillan, 1954.

Lilli Sentz

## Mary Sewall Gardner

### 1871–1961

Mary Sewall Gardner was second only to Lillian Wald in the development of public-health nursing. Her textbook defined the newly emerging field and set standards for public-health nursing, and as president of the National Organization of Public Health Nursing and head of the American Red Cross Town and Country Nursing Service, she was in a position to implement many of her ideas.

Gardner was born in Newton, Massachusetts, on February 5, 1871, the only child of William Sewall and Mary Thornton Gardner. She had a stepbrother, Charles Thornton Davis, her mother's son by a previous marriage. The Gardner family was a prominent and wealthy one. One of her mother's ancestors, Matthew Thornton, had been a signer of the Declaration of Independence. Her father, William Gardner, was a judge of the superior court of Massachusetts, and her half brother also became a judge. Both her brother and her father were influential figures in her life.

Gardner's mother died when she was four, and her stepmother, a physician, was an invalid during much of the time that Gardner was growing up. This led her to assuming more responsibility than most girls with her social background. Educated at home by a French governess and in private schools, she was severely ill at age 16 with what she later believed to be tuberculosis. Shortly after this, in 1888, her father died.

Gardner recovered enough to attend Miss Porter's School in Farmington, Connecticut, between 1888 and 1890. She then returned home to Newton, where she cared for her invalid stepmother and engaged in voluntary work, first in Newton and then, after 1892, in Providence, Rhode Island, where the family moved. Although she had a growing interest in nursing, it was not until 1901 at the age of 30 that Gardner was able to fulfill her ambition by entering the Newport Hospital Training School of Nurses in Newport, Rhode Island. Although her original intention was to become a missionary, Gardner realized early in her nursing career that she could do missionary work among the urban populations in the United States without going to China or India.

Gardner moved into positions of leadership in nursing as soon as she graduated in 1905. She became director of the Providence District Nurses' Association and soon found herself seeking ways to upgrade and professionalize this emerging specialty. She visited Lillian Wald's Henry Street Settlement and became a close friend of Wald. She also visited with others in the public-health movement and began a series of innovations to upgrade and change the Providence system. Among other things, she started in-service training programs, introduced the wearing of uniforms, established a record-keeping system, and attempted to establish a model that other district nursing associations might emulate. She remained as director of the Providence association until 1931, although she took several leaves of absence to carry out other tasks.

Gardner and Lillian Wald joined together to persuade the American Society of Superintendents (forerunner of NLNE) to set up an organization committee for public-health nurses. This led in 1912 to the National Organization of Public Health Nurses (NOPHN). Wald was the first chairman, while Gardner was secretary. In 1913 Gardner herself became president and served until 1916.

Gardner helped to write the constitution for the organization and headed the committee in charge of the new journal, *Public Health Nurse*, which later became *Public Health Nursing*. Under her direction, the organization set standards for training and service and for the collection of data. In recognition of her service to the emerging organization, she was made an honorary president of NOPHN in 1922, as Wald herself had been earlier. She served as special consultant to the organization in 1925 and 1936.

On leave from her Providence organization, in 1916 Gardner became the temporary director of the American Red Cross Town and Country Nursing Service (later called the Bureau of Public Health Nurs-

ing) while a permanent director was being trained. She then was sent in 1918 as the chief nurse for the American Red Cross Tuberculosis Commission for Italy. While there, she was the leader of a group to set up training programs for Italian women interested in nursing as a profession.

Returning to Providence in 1919, Gardner remained active in the Red Cross and, among other things, served on a committee to survey the future of the Bureau of Information for Nurses, which had acted as coordinator of nurses in World War I. She participated in a study of public-health nursing and child welfare in France and in Eastern Europe and served as chair of the International Council of Nurses from 1925 to 1933. She ended her term with a report for ICN on public-health nursing throughout the world. In 1931 on her retirement from the Providence District Nurses' Association, she was made an honorary director.

Gardner's textbook, *Public Health Nursing*, standardized what was expected of the public-health nurse. It went through two revisions and was translated into a number of languages. Always interested in writing, she had written a number of unpublished short stories and two novels. The novels try to convey the concept of an ideal nursing career.

Gardner continued to be active as a consultant and an adviser. She died February 20, 1961, in Providence at the age of 90.

## PUBLICATIONS BY MARY SEWALL GARDNER

### BOOKS

*Nursing Management.* London: E. Nash [1914].

*Public Health Nursing.* New York: Macmillan, 1916; 2nd ed., 1924; 3rd ed., 1936.

*So Build We.* New York: Macmillan, 1942.

*Katherine Kent.* New York: Macmillan, 1946.

### ARTICLES

"Problems Met by the Public Health Nurse." *Providence Medical Journal* (March 1913).

"A Report of Six Months' Study of the NOPHN." *Public Health Nursing.* (July 1926).

"Twenty-five Years Ago." *Public Health Nursing* (March 1937).

"Functions of NOPHN." *Public Health Nursing* (April 1938).

## BIBLIOGRAPHY

Fitzpatrick, M.L. *The National Organization of Public Health Nursing (1912–1952): Development of a Practice Field.* New York: National League for Nursing, 1975.

Gardner, M.S. Papers. Schlesinger Library, Radcliffe College, Cambridge, Mass.

Kantrov, I., and K. Wittenstein. "Mary Sewall Gardner." *Notable American Women.* Vol. 4, edited by Barbara Sicherman and Carol Hardgreen. Cambridge: Harvard University Press, 1980.

Mainero, L., ed. *American Women Writers.* 4 vols. New York: Frederick Ungar, 1980.

Monteiro, L.A. "Insights from the Past: Mary Gardner's Fictional Accounts." *Nursing Outlook* 35 (March–April 1987): 65–69.

Nelson, S. "Mary Sewall Gardner." *Nursing Outlook,* December 1953, January 1954.

Patterson, F.M. "As Her Colleagues Know Her." *American Journal of Nursing* 31 (1931): 707.

Vern L. Bullough

# Alma Elizabeth Gault

## 1891–1981

For over 50 years, Alma Elizabeth Gault was a leader in nursing, particularly in the state of Tennessee. She first served as dean of Meharry Medical College School of Nursing and later as dean of the school of nursing at Vanderbilt University, both in Nashville. She is known for her significant contributions to the racial integration of the nursing profession. She was inducted into the American Nurses' Association's Nursing Hall of Fame in 1984.

Gault was born September 28, 1891, in Fernwood Ohio, one of several children of Davison Stewart and Nancy Emma Stark Gault. She graduated from the Wells High School of Steubenville, Ohio, in 1910.

In 1916 Gault received a bachelor in philosophy degree from the College of Wooster in Wooster, Ohio and in 1918 attended Vassar Training Camp for Nurses. She received her basic nursing education from Philadelphia General Hospital School of Nursing, graduating in 1920. In 1936 and 1937 she did graduate study at the University of Chicago.

Soon after receiving her diploma, Gault became a head nurse at Philadelphia General Hospital where she was assigned to care for patients in two units isolated for erysipelas. She recounted her experiences in the *American Journal of Nursing* in 1926 in an early article on clinical nursing.

Between 1920-44 Gault assumed many other nursing roles, including clinic nurse in tuberculosis for the Ohio State Department of Health and clinic nurse in pediatrics at Johns Hopkins Hospital. She also taught public-health nursing at the Illinois Training School and the Cook County School of Nursing, Chicago, for ten years (1927–37); director of the Union Memorial Hospital School of Nursing in Baltimore; and director of nursing service at the Memorial Hospital in Springfield, Illinois.

Gault became dean of Meharry Medical College School of Nursing in Nashville in 1944. As a white person in a black school, she became a social activist as she protested injustices and sought social and professional equality for black nurses. Some of her activities included campaigning for desegregation of buses and integration at lunch counters and in hospital cafeterias. Other social interventions she proposed included day-care centers, school lunch programs, and traffic lights installed to aid the elderly. She was seen as a diplomat and served as an arbitrator between the black and white communities in Nashville during the difficult times following the assassination of Martin Luther King, Jr.

Gault was dean at Meharry from 1944 to 1953. She developed a diploma school of nursing that received accreditation, and later she established a baccalaureate program. This allowed the school to be the first segregated black school to hold membership in the American Association of Collegiate Schools of Nursing. The school was rated in the top one-third of schools of nursing in the nation. During this time, Meharry was a study site for Rockefeller Foundation nursing fellows. Many nurses from other countries were sent to study education in a collegiate setting, and black nurses received fellowships to study in Canada.

From 1953 to 1967 Gault was associated with the school of nursing at Vanderbilt University in Nashville. She held the positions of associate professor, acting dean, and associate professor emerita, and from 1965 to 1967 she served as dean. On her retirement, the mayor of Nashville proclaimed May 21, 1967, as Alma Gault Day. This tribute was organized by the North Central Tennessee League for Nursing.

During her time in leadership positions, Gault was concerned with regional planning for nursing. To this end, she worked through the Southern Regional Education Board to encourage the project to study the needs of the profession in that geographic area. Much of the advancement in nursing education and research has been attributed to these efforts.

Gault had many personal and professional friends. Among these were Julia Hereford, who was dean at Vanderbilt University from 1949–1965, and then professor of nursing emerita. However, according to Laurie Gunter, a personal friend until her death, Gault maintained her own home.

She received many awards and titles during her long professional career. These included the Certificate of Merit of the American Cancer Society, the Distinguished Alumni Award of Wooster College, the Distinguished Service Award of the National League for Nursing, and honorary recognition in the American Nurses' Association. She was also a member of Sigma Theta Tau, an honor society for nursing, and Delta Kappa Gamma, an honor society for professional educators.

Gault served as an officer and/or member of the American Nurses' Association, the National League for Nursing, the Tennessee Board of Nursing, and the Tennessee Council on Aging. She was a member of the American Association of University Women. Even as an older person, she maintained her activities, and in 1971 as a member of the Senior Citizens, Inc. of Nashville, she helped establish a multiphasic screening program.

In her later years, Gault lived in a teachers' retirement facility in Nashville. Finally, she moved to Westminster Terrace, a retirement home in Columbus, Ohio, where she died July 12, 1981, at the of 89, and was buried. She was survived by a nephew, John Gault, who had managed her personal matters, as well as many other nephews and nieces.

## PUBLICATIONS BY ALMA ELIZABETH GAULT

"The Adjustment of the Affiliating Student in the Teaching Program." *Hospital Management* 44 (October 1937): 48–50.

"Basic Requirements for Intelligent Nursing." *Modern Hospital* 40 (February 1933): 60–64.

"How Do People Respond to Health Film?" *Nursing Outlook* 7 (September 1958): 536–37.

"The Library in the School of Nursing." *Hospital Management* 43 (March 1937): 41–42.

"Nurses and Budget Making." *Modern Hospital* 43 (July 1934): 62–64.

"The Nursing Care of Erysipelas." *American Journal of Nursing* 26 (April 1926): 287–88.

"Nursing's Professional Reach." *Nursing Outlook* 2 (July 1954): 375–77.

"Student Government in Forms of Government in Schools of Nursing." *American Journal of Nursing* 26 (December 1926): 877–79.

## BIBLIOGRAPHY

American Nurses Association. *Nursing Hall of Fame.* Kansas City, Mo.: American Nurses Association, 1984.

Gunter, L.M. Telephone interview with author, July 1986. Professor of Nursing and Human Development, The Pennsylvania State University.

Caldwell, E. "Meet Miss Alma Gault: Today's Her Day, also Her Moment." *The Nashville Tennessean,* 21 May 1967.

Gault, A. E. Papers. School of Nursing, Vanderbilt University, Nashville.

Patricia E. Baldwin

## Janet M. Geister

### 1885–1964

Janet M. Geister was a researcher, journalist, editor, nurse executive, and consultant. In 1917 the United States Children's Bureau based its "Save 100,000 Babies" campaign on research in which she had a major role, and she also teamed with an engineer to design the "Child Welfare Special," a mobile clinic that brought child health care to remote rural areas. An editor of the *Trained Nurse and Hospital Review* for eight years, she authored over 300 professional articles.

Geister was a native of Elgin, Illinois, and little is known of her childhood. She took nurse's training at Elgin's Sherman Hospital, graduating in 1910. After working as a private-duty nurse for one year, she entered the Chicago School of Civics and Philanthropy, which later became the School of Social Service Administration of the University of Chicago. She completed a course of study on social work and social research there under such notables as Jane Addams, Julia Lathrop, Graham Taylor and Alice Hamilton. However, she still felt inadequately prepared for vocational life, believing that schooling was not a substitute for experience.

For the next few years, Geister worked for Michael Reese Hospital as an infant-welfare nurse among Chicago's poor, as a medical social worker at Cook County Hospital, and as a supervisor for the Chicago Visiting Nursing Association. In 1917 she was offered a challenge that matched her professional goals and skills. Julia Lathrop, then chief of the United States Children's Bureau, wanted to learn why so many infants and mothers were dying. Geister joined other researchers who surveyed homesteaders living in poverty and hardship in northern Montana. This was the beginning of a long career in service through research.

In 1918 Geister worked in cooperation with several visiting nursing associations on a study that showed how parents often neglected their children's need for milk. These research projects led the children's bureau to launch its "Save 100,000 Babies" campaign, which did much to improve the health care of young children. She also was loaned briefly to the Child Welfare Association of New Orleans to help reorganize public-health nursing work and set up clinics in rural areas.

In the late spring of 1918, Lathrop recalled Geister and gave her a new assignment. The bureau needed a mobile child-health clinic for use in remote areas. Geister and an engineer designed a clinic room mounted on a truck body. The "Child Welfare Special" was staffed by a doctor and a nurse and was met with overwhelming crowds. It shed new light on the health needs of rural children, in one case revealing the onset of a polio epidemic.

In 1919 Geister resigned from the bureau and joined the National Organization for Public Health Nursing (NOPHN), first as field secretary and later as educational secretary to evaluate courses. At other times she also served NOPHN as a director and first vice-president. The organization loaned her to help with the Winslow-Goldmark study of nursing education and with a health and hospital survey being conducted by the city of Cleveland.

At this period, illness temporarily interrupted her career, but in 1923 she returned to New York and joined the staff of the Committee on Dispensary Development, a six-year survey of out-patient philosophies and systems. She was with the committee for four years and concurrently worked on two other projects. She assisted a medical society committee that was considering a bill to establish a one-year "Nightingale" nurse-training program to help alleviate the nurse shortage. She also organized an independent survey of 1,400 private-duty nurses in two districts of the New York State Nurses' Association. At the 1926 American Nurses' Association (ANA) convention, she presented a paper on private-duty nursing that was reprinted widely and enhanced public understanding and appreciation of the role of private-duty nurses.

When the dispensary survey was finished, Geister became executive director of the American Nurses' Association in January 1927. At that time, fewer than half of the 550,000 active nurses belonged to any professional nursing organization. By the end of her six-year tenure, ANA membership had doubled.

In 1933 Geister became associate editor and then editor of *Trained Nurse and Hospital Review*, and she remained there for eight years. She wrote a regular column called "Plain Talk" for the journal, and later her "Candid Comment" column appeared in *RN* magazine for almost nine years. In total, she wrote over 300 professional articles. One article, published in 1949, won her *The Modern Hospital* Gold Medal.

Ordered by her doctor to ease her work load, Geister nevertheless continued to write and to participate actively in the ANA, the Illinois League of Nursing, and other professional organizations. In gratitude for her service, the Illinois league awarded her a life membership and the Student Nurse Association of Illinois made her an honorary member. She died December 8, 1964, in the Evanston (Illinois) Hospital at age 79 after a brief illness. She was survived by three sisters, Laura Karsten, Harriet Dolby, and Mary Tuthill, and two brothers, Edward A. and Ray Geister, all of Elgin.

## SELECTED PUBLICATIONS BY JANET M. GEISTER

"Hearsay and Facts in Private Duty." *American Journal of Nursing* 26 (July 1926): 515–28.

"Nurses out of Work." *Survey* 65 (December 15, 1930): 320–21.

"More about General Duty." *Trained Nurse and Hospital Review* 107 (1941): 346.

"The Flu Epidemic of 1918." *Nursing Outlook* 5 (October 1957): 582–84.

## BIBLIOGRAPHY

"About People You Know: Janet M. Geister." *American Journal of Nursing* 41 (November 1941): 1335.

"Candidates for ANA Election: Geister, Janet M." *American Journal of Nursing* 50 (April 1950): 253.

"Geister, Janet M." *American Journal of Nursing* 34 (March 1934): 286.

Geister, J.M. "This I Believe." *Nursing Outlook* 12 (March 1964): 58–61.

"Janet M. Geister." Obituary. *New York Times*, 10 December 1964.

"Janet M. Geister 1885–1964." In *Nursing Hall of Fame*, by the American Nurses' Association. Kansas City, Mo.: American Nurses' Association, 1984.

"Miss Geister Resigns." Editorial. *American Journal of Nursing* 33 (March 1933): 243.

Alice P. Stein

## Leila Ione Given
### 1884–1959

Leila Ione Given was an author, educator, public employee, and American Nurses' Association (ANA) staff member. She is also known as the founder of the school of nursing at South Dakota State College (now South Dakota State University).

Given was born December 18, 1884, the second child of Thomas and Julia Given. Her father, a grocer, and her mother were both born in Ottumwa, Iowa. The other children in the family were Edna Muriel, the oldest, and Genevieve, Sidney, and Harold.

Given was graduated from the Creston, Iowa, high school in 1902. Some time later, she enrolled in the Cottage Hospital School of Nursing in Creston, completing its program in July 1911. Her first nursing employment was as a laboratory assistant and X-ray nurse for the Cottage Hospital. Later, she was appointed an assistant superintendent and instructor in its school of nursing.

Given became well-known for her work with state boards of nursing, but she had an extensive nursing career before that. Following completion of a postgraduate course at Women's Hospital in New York, she was appointed assistant superintendent and instructor at Women's Hospital in Nashville, Tennessee, in 1915. During World War I she served with the Army Nurse Corps in base hospital unit 27 in France. She also had eight weeks of volunteer service in a poliomyelitis epidemic in New York City sometime prior to 1920.

Given was appointed an instructor and director of instruction at the Connecticut

Training School of the New Haven Hospital and served there 1920–23. Following this experience, she enrolled in Teachers College, Columbia University, receiving her B.S. degree in 1926. While at Columbia University, she was employed as a laboratory assistant in the chemistry department.

Given was next employed as an instructor and later promoted to an assistant professor of microbiology at the school of nursing at Western Reserve University in Cleveland in 1925–32. By attending summer sessions at Columbia University, she was able to complete the requirements for her M.S. degree in 1929.

The first edition of the microbiology book she wrote with Jean Broadhurst was published in 1930 while Given was at Western Reserve University. First titled *Bacteriology Applied to Nursing* and subsequently titled *Microbiology Applied to Nursing*, it was published in five editions and was widely used in nursing schools.

Given left Western Reserve to accept a position as assistant to the principal of the Michael Reese Hospital School of Nursing in Chicago, where she stayed until 1934. She then was appointed science instructor of the Kahler Hospital School of Nursing in Rochester, Minnesota.

In 1935 Given was appointed professor of nursing education and director of the department of nursing education at South Dakota State College in Brookings, where she served for four years. The program she established was unique in several ways, for the department of nursing education was initially housed in the division of pharmacy. It began by providing two years of liberal arts, with students sent elsewhere for their clinical practice. One of Given's major responsibilities was to find suitable nursing programs to which the students could transfer. She also taught courses in nursing administration and principles of teaching to registered nurses, usually in the summer session. These early developments eventually led to the establishment of the college of nursing at South Dakota State University. Evidence suggests that nurses urged the university to establish the program and that some financial support was provided by the state nurses' association.

In 1939 Given left South Dakota to become director of the Wisconsin Bureau of Nursing Education. She served in this post during the troublesome war years and is credited with maintaining high standards of nursing in the state in spite of critical shortages of staff nurses in hospitals and faculty members in schools of nursing. She also implemented Wisconsin's participation in the newly organized national State Board Test Pool for licensing examinations. She served on the National Nursing Council for War Service and for some years was on the committee on tests of the National League of Nursing Education. Given is credited with having a major role in the development of the State Board Test Pool Examinations.

In 1947 Given left Wisconsin and went to New York City as an associate executive secretary of the American Nurses' Association (ANA), where she worked with the ANA's bureau of nurse examiners and its committee on legislation. She retired in 1952 and continued to live in New York until her death on February 13, 1959. She was survived by a brother, Sidney.

An ANA memorial resolution to her praised her concern for nursing education and her devotion to the nursing principles, her integrity, her readiness to assist, and her thoroughness in every task.

## PUBLICATIONS BY LEILA IONE GIVEN

### BOOKS

With J. Broadhurst. *Microbiology Applied to Nursing.* Philadelphia: J.B. Lippincott, 1930; 5th ed. 1945.

With C. Fevreau. *A Guide for Supervisors of State Approved Schools of Nursing.* New York: American Nurses' Association, 1948.

### ARTICLES

"Blind Spots in Testing and Grading." *American Journal of Nursing* 42 (March 1942): 305–9.

With M. Jacobsen. "Nursing Practice Acts." *American Journal of Nursing* 49 (April 1949): 207–8.

"Licensure for Nursing—Professional and Practical." *Nursing World* 125 (May 1951): 186–87.

## BIBLIOGRAPHY

Given, L.I. Papers. Archives State Historical Society of Wisconsin, Madison.

Given, L.I. Personnel record. South Dakota State University, Brookings, S.D.

"Leila I. Given." Obituary. *American Journal of Nursing* 59 (May 1959): 629.

"Leila I. Given." Obituary. *New York Times*, 14 February 1959.

Miller, I.M. Letter to author, 13 April 1986.

Signe S. Cooper

## Mary Elizabeth Gladwin

### 1861–1939

Mary Elizabeth Gladwin served as a war nurse in Cuba, the Philippines, Serbia, and Japan. For these services, she was decorated by the governments of Japan, Serbia, Russia, and the United States.

Born in Stoke-upon-Trent in Staffordshire, England, on December 24, 1861, Gladwin was the daughter of Francis and Sarah Cooper Gladwin. Brought to the United States in her childhood, she grew up in Ohio. After graduation from Buchtel College in Akron, Ohio, in 1887, she worked as a science teacher in the Norwalk (Ohio) High School from 1887–93.

Dissatisfied with teaching, Gladwin began nurse's training at Boston City Hospital in 1896, but left to serve as a nurse with the United States Army during the Spanish-American War, first in Cuba and then with the American Red Cross in the Philippines. She returned to Boston City Hospital after her Philippines service and graduated cum laude in 1903.

Between 1903–4 and 1905–7, Gladwin served as superintendent of the Beverly (Massachusetts) Hospital. Her service was interrupted by another war, this time the Russo-Japanese war. Gladwin served with the Red Cross in Hiroshima, Japan, as a nurse.

In 1907–8 she moved to New York City to be superintendent of nurses at Women's Hospital, and this was followed by a short stint as superintendent of Cleveland City Hospital in Ohio. She then moved back to Akron, Ohio, to work as a welfare worker for women with the B.F. Goodrich Rubber Company. While there, she organized the George T. Perkins Visiting Nurse Association, in which she served from 1912 to 1914.

Gladwin continued her Red Cross ties and during the Dayton, Ohio, floods of 1913, she served as chief nurse. With the outbreak of World War I, she again entered the battle zone, serving as a nurse in Belgrade, Serbia, and Salonika, Greece, from 1914 to 1919.

Upon her return to the United States, Gladwin lectured and taught for the Red Cross in Ohio. She left this position to become director of nursing education for the state of Indiana (1922–23) and from there went to Minnesota for a similar position with the Minnesota State Board of Nurse Examiners. In 1927 she became superintendent of St. Mary's Hospital in Minneapolis, and in 1928 she assumed the position of director of St. Mary's Hospital in Rochester, Minnesota.

The recipient of many honors, Gladwin was awarded the Japanese Order of the Crown and the Port Arthur Medal for her service in Japan, the Serbian Royal Red Cross Order of St. Sava, La Croix de Charité, the Russian Imperial Medal and Ribbon of St. Anne, the Florence Nightingale medal of the International Red Cross, and a special medal from the United States in 1934 for her services in the Spanish-American War.

Gladwin was active in the American Nurses' Association, serving on its board of directors, as well as president of the Ohio Nurses' Association.

Gladwin died November 22, 1939 in Akron, Ohio.

### PUBLICATIONS BY MARY ELIZABETH GLADWIN

*Ethics, Talk to Nurses.* Philadelphia: W.B. Saunders, 1930, rev. ed.

*Ethics: A Textbook for Nurses*, 1937.

*Red Cross and Jane Arminda Delano.* Philadelphia: W.B. Saunders, 1931.

**BIBLIOGRAPHY**

"Mary E. Gladwin." Obituary. *American Journal of Nursing* 40 (January 1940): 105–06.

Vern L. Bullough

# Elizabeth Conde Glenn

## 1859–1920

Elizabeth Conde Glenn was an innovator in nursing education in Illinois. In administrative positions in the Rockford and Passavant hospital training schools for nurses, she effected significant curriculum improvements and was noted as a strict disciplinarian. During her career, she also sought federal inspection and national standards for nursing schools and improved benefits for retired nurses.

Glenn was born in 1859, one of a family of five children. Her parents were Presbyterians, and her father Gilbert worked as a painter, teacher, travel agent, and notions peddler after moving the family to Rockford, Illinois, in 1872.

In October 1885 at the age of 26, Glenn entered the two-year program of the Illinois Training School for Nurses in Chicago. She worked under Isabel Hampton, whose curriculum integrated scientific and practical work. Students studied anatomy, physiology, and *materia medica*; at the same time they worked in the wards or did private duty in the city.

As her training drew to a close, Glenn sought to return to Rockford, where she had spent most of her childhood. Hampton had written enthusiastically to the Rockford trustees about Glenn's work, which had included being head nurse on the women's ward in her last year. She had distinguished herself, especially with two women private patients whose husbands also wrote glowingly of her.

In February 1888 she began work as superintendent of nurses at Rockford City Hospital and helped in the move into a new building for the three-year-old hospital, where she soon urged the establishment of a training school for nurses. In April 1889 Glenn requested that the medical staff arrange a course of lectures that would lead to some form of certification for the two nurses then employed at the hospital. The hospital advanced the idea to the trustees. The trustees agreed that Glenn and the physicians would provide for the education and training of the nurses employed in the hospital.

The lectures Glenn had requested from the physicians began in October 1889, a few months before graduation of the first class in the 18-month course, and provided rudimentary knowledge of anatomy, physiology, and *materia medica*. Because the students already worked in the hospital, their practical experience had begun even before the trustees had approved the program.

Glenn taught and supervised nurses at the Rockford Hospital until 1901. Her tenure ended after a year of political conflict as physicians sought more authority over hospital practices. The medical staff wanted some voice in who should go, stay, or even be admitted to the school, rather than allowing that authority to rest with one person, Glenn. The trustees accepted Glenn's resignation, regretting that circumstances impelled her to resign.

Glenn left Rockford for Chicago and the superintendency of Passavant Hospital Training School for Nurses. There, she added a theoretical aspect to a three-year-old practical program. She phased new subjects into the curriculum and extended the program to three years in 1905, when Passavant affiliated with the Illinois Training School.

Glenn believed education and a proper public front would lead to professional respectability. She kept her program up to date, advocated an even more theoretically oriented curriculum, and participated in progressive efforts that would distinguish between trained and untrained nurses.

Glenn also defended a tradition in organized nursing when reform threatened it and the security of older nurses. Nurses had long organized in alumnae associations. Such local associations provided social intercourse and helped nurses in time of trouble. However, a new structure for the American Nurses' Association (ANA) imposed higher dues on alumnae associations and jeopardized the benefits of these local groups to retired nurses.

Glenn, who had chaired the revision committee for her alumnae association in 1915, opposed the idea, for it threatened in particular retired nurses. She claimed that these women, who had served the profession well, could not afford the new dues in their retirement and would lose membership in the association and the benefits of it. Nonetheless, the alumnae association adopted a revised constitution in 1919 that reflected the new relationship to the ANA.

Glenn had always supported a higher standard of professionalism for nurses. She had been a charter member of the Illinois State Association of Graduate Nurses in 1901 and on the legislative committee in 1905 as that group worked for a state board of examiners for registered nurses. She believed in a legal route for reform and also that nurses in uniform must behave differently in order to gain public respect.

Glenn also advocated federal inspection and national standards to reduce the problem of poor nursing schools. The government could eliminate undesirable training schools. The larger and better schools that remained could then upgrade education and conditions. Less routine and more professional responsibilities would attract more desirable women, and that professional condition would exist when nursing schools devoted more time to study and lectures and less time to practical work.

Some months after she had defended the benefits of retired nurses, Glenn fell seriously ill with pneumonia after a bout with influenza in the epidemic of 1918. She went to Florida to recuperate, returning the following February to Passavant. However, her heath did not improve. She went to Glockner Sanitarium in Colorado Springs, Colorado, where she died on August 18, 1920. After services in Chicago, she was buried in Rockford. She was survived by her sister Josephine of Milwaukee, Wisconsin.

## BIBLIOGRAPHY

Dunwiddie, M. *A History of the Illinois State Nurses' Association, 1901–1935.* N.p.: Illinois State Nurses' Association, 1937.

"Elizabeth Conde Glenn." Obituary. *Chicago Daily News,* 19 August 1920.

"Passing of Miss Glenn." Obituary. *Rockford Register-Gazette,* 19 August 1920.

Illinois Training School for Nurses. *Seventh Annual Report of the Illinois Training School for Nurses.* Chicago: Fergus Printing, 1887.

Illinois Training School for Nurses Alumnae Association. *Monthly Report,* April 1907, March 1912, February 1918, November 1918, March 1919.

Illinois Training School for Nurses Records. Special Collections. The University Library, University of Illinois at Chicago.

Passavant Memorial Hospital Alumnae. Minutes. Northwestern Memorial Hospital Archives. Northwestern Memorial Hospital, Chicago.

Passavant Memorial Hospital Training School for Nurses. Nurses' records, January 1, 1898. Northwestern Memorial Hospital Archives, Chicago.

Rockford City Hospital. Minutes of the trustees, book 1. Rockford, Ill.

Rockford Hospital Association. *Second Annual Report of the Rockford Hospital Association.* Rockford: Horner Printing, 1893.

Rockford Hospital Training School. Nurses' records, 1898. Rockford, Ill.

Rockford, Ill. City directories, 1872–90. Rockford Public Library.

Rockford Memorial Hospital. Minutes of the medical board, 1885–1920. Rockford, Ill.

James Monahan

## Hazel Avis Goff

### 1892–1973

Hazel Avis Goff achieved distinction in a variety of international positions in nursing, serving with the Red Cross and with the Rockefeller Foundation. She was the first nurse to be appointed to the health section of the League of Nations, the predecessor of the United Nations.

The daughter of Frederick J. and Barbara McGinnis Goff, she was born August 1892 in Leeds, Quebec, Canada, and moved to Massachusetts with her family when she was quite young. Goff was graduated from the Grafton High School and the Framingham Normal School, specializing in teaching home economics. She then entered the Massachusetts General Hospital Training School, graduating in 1917.

Goff began her nursing career as a private-duty nurse in the Boston area. In 1918 she joined the Red Cross and became an army nurse, serving with a base hospital in Toul, France.

Upon her return home from military service, she was appointed superintendent of nurses at Blodgett Memorial Hospital in Grand Rapids, Michigan. In 1922 she returned to Europe under the auspices of the Red Cross and went to Sophia, Bulgaria, as assistant to Rachel Torrence in establishing a Red Cross school of nursing. The next year, Goff was appointed director of the school.

This work was a real challenge in a country with 97 hospitals and only 165 nurses, as Goff described in a 1926 article in *Modern Hospital*. After three years in Bulgaria, she went to Paris as field director for the European office of the Rockefeller Foundation, a post she held for three years. As field director, she did consulting and advisory work in nursing in Bulgaria, France, Greece, Poland, Yugoslavia, and other countries.

Goff returned to the United States and in 1930–31 completed work for her B.S. degree at Teachers College, Columbia University, in public-health nursing administration. In 1931, she was appointed the only nurse in the health section of the League of Nations, composed of 17 health officers from as many countries. This appointment came about through the International Council of Nurses (ICN) after a nurse made an anonymous contribution of the salary of a nurse for two years for that purpose.

The ICN had high hopes for this position and called the appointment one of the greatest events in its history. It was hoped that the position would be continued after the two-year period, but funds were not available.

Goff's pioneer work in her two years with the League of Nations included a survey of public-health nursing in ten countries, which she reported at the ICN's congress in Paris in 1933. Her recommendations included the improvement of basic nursing education, the inclusion of public-health content in nursing curricula and postgraduate education in public-health nursing.

Following this experience, Goff returned to the Balkans, where she organized a rural public-health nursing center in Bulgaria, for which she received special recognition from the queen of that country. In 1936 the minister of health of Turkey invited her to Istanbul to reorganize its Red Crescent School of Nursing. Writing about this experience later, she described an intercontinental course: some of the students were in a hospital across the Bosporus in Asia, but the school was in Istanbul in Europe. Three years later, the threat of a European war forced her to return home.

Upon her return to the United States, Goff served as director of nursing at St. Luke's Hospital in Cleveland, Ohio. In 1942 she was invited to give one of a series of lectures on international aspects of nursing at Teachers College, Columbia University, later published in the *American Journal of Nursing*. She spoke on preparing for postwar work abroad, for even during the war, nurses were recalling contributions made by American nurses in the reconstruction of Europe following World War I. She shared her belief that nursing knowledge should be used to help people help themselves.

In 1945 and again under assignment for the Rockefeller Foundation, Goff reorganized the Portugal School for Technical Nurses in Lisbon. Two years later, she joined the staff of the National League of Nursing Education, working with Julia Miller on temporary accreditation of schools of nursing in the developing years of the league's accreditation program.

Goff served for a time as director of nursing at Allegheny General Hospital, Allegheny, Pennsylvania, and in 1954 was appointed director of nursing at Madison General Hospital, Madison, Wisconsin, where she served a short time. Her last position was as a lecturer at the University of Pennsylvania School of Nursing.

Goff was described as having a charming personality and an inquiring mind. She had a special facility with languages, an important asset for the kinds of positions she held. She had a colorful nursing career, and her contributions to nursing in Europe were extensive, covering many countries.

Goff was a member of Sigma Theta Tau and Chi Eta Phi, both honorary nursing sororities. In 1964 she was presented the Honorary Recognition Award of the Pennsylvania Nurses' Association.

Goff died September 10, 1973, at the Albert Einstein Hospital in Philadelphia, and was buried in Riverside Cemetery, Grafton, Massachusetts. She was survived by a brother, Winslow H. Goff.

## PUBLICATIONS BY HAZEL AVIS GOFF

"Bringing Health and Happiness to Bulgarian Peasants." *Modern Hospital* 27 (December 1926): 71–76.

"Trends in the Development of Public Health Nursing in Europe." Editorial. *International Nursing Review* 6 (September 1931): 395–97.

"A Comparative Study of Standards for Nursing." *Trained Nurse and Hospital Review* (October, November, December 1931): 477–82, 608–12, 740–52.

"The Influence of American Ideals and Traditions on Nursing Education in the Slav Countries." In *International Aspects of Nursing Education.* New York: Teachers College, Columbia University, 1932.

"The Hospital Nursing Service." *Trained Nurse and Hospital Review* 89 (August 1932): 169–73.

"Report of a Study of Public Health Nursing in Europe." *Public Health Nursing* 25 (November 1933): 600–04. Also published in *International Nursing Review* 9 (January 1934): 31–45.

"Preparing for Postwar Work Abroad." *American Journal of Nursing* 43 (February 1943): 169–80.

With M.W. Hall. "Alternating Theory and Practice." *American Journal of Nursing* 46 (March 1946): 189–91.

## BIBLIOGRAPHY

Bridges, D.C. *A History of the International Council of Nurses 1899–1964.* Philadelphia: J.B. Lippincott, 1967.

"Hazel A. Goff." Obituary. *American Journal of Nursing* 73 (December 1973): 2140.

"Hazel A. Goff." Obituary. *Worcester* (Mass.) *Telegram*, 12 September 1973.

Kernodle, P.B. *The Red Cross Nurse in Action, 1882–1948.* New York: Harper and Brothers, 1948.

"Nursing and the League of Nations." *American Journal of Nursing* 31 (November 1931): 128–34.

"A Nursing Expert Appointed to the Health Section of the League of Nations." *The ICN* 6 (September 1931): 483–84.

Pennock, M.R. "Hazel Goff." In *Makers of Nursing History*, edited by M.R. Pennock. New York: Lakeside Publishing, 1940.

Signe S. Cooper

# Emma Goldman

## 1869–1940

Emma Goldman's contributions as a nurse are often ignored in the accounts of her life, which emphasize her role as anarchist, rebel, lecturer, publicist, agitator for free speech, feminist, and advocate of birth control. However, her life illustrates the complexity of those individuals, mainly women, who entered nursing in the latter part of the nineteenth century. Goldman, popularly known as "Red Emma," was one of the most infamous women during that period.

Born in Kovno (Kaunas) in Lithuania on June 27, 1869, Goldman was the first child of the marriage of Abraham and Taube Bienowitch Goldman. Her mother, who had two daughters from a previous marriage, had not wanted another daughter, while her father, anxious for a son, never quite forgave his daughter for her gender, even though he later had two sons. The marriage was strained because Abraham Goldman had lost his wife's inheritance in a business venture. A lower middle-class shopkeeper, Goldman's father failed several times and each time moved on to another city or another job. The family moved from Kovno to Popelan, then to Konigsberg, Germany, and finally to St. Petersburg in Russia, each time with little success. While in Germany, Goldman, with the aid of a rabbi relative, was enrolled in a *Realschule*, and was preparing to attend a secondary school when she got into trouble with her teacher of religion. In St. Petersburg she had six more months of formal schooling, after which she went to work in a glove factory owned by a cousin. In order to escape her father's plans for an arranged marriage, she emigrated in 1885 to America with her half-sister Helena Zodokoff and settled in Rochester, New York, with her other half-sister, Lena.

In Rochester Goldman quickly found work in a clothing factory, where she met and in 1887 married Jacob Kersner (also Kershner), a naturalized citizen. Kersner proved to be impotent, and the result was a quick break-up of the marriage by divorce, followed by a short-lived reconciliation and a permanent divorce. After the divorce in 1889, Goldman moved to New York City. She stated that her only assets were her youth, her good health, and her ideals, which translated into dedication to the socialist cause.

Goldman fell in love with Alexander Berkman, and she accepted his view that individual acts of violence could bring about social change. She apparently helped Berkman in 1892 prepare to kill Henry Clay Frick, the steel magnate who was held responsible by her fellow anarchists for the Homestead strike at steel mills in the Pittsburgh area. Though Berkman shot and wounded him, Frick survived, and Berkman was sent to jail.

The next year Goldman was sent to jail for inciting a riot when she told an audience of unemployed men that it was their right to take bread if they were starving and their demands for food went unanswered. It was while in prison on Blackwell's Island in New York that she became acquainted with nursing and received training as a practical nurse. Her description of the penitentiary hospital to which

she was assigned was gruesome; nevertheless, she loved her job and eventually was given charge of the hospital ward.

After her release from prison, Goldman went to Europe in 1895 to gain further training. She studied at the Allgemeines Krankenhaus in Vienna, an institution recommended to her by Edward Brady, who was also her lover for a time. She received both a certificate in nursing and one in midwifery after one year's study in Vienna. Upon her return to New York City, Goldman began delivering babies. Her anger mounted at the number of unwanted pregnancies. She became close to other "radical" nurses, including Lillian Wald and Lavinia Dock, and although she disagreed with what she called their piecemeal, pragmatic approach, she got along well with them. She became an active campaigner for women's rights and women's reproductive freedom.

When Berkman was released from jail in 1906, Goldman toured the United States with him. They founded the journal *Mother Earth*, and in 1917 they were arrested for opposing the draft. They were first imprisoned and then in 1919 deported, to the Soviet Union.

Goldman quickly became disillusioned with the Soviet state and after a two year residence there fled to England, where she continued her activities on behalf of women, contraception, and socialist causes. In order to obtain British citizenship, she married James Colton, a Welsh collier. She continued to support herself through lectures and royalties from her books and from her autobiography, *Living My Life*, which she wrote in 1931.

In 1934 Goldman was granted a 90-day stay in the United States. In 1936 Berkman, her long-time lover, committed suicide. Goldman then devoted herself to the Loyalist cause of the Spanish civil war and traveled to Canada to raise money and also to visit with relatives, who came over from the States. In February 1940 she suffered a stroke, and she died on May 14, 1940, in a Toronto hospital. She was buried in Chicago's Waldheim Cemetery near the graves of the Haymarket "martyrs," those killed by the police in 1887 during the Haymarket riots.

Goldman loved helping people and wrote that it was in the prison hospital that she first had seen the complexities of the human soul. As a nurse, she became so upset at the way the poor and helpless were treated that she felt she needed to address the cause of this treatment. As a result, much of her life was spent involved in conflict. Nevertheless, she was influential, and in 1922 the *Nation* insisted that her name should be on any list of the greatest living women.

## PUBLICATIONS BY EMMA GOLDMAN

### BOOKS

*Anarchism and Other Essays*. New York: Mother Earth Publishing Association, 1911.

*The Social Significance of Modern Drama*. Boston: G.R. Badger, 1914.

*My Disillusionment in Russia*. Garden City, N.Y.: Doubleday, Page, and Co., 1923.

*My Further Disillusionment in Russia*. Garden City, N.Y.: Doubleday, 1924.

*Living My Life*. New York: Alfred A. Knopf, 1931.

### PAMPHLETS ( SELECTED )

Many of her articles were published in *Mother Earth* and separately published as pamphlets.

*Patriotism*. New York: Mother Earth, 1908.

*Marriage and Love*. New York: Mother Earth, 1911.

*Psychology of Political Violence*. New York: Mother Earth, 1911.

*Sydicalism: The Modern Menace to Capitalism*. New York: Mother Earth, 1914.

### ARTICLES ( SELECTED )

*The Truth about the Bolshevik*. New York: Mother Earth, 1918.

"Trotsky Protests Too Much." *Vanguard*, July 1938.

### BIBLIOGRAPHY

Drinnon, R. *Rebel in Paradise: A Biography of Emma Goldman*. Chicago: University of Chicago Press, 1961.

Goldman, E. Files. Justice Department, U.S. State Department, U.S. Post Office, and the National Archives, Washington, D.C.

Goldman, E. Papers. International Institute for Social History, Amsterdam.

Goldman, E. Papers. Labadie Collection. University of Michigan, Ann Arbor.

Goldman, E. Papers. New York City Public Library, New York.

Harris, F. *Contemporary Portraits, Fourth Series*. New York: Brentano's, 1923.

Mannin, E.E. *Red Rose: A Novel Based on the Life of Emma Goldman*. London: Jarold's, 1941.

Vern L. Bullough

# Minnie Goodnow

## 1875–1952

Minnie Goodnow was one of the more prolific nurse authors of the first half of the twentieth century. She held major administrative positions at hospitals throughout the United States.

Born in Albion, New York, on July 10, 1875, Minnie Goodnow was the daughter of Franklin and Elizabeth Arnold Goodnow. Her father was an architect, a profession that Goodnow at one time hoped to enter. The family moved to Denver, Colorado, when Goodnow was in her teens, and she attended Denver High School. After her graduation, she attended the University of Denver, where she won two prizes for her studies in Greek. She left college without graduating to work in her father's office doing drafting, then a necessary first step to becoming an architect.

Financial difficulties in the family initially led Goodnow to nursing. She received her diploma from the Las Vegas Hot Springs Sanitarium School of Nursing in New Mexico in 1899. From there she went on to take a postgraduate course at General Memorial Hospital in New York City as well as the New York Infant Asylum.

Goodnow began her nursing career in 1900 as a private-duty nurse, a position she soon left to become superintendent of Denver Woman's Hospital, the first of her many administrative positions. From Denver she moved to Milwaukee, Wisconsin, to be superintendent of nurses at the Milwaukee County Hospital and then back to Denver for a similar position at Park Avenue Hospital. In neither of these two positions did she stay for more than a year. Her next move took her to Kalamazoo, Michigan, where she served as superintendent of the Bronson Hospital for two and one-half years.

Goodnow then left nursing to serve with a firm of hospital architects in Boston, a job she held for two years. The firm she worked with was the first to devote itself to full-time hospital planning, and Goodnow played an important role in planning hospitals from a nursing point of view. She also developed, selected, and placed suitable hospital and nursing equipment.

With the outbreak of World War I, Goodnow returned to nursing. In 1915 she went to France with a Harvard ambulance unit. While in France, she wrote a handbook for nurses' aides, *War Nursing.*

Goodnow returned to the United States in 1917 to upgrade her skills in occupational therapy in order to care for and treat handicapped veterans after the end of the war. She worked briefly with the United States Army in a hospital in Wheeling, West Virginia, and at the Institute for Crippled Men in New York City.

In 1920 Goodnow returned to nursing administration as the superintendent of nurses at the Children's Hospital in Washington, D.C., where she also took classes at George Washington University. From 1925 to 1928, she was director of nurses at General Hospital in Philadelphia. She also took classes at the University of Pennsylvania. In 1929 Goodnow moved to Newport, Rhode Island, where she was superintendent of nurses at Newport Hospital.

Goodnow resigned from this position in 1935 to take a two-year trip around the world. She visited with nurses in New Zealand, Thailand, China, India, Japan, Palestine, Turkey, Greece, and western Europe, and she met with officials of the International Council of Nurses in England and Scotland.

Goodnow's first textbook appeared early in her career. Titled *Ten Lessons for Nurses in Chemistry,* it has the distinction of being the first chemistry text specifically designed for nurses. Since Goodnow was not a chemist, it of necessity was elementary in nature. This was followed by *First Year Nursing,* especially designed for schools in small hospitals. However, Goodnow is best remembered for her historical works. Her *History of Nursing* appeared in 1916 and was revised every four years, with the ninth edition appearing shortly after her death in 1953. She also wrote for several nursing journals, and a series of articles she wrote for *Trained Nurse and Hospital Review* appeared in book form as *The Nursing of Children.*

Although she contemplated retirement after her world travels, Goodnow reconsidered and became superintendent of nurses at Somerville Hospital in Somerville, Massachusetts. She stayed there until 1941, when she became supervisor of schools of nursing for Massachusetts. She left this post in 1943 to be superintendent of nurses at Pratt Diagnostic Hospital in Boston, from which she retired. She died in Pratt Diagnostic Hospital on February 9, 1952.

## PUBLICATIONS BY MINNIE GOODNOW

*Ten Lessons for Nurses in Chemistry.* New York: Lakeside Publishing, 1911; 5th ed., 1919.

*First Year Nursing.* Philadelphia: W.B. Saunders, 1912; 2nd ed., 1916; 3rd ed., 1921.

*History of Nursing* (first six editions listed as *Outlines of Nursing History*). Philadelphia: W.B. Saunders, 1916, 1920, 1924, 1928, 1932, 1936; 9th ed., 1953.

*War Nursing.* Philadelphia: W.B. Saunders, 1918.

*Practical Physics for Nurses.* Philadelphia: W.B. Saunders, 1919.

*Technique of Nursing.* Philadelphia: W.B. Saunders, 1923; 2nd ed., 1930; 3rd ed., 1935; 4th ed., 1941.

*Nursing History in Brief.* 3rd ed. Philadelphia: W.B. Saunders, 1950.

*The Nursing of Children.* Detroit: Trained Nurse and Hospital Review, n.d. This contained a number of articles that had been published in *Trained Nurse and Hospital Review.*

## BIBLIOGRAPHY

"Minnie Goodnow." Obituary. *American Journal of Nursing* 52 (April 1952): 54.

Pennock, M.R. *Makers of Nursing History.* New York: Lakeside Publishing, 1940.

Vern L. Bullough

# Annie Warburton Goodrich

## 1866–1954

Annie Warburton Goodrich envisioned the nursing and medical professions as equals, independent yet interdependent, each possessing a unique body of knowledge. In an age when nurses received their training in hospital schools of nursing, she charted a course for recognition of nursing's status and dignity. Goodrich's efforts introduced nursing to the university and pioneered the inclusion of preventive-medicine and community-nursing courses in the curriculum.

Goodrich was born February 6, 1866, in New Brunswick, New Jersey, the second of seven children. Her father, Samuel Goodrich, was an insurance executive and a descendant of Charles Chauncey, second president of Harvard University. Her mother, Annie Williams Butler, was the daughter of physician John S. Butler, a pioneer in progressive psychiatry who founded the Hartford Retreat, an institution for the treatment of the mentally ill. Samuel Goodrich provided well for the family, allowing the Goodrich children to be taught by tutors and in private schools. They continued study in private schools, first in New York City and in 1880 overseas, when their father's work took the family to London.

Due to poor health, Samuel Goodrich's fortunes faded, and the family returned to Hartford, Connecticut, in 1885. Because Goodrich felt responsible for her own support, for a brief time she became a companion to a woman living in Boston. This exposure to Boston society and an opportunity to travel contributed to her lifelong reputation for poise and hospitality. During the illnesses of her grandparents, in 1890, Goodrich returned to Hartford. Although she did not perform many of the nursing duties for her family during this time, her grandparents' illnesses had a profound effect on her. As she watched an untrained nurse attempt to help her family, she came to believe that if a nurse possessed a general education and scientific background, she could offer much more compassion and skill to the patient and thereby develop the patient's trust.

It was not a love of nursing (for she abhored sickness and death) that brought Goodrich to apply to a training school for nurses. Rather, it was the practical need to support herself, combined with the lack of vocational options open to women of the time. In 1890 she entered New York Hospital's Training School for Nurses. Students normally worked 12 hours each day on the wards of the hospital and attended a few evening lectures on clinical subjects. Senior nursing students served as head nurses, guiding the new students through their initial experiences on the wards. Lillian Wald was the senior student on ward 6, where Goodrich began her training. This partnership continued in later years as Wald, founder of the Henry Street Settlement, a community health center, drew Goodrich into the work of public-health nursing. The superintendent of nurses at New York Hospital, Irine H. Sutliffe, was another outstanding influence during Goodrich's formative school years. She served as both confidante and mentor when Goodrich later was a superintendent of training schools.

After graduation, Goodrich remained at New York Hospital until 1893, when she departed to become superintendent of nurses at New York Postgraduate Hospital. Although not responsible for nurse education, she became involved by holding weekly "class nights" at the nurses' home. Goodrich reduced student work hours and promoted a cooperative relationship between nurses and physicians. In 1897 the program was reorganized to place the training school under the control of hospital administration, and Goodrich became the superintendent of nursing and the training school.

In 1900 Goodrich became the superintendent of nurses at St. Luke's Hospital in New York. She strove to improve the working and educational environment for the students and to develop a new system for the delivery of patient care. Her concept of assigning a nurse to the complete care of a small group of patients replaced the older system of assigning a nurse to a specific functional duty performed for all patients on a ward. This concept represented an early introduction to primary-care nursing.

When Sutliffe retired in 1902, Goodrich replaced her as superintendent of nurses at New York Hospital. Continuing her efforts to enhance nursing education, she shifted students' classes to daytime hours and established affiliations with other local hospitals to offer clinical experiences for the students, experiences that were unavailable at New York Hospital. After five years, Goodrich left New York Hospital in 1907, when the hospital's board of governors discontinued many of her reforms.

Undiscouraged, Goodrich became general superintendent at the Bellevue and Allied Training Schools for Nursing in New York City. In her three years at Bellevue, 1907 to 1910, she institutionalized a formal student probationary period, which included standardized instruction and tests. As superintendent, Goodrich consistently endeavored to raise educational requirements for entry into the nursing school, achieve an expanded and systematic nursing curriculum, develop broader clinical experience in such areas as obstetrics and public health, and graduate students who valued high professional standards.

The irregular quality of nursing education led the state of New York to establish a position, state inspector of nurse training schools, to oversee educational standards. In 1910 Goodrich became the second person to hold that position. She fought to raise the standards in nursing education and training by working to win compulsory state registration of nurses, minimal acceptable educational standards for professional education, and licensing examinations. She did not achieve all these goals during her tenure, but she illuminated problem areas and continued to press for reforms in the years that followed.

From 1904 through 1914, Goodrich also lectured at Teachers College, Columbia University, on the subject of hospital economics. The American Society of Superintendents of Training Schools for Nurses underwrote this course, a pioneering step to place nursing into the academic setting. In 1914 she joined the full-time faculty of Columbia as an assistant professor, teaching administration of schools of nursing.

In 1917 Goodrich embarked on yet another professional venture. Lillian Wald asked Goodrich to join her at the Henry Street Settlement, an organization she founded in 1893 to bring basic health care and preventive medicine into the community. She hoped Goodrich's superior executive abilities could provide the leadership Henry Street Settlement needed to develop its community service. Goodrich accepted the challenge with goals of her own. With the cooperation of M. Adelaide Nutting, head of the department of nursing and health at Teachers College, Goodrich became the director of nurses at Henry Street Settlement, a position she held concurrently with her teaching appointment.

Goodrich was a logical choice to carry the torch for the Henry Street Settlement during its critical years of rapid growth. While with the Henry Street Settlement, she enhanced its reputation and the quality of its work by improving the pay and conditions there. She stressed the importance of preventive medicine in nursing, and under her direction, students from schools of nursing became affiliated with Henry Street Settlement to gain public-health nursing experience.

The United States entry into World War I in April 1917 brought rapid movement within the professional nursing community to plan for the immense requirements for nurses in wartime. The Emergency Committee on Nursing, formed in June 1917, included Goodrich. Although an avowed pacifist, she accepted her role in government service. The committee later assumed an official capacity as the National Committee on Nursing of the Council of National Defense.

Senior medical officers in Europe issued several pleas for Goodrich's help to direct American Red Cross nurses on the continent. She declined the requests, feeling that her work at the Henry Street Settlement was too critical and that American Red Cross efforts could be handled properly only if she could conduct a comprehensive survey of both the military and American Red Cross facilities in Europe. In February 1918 at the request of the surgeon general of the army, Goodrich did take a leave of absence from the Henry Street Settlement to become chief inspecting nurse of the United States Army's hospitals.

Goodrich's overwhelming task in this new position was to devise a solution to the problem of providing enough trained nurses to meet wartime requirements. Conflicting opinions existed inside and outside the nursing profession over how to meet the demand. Goodrich proposed that the army establish its own school of nursing, which would maintain a standardized curriculum at several military hospitals around the country. The students would ease the labor shortage at army hospitals and thereby free graduate nurses for service overseas. Opponents decried this idea on the grounds that it would deplete the pool of nurses attending civilian nursing schools and thus their source of cheap labor while creating a surplus of nurses after the war. Finally, due largely to Goodrich's arguments, the American Nurses' Association, the National League for Nursing Education, and the National Organization for Public Health Nursing supported the plan on the condition that it should not be allowed to interfere with enrollment in civilian schools of nursing. The Surgeon General and the Secretary of War approved the plan in May 1918.

With the Army School of Nursing, Goodrich saw the opportunity to build the model nursing program of her dreams. Standardized curriculum and equipment and the introduction of modern teaching methods demonstrated that centralized nursing education could ensure the quality of nursing instruction and, ultimately, nursing care. Student life at the school also improved with an eight-hour work day for students and a responsible student government.

As its dean, Goodrich guided the Army School of Nursing through its first year. With the school well established, she returned to Henry Street Settlement in July 1919 to resume her work there. In 1923 the United States War Department recognized her wartime efforts by awarding her the Distinguished Service Medal.

Goodrich's return to the Henry Street Settlement initiated a flurry of institu-

tional reforms and improvements in the standard of care. Fittingly, the Army School of Nursing joined the growing list of nursing schools affiliated with the Henry Street Settlement.

From her earliest entry into nursing practice, Goodrich was active in nursing's professional organizations, including the American Society of Superintendents of Training Schools for Nurses (later the National League of Nursing Education). She served on committees for education, publication, and hospital economics. In 1909 she served as president of the American Federation of Nurses and from 1912 to 1913 was president of the International Council of Nurses. Early in her presidency of the American Nurses' Association, 1915 to 1918, that organization surveyed nursing resources in anticipation of the coming war. Goodrich advocated state registration and licensing of nurses and, believing nurses would be unable to affect the laws that governed them until they had the right to vote, became involved in the women's suffrage movement.

In 1918 the Rockefeller Foundation named Goodrich to a committee to study nursing education. This committee issued recommendations that included entrance requirements to schools of nursing, including training in the basic sciences, and affiliation of schools of nursing with multiple hospitals in order to provide well-rounded clinical experience. The recommendation dearest to Goodrich encouraged funds be provided for the endowment of nursing education and stipulated that the place of nursing education was in the universities.

In response to the committee's 1923 report, known as the Goldmark Report, Yale University offered its facilities for the first experimental university-based independent school of nursing. In 1923 at the request of the university, Goodrich became dean and professor of nursing education. The nursing school was the first to have its own faculty, classrooms, and budget, and the experiment was so successful that after only five years, the Rockefeller Foundation presented Yale with a $1 million endowment to assure the permanence of the Yale School of Nursing.

During the 11 years of Goodrich's leadership, the Yale School of Nursing established progressively stricter entrance requirements. Indeed, by 1934 the entering nursing student already possessed a college degree. After completion of course work at Yale, the student graduated with a master's degree in nursing.

Goodrich retired to Colchester, Connecticut, in 1934, just before the first nurse graduated from the Yale master's granting program. This was retirement in name only, however, as she continued her energetic involvement in professional organizations, with Yale, and as a nursing consultant. At the request of the Rockefeller Foundation, she toured England and the Baltic countries in 1935 to study their hospital systems. From 1938 to 1941, she assisted the Institute of Living, the organization her grandfather founded as the Hartford Retreat, as consulting director of nursing service.

As consultant to the school of nursing at Western Reserve University, Goodrich taught courses in community-nursing service trends and administration of schools of nursing and nursing service. Her last official appointment was as special nursing education consultant to the United States Public Health Service in 1942. In this capacity, she helped develop the Cadet Nurse Corps, a response to the enormous requirement for nursing services as the United States entered World War II.

Goodrich's awards include the Medal of the Institute of Social Sciences in 1920, the U.S. Distinguished Service Medal in 1923, the Médaille d'honneur de l'hygiène publique from France in 1928, the Walter Burns Saunders Medal from the American Nurses' Association in 1932, the Silver Medal of the Ministry of Social Welfare from France in 1933, the Bronze Medal of Belgium in 1933, a citation from the International Council of Nurses in 1947, a fellowship with the American College of Hospital Administrators in 1948, and the National League of Nursing Education's Mary Adelaide Nutting Award in 1948. She received honorary degrees from Mount Holyoke College in 1921 (doctor of science), Yale University in 1923 (master

of arts), and Russell Sage College in 1936 (doctor of laws).

Goodrich died in a nursing home in Cobalt, Connecticut, on December 31, 1954, after a brief illness and was buried at Cedar Hill Cemetery, Hartford. Two of her sisters, Grace Markham of Fitchville, Connecticut, and Katherine Hawkes of Bryn Mawr, Pennsylvania, survived her. Through her lifelong efforts, she endowed nursing with her sense that the public has a right to expect professional nursing care and that knowledge remains the foundation of professional nursing and its responsibility.

## PUBLICATIONS BY ANNIE WARBURTON GOODRICH

### BOOKS

*The Social and Ethical Significance of Nursing.* New York: Macmillan, 1932.

### ARTICLES

"The Introduction of Salaried Instruction in the Training-Schools." *American Journal of Nursing* 5 (1905): 597.

"The Nurse and the Public Health." *Boston Medical and Surgical Journal* 164 (1911): 43–45.

"Some State Regulations upon the Appointment of the Faculties of Nursing Schools, Their Number, Preparation and Status." *American Journal of Nursing* 15 (1915): 950.

"The Trained Nurse." *Modern Hospital* 9 (1917): 431–36.

"The Nursing Program of the Army." *Modern Hospital* 9 (1918): 410–13.

"The Introduction of Public Health Nursing into the Training of the Student Nurse." *Public Health Nursing* 12 (1920): 580–89.

"The Vanguard of an International Army." *American Journal of Nursing* 21 (1921): 855–63.

"Education versus Training." *Modern Hospital* 16 (1921): 441.

"A Plan for Centralizing Schools of Nursing." *American Journal of Nursing* 22 (1922): 548.

"Role of Hospital Nursing Department in Community Health Program." *Modern Hospital* 19 (1922): 437–40.

"The Problem of the Care of the Child in the Public Health Field." *American Journal of Nursing* 23 (1923): 627.

"The Part of the Nurse in the Social Integration." *American Journal of Nursing* 25 (1925): 821.

"The Evolution of the Nurse: Building Our Future on Our Past." *Trained Nurse* 74 (1925): 142–47.

"The Nurse as a Teacher of Positive Health." *American Journal of Nursing* 26 (1926): 601.

"The Community's Relation to Nursing Education and Nursing Activities." *Hospital Social Service* 19 (1929): 37–49.

"The Responsibility of the Community for Nursing and Nursing Education." *American Journal of Nursing* 29 (1929): 1349.

"A New Epoch in Nursing." *American Journal of Nursing* 29 (1929): 1110.

"The Teaching of Prevention Through the Curriculum of the Undergraduate Nurse." *American Journal of Nursing* 29 (1929): 1549.

"The Past, Present, and Future of Nursing." *American Journal of Nursing* 31 (1931): 1385.

"Fundamental Principles Underlying the Training of a Nurse for Public Health Work." *Review and Information Bulletin* 12 (1931): 446.

"The School of Nursing and the Future." *American Journal of Nursing* 32 (1932): 676–80.

"Yale University School of Nursing—Methods and Problems." *Medical Education,* 21st Series (1932): 1–15.

"The Changing Order and Nursing." *American Journal of Nursing* 34 (1934): 517.

"Modern Trends in Nursing Education." *American Journal of Public Health* 26 (1936): 764–70.

"Nursing and the Art of Living." *Educational Outlook* 15 (1941): 93–97.

"Nursing and National Defense." *American Journal of Nursing* 42 (1942): 11–16.

"Honors to Whom Honor Is Due." *School and Society* 63 (1946): 185.

## BIBLIOGRAPHY

"Annie Warburton Goodrich." Obituary. *American Journal of Nursing* 55 (February 1955): 158–59.

"Annie Warburton Goodrich." Obituary. *New York Times,* 1 January 1955.

"Annie W. Goodrich—Crusader." *American Journal of Nursing* 34 (July 1934): 669.

Cary, E.H. "For Distinguished Service in the Cause of Nursing." *American Journal of Nursing* 32 (May 1932): 546–48.

Christy, T.E. "Nurses in American History: The Fateful Decade, 1890–1900." *American Journal of Nursing* 75 (July 1975): 1163–65.

Dock, L.L., et al. *History of American Red Cross Nursing.* New York: Macmillan, 1922.

"Goodrich, Annie Warburton." In *National Cyclopedia of American Biography.* Vol. 42. Clifton, N.J.: J.T. White, 1984.

Goodrich, A.W. Papers. Department of Archives, Teachers College Library, Columbia University, New York.

Goodrich, A.W. Papers. Nursing Archives. Mugar Library, Boston University.

Goodrich, A.W. Papers. School of Nursing, Yale University, New Haven.

Henderson, V. "Annie Warburton Goodrich." *American Journal of Nursing* 55 (December 1955): 1422–88.

Henderson, V. "Goodrich, Annie Warburton." In *Dictionary of American Biography.* Supplement 5, 1951–1955, edited by John Garraty. New York: Scribner's, 1955.

Koch, H.B. *Militant Angel.* New York: Macmillan, 1951.

Roberts, M.M. "Annie Warburton Goodrich, 1866–1954." *American Journal of Nursing* 55 (February 1955): 163.

Tomes, N. "Goodrich, Annie Warburton, Feb. 6, 1866–Dec. 31, 1954." In *Notable American Women: The Modern Period, A Biographical Dictionary,* edited by Barbara Sicherman, Carol Hurdbreen, Ilene Kantrov, and Harriette Walker. Cambridge, Mass.: Belknap Press of Harvard University Press, 1980.

Werminghaus, E.A. *Annie W. Goodrich, Her Journey to Yale.* New York: Macmillan, 1950.

Yost, E. "Goodrich, Annie Warburton." In *American Women of Nursing.* 3rd ed. Philadelphia: J.B. Lippincott, 1965.

Cindy Gurney

# Stella Goostray

1886–1969

The contributions of Stella Goostray to the nursing profession spanned the length of her career and strongly influenced the future of nursing. Professional standards, accreditation for nursing schools, pediatric care, and nursing education are only a few areas affected by her activities. Her lifelong commitment to the professionalization of nursing was evident in each of her varied endeavors.

Goostray was born July 8, 1886, in Boston, Massachusetts. Her father, Job Goostray, came to the United States from England and soon gained national recognition for improving foundry practice in the iron industry. Jane Wyllie Goostray, her mother, was of Scotch-Canadian descent. Stella Goostray had two older half-brothers and a half-sister, Ida, from her father's first marriage. Her younger brother, Frank, was born when she was six years old.

Following her education in the Boston public school system, Goostray pursued secretarial work and also served as assistant to the editor of an Episcopal church magazine. The editor's decision to relocate the offices from Boston to Philadelphia combined with the demands of World War I to heighten Goostray's interest in a nursing career. In December 1915 at the age of 29, she entered the Children's Hospital School of Nursing in Boston. An acquaintance, Mary Norcross, entered earlier that year, and the two women eventually became professional associates and close personal friends.

After a bout with typhoid fever interrupted her nursing education, Goostray returned to the school in 1917. She successfully completed the program in 1919 and received her diploma in January 1920. Teachers College of Columbia University awarded her a B.S. degree in 1926. She earned an M.Ed. degree in 1933 from Boston University, which also awarded her an honorary doctor of science degree in 1967.

Goostray's career as a nursing educator began in 1920, when she entered Teachers College and spent a semester practice teaching at St. Mary's Children's Hospital School of Nursing in New York City. Employment as assisting scholar in the department of nursing and health at Teachers College followed. She worked closely with Isabel Stewart, assisting with research and teaching courses in drugs and solutions to students from the joint program of Teachers College and the Presbyterian Hospital School of Nursing.

Goostray's six-year affiliation with the Philadelphia General Hospital School of Nursing began with her 1921 appointment as instructor in sciences. S. Lillian Clayton, director of the school and nursing service, appointed her educational director of the school in 1922. Rigorous curricular standards, high-quality teaching, and a genuine concern for students characterized Goostray's administration.

Throughout her tenure as educational director, Goostray taught courses in drugs and solutions as well as in chemistry. She perceived a need for improved texts in nursing and wrote *Drugs and Solutions for Nurses* and *Applied Chemistry for Nurses*. Both publications were widely used in nursing education programs. She utilized her writing skills throughout her career and contributed many articles to professional journals.

As a result of her success in Philadelphia, Goostray returned to Boston in August 1927 to become principal of the school and director of the nursing service at Children's Hospital. She remained in the position until 1946 and initiated many important changes during her administration. Emphasizing the quality of patient care and her lifelong concern for children, Goostray humanized and updated nursing procedures used in the hospital. She worked to upgrade the duties of nurses by increasing the number of graduate nurses and auxiliary workers available for duty. Goostray's emphasis on the quality of nursing education was reflected in her efforts to broaden the involvement of the nursing faculty in national associations as well as in the decision-making process of the school. As in Philadelphia, rigorous curricular standards were enforced throughout the school.

Additional activities during her administration included defining the role of the director in the administrative structure, clarifying the duties of affiliating students, and instituting a requirement that all affiliating students have high-school diplomas. She also established a program of international exchanges of people and ideas between Children's Hospital and other hospitals throughout the world. Goostray also taught in the Boston University School of Nursing during this period (1939, 1941–42, and 1946–47).

Goostray's involvements in professional associations began in 1925, when she was appointed to the board of directors of the American Journal of Nursing Company (1925–27). She later became secretary (1928–30) and president (1931–37) of the organization and participated in the decision to broaden the scope of the publication to encompass all areas of nursing interest. Equally important was Goostray's participation in the National League of Nursing Education. In this endeavor, she served as secretary (1928–39), president (1940–44), and director (1939, 1944–48).

In 1930 Goostray took a brief leave of absence from Children's Hospital to work with a committee charged with evaluating schools of nursing. The Joint Committee on Educational Policies included representatives from the American Nursing Association, the National League of Nursing Education, and the National Organization of Public Health Nursing and worked closely with the Committee on the Grading of Nursing Schools. Goostray served as full-time and, later, part-time adviser from 1930 through 1934. Her main responsibility was to evaluate curricular standards of various nursing schools and act as a liaison between the two committees. She became an ardent advocate of accreditation as a result of her activities and integrated this interest into her master's degree thesis. Additional accreditation activities included service on the board of registration in nursing of the Commonwealth of Massachusetts (1930–34, 1938–48) and as a part-time visitor for the accreditation service of the National League of Nursing Education (1946–47).

Goostray earned national respect for her activities geared toward improving the quality of nursing and nursing education. She served as chairman of the subcommittee on nursing at President Hoover's White House Conference on Child Health and Protection. This conference helped improve nursing education in pediatric care.

During World War II, Goostray worked with nursing, government, and relief organizations in establishing the Nursing Council for National Defense. She served

on its board of directors (1940–42) and, after the council's reorganization, as president of the National Nursing Council for War Service, Inc. (1942–46). These wartime organizations were instrumental in upgrading the status of nurses in the military and in encouraging full participation by black nurses in national defense efforts.

In 1946 Goostray retired from the Children's Hospital. Retirement allowed her more time for involvement in community affairs, including extensive work in establishing United Community Services of Boston and its nursing council (1947–53). As chairman of an advisory committee on a regionalization project in nursing education for the nursing council (1956–59), she helped establish the Newton Junior College Program in Nursing. She also used her retirement to serve as editor of *The Journal* of St. John's Episcopal Church of Roxbury Crossing, Massachusetts from 1952 to 1962.

Goostray's leadership in nursing was nationally recognized in 1955, when she received the Mary Adelaide Nutting Award from the National League for Nursing Education. Regionally, she was cited by the Massachusetts League for Nursing (1955), the Massachusetts Nurses' Association (1956, 1965), and United Community Services of Metropolitan Boston (1962) for her widespread contributions to nursing and nursing education.

Her avid interest in preserving materials relevant to the study of nursing history led Goostray to become involved with the National League of Nursing's committee on historical source materials in nursing. From 1952 to 1964, she served as regional consultant for the North Atlantic area. She also was invited to be a member of the committee of consultants for *Notable American Women, 1607–1950*, a member of the committee on nursing archives of the Mugar Library of Boston University (1966–69), and nurse historian/consultant at Boston University School of Nursing (1967–69). Radcliffe College appointed her a member of the Schlesinger Library's advisory board from 1967 to 1968.

In 1967 Goostray received the R. Louise McManus Medal from Teachers College in recognition of her distinguished service to nursing. She was also awarded an honorary D.Sc. degree from Boston University in 1967. On May 8, 1969, she died in Children's Hospital, Boston, after a long illness. She was 82 years old, and at the time of her death, she was survived by her sister, Ida Goostray, and a sister-in-law, Mrs. Frank Goostray. She was buried in Mt. Auburn Cemetery, Cambridge, Massachusetts.

## PUBLICATIONS BY STELLA GOOSTRAY

### BOOKS

*Drugs and Solutions for Nurses.* New York: Macmillan, 1924.

With W.G. Karr. *Applied Chemistry for Nurses.* New York: Macmillan, 1924.

*Problems in Solutions and Dosage: Arithmetic Review.* New York: Macmillan, 1949.

*Mathematics and Measurements in Nursing Practice.* New York: Macmillan, 1963.

*Fifty Years; A History of the School of Nursing, The Children's Hospital, Boston.* Boston: The Alumnae Assn. School of Nursing, 1940.

*Memoirs: Half a Century in Nursing.* Boston: Nursing Archive, Boston University, Mugar Memorial Library, 1969.

### ARTICLES (SELECTED)

"The Nursing Care in Pneumonia." *American Journal of Nursing* 26 (January 1926): 4–8.

"Nursing Care in Cerebrospinal Meningitis." *American Journal of Nursing* 27 (April 1927): 252–54.

"The Nursing Care in Typhoid Fever." *American Journal of Nursing* 27 (September 1927): 719–22.

"Why Teach Psychology, Chemistry, and Bacteriology?" *Trained Nurse and Hospital Review* 77 (October 1926): 393–95.

"What Lies Ahead for the Nursing Profession?" *American Journal of Nursing* 35 (August 1935): 765–71.

"Susan C. Francis." In *Biographic Sketches, 1937–1940.* New York: National League of Nursing Education, 1940.

"Problems of Cadet Nurse School Curriculum; Glamour Not Enough—the Job Is to Educate." *Hospitals* 17 (October 1943): 65–67.

"Pediatric Nursing at the Turn of the Century." *American Journal of Nursing* 50 (October 1950): 624–25.

"A Time to Every Purpose." *American Journal of Nursing* 52 (July 1952): 818–20.

"Isabel Maitland Stewart. The Story of a National and International Leader in Nursing Education." *American Journal of Nursing* 54 (March 1954): 302–06.

"Mary Adelaide Nutting." *American Journal of Nursing* 58 (November 1958): 1524–29.

"Sophie Nelson: Public Health Nurse." *American Journal of Nursing* 60 (September 1960): 1268–69.

"Nationwide Hunt for Nursing's Historical Treasures." *Nursing Outlook* 13 (January 1965): 26–29.

## BIBLIOGRAPHY

American Journal of Nursing Company. Records. Nursing Archive. Mugar Memorial Library, Boston University.

Bliss, M.E.G. "Stella Goostray." *National League of Nursing Education: Biographic Sketches, 1937–1940.* New York: National League of Nursing Education, 1940.

Goostray, S. Papers. Nursing Archive. Mugar Memorial Library, Boston University.

Goostray, S. Papers. Schlesinger Library, Radcliffe College, Cambridge, Mass.

"Ladies with Lamps." Editorial. *New England Journal of Medicine* 253 (Dec 1955): 989–90.

Roberts, M.M. "Stella Goostray ... Distinguished Administrator, Professional Leader, and Good Neighbor." *American Journal of Nursing,* 58 (March 1958): 352–55.

"Stella Goostray, at 82, Headed Nursing School. Obituary. *Morning Globe* (Boston, Mass.), 10 May 1969.

Margaret R. Wells

# Sister Mary Olivia Gowan

## 1888–1977

Sister Mary Olivia Gowan was a Benedictine nurse who campaigned for higher standards of nursing in Catholic hospitals, improvement of Catholic hospital schools of nursing, and inclusion of nursing subjects in the curricula of Catholic institutions of higher learning. She established and served as dean of the School of Nursing Education of the Catholic University of America in Washington, D.C., and was sister superior of St. Gertrude's School of Arts and Crafts for retarded children, an adjunct of the university.

Sister Gowan was born March 15, 1888, the oldest of seven children of William and Margaret Lawler Gowan of Stillwater, Minnesota. Her maternal great-grandmother, Margaret Robinson, had been well known in her native Edinburgh, Scotland, as a zealous, though untrained, nurse. Sister Gowan was inspired from early childhood by tales of her ancestor's devotion to helping the sick and was pressed to follow her lead by her frail mother's frequent need for care. Her father was a stern taskmaster, demanding that she carry a heavy load of domestic responsibility as well as develop her intellectual capabilities.

Sister Gowan began her education in the schools of the Sisters of St. Joseph in Stillwater, but when she was eight, the family moved north. She graduated from Roosevelt High School in Virginia, Minnesota, in 1908, having lost some time to family duties.

In 1909 at age 21, Sister Gowan became a member of the first class at St. Mary's School of Nurses in Duluth, Minnesota. She graduated and became an R.N. in 1912.

One month after graduation, she entered the novitiate of the Sisters of St. Benedict in Duluth. During the early part of her three-year term, she served the College of St. Scholastica as school nurse and also taught dietetics, anatomy, and physiology in the normal school connected with it. She then supervised the operating room of St. Joseph's Hospital in Brainard and finally taught at St. Mary's, where she had been trained. She made her final vows in 1916.

During her nurse's training and novitiate, Sister Gowan had shown such exceptional teaching, nursing, and administrative skills that she was appointed assistant superintendent of St. Mary's Hospital and one year later became superintendent. At that time, the American College of Surgeons was establishing an annual list of approved hospitals, and Sister Gowan focused on putting St. Mary's on that select list. She studied the minimum requirements and began making changes. She addressed staff training deficiencies, bought new equipment and enhanced the

X-ray and laboratory facilities, instituted departments of pathology and medical records, and reorganized the hospital medical staff. The result was that St. Mary's became one of only 80 of over 7,000 applying hospitals to win approval the first time.

During Sister Gowan's decade at St. Mary's, the hospital also gained a six-story addition with 100 new beds and a larger, improved nurses' home. Yet despite her heavy administrative responsibilities, Sister Gowan regularly found time for two personal activities she cherished: visiting patients on the wards and taking classes at the College of St. Scholastica.

One year after receiving her bachelor's degree from St. Scholastica, Sister Gowan was asked in 1926 to become sister superior of St. Gertrude's School of Arts and Crafts. The school for retarded children was being established by the Catholic University of America in Washington, D.C., in connection with the work of Thomas Verner Moore, another Benedictine, in psychology and psychiatry. On a farm just outside Washington, the school was designed to prepare its students to be minimally self-supporting.

Like many other nursing leaders of her day, Sister Gowan spent her summers studying professional subjects at Teachers College, Columbia University. She finished requirements for her master's degree in the winter of 1932.

At that time, no Catholic institutions of higher learning offered courses in nursing, but the Catholic University of America asked Sister Gowan to offer one nursing course in a summer session. Based on its success, a division of nursing was added to the department of psychology in the University Graduate School of Arts and Sciences, and Sister Gowan was named director. However, she continued to live at St. Gertrude's and serve as a trustee. Within a few years, the division was made a separate school in the university, with Sister Gowan as its dean and professor of nursing education.

With guidance from her old mentor, Isabel Stewart of Teachers College, Sister Gowan created three curricula for the school: administration, public-health nursing, and a combined bachelor's degree-R.N. program. She also helped develop the Providence (Hospital) division of the school; in 1945 it was one of a dozen Catholic schools of nursing to be accredited by the National League of Nursing Education.

Active in the league for many years, Sister Gowan served as chairman of its sisters' committee and a member of its curriculum committee and board of directors. She also was treasurer and then president of the Association of Collegiate Schools of Nursing, which later merged with the league.

Other professional offices she held include chairman of the curriculum committee and director, District of Columbia League of Nursing Education; member, subcommittee on nursing, health and medical committee of the Council of National Defense; and member, Nursing Council on National Defense. She also was a consultant to the training committee on psychiatric nursing of the United States Public Health Service, a member of the advisory council of the Veterans Administration Nursing Service, an honorary civilian consultant to the U.S. Navy Bureau of Medicine and Surgery, and an honorary fellow of the American Hospital Association. She attended the International Council of Nurses in Rome in 1957 and made a survey of Catholic nursing schools in Brazil.

Sister Gowan retired in 1957 to the College of St. Scholastica in Duluth, where the mother house of her order was, and died there April 2, 1977.

## PUBLICATIONS BY
## SISTER MARY OLIVIA GOWAN

### BOOKS

*The Nursing Program in the General College.* Washington, D.C.: Catholic University of America Press, 1954.

### ARTICLES

With Sister M. Maurice Sheehy. "Contribution of Religious Communities to Nursing Education." *Trained Nurse and Hospital Review* 100 (1938): 404–09, 652–55, 700.

### BIBLIOGRAPHY

"Candidates for Election at League Convention." *American Journal of Nursing* 43 (March 1943): 315.

"Candidates for NLNE Offices." *American Journal of Nursing* 41 (March 1941): 366–67.

"Gowan, Sister M. Olivia." In *Who's Who of American Women.* Vol. 2(1961–62). Chicago: Marquis Who's Who, 1962.

Scheerer, A.E. "Gowan, Mary Olivia." In *Biographical Dictionary of American Educators*, edited by John Ohles. 3 vols. Westport, Conn.: Greenwood Press, 1978.

Yost, E. *American Women of Nursing.* Philadelphia: J.B. Lippincott, 1965.

Alice P. Stein

# Elinor Delight Gregg
## 1889–1970

Public-health nursing and the care of the North American Indians would not be what it is today if it were not for Elinor Delight Gregg. As the first supervisor of nurses for the Bureau of Indian Affairs, she organized and developed a service and programs that greatly improved the health conditions of the Indians and the Eskimos. Her dedication to the nursing profession led to better working conditions for public-health nurses, and her active concern for tribal culture led to the preservation of Indian art.

Born in Colorado Springs, Colorado, in 1889, Gregg was the sixth of seven children. Her parents had traveled to Colorado from Connecticut after her father, James, a minister, had been assigned to the First Congregational Church there. Her mother, Mary, was an accomplished musician.

James and Mary Gregg had three children when they left Connecticut—James Jr., Faith, and Donald. Marjorie, Richard, Alan and Elinor were born in Colorado Springs. Alan, a surgeon, became the most well known of the siblings, when he became a vice president of the Rockefeller Foundation. Gregg's other brothers and sisters were also active in serving others and throughout their lives offered encouragement and support to one another.

Gregg spent the first 20 years of her life in Colorado Springs. In 1911, after attending Colorado College, she went to Waltham, Massachusetts, where she received her nursing education at the Waltham Training School for Nurses. She worked as an industrial nurse in a cotton manufacturing plant, and then continued with postgraduate study in institutional management at Massachusetts General Hospital in Boston. Her other experiences during these years included administrative work at the City Hospital in Cleveland and supervisory duties at the Infants' Hospital in Boston.

During World War I, Gregg joined the Red Cross and had the distinction of being selected to appear on a national recruiting war poster dressed in her nurse's uniform. In France she served on two fronts and was stationed at the same base hospital at Dannes-Camiers as her brother Alan, who was a physician.

After returning to the States in 1919, Gregg remained with the Red Cross, serving as a lecturer on the Chautauqua circuit. For over a year, she traveled throughout the Mid- and Southwest, giving speeches on her war experiences and on public-health topics. In 1920 she returned to Boston to take a four-month public-health nursing course at Simmons College and put this training into practice as a home nurse in rural areas of New Hampshire.

It was in 1922 that Gregg's various jobs, experiences, and background proved especially valuable, for she again joined the Red Cross and worked as a public-health nurse on the Rosebud and Pine Ridge reservations in South Dakota. From then on her career and life were bound up with the Indians and public-health nursing.

She arrived at the Rosebud Agency in her Model-T Ford and was given a three-room cottage, one room of which she used for a clinic. She began with examinations of the children who lived in the boarding schools, and visited the families to make sanitary check-ups across the reservation. Tuberculosis and trachoma were the main diseases, and there was high rate of infant morality.

She also taught the Indian women basic health care, drove patients to Omaha for special treatment, and persuaded the South Dakota State Anti-Tuberculosis Society to give a diagnostic clinic. Troubled by the lack of materials which the Indians could use to develop their talents, she either purchased them from her own funds or secured donations of materials for the children, especially for those who were hospitalized.

Gregg moved from the Rosebud Agency to the Pine Ridge Agency. There she found medical conditions so bad that she stayed only two months, feeling it futile to start any kind of program without greater support from the Red Cross or the federal government.

In 1924 Gregg left the Red Cross to become the first supervisor of Public Health Nursing for the Bureau of Indian Affairs. Her main task was to recruit nurses for the service, and this she did effectively for the next 12 years. She established qualifications for public-health nurses, assisted in developing a course of training at Lawton, Oklahoma, for nurse attendants, initiated the first labor turnover study for the Department of the Interior, outlined proposals to build new hospitals to replace the dilapidated ones on the reservations, helped to introduce health-education programs and the use of vitamins, which had lately been discovered, to the reservations, and publicized the plight of the Indians. She continued to make field trips throughout the country, particularly to the Northern and Southwestern agencies. At her retirement there were 650 nurses in the Indian service providing nursing service from Florida to Alaska. Part of this was due to the rapid expansion of the bureau under the Roosevelt New Deal but it was Gregg who was in the forefront of the movement.

She fought to preserve the old Indian culture and, for example, opposed the establishment of a birth-control program on the reservations and refused to implement it because she felt it was contrary to their culture. Although not involved in any other major controversy, she ridiculed many of the government's programs that attempted to change the Indians. She did support programs such as the "Preservation of Indian Art," as well as cooperative medical efforts to decrease the number of tuberculosis cases. In 1935 she made a field trip to Alaska to visit many of the nurses, checking on the health of the Indians and Eskimos. It was her final one for the bureau. She traveled to and in Alaska by boat, plane, and dogsled and found it so exhausting that it encouraged her to plan for her retirement.

In 1938, in part because of the promise of an annuity from a sister, Gregg retired from the service. In 1939 she moved to the Southwest and settled into private life. She devoted her time to gardening, travel, and working with her hands. In 1965 she related her experiences of the Indian reservations and her supervisory position in a book entitled *The Indians and the Nurse.* The last words in the book express her thoughts and feelings about her life and career, "I was happy and knew it." She was a fellow of the American Public Health Association and had been adopted into the Sioux tribe with the name of the "Helper Woman."

Gregg died in Santa Fe, New Mexico, on March 24, 1970.

## PUBLICATIONS BY ELINOR D. GREGG

### BOOKS

*The Indians and the Nurse.* Norman: University of Oklahoma Press, 1965.

### ARTICLES

"A Federal Nursing Service Above the Arctic Circle." *American Journal of Nursing* 36:2 (February 1936): 128–34.

## BIBLIOGRAPHY

*American Women 1935–40: A Composite Biographical Dictionary*, edited by D. Howes. Detroit: Gale Research Company, 1981.

Gregg, E.D. Personal papers. Mugar Memorial Library, Boston University, Boston, Mass.

*Makers of Nursing History*, edited by M.R. Pennock. New York: Lakeside Publishing Co., 1928 (photograph included).

"Miss Gregg Resigns from the Indian Service." *American Journal of Nursing* 39 (January 1939): 84.

Penfield, Wilder. *The Difficult Art of Giving: The Epic of Alan Gregg.* Boston: Little, Brown and Co., 1967.

Jerome O. Earley

## Lystra Gretter

1858–1951

Lystra Gretter was known as the dean of Michigan nurses because she served for many years as the principal of the Farrand Training School for Nurses, Harper Hospital, Detroit, and as the Superintendent of the Detroit Visiting Nurse Association from 1908 to 1923. She also was one of the authors of the Florence Nightingale Pledge.

Gretter was born in 1858 in Bayfield, Ontario, Canada. Her parents were Dr. and Mrs. Eggert. Her maternal grandfather was a Mennonite bishop and had come to the United States from Holland at the beginning of the nineteenth century. Her father was of Swiss descent and came to the United States to study medicine and to secure a medical degree. The family lived in Ontario for a time, then moved to North Carolina, near Greensboro, after the Civil War.

In 1877 at the age of 19, Gretter married John Birney Gretter, a Virginian and Civil War veteran who had served with General Robert E. Lee's army for four years. She had one daughter, Birney, born one month after her husband died in 1884. Gretter moved shortly afterward to North Collins, New York, along with her mother and sister. In 1886 she began her distinguished nursing career at the age of 28, when she entered the Buffalo General Hospital Training School for Nurses. She graduated in 1888.

The Farrand Training School for Nurses at Harper Hospital in Detroit was searching for a principal in 1888, and Gretter was highly recommended by Frank Abbett, a member of the training school committee at the Buffalo General Hospital. She was to hold that position for the next 18 years.

One of the first areas Gretter addressed was the lengthy hours of service expected of nurses in training. At that time, as was the custom, students at Farrand worked 12 hours each day, and the length of the program was 18 months. There was little supervision on the wards except that by senior students, and the few classes were given by the medical staff and the principal. In 1891 Gretter proposed an eight-hour day, an increase to two years in the length of the program, that the hospital no longer pay students, that a graduate nurse be employed on every floor to supervise students, and that private-duty nursing outside the hospital be included in the training. Because hospitals depended on students to staff their units, these changes had far-reaching economic implications. Despite this, the recommendations were implemented over the next five years.

In December 1892 Gretter called together the graduates of Farrand for the purpose of establishing an alumnae association, which was formally organized in January 1893. This was the first of similar efforts to organize people that would highlight her nursing career as organizer and innovator. She gave support in 1893 to the formation of a Detroit women's club for nurses. This occurred at a time when clubs for women were unusual and controversial.

During 1893 Gretter also began the reference and fiction library at Farrand and reorganized the nurses' registry. Because few textbooks existed for nurses, Gretter developed outlines of lectures and courses in handwritten volumes, which became part of the historical collection of the school.

The Florence Nightingale Pledge was the work of a committee that was chaired by Gretter, who was said to be the spirit behind the idea. The original pledge was first administered to the graduating class at Farrand on April 25, 1893. Colleagues of Gretter state that she felt responsible for graduate nurses' attitudes after graduation, and this was strongly manifested when she wrote the pledge. It since has been used universally by schools of nursing, usually during graduation exercises.

In 1893 Gretter helped organize the Society of Superintendents of Training Schools for Nurses, of which she was to become president in 1902. As an early member of the society, she supported a uniform curriculum for nursing, the separation of teaching and ward service, and the preparation of graduate nurses as teachers after they received postgraduate education.

The Farrand program under Gretter's influence reflected these trends, and in 1896 it extended its program from two to three years, the teaching components were strengthened, and in 1898 a resident teacher of dietetics was added to the faculty. On Gretter's recommendation, a probation period of three months was initiated in order to improve care of patients and to make more efficient use of faculty time and energy. Due to her mother's failing health, Gretter resigned from her position in 1897 to care for her and returned one year later after her mother's death.

In 1904 Gretter, along with J. Lennex, Mary E. Smith, J. Regan, and A.G. Deans (all nursing leaders in Michigan), called together nurses statewide in order to form a state nurses' association. Gretter became the first president of the Michigan State Nurses' Association in 1904. Again, her skills at organization formation were called upon at the beginning of a new phase of professionalism in nursing in Michigan.

In 1907 Gretter once again resigned from her position at Farrand, this time permanently in order to become superintendent of the Detroit Visiting Nurse Association (VNA), where she remained until 1923. Under her direction, the agency grew from 8 to 67 nurses. The Detroit VNA was a direct outgrowth of the work of Alice Bowen, a Farrand graduate of 1889. Since the 1890s, Bowen had cared for the sick poor with the assistance of a group of young women who called themselves the District Nursing Society and who met in Gretter's rooms to sew for Bowen's patients. Gretter, therefore, had been directly involved in this agency and served on its board of directors and as chair of its nurses' work committee from its inception until her appointment in 1907.

Gretter's interests in nursing education continued while her work in community health expanded. She felt that graduate nurses required additional education for advanced work and was interested in the hospital economics course, which the American Society of Superintendents of Training Schools for Nurses had established at Teachers College, Columbia University. She helped to sustain the commitment of Michigan nurses in raising funds to support the course.

Gretter was one of five nurses who urged the establishment of a training program in public-health nursing at the University of Michigan. The request was granted in 1918. It was also largely due to Gretter's work that the University of Michigan established a chair of public-health nursing.

In 1908 Gretter initiated a state committee on Red Cross work with herself as chair. The work later included recruiting nurses for World War I. Gretter continued her involvement with the group for the next 20 years.

In 1913 Gretter organized the Michigan League of Nursing Education. Her skills in encouraging groups and individuals to work together was again in evidence when in 1917 she invited the directors of four community agencies that were providing nursing services in Detroit to form the Detroit Council on Community Nursing.

Gretter's distinguished career at the VNA of Detroit was highlighted in the organization's anniversary report of 1933. Her various posts with the agency include counselor, 1894–98 and 1923–33; board member, 1898–1907 and 1923–33; and superintendent, 1907–22. Her charter memberships include first district of the Michigan State Nurses' Association, Michigan State Nurses' Association, National League of Nursing Education, and National Organization of Public Health Nurses. She held many leadership posts in all of the above organizations and was most productive from 1902 to 1928, when she served on numerous committees, both in the community and in nursing.

In 1937 Gretter was awarded an honorary M.S. degree from Wayne University. She died on February 27, 1951, at Grosse Point, Michigan.

### BIBLIOGRAPHY

American Society of Superintendents of Training Schools for Nurses. *3rd Annual Convention . . . 1896.* Harrisburg, Pa.: Harrisburg Publishing Company, 1896.

Deans, A.G.S. "Who's Who in the Nursing World." *American Journal of Nursing* 24 (June 1924): 736.

Germain, L. Papers. Nursing Archives. Mugar Memorial Library, Boston University.

"Lystra Gretter—Dean of Michigan Nurses." *The Michigan Nurse* 4 (May 1954): 63–68.

Munson, H. "Lystra E. Gretter." *American Journal of Nursing* 49 (June 1949): 2–7.

*Leaders of American Nursing.* National League of Nursing Education 1923 Report. New York: 1923.

Sargent, E. Personal recollections of Lystra Gretter. Nursing Archives. Mugar Memorial Library, Boston University.

Valerie Hart-Smith

## Carrie May Hall

### 1873–1963

Carrie May Hall's main concern in nursing lay in improving the educational standards and economic security of nurses. As superintendent of nurses and principal of the nursing school at Peter Bent Brigham Hospital in Boston, she helped implement a three-year program that had a high-school diploma as its prerequisite and a six-month probationary period. During World War I she earned many honors for her work as chief nurse of the American Red Cross in England and later in France and at a base hospital. As president of the Massachusetts Nurses' Association and the National League of Nursing Education (NLNE) and a member of the American Nurses' Association, she pressed on many fronts to better the lot of nurses. During her presidency, the NLNE conducted a major study of nursing education in the 1920s that pointed up the economic problems of nurses. She was instrumental in developing and promoting the Harmon Association for the Advancement of Nursing, a retirement insurance plan designed specifically for nurses.

Born in Nashua, New Hampshire, on July 5, 1873, Hall (known as May to her friends and family) was the oldest of three children and the only daughter of John K. and Caroline Rogers Hall. Her grandfather was an early mayor of Nashua, and her father was a ticket agent with the Boston and Maine Railroad. While there is little information about Hall's childhood and early adult years, it is known that she grew up in Nashua and was educated in its public schools. She left high school after the third year to complete her senior year at a private seminary for girls near Amherst, Massachusetts.

Following the completion of her education, Hall remained at home to care for her invalid mother. When her mother died, she was left at age 20 to care for her two younger brothers. In 1901, when she was 28 years old and her services at home were no longer needed, Hall entered nurses' training at Massachusetts General Hospital in Boston. Her interest in nursing was sparked by having nursed her invalid mother.

Hall was successful during her three years at Massachusetts General. When she entered the training school, she was mature and had organizational and executive skills that had been honed in part by the necessity of managing her home and caring for her brothers. These abilities were recognized early in her training. By the time she graduated, she had already worked as a head nurse, a situation that was not uncommon in training schools.

Upon completion of her training, Hall stayed on at the hospital as a head nurse. This was followed by an appointment as assistant matron at Quincy Hospital in Quincy, Massachusetts. From 1906 to 1911, Hall served as superintendent of the Margaret Pillsbury General Hospital in Concord, New Hampshire, where she began to recognize and understand the limitations of nursing education. This influenced her decision to leave her post in 1911 for one year of postgraduate education at Teachers College, Columbia University, New York.

Although the department of hospital economics, which later became the nursing department, at Teachers College was still in its infancy in 1911, it was the center of the professionalization reform movement in nursing and nursing education. In addition, it was the only college-based program for nursing at the time. While she was at Teachers College, Hall was immersed in the values and ideology of the professionalization movement as propounded by M. Adelaide Nutting, Isabel M. Stewart, and other nursing leaders who taught in the program.

In early 1912, while she was still at Teachers College, Hall accepted a position as the first superintendent of nurses and principal of the nursing school of the new Peter Bent Brigham Hospital in Boston. Because the hospital and school were new, Hall was provided with a rare opportunity to implement some of the professionalizing strategies that were being promoted by the nursing leadership. These included the development of a three-year curriculum with a six-month probationary period, the first four months of which constituted the preliminary course. Affiliations were established for obstetrics and pediatrics rotations, as these services were not offered at Brigham Hospital. An elective affiliation in public-health nursing also was arranged. Finally, a high-school education was required for admission to the school. With the development of this foundation, the Peter Bent Brigham Hospital School of Nursing soon gained recognition as one of the top nursing schools in the country.

Although Hall was one of the group of nursing leaders who believed in the need for reform in nursing education, there is no evidence to indicate that she questioned the relationship that existed between hospitals and training schools and the use of the pupil nurses to staff hospital wards. She did believe that the education of the students should not be sacrificed to the needs of the hospital. To this end, she worked to ensure that the women who entered the Brigham nursing school received the best in nursing education.

In 1917, when the United States entered World War I, there was an immediate need to increase enrollment to meet the demands of the emergency. Hall was called to serve as chief nurse of the Harvard Unit Base Hospital 5, which took her away for the duration of the war. She left Leone N. Ivers, a trustworthy and loyal officer of the school since it opened, in charge as acting superintendent.

Beginning with a small core of Brigham nurses, Hall put together a unit of nurses who were to serve under her supervision at a base hospital stationed in France. Although she served in this position for only one year, her executive abilities were noticed. In May 1918 she was called to London to serve as chief nurse of the American Red Cross in England. The following October, she went to Paris to serve as assistant to Julia Stimson, chief nurse of the American Red Cross in France, and in November Hall succeeded her in that post.

Because of her outstanding service to her country and to the cause of the war, Hall was decorated with the British Royal Red Cross for meritorious service by the British government, received honorable mention from General Neil W. Haig, was awarded the Médaille de la Reconnaisance by the French government, and the Florence Nightingale Medal by the International Red Cross.

On her return from the war, Hall resumed her post at the Brigham hospital. She also turned her attention to addressing nursing issues at state and national levels through the Massachusetts Nurses' Association, the American Nurses' Association, and the National League of Nursing Education (NLNE). During the 1920s, she served as president of the Massachusetts Nurses' Association for five years (1921–25) and as president of the NLNE for three years from 1925 to 1927. She also was on the board of directors of the NLNE for ten years (1922–32).

While Hall was president of the NLNE, a committee for grading nursing schools was established and began the task of surveying nurse training schools around the country. The data collected by this committee provided a wealth of information about the status of nursing education in the 1920s. It also highlighted the predicament of many nurses who were faced with either underemployment or unemployment. From these data, it was clear that nurses were faced with an economic depression.

In addition to her concerns about providing high-quality nursing education to the women who chose a nursing career, Hall also was deeply concerned about the economic plight of nurses, especially following their retirement. She was, therefore, involved in the development and promotion of the Harmon Association for the Advancement of Nursing. This was an annuity insurance plan in which nurses could invest for their retirement. In 1930–31 Hall took a five-month leave of absence from Brigham Hospital to travel around the country promoting the Harmon Association. She particularly encouraged young graduate nurses to begin planning and investing for their future security soon after they graduated and began working.

Hall retired from her position as superintendent of nurses and principal of the nursing school at Brigham Hospital in 1937 after 25 successful and productive years. In recognition of her many contributions to the school, the board of trustees of the hospital honored her with the status of director emeritus of the school of nursing.

Although she was retired, Hall did not stop working. She maintained her ties with the hospital and school through active involvement in the Friends of the Peter Bent Brigham Hospital. Her other postretirement activities included a survey of privately run nursing homes in Greater Boston for the Hospital Council of Boston, war preparation work prior to World War II under Massachusetts governor Leverett Saltonstall and with Elliot Cutler's medical committee, and in collaboration with Helen Wood, a survey of the school of nursing and nursing service of the infirmary at the state institution at Tewksbury, Massachusetts, which resulted in its closing.

After a full and productive life, Hall died on Nov. 17, 1963, at the age of 90. She left behind many friends and a legacy of quality in nursing education.

## PUBLICATIONS BY CARRIE MAY HALL

### BOOKS

*Memoirs of the School of Nursing.* Boston: Peter Bent Brigham Hospital, 1954.

### ARTICLES

"Sally Johnson." *National League of Nursing Education: Biographical Sketches, 1937–1940.* New York: The League, 1940.

"The Teaching of Hospital Housekeeping to Pupil Nurses." In *First Annual Report of the National League of Nursing Education.* New York: National League of Nursing Education, 1915.

### BIBLIOGRAPHY

Christian, H.A. Papers. Archives. Countway Library, Harvard Medical School, Boston, Mass.

Gerrard, G.M. "Miss Hall's War Service." *Alumnae Journal, Peter Bent Brigham School of Nursing* (June 1937).

Gilmore, M.C. "Miss Hall—An Appreciation." *Alumnae Journal, Peter Bent Brigham School of Nursing* (June 1937).

Hall, C.M. Papers. Schlesinger Library, Radcliffe College, Cambridge, Mass.

Johnson, S. "The Arrangement of Subjects Taught in the School of Nursing of the Peter Bent Brigham Hospital." In *Twentieth Annual Report of the National League of Nursing Education.* New York: National League of Nursing Educator, 1914.

Johnson, S. "Carrie M. Hall." *Quarterly Record of the Massachusetts General Hospital Alumnae Association.* (Boston) (September 1937).

Peter Bent Brigham Hospital School of Nursing. Records. Nursing Archives. Department of Special Collections, Mugar Memorial Library, Boston University.

Marilyn Givens King

# Lydia Eloise Hall

## 1906–1969

Nurse educator, consultant to the United States Public Health Service, and expert in clinical nursing and rehabilitation, Lydia Eloise Williams Hall is best known for her professional nursing care model. She initiated this model in 1962 at the Loeb Center for Nursing and Rehabilitation, Montefiore Medical Center, New York.

Born in New York City on September 21, 1906, Hall was the first child of Louis U. and Anna Ketterman Williams. She and her younger brother, Henry, grew up in York, Pennsylvania, where her father, a physician, practiced as a surgeon.

Following the divorce of her parents, she remained in York, residing with her mother and maternal grandmother.

In 1927 Hall received a diploma in nursing from the York Hospital School of Nursing. Previously, she had earned credits in liberal arts at Gettysburg College, Gettysburg, Pennsylvania. In 1937 she received a B.S. degree in public-health nursing from Teachers College, Columbia University. Continuing to study there, she was awarded the M.A. degree in the teaching of natural life science in 1942 and subsequently enrolled in the doctoral program, completing all but the dissertation.

During the early years of her career, Hall held a variety of positions in nursing, first in Pennsylvania and then in New York. From 1930–35 she was employed by the Life Extension Institute of the Metropolitan Life Insurance Company in New York City, from 1935–40 she was a member of the research field staff of the New York Heart Association, and between 1941 and 1947 she advanced from staff nurse to supervisor with the Visiting Nurse Service of New York. In 1947 she was appointed to the nursing faculty at Fordham Hospital School of Nursing and later returned to the New York Heart Association as executive assistant.

In August 1945 she married Reginald A. Hall, who was employed by the Hallmark Greeting Card Company. The couple made their home in New York City, and in February 1950 Hall was appointed to a combined instructional/research position with the division of nursing at Teachers College. She assisted with the development of a major new program and in 1953 helped implement that program. Designed to prepare nurses for positions as consultants, the program's curriculum centered on problem-solving skills, research methods, and the consultation process as it related to various disease modalities. Concurrently, Hall was serving as research analyst in cardiovascular-disease nursing for the heart disease control branch of the United States Public Health Service and as project director in the division of chronic diseases and tuberculosis, also part of the United States Public Health Service.

As visiting professor at the University of North Carolina School of Nursing and Marquette University College of Nursing in Wisconsin, Hall lectured and conducted a variety of conferences on cardiovascular nursing. In addition to her career commitments, she was actively involved in many professional organizations, including the American Nurses' Association, the National League for Nursing, the National Organization for Public Health Nursing, and the New York State Nurses' Association. She also was a committee member of New York City's board of education, served as secretary to the board of directors of Youth Aid in New York, and participated on a number of health-related voluntary committees in the New York area. Additionally, she was a member of Kappa Delta Pi, the national honor society in education.

Hall's most conspicuous contribution to health care was the conceptual model for nursing practice that she created and successfully implemented at the Loeb Center of Montefiore Medical Center. Her association with the Loeb Center was the culmination of a chain of events that began in 1947. That year, Martin Cherkasky was appointed director of the new hospital-based home-care program at the Montefiore Medical Center. Hall, who was then with the Bronx office of the Visiting Nurse Association, had professional connections with the Montefiore program. Cherkasky and Hall shared similar health-care philosophies; this formed the basis of a collegial relationship that survived more than 20 years.

During the 1950s, traditional convalescent homes began to lose popularity due to new medical advances in convalescent treatment. One of the homes that closed was the Solomon and Betty Loeb Memorial Home in Westchester, New York. Cherkasky, recognizing a unique opportunity, enlisted the help of Hall in convincing the board of the Loeb Home to join with Montefiore in the establishment of the Loeb Center for Nursing and Rehabilitation.

Planning and construction took place over a five-year period, during which Hall functioned first as project director and later as administrative director. The Loeb Center was dedicated in November 1962.

An 80-bed unit staffed by 40 professional nurses over 24 hours, the Loeb Center was unique in that its patients were selected by nurses for their potential to be rehabilitated. Opened to patients in 1963, it became a proving ground for Hall's philosophy, which focused more on personalized professional care than on routine care and thus streamlined the rehabilitation process. Influenced by the ideas of Carl Rogers and Harry Stack Sullivan, Hall was convinced that her conceptual model for professional nursing practice was the key to recovery for the patients at Loeb. Her model started with the patient's needs, continued with the concept of nursing as the essential ingredient for meeting those needs, and identified professionally prepared nurses as the only persons who could carry out nursing effectively. At a time when most institutions used team nursing, Hall implemented a one-on-one nurse-patient relationship.

Hall was a frequent contributor to the nursing literature, through which she shared her experience and her theoretical framework with the larger nursing community. A much sought speaker, her presentations drew large audiences. In 1967 she was honored by her peers when she received the Teachers College Nursing Alumni Award for Distinguished Achievement in Nursing Practice.

On February 27, 1969, Hall died at Queens General Hospital. Cremated at her own request, she was survived by her brother and her husband. Memorial services were held in the Rosenthal Auditorium at Montefiore Medical Center on March 11, 1969.

In 1974 Doctor's Hospital in Freeport, New York, was renamed Lydia E. Hall Hospital in her honor. In June 1984 at special ceremonies held in conjunction with the American Nurses' Association convention, Hall was inducted posthumously into the American Nurses' Association Hall of Fame.

### PUBLICATIONS BY LYDIA ELOISE HALL

"A Center for Nursing." *Nursing Outlook* 11 (November 1963): 805–6.

"Nursing—What Is It?" *Canadian Nurse* 60 (February 1964): 150–54.

"The Loeb Center for Nursing and Rehabilitation." *International Journal of Nursing Studies*, 6 (1969): 81–95.

## BIBLIOGRAPHY

Alfano, G. "Healing or Caretaking—Which Will It Be?" *Nursing Clinics of North America* 6 (June 1970): 273–80.

Alfano, G. "Hospital-based Extended Care Nursing: A Case Study of the Loeb Center." In *Nursing in the 1980s*, edited by L. Aiken. Philadelphia: J.B. Lippincott, 1982.

Alfano, G. "The Loeb Center for Nursing and Rehabilitation." *Nursing Clinics of North America* 4 (September 1969): 487–93.

Alfano, G. Telephone conversation with author. August 1985, July 1986.

Bowar-Ferres, S. "Loeb Center and Its Philosophy of Nursing." *American Journal of Nursing* 75 (May 1975): 810–15.

Cherkasky, M. Telephone conversation with author. July 1986.

Department of Nursing Education. Archives. Teachers College, Columbia University, New York.

Hall, L.E. "Another View of Nursing Care and Quality." Address delivered at Catholic University, Washington, D.C., 1965.

Hall, R.A. Telephone conversation with author. July 1986.

Henderson, C. "Can Nursing Care Hasten Recovery?" *American Journal of Nursing* 64 (June 1964): 80–83.

Levenson, D. *Montefiore—The Hospital as Social Instrument.* New York: Farrar, Straus and Giroux, 1984.

Levenson, D. Telephone conversation with author. August 1985 and July 1986.

"Lydia Hall." Obituary. *American Journal of Nursing* 69 (April 1969): 830.

"Lydia Hall." Obituary. *New York Times*, 28 February 1969.

"Montefiore Cuts Readmissions 80%." *New York Times*, 23 February 1966.

Montefiore Medical Center Archives. Montefiore Medical Center, Bronx, New York.

"News." *American Journal of Nursing* 74 (October 1974): 1774.

Nursing Archives. Mugar Memorial Library, Boston University.

Stevens, B. *Nursing Theory.* Boston: Little, Brown, 1979.

*Tempo.* Montefiore publication, February 1959.

Wiggins, L.R. "Lydia Hall's Place in the Development of Theory in Nursing." *Image* 12 (February 1980): 10–12.

Nettie Birnbach

# Anne Lyon Hansen
## 1878–1938

Anne Lyon Hansen made her career in public-health nursing and was director of the Visiting Nursing Association of Buffalo, New York, for 23 years. Other groups that she served as president include the National Organization of Public Health Nurses and the New York State Nurses' Association.

Hansen was born in Leeds, England, January 4, 1878, to Anna Lyon and Joseph L. Nichols. She received her early education in English private schools. She graduated from the Children's Hospital School of Nursing in Buffalo in 1897, and then did 18 months of graduate work at Buffalo General Hospital.

She began her career as a staff nurse for the Visiting Nursing Association of Buffalo from 1905–10. From 1910–13, Hansen held various positions in the North American Civic League for Immigrants, at one time heading the organization. From 1913–15 she was district secretary of the Charity Organization Society of Buffalo. In 1915 she became director of the Visiting Nursing Association of Buffalo and held that post until her death.

Hansen was a charter member of the National Organization of Public Health Nurses, serving as its president from 1926–30. At the time of her death she was on its board of directors and finance committee.

Hansen was president of the New York State Nurses' Association for three years and a director for eight years. During a long career of nursing leadership, she also served the following organizations as president: Middle Atlantic division of the American Nurses' Association, New York State Organization for Public Health Nursing (four years), and the Children's Hospital Alumnae Association of Buffalo (one year).

She was a fellow of the American Public Health Association and a member of the national committee on Red Cross Nursing Service and of the White House Conference on Public Health Nursing called by President Herbert Hoover. She was treasurer and a director of the American Journal of Nursing Company from 1931–37.

Hansen published several articles in such professional journals as the American Journal of Nursing and *Public Health Nursing.* Always concerned with the changing role of the nurse in society, she took part in hearings in Albany, New York, on proposed nurse practice acts.

From 1934, when it was created, until her death, she was a member of the nursing advisory committee of the Metropolitan Life Insurance Company. She was one of the first to work with Lee Frankel in establishing a nursing service for the company. In October 1937 the New York State Nurses' Association honored her by designating its loan fund the Anne L. Hansen Loan Fund.

The wife of Viggo Hansen, Hansen died at age 60 at her home in Buffalo on March 11, 1938, of a heart ailment. The funeral was held in St. Paul's Cathedral in Buffalo and burial was in Toronto, Ontario. She was survived by a son, Viggo, and three brothers, Dr. W.F. Nichols of Windsor, Ontario, J.L. Nichols of Buffalo, and J.W. Nichols of Toronto.

## PUBLICATIONS BY ANNE LYON HANSEN

"Miss (Jane C.) Allen's Resignation." *Public Health Nursing* 20 (August 1928): 397.

"Katherine Tucker." *Public Health Nursing* 21 (January 1929): 1–2.

## BIBLIOGRAPHY

"Anne L. Hansen." Obituary. *Buffalo Evening News*, 12 March 1938.

"Mrs. Anne L. Hansen." *American Journal of Nursing* 38 (April 1938): 498–99.

"Public Health Nursing Group Official Dies." *Buffalo Courier-Express*, 13 March 1938.

"Who's Who in the Nursing World 53. Anne Lyon Hansen." *American Journal of Nursing* 25 (1925): 1003.

Alice P. Stein

## Bertha Harmer

### 1885–1934

As early generations of trained American nurses grew up with Clara Weeks's 1885 *Textbook of Nursing,* so succeeding generations of nurses were indelibly influenced by Bertha Harmer's *Textbook of the Principles and Practice of Nursing,* first published in 1922. Various editions were used extensively in the United States and Canada as well as in Australia, China, Persia, France, and other European countries. The endurance of this classic is a powerful reflection of Bertha Harmer's lasting influence as an extraordinary nurse educator and administrator.

Bertha Harmer, daughter of Mr. and Mrs. John Harmer was born on March 2, 1885, in Port Hope, (Ontario) Canada. While still young, she moved with her family to Toronto, where she grew up with her brothers, Harry and Arthur, and her sisters, Emily and Mary. In 1899 Harmer graduated from the Jarvis Collegiate Institute of Toronto with the intention of pursuing a career in teaching.

However, when she agreed to relieve an ill friend who worked for a large business concern, she became interested in the various aspects of business administration. Yet despite the fact that the field of business promised success from certain worldly standpoints, Harmer found it limited in both appeal and opportunities after a few years. Wishing to provide a more personal service to others, in 1910 at age 25 Harmer began studies at the Toronto General Hospital School of Nursing. Her administrative talent resulted in her being placed in charge of various wards for most of her final year there. Her ability was further recognized when she was selected to receive the first prize in her graduating class of 40 students.

With such an outstanding record, Harmer upon graduation was immediately appointed supervisor and instructor at the Toronto General Hospital School of Nursing. In addition to fulfilling her administrative duties, she taught *materia medica,* the sciences, and the principles and practice of nursing.

In 1915 Harmer joined the class of 84 students enrolled for the academic year at Teachers College, Columbia University. Supported by such faculty as M. Adelaide Nutting, Isabel M. Stewart, Annie W. Goodrich, Anne Hervey Strong, and Charles-Edward A. Winslow, Harmer majored in administration, completed a full course in education, and studied public health and social casework. Committed to the philosophy of testing and promoting the relationship between theory and practice, Harmer spent her summer vacations as a head nurse at St. Luke's Hospital in New York City involved with specialty services in which she had no previous experience. During the school terms, she taught advanced principles and practice of nursing at the same hospital. In June 1918 Harmer was awarded a B.S. degree from Teachers College.

From May to September 1918, Harmer served as an instructor in the wartime experiment to prepare college graduates for admission to shortened courses of study at selected schools of nursing. Called the Vassar Training Camp because of its support by and location on the campus of Vassar College, the idea for the program had originated at Teachers College, which also recruited much of the camp's faculty from its alumnae.

Harmer returned to St. Luke's in late 1918 as a full-time instructor, teaching sciences, pathology, *materia medica*, history of nursing, and the principles and practice of nursing. It was during her five year tenure at St. Luke's that she wrote her first book about nursing.

Nursing authorities have noted that Harmer was the first nurse author to base and present nursing care on documented knowledge of physiology. Harmer's unassisted completion of *The Principles and Practice of Nursing* in one year attests to her mastery of the subject, her organizational acumen, her deep convictions and wisdom, and her unusual perseverance.

Harmer's widely adopted book brought further attention to her expertise as a nurse educator from sources in both Canada and the United States. In 1923 Harmer was appointed assistant professor of nursing at the new Yale School of Nursing. In addition, the New Haven Hospital appointed her assistant superintendent of nurses.

Once at Yale, Harmer, as chair of its first curriculum committee, was charged with the task of shaping a new program of study. The overall plan was to develop a program of education that would make a significant contribution to the preventive aspects of health care while giving due consideration to the more commonly attended curative elements. Included in the 28-month curriculum were planned experiences in public health, community work, and hospital services, all of which were correlated with pertinent theory. Harmer's position at Yale provided her with the circumstances to apply to nursing her interpretations of John Dewey's educational philosophy.

Harmer's second book *The Methods and Principles of Teaching the Principles and Practice of Nursing*, was published in 1926. It was the first book written specifically to assist and guide teachers of nursing.

In the fall of 1926, Harmer resigned from Yale due to ill health. Despite her fatigue, she returned that spring to Teachers College for further graduate study in administration. In October 1927 she was awarded the master of arts degree. Although still unwell, she completed the 1928 revision of her first book, increasing the emphasis placed on the role of the nurse as a teacher of health.

In March 1928 Harmer agreed to a request by McGill University in Montreal and in 1929 returned to Canada to assume the directorship of the University's school of graduate nurses. Harmer directed the school's programs in teaching, supervision, and administration of schools of nursing as well as programs in public-health nursing. She also exercised her capacity for research and enthusiastically promoted and planned investigatory projects, particularly as they related to increasing understanding of the nursing care needs of patients.

However, her administrative responsibilities became increasingly more difficult. The financial effects of the depression were so great that an energetic campaign to raise funds was needed to prevent the school from closing its doors. The crisis occurred as Harmer's health again declined. In the summer of 1934 on the insistence of her medical advisors, she resigned from McGill with plans to visit her family in Toronto before traveling to Jamaica in the fall.

Frailty, weakness, and pain kept Harmer in Canada where she managed to complete the third edition of *The Principles and Practice of Nursing.* Prominent among her friends, was her mentor and colleague of many years, Annie W. Goodrich, whose picture had occupied a conspicuous place on Harmer's desk. On December 14, 1934, at the age of 49, Harmer succumbed to cancer in the Toronto home of her sister Mary Hossack. In addition to Mary, she was survived by another sister, Emily Harmer, two brothers, Harry and Arthur Harmer, and two nephews.

## PUBLICATIONS BY BERTHA HARMER

### BOOKS

*Textbook of the Principles and Practice of Nursing.* New York: Macmillan, 1922; 2nd ed. 1928; 3rd ed., 1934.

*The Methods and Principles of Teaching the Principles and Practice of Nursing.* New York: Macmillan, 1926.

### ARTICLES

"Inspection of Training Schools." *Modern Hospital* 8 (April 1917): 281–84.

"The Teaching of Practical Nursing." *Modern Hospital* 23 (June 1923): 587–90.

"Teaching and Learning Through Experience." *Annual Report of National League for Nursing Education* (1925): 124–32.

### BIBLIOGRAPHY

"Bertha Harmer." Obituary. *American Journal of Nursing* 35 (January 1935): 90–91.

"Bertha Harmer." Obituary. *New York Times,* 15 December 1934.

Bhatt, D. Letter to author, 28 April 1986.

Brown, N. Review of *Methods and Principles of Teaching the Principles and Practice of Nursing,* by B. Harmer. *American Journal of Nursing* 26 (September 1926): 737–38.

*Bulletin of Yale University School of Nursing.* New Haven: Yale University, 1924–25, 1925–26, 1926–27.

Christy, T. *Cornerstone for Nursing Education.* New York: Teachers College Press, 1969.

Editorial. *Canadian Nurse* 29 (May 1933): 249–50.

Goodrich, A. Letters, 1923–28. Archives. Yale School of Nursing, New Haven, Conn.

Harmer, B. Letters, 1923–34. Archives. Yale School of Nursing, New Haven, Conn.

Henderson, V. Interviews with author. New Haven, Conn. 31 March 1981, 20 April 1985.

Hossack, M. Letters, 1934. Archives. Yale School of Nursing, New Haven, Conn.

Martin, C. Review of *Principles and Practice of Nursing,* by B. Harmer. *American Journal of Nursing* 22 (June 1922): 781–82.

"The McGill School for Graduate Nurses." *Canadian Nurse* 29 (July 1933): 355–57.

"Miss Bertha Harmer." *Canadian Nurse* 24 (September 1928): 463.

"Miss Harmer Goes to McGill." *American Journal of Nursing* 28 (May 1928): 465.

Pennock, M., ed. *Makers of Nursing History.* New York: Lakeside, 1940.

"Scholar and Teacher." *Canadian Nurse* 30 (September 1934): 415.

Shaw, H., trans. *Heritage,* by E. Desjardins, E. Flanagan, and S. Giroux. Quebec: Association of Nurses of Province of Quebec, 1971.

Tracy, M. Review of *Textbook of the Principles and Practice of Nursing,* by B. Harmer. *American Journal of Nursing* 28 (December 1928): 1286–87.

Werminghaus, E. *Annie W. Goodrich—Her Journey to Yale.* New York: Macmillan, 1950.

Eleanor Krohn Herrmann

## Esther Voorhees Hasson

### 1868–1942

Esther Voorhees Hasson was the first superintendent of the female Navy Nurse Corps. She was also one of the first professional nurses to serve under contract with the army during the Spanish-American War and was one of the original members of the Army Nurse Corps when it was organized in 1901.

Hasson was born in Baltimore, Maryland, on September 20, 1868, the youngest of two children of Alexander B. and Hetty A. Hasson. Most of her childhood and early adult years were spent in New London, Connecticut. Her father was a surgeon who had served with the U.S. Army during the Civil War; her brother, Alexander R. Hasson, was a graduate of the U.S. Naval Academy in 1881; her grandfather served in the War of 1812; and two of her great-grandfathers fought in colonial and revolutionary wars. Much of her own life was spent in some form of military nursing.

At age 28, Hasson graduated from the Connecticut Training School for Nurses at the New Haven Hospital in May 1897. During the year following graduation, she served as head nurse of the operating room and two surgical wards at the New Haven Hospital.

Shortly after the Spanish-American War broke out in 1898, she took the oath of office as a contract nurse for the army. She served first on the army hospital ship *Relief*. In April 1900 she reported to Vigan Hospital in the Philippines as chief nurse. She continued in this capacity until February 1902, when at her own request, she was ordered home for discharge. While enroute, Hasson served briefly at hospitals in Manila and at the Presidio in San Francisco. Her total tour of duty was three years and two months.

The Navy Nurse Corps was approved by an act of congress on May 13, 1908, but the effort to establish it had taken five years. Hasson, aware of the probable passage of the legislation, had applied for the position of superintendent of the Navy Nurse Corps as early as July 1903. She was one of three final candidates for the position; the finalists had to undergo a physical examination and undertake written and oral examinations on first aid, pharmacology, nursing therapeutics, and general knowledge. She was appointed superintendent in August 1908. A total of 20 nurses were appointed at the same time, and they later became known as the "sacred twenty." These women were graduates of hospital training schools with at least two years of instruction and had passed examinations on professional, moral, mental, and physical fitness. Recognized as members of the military, they were not given the rank of officer nor the rate of enlisted personnel.

Primary duties of the nurses included supervising patient care, teaching hospital apprentices basic nursing principles, and ensuring that these apprentices carried out orders promptly and intelligently. The duties of the superintendent were generally administrative tasks that promoted good management, efficient performance, and discipline for the betterment of the Navy Nurse Corps. During Hasson's administration, the corps grew to more than 100 nurses assigned to various areas throughout the world. Hasson regarded the first nurses as pioneers who were to set the pace for those to follow.

Hasson clashed with Admiral Stokes, the Surgeon General, in March 1910, and although she continued to serve, Stokes asked for her resignation. Hasson resigned in January 1911. She did not lose her interest in military nursing, however, and in World War I, she volunteered her services to the Army Nurse Corps, spending most of her time as chief nurse in hospitals in France. For her service, she received the Médaille d'Honneur des Epidemics from the French government.

Hasson died March 8, 1942, at the Emergency Hospital in Washington, D.C. She was buried in Arlington National Cemetery, and she left no survivors.

## PUBLICATIONS BY ESTHER VORHEES HASSON

"The Navy Nurse Corps." *American Journal of Nursing* 9 (November 1908): 91–92.

"The New Navy Nurse Corps Superintendent." *American Journal of Nursing* 11 (May 1911): 474.

## BIBLIOGRAPHY

Arlington National Cemetery. Interment records, Esther V. Hasson, March 10, 1942.

Editorial. *American Journal of Nursing* 11 (1910–11): 165.

Hickey, D.V. "The First Ladies in the Navy: A History of the Navy Nurse Corps, 1908–1939." Unpublished Ph.D. diss., George Washington University, 1963.

U.S. Navy Archives. Circular of Information, Embodying Regulations, Extract from Act of Congress, May 13, 1908. Record Group 52, File 115148. Washington, D.C.

U.S. Navy Archives. Letter, Esther V. Hasson to Secretary of Navy, July 16, 1903. Record Group 52, File 80896, Box 169. Washington, D.C.

U.S. Navy Archives. Letter, J.D. Pillsbury to Esther V. Hasson, August 17, 1908. Record Group 52, File 115738. Washington, D.C.

U.S. Navy Archives. Letters Sent by Superintendent of Nurse Corps, U.S. Navy (1908–1925). 3 vols. Record Group 52, File 115738. Washington, D.C.

U.S. Navy Archives. Memorandum, Esther V. Hasson to Secretary of Navy, January 14, 1911. File 80896, Box 169, File 115738.

U.S. Navy Archives. Memorandum, Esther V. Hasson to Secretary of War, May 25, 1927. Record Group 112, Entry No. 150, Box 553.

U.S. Navy Archives. Personal Record of Esther V. Hasson, M. and S. No. 115148, Record of Proceedings of Board of Medical Officers, August 3, 1908. Record Group. File 115738.

U.S. Navy Archives. Register of Service of Spanish-American War Contract Nurses, 1898–1900. Record Group 112, Entry No. 148, pp. 60–61, 65.

*Washington Post*, March 30, 1920, Record Group 112, Entry No. 150.

Betty T. Johnson
Rosemary T. McCarthy

# Alma Cecelia Haupt

## 1893–1956

Alma Cecelia Haupt is well known for her many contributions to the improvement of public-health nursing. From her first nursing position with the Minneapolis Visiting Nurse Association, she was invited by the Commonwealth Fund to become associate director of its child welfare demonstration in Vienna, Austria, where she was recognized for distinguished service. She then became associate director of the fund's division of rural hospitals. She also served as associate director and acting director of the National Organization of Public Health Nursing, and in 1935 she became director of the nursing bureau of the Metropolitan Life Insurance Company. Under her 17-year administration of this service, it became a model of its type for community and state agencies. During the war years, Haupt served as consultant and executive secretary of the nursing subcommittee of the Office of Defense Health and Welfare Services, helping to coordinate the wartime nursing activities of 12 governmental agencies.

Haupt, born March 19, 1893, in St. Paul, Minnesota, came from a long line of citizens prominent in the religious and cultural life of St. Paul, Minnesota. She was a granddaughter of Brigadier General Herman Haupt, who was in charge of military railroads for the Army of the Potomac during the Civil War. Her parents were Charles Edgar Haupt, an Episcopal minister, and Alexandra Dougan Haupt. Her brother, Theodore Haupt, was an art student who joined her for a European trip during her Austrian assignment from 1924 to 1927.

Haupt completed her secondary education at West High School in St. Paul and entered the Liberal Arts College at the University of Minnesota in 1911. She graduated in 1915 with a degree in physical education. After working for a year as a social worker in Minneapolis and a playground instructor in St. Paul, she returned to the university to enroll in its school of nursing.

Like several of her classmates, Haupt resented the restrictions on nursing students, particularly the rigid dormitory rules and the restrictions against social associations with medical students and staff. She was the leader of a small group who insisted on having student government for nursing students. Haupt was one of the students selected for a six-month psychiatric-nursing affiliation at the Johns Hopkins Hospital School of Nursing, an experience not then available at the University of Minnesota hospitals.

After graduating from the school of nursing in 1919, Haupt was employed as a supervisor in the Minneapolis Visiting Nurse Association (VNA). While in this position, she also worked with university faculty to develop courses in public-health nursing. During her last two years (1922–24) with the VNA, she served as general superintendent.

In 1924 she was invited by the Commonwealth Fund to become associate director of its child welfare demonstration in Vienna, Austria. Here she helped to reshape the war-shattered country by introducing into its rural districts American ideas of public service. In recognition of her distinguished service in this role, she was awarded the Gold Cross of Austria.

Following this assignment, Haupt returned to the United States in 1927 and was named associate director of the Commonwealth Fund's division of rural hospitals. She was concerned about adequate nursing service in these hospitals and made recommendations regarding nursing's responsibilities to meet these needs.

In 1929 Haupt accepted a position as assistant director of the National Organization for Public Health Nursing (NOPHN). She remained with this organization for six years, in the last few years serving as acting director. Her many publications in the area of public health reflected her administrative experiences with NOPHN.

Having attained national recognition through her writings and organizational activities, Haupt was named director of the nursing bureau of the Metropolitan Life Insurance Company, a pioneer in provision of home nursing care, in October 1935. Under her 17-year administration, this service became a model for community and state agencies. According to an article by Haupt in the June 1939 issue of the *American Journal of Nursing*, the Metropolitan Life Insurance Company had initiated home nursing service in 1909 through an affiliation with nurses of the Henry Street Settlement in New York City. The concept spread more rapidly than the company could find visiting nurse associations or similar agencies with which to affiliate and became too complex for the physician in charge to adequately supervise. Haupt was employed to coordinate and extend the nursing services, including improving the methods of record-keeping, cost-analysis studies, and concern for quality of nursing service.

During World War II, Haupt played an important role in providing adequate civilian and military nursing care. In 1941 she was granted a leave of absence to serve as nursing consultant and executive secretary of the nursing subcommittee of the Office of Defense Health and Welfare Services in Washington, D.C. In this dual capacity, she helped to coordinate the wartime nursing activities of 12 government agencies, including the nursing advisory committee of the procurement and assignment service of the War Manpower Commission, the American Red Cross, and the National Nursing Council for War Service. She returned to Metropolitan Life in 1943, but remained a consulting member of these national committees until the end of the war.

In July 1949 after a visit to Great Britain to study the British National Health Service, Haupt and Alice Girard of the Canadian Metropolitan Life Insurance Company's nursing staff attended the meeting of the International Council of Nurses in Stockholm, Sweden. They presented an address concerning their observations on the practical aspects of home health care in the United States.

From 1950–51 Haupt taught administration of public health-nursing at New York University. She was deeply involved in extending the frontiers of providing adequate health care. She was a prolific writer, and her many articles appeared in nursing and public-health publications. Several themes recur in her writings, including the importance of continuing in-service education, concern for the improvement of opportunities for black nurses, the extension of adequate nursing care to all in need, and organized nursing's stewardship responsibilities to the profession.

Haupt was loyal to her alma mater, the University of Minnesota School of Nursing, lauding the scientific basis of its medical and nursing instruction, its social and public-health viewpoint, and its encouragement of a mix of work and play for students. She received many honors, among them the Gold Cross of Austria and the Outstanding Achievement Award of the University of Minnesota, conferred October 8, 1951.

Haupt never married. She died in San Francisco, California, on March 15, 1956, three years after her retirement from Metropolitan Life.

### PUBLICATIONS BY
### ALMA CECELIA HAUPT

"Meeting the Need of the Small and Rural Hospital." *American Journal of Nursing* 29 (January 1929): 42–46.

"Nursing Councils: An Aid to Understanding Nursing." *Public Health Nursing* 32 (April 1932): 410–414.

"A Pioneer in Negro Nursing." *American Journal of Nursing* 35 (September 1935): 857–859.

"Why Study the Community's Nursing Service?" *American Journal of Nursing* 39 (January 1939): 41–43.

"Thirty Years of Pioneering in Public Health Nursing." *American Journal of Nursing* 39 (June 1939): 619–626.

"Accidents in the Home." *American Journal of Nursing* 41 (April 1941): 391–396.

"Organization of Nursing in Defense." *American Journal of Nursing* 41 (December 1941): 1415–1416.

"Forty Years of Teamwork in Public Health Nursing." *American Journal of Nursing* 53 (January 1953): 81–84.

### BIBLIOGRAPHY

"Alma C. Haupt." Obituary. *American Journal of Nursing* 56 (1956): 564.

"Alma C. Haupt." Obituary. *New York Times*, 17 March 1956.

Gray, J. *Education for Nursing, A History of the University of Minnesota School of Nursing.* Minneapolis, Minn.: University of Minnesota Press, 1960.

University of Minnesota Archives. University of Minnesota Library, University of Minnesota, Minn.

University of Minnesota, School of Nursing, Minneapolis. Student Records.

M. Isabel Harris

# I. Malinde Havey

## 1887–1938

A decorated nurse in World War I, I. Malinde Havey became the national director of public health, nursing, and home hygiene for the Red Cross, a position she held at her death. She was in charge of disaster work during the 1927 Mississippi flood as well as during the floods of 1937.

Havey was born in Stoughton, Wisconsin, in 1887. She graduated from the Illinois Training School for Nurses in 1910. Following graduation, she was employed by the Western Electric Company in Chicago as an industrial nurse, and from there she moved to Ann Arbor, Michigan, to work as a staff nurse with the Visiting Nurse Association. She had attended the University of Wisconsin before entering nursing school, and she did graduate work in social work and public-health nursing at the Chicago School of Civic and Philanthropy and at Teachers College, Columbia University.

Havey joined the Red Cross nursing service with the United States entry into World War I and became assistant chief nurse in the base hospital at Vittal, France, in the Vosges mountains. During the German offensive in the spring of 1918, she served under fire with the field nursing forces at Compiegne. For her courage and devotion to duty, she was decorated by the British Red Cross and the French government.

After the war, Havey remained with the Red Cross, becoming first the Red Cross supervising nurse for Michigan and then regional director for the lake division of the Red Cross, with headquarters in Cleveland, Ohio. In 1922 she became assistant national director of the American Red Cross Public Health Nursing Service in Washington, D.C., and in 1929 she was named national director. Later the Red Cross Home Hygiene and Care of the Sick Service was also placed under her direction. She was particularly interested in rural nursing. She was responsible for supervising the work of nurses in the Mississippi flood of 1927, the Puerto Rico hurricane of 1928, and the Ohio-Mississippi Valley flood of 1937, as well as in numerous smaller disasters.

Active in various professional circles, Havey was a fellow of the American Public Health Association; a member of the joint committee of the American Nurses' Association, the National League of Nursing Education, and the National Organization for Public Health Nursing on Subsidiary

Workers; and a member of the advisory committee of the Metropolitan Life Insurance Company, the board of directors of the Frontier Nursing Service, and numerous other groups.

Havey died September 7, 1938, at Baker Memorial Hospital in Boston. She was buried with military honors in Arlington National Cemetery. She was survived by her mother, two sisters, and two brothers. A memorial loan fund was established in her honor.

## PUBLICATIONS BY
## I. MALINDE HAVEY

"American Red Cross Meets the Challenge of Rural Nursing." *American Journal of Nursing* 32 (1932): 1129.

"Civilizing Rural Health." *American Journal of Nursing* 37 (1937): 513.

## BIBLIOGRAPHY

"I. Malinde Havey." Obituary. *Public Health Nursing* 30 (October 1938): 602–5.

"I. Malinde Havey." Obituary. *New York Times*, 8 September 1938.

Vern L. Bullough

## Sally Cain Hawkins
### 1883–1959

In 1959 when Sally Cain Hawkins was 72, she was named "Woman of the Year" for outstanding service to her community and fellow citizens of McCook, Nebraska. She spent most of her career providing nursing services to the community and was particularly well known for her assistance during the depression years.

Hawkins was born December 26, 1883, in Mead County, Kentucky. Her father, Keleb Hawkins, owned a farm in Mead County and had seven children from his first marriage. He was 35 years old when he married Florence Townsend Hardaway, age 17, with whom he had Sally and another daughter.

After graduating from high school in Kentucky, Hawkins became a teacher in a rural Kentucky grade school. In 1906 at her brother Benjamin's request, the whole family moved to a sod house 17 miles from McCook, Nebraska, where they farmed the land with Benjamin. Hawkins taught elementary school in Mendin, Nebraska, where only a high-school diploma was required for teaching. She attended the normal school in McCook and State Teachers' College in Kearney, Nebraska, to further her education.

Hawkins's interest in nursing began soon after she finished high school when she was called to Texas to nurse her cousins back to health after a bout with yellow fever, from which their mother had died. She also became involved in the Methodist church and its missionary work during this time, hoping to change her career from education to nursing and serve in Africa as a medical missionary.

Hawkins attended nursing school at the Illinois Training School in Chicago from 1918 to 1921. After nursing school, she volunteered as a missionary to Africa for the Memorial Methodist Church. Although she never made it to Africa, her missionary zeal brought her to the Philippines instead. From 1921–26 she was in charge of an obstetrical ward at the Mary Johnston Hospital in a slum area of Manila. Along with nursing care, she taught conversational English, massage, obstetrics and gynecology, and the concepts of Christianity to the Filipino nurses.

In 1926 Hawkins was called back to Nebraska when her parents' health failed. She bought a house and moved the family from the farm into McCook, and she paid the mortgage payments by working as a private-duty nurse at St. Catherine's Hospital. She remained in this capacity from 1928 to 1934.

From 1934 to 1935 Hawkins was a nursing case worker in Red Willow County, Nebraska. She bought a car so she could help the destitute farmers during the depression.

In 1935 at age 52, Hawkins began a career as a school nurse that would span the next 17 years. Her time was divided among three schools in McCook. Because many families were poor during these depression years, many children could not afford to come to school. Hawkins would often arrange for clothing, food, and transportation to be provided for them.

In 1952, 69-year-old Hawkins fell and broke her hip while running to an injured child. She became one of the first recipients of a femur recap. Because she had to wear an iron brace after months of recovery, she was unable to continue working for the school system. However, the townspeople and her former students presented her with a new car, which enabled her to continue working. She did private-duty nursing until 1956, when it became impossible for her to walk.

Hawkins remained active in community and social-work projects until her death on November 21, 1959 at the age of 76. She was buried in Memorial Park, Red Willow County, Nebraska. She is survived by a nephew, Douglas Austin of McCook, Nebraska.

### BIBLIOGRAPHY

Austin, D. Phone Interview. McCook, Nebraska. April 27, 1986.

"Hawkins, Sally." *Biographical Index.* Vol. 4. (1955–58). New York: H.W. Wilson, 1960.

Minny, D. "A Nebraska Nurse Looks Ahead." *Independent Women* 35 (1956): 15, 27.

Susan Peterson

# Nellie Xenia Hawkinson

## 1886–1971

Strong professional commitment and major contributions to baccalaureate nursing education characterize Nellie Xenia Hawkinson's importance to the field of nursing and distinguish her as one of nursing's visionaries. Accepting the presidency of the National League for Nursing Education, Hawkinson chose the task of helping to guide the education of student nurses because of its beneficial effect on the future health of the United States.

Webster, Massachusetts, was the site of Hawkinson's birth on May 29, 1886. She was the youngest of four daughters born into the family of Sven and Agnes Olson Hawkinson, immigrants from Sweden. Her father worked as a woolen weaver in the mills, and two of her sisters as teenagers also worked in the mills.

Framingham Hospital School of Nursing in Framingham, Massachusetts, just a short distance from Webster, was the school from which Hawkinson graduated in 1909. She then entered Teachers College, Columbia University, New York, where she was considered an outstanding member of her class. She received a B.S. degree in 1919 and an M.A. degree from the same institution in 1923. Later, under a traveling fellowship from the Rockefeller Foundation, Hawkinson spent one year, 1932–33, studying nursing schools and public-health centers in Europe. On her return, she spent one year in postgraduate study at Columbia University.

The beginning years of Hawkinson's nursing career were spent in bedside nursing at Framingham General Hospital. In 1918 Hawkinson took a position as an assistant instructor in the Vassar Training Camp for Nurses. The following year, she took a similar teaching assignment at Teachers College, where she taught home nursing and child care. A teaching position at Massachusetts General Hospital School of Nursing followed.

Hawkinson continued her teaching career when she became assistant professor of nursing at Western Reserve University, Cleveland, Ohio. This began ten years, 1923–32, of increasing responsibility at Western Reserve, leading to the position of professor and dean of the school of nursing. The school of nursing was generously endowed by Frances Payne Bolton, including provisions for a new nursing school to be built in 1930.

The hope for nursing to become regarded as a profession rested heavily on schools of nursing being established in institutions of higher learning instead of in hospitals. The acknowledgment by academia of nursing's right to base its work on scientific facts was sought by the Illinois League of Nursing when in 1924 they requested that the University of Chicago establish academic courses for nurses. In 1925 the first summer course at the University of Chicago was taught by Laura Logan of the Illinois Training School, and in 1926 the tangible resources of that famous school (then appraised at $420,000) were given to the University of Chicago to further its educational project for nurses.

An understanding that the University of Chicago would establish a school of nursing and a course of instruction leading to the bachelor of science in nursing degree accompanied the awarding of the assets of the Illinois Training School for Nurses. The purpose of this course of study was to prepare nurses for instruction or administration in a school of nursing. To implement this program, Hawkinson was appointed professor of nursing education at the University of Chicago in 1934. This establishment of nursing studies in an institution of higher learning was hailed by nursing educators as a forward step in nursing.

Throughout her career, Hawkinson remained in close touch with her instructors at Teachers College, M. Adelaide Nutting and Isabel Stewart. She continued as head of the University of Chicago's nursing education department until her retirement in 1951. At that time, she was awarded the title of professor emeritus of the University.

Hawkinson devoted much of her time to service. During her tenure at the University of Chicago, she was twice elected president of the National League for Nursing Education, serving from 1936 to 1940. Prior to that, she served as member and chair of many league committees, as well as serving as a member of the board of directors of the league. She also served as a board member of the Association of Collegiate Schools of Nursing and on many national and state committees.

Many of the same issues that the members of the National League for Nursing Education grappled with during the late 1930s remain issues of concern to today's nursing educators. Curriculum revision, qualifications of nursing faculty, accreditation of nursing schools, the cost of nursing education, the administration of nursing schools, the supply of staff nurses, and the role of subsidiary workers were some of the areas of concern to league members during Hawkinson's terms as president.

Hawkinson considered the third revision of the *Curriculum for Schools of Nursing*, published in 1937, to be one of the most significant projects of the league. She expressed hope that the curriculum guide would provide a stimulus to schools of nursing to reexamine their curricula and would supply guidance in planning programs of revision. Hawkinson's philosophy of nursing education took into account social and student needs as well as hospital needs. According to Hawkinson, acceptance of this philosophy would result in schools of nursing providing students with more adequate preparation for community service through broadened curricula. Her philosophy was further exemplified in an address to students at Milwaukee County School of Nursing in 1938, when she encouraged students to incorporate humanitarianism into nursing service.

During Hawkinson's terms as president, the National League for Nursing Education agreed to accept the responsibility of accrediting nursing schools. The first step leading to this acceptance of responsibility was taken 26 years earlier, when funding was sought to study the issue. After years of careful study and thoughtful consideration, means to implement accreditation were finally approved in 1936.

Though the school of nursing at the University of Chicago never flourished as nursing educators hoped it would, Hawkinson's contributions to nursing education were acknowledged, and she received many honors throughout her lifetime. In 1941, the Sigma Theta Tau Scholarship Society conferred honorary membership upon her. She also was a recipient of a citation as one of Chicago's 100 outstanding citizens, awarded during the Jesuit centennial in 1957. Hawkinson also earned inclusion in the first edition, published in 1959, of *Who's Who of American Women: A Biographical Dictionary of Notable Living American Women*.

Hawkinson lived to the age of 85 years, with her last few years spent in the Westminster Retirement Home in Evanston, Illinois. She died October 7, 1971, at Westminster after an illness of several months. She was survived by one niece, a grand-nephew, and two grandnieces. Services were held in the Elliott Chapel of the Presbyterian Home in Evanston, and she was buried in Webster, Massachusetts.

## PUBLICATIONS BY NELLIE XENIA HAWKINSON

"A Task and a Vision Is Joy Unspeakable." Nursing Education Department: The President's Address. *American Journal of Nursing* 37 (1937): 627–32.

"The Outlook in Nursing Education." Nursing Education: The President's Address. *American Journal of Nursing* 38 (1938): 573–80.

## BIBLIOGRAPHY

Hawkinson, N.X. "Capping Ceremony Address." Manuscript, 1938. Historical Room, Milwaukee County Medical Complex School of Nursing.

Hawkinson, N.X. Letter to M. Adelaide Nutting, no date. No. 2443. In *The History of Nursing: An Index of the Microfiche Collection, Vol. 2: The Archives of the Department of Nursing Education of Columbia University.* Ann Arbor: University Microfiche, International, 1985.

"Nellie X. Hawkinson." Obituary. *Chicago Tribune*, 8 October 1971.

"News About Nursing." *American Journal of Nursing* 41 (1941): 606–7.

Nutting, M.A. Letter to Nellie X. Hawkinson, 1930. No. 2443. In *The History of Nursing: An Index of the Microfiche Collection, Vol. 2: The Archives of the Department of Nursing Education of Columbia University.* Ann Arbor: University Microfiche, International, 1985.

Pennock, M.R. *Makers of Nursing History.* New York: Lakeside Publishing, 1940.

Stewart, I. Letter to Margaret Carrington, 1930. No. 2060. In *The History of Nursing: An Index of the Microfiche Collection, Vol. 2: The Archives of the Department of Nursing Education of Columbia University.* Ann Arbor: University Microfiche, International, 1985.

*Who's Who of American Women: A Biographical Dictionary of Notable Living American Women.* Chicago: A.N. Marquis, 1959.

Geri L. Dickson

# Helen Scott Hay

## 1869–1932

Helen Scott Hay is best known for her Red Cross service in eastern Europe during World War I. Her work was closely interwoven with the project in nursing education that first linked the American Red Cross with the development of foreign nursing. Hay also was a leader in organized nursing on local, state, national, and international levels. A prolific writer and speaker, she was instrumental in the standardization of nursing school curricula both in the United States and abroad, with special emphasis on nursing ethics and psychiatric nursing.

Hay was born on a farm near Lanark, Carroll County, Illinois, on January 5, 1869. While she was still young, the family moved to Kansas, returning to Illinois a few years later to settle in Savanna. Hay's mother was from Pennsylvania, and her Scottish father was one of the organizers of the First National Bank of Savanna. The Hays had two daughters and one son in addition to Helen.

Hay attended the Savanna schools and was graduated from high school in 1886. She taught school for a while, graduated from Northwestern Academy in 1889, and received a bachelor's degree with Phi Beta Kappa honors from Northwestern University in 1893.

Hay then entered the Illinois Training School for Nurses (ITS), graduating in 1895. In 1900 Hay did one year of postgraduate work at the University of Chicago.

In the first 17 years of her nursing career, Hay demonstrated skill as an administrator and educator and as a speaker and writer. Following her graduation from ITS, Hay's first practical experience as an administrator came as chief nurse at the Southwestern Iowa Hospital for the Insane at Clarinda, Iowa. Hay also served as superintendent of nurses at the County Institute for the Insane and Indigent in Chicago and later worked in the same capacity at Pasadena Hospital and School of Nursing in Pasadena, California, where her sister, Rachael Johnson, lived. In addition, Hay worked in an executive capacity in private sanatoriums in Los Angeles. She spent one year as high-school principal in her native Savanna; private nursing also claimed her attention at intervals.

Hay reluctantly left her position in Pasadena in 1906 to serve as superintendent of nurses for the ITS. During Hay's six-year tenure, ITS was one of the first training schools to offer affiliation with other schools of nursing, psychiatric nursing as an elective, and postgraduate nursing education. In reviewing the history of her tenure, Hay summarized such routine problems as her yearly contract with the Cook county board which controlled the hospitals, a linen shortage, and epidemics of scarlet fever, smallpox, and flu.

In addition to her work as an administrator and educator, Hay was instrumental in the development of local, state, and national nursing organizations as nurses began to organize at the turn of the century. She attended the first meeting called by representatives from the St. Luke and Illinois training schools to discuss the need for an Illinois Graduate Nurses' Association. At a meeting in July 1901, a 30-member executive committee was chosen and appointed Hay as chair to draft a constitution and bylaws.

The primary goal of the nurses' association was to initiate state registration procedures, and in 1908 the first board of nurse examiners was appointed. Hay was one of five nurses selected to serve on the board and was elected its president, serving until August 1913.

Hay also was appointed by the Illinois Board of Charities to serve on a state committee promoting uniform curricula for nurses in hospitals for the insane. In addition, while in California she assisted in the organization and development of the California Nurses' Association.

In Chicago Hay was active in the Illinois Training School Alumnae Association, and her signature was one of three on the document of incorporation of the association in May 1903. She served as one of five directors on the alumnae association's board of directors that same year and as one of seven directors in 1910.

At the national level, Hay served as chair of the education committee of the American Society of Superintendents of Training Schools (1910). As a writer and public speaker, she addressed a number of national nursing issues. In 1914 she spoke on the arrangement of subjects in training school curricula and emphasized the importance of balancing course work with practical experience, the self-care of nursing students through physical training, and postgraduate education in nursing administration.

The years 1912–14 were a transition time for Hay. She resigned as superintendent of the ITS in 1911, and in 1912 she took a much-needed rest of 18 months and enjoyed a tour of the world. On her return to Chicago, Hay became involved in the founding of West Suburban Hospital and School of Nursing in Oak Park, a suburb of Chicago, and became its first superintendent in February 1914. ITS students staffed the hospital as part of their private-duty experience, and West Suburban students affiliated with ITS by participating in a six-month elective in pediatrics and medical nursing at Cook County Hospital.

Hay resigned in July 1914 and in August planned to set sail for Bulgaria as a representative of the American Red Cross, which had responded to the appeal of Queen Eleanora of Bulgaria to organize a school of nursing in Sofia. However, the declaration of war in Europe delayed these plans, allowing the American Red Cross to assign Hay to duty on the USS *Red Cross*, a mercy ship sending relief supplies and medical personnel to Europe. This highly popular and well-publicized excursion exemplified the neutrality ideal of the Red Cross.

Jane Delano, head of the American Red Cross, recruited Hay to help in the selection and organization of the nurses to serve in Europe. As director of nursing personnel for the USS *Red Cross*, Hay was responsible for harmonizing the aims and ambitions of 126 nurses from 12 states who would be divided into 10 units. In England, the medical units separated, and Hay became senior supervising nurse for the two units heading for Russia. In Kiev, the 24 nurses served the wounded and refugees by creating a 400-bed hospital in a large school building.

In June 1915 Hay resigned and traveled to organize the Bulgarian training school proposed in 1913, which first linked the American Red Cross with the development of foreign nursing. The training school started with eight students in September 1915. However, soon Bulgaria joined forces with the Axis powers and the Germans took over the administration of the hospital. Hay then travelled to Philippopolis at the request of the queen to do public-health and child-welfare work among the refugees until the United States entered the war.

In July 1917 Hay was called back to serve the American Red Cross in Washington, D.C., joining the group of nursing leaders brought by Delano to the national headquarters. As a member of the national committee on nursing service and director of the newly created Bureau of Instruction in Elementary Hygiene and Home Care of the Sick, Hay was instrumental in the selection and assignment of nursing personnel for the base hospitals serving the U.S. soldiers overseas.

In January 1918 Hay resigned from the Red Cross Nursing Service to assist Annie W. Goodrich in establishing an army school of nursing at the request of the surgeon general. In October Hay was appointed chief nurse of the American Red Cross Commission to the Balkan States, and she sailed for Europe shortly after the armistice. By December Hay was recruiting from the Army Nurse Corps in France and the nurses' bureau of the former Commission for France to create a large staff of experienced and able nurses for duty in the Balkan States.

Hay continued to coordinate American Red Cross nursing in the Balkans until 1920, when she was appointed director of nursing services for the American Red Cross in Europe. Her duties included supervision of the American Red Cross nurses in the Baltic Provinces, Poland, Czechoslovakia, Austria, and Hungary, as well as the Balkans. Hay assisted in establishing programs for child welfare and for several schools of nursing and in preparing groups to take over this work.

In 1922 Hay returned to the United States to care for her ill brother, John Hay. She had received medals and decorations from Bulgaria, England, France, Poland, Romania, Russia, and Serbia. Her most treasured decoration was the Florence Nightingale Medal, one of six awarded to American nurses who served in the war. In addition, Northwestern University awarded her the honorary degree of doctor of humane letters in 1923.

Hay spent her remaining ten years in Savanna. Despite failing health, she worked in local Red Cross drives, civic movements, and the Federated church. She was also active in a women's club, reading clubs, and the American Legion.

In 1925 Hay was to have taken the position of regional director of the division for home hygiene and care of the sick at the branch office of the American Red Cross in St. Louis. However, she was stricken by illness en route. According to Elsbeth Vaughan, a Red Cross colleague, in addition to developing cancer of the groin and pelvis, Hay had suffered mental and physical problems that were belatedly traced to a fractured skull, apparently from an accident in Europe.

Hay suffered a stroke in April 1932 and died at age 63 at her home in Savanna on November 25, 1932. She earlier had declined that she be buried in Arlington National Cemetery, preferring to join her parents in the small family cemetery near Savanna. She was survived by her sisters, Mrs. Arthur P. Woodruff of Freeport, Illinois, and Rachael Johnson of Pasadena, California, and a brother, John Hay of Savanna, Illinois. Memorial services also were held in the Evangelical church in Sofia, Bulgaria, on December 18.

## BIBLIOGRAPHY

Barclay, D.W., *In Memoriam: Helen Scott Hay: Red Cross Nurse.* Savanna, Ill. April 6, 1933.

"Dedication to Helen Scott Hay." *Illinois Training School Alumnae Report* (December 1932).

Dock, L. et al. *History of American Red Cross Nursing.* New York: Macmillan, 1922.

Dunwiddie, M. *A History of the Illinois State Nurses' Association 1901–1935.* Chicago: Illinois State Nurses' Association, 1937.

"Helen Scott Hay." Obituary. *American Journal of Nursing* 33 (1933): 87–88.

*Illinois Training School Alumnae Report,* 1909–10, 1924–25. Midwest Nursing History Research Center, Chicago.

Kleinfall, B. *History of West Suburban Hospital.* Diss., University of Chicago, 1959.

National League of Nursing Education. *Annual Reports of the National League of Nursing Education.* Baltimore: Williams and Wilkins, 1914.

Noyes, C. "Department of Red Cross Nursing." *American Journal of Nursing* 33 (1933): 67–68.

Schryver, G.F. *A History of the Illinois Training School for Nurses 1880–1929.* Chicago: Illinois Training School, 1930.

Vaughn, E. Letter about Helen Scott Hay. *Illinois Training School Alumnae Report* (January 1933).

Volk, K. *Buddies in Budapest.* Los Angeles: Kellaway-Ide, 1936.

Janet Milauskas

# Mary Eugenie Hibbard

## 1856–1946

Mary Eugenie Hibbard was a dedicated, highly esteemed nursing educator, administrator and organizer. Her distinguished international career spanned 40 years.

Hibbard was born in the Montreal area in 1856. She was a Canadian citizen of American and Canadian descent. Although little is known about her family and early years, she had at least one brother, Omri F. Hibbard, who became an attorney in New York City. She graduated in 1886 from the Mack Training School for Nurses, associated with the General and Marine Hospital, St. Catharine's, Ontario, Canada.

Hibbard then began what was to be the first of many administrative positions when she became superintendent of the Mack Training School, remaining there until 1888. Continuing her work in nursing schools, she moved to the new Grace Hospital in Detroit, Michigan, where she became the first principal of the Newberry Training School for Nurses. The 100-bed hospital opened in December 1888, and in January 1889 the school opened, offering a two-year course of study. During Hibbard's eight-year tenure, the program grew into a successful, well-organized nursing school. In 1897 Hibbard left the school to serve as the superintendent of the Homeopathic Hospital in Trenton, New Jersey, until 1898.

On August 1898, after the outbreak of the Spanish-American War, Hibbard wrote to Anita Newcomb McGee, the wartime head of nursing, offering her services. As required by the Daughters of the American Revolution, she connected herself to the Revolutionary War by stating that her great-grandfather had been a chaplain in the American army. Hibbard was employed at the time and only offered to work for the two weeks of her vacation. She expressed her willingness to take charge of a department or a detachment of nurses. She was assigned to Camp Cuba Libre in Jacksonville, Florida.

Due to a mix-up in communications, Hibbard found her enlistment had been accepted for a longer period and she remained at Jacksonville for several months. Although she was scheduled in November to be appointed chief nurse, a position she had filled since her arrival at the camp, she was given leave in late October because she contracted typhoid fever.

In March 1899, after her recovery, Hibbard signed a contract to work as chief nurse at the U.S. General Hospital in Savannah, Georgia. She remained there until June 23, 1899, when she was transferred to General Hospital, Fort Meyers, Virginia. She became an assistant to McGee in the surgeon general's office in nearby Washington, D.C. McGee's journal indicates Hibbard assisted with immune lists, went over efficiency reports, and sorted correspondence. Hibbard and McGee often socialized together, and a monument to Spanish-American War nurses in Arlington National Cemetery cites the joint efforts of these two nurses.

In October 1899 Hibbard was relieved from duty at Ford Meyers and transferred first to New York and then to her home in Manchester, New Hampshire. Her next service was overseas. She set sail for London on the American hospital ship *Maine*, which had been outfitted by American women living in England for service during the Boer War. In December she was one of five nurses and five physicians invited to lunch at Windsor Castle and an audience with Queen Victoria. In late December the *Maine* embarked for South Africa with Hibbard as superintending nurse. Lady Randolph Churchill, chair of the American Hospital Ship Fund, accompanied the ship.

Hibbard's experiences were chronicled in a series of articles, the first appearing in the first issue of the *American Journal of Nursing*. These articles described the ship's departure from London, its stop in the Canary Islands, and its arrival at Capetown. For their nursing services in South Africa in 1900, Hibbard and four other nurses were awarded medals by the English government.

On her return from South Africa, Hibbard was assigned to duty in the Philippines. However, Hibbard declined the position because it required a nurse, not a chief nurse, and she believed other candidates were available.

Hibbard spearheaded the development and organization of the Order of Spanish-American War Nurses' Association, which held its first meeting at New York Hospital early in September 1900. Throughout her lifetime she maintained her activity in this association, serving as vice-president in 1916.

Hibbard was soon involved in new work. On September 29 she sailed for Cuba in response to a cablegram offering her the position of superintendent of the training school for nurses at Santa Isabel Hospital in Matanzas, Cuba. Conditions in Cuban hospitals after the Spanish-American war were poor. Hibbard described filth, disease, and apathy, and she contracted yellow fever soon after her arrival. However, nursing education progressed quickly under Hibbard and others such as Lucy Quintard and Mary Agnes O'Donnell. Well organized and experienced, these leaders immediately set high standards for the Cuban schools. Both Quintard and Hibbard were members of the committee that established nursing rules and regulations. Legal status for nursing in Cuba was achieved in 1902, one year before the first licensing laws were passed in the United States.

Hibbard's writings reveal her philosophy of nursing. She wrote of nursing's close work with medicine, and she described three classes of qualifications necessary for nursing: general culture, practical knowledge, and theoretical knowledge. She described the role of the nursing school and superintendent as pivotal to building character and educating nurses in self-control, obedience, accuracy, cheerfulness, humor, patience, and tact.

Hibbard spent three years in Cuba, moving from Matanzas to Havana in 1902–1903. In July 1904, Hibbard sailed for the Panama Canal, having been appointed chief nurse at Ancon Hospital, Panama. At that time, the recommended management of yellow fever was unknown in Panama, and the nursing aspects of this problem were left to Hibbard. After three years, her task was complete, and she returned to her home in Manchester. Her work in the Canal Zone was recognized when a plaque was dedicated to her there in 1951.

From 1907–8 Hibbard served as superintendent of Leonard Hospital in Landisburgh, New York. In October 1908 she again sailed for Cuba, having been appointed inspectress general of Cuba. In this capacity she served in the Department of Charities and was responsible for everything related to nursing and nursing schools, making inspections of hospitals employing graduates and keeping records of all nurses.

During 1909–19 Hibbard served as head of the Department of Nursing Tuberculosis Section in Havana. She worked initially with Mary O'Donnell organizing a dispensary in Havana, and she trained seven graduate nurses at the tuberculosis sanatorium. In 1919 Hibbard was appointed, by presidential decree, chief of the bureau of nurses of Cuba.

On June 15, 1927, at the age of 71, Hibbard retired on a pension from the

Cuban government. She died on June 7, 1946, in Melverne, Jamaica.

### PUBLICATIONS BY
### MARY EUGENIE HIBBARD

"With the *Maine* to South Africa." *American Journal of Nursing* 1 (1900): 1.

"The Queen's Reception of American Nurses and Doctors." *American Journal of Nursing* 1 (1900): 401.

"The Establishment of Schools for Nurses in Cuba." *American Journal of Nursing* 2 (September 1902): 986.

"General Culture in the Education of the Nurse." *British Journal of Nursing* 2 (August 30, 1902): 175.

"Cuba: A Sketch." *American Journal of Nursing* 4 (1903–04): 696–702.

### BIBLIOGRAPHY

Dock, L. *A History of Nursing.* Vol. 4. New York: G.P. Putnam's Sons, 1912.

Freeland, I. "Nursing in the Canal Zone." *American Journal of Nursing* 7 (1906–07): 697–99.

Guevara, M. "Tuberculosis Nursing in Cuba." *American Journal of Nursing* 40 (1940): 1219–20.

Hibbard, M.E. Curriculum vitae. St. Catharine's General Hospital, Ontario.

Kalisch, P.A. "Heroines of '98: Female Army Nurses in the Spanish-American War." *Nursing Research* 24 (November–December 1975): 411–29.

"Mary Eugenie Hibbard." Obituary. *American Journal of Nursing* 46 (1946): 640.

"M. Eugenie Hibbard Retires." *American Journal of Nursing* 27 (1927–28): 660.

National Archives. Office of the Surgeon General, Document Files 1894–1917. Record Group 112, File. Washington, D.C.

*National Archives.* Public Health and Marine Hospital Service Records. Record Group 90, File. Washington, D.C.

Phyllis Foster Healy

## Mary Agnes Hickey
### 1874–1954

As superintendent of the nursing service at the Veterans Bureau, Mary Agnes Hickey organized the department. She also became an authority on federal nursing services.

Mary Agnes McCarthy Hickey was born in Ireland on December 1, 1874. She grew up in Springfield, Massachusetts, where she graduated from Cathedral High School. She entered the school of nursing at St. Mary's Hospital, Brooklyn, New York, and after receiving her nursing diploma in 1900, did postgraduate work at the Lying-in-Hospital in New York City.

She married James Eli Hickey, a physician and a former high-school classmate, following her graduation. She became the first school nurse in Springfield and also served as a tuberculosis and child-welfare nurse, assisting in the organization of the first nutrition classes for children in the public schools in Springfield.

In 1917 Hickey resigned her position, held since 1910, as supervisor of public-health nursing in the Massachusetts department of health to enter overseas service with the American Red Cross. One of the first nurses to go overseas, she later transferred to the Army Nurse Corps and served with surgical units at the front lines. She was assigned to the Fourth French army in the sector north of Châlons-sur-Marne and, working directly behind the front-line trenches, was continually under fire.

After the war, Hickey entered the United States Public Health Service in November 1918 as a staff nurse. In 1921 she was promoted to assistant superintendent of nurses and served in the eastern states as a nurse representative in charge of recruiting nurses for service, making professional contacts with schools of nursing and with state and local nursing organizations in the interest of former service men and women.

In 1922 when the 47 hospitals for the care of veterans were transferred to the Veterans Bureau, forerunner of the Veterans Administration, Hickey was appointed superintendent. The nursing service at that time was composed of 1,442 nurses assigned to hospitals and 400-public health nurses in the 14 regional districts of the bureau. Hickey worked to improve the nursing service to patients and strongly supported higher educational standards for nurses, including instruction in such specialties as tuberculosis and psychiatric nursing.

Hickey's retirement from the Veterans Administration marked the completion of 20 years as superintendent of nurses. She continued her interest in nursing activities, serving in a volunteer advisory capacity with the procurement and assignment service of the War Manpower Commission throughout World War II.

Hickey was the author of articles on nursing procedures and techniques and nursing activities in mental hospitals and of a bulletin on tuberculosis nursing. She was a frequent guest lecturer at Catholic University in Washington and at Teachers College, Columbia University.

She served as secretary and board member of the American Nurses' Association, as president of District of Columbia League of Nursing Education (1927–29), and on numerous committees. She was also commander of the Jane A. Delano American Legion post.

Hickey's experience during World War I and in the United States Public Health Service made her ideally suited to head the nursing service of the Veterans Bureau. Characterized as possessing a rare friendliness and optimism, she was able to build a strong, progressive service. She died on February 14, 1954, at the Veterans Administration Hospital at Ft. Howard, Maryland, at the age of 80 following a lengthy illness.

## PUBLICATIONS BY
## MARY AGNES HICKEY

"The Development of High Standards of Nursing in the United States Veteran's Bureau." *United States Veteran's Bureau Medical Bulletin* 3 (May 1927): 494–99.

"Nurses in the American Legion." *American Journal of Nursing* 28 (June 1928): 590–91.

"Narrative Reports of Follow-up Nurses." *United States Veteran's Bureau Medical Bulletin* 5 (July 1929): 544–47.

"Nursing Procedures and Technique as a Guide for Follow-up Nurses." *United States Veteran's Bureau Medical Bulletin* 5 (August 1929): 622–25.

"Educational Program for Nurses." *United States Veteran's Bureau Medical Bulletin* 6 (February 1930): 155–56.

"Postgraduate Course in Neuropsychiatric Nursing." *United States Veteran's Bureau Medical Bulletin* 6 (April 1930): 328–30.

### BIBLIOGRAPHY

American Red Cross Archives. American Red Cross National Headquarters, Washington, D.C.

Bytheway, R.E. "History of the Development of the Nursing Service of the Veterans Administration under the Direction of Mrs. Mary A. Hickey 1919–1942." Ph.D. diss., Columbia University, 1972.

"Mary A. Hickey." Obituary. *American Journal of Nursing* 54 (November 1954): 1324.

"Mrs. Mary Hickey." Obituary. *New York Times*, 16 February 1954.

Pennock, M.R. *Makers of Nursing History.* New York: Lakeside, 1928.

Roberts, M.M. *American Nursing History and Interpretation.* New York: Macmillan, 1954.

Lilli Sentz

## Agatha Cobourg Hodgins
### 1877–1945

Agatha Cobourg Hodgins is primarily known for her work in anesthesia. She served as physician George Crile's anesthetist in Cleveland, Ohio, and in France during World War I. In 1915 she was instrumental in the opening of the Lakeside School of Anesthesia in Cleveland. In 1931 she became a founding member and the first president of the International Association of Nurse Anesthetists (now the American Association of Nurse Anesthetists).

Hodgins was born in Ontario, Canada, in 1877 and was raised in Toronto. In 1898 she left Toronto and emigrated to Boston, Massachusetts, where she attended the Boston City Hospital Training School for Nurses. She entered the training school at age 21.

Hodgins graduated from the training school in 1900. Her teachers described her as intelligent, self-possessed, patient, and earnest. Upon graduation, she and two classmates moved to Cleveland, where she worked for eight years as a head nurse at the Lakeside Hospital. In 1908 George Crile, a preeminent surgeon, invited her to be his chief anesthetist.

In choosing a nurse as a permanent anesthetist, Crile was following the model of the Mayo brothers, surgeons in Rochester, Minnesota. Hodgins was sent to Minnesota to learn their methods and was also given preliminary practice on animals under Crile's guidance.

Crile was one of the first surgeons to use nitrous oxide anesthesia, and by 1911 he and Hodgins had performed a large number of operations without any fatalities. Because of their outstanding record, Crile and Hodgins became known as experts in the field. Many nurses and other medical personnel came to Lakeside Hospital to study the administration of nitrous oxide under their tutelage.

In 1911 a survey to determine who was administering anesthesia in hospitals determined that 25 percent used nurse anesthetists, 28 percent used interns, and 20 percent used physician specialists. Anesthesia, which at one time had been considered a distasteful task, had become a coveted profession. There was already contention about which profession should have the legal right to administer anesthesia, but for a time nurse-administered anesthesia was allowed to continue unchallenged. Hodgins was able to meet, train, and keep in contact with many of these nurses.

World War I gave nurse-administered anesthesia a tremendous boost. In 1914 Hodgins, Crile, and other health-care professionals organized a surgical unit that volunteered to go to France, where they helped establish a hospital in the city of Neuilly. Nitrous oxide anesthesia proved to be well suited to rapid and safe surgery. It was especially useful with poison-gas victims, who were unable to use other types of anesthesia. Since it soon became apparent that there were too few trained practitioners, Hodgins remained in France training anesthetists and performing battle-line service.

In 1915 she returned to the United States to increase the size of the nation's anesthesia service. In that same year, she began plans to open a school of anesthesia at Lakeside Hospital. The school opened later that year.

In 1916 the school had a small graduating class comprised mostly of nurses, but shortly after this, the school was closed in a dispute with Ohio's medical board over the legality of nurses administering anesthesia. In 1918 the school reopened when the medical board withdrew its complaint, but the controversy was far from over.

The influence of the graduates from the Lakeside school was great. Many served overseas as instructors of anesthesia and as clinical practitioners. The Lakeside school was the first postgraduate school of anesthesia for registered nurses in the United States. It combined rigorous classroom instruction with extensive clinical practice.

With the success of the Lakeside school, many other schools began to appear. By 1931 over 20 postgraduate schools of anesthesia were in operation. The quality of these schools varied, as no accreditation process regulated the schools. This situation and the continued controversy about the legal status of nurse-administered anesthesia were Hodgins's primary concerns during the next two decades. In 1923 she initiated the formation of the Alumnae Association of the Lakeside School of Anesthesia, an organization she envisioned as the foundation on which to build a national nurse anesthetist group.

It was not until 1931 that such an organization was founded, in part because the 1920s had been a difficult period for nurse-administered anesthesia. Although the profession had grown during the economic boom that characterized the decade, several states, including Kentucky and California, had declared the profession illegal. However, in 1931 the American Nurses' Association decided to organize the nurse anesthetists into a section with office nurses. Hodgins did not feel that this arrangement would best serve the field. Calling upon all the contacts she had maintained over the years, Hodgins organized a meeting attended by 40 nurses representing 12 states. At this meeting, the International Association of Nurse Anesthetists was established with Hodgins elected president. The objectives for the organization were the advancement of the science of anesthesia by publication of periodicals and creation of an information bureau, the development of an accreditation program to standardize and upgrade training, and the establishment of legal status for nurse anesthetists throughout the United States.

The association was formed at a critical time, as the economic upheaval of the depression years was a factor in the need to defend nurse-administered anesthesia. Both physicians and nurses were hard hit by the depression, and since the nurse anesthetists were occupying a money-making niche, many physicians felt the anesthetist jobs should be theirs. The result was an increase in legal cases against the nurses.

In addition to serving as a defense organization, the association became the base for creating nurse-administered anesthesia as a separate profession. Hodgins felt that nurses should have status within the American Nurses' Association (ANA) similar to that of public-health nurses. To this end, the association petitioned the ANA for membership as a specialty organization in 1931. During negotiations, the International Association of Nurse Anesthetists became the National Association of Nurse Anesthetists, and several new constitutions were drafted. By 1933 with association membership over 550, negotiations ended. The ANA rejected the association's bid, stating that association members could join the ANA on an individual basis. Apparently, the ANA did not feel prepared to take up the legal battle that would be implicit in recognizing the nurse anesthetists.

In 1933 Hodgins suffered a heart attack. Forced to cut back on her work, she gave up her clinical practice and resigned as director of the school of anesthesia. For the remaining years of her life, Hodgins continued to support the nurse anesthetists' cause by writing articles and giving speeches. She died in Chatham, Massachusetts, on March 24, 1945.

## BIBLIOGRAPHY

American Association of Nurse Anesthetists. *A 50 Year Retrospective of the American Association of Nurse Anesthetists.* Park Ridge, Ill.: American Association of Nurse Anesthetists, 1981.

Bullough, B. "Clinical Specialization in Nursing: Historical Overview." In *Conference Proceedings: Historical Basis of Clinical Nursing Practice in the United States,* ed. S. Fondiller. Chicago: American Association for the History of Nursing, 1985.

Thatcher, V. *History of Anesthesia: With Emphasis on the Nurse Specialist.* New York: Lippincott, 1953. Reprint. New York: Garland Publishing, 1984.

Michael Stein

## May Shiga Hornback
### 1924–1976

May Shiga Hornback was an early leader in continuing education in nursing. A pioneer in the development of innovative educational materials in nursing, she was among the first nurse educators to recognize the potential of and to use television in teaching nursing. She was also among the first to use the telephone for teaching.

Hornback was the fifth and youngest child born to Henry Juro and Sumi Hirano Shiga. She was born on May 4, 1924, in Seattle, Washington, where she attended public schools. After regular school hours, she also attended Japanese school. Her mother was ill during much of her childhood and her father often away from home on business, but she and her sister Saki were close. The family was financially secure.

In 1941 Hornback enrolled in Seattle

College, but during World War II, she moved hastily inland to avoid internment in one of the relocation camps set up to confine West Coast Japanese-Americans. She enrolled in the nursing program at St. Xavier's College in Chicago, which she attended for two years. On May 2, 1944, while still a student, she married Vernon Hornback, then serving in the army, and because of the marriage, was not allowed to continue in the nursing program, a practice then common.

The couple's son, Vernon Junior, was born in 1945 in Pennsylvania. After the war, the family moved to Madison, Wisconsin, where their daughter, Frances, was born. Hornback found employment as a nursing aide at the Lakeview Tuberculosis Sanitarium. Staff members were so impressed with her nursing skills that they encouraged her to enroll in the University of Wisconsin School of Nursing. She received her B.S. degree in 1954.

Hornback's first nursing employment was as a staff nurse at the Veterans Administration Hospital in Madison. In 1956 she was appointed an instructor in nursing at the University of Wisconsin-Madison School of Nursing, teaching fundamentals of nursing and later medical-surgical nursing.

Hornback took a leave of absence in 1957 from her teaching position to enroll in the graduate program at the Frances Payne Bolton School of Nursing in Cleveland. During this time, her husband was employed in Greenland, and Hornback took her two children with her to Ohio. She was awarded her M.S. degree from Case-Western Reserve in 1958.

Returning to Madison and the University of Wisconsin, Hornback soon began the first of several teaching innovations. She was among the earliest nurse educators to design a televised nursing course; it consisted of 17 half-hour videotapes for a fundamentals of nursing course, completed in 1963. She produced a number of other videotapes, primarily designed for continuing education. One of these, "A Talk with Linda," was an interview with a young patient with leukemia and was produced in 1970. She also produced a series of educational films for the Lippincott Company.

In 1965 Hornback joined the staff of the department of nursing in the University of Wisconsin-Extension and enrolled in the doctoral program in adult education of the University of Wisconsin-Madison. She completed her doctorate in 1970. She was awarded tenure as an associate professor in the university in 1970; two years later she was promoted to full professor.

From 1966 to 1976 Hornback directed the continuing education courses in nursing presented over the Wisconsin statewide Educational Telephone Network. Nurses from around the country sought her advice before starting similar programs.

She served as a project director for a number of innovative projects, including "Nursing Dial Access", a taped library on nursing topics; two projects on institutional sharing of an in-service coordinator; one on developing audio-cassette courses for self-directed learning; and another on physical assessment skills in nursing care. She also served as codirector of a joint cancer nursing training project with the University of Wisconsin-Madison School of Nursing.

Hornback's expertise as a consultant was sought by several national groups, including the nursing department of the National Institutes of Health and the education division of Hoffman-LaRoche Company. She served on the curriculum advisory committee of Video Nursing, Inc., of Evanston, Illinois, and as an editorial consultant for nursing films for J.B. Lippincott Company.

An active member of state, local, and national nursing organizations, Hornback served as a member of the American Nurses' Association's commission on nursing education (1972–74) when it produced the first draft of its standards for nursing education. In 1975 she was appointed the first chair of the American Nurses' Association's national accrediting board for continuing education.

She was recognized as an honored national leader in continuing education in nursing at the Sixth National Conference on Continuing Education in Nursing, held in Milwaukee in 1974. She was elected to Pi Lambda Theta, the honorary education sorority, and Sigma Theta Tau, the honorary nursing society. For her contributions to the Wisconsin Nurses' Association, Hornback received the organization's first service award, presented posthumously at its 1976 convention and accepted by her husband.

Hornback died of cancer of the pancreas July 6, 1976, at University Hospital, Madison, Wisconsin, and her husband died the following year. A Japanese-American, she was proud of her Japanese heritage, but she was equally proud to be an American. Her last goal was to live to see the American bicentennial celebration on July 4, 1976. She was survived by her two sisters, a brother, her daughter, her son, and five grandchildren. After her death, her colleagues established the May Shiga Hornback Scholarship with a generous contribution from her husband. The fund permits the annual award of scholarships to nurses seeking doctoral degrees in adult education.

Hornback's contributions to her profession were exemplary. She was a creative teacher with a practical and down-to-earth approach. Hornback was an ardent supporter of civil and human rights. She had unusual abilities and talents and she is remembered for her persistence and determination, her sense of humor, her cheerful disposition, and her calm and common-sense approach to life's problems.

## PUBLICATIONS BY MAY SHIGA HORNBACK

### BOOKS

With S.S. Cooper. *The Continuing Learner in Nursing: A Description of Nurses Enrolled in Institutes and Conferences Offered by the University of Wisconsin-Extension Division, September 1962–August 31, 1963.* Madison, Wis.: University of Wisconsin-University Extension, 1966.

With S.S. Cooper. *Continuing Nursing Education.* New York: McGraw-Hill, 1973.

### ARTICLES

With B. Westley. "An Experimental Study of the Use of Television in Teaching Basic Nursing Skills." *Nursing Research* 13 (Summer 1964): 205–209.

With S.S. Cooper. "Profile of the Continuing Learner in Nursing." *Nursing Outlook* 4 (December 1966): 28–31.

With H. Brunclik. "Party Line for Nurses." *Nursing Outlook* 16 (1968): 30–31.

"University Sponsored Staff Education in Nursing via a Telephone/Radio Network." *International Journal of Nursing Studies* 6 (September 1969): 217–23.

"Diabetes Mellitus—The Nurses' Role." *Nursing Clinics of North America* 5 (March 1970): 3–12.

"Continuing Education—Whose Responsibility?" *Journal of Continuing Education in Nursing* 2 (July–August 1971): 9–13.

"Measuring Continuing Education." *American Journal of Nursing* 73 (September 1973): 1576–78.

## BIBLIOGRAPHY

Hornback, M. "The Nature and Extent of Inservice Programs for Professional Nurses in General Hospitals in Wisconsin." Ph.D. diss., University of Wisconsin-Madison, 1970.

"May Hornback." In *Who's Who of American Women, 1972–1973.* 7th ed. Chicago: A.N. Marquis, 1973.

"May Hornback." Obituary. *American Journal of Nursing* 76 (August 1976): 1388.

Hornback, M. Papers. University Archives. University of Wisconsin-Madison.

"Memorial Resolution for May Shiga Hornback." Faculty Document, University of Wisconsin-Extension.

Signe S. Cooper

## Thelma Marguerite Ingles

### 1909–1983

Thelma Marguerite Ingles was a distinguished nurse educator and writer who pioneered the development of the first nurse clinical specialist program at the master's-degree level. She also was instrumental in upgrading health care in undeveloped countries.

Ingles was born December 16, 1909, in Redfield, South Dakota. Her father was Thomas Jefferson Ingles, real estate and insurance broker, city alderman, and state representative from Redfield. Her mother was Della Hooker Ingles, a practical nurse. Ingles had two older brothers, Glen and Bernard, and one younger sister, Virginia.

In 1918 Ingles and her family began an almost annual commute to California for the school months because her sister had poor health, because schools were better in California, and because of the prestige of living there. Thus, adaptation and change became a lifestyle that continued into Ingles's choice of career opportunities. Her last three years of high school were spent in Redfield, and during this period of her education, she became fond of English. This, together with her father-initiated elocution lessons, was probably responsible for her several childhood speech and literary awards.

Upon graduation from high school in 1927, Ingles attended junior college in Glendale, California. She received a B.A. degree from the University of California-Los Angeles with a major in English literature and a minor in education in 1931. Although the depression years were a poor time for journalists, Ingles's brother, an editor of a small weekly newspaper in Los Angeles, gave her a reporting job. She later obtained employment in a dining room at a ranch in Montana, where after one summer she had saved enough money to feel some financial security. After flipping a coin to make her decision, she decided to return to her father in South Dakota rather than returning to California and an old boyfriend.

Ingles soon became restless, and after hearing about a new acquaintance's experiences in nursing, she applied to several nursing schools. She chose to attend Massachusetts General Hospital (MGH) in Boston because of its historical strength and fame. Ingles was impressed and ex cited by the course in anatomy and physiology, taught by Annabel McCrae, who after 40 years was teaching her last class of students. Ingles's subsequent respect for the way the body functions and its ability to make adaptations became the centerpiece for her future teaching of nursing to students in the United States and foreign countries.

After graduation in 1936 from MGH, Ingles was an assistant teacher there for 8 months. She then worked for one year at the Boston Nursery for Blind Children. Needing more of a challenge, she accepted a nursing arts instructorship at Fitchburgh Hospital School of Nursing in Fitchburg, Massachusetts. This was followed by employment with a group of physicians in private practice in Cleveland, Ohio from 1940 to 1942. During this time, she learned how to do tests on blood and urine, as well as how to do electrocardiograms and diathermy. She also revived her love for English literature and completed requirements for an M.A. degree in 1942 at Western Reserve University.

When World War II erupted, the doctors in the group practice were called to service. Ingles moved to St. Luke's Hospital in Cleveland to be in charge of an understaffed surgical intensive care unit. After one year of shouldering these responsibilities, she decided to join the navy. However, she was refused because she held teacher's qualifications, and faculty personnel were needed to provide additional nurses for the military and for civilians.

A conversation with a Georgia woman in the Cleveland library led to Ingles's next position as director of nursing education at the University of Virginia from 1942 to 1945. Her institution of preadmission requirements for nursing applicants resulted in fewer students failing the first semester of study.

With the war over in 1945, Ingles felt she had done her duty at home and wanted to work overseas. She contacted the American Red Cross, which had a teaching position available with the Admiral Bristol Hospital in Istanbul, Turkey. She accepted the position without knowing that she would be the only faculty member to teach in the nursing program. Only one of the nine student nurses spoke English, so Ingles used gestures and a chalkboard as communication links. She created what may have been the first integrated nursing curriculum, combining courses in anatomy, physiology, pathology, nutrition, psychology, nursing, and public health.

After Ingles had completed her three-year assignment in Turkey (1945–48), she accepted a faculty position at Duke University School of Nursing in Durham, North Carolina. Between 1949 and 1961, Ingles taught in Duke's bachelor of science in nursing education program, assisted in the development of the bachelor of science in nursing program, participated in phasing out the diploma program, and developed the first nurse clinical specialist program at the master's degree level in the country. During much of this time, she served as chair of the department of medical-surgical nursing.

Ingles instituted the teaching of medical-surgical nursing courses by nurse faculty, with physicians who were heads of divisions or departments invited to attend the lectures. This provided a basis for nursing-medical interactions between and among nurses and physicians in the clinical area, including clinical teaching rounds and clinical conferences.

In 1956 Ingles accepted the invitation of physician Eugene Stead, chair of the department of medicine, to spend a year of clinical study with him. This period resulted in a mutual learning experience in how closer collaboration of nurses and physicians could improve patient care and increase respect between the two professions. A result of this experience was the development of a master's degree program in nursing that would focus on clinical specialization, rather than on teaching or administration. A grant to support this pioneering program was submitted to the Rockefeller Foundation and funding for five years was awarded. However, the program was not accredited by the National League of Nursing because it lacked "functional preparation" and because there were no positions available for clinical specialists.

In 1961 Ingles decided to attend the University of California-Berkeley for additional courses. In California, she continued writing for professional journals, which she had begun in the 1950s.

She also spoke at professional meetings and university schools of nursing about her beliefs that nurses should assume increased responsibility for the advanced clinical care of patients. A few nursing and medical colleagues shared her philosophy and joined her in working against the traditional ideas of nursing. Lydia Hall was supportive of Ingles's ideas; Hall had initiated the Loeb Center for Nursing at Montefiore Medical Center, where nurses were in charge of the care given patients and physicians called in on a consultant basis. Frances Reiter also offered encouragement in the clinical specialization program and began a similar one at Flower-Fifth Avenue Hospital in New York City. Through Ingles's persistant efforts, the clinical specialization graduate program at Duke University persevered without National League of Nursing accreditation and became the pilot venture for the redirection of graduate nursing education across the country.

Discouraged with nurses who were unwilling to accept changes in nursing, Ingles discontinued her studies at Berkeley in 1962 and accepted a field staff position with the Rockefeller Foundation. Her nursing consultant activities were concentrated for several years at University del Valle in Cali, Colombia, South America. From 1962–74 she traveled to other Latin American countries, the Middle and Far East, and Africa under the auspices of the Rockefeller Foundation, emphasizing the importance of the clinical nurse. Prior to her retirement in 1978, she also was a consultant with the Peace Corps and Project HOPE. She was a consultant to the senior staff of the Robert Wood Johnson Foundation and influenced the development of programs for nurses.

During her career on the international scene, she repeatedly emphasized the need to examine carefully the curricula for each health work group since no one curriculum in her opinion could satisfy the need of all areas of the world or the various kinds of workers. Everywhere she taught she emphasized that nursing education should not only teach students what nursing was in an ideal setting, but how nursing was in the workplace in order that the students could act responsibly and independently in any situation that might arise. Her early efforts in establishing the clinical specialist program marked a turning point in nursing and helped change the nature of graduate education. In recognition of Ingles's varied and valuable contributions to the profession of nursing and to the School of Nursing at Duke, the Beta Epsilon Chapter of Sigma Theta Tau at Duke University in 1973 established the Thelma Ingles Writing Awards Program. The program continues in her memory.

Ingles enjoyed having colleagues, friends, and students in her home, and many of these interactions resulted in fruitful discussions. Her home in Blue Hill, Maine, provided restful but stimulating vacations for a number of professional friends.

A chronic respiratory condition forced Ingles's early retirement in 1978 from professional activities. She died from emphysema in La Jolla, California, July 23, 1983. She was survived by a brother, Bernard, a sister, Virginia, and several nieces and nephews. At her request, she was cremated and a ceremonial burial was held by her surviving family members from a boat in the Pacific Ocean.

## PUBLICATIONS BY THELMA MARGUERITE INGLES

### BOOKS

With H. Turk. *The Nurse in the Clinic.* Philadelphia: F.A. Davis, 1963.

### ARTICLES

"Action within Action." *Nursing Outlook* 2 (May 1954): 242–44.

With Rebekah Conrad et al. "One Method of Teaching Medical and Surgical Nursing," *American Journal of Nursing* 54 (August 1954): 956–58.

"Understanding Instructors." *Nursing Outlook* 4 (December 1956): 692–94.

"An Experience in Learning." *Nursing Research* 6 (October 1957): 77–78.

"The Worst Patient on the Floor." *Nursing Outlook* 6 (February 1958): 99ff.

"Mrs. Belmont—A 'Good' Patient: A Case Study." *Nursing Outlook* 6 (March 1958): 163.

"Mr. Parker—A 'Bad' Patient: A Case Study." *Nursing Outlook* 6 (April 1958): 209.

"Margaret—An 'Uncooperative' Patient: A Case Study." *Nursing Outlook*, 6 (May 1958): 289.

With Emily Campbell. "The Patient with a Colostomy." *American Journal of Nursing*, 58 (November 1958): 1544+.

"Cora—Who Didn't Understand: A Case Study." *Nursing Outlook* 6 (December 1958): 709.

"The Nurse Today." *Maryland State Medical Journal*, January 1959, pp. 38–42.

With John McKinney. "The Professionalization of Nurses." *Nursing Outlook* 7 (June 1959): 365ff.

"The Patient, the Student, and the Teacher." *Nursing World*, September 1959, pp. 9–11.

"What Is Good Nursing?" *American Journal of Nursing* 59 (September 1959): 1246–49.

"Do Patients Feel Lost in a General Hospital?" *American Journal of Nursing* 60 (May 1960): 648–51.

"On Developing Skilled Practitioners." *American Journal of Nursing* 60 (October 1960), 1482–84.

"Understanding the Nurse-Patient Relationship." *Nursing Outlook* 9 (November 1961): 698ff.

"The University Medical Center as a Setting for Nursing Education." *Journal of Medical Education* 37 (May 1962): 411–20.

"Death on a Ward." *Nursing Outlook* 12 (January 1964): 28.

With Inez Durana. "The University del Valle School of Nursing in Cali, Colombia." *Nursing Outlook* 13 (October 1965): 42ff.

"Maria—The Hungry Baby." *Nursing Forum* 5 (1967): 36ff.

"WHO Inter-country Conference on Nursing Curriculum: A Concept of Nursing Practice." *Nursing Journal of India* 57 (March 1966): 75ff.

"A Concept of Nursing Practice." *International Nursing Review* 13 (March/April, 1966): 7–12.

"Maria." *The Rockefeller Foundation Quarterly*, July–August 1967, pp. 14–19.

"A New Health Worker." *American Journal of Nursing* 68 (May 1968): 1059–61.

"A Proposal for Health Care Education." *American Journal of Nursing* 68 (October 1968): 2135–40.

With Nelson Ordway et al. "Interpersonal Factors in Failure to Thrive." *Southern Medical Bulletin* 57 (December 1969): 23–28.

"An American Nurse Visits the Soviet Union." *American Journal of Nursing* 70 (April 1970): 754–62.

"Where Do Nurses Fit in the Delivery of Health Care?" *Archives of Internal Medicine* 127 (January 1971): 73–75.

"Mobility in Nursing." *Rhode Island Medical Journal* 54 (June 1971): 313–15.

"Debate: Ladder Concept in Nursing Education." *American Journal of Nursing* 71 (November 1971): 726–30.

"St. Christopher's Hospice." *Nursing Outlook* 22 (December 1974): 759–63.

"The Physician's View of the Evolving Nursing Profession—1873–1913. *Nursing Forum* 15 (1975): 123–64.

"You Can Come Home Again." *Nursing Outlook* 24 (August 1976): 494–95.

### BIBLIOGRAPHY

Ingles, T.M. Autobiography, unpublished.

Ingles, T.M. Papers. Duke University School of Nursing, Durham, N.C.

Wilson, R. Personal reminiscences.

Ruby L. Wilson

## Anna C. Jammé

d. 1939

Anna C. Jammé was influential in the organization of California nurses. She encouraged nursing reform and was a founder of nursing schools.

Jammé's father was a mining engineer, and her early life was spent in several different places, which may have stimulated her interest in both travel and people. She graduated from the Johns Hopkins Hospital School of Nursing in Baltimore, Maryland, in 1897, and she stayed at Johns Hopkins in various head nursing positions for three years after her graduation. As head of outpatient maternity services, she became the first American nurse to make prenatal visits in the home.

From Baltimore, Jammé moved to Boston to be superintendent of nurses at the New England Hospital for Women and Children. While there, she established the eight-hour workday system and encouraged the development of a permanent and strong alumnae group. In 1906 she moved to Rochester, Minnesota, where she founded the school of nursing at St. Mary's Hospital.

In 1912 Jammé moved to California, where she became active in the legislative campaign that secured the passage of the nurse practice act in 1913. She was appointed the first director of the Bureau of the Registration of Nurses in California's department of public health and held this position until 1928. At that time, she became director of the California State Nurses' Association and editor of the association's publication, the *Pacific Coast Journal of Nursing*.

In 1918 Jammé was given a leave of absence to serve in the office of the surgeon general as assistant to Annie Goodrich, the dean of the Army School of Nursing. She served as inspector of the units of the school and of the base hospital in which schools either had been or were to be established.

Jammé was active in nursing organizations, as director of the American Nurses' Association and of the American Journal of Nursing Company, and as president of the National League of Nursing Education from 1920 to 1922. She retired as director of the California State Nurses' Association in 1936. She died on July 4, 1939, at Stanford Hospital, Stanford, California, of a heart attack.

### PUBLICATIONS BY ANNA C. JAMMÉ

*Textbook of Nursing Procedures.* New York: Macmillan, 1921.

### BIBLIOGRAPHY

"Anna C. Jammé." Obituary. *American Journal of Nursing* 39 (1939): 939.

Vern L. Bullough

## Sally Lucas Jean

1878–1971

Sally Lucas Jean was a leader in the development of health education and has been credited with creating the term *health education*. She devoted her career to interpreting and putting into practice the full meaning of health education.

Born in Towson, Maryland, on June 18, 1878, Jean was the daughter of George B. and Emilie Watkins Selby Jean. She attended local schools and the Maryland State Normal School in Towson, from which she graduated in 1896. She then entered the Maryland Homopathic Hospital Training School for Nurses and graduated in 1898. During the Spanish-American War, she served as a nurse in army hospitals in Lexington, Kentucky, and Chikamauga, Georgia. She then returned to her native Maryland, first as a private-duty nurse and then as a school nurse for the Baltimore public school system.

It was as a school nurse that Jean began her lifelong work in the coordination of public and school health education. At first she worked with teachers and children in the classroom. In 1915 she was appointed by the Baltimore Health Department as a playground nurse, and she utilized this opportunity to extend her work.

In 1917 Jean was invited to join the People's Institute in New York City to promote the same type of health education programs she had begun in Baltimore as well as to create a program of health education for school children. In that same year, she was appointed to serve on the Committee on Wartime Problems of Childhood set up by the New York Academy of Medicine. This committee reported that one in five children in New York City was suffering from serious malnutrition, a finding that in 1918 led to the formation of the Child Health Organization.

Jean became director of the new agency and began devising new ways of interesting children and teachers in health. She continually emphasized the pivotal role of schoolteachers in health education and was instrumental in influencing teacher training institutions throughout the United States to introduce health-education courses into their curricula.

Jean served as specialist in health education with the United States Bureau of Education from 1919 to 1921. Her contacts with the Child Health Organization and the United States Bureau of Education enabled her to organize the Lake Mohawk Conference in 1922, which emphasized the proper training of health-education teachers. By 1922, the year of the conference, workers in health agencies concerned with health education had become numerous enough to establish a separate section within the American Public Health Association. Jean served as chair and secretary of the section and remained active in the section throughout most of her life.

In 1923 the Child Health Organization merged with the American Child Hygiene Association to form the American Child Health Association, with Jean as director of the health education division, a position she held until 1924. She entered the international arena of health education in 1922, when she served on a special mission to Belgium for the Commission for Relief of Belgium Educational Foundation. In 1924 she took on the development of health-education programs for the schools of the Panama Canal Zone, and this was followed by similar missions to the Philippines, Japan, and China in 1929 and to the Virgin Islands. From 1933 to 1936, she was supervisor and health-education coordinator for the Navajo division of the United States Indian Service.

Jean saw no reason why public-health disciplines and business enterprises could not cooperate on tasks affecting the health and hygiene of children, and she became a consultant for several of them. Most notably, she was the consultant responsible for the establishment of a school health bureau by the Metropolitan Life Insurance Company, and for 40 years, she acted as a member of its advisory education group. In 1944 when she was 66, she was invited to organize work in health education for the National Foundation for Infantile Paralysis.

Jean wrote numerous articles and an account of her trip to China, Japan, and the Philippines. During her lifetime, she was decorated by the Belgium Red Cross (in 1923) and other organizations, many of which she served as an officer. For many years, her summer home was at Pemaquid Point, Maine, while she spent her winters in New York City.

Jean died July 5, 1971, at the age of 93 in New York City.

Among her awards was a medal from L'Oeuvre Nationale de l'Enfance (France, 1922), Belgian Red Cross, 1923; State Service Award, New York State Association for Health, Physical Education and Recreation, 1948; the William Howe Award, American School Health Association, 1948. She also received an honorary M.A. from Bates College in 1924.

## PUBLICATIONS BY SALLY LUCAS JEAN

### BOOKS

*Spending the Day in China, Japan, and the Philippines.* New York: Harper and Brothers, 1932.

### ARTICLES

"Health Education." *Addresses and Proceedings, National Education Association of the United States,* 1920, pp. 318–19.

"Health Organization Work in Public Schools." *Addresses and Proceedings, National Education Association of the United States,* 1920, pp. 369–71.

"Health Problems in Education." *Addresses and Proceedings, National Education Association of the United States,* 1918, pp. 443–46.

"Laying the Cornerstone of Tomorrow's Healthy Citizen." *Addresses and Proceedings, National Education of the United States,* 1928, pp. 79–87.

### BIBLIOGRAPHY

"Sally Lucas Jean." Editorial. *American Journal of Public Health* 61 (November 1971): 2153–54.

"Sally Lucas Jean." *Who Was Who 1969–73.* Vol. 5. Chicago: A.N. Marquis, 1973.

Vern L. Bullough

# Deborah MacLurg Jensen

## 1900–1962

Deborah MacLurg Jensen was a prominent nurse educator and author of over 20 nursing books and numerous articles and papers. She founded and edited a journal for student nurses, *Tomorrow's Nurse,* the first periodical of its kind.

Jensen was born on November 4, 1900, in County Tyrene, Northern Ireland, one of six children of the Reverend and Mrs. Alexander MacLurg. Her father, a Presbyterian minister, moved his family to Canada, then to Pennsylvania in 1915, and later returned to Canada.

Jensen attended grade school in Northern Ireland and completed high school and one year of college in Canada. She then taught school for a short time in Frenchburg, Kentucky. She entered the Johns Hopkins Hospital School of Nursing in Baltimore, Maryland, graduating in 1924.

Her nursing career began with her appointment as head nurse of a surgical ward at Johns Hopkins Hospital in 1924; the next year she was appointed assistant night supervisor. In 1926 she became assistant admitting officer for the hospital.

Jensen then enrolled in Teachers College, Columbia University, New York City. To support herself and pay for her education, she did private-duty nursing at night. She received her B.S. degree in 1927.

That year she went to Minneapolis, where she served as supervisor of clinical instruction at the University of Minnesota School of Nursing. She then moved to St. Louis, Missouri, where she was assistant admitting officer of the Washington University clinics (1929–30) and assistant director of the Washington University School of Nursing (1930–32).

After her marriage to Julius Jensen, a physician, and while employed in various administrative and teaching positions, she undertook graduate study at Washington University. She was awarded an M.A. degree in 1941.

Unlike most women of her time, Jensen continued to practice her profession after her marriage. After her first son, Julius III, was born in May 1933, she continued to keep professionally active with various part-time and short-term positions. She taught summer sessions at the University of Chicago (1932–34) and at Simmons College, Boston (1942–49). She served as a medical social worker at Washington University clinics and allied hospitals in the summers of 1935 and 1936; she was social-service consultant to the St. Louis Visiting Nurse Association in 1936–39.

Two more sons were born to the Jensens: John Alexander, born in March 1939, and Arne MacLurg, born in December 1943. Later, the couple was divorced.

From 1939 to 1944, Jensen served as a lecturer in nursing supervision, ward management, and teaching at Washington University. The next year, she was appointed assistant director of the school of nursing at the St. Louis City Hospital, where she served for five years. During some of this time, she was also employed as a part-time instructor in nursing education and sociology for the extension division of the University of Missouri.

At St. Louis City Hospital, Jensen worked diligently to improve the curriculum of the school. She also began a student-nurse internship program, which was the first of its kind in the state and perhaps the nation.

Jensen's special contribution to nursing was in her publications; she wrote professional books at a time when few nurses were doing so. Her first book, *Handbook on Nursing Case Studies*, was published in 1929, and from then until her death, she continued to write and edit professional books. A few of her books were coauthored with her physician husband. The first of these, *Medical Nursing*, was published in 1932. They coauthored *Nursing in Clinical Medicine*, which was published in four editions.

In addition to her books, she wrote a number of articles for nursing journals. Believing that student nurses needed a journal designed for them, in 1960 she founded and edited *Tomorrow's Nurse* and was its editor at the time of her death.

Jensen was active in professional associations, serving as president of both the Missouri Nurses' Association (1947–48) and the Missouri League of Nursing Education (1948–52). At the national level, she served as board member (1944–48) and vice-president (1948–52) of the National League of Nursing Education. She also served on the board of trustees of Nurses' Educational Funds (1954–62).

Recognized as an outstanding educator, Jensen frequently was invited to speak at national nursing meetings. She conducted workshops and seminars for the Veterans Administration and numerous schools of nursing throughout the country. In 1958, she was presented the Woman of Achievement Award of the St. Louis *Globe Democrat* newspaper.

Jensen moved to Nantucket, Massachusetts, in 1960 after having been a summer resident there for several years. She died following abdominal surgery on July 31, 1962, and was buried in Nantucket. She was survived by her three sons and a grandson.

## PUBLICATIONS BY DEBORAH MACLURG JENSEN

### BOOKS

With J. Jensen. *Medical Nursing*. New York: Macmillan, 1932.

*An Introduction to Sociology and Social Problems*. St. Louis, Mo.: C.V. Mosby, 1939.

*Nursing Care Studies*, 3rd ed. New York: Macmillan, 1940.

With J. Jensen. *Nursing in Clinical Medicine*. 2d ed. St. Louis, Mo.: C.V. Mosby, 1945.

*Mosby's Comprehensive Review of Nursing*. St. Louis, Mo.: C.V. Mosby, 1949.

*History and Trends in Professional Nursing*, 2d ed. St. Louis, Mo.: C.V. Mosby, 1950.

*Mosby's Comprehensive Review of Practical Nursing*. St. Louis, Mo.: C.V. Mosby, 1956.

*Principles and Technics in Rehabilitation Nursing*. St. Louis, Mo.: C.V. Mosby, 1957.

*Practical Nursing: A Textbook for Students and Graduates*. St. Louis, Mo.: C.V. Mosby, 1958.

*Nursing Service Administration: Principles and Practice*. St. Louis, Mo.: C.V. Mosby, 1962.

With J.C. Barbata and W.G. Patterson. *A Textbook of Medical-Surgical Nursing*. New York: G.P. Putnam's Sons, 1964.

### ARTICLES

"Case Study in Schools of Nursing." *American Journal of Nursing* 29 (July 1929): 851–55.

"Case Study as a Method of Teaching Nursing." *Trained Nurse and Hospital Review* 88 (January 1932): 61–64.

With J. Jensen, "Medical Nursing Brought Up to Date." *American Journal of Nursing* 46 (August 1946): 539–42.

### BIBLIOGRAPHY

"Deborah Jensen." In *Who's Who of American Women*. 2nd ed. Chicago: Marquis Who's Who, 1962.

"Deborah MacLurg Jensen." Obituary. *American Journal of Nursing* 62 (September 1962): 124.

Jensen, D.M. Papers. Johns Hopkins Nurses' Alumni Association, Baltimore, Md.

Morrin, H.C. "In Memoriam." *Tomorrow's Nurse* 3 (October–November 1962): 4.

"Tribute to Deborah MacLurg Jensen." *Alumnae Magazine* (Johns Hopkins Hospital School of Nursing) 61 (December 1962): 103–04.

Signe S. Cooper

# Florence Merriam Johnson

## 1875–1954

Florence Merriam Johnson made contributions to nursing in public service. She was best known as "the nurse on the docks" who greeted and sent off the thousands of nurses who passed through New York Harbor from the beginning of the First World War until after World War II. Johnson also pioneered unique welfare programs for nurses of the New York chapter of the American Red Cross.

Johnson was born in 1875 in Montclair, New Jersey, the fourth of five children. In her childhood home, religious activities were prominent.

Johnson attended private elementary schools in Montclair and Montclair High School. She graduated from Smith College in 1897. After her graduation, she participated in church and welfare activities. Undeterred by her parents' disapproval of her wish to become a nurse, Johnson took community courses in home nursing and first aid. Then, under the auspices of an organization called the New England Women, she volunteered as Montclair's first visiting nurse, riding a bicycle on her rounds. Her performance in this job paved the way for the hiring of a professional nurse based on the qualifications Johnson had specified. In addition, Johnson had overcome her mother's opposition to her attending nursing school. Johnson was admitted by Annie Goodrich to the New York Hospital School of Nursing. There she was a classmate of Julia C. Stimson, with whom she was in friendly competition. During her training, Johnson was in charge of the surgical and medical dispensary.

Following her graduation in 1908, Johnson served as director of the medical service at Cornell Clinic and as a member of the staff of the Association for Improving the Condition of the Poor. From 1910 to 1915 she established and became director of the social service department of Harlem Hospital in New York City. During the time she was at Harlem Hospital, Johnson's guide, counselor, and friend was Mary E. Wadley, the pioneer organizer of the social service department at Bellevue Hospital. Long after Johnson had gone on to other work, she remained interested in the social service department at Harlem and later became a member of its board of directors.

Johnson left Harlem to teach in the department of nursing and health at Teachers College, Columbia University, where she worked under Adelaide Nutting. Johnson was popular and admired as a teacher, but she decided that personal service, not teaching, was her main interest. In January 1918 she accepted an appointment as director of the bureau of the nursing service of the Atlantic division of the American Red Cross. From that time until her retirement in 1952, Johnson dedicated her life to the Red Cross.

As director of nursing services, Johnson was responsible for the recruitment of nurses for military service. But the most important part of her job, a duty delegated to the Red Cross by the United States War Department, was the mobilization, equipping, interviewing, and embarkation of over 10,000 army, navy, and Red Cross nurses sailing from New York. Johnson not only spoke to nurses about their responsibilities, but also saw them aboard their ships. She scheduled her work according to ship arrivals and departures, regardless of time of day or weather conditions.

It was for her work on the docks during World War I that Johnson was awarded the Florence Nightingale Medal in 1921. She was one of the first recipients of the medal and the only one who had not served overseas. It was felt that her service to those nurses who did serve abroad compensated for her lack of overseas service.

Following World War I, Johnson worked in the Atlantic headquarters of the Red Cross in New York. As the official representative of the United States Public Health Service, she was in charge of informing former service nurses of their welfare and educational benefits. Assisted by Christine Nuno and her staff, Johnson worked to ensure that each nurse had claimed and received the care and benefits designated by federal law for army or navy nurses or by the National Red Cross for nurses under special Red Cross service overseas.

Johnson was also active in establishing nurses' convalescent homes at Bayshore and Babylon, Long Island. At these homes, returning nurses could convalesce and recuperate before reentering civilian life. A close colleague in this endeavor was Alta E. Dines. To identify such nurses in need more effectively, Johnson sent out a questionnaire to every former service nurse. So effective was Johnson's questionnaire that all division nurses were authorized to send out such questionnaires.

In 1922 the Atlantic division was absorbed by the National Red Cross, and Johnson became director of nursing service of the New York chapter. In this position, she encouraged enrollment in the Red Cross by speaking to senior classes and graduate nurses. She also developed a program for sick, aged, lonely, or displaced nurses. Johnson's program provided such services as sick visits, small courtesy gifts, income management, and even burial plots. Johnson also served as secretary of the New York City committee on Red Cross nursing services and chair of the Red Cross state committee.

Johnson's work on the docks continued until the end of her life. She was continually meeting and sending off such groups as military nurses or international nurses coming to the United States for practical experience or study grants. Her service was first conducted under the auspices of the American Red Cross and later the American Nurses' Association, for which she served as chair of the transportation committee from 1931 until 1947.

In 1948 the American Association of Nurses awarded Johnson a special tribute as the official and unofficial hostess of New York Harbor. Johnson was also an honorary member of the Old Internationals Association, a society of those who had graduated from a special one-year study course in London. In 1950 the class of Columbia-Presbyterian School in New York awarded her an honorary membership, accorded to the "best-loved" nurse in New York.

Throughout her career, Johnson was considered to be a born leader with high standards. Her cheerful and buoyant nature was said to have uplifted the morale of those around her. She possessed excellent organizational and executive talents and an unprejudiced mind, and she was selected by Ida F. Butler as an assistant when Butler was acting director of the National Red Cross in Washington, D.C. With the exception of her service in Washington, Johnson remained director of the New York division. In 1949 Johnson was named dean of nursing services, New York chapter, American Red Cross.

After her retirement in 1952, Johnson continued to volunteer at the New York chapter, meeting incoming foreign nurses until the week of her death. She also corresponded with her many friends from all parts of the globe. She shared an apartment in New York City with Mary M. Roberts, editor of the *American Journal of Nursing.*

Johnson died suddenly at age 77 of a cerebral hemorrhage on March 22, 1954, in Mountainside Hospital, Montclair, New Jersey, where she had gone to visit her two sisters. She was survived by her sisters, Mrs. Oliver Huckel and Edith Johnson. To honor Johnson for her unique and devoted service to the Red Cross and to ensure that the welfare programs that she had developed would be continued, the board of directors of the New York chapter of the American Red Cross renamed its benevolent fund the Florence M. Johnson Memorial Fund.

## BIBLIOGRAPHY

American Red Cross Archives. American Red Cross Headquarters, Washington, D.C.

Dock, L. *The History of American Red Cross Nursing.* New York: Macmillan, 1922.

"Florence Merriam Johnson." Obituary. *American Journal of Nursing* 54 (May 1954): 556, 558.

"Florence Merriam Johnson." Obituary. *New York Times*, 23 March 1954 and 25 March 1954.

"Florence Merriam Johnson." Obituary. *Nursing Outlook* 2 (April 1954): 218

Kernodle, P. *Red Cross Nurse in Action.* New York: Harper and Brothers, 1949.

New York Hospital-Cornell Medical Center Archives. Cornell Medical Center, N.Y.

Nursing Education Department Archives. Columbia University, N. Y.

Roberts, M.M. "Nurse on the Docks." *American Journal of Nursing.* 54 (July 1954): 854–57.

Dorothy S. Tao

## Joanna Mabel Johnson

### 1891–1971

Joanna Mabel Johnson was a pioneer industrial (occupational health) nurse. As the first nurse employed by Employers Mutuals Insurance Company (now Wausau Insurance Companies), she helped establish a significant role for nurses employed in industry. She wrote numerous articles and was editor of the first standards and guidelines for industrial nurses.

Johnson was born August 16, 1891, in Shawano County, Wisconsin. Her parents were Thorwald and Julia Wahl Johnson, both of Norwegian ancestry and born in Wisconsin. Johnson was the fourth of six children: Inge, Alfred, Rudolph, Elmer, and Ethel.

Johnson attended Oshkosh State Normal School (now University of Wisconsin-Oshkosh) from 1907 to 1911. A bout with

pneumonia convinced her that she wanted to be a nurse, and she enrolled in St. Mary's Hospital School of Nursing in Rochester, Minnesota. She received her nursing diploma in 1919.

Her first nursing position was supervisor of the surgical unit in Columbia Hospital, Milwaukee, Wisconsin (1919–21). This was followed by general staff nursing in Milwaukee from 1921 to 1922 and in Pasadena, California, from 1922 to 1923.

Johnson's first job as an industrial nurse was in 1923, when she was employed by the Northwestern Malleable Iron Company in Milwaukee. In 1927 and 1928 she did public-health nursing in Waukegan, Illinois.

Johnson came to Employers Mutuals in 1928, the first nurse to be employed by the company and the first person to fill such a post at any insurance company. Her role was to help the firm's policyholder companies to become safer and healthier places to work by preventing disease and accidents, reducing disability, and contributing to the welfare of the employees. She held various titles in the company, including senior nurse, supervising nurse, and director of industrial nursing until 1952, when her title became director of the nursing division.

In this position, Johnson determined the role and function of the nurse. She began by helping companies develop their own health and safety programs, establish record-keeping systems, and initiate first-aid training. She visited injured workers in the hospital and encouraged their employers to give them personal attention as an aid to their recovery.

As the demand for her services increased, the industrial nursing division at Employers Mutuals grew steadily in size and accomplishments. In the 1940s safety education was expanded and the nursing staff enlarged to deal with the influx of inexperienced industrial workers in the war years. Programs were expanded to include health problems such as silicosis, hearing and sight conservation, and back injuries, as well as increased rehabilitation services. The expansion of programs led to an increase in nursing services.

Through the years, Johnson traveled

throughout the United States helping with programs relating to industrial nursing for such organizations as the American Red Cross, the National Society for the Prevention of Blindness, the National Organization for Public Health Nursing, and various visiting nurses' associations.

In addition to her work with nursing groups, Johnson laid the groundwork for the creation of the industrial nursing section of the National Safety Council. Her work was recognized in the May 1953 issue of the section's safety newsletter.

Johnson also was instrumental in organizing various educational programs. She provided consultation and assistance in the development of the industrial nursing and occupational health programs at Case Western University in Cleveland, Wayne State University in Detroit, Marquette University in Milwaukee, Teachers College, Columbia University, in New York City, and the universities of Illinois and Pennsylvania.

Johnson was a participating member of many organizations, including the American Nurses' Association and the Industrial Health Council of the American Medical Association. She was an advisory member of the National Society for the Prevention of Blindness.

A member of the National Safety Council, she served as chair of its nurses' advisory committee (1937–39) and was organizer and general chair of its industrial nursing section from 1944 to 1956. She served as chair of the Chicago Industrial Nurses' Club in 1937 and on the executive committee of the Milwaukee Industrial Nurses' Club.

Much of Johnson's influence on the development of industrial nursing was through her frequent contributions to the nursing literature. For several years she edited *Industrial Nursing*, a newsletter sponsored by Employers Mutuals. Her articles appeared in many nursing journals and in *Industrial Medicine*. She also served as editor of the first published standards and guidelines for industrial nurses, particularly important since so many nurses entered the field with little understanding of their role in industry. In addition, during her career she gave nu-

merous speeches, including many to congresses of the National Safety Council and to nursing groups in various parts of the country.

In her lifetime, Johnson received several honors and awards. The April 1953 issue of *Nursing World* was dedicated to her in honor of her 25th anniversary with Wausau Insurance Companies. In 1962 she received an award of appreciation from the Los Angeles County Heart Association.

But perhaps her greatest honor came after her death, when the Joanna Johnson Professional Chair in Occupational Health Nursing was established in 1978 at the University of Wisconsin-Milwaukee School of Nursing. The nation's first professional chair in occupational health nursing, it was funded by Wausau Insurance Companies.

Johnson retired in 1954 and moved to California. However, she became bored with retirement and returned to Wisconsin in 1955 to become executive director of the Green Bay Visiting Nurse Association. After a short time, she retired from this position and returned to Pasadena, California, where she lived until her death on November 30, 1971. She was buried in Mountain View Cemetery in Pasedena.

## PUBLICATIONS BY JOANNA MABEL JOHNSON

### ARTICLES

"Nursing Problems when Farming Becomes an Industry." *Public Health Nursing* 23 (February 1931): 81–82.

"Nursing Service for Industry." *Industrial Medicine* 5 (April, May, June 1936): 183–85, 256–68, 295–97.

"Health Service and Accident Prevention Program." *Trained Nurse and Hospital Review* 98 (January 1937): 59–60.

"Prevention of Accidents in the Restaurant Business." *Public Health Nursing* 29 (May 1937): 308–9.

"Industrial Hygiene and the Nurse." *Industrial Medicine* 7 (July 1938): 385–88.

"You and Your Annual Report." *Nursing World* 127 (April 1953): 28–40.

### BIBLIOGRAPHY

Cooper, S.S. "Joanna Johnson." In *Wisconsin Nursing Pioneers*. Madison, Wis.: University of Wisconsin-University Extension, 1968.

"Joanna M. Johnson ... An Employers Original." *Good People* (Employers Insurance of Wausau), March 1978, 4.

Johnson, J. Papers. Corporate Archives. Wausau Insurance Companies, Wausau, Wis.

"Nursing Director Has Anniversary." *Coverage* (Employers Insurance of Wausau), April 1948, 15.

Streigel, B. "Joanna M. Johnson: Industrial Nursing Pioneer." *Nursing World* 127 (April 1953): 27.

Signe S. Cooper

# Julia Crystine Kasmeier

## 1899–1979

Julia Crystine Kasmeier's most valuable contributions to nursing were those in the realm of nursing education. She was employed in hospital management and in a school of nursing for several years. However, most of her accomplishments came as a result of her position of education secretary for the Board of Nurse Examiners (BNE) for the state of Texas for 36 years.

Kasmeier was born May 27, 1899, in Florence, Alabama, to John and Betty Steinbeck Kasmeier. She had at least one sister and one brother. She was raised in the Roman Catholic faith and steadfastly practiced that religion until her death.

Kasmeier attended St. Mary's Academy in Beeville, Texas. After high-school graduation, she entered Santa Rosa Hospital School of Nursing in San Antonio, Texas, in 1919 and was graduated in 1922. While a student, she caught the attention of Sister Fedalia Foley, the director of the school, who saw considerable promise in the young woman. Sister Foley helped promote Kasmeier and direct her energies.

After graduation, Kasmeier became departmental supervisor at Santa Rosa Hospital. From 1923 to 1925 she was administrative night supervisor. She then became educational director of the Santa Rosa Hospital School of Nursing, where she remained until 1928.

In 1928 the position of educational secretary for the Board of Nurse Examiners for the state of Texas was vacated by A. Louise Dietrich. Although Kasmeier met neither of the age nor experience requirements, she was appointed to the position in 1928.

The position she assumed was a poorly defined one. In addition, the accreditation requirements for schools of nursing were low. As a result, Kasmeier embarked upon a crusade to improve the status of nursing education in Texas. The first years of her tenure were spent making a thorough assessment of the status of nursing education in the state. Radical decisions, such as recommending the closing of extremely poor schools, were made only when necessary for the well-being of students. However, in keeping with the Goldmark Report of 1923, a total of 77 of the worst nursing schools throughout the state were closed between 1928 and 1932. For the remaining schools, Kasmeier set a definite plan of action into motion.

The written regulations enacted by the BNE were upgraded periodically and disseminated to schools throughout the state so they would know the standards expected, but not necessarily required. As she visited every school in the state yearly, Kasmeier set reasonably attainable goals for schools to work toward. Her recommendations were written into her annual report of the schools, and she personally reviewed the report with each hospital administration and school superintendent.

Feeling both a vocational and personal need for a formal academic background, Kasmeier attended summer school at Incarnate Word College in San Antonio, Texas. By 1939 she had earned a degree in biology from that college.

Throughout the 1930s, Kasmeier kept close track of the state's unemployment and underemployment of nurses, a situation resulting from the Depression. As a result of her findings, she endeavored to reduce and improve the supply of nurses.

As early as 1933, the BNE encouraged the affiliation of nursing schools with junior colleges. Such a move had distinct advantages to the hospital owning the school and to its students. It decreased the cost to the hospital training school by eliminating the need for maintaining science laboratories, and it ensured that students entering nursing schools were prepared to undertake college work. By 1936 three schools in Texas had begun such affiliations.

In 1938 Kasmeier began to attend the annual conventions of the Texas Hospital Association. Her continued presence at these conventions made nursing visible, and Kasmeier was given an honorary lifetime membership in the association.

Political astuteness was one of Kasmeier's strongest traits. This ability enabled her to manipulate the system to achieve her ends in raising the educational standards of nursing schools in the state.

In the late 1930s, the University of Texas began accrediting schools of nursing. The graduates of those schools accredited were automatically granted 30 semester hours credit at the university should they choose to pursue a degree there. By 1939 fourteen schools met the university's accreditation standards. Kasmeier openly encouraged schools to strive for and maintain that accreditation. Simultaneously, she encouraged nurses whom she had identified as showing promise to return to college to earn degrees.

During the 1940s, educational standards were still an issue. The American Red Cross rejected some graduates from Texas-accredited schools. In addition, nursing needs for World War II put many pressures on nursing. The Texas BNE tried to comply with requests from nursing's collective leadership to increase the number of nurses in the nurse pool while maintaining standards. Despite the pressures of the war years, Kasmeier completed her master of arts degree at George Peabody College for Teachers in Nashville, Tennessee, in 1943.

Kasmeier remained educational secretary for the BNE until her retirement in 1964. For a retirement gift, individuals within the Texas Hospital Association gave her a trip to Ireland. Kasmeier retired to San Antonio, where Catherine Maley, another nurse, resided with her.

Kasmeier died in 1979. She was buried in Shanence, Oklahoma, next to her father and mother.

## BIBLIOGRAPHY

Board of Nurse Examiners for the State of Texas. *Curriculum and Requirements for Accredited Schools of Nursing.* Austin, Tex., 1925.

Board of Nurse Examiners for the State of Texas. Educational secretary's personal report of time and expense 1931–1932. Appended to minutes, 4 June 1932. Austin, Tex.

Board of Nurse Examiners for the State of Texas. Minutes, 1928–1964. Austin, Tex.

Cole, A.L. Interview with author. Temple, Tex., 2 February 1983.

Committee on Education of the National League for Nursing Education. *A Standard Curriculum for Schools of Nursing.* New York: National League for Nursing Education, 1917.

Committee on Education of the National League for Nursing Education, *A Curriculum for Schools of Nursing.* New York: National League for Nursing Education, 1927.

Frank, C.M. Interview with author. San Antonio, Tex., 4 May 1982.

*The General Laws of the State of Texas, 1923.* Austin: A.C. Baldwill and Sons, 1923.

Maley, C. Interview with author. San Antonio, Tex., 4 May 1982.

Sherry, B. Eulogy for Julia C. Kasmeier, 1979. Austin, Tex. Copy given to author by B. Sherry.

"Julia Crystine Kasmeier." Texas League of Nursing Archives. Southwest Center for Nursing History, University of Texas at Austin School of Nursing.

"Julia Crystine Kasmeier." *Who's Who of American Women.* Chicago: A.N. Marquis, 1958–59.

Eleanor L.M. Crowder

# Sister Elizabeth Kenny

## 1886-1952

Sister Elizabeth Kenny was an Australian nurse who devised a treatment for polio that became the subject of worldwide controversy. Although the development of polio vaccines has lessened the demand for her treatment, she made a lasting impact by drawing public attention to the value of physiotherapy in medical practice.

Sister Kenny was born September 20, 1886, in Warialda, New South Wales, Australia, to Michael and Mary Moore Kenny. Her father was an Irish immigrant veterinary surgeon, and there were six girls and five boys in the family. One of the boys was very weak, and when Sister Kenny was 14, she studied the composition, development, relationship, and function of muscles in an effort to help him gain strength. His improvement sparked a career interest that was encouraged by a physician acquaintance, Aeneas McDonnell.

Sister Kenny graduated from the nursing school of St. Ursula's College in 1902 and entered practice as a visiting nurse in the Clifton area of New South Wales. A lover of the outdoors and a skilled horsewoman, she made her rounds on horseback and exercised her nursing resourcefulness in homes miles removed from doctors, hospitals, and medicines.

At age 23, Sister Kenny was called to Pilton Hills, where she encountered a two-year-old girl whose limbs were fixed in grotesque positions. McDonnell, whom she wired for advice, diagnosed infantile paralysis and told her there was no known cure. Sister Kenny was unaware of the common medical practice to immobilize the affected areas. After unsuccessfully trying to relieve the patient by applying bags of heated salt and linseed poultices, she dipped strips of wool blanket in hot water and wrapped them around the child's limbs. This treatment brought relief.

Sister Kenny reasoned that she had succeeded because infantile paralysis was not a paralysis but a spasm of the muscles. The muscles were not dead, just temporarily contracted, and the nerves that controlled the muscles were also alive and able to resume their function. Thus the treatment should be to massage and exercise the weakened muscles—the opposite of what physicians were doing at the time.

Soon after this experience, Sister Kenny opened a small clinic for infantile paralysis victims. However, her work was interrupted by World War I. In the Spring of 1914 she enlisted as a nurse in the transport service that shuttled troops between Australia and Europe, served four years, and made 15 round trips. It was here that "Sister" was added to her name, as it was to those of all Australian nurses who achieved the rank of naval officer. During the war years, Sister Kenny invented and patented an improved stretcher and a device for stabilizing wounded bodies in transport. One of her legs was shattered by shrapnel, and overwork caused a heart condition that resulted in a series of heart attacks.

Following her first heart attack in 1919, Sister Kenny traveled to England, Ireland, and continental Europe to regain her health. Returning home, she took up her old work and was successful in treating a child who suffered from cerebral diplegia, a paralysis of both legs. She wrote on this subject and in 1937 published *Infantile Paralysis and Cerebral Diplegia: Methods Used for the Restoration of Function*. In 1933 she opened an infantile paralysis clinic in Townsville, Queensland.

For two decades, Sister Kenny fought to have her treatment accepted by the medical community. She met with constant rebuffs. When she explained her theories to a group of physicians in Brisbane, she was ridiculed. However, popular demand caused the government health department to open the Elizabeth Kenny Clinic and Training School in Brisbane in June 1934. From 1934 to 1937, she helped set up clinics in both Australia and England. Always she insisted that a physician examine each patient before and periodically during treatment. She stressed that her method was not a cure, but a means of relieving the painful aftereffects of the disease.

Sister Kenny's success with the English niece of an Australian physician led to an invitation to demonstrate her methods in England in 1937. A committee of British physicians appointed to study them observed that her cases had been cured. However, the Australian Royal Commission issued a 120-page statement against the treatment. In the face of extensive debate on the subject in the Australian House of Parliament, the government continued to maintain the Kenny Clinic. Australian opposition was relaxed somewhat after the British reports became known.

In 1940 Sister Kenny was invited to the United States to demonstrate her methods at the Mayo Clinic and at Children's Hospital in St. Paul, Minnesota. The president of the University of Minnesota was sufficiently impressed that he invited her to deliver a series of lectures at the university. Though skeptical, some of the physicians believed that the cause of pain associated with acute anterior poliomyelitis might result from a muscle spasm that could be helped by her techniques. With the cooperation of the university's department of orthopedic surgery, the city of Minneapolis opened the Elizabeth Kenny Institute in 1942. Sister Kenny regarded her treatment not as a cure but as a palliative, a view shared by many of her physician supporters interested in preventing deformities.

Her acceptance in Minnesota forced others to reevaluate their opposition. The National Foundation for Infantile Paralysis offered her support, the *Journal of the American Medical Association* encouraged further experimentation, and fame and honor followed in rapid succession. The American Congress of Physical Therapy awarded her a gold key, the University of Rochester and New York University gave her honorary doctorates, a biography appeared, and in 1946 her status as a nurse heroine was established by the movie *Sister Kenny*, starring Rosalind Russell.

Though a 1944 report based on about 650 cases failed to support her theories, it also failed to detract from her reputation. It did, however, cut off funds from the National Foundation for Infantile Paralysis. A new foundation, the Sister Kenny Foundation, was established by supporters. Based in Illinois and with Bing Crosby as national chair, it began a national fundraising campaign. Clinics using her methods opened in Pontiac, Michigan; Buffalo, New York, Jersey City, New Jersey; and El Monte, California.

However, the foundation's accounting techniques, over which Sister Kenny had no control, were not rigorous. Funds were diverted by some of the fund-raisers, and in 1952 one of them, Henry Von Morpurgo, was convicted of diverting funds for his personal use. The scandal eventually forced the foundation to close.

Sister Kenny had returned to Australia in 1950 and was untouched by the scandal. Throughout her adult life and in spite of health problems, she maintained a grueling schedule, often working 18-hour days. She accepted no salary, fees, or grants for her work, but met her modest needs with royalties on her two wartime patents and her books. In spite of the controversy over the success of her treatment, she had managed to bring physical therapy into the mainstream of medical and nursing practice.

Sister Kenny died November 30, 1952, of cerebral thrombosis in Toowoomba, Queensland, Australia. During the last few weeks of her life, she was completely paralyzed on her right side and was unable to talk.

## PUBLICATIONS BY SISTER ELIZABETH KENNY

*Infantile Paralysis and Cerebral Diplegia: Methods Used for the Restoration of Function.* Sydney, Australia: Angus & Robertson, 1937.

*The Treatment of Infantile Paralysis in the Acute Stage.* Mpls-St. Paul: Bruce Publishing, 1941.

With J. Pohl. *The Kenny Concept of Infantile Paralysis and Its Treatment.* MPLS-St. Paul: Bruce Publishing, 1942.

With M. Ostenso. *And They Shall Walk.* New York: Dodd, Mead, 1943.

## BIBLIOGRAPHY

"Crosby Says He Let Polio Fund Use His Name." *New York Times*, 11 April 1952, p. L-9.

"Convicted in Polio Fraud," *New York Times*, 27 April 1952, p. 61.

Kalisch, P.A., and B.J. Kalisch. *The Changing Image of the Nurse.* Menlo Park, Calif.: Addison-Wesley, 1987.

"Sister Kenny Dies in Her Sleep at 66." Obituary. *New York Times*, 30 November 1952.

Thomas, H., and D.L. Thomas. "Sister Elizabeth Kenny." In *50 Great Modern Lives*. Garden City, N.Y.: Hanover House, 1946

Alice P. Stein
Vern L. Bullough

# Alice Magaw Kessel

## 1860–1928

The history of anesthesia care in the United States has as its foundation the involvement of nurses who specialized in its delivery. Between 1860 and 1900, surgeons began to demand a higher quality of anesthesia care, and specially trained nurses soon began to replace a largely unskilled body of anesthesia providers. Alice Magaw Kessel brought both the Mayo Clinic and the nurse anesthesia specialty acclaim at a time when the poor outcome often associated with anesthesia was a major concern of surgeons.

Born in Rochester, Minnesota, in 1860, the daughter of a grocer, Kessel later attended the school of nursing at Woman's Hospital in Chicago. She apparently was following the example of her good friend, Edith Graham. Edith and her sister Dinah Graham had both completed their nursing training at the Woman's Hospital in Chicago. Upon returning to Rochester as the first trained nurses in town, the Grahams soon assumed the responsibility for the administration of anesthesia at St. Mary's Hospital after receiving instruction from William W. Mayo. After the Grahams left the hospital, Kessel began working for William Mayo and his brother, Charles, and they trained her in anesthesia to the extent that they could. She was mostly self-taught.

Kessel used an "open-drop" technique of administering both chloroform and ether, although ether was the agent preferred both by Kessel and the surgical staff at the Mayo Clinic. The method she employed was developed in 1897 by the German military surgeon, Johannes Friedrich August von Esmarch. Though neither she nor the Mayos were the first to use this open-drop Esmarch mask technique, it was her remarkable proficiency that popularized it in the United States.

In 1900 Kessel reported in the *St. Paul Medical Journal* on 1,092 patients for which she had used the Esmarch mask with two thicknesses of stockinette. Ether was used in 674 cases, chloroform was used in 245, and in 173 cases both agents were used. These anesthetics were administered without accident or serious results. By 1904 the total had increased to 11,000 cases and to 14,000 by 1906 without a death directly attributable to anesthesia.

In her writings, Kessel stressed the proper technique for slow ether administration and provided great detail about the induction of ether anesthesia and the management of the airway. In addition, she provided observations about the choice of specific anesthetic techniques based on specific surgical and patient considerations. Her writings illustrated the importance that she attached to individualized care.

Kessel felt strongly that patient preparation was an important element of the anesthesia experience. Unlike the common practice of anesthetizing patients in another location and transporting them to the operating room in the anesthetized state, patients at the Mayo Clinic were anesthetized in the operating room. It was felt that this had a positive psychological effect on the patients, who could actually see their surgeons and the operating room.

Early in its history, St. Mary's Hospital had become a meeting place for surgeons who had come to observe the outstanding skill of the Mayo surgeons. These surgeons also had the opportunity to witness Kessel's skillfully conducted anesthesia. Word of the Mayos' use of nurses as anesthetists spread, and testimonials appeared in the medical literature both in the United States and Great Britain.

By 1900 the Mayos began to seek another individual who could act as the anesthetist for Charles Mayo, who had shared the abilities of Kessel with his brother William. This began the expansion of the Mayo Clinic's staff, which continued to rely on nurses for the provision of anesthesia care. In 1905 Mary Hines was added to the anesthesia staff; she was trained by Kessel and became Charles Mayo's anesthetist when Kessel married physician George Kessel about 1908. After her marriage, Kessel left nursing.

Throughout her career at the Mayo Clinic, Kessel reported her findings, usually in medical journals. In 1901 for example, she reported on the efficacy of nitrous oxide as a supplement to ether anesthesia.

Kessel died in 1928.

## PUBLICATIONS BY ALICE MAGAW KESSEL

"Observations on 1092 Cases of Anesthesia from Jan., 1, 1899 to Jan. 1, 1890." *St. Paul Medical Journal* 2 (1900): 306.

A Report of 245 Cases of Anesthesia by Nitrous Oxide Gas and Ether." *St. Paul Medical Journal* 3 (1901): 231.

"Observations Drawn from an Experience of Eleven Thousand Anesthesias." *Transactions of the Minnesota Medical Association* (1904): 91–102.

"A Review of Over Fourteen Thousand Surgical Anesthesias." *Surgery, Gynecology, and Obstetrics* 3 (1906): 795.

## BIBLIOGRAPHY

Clapesattle, H. *The Doctors Mayo*. Minneapolis, Minn.: University of Minnesota Press, 1941.

The *Collected Papers by the Staff of St. Mary's Hospital, Mayo Clinic*. 1905–1909, edited by M.H. Mellish. Philadelphia: W.B. Saunders, 1911.

Pougiales, J. "The First Anesthetizers at the Mayo Clinic." *Journal of the American Association of Nurse Anesthetists* 38 (June 1970): 235–41.

Thatcher, V. *A History of Anesthesia with Emphasis on the Nurse Specialist*. Philadelphia: J.B. Lippincott, 1953.

Thomas E. Obst

# Dita Hopkins Kinney
## 1854–1921

One of the vanguard of contract nurses employed during the Spanish-American War period, Dita Hopkins Kinney became the first superintendent of the Army Nurse Corps in March 1901.

The daughter of C.T. and Myra Burtnett Hopkins, Kinney was born September 13, 1854, in New York City. She grew up in California and was graduated from Mills Seminary, now Mills College, in California. In 1874 she married Mark Kinney, whose early death in 1878 left her with a young son to support. She graduated from the Massachusetts General Hospital Training School for Nurses in August 1892.

Following graduation, Kinney lectured throughout New England, taught home nursing for the Young Women's Christian Association of Boston. She also trained young women to be nursing assistants. Kinney subsequently became superintendent of the Long Island Almshouse at Boston Harbor from 1892 to 1896, and for six months in 1887 of the City and County Hospital of St. Paul, Minnesota. She gained recognition for her attack on fraudulent nursing schools. In 1898 she worked at the French Hospital in San Francisco.

Although the Spanish-American War ended in August 1898, Kinney joined the army in September as a paid contract nurse to care for soldiers who were victims of malaria, typhoid, and dysentery. She was immediately assigned to General Hospital, the Presidio, in San Francisco. Six days later, at the request of the Oakland, California, Red Cross Society, she resigned to take charge of that organization's convalescent home for soldiers. When the unit closed, she returned to French Hospital for eight months.

Dissatisfied with the work, Kinney signed a new army contract in October 1899 and was placed in charge of the hospital operating room until the following October. On the recommendation of the head nurse, commanding officer, and chief surgeon of the division, she was selected as chief nurse for a proposed hospital in Nagasaki, Japan. The plan never materialized, and she was assigned to the United States Army Hospital at Fort Bayard, New Mexico.

In August 1900 Kinney was transferred to the Office of Surgeon General George M. Sternberg in Washington, D.C., and assigned to the staff of acting assistant surgeon Anita Newcomb McGee. McGee was a practicing gynecologist and vice-president general of the Daughters of the American Revolution (DAR). Sternberg was indifferent to administrative details and had cooperated with conservatives to block the recruitment of female nurses. However, when tropical fever mounted in Cuba, Sternberg acquiesced to McGee's suggestion that members of the DAR screen nurse recruits for the army.

The call for nurses far exceeded Sternberg's expectations, and systematic direction of the nursing division was paramount. Most contract nurses were subject to army control, but others had been paid by private sources or were under the auspices of voluntary organizations, which created difficult administrative problems.

Following the war, the president appointed a commission to investigate the conduct of the war department. The commission's findings indicated that the high mortality had been the result of mismanagement, the inability of the army to recruit 6000 or more men qualified to perform patient-care duties, the thwarting of efforts to include trained female nurses in the military setting, and the lack of knowledge and use of adequate field sanitation measures. The scandal resulted in a campaign to promote better medical and nursing organization in the armed forces. The outcome was the Army Reorganization Act of 1901, which reorganized the medical department of the army.

At the request of the surgeon general, McGee wrote the section of the bill that established the Army Nurse Corps (Female) under the direction of a nurse superintendent, a graduate of a two-year hospital training program. Kinney, McGee's nominee, was appointed first superintendent of the Army Nurse Corps on March 15, 1901.

The reorganization act had no provision for rank, but did authorize a reserve corps for nurses with a record of six months' satisfactory military service. In June 1901 there were 37 names on the reserve list; by December only six names remained. Nurses were uninformed or indifferent to the corps because of the undefined status of the army nurse, which was below that of a private. Moreover, nurses were not accepted socially by officers and their wives and were tolerated in the army as a questionable good. The low salary and the requirement that nurses be graduates of hospital training schools, not two-year training schools, caused the corps to stagnate for the next ten years.

As superintendent, Kinney had little power. Her general superivsory duties were subject to the orders of The Surgeon General. She could not change the rules regarding nurses' duties, nor could she designate and evaluate chief nurses. She could not visit, inspect, or communicate with nurses without the approval of the Surgeon General.

In spite of this, Kinney made many recommendations to improve the status of the army nurse. On one occasion, she revised and upgraded a proficiency examination for promotion to chief nurse. The Surgeon General curtly rejected it; promotion was to be contingent upon the qualities of tact, efficiency, and respect rather than the ability to answer questions about mathematics, chemistry, and therapeutics.

Kinney attempted to establish an indoctrination course for nurses to familiarize them with army protocol, regulations, and military correspondence in order to observe and evaluate them before permanent assignment to the Corps. She sought authorization to visit nurses stationed in the Philippines in order to promote coordination between the nurses and staff headquarters in Washington, D.C. None of this was accomplished. Her aspirations for nurses' pensions, pay increases, and standardization of the uniform and laundry service were never realized.

Kinney served as superintendent under three surgeons general without notable incident until Surgeon General George H. Torney requested Kinney's resignation. Torney stated that Kinney's greatest failing had been her inability to recruit nurses for the army reserve for emergency service. However, plans to replace Kinney had probably been made as early as 1906. Kinney had never been told that the quality of her work was unsatisfactory, nor could she control the dwindling reserve list, given the poor salary and working conditions and the low social status of the army nurse. Kinney submitted her resignation in July 1909, protesting that she had been denied authorization to visit army hospitals. Her successor, Jane Delano, secured cumulative leave, first-class transportation, and improved living quarters for nurses, all of which had been recommended by Kinney.

Following her resignation, Kinney took a course in hospital administration at the Massachusetts General Hospital and secured an appointment as superintendent of the Addison Gilbert Hospital in Gloucester, Massachusetts. In March 1912 she resigned due to failing health.

Kinney was described as having a good sense of humor and a remarkable talent as a teacher. Her creative endeavors included the writing of several books. During World War I, she taught home nursing, despite a serious heart impairment, for the Penobscott, Maine, Red Cross and taught at the Eastern Maine General Hospital.

Kinney died in Bangor, Maine, on April 16, 1921. She was buried beside her husband in Trinity Cemetery in New York City.

## PUBLICATIONS BY
## DITA HOPKINS KINNEY

"Dr. Anita Newcomb McGee and What She Has Done for the Nursing Profession." *Trained Nurse* 26 (March 1901): 129–34.

"Some Christmas Days in Army Hospitals." *American Journal of Nursing* 2 (December 1901): 155–59.

"Nursing in the United States Army and the Legislation Effected in Connection with." *Trained Nurse* 27 (December 1901): 337–40; 28 (January 1902): 27–31.

"The Trained Nurse in the Philippines." *Trained Nurse* 29 (August 1902): 99–101.

"The Ounce of Prevention." *American Journal of Nursing* 3 (December 1902): 183–85.

"The Year's Progress in Army Nursing." In *Report to the Tenth Annual Convention of the National League of Nursing Education*, 7 October 1903, 32–36.

"Some Questionable Nursing Schools and What They Are Doing." *American Journal of Nursing* 5 (January 1905): 224–29.

"Inoculation Against Typhoid Fever." *Trained Nurse* 43 (July 1909): 5–9.

## BIBLIOGRAPHY

Addison Gilbert Hospital Board of Trustees. Records, September 1910–12. Addison Gilbert Hospital, Gloucester, Mass.

Aynes, E.A. *From Nightingale to Eagle*. Englewood Cliffs, N.J.: Prentice-Hall, 1973.

Blanchfield, F.A., and M. Standlee. "Organized Nursing and the Army in Three Wars." Manuscript. United States Army Center of Military History, Washington, D.C.

Cosmos, G.A. *An Army for Empire*. Columbia, Mo.: University of Missouri Press, 1971.

"Dita Hopkins Kinney." Obituary. *Bangor Daily News*, 17 April 1921.

Dock, L. et al. *History of American Red Cross Nursing*. New York: Macmillan, 1922.

Fitzpatrick, M.L. ed. *Prologue to Professionalism*. Bowie, Md.: Robert J. Brady, 1983.

"Further Information about D.H. Kinney." Letter to editor. *American Journal of Nursing* 21 (November 1921): 122.

Kernodle, P.B. *The Red Cross Nurse in Action, 1882–1948*. New York: Harper and Row, 1949.

Kinney, D. Red Cross membership application form, May 1917. American Red Cross, Washington, D.C.

Maxwell, P.E. "History of the Army Nurse Corps 1775–1948." Manuscript. United States Army Center of Military History, Washington, D.C., 1976.

McGee, A.N. "Legislation for Army Nurses." *Trained Nurse and Hospital Review* 26 (April 1901): 207–9.

National Archives. Comment, Surgeon General William H. Forwood to Dita Kinney, 1902. Record Group 112, E 26.

National Archives. Letter, J.W. Seligman & Co., 11 March 1901. Record Group 112, E26.

National Archives. Letter, Surgeon General Sternberg to secretary of war, 25 January 1902. Record Group 112, E26.

National Archives. Letter, Surgeon General Torney to Secretary of War Jacob M. Dickinson, 4 February 1910. Record Group 112, E 26.

National Archives. Memorandum, Dita Kinney to Surgeon General William H. Forwood, June 1902. Record Group 112, E 26.

National Archives. Memorandum, Surgeon General Torney for assistant and chief clerk of war department, 3 February 1910. Record Group 112, E 26.

National Archives. Statement, Dita Kinney to surgeon general, 27 October 1903. Record Group 112, E 26.

Roberts, M.M. *The Army Nurse Corps: Yesterday and Today*. Report prepared for surgeon general, United States Army Medical Department, Historical Unit, Washington, D.C., 1957.

Shields, E.A. "A History of the United States Army Nurse Corps (Female) 1901–1937." Ph.D. diss., Teachers' College, Columbia University, 1980.

Shields, E.A., ed. *Highlights in the History of the Army Nurse Corps*. Washington, D.C.: United States Government Printing Office, 1981.

Sleeper, R. Letter to S.C. Gholson, 4 March 1948. Francis A. Countway Library of Medicine, Boston, Mass.

Eileen M. Danis
Rosemary T. McCarthy

# Ellen Newbold LaMotte

## 1873–1961

Ellen Newbold LaMotte was an early public-health nurse who achieved her greatest fame as a writer and as a crusader against opium. She began writing in World War I while serving as a nurse in Belgium with the French army and thereafter continued to publish widely.

LaMotte was born in Louisville, Kentucky, on November 7, 1873, the daughter of Ferdinand and Ellen Newbold LaMotte. She graduated from the Training School of Johns Hopkins Hospital in 1902, after which she joined the Instructive Visiting Nurse Association of Baltimore. She participated in the development and organization of nurses for the Baltimore Health Department, and from 1910 to 1913 she served as superintendent of the tuberculosis division. From this experience she wrote a text, *The Tuberculosis Nurse*.

With the outbreak of World War I, LaMotte served as a nurse with the French army in Belgium during 1915 and 1916. She published her account of this experience as the book *Backwash of War: The Human Wreckage of the Battlefield as Witnessed by an American Hospital Nurse*.

In 1916 after the publication of her book, she left wartime nursing to travel throughout the Far East, where she became aroused by the sale and use of opium. Through a series of magazine articles and by her books she sought to alert the public. Among her books on this subject are *Peking Dust* and *The Ethics of Opium*. A series of articles she wrote for the *Nation* was issued separately as *Opium at Geneva: Or How the Opium Problem is Handled by the League of Nations*. In all her books she tried to inform the public of the dangers of opium.

LaMotte also wrote fiction, and one of her stories was included in a 1918 collection of the best short stories of that year. In 1930 she received the Lin Tse Hsu Memorial Medal from the national government of China for her work in trying to limit opium sales. She also received a special order of merit from the Japanese Red Cross.

LaMotte died March 2, 1961, and was buried in the Oakhill Cemetery in Washington, Delaware. She was survived by a brother, Ferdinand LaMotte of Wilmington, Delaware.

## PUBLICATIONS BY ELLEN NEWBOLD LAMOTTE

### BOOKS

*The Tuberculosis Nurse*. New York: G.P. Putnam's Sons, 1915.

*Backwash of War: The Human Wreckage of the Battlefield as Witnessed by an American Hospital Nurse*. New York: G.P. Putnam's Sons, 1916.

*Peking dust*. New York: Century, 1919.

*The Opium Monopoly*. New York: Macmillan, 1920.

*Civilization: Tale of the Orient*. New York: Century, 1922.

*The Ethics of Opium*. New York: Century, 1922.

*Snuffs and Butters*. New York: Century, 1925.

*Opium at Geneva: Or How the Opium Problem is Handled by the League of Nations*. New York: N.P., 1929.

### ARTICLES (SELECTED)

"Golden Stars." *Century* 98 (October 1919): 787–94.

Elinor Delight Gregg     Carrie May Hall

Lydia Eloise Hall     Ester Voorhees Hasson

Alma Cecelia Haupt

Nellie Xenia Hawkinson

Mary Eugenie Hibbard    May Shiga Hornback

Thelma Marguerite Ingles    Debora MacLurg Jensen

Joanna Mabel Johnson    Dita Hopkins Kinney

Mathild Helen Krueger Lamping

Rose Hawthorne Lathrop (Mother Alphonsa)

Eleanor Lee

Mary Ashton Rice Livermore

Laura Rebekah Logan

Clara Louise Maass

Anita Newcomb McGee

Pearl L. McIver    M. Helena McMillan

Mary Eliza Mahoney

Ada Mayo Stewart Markolf

Stella S. Mathews

Anna Caroline Maxwell

"America and the Opium Trade." *Atlantic Monthly* 129 (June 1922): 732–39.

"Opium and England." *Nation* 119 (September 3, 1924): 232–34.

"Deadlock at Geneva." *Nation* 120 (February 4, 1925): 113–114.

"Opium Smoking in the Far East." *Nation* 127 (December 5, 1928): 610–12.

"Coronation in Abyssinia." *Harper's Magazine* 162 (April 1931): 574–84.

"Manchuko and the Opium Trade." *Nation* 138 (February 28, 1934): 246–47.

## STORIES AND FICTION (SELECTED)

"Desert Owl." *Atlantic Monthly* 139 (January 1927): 81–86.

"Hidden Treasure." *Atlantic Monthly* 142 (August 1928): 234–39.

### BIBLIOGRAPHY

Pennock, M.R. *Makers of Nursing History.* New York: Lakeside Press, 1940.

"LaMotte, Ellen Newbold." *Who Was Who in America, 1961–1968.* Vol. 4., Chicago: A.N. Marquis, 1968, p. 551.

Vern L. Bullough

# Mathild Helen Krueger Lamping

## 1869–1948

Mathild Helen Krueger Lamping was a pioneer public-health nurse in Wisconsin and North and South Carolina. Prior to the entry of the United States into World War I, she headed a contingent of Red Cross nurses sent to Serbia, where they gave outstanding service in a typhus epidemic.

Lamping was born August 21, 1869, in Wolf River Township, Winnebago County, Wisconsin. She was the oldest child of August and Louisa Williams Krueger, both natives of Germany. The other children were Emilee, Otto, Emma, and John. The family lived on a farm.

Lamping was graduated from Neenah High School and later enrolled in the Illinois Training School in Chicago, receiving her diploma in 1897. She also attended Teachers College, Columbia University from 1902 to 1904 and from 1913 to 1914.

Employment records reveal that from 1907 to 1913 she served as principal of the Farrand Training School for Nurses, associated with the Harper Hospital in Detroit. During her tenure, entrance requirements were raised to two years of high school, and student enrollment increased. Arrangements were made for student affiliations with other agencies and institutions, including the Detroit Visiting Nurse Association. While she was in Detroit, Lamping was among the nurses who worked for the passage of the first Michigan nurse practice act.

In 1914 Lamping headed a contingent of American Red Cross nurses sent to Serbia, where they provided service under difficult conditions in an improvised hospital. They worked in unsanitary locations lacking modern equipment and nursed surgical patients and wounded soldiers. Lamping developed typhus and was sent home in 1915. She was later awarded the Cross of Mercy and Diploma by King Alexander of Yugoslavia for her service to the country.

Not one to avoid challenges, Lamping next was appointed county nurse in Dunn County, Wisconsin—the first nurse to hold this position. In her first report to the county board of supervisors, she noted that she had conferred with ministers, physicians, educators, health officials, club women, and the press about the health needs in the county. In less than two months, she had visited 53 rural schools and examined 1,466 pupils to detect health problems. She had also given talks to the school children and to various community groups.

At the conclusion of this public-health demonstration project, she was appointed superintendent of the La Crosse, Wisconsin, Lutheran Hospital. She had previously been appointed to the committee of nurse examiners (predecessor of the present state board of nursing) and served as its president from 1916 to 1919. At that time, the committee members were responsible for writing the state licensing examination questions, administering the examination, and registering the state's nurses. This was accomplished without paid staff, and as president Lamping carried much of the responsibility for these tasks. In addition, committee members were called upon to confer with appropriate groups on the advisability of establishing schools of nursing in their communities.

During World War I, Lamping served for a short time as a public-health nurse at a military cantonment at Waco, Texas. In 1918 she was appointed field secretary for the central division of the Red Cross Nursing Service.

Throughout her professional career, Lamping was active in the American Nurses' Association (ANA), often serving as a delegate to biennial conventions. She was ANA secretary (1913–1914) and on its board of directors (1914–1917). She was a member of several ANA committees and represented the association on the nursing committee of the Town and Country Nursing Service of the American Red Cross. She continued her active participation in the ANA for some time after her marriage, when she was no longer employed in nursing.

She married Lt. Thomas Lamping on March 1, 1919, and moved to Illinois. She maintained her interest in her profession and served for four years on the board of directors of her alma mater, the Illinois Training School for Nurses. She was a member of the Infant Welfare Association of Oak Park and a life member of the Art Institute of Chicago.

Lamping and her physician husband lived in Illinois until 1946, when they moved to Neenah, Wisconsin. He died shortly after that, and Lamping then lived with her niece, Ruth Falvey. She died on March 17, 1948, of complications following a hip fracture resulting from a fall at home. She was buried in Oak Hill Cemetery, Neenah. She was survived by a niece.

## PUBLICATIONS BY MATHILD KRUEGER LAMPING

### ARTICLES

"Personal Experience in Serbia." *American Journal of Nursing* 15 (August 1915): 1012–16.

"First Report on Pioneer Health Work in Rural Districts in County." *Dunn County News*, 7 December 1916.

### BIBLIOGRAPHY

Cooper, S.S. "Mathild Krueger—World War I Heroine." In *Wisconsin Nursing Pioneers*. Madison, Wis.: University of Wisconsin-University Extension, 1968.

Deans, A., and A.L. Austin. *The History of the Farrand Training School for Nurses.* Detroit: Alumnae Association of the Farrand Training School, 1936.

Dock, L.L., et al. *History of American Red Cross Nursing.* New York: Macmillan, 1922.

Kernodle, P.B. *The Red Cross Nurse in Action, 1882–1948.* New York: Harper and Brothers, 1949.

"Mathild Krueger, Rural Health Nurse, Dunn County." *Wisconsin Medical Journal* 15 (December 1916): 208.

"Mathild Krueger Lamping." Obituary. *American Journal of Nursing*, 48 (May 1948): 46 adv.

"Mathild Krueger Lamping." Obituary. *Milwaukee Journal*, 19 March 1948.

Schryver, G.F. *A History of the Illinois Training School for Nurses, 1880–1929.* Chicago: Illinois Training School, 1930.

Signe S. Cooper

## Rose Hawthorne Lathrop (Mother Alphonsa)

### 1851–1926

Rose Hawthorne Lathrop (Mother Alphonsa) was a humanitarian who introduced to America the hospice concept of nursing care for terminally ill patients. She founded the Servants of Relief for Incurable Cancer, whose mission was to make as comfortable as possible the last days of destitute cancer patients. In order to create an effective framework for the group's activities, New York's Roman Catholic archbishop Michael A. Corrigan permitted the women to become lay sisters of the Dominican Third Order. Lathrop, who became Mother Alphonsa in 1900, supervised the establishment of nursing homes where she tried to create a home-like atmosphere for the terminally ill.

The youngest daughter of author Nathaniel Hawthorne and Sophia Peabody Hawthorne, Lathrop was born May 20, 1851, near Lenox, Massachusetts. In November her father, who never stayed in one place very long, moved his family to West Newton and when Lathrop was one year old to Concord, where he purchased Wayside, the former home of Amos Bronson Alcott, Louisa May Alcott's father. In addition to the Alcotts, the Hawthornes' friends included many prominent literary figures of the day, such as Ralph Waldo Emerson, Henry David Thoreau, Herman Melville, and Henry Wadsworth Longfellow.

By the time Lathrop was born, her father's literary reputation was established. In 1852 when his Bowdoin College friend Franklin Pierce ran for president of the United States, Hawthorne assisted by publishing a campaign biography of the candidate. After Pierce won the election, he appointed Hawthorne the American consul in Liverpool in 1853. Two-year-old Lathrop went to England with her parents, her nine-year-old sister Una, and her seven-year-old brother Julian. When Hawthorne resigned his post in 1857, the family spent over one year in Rome.

Although Lathrop had only a few years of formal schooling, she had lived in several countries and was imbued with the literary and cultural tradition of her parents. With the help of governesses, they taught her at home.

The Hawthorne family returned to the United States in 1860, just before the outbreak of the Civil War. After Nathaniel Hawthorne's death in 1864, Lathrop's mother sold Wayside and in 1868 took the family to Dresden, Germany. There Lathrop met her future husband, George Parsons Lathrop. By 1870 the Hawthornes had moved on to London, where Sophia Hawthorne died in 1871.

Lathrop surprised her friends and family by getting married September 11, 1871. The couple returned to Massachusetts, where George Lathrop worked for the *Atlantic Monthly* magazine and later became editor of the Boston *Sunday Courier*.

Though brought up as a Unitarian, Lathrop had become interested in Catholicism during her stay in Italy in 1857, and when her only child Francis was born in November 1876, she baptized him in the Catholic church. After the child died at the age of five, the Lathrops moved to New York City, where they became Catholics. However, religious conversion did not alleviate their marital problems. They frequently quarreled and lived apart from each other, and in 1895 they separated permanently.

During the years of her marriage, Lathrop had published short stories, a poetry book, *Along the Shore*, and in collaboration with her husband, *A Story of Courage: Annals of the Georgetown Visitation Convent*. However, after the couple's separation, Lathrop decided to devote her life to a cause. A concern for human suffering had been a legacy from her father, and when her friend Emma Lazarus died of cancer, Lathrop became aware of the devastation the disease caused. She learned that destitute cancer patients often died in the poorhouse, which added to their misery. Hospitals did not provide charity beds for the poor with incurable cancer, and public interest in the disease lagged. Lathrop decided to dedicate her life to helping these patients.

Lathrop asked to serve as a nurse for three months in the New York Cancer Hospital, later Memorial Hospital. While working on the women's ward, she learned that the physicians carefully monitored the condition of their patients. When they pronounced cases inoperable, the hospital discharged patients who were unable to pay for further care.

After Lathrop finished her training period in 1896, she rented a few rooms in the slums of New York City. She began her work by making house calls and changing the dressings of patients who came to her flat, but she soon realized that what she needed most was space for the homeless. Using the royalties from the *Memories of Hawthorne*, which she had published in 1897, she moved to a larger apartment where she could house seven needy women. Seeking publicity, she soon gained support. Friends and others who recognized the Hawthorne name gave her money and help in caring for the patients. Women who came to work as volunteers for her began calling themselves the Servants of Relief for Incurable Cancer.

Lathrop gained a permanent associate and lifelong co-worker in December 1897 when Alice Huber joined the group. However, Lathrop soon realized that affiliation with a religious organization was the best way to maintain her work. After George Lathrop's death in 1898, she and Huber began dressing in uniforms similar to a religious habit. In 1899 Archbishop Corrigan gave them permission to become lay sisters of the Dominican Third Order. The next year, when they were given permission to wear the Dominican habit, Lathrop became Mother Alphonsa, taking her name from St. Alphonsus Liguori, an Italian who worked among the rural poor.

In 1899 the group purchased a house, which they called St. Rose's Free Home, large enough for 15 resident patients. They continued to expand their work, and two years later the community purchased Rosary Hill Home in Westchester County, New York. Lathrop moved to the new facility where, with 60 rooms on nine acres of land, the order could extend its services to men as well as to women. During 1901 the charity took care of 65 patients. In 1912 St. Rose's Free Home moved to a new building with room for 75 cancer victims; Rosary Hill had 40 beds and, in addition, housed the novitiate of the order.

From the beginning, Lathrop had insisted that the Servants of Relief for Incurable Cancer devote themselves not only to nursing the patients, but also to making them as comfortable and happy as possible. She encouraged entertainment to keep patients from becoming depressed and took special pride in the fact that the homes served good, well-cooked food. She allowed no shrinking on the part of any nurse from close contact with the patients and no experimental surgery or radium treatments to be performed on incurable patients. The nurses' mission was to alleviate feelings of being unloved and abandoned and to lessen physical suffering as much as possible.

The National Institute of Social Science

gave Lathrop its medal in 1914; in 1925 her father's college, Bowdoin, bestowed on her an honorary master of arts degree. One year later, the New York Rotary Club awarded her its gold medal for outstanding service to humanity.

On July 9, 1926, Lathrop died at Rosary Hill of a cerebral hemorrhage. She was buried at the Gate of Heaven Cemetery in Hawthorne, and she was survived by her brother Julian. The Servants of Relief for Incurable Cancer continued her work after her death.

## PUBLICATIONS BY ROSE HAWTHORNE LATHROP

### BOOKS

*Along the Shore.* Boston: Ticknor and Company, 1888.

With G.P. Lathrop. *A Story of Courage: Annals of The Georgetown Visitation Convent.* Boston: Houghton, Mifflin, 1894.

*Memories of Hawthorne.* Boston and New York: Houghton, Mifflin, 1897.

*Christ's Poor.* Hawthorne, N.Y.: Servants of Relief for Incurable Cancer, 1901–04.

*Reports.* Hawthorne, N.Y.: Servants of Relief for Incurable Cancer, 1920–26.

### ARTICLES

"At Heart." *Harper's Monthly* 80 (January 1890): 311.

"Cheerful View of a Hard Problem." *Catholic World* 68 (February 1899): 659–69.

"The Hawthornes at Lenox, Told in Letters by Nathaniel and Mrs. Hawthorne." *Century Magazine* 27 (November 1894): 86–98.

"Pure Hearts." *Harper's Weekly* 34 (May 31, 1890): 430.

"Some Memories of Hawthorne." *Atlantic Monthly* 77 (February 1896): 173–86; (March): 373–87; (April): 492–507; (May): 649–60.

"Troth." *Harper's Monthly* 85 (August 1892): 341–50.

### BIBLIOGRAPHY

Burton, K. *Sorrow Built a Bridge: A Daughter of Hawthorne.* New York: Longmans, Green, 1937.

"The Death of Mother Lathrop." *Catholic World* 123 (August 1926): 699–700.

Hawthorne, J. "A Daughter of Hawthorne." *Atlantic Monthly* 142 (September 1928): 372–77.

Hinding, A., A.S. Bower, and C.A. Chambers, eds. *Women's History Sources: A Guide to Ar-*

*chives and Manuscript Collections in the United States.* New York: R.R. Bowker, 1979.

"Honor to Mother Alphonsa." *Catholic World* 123 (May 1926): 269.

Johnson, A., ed. *Dictionary of American Biography*, Vol. I. New York: Scribner's, 1928.

Klinkhamer, M.C. "Lathrop, Mother Mary Alphonsa." In *Notable American Women: A Biographical Dictionary, 1607–1950*, Vol. 2, edited by E.T. James. Cambridge, Mass.: Belknap Press of Harvard University, 1971.

Maynard, T. *A Fire Was Lighted: The Life of Rose Hawthorne Lathrop.* Milwaukee, Wis.: Bruce Publishing, 1948.

Walsh, J.J. *Mother Alphonsa: Rose Hawthorne Lathrop.* New York: Macmillan, 1930.

Mary Van Hulle Jones

# Eleanor Lee

1896–1967

On the occasion of her retirement, Eleanor Lee was described as a scholar, educator, author, historian, and administrator. For nearly 40 years, she was responsible for the educational program at Columbia University's department of nursing at Presbyterian Hospital in New York.

Lee was born January 5, 1896, in Jamaica Plain (Boston), Massachusetts, to Daniel David and Mabel Morse Lee. She was the second child; she had an older sister, three younger sisters, and a younger brother. Her father had trained as a physician but due to increasing deafness had become a veterinarian. All six of the Lee children attended the Windsor school in Boston. From there Lee went on to Radcliffe College in Cambridge, Massachusetts, from which she received her A.B. degree in 1918. She began her nursing education in the special three-month wartime program organized for college graduates at Vassar College. She finished the course in 1918. The Vassar College Training Camp for Nurses produced several of the most influential leaders of nursing in America.

After leaving the Vassar camp, Lee went on to complete her nursing studies at the School of Nursing at Presbyterian Hospital in New York City, from which she graduated in 1920. She remained at Presbyterian Hospital as head nurse on a surgical floor from January to September 1921.

Early in her nursing career, Lee had developed an interest in nursing education and in September 1921 she moved to Boston to become an instructor at the Peter Bent Brigham Hospital. In 1924 she returned to Presbyterian Hospital and Teachers College, Columbia University, as a nursing instructor and educational director, holding these two appointments until 1937.

Lee laid the foundation for the eventual affiliation agreement between Presbyterian Hospital School of Nursing and Columbia University, which was finally signed in 1937. Thereafter, all nursing students were admitted as university students enrolled in one of three different academic nursing programs. Lee was appointed as an assistant professor of nursing, a position she held until 1955. In 1950 she also took on the additional position of acting executive officer of the department of nursing at Columbia-Presbyterian Hospital. (The department of nursing was part of the Faculty of Medicine at Columbia University.)

In June 1955 Lee was appointed professor of nursing and executive officer of the Department of Nursing (Faculty of Medicine) at Columbia University and director of nursing at Presbyterian Hospital. She was the fourth person to lead the school of nursing at Presbyterian Hospital. In 1958 her title was changed to Associate Dean (Nursing), Faculty of Medicine. She served in this position until her retirement in June 1961. She then was appointed the first professor emeritus of nursing at Columbia University.

Lee was responsible for the school's education program for nearly 40 years (1924–61). Due to her interest in curriculum planning and development, many new educational opportunities became available for nursing students. After 1957 all nursing students became candidates for the baccalaurate degree from Columbia University.

Lee also made important contributions to the war effort during World War II. In 1943 and 1944 she took a leave of absence from Columbia University to serve as director of the nurse recruitment program of the Army and Navy Nurse Corps for the New York chapter of the American Red Cross. She also directed the college recruitment program of the National Nursing Council, bringing many college women into nursing who might not otherwise have considered nursing as a career.

Lee was active on various Presbyterian Medical Center and Nursing School Alumnae Association committees. In 1953 she was chair for the 25th anniversary celebration of the Columbia-Presbyterian Medical Center, and in 1954 she was chair of the program committee for the bicentennial conference held by the Department of Nursing Education, Teachers College, and the Faculty of Medicine, Columbia University.

Throughout her career, Lee was active as an officer and member of numerous professional organizations. She served as treasurer and vice-president of the New York Counties Registered Nurses Association. She was for ten years a member of the Board of Nurse Examiners of the University of the State of New York. Lee also was a member of the committee on historical source materials in nursing of the National League for Nursing (1924–67).

Beyond her primary interest in nursing education, Lee built a reputation as an author and editor. She coedited two widely used textbooks for nurses, *Essentials of Nursing* and *Lippincotts' Quick Reference Book for Nurses* and was the coauthor with Helen Young of the 1948 edition of *Essentials of Nursing*. Lee published several articles on nursing curriculum in professional journals.

To the general public, Lee was perhaps best known as a historian. She taught nursing history for many years and was the curator of the school archives. She wrote the first histories of the Presbyterian Hospital School of Nursing, published in 1942 and in 1967. She organized the extensive collection of Florence Nightingale memorabilia, given to the school of nursing by Hugh Auchincloss in May

1932. She was appointed the collection's curator, serving in that capacity for many years.

Lee spent much of her spare time with her family and friends in Boston and maintained an apartment in Cambridge during her tenure in New York City. Her summers were spent at the Lee family complex in Falmouth, Massachusetts, where she enjoyed gardening and beach life with her ten nieces and nephews and their parents. Her closest nursing friend was Margaret Elliott, an alumnae and colleague on the Columbia University-Presbyterian Hospital faculty. In addition, she served as the permanent secretary of the class of 1918, Radcliffe College; chair of the personnel committee and member of the board of managers of the Home for Aged Women, Boston; and on the membership committee, the College Club of Boston.

In 1943 Lee was elected to membership in Phi Beta Kappa. She received the Columbia University Bicentenial Medal in November 1954 for her service as chair of the Department of Nursing Fund of Columbia's bicentennial fund for the medical sciences. On her retirement, the Eleanor Lee Scholarship Fund for nursing students was established and endowed in her honor.

Lee died on May 31, 1967, of a heart attack while visiting Maxwell Hall, Columbia-Presbyterian School of Nursing. A memorial service was held on June 15, 1967, at Pauline A. Hartford Memorial Chapel, Presbyterian Hospital and burial was at Mount Auburn Cemetery, Boston. She was survived by two sisters and ten nieces and nephews.

## PUBLICATIONS BY ELEANOR LEE

### BOOKS

*Essentials of Nursing by Helen Young*. New York: G.P. Putnam's Sons, 1942: 2nd ed., 1948. Title changed to *Lippincott's Quick Reference Book for Nurses*. Philadelphia: Lippincott, 1950, 7th ed. 1955, 8th ed., 1962.

*History of the School of Nursing of the Presbyterian Hospital, New York 1892–1942*. New York: G.P. Putnam's Sons, 1942.

With H. Young. *Essentials of Nursing*. New York: G.P. Putnam's Sons, 1948.

With H. Young. *Lippincott's Quick Reference Book for Nurses*. Philadelphia: J.B. Lippincott, 1950, 1955, 1962.

*Report on Public Health Nursing Field Work in Basic Baccalaureate Programs*. New York: Columbia University, Faculty of Medicine, Department of Nursing, 1960.

*Neighbors 1892–1967: A History of the Department of Nursing, Faculty of Medicine, Columbia University 1937–1967 and Its Predecessor The School of Nursing of the Presbyterian Hospital, New York 1892–1937*. New York: Columbia University Press, 1967.

## ARTICLES

"Block System." *American Journal of Nursing* 31 (August 1931): 935–39.

"Year's Survey of Ward Teaching." *American Journal of Nursing* 32 (April 1932): 445–51.

"Examinations in Nursing Arts." *American Journal of Nursing* 37 (November 1937): 1253–56.

"A Florence Nightingale Collection." *American Journal of Nursing* 38 (May 1938): 555–61.

## BIBLIOGRAPHY

Buckley, Mrs. John H., niece of Eleanor Lee. Telephone interviews, July 9 and 10, 1987.

Clappison, G.B. *Vassar's Rainbow Division, 1918: The Training Camp for Nurses at Vassar College*. Lake Mills, Iowa: Graphic Publishing Company, 1964.

Columbia University, Faculty of Medicine, Department of Nursing. Records, 1937–67. Columbia University, N.Y.

"Eleanor Lee, 71, Nursing Director." Obituary. *New York Times*, 1 June 1967.

"Helen Young." *National League of Nursing Education: Biographic Sketches, 1937–1940*. New York: National League of Nursing Education, 1940.

Lee, E. Papers. Schesinger Library, Radcliffe College, Harvard University, Cambridge, Mass.

"Miss Eleanor Lee Retires." *Quarterly Magazine*, Columbia University-Presbyterian Hospital School of Nursing Alumnae Association 56 (August 1961): 18–21.

"Miss Lee's Appointment." *Quarterly Magazine*, Columbia University-Presbyterian Hospital School of Nursing Alumnae Association 50 (August 1955): 24–26.

Pettit, H. "A 'Neighbor' Passes Away. Eleanor Lee—Working Till the Last for the School She Loved." *Alumnae Magazine* (Columbia University-Presbyterian Hospital School of Nursing Alumni Association) 62 (Summer 1967): 103–09.

Presbyterian Hospital School of Nursing Records, 1918–37. Presbyterian Hospital School of Nursing, N.Y.

Taggard, Mrs. Henry P., sister of Eleanor Lee. Telephone interviews, July 9 and 10, 1987.

Joan LeB. Downer

## Mary E. Lent
### 1869–1946

An innovative leader in the field of public-health nursing, Mary E. Lent served as superintendent of the Visiting Nurse Association of Baltimore. She also directed the wartime effort against communicable diseases.

Born in New York State on October 24, 1869, Lent graduated from the Johns Hopkins School of Nursing in 1895. Her first position was as head nurse at the Johns Hopkins Hospital. She joined the staff of the Instructive Visiting Nurse Association of Baltimore in 1898 as a head nurse and in October 1903 was promoted to superintendent of nurses, a position she retained for 13 years.

During that 13-year period, the work of the association grew and broadened in many directions. The development of tuberculosis nursing was one of its most important activities. Another was the establishment of classes in hygiene and home nursing. Lent realized the great need that existed for teaching health to young women in industry. She visited department stores and other industrial concerns in Baltimore and gained the permission of employers to speak to groups of women workers. The classes she organized were similar to the training given by the Red Cross today.

Another innovative program was carried out by Lent in connection with the Public Athletic League of Baltimore. Before being allowed to take part in the athletics programs, all young men were required to undergo a medical examination. These examinations revealed many health problems, including serious cardiopulmonary defects.

In 1916 Lent spent six months in Los Angeles as organizer for the nursing division of the public health department. The plan she developed was adopted by the city and served as a model for other cities as well. Its original feature was the provision of general nursing in the districts, in addition to specialized supervision.

When the federal public health service decided to appoint a general supervising nurse, Lent was chosen at the recommendation of the Red Cross. In November 1917 she became an officer of the U.S. Public Health Service and started on a tour of inspection of public-health nursing in the various sanitary zones throughout the country. The concentration of troops and the establishment of war industries created special health problems, and sanitation zones surrounding mobilization and training camps were established to prevent the spread of communicable diseases. The role of the public health nurses assigned to these zones was to educate the public in preventing the spread of disease, and during the first nine months of her service, Lent traveled nearly 12,000 miles, cooperating with local agencies in an effort to achieve this goal.

By January 1919 the war was over, and Lent resigned her position. She had organized the nursing activities in 37 zones and directed a staff of 200 nurses. The surgeon general praised the work of the nurses, and Ella Phillips Crandall, executive secretary of the National Organization of Public Health Nursing, stated that Lent's work was the greatest single war service rendered by the organization to the government and the public.

The author of many articles on public-health nursing, Lent also held the office of associate secretary and financial secretary with the National Organization for Public Health Nursing. In addition, she helped raise endowment funds for the Johns Hopkins School of Nursing.

Wearied by years of intense mental and physical effort, Lent retired in 1922 and opened an antique shop in New York City. She continued to encourage students to develop their talents, not only to enrich their own lives and broaden their horizons, but to add quality to the nursing care of their patients. She died at her home in Wallington, New York, on November 11, 1946.

## PUBLICATIONS BY MARY E. LENT

"True Function of the Tuberculosis Nurse." *British Journal of Nursing* 41 (November 1908): 367–69.

LaMotte, Ellen N. "The Present Status of Tuberculosis Work Among the Poor." *Maryland Medical Journal* 52 (April 1909): 147–60.

"The Organization of District Work." *American Journal of Nursing* 9 (September 1909): 967–77.

"The History and Development of Public Health Nursing." *Pacific Coast Journal of Nursing* 13 (March 1917): 148–53.

"Public Health Nursing Service in Extra-Cantonment Zones." *Public Health Nurse Quarterly* 10 (July 1918): 264–75.

"The Fundamental Importance of Bedside Care in Public Health Nursing." *Public Health Nurse* 12 (September 1920): 774–81.

## BIBLIOGRAPHY

Alan Mason Chesney Medical Archives. Johns Hopkins Medical Institutions, Baltimore, Md.

Brainard, A.M. *The Evolution of Public Health Nursing.* Philadelphia: W.E. Saunders, 1922.

Nutting, M.A. *A History of Nursing.* New York: G.P. Putnam's Sons, 1935.

Roberts, M.M. *American Nursing: History and Interpretation.* New York: Macmillan, 1954.

"Mary E. Lent, a Pioneer in Public Health Nursing." *Johns Hopkins Nurses Alumnae Magazine* 46 (1947): 60–62.

Lilli Sentz

# Mary Ashton Rice Livermore

## 1820–1905

A dynamic speaker and prolific writer Mary Ashton Rice Livermore achieved a permanent place in the history of nursing because of her relief work during the Civil War. Her book on Civil War nursing experiences has become a classic.

Livermore was born in Boston, Massachusetts, December 19, 1820, the fourth of six children to Timothy Rice and Zebiah Vose Glover Ashton Rice. She was the first of their children to survive infancy. Her parents provided a strict Calvinist Baptist background, which affected her values and goals throughout her life. She received her basic education in Boston public schools and later attended Miss Martha Whiting's Female Seminary in Charleston, Massachusetts. She graduated from the seminary in 1836 and remained there for two more years, teaching French, Latin, and Italian.

Livermore then spent three years (1839–1842) in the South tutoring the children on a plantation near Ridgeway, North Carolina. This experience influenced her attitudes toward slavery and stimulated her strong abolitionist beliefs, and she became a staunch supporter of emancipation. Her later writings often reflected her outrage and despair over the conditions of slavery as she perceived them during her teaching experience.

After returning north, Livermore taught in a private school in Duxbury, Massachusetts, sponsored by a local church and under the direction of her future husband, the Reverend Daniel Parker Livermore, a Universalist minister. The couple married on May 6, 1845. Daniel Livermore strongly supported women's rights and encouraged his wife's activities outside the home. The couple had three daughters, two of whom survived to adulthood, Henrietta White and Maria Elizabeth. Livermore continued to work in church and social activities with her husband.

The family moved to Chicago in 1857, relocating for a new church ministry for Daniel Livermore and to purchase a church newspaper for the western area of the Universalist church. Livermore assisted her husband in writing and editing the newspaper for 11 years before the Civil War. She gradually became aware of the plight of women in nineteenth-century America and developed strong beliefs in suffrage for women.

During the Civil War years, Livermore served the Western Sanitary Commission. Her work for this group called her to tour hospitals, reorganize supply systems, and review the needs of injured soldiers and other war victims. In this era before the establishment of the American Red Cross, providing sanitary supplies and medical equipment required the women of the Sanitary Commission to raise the money themselves before the materials could be purchased and shipped. Livermore and her colleagues made speaking tours, initiated letter-writing campaigns, and organized fairs to raise funds for war relief.

Livermore met and worked with many volunteer nurses whom she described in her war memoir, *My Story of the War*. The book described hospital life and the activities of nurses involved in the Union cause. Illustrated with prints of actual clinical settings and specific activities of nurses, the book proved to be enormously popular. After the war, many of the nurses mentioned continued to serve the veterans and victims left handicapped by their injuries.

In the postwar period, Livermore returned to her literary and public-speaking activities but devoted increasing energy to the suffrage movement. Her war experiences had changed her opinions about the progress of and the need for higher education for women.

Livermore retired from lecturing and public life in 1895. She continued her private social life back in her native New England and enjoyed extensive family relationships. The death of her husband in 1899 left a void, and soon her physical stamina began to fail. She died on May 19, 1905, of bronchopneumonia and heart failure. She was buried in Melrose, Massachusetts in the Wyoming Cemetery. She was survived by two daughters and several grandchildren.

## PUBLICATIONS BY
## MARY ASHTON RICE LIVERMORE
### BOOKS

*Pen Pictures; or, Sketches from Domestic Life.* Chicago: S.C. Griggs, 1862.

*Thirty Years Too Late: A True Story: And One in a Thousand.* Boston: Longwood and Brooks, 1878.

*What Shall We Do with Our Daughters?* Boston: Lee and Shepard, 1883.

*My Story of the War.* Hartford, Conn.: A.D. Worthington, 1889.

*The Story of My Life.* Hartford, Conn.: A.D. Worthington, 1899.

### ARTICLES

"Women: Superfluous." *Chautauguan* 7 (1888): 216.

"Homes Builded by Women." *Chautauguan* 7 (1888): 408, 473.

"Womanhood, Co-Operative, in the State." *North American Review* 153 (1896): 283.

"Wrongs of Women: Centuries of Dishonor." *Arena* 1 (1890): 82.

### EDITED JOURNALS

*The New Covenant* (as Assistant Editor), 1858–1869. A Universalist publication printed in Chicago.

*The Woman's Journal,* 1870–1872. Published in Boston by the Women's Suffrage Organization.

*The Agitator,* 1869–1870, when it merged with *The Woman's Journal.* Published in Chicago by the Illinois Women's Suffrage Association.

## BIBLIOGRAPHY

Brockett, L.P., and M.C. Vaughn. *Woman's Work in the Civil War: A Record of Heroism, Patriotism and Patience.* Philadelphia: Seigler, McCurdy, 1867.

Livermore, M. Letters. Kate Field Collection. Boston Public Library, Boston, Mass.

Livermore, M. Letters. Sophia Smith Collection. Smith College. North Hampton, Mass.

"Mary Ashton Rice Livermore." Obituary. *Boston Transcript,* 23 May 1905.

"Mary Ashton Rice Livermore." Obituary. *New York Times,* 24 May 1905.

"Mary Ashton Rice Livermore." Obituary. *New York Tribune,* 24 May 1905.

"Mary Ashton Rice Livermore." Obituary. *The Woman's Journal,* 27 May 1905.

"Mary Ashton Rice Livermore." Obituary. *Arena* 34 (August 1905): 185–88.

Riegel, R. "Mary Ashton Rice Livermore." In *Notable American Women 1607–1950: A Biographical Dictionary,* edited by E.T. James. Cambridge, Mass.: 1971, pp. 410–13.

Linda E. Sabin

## Laura Rebekah Logan
### 1879–1974

Laura Rebekah Logan made major contributions to nursing education as the director of various schools of nursing. She is recognized as responsible for the emergence of the first five-year baccalaureate diploma nursing program in the United States, which was established at the University of Cincinnati in 1916. Logan was the second professor of nursing in the United States.

Logan was born on September 15, 1879, in Amherst Point, Nova Scotia, Canada. Her family was of Scottish, English, and Welsh descent. In addition to Laura, there were four boys in the family. On the family farm, all the children enjoyed outside activities, and they were influenced by kindly discipline and religious service. Logan received her childhood education at Amherst Academy, a private school.

In 1901 Logan received a B.A. degree in English from Acadia University in Wolfville, Nova Scotia. She decided to enter nursing school so that she could eventually become a doctor. In 1904 she received her diploma from Mt. Sinai Hospital School of Nursing in New York City. While working as a private-duty nurse to earn money to study medicine, Logan decided to remain in nursing. She earned a B.S. degree in hospital economics from Teachers College, Columbia University, in 1908. Later, Logan would receive three honorary degrees: an M.A. degree (1929) and a D.C.L. degree (1938) from Acadia University and a D.Sc. degree (1954) from the University of Cincinnati.

Logan chose to pursue a career in nursing education. Her first position was that of instructor and supervisor at Mt. Sinai Hospital in New York City (approximately 1907–11). She became the superintendent of Hope Hospital and the principal of the Hope School of Nursing in Ft. Wayne, Indiana (1911–14). From 1914 to 1924 Logan was in Ohio, first as the director of nursing at the school at Cincinnati General Hospital and later as the first director and professor at the University of Cincinnati School of Nursing and Health. Appointed in 1916, Logan is believed to have been only the second professor of nursing in the United States (the first being M. Adelaide Nutting).

Logan's efforts resulted in the creation of the University of Cincinnati's nursing school, which claimed the first five-year combined nursing and liberal-arts course leading to a B.S. degree and a diploma in nursing. In 1924 Logan was recruited as the dean of the Illinois Training School in Chicago in the hopes that she would also create a university nursing program there. Although this did not occur, Logan did remain as dean when the Cook County School of Nursing was formed in 1929. Logan left this position in 1932.

After an extended visit to Europe where, under the auspices of the Rockefeller Foundation, she studied schools of nursing, Logan reportedly spent two years caring for her ill mother. In 1936 she accepted the position of director of the nursing service and principal of the school of nursing at Flower-Fifth Avenue Hospital in New York City. Not finding an atmosphere conducive to what she thought she needed to do, Logan stayed less than one year. Remaining on the East Coast, Logan next took the position of director of nursing at Boston City Hospital (1937–40).

In 1941 Logan returned to the Midwest as director of the nursing services and the school of nursing at St. Louis City Hospital. She retired from her career in this position in 1953. In addition to her regular positions, Logan also taught nursing courses in summer sessions at Stanford University (1924), the University of Chicago (1925), and Marquette University (1927).

Logan was widely recognized as a leader in nursing education, and her expertise was utilized to improve schools of nursing and their faculties. The schools where Logan was in charge were known for their advanced curricula. These programs included the early introduction of neurologic and mental-health nursing, communicable-disease nursing, tuberculosis nursing, and public-health nursing. Nurses who worked with Logan at the University of Cincinnati and the Illinois Training School eventually became leaders in nursing, acknowledging Logan as a

mentor. This group included Katharine Densford, Gladys Sellew, Ella Best, and Alma Gault.

Logan's major organizational involvement was with the National League of Nursing Education. In addition to serving as president from 1922 to 1925, Logan also held the positions of secretary, first vice-president and board member from 1918 until 1935. Another long-term assignment was that of editor for the department of nursing education for the *American Journal of Nursing* from 1920 until 1929. Logan also was a member of the national committee of the Red Cross Nursing Service, the National Committee for the Grading of Nursing Schools, the National Organization of Public Health Nurses' education committee, the American Nurses' Association's committee on the Florence Nightingale International Foundation, and the advisory committee of nurses to the U.S. Veterans Bureau.

Early in her career, Logan was the president of the Ohio State Nurses' Association and the Ohio League of Nursing Education. During World War I, she recruited nurses for base hospital 25, was chair of the state and local branch of the nursing section-woman's committee of the Council of National Defense, and recruited 600 women for the U.S. Student Nurse Reserve.

In her retirement, Logan enjoyed painting landscapes and portraits in oils and visiting and corresponding with her friends. In 1954 she was honored by the University of Cincinnati when the nurses' residence was named Logan Hall. Logan's publications appeared in the *American Journal of Nursing*, *Lancet Clinic*, *Modern Hospital*, *Hospital Management*, and *Hospital Progress*.

Logan died July 16, 1974, in a nursing home in Sackville, Nova Scotia, Canada. She was survived by a niece, Elizabeth Logan.

## PUBLICATIONS BY LAURA REBEKAH LOGAN

### BOOKS

*National League of Nursing Education: Annual Report 1923 and Proceedings of the 29th Convention.* Baltimore: Williams & Wilkins, 1923.

### ARTICLES

"Retrospect and Prospect." *American Journal of Nursing* 23 (August 1923): 917–23.

"A Review of the Progress of Nursing and Nursing Education in 1924." *Modern Hospital* 24 (January 1925): 18–22.

"The Goal of Nursing Education." *American Journal of Nursing* 25 (July 1925): 539–44.

"A Program for the Grading of Schools of Nursing." *American Journal of Nursing* 25 (December 1925): 1005–13.

"Cooperative Arrangements between Schools of Nursing." *American Journal of Nursing* 31 (August 1931): 961–66.

"The Cook County School of Nursing, Chicago, Illinois." In *Methods and Problems of Medical Education.* New York: Rockefeller Foundation, 1932.

"A School of Nursing Faculty." *American Journal of Nursing* 43 (May 1943): 477–83.

### BIBLIOGRAPHY

Cook County Hospital Archives, Personnel files. Cook County Hospital, Chicago.

Densford, K.J. *Laura R. Logan.* New York: National League of Nursing Education, 1940.

Densford, K.J. "Laura R. Logan." In *Makers of Nursing History,* edited by M.R. Pennock. New York: Lakeside, 1940.

Densford, K.J. "Laura R. Logan, A.M., R.N." *Trained Nurse and Hospital Review* 91 (July 1933): 23–24.

Dreves, K.D. Papers. University of Minnesota Archives. University of Minnesota, Minneapolis, Minn.

"Laura Logan Dies." *American Journal of Nursing* 74 (September 1974): 1722, 1724.

"Who's Who in the Nursing World, Laura Logan." *American Journal of Nursing* 22 (August 1922): 913.

Laurie K. Glass

# Clara Louise Maass

## 1876–1901

As a contract army nurse during the Spanish-American War, Clara Louise Maass committed herself to serving humanity. Motivated to reduce the suffering caused by yellow fever, Maass died after she volunteered to be bitten by a mosquito in an experiment to prove the cause of yellow fever.

Maass was born on June 28, 1876, in East Orange, New Jersey, to Robert and Hedwig Maass. The oldest of nine children, (four boys and five girls), she assumed a serving role early in life. Her father, a hat maker, was barely able to support the family. While still in grammar school, Maass left home to become a mother's helper. After completing three years of high school, she took a full-time job at the Newark Orphans' Asylum and sent her earnings home to her mother.

In 1893 Newark German Hospital started the Christina Trefz Training School for Nurses, and Maass entered as a probationer at age 17. She completed the two-year program in 1895. For the next three years, Maass provided private-duty nursing at German Hospital and in 1898 was appointed a head nurse.

When the Spanish-American War was declared in 1898, Maass was quick to volunteer as a contract nurse for the United States Army. She was sent to the field hospital of the Seventh U.S. Army Corps at Jacksonville, Florida, to Savannah, Georgia, and later to Santiago, Cuba. She nursed soldiers with malaria, typhoid fever, and dysentery until her honorable discharge in February 1899.

Maass returned to Newark German Hospital until November 1899, when she again responded to a call for contract nurses. This time, she was sent to the Philippines to care for soldiers with smallpox, typhoid fever, and yellow fever. She worked in the Philippines until May 1900, when she became ill and was sent home to recuperate.

During the Spanish-American War, more soldiers died of yellow fever than were killed in battle. As part of an effort to determine the cause of yellow fever, William Gorgas, Havana sanitary officer, sent out a call for volunteer nurses. Knowing firsthand of the devastation caused by yellow fever, Maass volunteered in October 1900.

Maass worked as a civilian for the Cuban government and was assigned to Las Animas Hospital in Havana. She wrote to tell her mother of her engagement to a businessman from New York, however, nothing further is known about her fiance.

In the spring of 1901, hospital workers who were considered not immune to yellow fever were sought as volunteers in experiments to determine if the mosquito was the carrier for the dread disease. Six Spanish immigrants had been bitten, and two had died in the experiments. Maass, the only American woman and the only nurse to participate, was paid $100 for volunteering. She sent the money to her mother, telling her that she expected to contract a mild form of yellow fever and thereafter be immune and able to nurse other yellow-fever victims.

As a result of the experiment, Maass contracted a mild form of the illness, from which she quickly recovered. Physicians did not believe that she could have become immunized by such a mild attack, and she agreed to be bitten again on August 14, 1901. She contracted a virulent case of yellow fever and died on August 24, 1901, at the age of 25. Her death proved that the mosquito was the carrier of yellow fever, and no further experiments were conducted.

Maass was buried initially in Havana, but the U.S. Army moved her body to the Fairmount Cemetery in Newark. Two years after her death, Congress granted her mother a pension in recognition of her daughter's service.

For many years, the sacrifice of this young nurse went largely unheralded. In 1923 Leopoldine Guinther became the superintendent of Newark Memorial (formerly German) Hospital. Intrigued by the portrait of Maass in the nurses' sitting room, she learned only that Maass was a former superintendent. Through two trips to Havana and extensive research, Guinther uncovered the complete story of Clara Maass. A memorial fund was started, and a pink granite memorial with a bronze plaque replaced the worn gravestone in Fairmount Cemetery.

In 1952 Newark German Hospital was renamed the Clara Maass Memorial Hospital. It has since moved to Belleville, New Jersey. Cuba issued a postal stamp honoring Maass in August 1951, the 50th anniversary of her death. In 1976, the 100th anniversary of her birth, the United States Postal Service issued a commemorative stamp honoring Maass, the only individual nurse so honored.

### BIBLIOGRAPHY

Cunningham, J.T. *Clara Maass: A Nurse, A Hospital, A Spirit.* Belleville, N.J.: Rae Publishing, 1968.

Guinther, L. "A Nurse Among the Heroes of the Yellow-Fever Conquest." *American Journal of Nursing* 32 (February 1932): 173–76.

Herrmann, E.K. "Clara Louise Maass: Heroine or Martyr of Public Health?" *Public Health Nursing* 2 (March 1985): 51–57.

Janet L. Fickeissen

## Anita Newcomb McGee

1864–1940

Although not a nurse, Anita Newcomb McGee fostered the establishment of the Army Nurse Corps. Throughout her life, she challenged women to assume a stronger intellectual role and personified that ideal through her many scholarly works and executive positions in scientific, anthropological, and service organizations.

McGee was born November 4, 1864, in Washington, D.C., to Simon and Mary Caroline Hassler Newcomb. Her father, a graduate of Harvard University, was a noted astronomer and mathematician. Her mother, also a strong intellectual influence, was a granddaughter of Ferdinand Rudolph Hassler, founder and first superintendent of the United States Coast and Geodetic Survey. The Newcombs had three daughters.

McGee was educated in private schools in Washington, D.C. She later traveled for three years in Europe, taking courses at Newnham College, Cambridge, England, and at the University of Geneva, Switzerland. In 1892 she graduated from Columbian University (now George Washington

University) in Washington, D.C., with a degree in medicine. She followed this with postgraduate study in gynecology at Johns Hopkins University. During the next four years, she maintained an active medical practice in Washington.

In February 1888 she married W.J. McGee, geologist-in-charge of the Atlantic coastal plain division of the U.S. Geological Survey. She participated with him on a geologic survey of the country shortly after their marriage. He left geology in 1903; in 1907 he became vice-chair and secretary of the U.S. Inland Waterways Commission.

The McGees' oldest child, daughter Klotho, was born in 1889 and was primarily raised by a private nurse. Her brother Donald died of meningitis at age nine months. The youngest boy, Eric Newcomb, was born in 1902.

McGee always possessed a profound interest in scholarly subjects, but her drive toward intellectual challenge was increasingly evident upon her return following studies in Europe. She studied and wrote on subjects related to geneology and history and was published in *Appletons' Cyclopedia of American Biography.* A group of women formed a society in 1885 called the Women's Anthropological Society of America, and in 1889 McGee served as its recording secretary. Publication of a study on the evolution of the Shaker community brought McGee professional renown.

McGee's medical practice from 1892–96 was thriving; nevertheless, she left active practice in 1896 to return to her first love, original research. But it was her executive skill that most influenced the future direction of her career. Active in the Daughters of the American Revolution (DAR), McGee served from 1894 to 1898 as its surgeon general, librarian general, vice-president general, and historian general. When relations between the United States and Spain threatened war, McGee charted a new course for herself and for professional nursing.

Before the war with Spain, the army surgeon general had endeavored to obviate the need for female nurses to support the military services by establishing and training a hospital corps of enlisted medics. When hostilities began in April 1898, the army continued to believe this hospital corps would meet its needs. Even so, hundreds of women wrote to offer their services as nurses to the army and navy. McGee suggested to the DAR that that organization develop its own hospital corps. Defined differently from the army's hospital corps, this body of trained nurses would be ready to answer the call to service. The DAR rallied behind McGee's proposal and appointed her director of its hospital corps.

An epidemic of yellow fever invaded the hastily constructed training camps and marshaling areas in the South and greatly intensified the need for hospital services. The surgeons general of both the army and navy readily accepted the DAR's offer and enlarged its scope from developing a body of trained nurses to full responsibility for examining and selecting all applicants. In August 1898 the surgeon general named McGee acting assistant surgeon in the U.S. Army, the only woman at that time to hold such a position. She was placed in charge of the Army Nurse Corps.

The surgeon general immediately requisitioned the first group of 30 nurses. Of these, 23 were found qualified and departed for Puerto Rico immediately. McGee's insistence on accepting only hospital-trained and well-referenced nurses placed stringent limitations on the number of nurses eligible to serve in the corps, but it also established a standard for safe, skilled nursing practice. Within slightly over two weeks, 1,200 nurses were on duty.

The DAR and McGee were not the sole source of nurses for the army. The Associated Alumnae of Trained Nurses of the United States and Canada also offered to assist the procurement of nurses; eventually, this organization and the American Red Cross became involved in supplying nurses. However, the surgeon general's initial decision to utilize the DAR created ill will between the organizations.

McGee served throughout the brief war and the year after screening women volunteers for hospital service. Upon the war's conclusion, she directed her attention to winning support for a permanently established nurse corps for service to the army. As early as November 1898, the surgeon general issued the first rules related to a corps of nurses. However, further progress was slow because of the general postwar turmoil in the military services. McGee continued to shape the nurse corps by setting and maintaining standards for qualification of nurses.

The permanent existence of a nurse corps required congressional action. The professional nursing organizations were the first to present a bill in Congress to establish a nurse corps. Though well intended, the bill was flawed in several areas. It did not establish a minimum size for the corps, a necessity for insuring its survival in peacetime. It also failed to mandate funding for the corps. McGee objected to the bill, seeing it as a diversion that delayed the permanent establishment of a nurse corps.

At the request of the surgeon general, McGee drafted Section 19 of the Army Reorganization Bill, which would establish an army nurse corps. After selecting her successor, McGee resigned at the end of December 1900, when the bill's passage appeared imminent. In February 1901, the president signed the Army Reorganization Act, creating the Army Nurse Corps.

Although McGee left government service, she continued to fight for the rights and privileges of the women who served during the Spanish-American War. Their contract status deprived them of veterans' benefits, including disability pay, pension, and health care. She founded the Society of Spanish-American War Nurses in 1898 and served as its president for six years. She kept close contact with the nurse veterans, and when war threatened between Russia and Japan in 1904, she offered her organization's assistance to the Japanese. With a group of trained nurses, she voluntarily served the Japanese army for six months. The Japanese minister of war appointed McGee "superior of nurses," giving her rank on par with officers in the Japanese army.

Following her return to the United States, McGee continued her studies in eugenics, lecturing on a variety of subjects, including the status of women. She also lectured on hygiene at the University of California. Through most of this period she lived in her homes in Woods Hole, Massachusetts, and Southern Pines, North Carolina, and in California with her daughter. Her son attended private schools. Her husband remained in positions in St. Louis and later Washington, D.C., succumbing to cancer in 1912.

McGee's son's education consumed much of her attention from this time until he died in 1930 at age 28 in an unexplained accident. Her correspondence is filled with letters from school directors and professors responding to her voluminous inquiries and discussions pondering his failure to succeed.

McGee received the Spanish War Medal for her services during the Spanish-American War. For her work in Japan, she was awarded the Japanese Imperial Order of the Sacred Crown, the Japanese Red Cross decoration, and two Russo-Japanese war medals from the Japanese government.

McGee died October 5, 1940, in a Washington, D.C., nursing home after suffering a cerebral hemorrhage. Her daughter, Mrs. David Madison Willis (Klotho), survived her. She was buried with full military honors beside her father in Arlington National Cemetery.

## PUBLICATIONS BY
## ANITA NEWCOMB MCGEE

"The Women's Anthropological Society of America." *Science* 13 (1889): 240–42.

"The Army Nurse Corps in 1899." *Trained Nurse and Hospital Review* 24 (February 1900): 119–24.

## BIBLIOGRAPHY

"Anita Newcomb McGee." Obituary. *Trained Nurse and Hospital Review* 105 (November 1940): 389.

"Anita Newcomb McGee." Obituary. *Washington Post*, 6 October 1940.

"Anita Newcomb McGee." Obituary. *Washington Star*, 6 October 1940.

Barton, C. Papers. Library of Congress, Washington, D.C.

Davies, W. *Patriotism on Parade*. Cambridge, Mass.: Harvard University Press, 1955.

Dock, L., et al. *History of American Red Cross Nursing*. New York: Macmillan, 1922.

Dulles, F. *The American Red Cross: A History*. New York: Harper, 1950.

Kernodle, P. *The Red Cross Nurse in Action, 1882–1948*. New York: Harper, 1949.

Kinney, D.H. "Dr. Anita Newcomb McGee and What She Has Done for the Nursing Profession." *Trained Nurse and Hospital Review* 26 (March 1901): 129–34.

McGee, A.N. Papers. Manuscript Room, Library of Congress, Washington, D.C.

"McGee, Anita Newcomb." In *Dictionary of American Biography*. Vol. 5, edited by John A. Garraty. New York: Charles Scribner's Sons, 1951–55.

"McGee, Anita Newcomb." In *American Men of Science*. 6th ed. Jacques Cattell Press ed. New York: Bowker, 1938.

"McGee, Anita Newcomb." In *National Cyclopedia of American Biography*. Vol 42. Clifton, N.J.: J.T. White, 1984.

"McGee, Anita Newcomb." In *Notable American Women 1607–1950*. Vol. 2, edited by Edward T. James. Cambridge: Belknap Press of Harvard University Press, 1971.

McGee. E.R. *Life of W.J. McGee*. Farley, Iowa: Private publication, 1915.

National Archives. Office of the Surgeon General. Record Group 112, Entry 201.

Newcomb, S. Papers. Manuscript Room, Library of Congress, Washington, D.C.

Spanish-American War Papers. File 900.2, 900.3. American National Red Cross, Washington, D.C.

U.S. Congress. Senate. Document, Series 3865, 23, no. 221, Vol. 7. 56th Cong., 1st sess., 1899–1900.

Cindy Gurney
Dolores J. Haritos

# Isabel McIsaac

## 1858–1914

Isabel McIsaac, who was sometimes called Belle, held leadership positions in the major nursing movements at the turn of the century and participated in the formation and development of nursing organizations as well as the *American Journal of Nursing* and the Army Nurse Corps, the expansion of the American Red Cross Nursing Service, the standardization of nursing education, and the state registration of nurses. In addition, she contributed three textbooks to the nursing literature, wrote a fourth book on hygiene in public schools, and coauthored with Jane Delano an international textbook for Red Cross classes in care of the sick in the home.

Of Scottish parentage, McIsaac was born in Waterloo, Iowa, in 1858. She had at least one brother and a younger sister, Euphemia May. The McIsaac sisters attended the Illinois Training School for Nurses in Chicago for two years, graduating in 1888. They were two of the first nursing students under the supervision of Isabel Hampton.

Upon graduation, McIsaac became second assistant superintendent to Hampton, in charge of nursing at Presbyterian Hospital. Hampton recently had finished arrangements for the Presbyterian Training School to be subsumed under the Illinois Training School (ITS). McIsaac served as assistant superintendent of ITS for seven and one-half years, the first year under Hampton. She was promoted to first assistant superintendent under Edith Draper in 1891 and then served for two years under Lavinia Dock. In 1905 McIsaac succeeded Dock, becoming the first ITS graduate to serve her alma mater as superintendent.

Under McIsaac's direction, ITS was one of the first training schools to increase its program from two to three years. In addition, McIsaac is credited with instituting the first clinical demonstrations to increase the uniformity of nursing technique. She spoke and wrote on the subject in 1902, modifying and elaborating further in her first book, *Primary Nursing Technique*. McIsaac also was one of the first to establish the custom of grading students' practical work and conduct as well as their regular theoretical course work. Other innovations during McIsaac's tenure as superintendent included lectures to seniors on administration and ethics, routine continuing education for ITS graduates during the summers, and the evolution of a more regular course of postgraduate work.

In 1891 McIsaac became a charter

member and first vice-president of the alumnae association of the Illinois Training School for Nurses, the first such association in the state. Under her leadership as president in 1893 and 1894, the association established a code of ethics, something the national association would not officially do for another 30 years.

At the 1893 Columbian Exposition in Chicago, McIsaac presented a paper on the benefits of alumnae associations to the first national and international gathering of nurses under the auspices of the International Congress of Charities, Correction, and Philanthropy. Here the foundation was laid for the formation of the American Society of Superintendents of Training Schools for Nurses, precursor of the National League of Nursing Education.

In 1896 the Superintendents Society appointed a committee of 10 delegates from the oldest alumnae associations to form an organization representing practicing bedside nurses and to be known as the Nurses' Associated Alumnae of the United States and Canada, or the Associated Alumnae. The Illinois Training School was represented by McIsaac, who became a charter member of the organization in 1897.

McIsaac became a national nursing spokesperson, serving as president of the Superintendents Society in 1898, vice-president in 1899, and a regular presenter at national nursing conventions. By 1901 McIsaac served as presiding officer of the Third International Congress of Nurses at the Pan American Exposition in Buffalo, New York. During this exposition, American nurses were first represented on the National Council of Women and the new International Council of Nurses. Nurse delegates attending these councils represented the newly formed American Federation of Nurses, a federation of the two national nursing organizations, with McIsaac serving the federation as president during the exposition.

In August 1901 the Illinois State Association of Graduate Nurses, an organization that McIsaac had urged be created, came into being. Its first order of business was to initiate legislation for the registration of nurses in the state, an attempt to control the quality of the trained nurse by establishing criteria for graduates of rapidly proliferating schools of nursing. McIsaac once again took a leadership role, this time as a consultant in the writing of the bill and as a lobbyist. Illinois finally gained a nurse registration law in 1907.

McIsaac was among several nurses called by M. Adelaide Nutting to Washington in 1900 to speak on behalf of an army nursing bill, the first nurse lobbying effort in Congress. McIsaac had also been a member of the Associated Alumnae committe that formulated a resolution expressing support of the bill. When passed in February 1901, the bill established the Army Nurse Corps, which McIsaac would later head.

During the first year of the *American Journal of Nursing*, McIsaac had charge of a department called "Practical Points on Private Nursing," for which she gathered several articles each month. In 1904 she became president of the American Journal of Nursing Company, serving again from 1910 to 1912. From the journal's inception in 1900 until her death in 1914, McIsaac contributed over 25 articles to the journal.

McIsaac retired from the ITS in 1904 and, with her sister Euphemia and her brother, took up fruit farming in Benton Harbor, Michigan. During her retirement, McIsaac published three nursing textbooks. The first, *Primary Nursing Technique*, outlined 10 clinical demonstrations as a basis for a preclinical course for students. The second, *Hygiene for Nurses*, published in 1908, covered the topics of environmental and public-health nursing, including the causes and prevention of disease. McIsaac's third textbook, *Bacteriology for Nurses* (1910), systematically reviewed the most up-to-date knowledge in bacteriology.

McIsaac was chosen by Jane Delano to help her complete a textbook for the lay public to accompany a class in home care of the sick and the prevention of disease. Their book, *Elementary Hygiene and Care of the Sick*, was published in 1913. They specified that this course and book were to teach only rudimentary home hygiene and not nursing. Nevertheless, some nurses refused to teach the course, fearing that graduates would call themselves trained nurses. Eventually, the course and text became among the most popular of Red Cross offerings.

In the fall of 1910, McIsaac left retirement to serve as traveling field secretary for the national nursing organizations, her salary paid by the Associated Alumnae, the Superintendents Society, the journal, and the nursing service of the Red Cross. She visited a cross-section of nursing schools, consulting with various nursing organizations. She spoke before conventions, local and state meetings, training-school graduating classes, and to high-school students who might consider nursing as a career.

McIsaac's home base was the *American Journal of Nursing*'s headquarters in Rochester, New York. At this time she also was functioning as president of the American Journal of Nursing Company, chair of the Robb Memorial Fund Committee, and a member of the executive committee and board of directors of the Associated Alumnae.

In 1912 McIsaac was called to Washington to replace Delano as head of the Army Nurse Corps when Delano took full-time charge of the nursing service of the American Red Cross. McIsaac served as vice-chair of the national committee on Red Cross Nursing Service and became secretary of the American Journal of Nursing Company, with Delano succeeding her as president. In addition, as first vice-president of the Associated Alumnae, McIsaac became acting president when Sarah Sly stepped down.

With all these responsibilities, McIsaac still found time to participate in the nursing section of the suffrage parade held in Washington, D.C., in 1913. However, the strain of her multiple roles began to wear on her, and on the urging of her colleagues, she tendered her resignation from the Army Nurse Corps in October 1914. The day following her replacement's arrival, McIsaac became seriously ill. She died 19 days later on September 21, 1914, at the age of 56. She was buried in Fairview Cemetery in Waterloo, Iowa, and was survived by her brother and sister.

The Isabel McIsaac Loan Fund for nursing education was established and was administered by the Robb Memorial Committee. McIsaac also had been honored at the International Congress of Nurses at the Pan American Exposition in September 1901, when she was named an honorary member of the Matron's Council.

## PUBLICATIONS BY ISABEL MCISAAC

### BOOKS

*Primary Nursing Technique for First-Year Pupil Nurses.* New York: Macmillan, 1907.

*Hygiene for Nurses.* New York: Macmillan, 1908.

*Bacteriology for Nurses.* New York: Macmillan, 1910; 2nd ed., 1914.

*The Elements of Hygiene for Schools.* New York: Macmillan, 1909.

With J. Delano. American Red Cross Textbook on *Elementary Hygiene.* Philadelphia: P. Blakiston's Son, 1913.

### ARTICLES

"The Benefits of Alumnae Associations." *Nursing of the Sick,* edited by I.A. Hampton. 1893. Reprint. New York: McGraw-Hill, 1949.

### BIBLIOGRAPHY

*American Red Cross Nursing Services.* Washington, D.C.: American National Red Cross, 1949.

*Annual Report of the National League of Nursing Education.* Baltimore: Williams and Wilkens, 1914.

*Constitution of the Alumnae Association of the Illinois Training School for Nurses.* Chicago: Fergus Printing, 1893.

Delano, J. *American Red Cross Textbook on Home Hygiene and Care of the Sick.* 4th ed. Washington, D.C.: American Red Cross, 1933.

Dock, L., et al. *History of American Red Cross Nursing.* New York: Macmillan, 1922.

Dunwiddie, M. *A History of the Illinois State Nurses' Association 1901–1935.* Chicago: Illinois State Nurses Association, 1937.

*Early Leaders of American Nursing.* New York: National League of Nursing Education, 1922.

*Eighth Annual Report of the Illinois Training School for Nurses Attached to Cook County Hospital, Chicago, Ill.* (1888–1889). Chicago: Fergus Printing.

Gladwin, M. *The Red Cross and Jane Arminda Delano.* Philadelphia: W.B. Saunders, 1931.

*In Memoriam: Miss Isabel McIsaac.* The University of Illinois Archives. Chicago.

Roberts, M. *American Nursing: History and Interpretation.* New York: Macmillan, 1959.

Schryver, G.F. *A History of the Illinois Training School for Nurses 1880–1929.* Chicago: Illinois Training School, 1930.

Janet Milauskas

# Pearl L. McIver

## 1893–1976

Pearl L. McIver was a celebrated nurse and pioneer in the federal health services. She served in the United States Public Health Service (USPHS) from 1933–1957, becoming the first chief of public health nursing for the USPHS in 1944. She was 15th president of the American Nurses' Association, 1948–50; chaired its structure steering committee, 1950–52; and after retirement from the USPHS in 1957, was executive director of the American Journal of Nursing Company for two years.

McIver was born in Lowry, Minnesota, on June 23, 1893. Her parents, Hugh and Anna Erickson McIver, were pioneer farmers. She was one of ten children, of whom three boys and three girls lived to maturity. After completing one year of high school in Lowry, she transferred to Mayville State Normal School in North Dakota, graduating in 1912. Later, she taught grade school in Hatton and in Webster, North Dakota, for four years.

McIver entered the University of Minnesota School of Nursing in Minneapolis, Minnesota, in 1916. During her student years, she advocated the establishment of a student government and sought alternatives to impractical aspects of traditional nursing practices.

After graduation in 1919, McIver spent two years as the University of Minnesota's campus visiting nurse, a predecessor of the student health service. In 1922 she was appointed director of public health nursing for the Missouri State Health Department. During her ten years in this position, she completed baccalaureate preparation in public health nursing (1930) and received a masters degree in public health nursing administration (1932), both at Teachers College, Columbia University, in New York City.

In 1933 McIver became the first public-health nurse appointed to the United States Public Health Service. She was public-health nursing analyst for three years with the research division before serving as senior nursing consultant for eight years. During the latter period, she organized the public-health nurse consultant services provided by the USPHS to states and to communities throughout the United States.

McIver was named chief of the USPHS's newly created Office of Public Health Nursing in 1944, with responsibility for providing leadership and consultation service to 23,000 public-health nurses in both rural and urban areas of the United States. In addition, the office developed studies to demonstrate the effectiveness of public-health measures and to evaluate techniques and methods of administration.

McIver was active in many prewar and wartime activities related to nursing. One of these was a national survey to ascertain the number of nurses available for both military and civilian needs. The survey, completed in 1941, used the records of approximately 300,000 registered nurses as a data base. The results assisted in the planning of refresher courses, were a source of information needed by Red Cross enrollment committees, and became a source of volunteer service for hospitals and clinics.

Throughout her professional career, McIver was active in many organizational activities. From 1948 to 1950, she was the 15th president of the American Nurses' Association and served during a dramatic period of postwar changes. In her opening address to the house of delegates at the 1950 biennial convention, McIver cited several critical decisions facing the organization: whether the six major nursing organizations should move to a two-organization structure, whether a proposed code of ethics should be adopted, and whether the American Nurses' Association headquarters should be moved. The decision on the first issue was to endorse the proposed structure, and McIver became chair of the structure steering committee appointed to implement the plan.

In 1957, the time of her retirement from the USPHS, the American Nurses' Association honored her by establishing the Pearl McIver Public Health Nurse Award, of which she was the first recipient. She was accorded many other honors: the Outstanding Achievement Award of the University of Minnesota; the American Public Health Association's Lasker Award for distinguished service in the field of public-health administration; the Florence Nightingale Medal, highest international Red Cross honor; and election as an honorary fellow of the Royal Society of Health in Great Britain.

After a two-year postretirement stint as executive director of the American Journal of Nursing Company, McIver returned to her childhood home in Lowry. Although plagued by failing vision, she continued to be interested in nursing and the issues facing nursing organizations until her death on June 3, 1976, in Lowry, Minnesota.

## PUBLICATIONS BY PEARL L. McIVER

"Rural Public Health Nursing Teaching Centers." *Public Health Nursing* 21 (February 1929): 72–77.

"Maternity Nursing Programs in Rural Health Departments." *Public Health Nursing* 28 (November 1936): 745–751.

"WPA Nursing Projects." *Public Health Nursing* 29 (January 1937): 50–51.

"Public Health Nursing in the United States Public Health Service." *American Journal of Nursing* 40 (September 1940): 996–1000.

"The National Survey: a Progress Report." *American Journal of Nursing* 42 (January 1942): 23–26

"Nurse in the Eye Health Program." *Public Health Nursing* 32 (January 1942): 34–37.

"Registered Nurses in the United States." *American Journal of Nursing* 42 (July 1942): 769–773.

"A National Health Service for England, Scotland and Wales." *American Journal of Nursing* 44 (September 1944): 845–846.

## BIBLIOGRAPHY

Fitzpatrick, M.L. *Prologue to Professionalism.* Englewood Cliffs, N.J.: Prentice-Hall, 1983.

Flanagan, L. *One Strong Voice.* American Nurses' Association, Kansas City: 1976.

Gray, J. *Education for Nursing, A History of the University of Minnesota School of Nursing.* Minneapolis: University of Minnesota Press, 1960.

"Noted Nurse Leader, Pearl McIver Dies." Obituary. *American Journal of Nursing* 76 (August 1976): 1234.

Roberts, M.M. *American Nursing, History and Interpretation.* New York: Macmillan, 1961.

University of Minnesota Archives. University of Minnesota Library, University of Minnesota, Minneapolis.

University of Minnesota School of Nursing, Minneapolis, Minn. Student records.

M. Isabel Harris

# M. Helena McMillan
## 1869–1970

Founder of two schools of nursing, M. Helena McMillan was a recognized leader in nursing education in the United States. An ardent supporter of university education for nurses, she worked diligently for the establishment of nursing courses at the University of Chicago.

McMillan was born in Montreal, Canada, in 1869. She was educated in private schools and received a B.A. degree from McGill University, Montreal, in 1891. She then enrolled in the Illinois Training School in Chicago and was graduated in the class of 1894.

The next year she was appointed superintendent at Kingston General Hospital in Kingston, Ontario, and served there three years. She then went to Cleveland, Ohio, as superintendent of nurses of the Lakeside Hospital, where she organized its school of nursing and served as its first principal. The faculty consisted of one night supervisor, eight head nurses, and McMillan, whose responsibilities included teaching classes in practical nursing. The first class of 16 was graduated in 1901. This school was the predecessor of the Frances Payne Bolton School of Nursing at Case Western Reserve University.

McMillan remained in Cleveland five years, then in 1902 went to New York City for a postgraduate course in public-health nursing at the Henry Street Settlement. The following year, she was appointed superintendent of the new Presbyterian Hospital in Chicago, where she organized its school of nursing and became its first principal. She served in this capacity until her retirement in 1938.

An active participant in nursing organizations, McMillan was one of the organizers and served as first president of the Cleveland Graduate Nurses' Association. She served five times (1905, 1906, 1907, 1915, and 1919–20) as president of the Illinois Nurses' Association. She served on the legislative committee to secure passage of the Illinois Nurse Practice Act, and appeared before the legislature many times before the bill creating the nurse practice act was passed. She also served as secretary, treasurer, and second vice-president of the National League for Nursing Education. She was a member of several important committees, including the committee on hospital economics, which guided the courses at Teachers College, Columbia University, before its department of nursing and health was established.

As an educator, McMillan was deeply concerned about the welfare of nurses. In an article in the 1907 *American Journal of Nursing*, she reported that the results of a survey she had conducted on the health of nursing students showed 16 deaths of students in the 23 reporting schools. It was common practice at the time for students to work 12 hours on the hospital wards in addition to attending all their classes in the evening. McMillan was an early advocate of the eight-hour day for students. McMillan's accomplishments at the Presbyterian Hospital School of Nursing also included the introduction of tuition fees, provisions for a preliminary period, providing students with some instruction and supervision for six months before they were expected to give total care to patients, and affiliations for student experiences not available at the Presbyterian Hospital.

McMillan was also a strong advocate of transforming so-called training schools into educational institutions. She believed that training schools needed to become associated with educational organizations and become part of an educational system.

In Chicago, McMillan chaired a university relations committee and helped stimulate the interest of both professional and lay groups in university education for nurses. It was largely through the work of this committee that courses for graduate nurses were established at the University of Chicago. Although the nursing programs at the University of Chicago closed down many years later, the school's impact on nursing, especially in the Midwest, was substantial. Its graduates have held leadership positions throughout the United States.

McMillan was presented the Saunders Medal Award at the 1936 American Nurses' Association convention in Los Angeles. She was described as a person with unusual initiative and high educational ideals characterized by her fairness, sincerity, and honesty.

McMillan died in Boulder, Colorado, on January 28, 1970, at the age of 101.

### PUBLICATIONS BY M. HELENA McMILLAN

"Practical Methods of Examination and Marking Pupils for the First, Second, and Third Years." In *Annual Report, American Society of Superintendents of Training Schools for Nurses.* Harrisburg, Pa.: Harrisburg Publishing, 1902.

"Schedule of Lectures for a Three Year Course of Training." *American Journal of Nursing* 3 (October 1902): 27–32.

"The Affiliation of Training Schools." *American Journal of Nursing* 6 (July 1906): 707–12.

"The Physical Effects of the Three Year Course." *American Journal of Nursing* 7 (July 1907): 767–70.

"What Nurses Need to Know About Food and Dietetics." *American Journal of Nursing* 22 (May 1922): 612–16.

"Recent Developments in Hospital Service." *American Journal of Nursing* 24 (October 1923; November 1923): 1–4, 89–93.

## BIBLIOGRAPHY

Dunwiddie, M. *A History of the Illinois State Nurses' Association, 1901–1935.* Chicago: Illinois State Nurses' Association, 1937.

Faddis, M.O. *A School of Nursing Comes of Age: A History of the Frances Payne Bolton School of Nursing.* Cleveland, Ohio: Alumni Association of the Frances Payne Bolton School of Nursing, 1973.

"M. Helena McMillan." Obituary. *American Journal of Nursing* 70 (April 1970): 864.

"News About Nursing." *American Journal of Nursing* 38 (October 1938): 1164–66.

"The Saunders Medal Award." *American Journal of Nursing* 36 (August 1936): 793–94.

"Who's Who in the Nursing World: M. Helena McMillan." *American Journal of Nursing* 23 (May 1923): 665.

Signe S. Cooper

# Mary Eliza Mahoney

## 1845–1926

Mary Eliza Mahoney was the first black professional nurse in America. Her professional career made her an example for nurses of all races; she gave more than 40 years of expert nursing service in addition to making contributions to local and national organizations. She worked for the acceptance of black women in the nursing profession and for improvement of the status of the black professional nurse.

Mahoney was born in Dorchester, a part of Boston, Massachusetts, on May 7, 1845, to Charles and Mary Jane Steward Mahoney. There were three children in the family; Mahoney was the eldest and her younger siblings were Ellen and Frank. Her parents had moved to Boston from North Carolina soon after their marriage.

Mahoney grew up in Roxbury, now part of Boston, and at the age of 18, she began to show an interest in nursing as a career. Between the age of 18 and 33, Mahoney worked as an untrained nurse. The New England Hospital for Women and Chil-

dren, located in Roxbury, was incorporated on March 18, 1863, by a group of women to counter the discrimination affecting women in medicine, to provide medical aid to women by female physicians, and to train nurses. Mahoney went to work there and was employed to cook, wash, and scrub. However, in 1878 she was accepted as a student nurse and entered on March 23 at age 33, two years above the top age limit. A female doctor was influential in her employment and subsequent acceptance to the nursing school.

As a student, Mahoney had 16-hour days and 7-day weeks, and night duty was required. Student nurses were given an allowance of one dollar a week during the first six months, two dollars a week during the second six months, and three dollars a week during the last four months. This allowance was to provide the required dress for hospital service, a calico dress and felt slippers.

Demands for performance at the school were high. Of 42 students who entered the school in 1878, only 4 students made the grade for graduation. Mahoney was one of these, and she was graduated on August 1, 1879.

Mahoney's attendance at this school of nursing was unique in contrast to American society during an era when black women were not admitted to white schools of nursing. Her graduation predated the existence of black schools of nursing. The New England Hospital for Women and Children was progressive in its philosophy, and took pride in a racially mixed patient population. By 1899 there were five other black graduates of the hospital's school of nursing.

Although Mahoney graduated with the full recommendation of the hospital, discrimination was pervasive in American society. Serious illness was often treated at home rather than in a hospital, however, and Mahoney was employed primarily as a private-duty nurse. After graduation, Mahoney registered with the Nurses Directory at the Massachusetts Medical Library in Boston to work as a private-duty nurse. This Directory, organized in 1879, provided a nurse's name and references upon request for a private-duty nurse. Graduate nurses frequently were expected to work 24 hours a day for as long as they were needed.

Mahoney had a "good temper, discretion and loyalty." Her references stated "high recommendation, no faults noticed" and that she was an "excellent nurse." Families who had employed Mahoney were eager to employ her again. Her well-known calm, quiet efficiency instilled confidence and trust, which in many instances overcame the racial barrier. Her reputation spread, and she was called to nurse patients in New Jersey, Washington, D.C., and North Carolina.

Mahoney became a member of the Nurses Associated Alumnae of the United States and Canada, organized in 1896, which later became the American Nurses Association. Mahoney was one of the few early black members of the ANA.

By 1908 she had become convinced that if black nurses were to have the same privileges that white nurses were granted, they would have to organize. She enthusiastically welcomed and supported the organization of the National Association of Colored Graduate Nurses (NACGN), founded by Martha Franklin in 1908. At the first meeting of the NACGN in New York City, Mahoney's friend, physician John B. Hall of Boston, invited the nurses to have their annual meeting in Boston. At the first convention of the NACGN in Boston in August 1909, Mahoney delivered the welcoming address.

In 1911 Mahoney was awarded life membership in the NACGN, and was elected the national chaplain. She was responsible for the induction of new officers, instructing them in their new duties and responsibilities. She rarely missed a national nursing meeting, and her local and national involvements were extensive. She was a strong force in convincing other nurses to join the NACGN. Through Mahoney's pioneering interest in the status of the black nurse, and her early support of the NACGN, she developed a professional bond and friendship with Martha Franklin and Adah Thoms.

In 1911 Mahoney relocated to New York to take charge of the Howard Orphan Asy-

lum for black children in Kings Park, Long Island. She held this position for only one year before retiring in 1912.

Mahoney was concerned about the progress of women as citizens and worked diligently for their equality. She was a strong supporter of the women's suffrage movement. In 1921, when Mahoney was 76 years old, she was among the first women in her city to register to vote.

Mahoney had many friends in Boston. She had ties with Boston's black medical circle through her good friends, physician John B. Hall and his wife. He was a prominent Roxbury physician and leader in the National Medical Association. Mahoney worked frequently for the Armes family. A lifetime friendship was established with them, and they were like family to her.

Mahoney became ill in 1923, suffering from metastatic cancer of the breast. In December 1925, she entered the New England Hospital for Women and Children in critical condition. She died there on January 4, 1926, at the age of 81, and was buried at Woodlawn Cemetery in Everett, Massachusetts. Mahoney never married; she was survived by her great-nephew, Fredrick Saunders, the grandson of her sister Ellen Mahoney, and his children.

Several local affiliates of the NACGN were named in honor of Mahoney. In 1936 the NACGN established an award in her name to honor her active participation in nursing organizations and her efforts to raise the status of black nurses in the nursing profession. When the NACGN merged with the ANA in 1951, the award was continued. The Community Health, Education, and Welfare Department established a center in Oklahoma in her memory. She was honored in 1954 by the ANA on the 75th anniversary of her graduation, and in 1976 she was admitted to nursing's prestigious Hall of Fame. The Dimock Community Health Center, previously the New England Hospital for Women and Children, houses the Mary Mahoney Health Care Clinics which is a comprehensive Health Care Center. Her grave was made into a shrine by Chi Eta Phi, a nursing sorority, and the American Nurses Association. On September 1, 1984, Chi Eta Phi and the American

Nurses Association organized a national pilgrimage to the grave in her honor.

## BIBLIOGRAPHY

American Nurses' Association. *Nursing Hall of Fame.* Kansas City, Missouri: American Nurses' Association, 1976.

*Annual Report of the New England Hospital for Women and Children.* New York: Academy of Medicine, 1865.

*Annual Report of the New England Hospital for Women and Children.* Boston, Mass.: Boston Public Library, 1879.

Chayer, M.E. "Mary Eliza Mahoney." *American Journal of Nursing* 54 (April 1954): 429.

Danett, S. *Profiles of Negro Womanhood.* New York: Educational Heritage, 1966.

Davis, A.T. "Architects for Integration and Equality: Early Black American Leaders in Nursing." Ed.D. diss., Teachers College, Columbia University, 1987.

Delend, W.L. *History of the New England Hospital for Women and Children, Boston.* New York: Academy of Medicine, 1876.

*Directory, The.* "References of Mary Eliza Mahoney." Countway Medical Library, Boston, Mass.

Gripando, G. *Nursing Perspectives and Issues.* 2d ed. New York: Delmar, 1983.

Kalisch, P., and B. Kalisch. *The Advance of American Nursing.* Boston: Little, Brown, 1978.

Logan, R., and M. Winston. *Dictionary of American Negro Biography.* New York: Norton, 1982.

"Mary Eliza Mahoney." Certificate of Birth # 1845, Vol. 17, No. 53, p. 107. The Commonwealth of Massachusetts, Boston State Archives.

"Mary Eliza Mahoney." Death certificate. Massachusetts Department of Public Health, Registry of Vital Records and Statistics, No. E 001828.

National Association of Colored Graduate Nurses. Minutes, 1908–17, 1917–37. Schomburg Center for Black Culture, New York Public Library, New York.

*Notable American Women, 1607–1950.* Vol. 2, edited by E. James. Cambridge, Mass.: Belknap Press of Harvard University Press, 1971.

Roberts, M. *American Nursing: History and Interpretation.* New York: Macmillan, 1954.

Saunders, F. Interview with author. Boston, Mass., 16 January 1987.

Sloan, P. "A Commitment to Equality: Early Afro-American Schools of Nursing." Ed.D. diss., Teachers College, Columbia University, 1978.

Staupers, M. *No Time for Prejudice.* New York: Macmillan, 1961.

Staupers, M. Telephone interviews with author. Washington, D.C., March, July, August 1984; February 1985; April 1986.

Thoms A.B. *Pathfinders.* New York: Kay Printing House, 1929.

Althea T. Davis

# Ada Mayo Stewart Markolf
## 1870–1945

Ada Mayo Stewart Markolf is credited with being the first nurse to be employed by an industrial concern in the United States. Although her career in industrial nursing was a brief one, it marked the beginning of an important nursing service. She accepted the challenge of working in an unexplored area of nursing practice, designed a role for herself, and was successful at it. Although her successors would establish the economic and social benefits of the employment of nurses in business and industry, she set a precedent for them to follow.

Markolf was born on December 2, 1870, in Braintree, Massachusetts. She had two sisters who also became nurses.

She was graduated from the Vermont Academy at Saxon's River in 1889 and from the Waltham Training School for Nurses in Waltham, Massachusetts, in 1893. The Waltham nursing school educated young women for both private-duty and "district" (public-health) nursing.

In 1895 Fletcher D. Proctor, president of the Vermont Marble Company of Proctor, Vermont, decided to employ a district nurse to care for the sick and injured employees of his company. Proctor directed his request for a nurse to the superintendent of nurses at the Waltham school. Markolf, a recent graduate who had special training in dispensary work, began employment with the company in March 1895.

Markolf wore the Waltham uniform and rode her bicycle as she made rounds of the community, visiting her patients. Her care was not limited to company employees, for the company took a benevolent attitude toward the people in the community. She also gave health talks at the village school after being invited by the teacher, a friend of hers. Eventually, Proctor decided that it would be a good idea for her to give similar talks in other schools in the area.

The success with the visiting-nurse service influenced the Vermont Marble Company to provide a hospital for its employees and other citizens in the community. The Proctor Hospital, a rebuilt private home, opened on August 6, 1896, with Markolf as its first matron. Five patients with typhoid fever were admitted the day it opened. Markolf had one assistant, and in addition to caring for the patients in the hospital, the two women also provided visiting nursing to the sick in the community.

Markolf stayed at the Proctor Hospital for two years, then moved to Troy, New York, where she practiced massage and taught the skill to nurses at the Samaritan Hospital Training School. Later, she worked at private-duty nursing and massage in Seattle, Washington; St. Augustine, Florida; and Lake Placid, New York.

In 1918 she married Henry J. Markolf, a retired businessman. The couple lived in West Rutland, Vermont.

Markolf was to have been honored by the American Association of Industrial Nurses in 1945 in recognition of her 50 years of industrial nursing, but ill health prevented her from attending the meeting. She died in the Eastern Star Nursing Home in Randolph, Vermont, on April 26, 1945.

### PUBLICATIONS BY
### ADA MAYO STEWART MARKOLF

"Industrial Nursing Begins in Vermont." *Public Health Nursing* 37 (March 1945): 125–29.

### BIBLIOGRAPHY

"Ada Stewart Markolf." Obituary. *Trained Nurse and Hospital Review* 115 (August 1945): 196, 198.

Arms, F.C. "The First Industrial Nurse in the U.S. Was a Vermonter." *American Association of Industrial Nurses Journal* 10 (October 1962): 20–22. Reprint. *Burlington Free Press*, 31 May 1962.

Felton, J.S. "The Genesis of Occupational Health Nursing, Part I." *Occupational Health Nursing* 33 (December 1985): 615–21.

McGrath, B. "Fifty Years of Industrial Nursing in the United States." *Public Health Nursing* 37 (March 1945): 119.

Roberts, M.M. American Nursing: History and Interpretation. New York: Macmillan, 1954.

Signe S. Cooper

## Stella S. Mathews
### 1868–1949

A Red Cross nurse in World War I and in the reconstruction of postwar Europe, Stella S. Mathews helped organize nursing associations. In addition, she worked for the passage of nursing legislation.

Mathews was born July 23, 1868, in Albion, Edwards County, Illinois. Her father, Amos Bickford Mathews, and her mother, Sarah Elizabeth Parker Mathews, were both natives of the state of Maine. She had a younger sister, Sarah, and two brothers, Roy and John. At the age of 14, Mathews moved with her family to Breckinridge, Minnesota.

Because her mother was opposed to her becoming a nurse, Mathews secured a position as clerk to the judiciary committee of the Minnesota legislature. This experience helped her gain insight into the political process, useful to her later when she worked for the passage of the Wisconsin Nurse Practice Act.

In 1889 and 1890, Mathews taught in rural schools in Minnesota and North Dakota. After taking a two-year course in kindergarten teaching, she went to Victoria, British Columbia, where she is credited with starting the first kindergarten in that city. She taught there fourteen months (1894–95) before returning home due to her mother's illness.

After the death of her mother, Mathews went to Milwaukee, Wisconsin, and entered the Knowlton (now Columbia) Hospital Training School, from which she was graduated in October 1906. After completing the program, she served for a short time as head nurse in the women's and children's ward at Allegheny General Hospital, Allegheny, Pennsylvania, then returned to Milwaukee as superintendent of the Milwaukee Children's Hospital, where she served for four years (1907–11).

While she was at the Children's Hospital, Mathews was instrumental in the establishment of the Wisconsin Association of Graduate Nurses, forerunner of the present Wisconsin Nurses' Association. She invited Milwaukee nurses to meet with her and discuss the possibility of establishing an association of nurses. The group decided to form a state association. Mathews was elected chair, and in 1909 the association came into being.

Much of the early work of its members was devoted to the passage of the Wisconsin Nurse Practice Act. With considerable involvement by Mathews, the group was able to introduce a stronger substitute bill for the original bill. The Wisconsin Nurse Practice Act was enacted by the state legislature in 1911.

At this time, John Yates, a Milwaukee surgeon, persuaded Mathews to go to Cleveland, Ohio, to observe the use of gas anesthesia. She enrolled in a short course in anesthesia at Johns Hopkins Hospital in Baltimore, Maryland, and subsequently worked with Yates for over two years. However, she found the work as anesthetist strenuous and decided not to make this field her career.

In 1913 Mathews left Milwaukee for San Francisco, where she enrolled in a year-long course in hospital management taught by Amy Pope at St. Luke's Hospital. Shortly after completing the course, she was called back to Ohio to care for her father during his final illness.

After her father's death, Mathews returned to Milwaukee, where she was appointed registrar for the Milwaukee County Nurses' Association (now the Milwaukee District Nurses' Association). She directed the first official nurses' registry and district headquarters in Wisconsin several years before the state association established its own headquarters.

In 1918 Mathews was appointed chief nurse of the Milwaukee Hospital unit (base hospital 22) which sailed for Europe in June of that year. The unit was sent to Beau Desert, France, about five miles from Bordeaux. One hundred nurses were assigned to the unit, and at times they cared for over 5,000 patients, many of whom had been wounded in the battle of Château-Thierry.

With the end of the war, Mathews returned to Milwaukee in May 1919. The next year she went to Warsaw, Poland, serving first as chief nurse of a typhus research unit, organized by the League of Red Cross Societies. In recognition of her administrative skills, she was later appointed chief nurse of the American Red Cross Commission for Poland, in charge of the 82 Red Cross nurses in Poland. These nurses were American, Australian, Canadian, English, and Irish.

Mathews traveled throughout Poland and helped establish schools of nursing in Warsaw and Poznan. She was especially interested in developing nursing schools and in establishing a children's health program. In their history of the Red Cross, Lavinia Dock and her colleagues identified these two programs as among the outstanding contributions of the Red Cross following the war, and credit much of their success to Mathews. The nurses were forced to leave Poland before their work was finished when the Russian revolutionary armies invaded the country.

But her work in Europe was not over, and from November 1922 until July the next year, Mathews served in Salonika, Greece, again under the auspices of the Red Cross. She assisted with refugee work in Greece's devastating war with Turkey.

Mathews received several awards for her services. From her own country, she received the Victory Medal for her war work in France. She was awarded the Silver Medal of the Polish Red Cross (1921), the Gold Cross of Merit from the president of Poland (1923), and the Chevalier of the Royal Order of George the First of Greece (1923). In 1939 she was awarded the Florence Nightingale Medal, the highest honor conferred on a nurse by the International Red Cross.

Still seeking adventure, in 1923 Mathews went to Hawaii, where her sister was teaching school. Appointed superintendent of Hilo Memorial Hospital, she had to cope with a rapid turnover of nurses and the difficulty of replacing them with native nurses. Five years later, she was appointed to the public-health nursing department in Honolulu, where she worked in the Paloma Settlement, one of the poorer outlying areas of the city. She retired after five years, but the city and county nurses' association of Honolulu persuaded her to set up a nursing bureau and registry, and she served as registrar from 1934 to 1938. As she had done in Wisconsin, she helped organize the state (then territorial) nurses' association.

Mathews was living in Honolulu when the Japanese bombed Pearl Harbor. She left Honolulu in January 1942 in response to the governor's request that all women not required to remain in Hawaii leave. She and her sister, Sarah, shared a home in Berkeley, California, until her death of a heart ailment on August 12, 1949. In addition to her sister, Sarah, she was survived by two brothers, Roy and John.

### PUBLICATIONS BY
### STELLA MATHEWS

With A.M. Owan. "Public Health Nursing in Honolulu." *Public Health Nurse* 22 (October 1930): 521–24.

"The Paloma Settlement and Public Health Nursing in Honolulu." *International Nursing Review* 6 (March 1931): 114–19.

### BIBLIOGRAPHY

Benedict, R., and S. Mathews. *Biography of Stella Mathews*. Milwaukee County Historical Society, Milwaukee. Manuscript.

Cooper, S.S. "Stella Mathews—Notable Nurse." In *Wisconsin Nursing Pioneers*. Madison, Wis.: University of Wisconsin-University Extension, 1968.

Dock, L.L., et al. *History of American Red Cross Nursing*. New York: Macmillan, 1922.

Jeffers, V. "Stella Mathews' Organizational Work in the Red Cross (1918–1923)." Master's thesis, University of Wisconsin-Milwaukee, 1982.

Kernodle, P.B. *The Red Cross Nurse in Action, 1882–1948*. New York: Harper and Brothers, 1949.

Kohler, R.D.Y. *The Story of Wisconsin Women*. Kohler, Wis.: Committee on Wisconsin Women, 1948.

Miller, V. *The History of U.S. Army Base Hospital No. 22*. Milwaukee, Wis.: Direct Press, 1940.

"Stella Mathews—A Modern Florence Nightingale." *Capital Times* (Madison, Wis.), 8 November 1949.

"News About Nursing." *American Journal of Nursing* 38 (December 1938): 1379–80.

"Stella Mathews." Obituary. *American Journal of Nursing* 49 (November 1949): 28 adv.

Signe S. Cooper

## Mary Lathrop Wright Matthews
### 1891–1955

An outstanding leader in the field of public-health nursing, Mary Lathrop Wright Matthews served in the Army Nurse Corps during World War I. She also organized and directed public-health departments in Florida for almost 20 years.

Matthews was born in Port Sanilac, Michigan, on June 23, 1891, the only child of Malan H. and Alice E. Lathrop Wright. Her father was a Congregational minister, and her mother was a descendant of the Reverend John Lathrop, who arrived in Boston on the *Griffin* in 1634. Soon after her birth, the family moved to Connecticut, later settling in Northfield, Massachusetts, where Matthews grew up in a home of strict discipline enforced by her religious parents. Throughout her life, but especially after the death of her mother in 1917 and her father in 1920, she was close to her maternal uncle, Dwight Lathrop, a businessman and amateur etymologist who influenced her greatly.

From 1904 to 1910, Matthews went to Northfield Seminary in East Northfield, Massachusetts, and in October 1910 began training at the Springfield Training School of Nursing. She received her nursing diploma in September 1913. In 1919 and 1920, she attended Teachers College,

Columbia University, studying public health, and in 1932 received a bachelor's degree and diploma as superintendent of hospitals from that institution. Her field work included duties at the Henry Street Settlement and at Presbyterian Medical Center in New York City.

After her graduation from Springfield Training School of Nursing in 1913, Matthews worked as night supervisor, probation instructor, and operating-room supervisor at Springfield Hospital. She also became assistant superintendent at the hospital.

In April 1917 Matthews was called to duty by the Army Nurse Corps. She arrived in France on May 13, and she served as operating-room supervisor and on surgical wards throughout World War I. In her diary, which was published in 1957, she gives an account of hospital life in France in 1917 and 1918.

Upon her return to the United States in March 1919 and after completing postgraduate study in public health at Teachers College, Matthews became superintendent of the Visiting Nurse Association, Waterbury, Connecticut. On a leave of absence in 1925, she spent several months in the hills of eastern Kentucky doing public-health work.

In 1926 she traveled to China to teach nursing at the Episcopal Mission, Shanghai, and to learn the language. She had previously joined the Episcopal church, a radical departure from her religious upbringing. Forced to leave China because of the revolution in 1927, she served in several temporary positions after her arrival in the United States, hoping to return to China.

In 1932 she married Alexander Matthews. The couple moved in March 1934 to Florida, where Matthews held a number of posts with public-health departments. She served as district supervisor with Florida's state board of health and as director of nurses for Dade County's health department. She retired on December 31, 1954, as director of nurses for the county health department of Palm Beach.

Matthews believed that nursing, to be effective, must be accepted as a call to serve the sick of all nations, not merely as a way to earn a living. She died, one month after her retirement, on February 2, 1955, from cancer in West Palm Beach and was survived by her husband.

### BIBLIOGRAPHY

"Mrs. Mary W. Matthews." Obituary. *Palm Beach Post*, 3 February 1955.

Matthews, A. *A Nurse Named Mary.* New York: Pageant Press, 1957. This was compiled by her husband.

Lilli Sentz

## Anna Caroline Maxwell

### 1851–1929

Anna Caroline Maxwell worked to advance the professionalization of nursing. She was superintendent of nurses at three American hospitals: Massachusetts General Hospital in Boston; St. Luke's Hospital; and Presbyterian Hospital in New York City. She established the nursing schools at both St. Luke's and Presbyterian hospitals. She directed the nursing service and training school at Presbyterian Hospital for nearly 30 years; she organized nurses to serve in wartime military hospitals during the Spanish American War; and she was active on behalf of American nurses during World War I.

Maxwell was born March 14, 1851, in Bristol, New York. Her father, John Eglinton Maxwell, was born in Scotland to a distinguished military family and ordained as a Baptist minister. Her mother, Diantha Caroline Maxwell, was an American of English descent. Maxwell was a young child when her family moved to King, Ontario, Canada, where her two younger sisters were born. She studied mainly at home under her father's guidance. There is some indication that she later attended boarding school for two years. She cared for her mother who was ill, thus developing her interest in nursing.

In 1874 Maxwell received three months' obstetrical training at New England Hospital for Women and Children, Boston, and subsequently served four years there as assistant matron. She resigned in order to study nursing under Linda Richards, the superintendent of nurses at the Boston Training School for Nurses, Massachusetts General Hospital. Maxwell entered the program in October 1878. She was graduated in October 1880.

Immediately after her graduation, Maxwell was called to establish a school of nursing at Montreal General Hospital in Canada. However, after a fruitless struggle with doctors and administrators opposed to the changes necessary for such a school and with few applicants for entrance as probationers, Maxwell left in June 1881. She traveled to Europe for three months to inspect hospitals, particularly those in England.

She returned to Boston in November 1881, planning to do private-duty nursing. While on her first case, Maxwell was offered the superintendency of the Boston Training School for Nurses, Massachusetts General Hospital, a position she held until 1889. She was made an honorary member of the school's alumnae association in 1895.

Maxwell's gift for leadership and organization were becoming well known. In the spring of 1889, she was appointed superintendent of nurses and completed the organization of the training school for nurses at St. Luke's Hospital, New York City. When she resigned in 1891, hospital administrators noted that the training school's success and permanent establishment were largely due to Maxwell's work.

Maxwell next accepted an appointment as superintendent of nurses at the Presbyterian Hospital in New York City, taking over her duties on January 1, 1892. She established the school of nursing of the Presbyterian Hospital, which opened in May 1892. Maxwell held this position for nearly three decades until her retirement in May 1921 at the age of 70. She received strong support from the trustees, hospital administration, and physicians at Presbyterian Hospital, support that enabled her to create the school she had long envisioned. To build her nursing staff, she at-

tracted the best-trained nurses available.

Maxwell set the highest standards for her profession and herself. To realize her goal of making nursing an honored profession for women, she consistently sought students of good background and education. She emphasized the need for highly qualified women in the nursing profession. During her tenure, there were 736 graduates from the Presbyterian Hospital School of Nursing, many carrying her high standards of nursing throughout the world. Maxwell believed that to overcome the low status of nursing's past, nurses must project professional dignity and a pride in personal appearance. She took great interest in nurses' uniforms, helping design attractive uniforms, caps, and pins for her student nurses and for the nurses who served in the army. (It is interesting, however, that Maxwell herself never wore a nurse's cap when in uniform.)

Soon after the United States entered the Spanish-American War in 1898, Maxwell wrote to the surgeon general of the army and urged him to allow trained female nurses to care for the sick and wounded. Trained nurses previously had not been permitted to serve during wartime in military hospitals in the United States. Maxwell was chosen to organize nurses to serve for the first time in the nation's history and was given a leave of absence by Presbyterian Hospital. She was placed in charge of 160 graduate nurses sent to Camp Thomas, Chickamauga Park, Georgia. The Red Cross Society for Maintenance of Trained Nurses assisted her in recruitment of the nurses.

On her arrival in Georgia in July 1898, Maxwell found chaotic conditions, inadequate supplies, overcrowding, poor sanitary conditions, severe heat, and extreme suffering and loss of life. However, her gift for organization and attention to detail soon established order. In addition to the wounded soldiers, more than 600 cases of typhoid fever developed along with malaria, yellow fever, and an epidemic of measles among the 50,000 men being trained at the camp. Once the nurses took charge, only 67 deaths occurred among 1,000 cases admitted to the camp hospital.

"When you were coming, we did not know what we would do with you. Now we wonder what we would have done without you" is a frequently quoted remark and it directly refers to Maxwell's Spanish-American wartime work.

When World War I began, Maxwell accepted the position of chief nurse of the Presbyterian Hospital unit (U.S. Base Hospital No. 2.) In 1916 she visited hospitals in the war zone, traveling to three fronts. She brought back valuable reports of the medical work and subsequently was active in preparations on the home front. However, when the United States entered the war in April 1917, Maxwell, at age 66, was prohibited from active duty at the front. In 1918 she again visited the war zone and the Presbyterian Hospital unit at Étretat and Auteuil, France. Maxwell was one of three American nurses decorated by the French government with the Médaille d'Honneur de l'Hygiène Publique in recognition of her war efforts.

Maxwell's two experiences in wartime gave added impetus to her efforts in three areas: to establish an army nurse corps, to secure officer rank for military nurses, and to recruit qualified nurses for emergency duty through the American Red Cross. After the Spanish-American War, Maxwell had been a member of the committee to establish a nurse corps within the military. Following many defeats in Congress, the committee succeeded in having the U.S. War Department bring out its own bill so that the Army Nurse Corps Female, under the direction of a graduate nurse, was established in 1901. The Navy Nurse Corps followed in 1908. However, even after World War I, the struggle to secure military rank for nurses in the armed forces continued for many years. It was not until June 1920 that, by an act of Congress, relative rank for military nurses became law.

Maxwell was a member of the committee that formulated plans for the reorganization of the American Red Cross (1905) to include nurse enrollment. She also served on the national committee on Red Cross Nursing Service, established in 1909, to evaluate credentials and set high standards for nurses accepted by the Red Cross as reserves for the army and navy nurse corps.

Maxwell was active in professional organizations. She was a charter member of the American Society of Superintendents of Training Schools for Nurses (1893) (renamed the National League of Nursing Education in 1912), the Nurses' Associated Alumnae of the United States and Canada (1897) (renamed American Nurses' Association in 1911), the American Red Cross Nursing Service, and the International Council of Nurses (1899). Early organizational minutes and proceedings are replete with her name and reports as chair and member of boards and committees. She actively worked to establish the *American Journal of Nursing*, the Hospital Economics course at Teachers College, and the Robb Scholarship Fund. She was the first nurse to standardize nursing techniques and procedures, and she was the first nurse to demonstrate nursing methods to non-nurses.

Columbia University conferred the honorary degree of master of arts on Maxwell in 1917, making her one of the first nurses so honored by a university. It was at this time that tentative relationships between Columbia University and Presbyterian Hospital Nursing School began.

Known for her keen intelligence, personal magnetism, enthusiasm, wit, energy, and self-discipline, Maxwell had many deep friendships both within and outside the field of nursing. Her closest nursing friends were Isabel Hampton Robb, M. Adelaide Nutting, Jane Delano, Lillian D. Wald, Sophia Palmer, and Annie W. Goodrich. She was an active member of the Cosmopolitan Club, the Woman's City Club of New York and the National Institute of Social Science. She regularly attended performances at the Metropolitan Opera House as well as the theater. With her tall, erect carriage and handsome appearance, and dressed in her black gown and scarlet Spanish shawl, Maxwell made an unforgettable impression on members of the medical and nursing staffs, from whom she earned the title of "The Queen." She could be stern and autocratic on occasion but her extensive social contacts proved helpful in winning respect for the nursing profession.

Maxwell's belief in the necessity for independent, endowed, university schools of nursing had started long before any such schools were established. Although Maxwell never faltered in her belief that some day the school of nursing of the Presbyterian Hospital would attain university affiliation and financial independence, it must have been a great disappointment to her that it did not occur during her lifetime. (The Columbia University affiliation officially began in 1937.) The only endowment to the school during Maxwell's life was for the Anna C. Maxwell Reference Library Fund, established in 1928.

Following her retirement in 1921, Maxwell remained active in her profession. She attended the ICN meeting in Helsingfors Finland in 1925 at which time she was made an honorary member of the Association of Nurses of Finland. She served as honorary chair of the Nurses' Campaign Committee, helping to raise over $1 million for the school of nursing residence to be a part of the new Columbia-Presbyterian Medical Center. Maxwell personally selected the site for the nurses' residence overlooking the Hudson River and the Palisades and was present at the 1928 ceremony dedicating the residence, Anna C. Maxwell Hall.

Maxwell was hospitalized in October 1927, at the (downtown) Presbyterian Hospital for a cardiac condition. When the Harkness Pavilion at the new Columbia-Presbyterian Medical Center opened in March 1928, she was the first patient to be transferred there. Though she was able to leave the hospital for brief visits, she remained a patient in the hospital until her death there on January 2, 1929. Funeral services were held at Maxwell Hall and the Chapel of Union Theological Seminary. She was buried with full military honors in Arlington National Cemetery, Washington, D.C.

The nation paid honor to Anna Caroline Maxwell as it never has to any other nurse. Two of New York's leading newspapers carried editorials honoring her in each of which she was called "the American Florence Nightingale" and "the Dean of American nurses."

## PUBLICATIONS BY ANNA CAROLINE MAXWELL

### BOOKS

With A.E. Pope. *Practical Nursing: A Textbook for Nurses.* New York: G.P. Putnam's Sons, 1st ed., 1907; 2nd ed., 1910; 3rd ed., 1914; 4th ed., 1923.

With A.E. Pope. *Physics and Chemistry for Nursing.* New York: G.P. Putnam's Sons, 1916.

### ARTICLES

"Struggles of the Pioneers. "*American Journal of Nursing* 21 (February 1921): 321–29.

"The Field Hospital at Chickamauga Park," *American Society of Superintendents of Training Schools for Nurses, Annual Report* (1900): 76–80.

### BIBLIOGRAPHY

"Anna Caroline Maxwell." Obituary. *New York Times,* 3 January 1929.

"Anna Caroline Maxwell, R.N., M.A." *American Journal of Nursing* 21 (July 1921): 690–93.

"Anna Caroline Maxwell, R.N., M.A., 1851–1929." *American Journal of Nursing* 29 (February 1929): 191–94.

Delavan, D.B. *Early Days of Presbyterian Hospital in the City of New York.* East Orange, N.J.: The Abbey Printshop, 1926.

Dock, L. and I.M. Stewart. *A Short History of Nursing.* New York: G.P. Putnam's Sons, 1920.

Editorial. *New York Herald-Tribune,* 5 January 1929.

*History of the St. Luke's Hospital Training School for Nurses, N.Y.* 50th Anniversary. May 28, 1888–May 28, 1938. New York: privately published, 1938.

James, E.T., et al., eds. *Notable American Women 1607–1958.* Cambridge, Mass.: Belknap Press of Harvard University Press, 1971.

Kalisch, P.A., and B.J. Kalisch. *The Advance of American Nursing.* Boston: Little, Brown, 1978.

Lamb, A.R. *The Presbyterian Hospital and the Columbia-Presbyterian Medical Center, 1868–1943.* New York: Columbia University Press 1955.

Lamb, A.R. *Recollections of Anna Caroline Maxwell, 1952.* Alumnae Office, Columbia University-Presbyterian Hospital School of Nursing, New York.

Lee, E. *History of the School of Nursing of the Presbyterian Hospital New York, 1892–1942.* New York: G. P. Putnam's Sons, 1942.

"Military Funeral for Anna Maxwell." *New York Times*, 6 January 1929.

"Miss Maxwell." Editorial. *New York Times*, 4 January 1929.

Parsons, S.E. *History of the Massachusetts General Hospital Training School.* Boston: Whitcomb and Barrows, 1922.

*Quarterly Magazine* (Alumnae Association of the Presbyterian Hospital) 23 (January 1929). Dedicated to Anna C. Maxwell, with 20 pages of reminiscences; excerpts published in 1938.

Riddle, M.M. *Boston City Hospital Training School for Nurses: Historical Sketch.* Boston: privately published, 1928.

Roberts, M.M. *American Nursing History and Interpretation.* New York: Macmillan, 1954.

Joan LeB. Downer

# Darius Ogden Mills

## 1825–1910

Darius Ogden Mills, a well-known philanthropist, banker, and financier, was instrumental in promoting the education of men in nursing in the late nineteenth-century United States. Although he was not a nurse, he invested heavily in nursing education as a means to improve the quality of nursing care provided to male patients. In 1888 he established the Mills Training School for Male Nurses, a companion to the Bellevue Training School for Nurses in New York City.

Mills was born on September 5, 1825, in North Salem, New York, the son of James and Hannah Ogden Mills. He was educated at North Salem Academy and then attended the Mount Pleasant Academy in Sing Sing, New York.

Mills began his professional career as a clerk in New York City. He moved to Buffalo in 1847, where he served as cashier in the Merchant's Bank of Erie County. In 1849 he went to Sacramento, California, where he founded the Bank of D.O. Mills and Company. He became the president of the Bank of California in 1864 in San Francisco, holding that position until

1878. In 1880 he returned to New York City. During this period, he was a director of the boards of 18 large New York City corporations. He was also viewed as a prominent philanthropist. He married Jane Templeton Gunningham of New York on September 5, 1854. The couple had two children, Ogden and Elizabeth.

The Bellevue Training School for Nurses, a program for educating women, was opened on May 1, 1873. It was intended that the student nurses would assume responsibility for providing nursing care to all patients hospitalized at Bellevue. Plagued by financial difficulties, however, the training school could not take charge of providing nursing care throughout Bellevue. In addition, a view prevailed that females could not provide all the nursing services required by sick men.

As a result, the female students provided nursing care to the women and children, and the male patients were cared for by orderlies, who received no special training. Mills felt that a training program for male nurses should be established to upgrade the level of care provided to male patients. Mills thought that as Bellevue had New York's first nursing school for women, it would be fitting to have New York's first school for men at Bellevue as well.

Mills donated money to the New York City Department of Public Charities and Corrections to establish the training school for male nurses. The announcement on Christmas Day, 1887, was hailed as an important step in improving the quality of hospital services to Bellevue patients. Named in honor of its benefactor, the Mills Training School was built on the Bellevue grounds. After the building was completed, the first class of students was admitted in December 1888.

The Mills School, under the direction of its first superintendent, Ada S. Willard, assumed responsibility for five male patient wards in Bellevue. Eventually, the entire male section of the hospital, including the Pavilion for the Insane, was placed under the care of the male student nurses.

The Mills School and the Bellevue Training School were operated independently, each with its own superintendent and faculty. In 1902 the two schools were placed under the general direction of Jane Delano. This reorganization was a result of two factors. First, many people felt that the female nurses provided better patient care, and the realignment was seen as an attempt to improve the care delivered by the males. In addition, a major scandal had made a severe impact on the reputation of the Mills School, and the reorganization was intended, in part, to help the school regain its former image.

The scandal began when Louis Hilliard, a psychiatric patient in Bellevue's Pavilion for the Insane, was found dead on December 15, 1900. Thomas J. Minnick, a news reporter who had posed as a psychiatric patient for the purpose of writing an exposé of the care of the mentally ill, alleged that he had witnessed Hilliard being beaten and strangled by three male student nurses. Minnick testified before a grand jury, and the three males were suspended from their duties. Following the inquest, Jesse R. Davis, the head nurse, was indicted for manslaughter. Mills posted bail for Davis and engaged Francis L. Wellman, a noted defense attorney, to defend him. Mills was concerned over the effect a possible conviction of a student nurse would have on the reputation of the Mills School.

The court case resulted in a citywide investigation of the care of all Bellevue patients, psychiatric patients in particular. As a result of the investigation, the hospital superintendent was dismissed, Ada Willard resigned, and several male nurses were suspended from the hospital.

The impact on the Mills School was devastating. At the beginning of the investigation, the Mills School had 85 male students. By January 12, 1901, 50 students had either resigned or been dismissed. Although Davis was eventually acquitted of manslaughter charges, the nursing system at Bellevue was badly crippled because of the negative publicity.

In 1911 the Mills School suspended the program for male nurses due to difficulties in recruiting students and replaced it with a course to prepare orderlies for service. In 1929 the program for male nurses

was resumed. Mills, who died in New York City on January 4, 1910, never saw his project resume its intended mission in American nursing education.

## BIBLIOGRAPHY

Alumnae Association of Bellevue, Pension Fund Committee. *Bellevue: A Short History of Bellevue Hospital and Training Schools.* New York: Bellevue Hospital, 1915.

Carlisle, R.J., ed. *An Account of Bellevue Hospital.* New York: Society of the Alumni of Bellevue Hospital, 1893.

Cooper, P. *The Bellevue Story.* New York: Thomas Y. Crowell, 1948.

Giles, D. *A Candle in Her Hand.* New York: G.P. Putnam's Sons, 1949.

Johnson, R., ed. *The Twentieth Century Biographical Dictionary of Notable Americans.* Boston: Biographical Society, 1904.

Malone, D., ed. *Dictionary of American Biography.* Vol. VII. New York: Scribner's, 1934.

Mottus, J.E. *New York Nightingales: The Emergence of the Nursing Profession at Bellevue and New York Hospital, 1850–1920.* Ann Arbor, Mich.: UMI Research Press, 1981.

*Who Was Who, 1897–1916.* London: A and C Black, 1920.

Richard Redman

# Lucy Minnigerode
## 1871–1935

Born into a family with a distinguished tradition of leadership, Lucy Minnigerode organized the nursing service of the United States Public Health Service (USPHS) in 1919 and had more than 1,700 nurses in 76 hospitals under her command. During World War I, she was decorated by Czar Nicholas of Russia for her work in organizing nurses stationed by the American Red Cross in Kiev. She also was a recipient of the Florence Nightingale Medal of the International Red Cross.

Minnigerode was born in Leesburg, Virginia, on February 8, 1871. Her parents were Charles and Virginia Cuthbert Powell Minnigerode. One of her brothers became an army colonel, and another became the director of an art gallery. Minnigerode was trained as a nurse at Bellevue Hospital, New York, receiving her diploma in 1899 and her R.N. certification in 1905.

From 1901 to 1910, Minnigerode worked as a private-duty nurse. She then served as superintendent of nurses at Episcopal Eye and Ear Hospital in Washington, D.C.; Savannah (Georgia) Hospital; and Columbia Hospital in Washington, D.C., from 1910–1912.

At the onset of World War I, Minnigerode became supervisor of the American Red Cross's unit C. She sailed with the organization's Mercy Ship, which was stationed at Kiev, Russia, from 1914 to 1915. While there, she received the Cross of St. Anne from the czar in gratitude for her services to the Russian people.

Minnigerode returned to Columbia Hospital from 1915 to 1917. When the United States entered World War I, she joined the staff of the American Red Cross Nursing Service and helped organize special units until 1918. During that year's influenza epidemic, she organized the nursing staff for a special emergency hospital in Washington under the sponsorship of the U.S. Public Health Service and the American Red Cross.

She was then delegated by the Red Cross to make a supervisory tour of USPHS hospitals. In 1919 she was named USPHS superintendent of nurses and put in charge of more than 1,700 nurses in the 76 hospitals the service was setting up to care for disabled war veterans. She turned her work over to the newly formed Veterans Bureau in 1922 but continued to serve the Veterans Administration as a member of the advisory committee of its medical council.

Minnigerode arranged for superintendents of nurses of the federal government nursing services to become members of the advisory council of the American Nurses' Association (ANA). She also helped establish and became the first chair of a section of the ANA for nurses in government service, thus drawing the attention of national nursing organizations to the special problems of this group.

From 1923 to 1928, Minnigerode represented the ANA both as chair of the committee on federal legislation and as a member of the Women's Joint Congressional Committee. During this same period, she was chair of the Delano Memorial Committee.

Having joined the national committee of the American Red Cross Nursing Service in 1919, she became chair of the service's local committee in 1931 and also served on the executive committee of the District of Columbia chapter. In recognition of her many services, the International Red Cross Committee awarded her its Florence Nightingale Medal in 1925. At the time of her death in 1935, she was in charge of reorganizing the USPHS nurses and dietetic corps.

During her career, Minnigerode contributed many articles to professional journals.

Minnigerode died of a stroke at age 64 on March 25, 1935, at the home of a niece in Alexandria, Virginia. She was buried in the family plot in Middleburg, Virginia. She was survived by five brothers: C. Powell, George M., Charles, Fitzhugh Lee, and Carl M. Minnigerode.

## PUBLICATIONS BY LUCY MINNIGERODE

*Survey of Public Health Nursing in the State Departments of Health.* Washington, D.C.: United States Public Health Service, 1925.

*Dietetics in Institutions and in the Field.* Washington, D.C.: United States Public Health Service, 1927.

*The Public Health Service Nursing Corps.* Washington, D.C.: United States Public Health Service, 1927.

*What the Government Is Doing for Tuberculous Persons.* Washington, D.C.: United States Public Health Service, 1927.

## BIBLIOGRAPHY

"Lucy Minnigerode." Obituary. *American Journal of Nursing* 35 (May 1935): 477, 499–500.

"Lucy Minnigerode, War Nurse, Is Dead." Obituary. *New York Times,* 25 March 1935.

"Minnigerode, Lucy." In *Who's Who in America.* A.N. Marquis, 1934.

Alice P. Stein

# Maude Blanche Muse

1879–1962

A dynamic and able teacher and writer, Maude Blanche Muse influenced nurses and nursing education for over three decades. She was particularly interested in the application of psychology in nursing.

Muse was born in Edinboro, Pennsylvania, on March 9, 1879, the daughter of William and Lydia Luella McCauslin Muse and the eldest of three children. Her mother was a descendant of a Scottish Presbyterian family; her father was of French ancestry. Both parents had studied with Horace Mann and were influenced by Emerson. The family moved frequently, and schooling often was interrupted. Muse attended kindergarten in San Francisco, elementary school in Kansas, Nebraska, Pennsylvania, and Washington, and high school in Ohio. Both parents died before Muse was 13 years old, and after that she lived with various relatives. While still in her teens, she started to teach in a small country school in Ohio, where she had students of all grades.

After three years of teaching, Muse entered the school of nursing at Lakeside Hospital in Cleveland, Ohio. She graduated in 1912 and spent two years in private-dute nursing. With a scholarship from the Lakeside school, in 1914 she enrolled at Teachers College, Columbia University, where she specialized in nursing education. She was an instructor at St. Luke's Hospital, New York City, from 1915 to 1917, and at Stanford-Lane Hospital School of Nursing in San Francisco from 1917 to 1921.

Returning to Teachers College in 1921, Muse finished her B.S. degree and, with the help of an Isabel Hampton Robb Scholarship in 1922, continued working on a master's degree. She became assistant professor at Columbia in 1927 and associate professor in 1937. She was especially interested in psychology and its application to nursing, and she also taught subjects such as pharmacology, the principles and methods of nursing education, and the history of nursing. Soon after becoming a full-time instructor, she took over the supervision of graduate nursing students.

Her book *Psychology for Nurses*, published in 1925, was a major contribution to the profession, and it went through five editions. Throughout her career, she made numerous contributions to the nursing literature, and her articles appeared in the *American Journal of Nursing*, the *Trained Nurse and Hospital Review*, and the *Pacific Journal of Nursing*. Her major goal in writing was to help student nurses master subject matter and gain the interpersonal skills required of their profession. She was an associate editor of *Physiotherapy Review* and a member of the National League of Nursing Education and the American Red Cross Nursing Service.

During her long association with Columbia University, Muse shared her campus home with Bess V. Cunningham, associate professor of education at Teachers College. She also was closely associated with Isabel M. Stewart.

Muse moved to Savannah, Georgia, in 1951 after her retirement. In 1955 she suffered a severe stroke, which left her incapacitated until her death in 1962 at the age of 83.

## PUBLICATIONS BY MAUDE BLANCHE MUSE

### BOOKS

*A Textbook of Psychology for Nurses.* Philadelphia: Saunders, 1925, 1930, 1934, 1939, 1945. Title varies: *Textbook of Psychology* and *Psychology for Nurses.*

*A Study Outline Designed to Assist Students of Nursing.* . . . Philadelphia: Saunders, 1928, 1930.

*An Introduction to Efficient Study Habits.* . . . Philadelphia: Saunders, 1929, 1930.

*Materia Medica, Pharmacology and Therapeutics.* Philadelphia: Saunders, 1933, 1936, 1940, 1944. Title varies: *Pharmacology and Therapeutics.*

*Guiding Learning Experience.* . . . New York: Macmillan, 1950.

### ARTICLES

"Teaching Probationers How to Study." *American Journal of Nursing* 20 (December 1919): 216–20.

"Endocrinology." *Trained Nurse* 65 (September 1920): 213–15.

"Newer Methods of Examination." *American Journal of Nursing* 27 (May 1971): 345–49.

**BIBLIOGRAPHY**

Cunningham, B.V., and I.M. Stewart. "Muse—Nurse, Educator, Author, and Creative Thinker." *American Journal of Nursing* 56 (November 1956): 1434–36.

Howes, D. *American Women.* Los Angeles: American Pub., 1947.

M.A. Nutting Collection. Teachers College, Columbia University, New York.

Pennock, M.R. *Makers of Nursing History.* New York: Lakeside, 1928.

Roberts, M.M. *American Nursing History and Interpretation.* New York: Macmillan, 1954.

Lilli Sentz

## Mildred Emily Newton

### 1901–1972

Mildred Emily Newton's contributions to nursing have been particularly notable in the areas of education, research, publication, and organizational development. However, her greatest contribution may have been to the development of individuals—faculty, students, and associates. Through her strong belief in the dignity and worth of human beings, she was able to encourage them to reach their potential.

Newton was born on July 1, 1901, in Cedar Falls, Iowa. Her parents, George Whitemore Newton and Marian Ross Newton, were affiliated with the Presbyterian church. She attended Iowa State Teachers College High School and studied during the summer at Colorado State Teachers College and at the University of California.

Newton earned a graduate nurse certificate from Evanston Hospital School of Nursing as well as a B.S. degree from Northwestern University in 1924. She obtained the M.A. degree in education in 1932 from the University of Southern California. Finally, in 1949 she received an Ed.D. degree from Stanford University. Her dissertation, "Florence Nightingale's Philosophy of Life and Education," was one of the early studies conducted by nurses in the field of historical research.

Newton held faculty and administrative positions in three institutions during her professional career. From 1925 to 1934, she served as supervisor, instructor and director of the Pasadena Hospital and Junior College. At the University of California, she was supervisor and instructor from 1934 to 1944, and from 1944 to 1951, she served as an assistant professor and assistant dean of its school of nursing. Her final position was professor and director of The Ohio State University School of Nursing until her retirement in July 1968.

Newton freely devoted her time and energy to numerous professional organizations at the district, state, and national levels. She was a member of the American Nurses' Association and the American Red Cross Nursing Service, but was particularly involved with the National League for Nursing from the time of its inception in 1951. She served this organization in various capacities, including the following: member of its first collegiate board of review for accreditation (1951–55); chair of the board of review (1954–55); member of the steering committee (1955–59); chair of its council of member agencies, department of baccalaureate and higher degree programs (1957–59); member of the board of directors (1957–65); chair of the interim committee on accrediting policies (1960–64); and member of the joint committee of the American Hospital Association and the National League for Nursing (1964–68).

Other organizations also benefited from Newton's participation. She was a member of the committee on civil defense and higher education of the American Council on Education (1953–54), which issued *Civil Defense and Higher Education* (1954). Her educational endeavors also included service as nursing consultant to the education and training division of the U.S. department of the Army, Office of the Surgeon General, and as a member of the defense advisory committee on women in the services to the U.S. Department of Defense (1960–63). For five years, Newton was a member of the nursing advisory committee to the W.K. Kellogg Foundation (1957–62) and was chair of the nurse scientist training grant committee in the division of nursing, U.S. Public Health Service (1962–67).

In 1953 Newton conducted a survey for the University of Florida to determine whether facilities were available for the establishment of a university school of nursing. In addition, she assisted with surveys of nursing programs at the University of Pennsylvania and Rutgers University (1958) as well as with similar surveys at Pennsylvania State College, Johns Hopkins University, and the University of Missouri.

Newton, a member of the National League of American Pen Women, was a member of the editorial board of *Nursing Research* from 1960 to 1966. She was a regular contributor to professional journals and collaborated in the writing of two nursing textbooks, *Principles and Practices of Surgical Nursing* (1932) and *Nursing: An Art and a Science* (1938). She also wrote a chapter on the history of nursing for the seventh edition of *Professional Nursing* (1965), a contribution consistent with her love of history and philosophy.

Newton was particularly interested in the lives of Florence Nightingale and early American nursing leaders. She was honored by being given a collection of nursing stamps in recognition of these historical interests. The stamp collection was begun by June A. Ramsey. Newton continued to add to the collection stamps that portrayed aspects of medicine and nursing, and she organized them into four volumes. This collection was donated to the Health Center Library at The Ohio State University shortly before her death.

Numerous awards were bestowed on Newton throughout her professional career. She was elected to Sigma Theta Tau and Alpha Tau Delta honor societies in nursing and to Pi Lambda Theta, an honorary education society, from which she received the central Ohio alumnae chapter's annual citation (1962) for contributions to teaching. In 1969 she was awarded the Mary Adelaide Nutting Award for leadership in nursing from the National League for Nursing. She was also frequently honored at The Ohio State University, including membership in Alpha Lambda Delta's freshman honorary and in Mortar Board's senior women's honorary (both awarded by student selection), a Centennial Achievement Award (1970), a fund begun to establish a chair in her name, and the naming of the school of nursing building, Mildred E. Newton Hall, in her honor in 1972.

Newton was the principal investigator of the first major research project for which The Ohio State University School of Nursing sought funds. The study involved an interdisciplinary effort to measure pain and to develop a device for simulating pain reactions.

Newton retired from her position as director of The Ohio State University School of Nursing in July 1968. While at Ohio State, she was credited with strengthening the baccalaureate degree program and inaugurating graduate degree programs in nursing. She was living in San Francisco at the time of her death on July 26, 1972.

## PUBLICATIONS BY MILDRED EMILY NEWTON

### BOOKS

With the Committee on Civil Defense and Higher Education of the American Council on Education. *Civil Defense and Higher Education.* Washington, D.C., 1954

With C.D. Lockwood. *Principles and Practice of Surgical Nursing.* 1st ed., New York: Macmillan, 1932.

With C.D. Lockwood and J.A. Wolfer. *Principles and Practice of Surgical Nursing.* 2nd ed. New York: Macmillan, 1943.

With M.A. Tracy and others. *Nursing, an Art and Science.* St. Louis: C.V. Mosby, 1938; 2nd ed., 1942.

### BOOK CHAPTER

"Historical Foundations of the Profession of Nursing." In *Professional Nursing,* edited by E.K. Spalding and L.E. Notter. Philadelphia: J.B. Lippincott, 1965, pp. 3–28.

### ARTICLES

"Ward Teaching in General and Advance Obstetrics Courses." *American Journal of Nursing* 27 (October 1927): 847.

"The Supervisor as a Member of the Faculty." *American Journal of Nursing* 27 (May 1927): 380.

"The Noiseless Perineal Dressing Cart." *American Journal of Nursing* 28 (July 1928): 667.

"The Prediction and Prognostic Value of Success in Nursing Theory." *American Journal of Nursing* 33 (October 1933): 985.

"Pressure Areas." *American Journal of Nursing* 38 (August 1938): 888.

"Leadership and Followership: The Two Needs in Nursing." *Nursing World* 125 (April 1951): 144.

"The Administrative Assistant." *Nursing Outlook* 5 (February 1957): 78.

"Developing Leadership Potential." *Nursing Outlook* 5 (July 1957): 400.

"The Relation of the Educational Unit in Nursing to Other Departments of the University." *Nursing Outlook* 6 (May 1958): 264.

"What Every Nurse Needs to Know about Nutrition." *Nursing Outlook* 8 (June 1960): 316.

"What's Ahead for Nursing and the NLN?" *Nursing Outlook* 9 (October 1961): 600.

"Nutrition in an Associate Degree Program." *Nursing Outlook* 9 (November 1961): 678.

"As Nursing Research Comes of Age." *American Journal of Nursing* 62 (August 1962): 46.

"The LPN in Obstetrics." *Practical Nurse* 13 (October 1963): 22.

"The Case for Historical Research." *Nursing Research* 14 (Winter 1965): 20.

"Communication with the Patient and Family." *International Nursing Review* 13 (May–June 1966): 37.

"NLN Accreditation: From Four Viewpoints." *Nursing Outlook* 14 (March 1966): 48.

"Nurses' Caps and Bachelors' Gowns." *American Journal of Nursing* 64 (May 1964): 73.

With others. "Nutritional Aspects of Nursing Care." *Nursing Research* 16 (Winter 1967): 46.

### BIBLIOGRAPHY

Hudson, N.P., ed. *The Ohio State University College of Medicine, 1934–1958.* Vol. 2. Columbus, Ohio: The Ohio State University, 1961.

The Ohio State University Archives. The Ohio State University, Columbus, Ohio.

"Research Solves Pain Determination." The *Ohio State University Monthly* (November 1964): 13.

*Who's Who of American Women.* Chicago: A.N. Marquis, 1958, 1961, 1964, 1966, 1968, 1970, 1972, 1974.

M. Patricia Donahue

## Clara Dutton Noyes

### 1869–1936

Clara Dutton Noyes contributed to the nursing profession with her skillful and energetic leadership for many years. As Jane Delano's assistant in the American Red Cross's bureau of nursing during the turbulent World War I years, she helped with the coordination of nurses' assignments in Europe. When Delano died in 1919, Noyes assumed the positions of director of the nursing service and chair of the national committee of the American Red Cross.

Noyes was born at Port Deposit, Maryland, to Enoch and Laura Lay Banning Noyes on October 3, 1869. She had one brother, Charles, who was several years younger. Both sides of her family were descended from pioneer settlers in the Old Lyme, Connecticut, area and on one side of her family she traced her ancestry to William Brewster who arrived on the Mayflower.

Noyes received her basic education in private schools in Maryland and was graduated from the Johns Hopkins Hospital School of Nursing in the class of 1896. She demonstrated leadership abilities during her student days and remained at Johns Hopkins as a head nurse after her graduation. She then assumed the position of superintendent of nursing at the New England Hospital for Women and Children in Boston. In the years that followed, she also directed nurses at St. Luke's Hospital in New Bedford, Massachusetts, and Bellevue and its allied hospitals in New York City.

Delano asked Noyes to leave New York in 1916 and join the American Red Cross in Washington, D.C., as its director of the bureau of nursing. In addition to coordinating nurse assignments, Noyes worked for standardized procedures and treatments within the nursing service.

In 1919 when she had to step into Delano's position, the United States and Europe had just begun to recover from the war and the influenza epidemic of 1918. Noyes initiated a vigorous inspection program to evaluate existing services of the Red Cross. She then designed and coordinated new services to meet rapidly changing problems in the target areas of greatest need. Her interventions had a significant impact on the development of Red Cross nursing programs in postwar Europe.

Noyes directed the bureau of nursing throughout the 1920s and into the troubled 1930s. She actively supported many Red Cross outreach programs for persons in acute need due to the Depression. She continued in the role of director at the American Red Cross until her death in 1936.

Throughout her busy career, Noyes served in many capacities in a variety of professional organizations. She served as president of the National League of Nursing Education from 1913 to 1918 and was twice elected to the position of first vicepresident of the International Council of Nurses in 1925 and 1929. She also accepted the presidency of the American Nurses' Association along with her heavy duties at the Red Cross from 1918 to 1922. Noyes remained a loyal member of her school's alumnae association, editing the group's journal and serving on the advisory board of the Johns Hopkins School of Nursing.

Noyes received the International Florence Nightingale Medal in 1923. She had also been honored with the American Red Cross Service Medal, the Bulgarian Red Cross medal, the Latvian Red Cross medal, and the French Médaille d'Honneur d'Hygiene Publique as well as the Médaille d'Argent Reconnaissance de la Française. She also received the Walter Burns Saunders Medal, given by the American Nurses' Association for excellence in nursing, in 1933.

The year before her death, Noyes received a "degree" pin of the Florence Nightingale School of Nursing in Bordeaux, France. The school had been built with Red Cross funds and in honor of her efforts, she was made an honorary graduate.

Noyes died unexpectedly while driving to American Red Cross headquarters on June 3, 1936. Her memory was honored in a Washington, D.C., Red Cross service at Georgetown Presbyterian Church and in a service in Old Lyme, Connecticut, where she was buried. She was survived by one brother, Charles, and several nieces and nephews.

## PUBLICATIONS BY CLARA DUTTON NOYES

"Post-Graduate Study for Nurses." *American Journal of Nursing* 5 (1905): 611.

"Small Hospital Laundry." *American Journal of Nursing* 6 (1906): 689.

"Modern Hospital Laundry." *American Journal of Nursing* 8 (1908): 513.

"Midwifery Problem." *American Journal of Nursing* 12 (1912): 466.

She wrote numerous reports about Red Cross activity for the *American Journal of Nursing* from 1917 to 1936.

## BIBLIOGRAPHY

American Red Cross Archives. Washington, D.C.

American Nurses' Association Archives. Mugar Memorial Library, Boston University, Boston.

"Clara Dutton Noyes." Obituary. *American Journal of Nursing* 36 (July 1936): 750–52.

Dock, L.L., et al. *History of American Red Cross Nursing*. New York: Macmillan, 1922.

Fitzgerald, A.A. "Clara D. Noyes—An Appreciation." *Trained Nurse and Hospital Review* 97 (July 1936): 18–21.

Flanagan, L. *One Strong Voice*. Kansas City, Mo.: American Nurses' Association, 1976.

Johns, E. and B. Pfefferkorn. *The Johns Hopkins Hospital School of Nursing, 1889–1949*. Baltimore: Johns Hopkins Press, 1954.

Kernodle, P.B. *Red Cross Nurse in Action 1882–1948*. New York: Harper and Brothers, 1949.

"Clara Dutton Noyes." National League for Nursing Archives. New York.

Roberts, M.M. "Clara Dutton Noyes." In *Proceedings, 30th Convention, American Nurses' Association*. New York: American Nurses' Association, 1936.

Linda E. Sabin

# Mary Adelaide Nutting
### 1858–1948

Strong foundations for the establishment of a system of nursing education and for nursing's professional advancement were laid by Mary Adelaide Nutting. She was an educator and administrator who was regarded by some as second only to Florence Nightingale in overall contributions to nursing. Her clarity of vision, high ideals, creativity, and educational experimentation affected nursing throughout the world. Nutting worked diligently to provide broad educational opportunities for nurses in institutions of higher learning, opportunities that would prepare them for their responsibilities.

Nutting was born on November 1, 1858, in Frost Village, Quebec, Canada. The fourth of five children, she was so frail that neighbors doubted that she would survive. Her parents, Vespasion and Harriet Sophia Peasley Nutting, were from New England families who had left the United States because of pro-British sentiments during the Revolutionary War period.

Most of Nutting's childhood was spent in Waterloo, Quebec, where she was reared according to English ideals, customs, and traditions. There was also a strong emphasis on music and intellectual development in the family, in spite of limited financial resources. Nutting's mother worked to create educational opportunities and to ensure that the girls would be schooled in social graces. Consequently, Nutting received special instruction in music and art and was considered to be an accomplished pianist and talented singer. She attended the village convent school to study French and music and a private school in Montreal, Bute House, which devoted attention to social accomplishments. Nutting then studied design and music for one year in Lowell, Massachusetts, where her parents had once briefly lived.

When the family moved from Waterloo to Ottawa in 1881, Nutting received additional training in music and art. For one year, she taught music at a school for girls in St. John's, Newfoundland, where her sister Armine was principal.

In June 1884 her mother became seriously ill, and Nutting assumed almost total responsibility for her care. This proved to be a turning point in her life, as she felt inadequate as a caregiver and instinctively knew that there was more to nursing than what she had experienced. While reading the newspaper one evening, she read an article that described the opening of a hospital and training school at Johns Hopkins University in Baltimore, Maryland. Three Canadians had been appointed to the staff: William Osler of McGill University in Montreal, Henri A. LaFleur, and Isabel Hampton. She immediately wrote for admission to the program, was accepted, and entered on her 31st birthday, November 1, 1889.

Upon graduation in June 1891, Nutting served as head nurse on Osler's medical ward and then as assistant superintendent of nurses. She became the new superintendent of nurses and principal of the school when Hampton was married in 1894. Here she spent half of her professional life, translating Hampton's dreams of a three-year course and an eight-hour day into reality.

However, Nutting was an innovator in her own right. She initiated and developed tuition fees, scholarships, and a six-month preliminary course to prepare new students for hospital experiences. In addition, she introduced social subjects into the curriculum, began payment of lecturers, and originated the use of full-time instructors and supervisors. Under her leadership, the Johns Hopkins school flourished and became known as one of the top schools of nursing in the country.

Nutting participated in the early professional organizations at the state, national, and international levels in the capacity of committee member or principal officer. Each of her organizational efforts advanced her crusade to put nursing education on a sound economic basis. While in Baltimore, she assisted with the organization of the Maryland State Nurses' Association and was its president when the Maryland legislature passed a bill for regulation of nurses. She was one of the founders of the American Home Economics Association and its *Journal of Home*

*Economics*, and she helped to organize the Nurses' Associated Alumnae of the United States and Canada. A list of her contributions to professional organizations includes the following: member of the committee on periodicals of the Nurses' Associated Alumnae, which established the *American Journal of Nursing*; president of the American Federation of Nurses; chair of the education committee of the International Council of Nurses; and member of the committee for the study of nursing education, which published the Winslow-Goldmark report, *Nursing and Nursing Education in the United States* (1923).

Nutting was twice president (1896, 1909) and twice secretary (1903, 1905) of the American Society of Superintendents of Training Schools for Nurses. But it was in her role of chair of its education committee that her visionary ideas emerged. In a 1911 report, she advised that an exhaustive study regarding the education of nurses was needed. When the president of the Rockefeller Foundation established an advisory group to study the education of public-health nurses, Nutting was included. Eventually, information about training schools for nursing began to be included in the report of the commissioner of education of the Federal bureau of education.

However, the American Society of Superintendents of Training Schools for Nurses was dissatisfied with the information being given about the status and condition of nursing schools, and worked to incorporate a series of articles by society members in the commissioner's report for 1906. Nutting wrote one of these articles, and by 1920 she had prepared two influential reports on nursing education that were issued through the United States Bureau of Education. One of these, the *Educational Status of Nursing* (1912), was regarded as an historic publication in the nursing profession. Complete with statistics that presented the status of 1912 nursing, the report also identified future directions for nursing. Nutting was also a member of the society's committee that worked with Dean James E. Russell to establish a postgraduate course for nurses at Teachers College, Columbia University, in New York City.

When Nutting took charge of the hospital economics course at Teachers College in 1907, she became the nursing profession's first professor of nursing. Her original title, professor of domestic administration (also listed as professor of institutional administration) was changed to professor of nurses' education in 1910.

In preparation for this position, Nutting had traveled through England, France, and Germany in the summer of 1907 to study institutional methods abroad. Under Nutting's administration and leadership, the Teachers College program prospered and attracted nurses from around the world.

Nutting remained at Teachers College until her retirement in 1925. The Adelaide Nutting Historical Nursing Collection was dedicated in her honor and is a special collection at the college.

Nutting's professional interests were varied. She participated in many nursing activities, including organizational work, committee work, government projects, publications, and international endeavors. During World War I, she served as chair of the National Emergency Committee on Nursing (1917), which became the Committee on Nursing of the General Medical Board of the Council of National Defense. The records of the committee on nursing later proved valuable to the National Nursing Council for Defense in World War II.

Aware of problems that were likely to occur as a result of the need for nurses in the war emergency, Nutting proposed that action be taken to attract young college graduates into legitimate nurses' training schools. This resulted in the establishment of the Vassar Training Camp of 1918, a three-month intensive theoretical training program for college graduates wishing to enter nursing schools.

During her tenure at Johns Hopkins, Nutting began collecting materials and books for an historical collection for the nursing school. These later became the nucleus for the first two volumes of the four-volume *A History of Nursing*, written with Lavinia Dock. A student and admirer of Florence Nightingale, Nutting also collected materials concerning Nightingale and outlined a plan for an international memorial in her honor. The Florence Nightingale International Foundation was established in 1934 with Nutting as honorary president. Her interest in history also led to the founding of the two history-of-nursing societies at Johns Hopkins and Teachers College.

Just as her historical writing demonstrated her keen analysis of the development of nursing, *A Sound Economic Basis for Schools of Nursing* (1926) demonstrated her prophetic ideas. This collection of speeches illustrates how her knowledge of the past assisted in the formulation of ideas for the future.

Poor health prevented Nutting from actively participating in professional activities after her retirement. She was constantly apprised, however, of nursing activities. In 1944 she was presented with the Mary Adelaide Nutting Medal. This award for leadership in nursing education had been created at the 50th anniversary of the National League of Nursing Education in 1943, and Nutting was the first to receive the award. She also received other honors that included an honorary master of arts degree from Yale University (1921) and the Liberty Service Medal for humanitarian and patriotic services.

Throughout her lifetime, Nutting had a wide circle of colleagues and friends. These included many male associates of stature and renown who admired and respected her abilities. These men frequently were enlisted by Nutting to assist with her many projects that forwarded the cause of nursing. Isabel M. Stewart, Lillian Wald, Isabel Hampton Robb, and Lavinia L. Dock were among her lifelong nursing friends.

Nutting died at the country branch of the New York Hospital on October 3, 1948, after a long illness. Although she had requested that her body be cremated and the ashes interred in her native Canada, the laws of Quebec prevented this. Therefore, her ashes were scattered from the George Washington Bridge, which spans the Hudson River above Columbia University. Nutting had enjoyed the view of the bridge from her window for over 30 years.

## PUBLICATIONS BY MARY ADELAIDE NUTTING

### BOOKS

With L.L. Dock. *A History of Nursing.* 4 vols. New York: G.P. Putnam's Sons, 1907–12.

*Geschichte der Krankenflege.* Translated by Agnes Karll. Vol. 1. Berlin: Dietrich Reimer, 1911.

*Educational Status of Nursing.* U.S. Bureau of Education Bulletin no. 7. Washington, D.C.: U.S. Bureau of Education, 1912.

*"A Sound Economic Basis for Schools of Nursing" and Other Addresses.* New York: G.P. Putnam's Sons, 1926.

### ARTICLES ( SELECTED )

"A Case of Typhoid Fever." *Trained Nurse and Hospital Review* (March 1891): 121.

"The Preliminary Course." *The Johns Hopkins Nurses Alumnae Magazine* (December 1901): 8.

"Education of Nurses." *American Journal of Nursing* (1902): 799–804. (Also printed in American Society of Superintendents of Training Schools for Nurses, *Annual Report,* 1902, p. 15.

"Visiting Nurses in the Homes of Tubercular Patients." *American Journal of Nursing* 5 (1904): 500–506.

"American Federation of Nurses." *American Journal of Nursing* (July 1905): 653–56.

"Social Service of the District Nurse." *Household Arts Review* (April 1910): 8–15.

"Nursing Conventions and the Nightingale Anniversary." *Survey* (June 4, 1910): 363–64.

"Isabel Hampton Robb: Her Work in Organizations and Education." *American Journal of Nursing* 11 (October 1910): 19–25.

"Nursing and Public Health." *Boston Medical and Surgical Journal* (March 14, 1912): 401–05.

"Work of the Department of Nursing and Health, Teachers College." *Public Health Nurses Quarterly* (January 1913): 87–91.

"Training of the Psychopathic Nurse." *Boston Medical and Surgical Journal* (September 24, 1914): 473–76.

"The Visiting Housekeeper." *Journal of Home Economics* 7 (April 1915): 167–70.

"Education of Nurses for the Home and the Community." *Modern Hospital* (March 1916): 196–200.

"War and Nursing Education." *Vassar Quarterly* (July 1917): 259–61.

"Relation of the War Program to Nursing in Civil War Hospitals." *Teachers College Record* (January 1919): 66–78.

"How to Educate the Nurse and at the Same Time Properly Care for the Patient," *Modern Hospital* (September 1923): 305–10.

"Florence Nightingale as a Statistician." *The Public Health Nurse* (May 1927): 207–09.

"The Future in Nursing Education." *World Health* (January–March 1930): 59–65.

"Clara Dutton Noyes," *The Johns Hopkins Nurses Alumnae Magazine* (July 1936): 163–66.

## BIBLIOGRAPHY

Christy, T.E. *Cornerstone for Nursing Education: A History of the Division of Nursing Education of Teachers College, Columbia University, 1899–1947.* New York: Teachers College Press, 1969.

Christy, T. E. "Portrait of a Leader: M. Adelaide Nutting." *Nursing Outlook* 17 (January 1969): 20.

*Dictionary of American Biography.* Supplement 4. New York: Scribner's, 1946–50.

Donahue, M.P. *Nursing: The Finest Art. An Illustrated History.* St. Louis, Mo.: C.V. Mosby, 1985.

Goostray, S. "Mary Adelaide Nutting." *American Journal of Nursing* 58 (November 1958): 1524.

The Johns Hopkins Hospital School of Nursing Archives, The Johns Hopkins Hospital, Baltimore.

Marshall, H.E. *Mary Adelaide Nutting: Pioneer of Modern Nursing.* Baltimore: Johns Hopkins University Press, 1972.

Mary Adelaide Nutting Historical Collection. Teachers College, Columbia University.

Nevins, G.M. "M. Adelaide Nutting As Known by Friends, Students and Co-workers". *American Journal of Nursing* 15 (June 1925): 456.

*Notable American Women,* edited by J.A. Garraty and E.T. James. Vol. 2. Cambridge, Mass.: Harvard University Press, 1971.

Nursing Education Department Archives. Teachers College, Columbia University.

Russell, J.E. "M. Adelaide Nutting As Known by Friends, Students and Co-workers." *American Journal of Nursing* 25 (June 1925): 445.

Stewart, I.M. "M. Adelaide Nutting As Known by Friends, Students and Co-workers." *American Journal of Nursing* 25 (June 1925): 450.

Stewart, I. M. "Mary Adelaide Nutting: Educator. Historian, Internationalist." *International Nursing Bulletin,* Winter 1948.

Stewart, I. M. "Reminiscences of Isabel M. Stewart." 1961. Oral History Office, Columbia University.

Wald, L.D. "M. Adelaide Nutting As Known by Friends, Students and Co-workers." *American Journal of Nursing* 25 (June 1925): 449.

M. Patricia Donahue

# Katherine M. Olmsted
## 1888–1964

Katherine M. Olmsted, an early public-health nurse, taught the first public-health nursing course in Wisconsin, one of the first such courses in the nation. She served as a Red Cross nurse in Romania during World War I and later was director of the department of nursing of the League of Red Cross Societies. She was decorated by 11 countries for her work in the reconstruction of Europe following the First World War.

Olmsted was born in February 1888, in Des Moines, Iowa, where she attended public schools. She won an art scholarship to the Art Institute of Chicago, but after one year, she enrolled in a Wisconsin college, which she attended for two years. She then attended the Chicago School of Civics and Philanthropy before enrolling in a nursing program.

A member of the class of 1912 of the Johns Hopkins Hospital School of Nursing, Olmsted accepted her first nursing position with the Baltimore Instructive Visiting Nurse Association. In 1913 she then returned to Johns Hopkins Hospital, where she served in its social service department. This was followed by two years (1914–16) of rural public nursing with the Morgan County, Illinois, Anti-Tuberculosis Association.

In 1916, Olmsted was invited by the Wisconsin Anti-Tuberculosis Association to organize and teach an eight-week course in public-health nursing. This was nearly 20 years before other such courses were offered by nursing programs in the state. Cosponsored by the state university's extension division, the course had a significant impact on the development of public-health nursing in Wisconsin.

The following year, Olmsted joined the Red Cross and was sent with a unit of 12 doctors and 12 nurses to fight typhus in Romania. To avoid submarines in the Atlantic, the unit sailed from Vancouver to Japan and then to Vladivostok, where the group boarded a train for Romania. The trip took five weeks, and when the health workers finally arrived in Romania, they were forced to abandon their typhus mission because the Germans had invaded the country.

Instead, the unit established a makeshift hospital, using limited supplies and equipment, in an old monastery. In March 1918, the Germans ordered them to leave the country. Their harrowing escape involved crossing Russia in a train they ran themselves, finally reaching Murmansk, and then sailing by ship to London.

On her return to the United States in 1919, Olmsted was employed as a public-health nurse in Wyoming, working with two tribes of Indians. She later served as executive secretary of the western office of the National Organization for Public Health Nursing.

In 1921 Olmsted returned to Europe as assistant to Alice Fitzgerald, director of nursing of the League of Red Cross Societies. The following year, Olmsted was appointed director and served in this capacity until 1927. As director, she traveled throughout Europe, organizing Red Cross schools of nursing.

Olmsted was instrumental in helping to establish an advanced nursing course at King's College, London (later at Bedford College). At the time, advanced courses were not available to nurses except in the United States. The need for well-prepared public-health nurses and for nurses with administrative skills was evident in the devastation of wartorn Europe, and the establishment of these courses was a milestone in nursing history. Nurses from around the world enrolled in the courses.

Olmsted was decorated by 11 countries for her work with the Red Cross. As director of its nursing division, she was instrumental in establishing nursing standards and policies. She received the Highest

Order of Merit from Hungary, medals from the King and Queen of Romania, King Albert of Belgium, from Latvia, Italy, and Norway, all now in the Alumnae House of the Johns Hopkins School of Nursing.

During World War II Olmsted served on the executive board of the New York State Nursing Council for War Service. She also taught Red Cross home nursing and nutrition classes. Throughout her nursing career, she contributed articles to American and international nursing journals.

Before returning to the United States, Olmsted enrolled in the famous Cordon Bleu cooking course at the University of the Sorbonne in Paris. In 1928 she then opened her well-known French restaurant, Normandy Inn, at Sodus, New York, which she continued to run until her death on April 7, 1964.

## PUBLICATIONS BY KATHERINE M. OLMSTED

### BOOKS

*Nursing as a Vocation for Women.* Madison, Wis.: University of Wisconsin-Extension Division, 1916.

### ARTICLES

"The Recruiting of Student Nurses." *American Journal of Nursing* 20 (September 1920): 974–79.

"An International Course for Public Health Nursing." *Public Health Nurse* 13 (June 1921): 297–300.

"International Aspects of Public Health Nursing." *Quarterly Journal Chinese Nurses* 6 (July 1925): 17–18.

### BIBLIOGRAPHY

Cooper, S.S. "Katherine Olmsted-Public Health Teacher." *Wisconsin Nursing Pioneers.* Madison, Wis.: University of Wisconsin-University Extension, 1968.

"Honors for Katherine M. Olmsted." Editorial. *Johns Hopkins Nurses Alumnae Magazine* 20 (May 1921): 50.

"Katherine Olmsted." Obituary. *American Journal of Nursing* 64 (July 1964): 152.

Olmsted, A.W. "The Story of an American Red Cross Nurse." 1965. Reprint. *Johns Hopkins Nurses Alumnae Magazine* 67 (June 1968): 40–47.

"University of Wisconsin Establishes Instruction in Preventable Diseases for Nurses." *Public Health Nurse Quarterly* 2 (May 1917): 6.

Signe S. Cooper

# Betty Ann Olsen

### 1934–1968

Betty Ann Olsen was a registered nurse and a missionary who devoted her life to the care of the lepers in South Vietnam. She died a prisoner of war in Vietnam at the age of 34. She received, posthumously, the Vietnamese citation for "Heroic Medical Work" for her care of the lepers in Ban Me Thuot.

Olsen was born October 22, 1934, at the mission station in Bouake, on the Ivory Coast of West Africa. Her parents, the Reverend Walter Olsen and Elizabeth Jane Kennedy Olsen, were missionaries for the Christian and Missionary Alliance. She had one sister, Marilyn.

Olsen was raised on the Ivory Coast. She attended Hampden-Dubois Academy, a Christian high school, and was under the influence and guidance of visiting ministers and missionaries. At approximately age 18, she dedicated her life to missionary service.

Olsen received her nurse's training at Methodist Hospital in Brooklyn, New York, from 1953 to 1956. After nurse's training, she was accepted at Nyack (N.Y.) Missionary College, which she attended from 1957 to 1962. During this period, she also worked as a nurse in obstetrics at Nyack Hospital.

However, Olsen was dissatisfied with her life. She moved to Chicago, working as an obstetrical nurse at West Suburban Hospital. After undergoing counseling, she rededicated her life to missionary work. In October 1963, she applied to the Christian and Missionary Alliance to become a missionary nurse.

One year later, she was sent to Hong Kong to train in a leprosarium before assuming assignment in Vietnam. Although her family and friends were concerned about her going to Vietnam under war conditions, Olsen remained dedicated to her task.

From Hong Kong, Olsen was sent to Da Nang, South Vietnam, to study the Vietnamese language and to work in the missionary hospital. Every Saturday morning, she served as a volunteer worker at the United Service Organizations (USO) building in the heart of the city. Volunteers were needed to keep the building open to provide a place for the servicemen to relax and rest. It was there that Olsen become known as the "Belle of Da Nang" to the American soldiers. She was highly praised by the director of the USO Club for her volunteer work.

After a year of studying in Da Nang, Olsen was sent to Dalat to continue her studies. From there she was transferred to Ban Me Thuot, 180 miles northeast of Saigon, to work with the leprosarium staff and to study the Raday language.

Thirteen American civilians, all missionaries, lived in Ban Me Thuot. When fighting neared the town, they decided not to leave the village and their patients. On January 30, 1968, the first day of the Tet offensive, the house of one missionary family was struck by a mortar shell or grenade; the next day, more bombing occurred. Several missionaries were killed, and Olsen provided medical aid to those who were injured.

Olsen was captured while she was preparing to move an injured missionary and obtain medical attention. Shortly after, another missionary, Hank Blood, was captured. They were joined by another prisoner, Michael Benge, an expert in agriculture, who had been captured two days before.

The prisoners were chained together and herded from one makeshift camp to another through South Vietnam. Slowly, they began to starve, and they contracted dengue fever and malaria. Olsen nursed them during their ordeals. After Blood died, Olsen and Benge were moved again from camp to camp, often without food or proper clothing. In August and September, they entered the dense jungle, drenched with the monsoon rains and armies of leeches.

On September 26, 1968, ten months after her capture, Olsen died and was buried in the jungle of Darlac province. She remained on the prisoner of war list from 1968 to 1972, when Benge was released from a Hanoi prison and confirmed her death. Of the original 13 only 5 survived and continued to work as missionaries.

***BIBLIOGRAPHY***

American Foreign Service. Death certificate. Report of Death of an American Citizen. Stephen J. Hobert, Vice Consul of the American Embassy, Saigon, Vietnam.

Bolye, H. "She's the Belle of Da Nang, This Former Nyack Girl." "*Journal-News*" (Nyack, N.Y.), 6 May 1965.

Cowles, H.R. "She Was a Wonderful Girl." *The Alliance Witness* (May 9, 1973): 15–16.

Enloe, C.F. "The Story of Michael Benge, Betty Ann Olsen, and Henry Blood." *Nutrition Today* 9 (May–June 1973): 5–11.

Enloe, C.F. "The Story of Michael Benge." *Saturday Evening Post* 245 (November–December 1973): 42–46, 100–101.

Olsen, B.A. Application for foreign missionary service, 1963. Christian and Missionary Alliance, Nyack, N.Y.

Olsen B.A. "Information for Sowers and Reapers." Personal file, 1965. Christian and Missionary Alliance, Nyack, N.Y.

Olsen, B.A. "Testimony." Personal file, 1964. Christian and Missionary Alliance, Jefferson Park Church, Chicago.

"Olsen, Betty Ann." In *Biographical Index 1973-1976*, edited by Rita Volmer Louis. New York: H.W. Wilson, 1977.

"Olsen, Betty Ann." In *N.Y. Times Index*. Vol 2. New York: New York Times Company, 1973.

Olsen, G. "Our Betty a Martyr?" *Adults Power for Living*, August 5, 1973, 2–3, 7.

Susan Lee Peterson

# Geneva Estelle Massey Riddle Osborne

## 1901–1981

Geneva Estelle Massey Riddle Osborne was the first black nurse in the United States to earn a master's degree and the first black instructor at New York University and the Harlem Hospital School of Nursing. She also was the first black superintendent of nurses and director of the nursing school at Homer G. Phillips Hospital in St. Louis, Missouri.

Osborne was born May 3, 1901, in Palestine, Texas, the eighth of 11 children born to Hall and Bettye Massey, 10 of whom lived to adulthood. All attended segregated schools in Palestine. Her father was one of the community's earliest settlers, and her mother worked hard for her children's education; all 10 completed at least two years of college. Osborne's brother Edward became a St Louis dentist and influenced his sister to enter nursing rather than dentistry, her original choice. Her 5 older sisters all became teachers.

After receiving her early education in Palestine, Osborne graduated from Prairie View State College in Texas. She taught in rural schools for two years, as had her older sisters. Deciding to give nursing a try, she entered the school of nursing at St. Louis City Hospital 2, a segregated facility, in October 1920 and was graduated in 1923. She received the highest score on that year's state nursing exam.

After graduation, Osborne served as head nurse in the male medical division of the hospital for two and one-half years, and for the next several years, she was a public-health nurse for the St. Louis Municipal Nursing Service. Barred from advancement in both jobs by racial discrimination, she resigned, determined to leave nursing. However, a friend directed her to Kansas City, where she taught hygiene and physiology in Lincoln High School and Junior College, with some of her students coming from the central nursing school of Kansas City municipal and Wheatley-Provident hospitals.

In the summers of 1927–29, Osborne borrowed money to take classes at Teachers College, Columbia University, and in 1929 she was awarded a scholarship by the Julius Rosenwald Fund to attend the New York City institution on a full-time basis. She received a B.S. degree in 1930 and an M.A. degree in 1931, both from Teachers College. She was the first black nurse to be awarded a master's degree. While working for her M.A. degree, she became the first black instructor at the Harlem Hospital School of Nursing.

Following her graduation from Columbia, Osborne was named educational director of the Freedmen's Hospital School of Nursing in Washington, D.C. After becoming increasingly aware of the problems caused by the serious underfunding of segregated schools, she developed enriching extracurricular activities, such as drama, music, and journalism, and helped establish closer ties with Howard University in order to improve the teaching of science subjects. She also managed to increase the budget for nursing education.

After three years in Washington, she resigned, married Bedford N. Riddle, an Akron, Ohio physician, and sought some means of addressing her concerns on a national level. Once again the Julius Rosenwald Fund provided the opportunity, calling on her to become 1 of 14 investigators participating in a two-year study of poverty and health conditions in the South. The group's findings formed a basis for remedial programs later undertaken by the federal government.

When the study was complete, Osborne returned to her home in Akron, where she worked as supervisor of adult education and was active in community affairs. She was elected president of the National Association of Colored Graduate Nurses, having previously served two years as chair of its institute committee. During her five-year tenure from 1934 to 1939, the organization structure was strengthened, the budget was stabilized, and membership increased. Osborne also strengthened the group's bonds with other national professional nursing organizations, worked to improve the quality of the association's national conferences, and conducted regional conferences.

In January 1940 Osborne became the first black superintendent of nurses and director of the nursing school at the Homer G. Phillips Hospital in St. Louis. The hospital was formerly City Hospital 2, from which she had graduated.

Osborne was called to New York City in 1943 to act as a consultant for the National Nursing Council for War Service and was retained in the post after the war, when the group became the National Nursing Council. In this job, she faced two problems: to convince the military to accept nurses without racial bias and to obtain better training for black nurses. Partly through her influence, the navy began to accept black nurses, the army accepted more than it had previously, and

the number of training schools admitting both blacks and whites grew from 14 to 38—all within two years.

She also was appointed to the advisory committee to the surgeon general. In 1943 Fisk University honored her by establishing the Estelle Massey Scholarship.

In 1945 Osborne became the first black instructor at New York University when she was named assistant professor of nursing education. She went on to the National League for Nursing in 1954 and served through December 30, 1966, first as associate general director and then as director of services to state leagues. Osborne's first marriage ended in divorce. She remarried while in New York, to Herman Osborne. There were no children from either marriage.

A member of the American Nurses' Association board of directors from 1948 to 1952, Osborne was one of its delegates to the 1949 congress of the International Council of Nurses in Stockholm, Sweden. She also was first vice-president of the National Council of Negro Women, an honorary member of the Chi Eta Phi sorority and the American Academy of Nursing, and a member of the National Urban League. Osborne was active in numerous civic and professional groups, including the National Council of Negro Women, the Legal Defense Fund of the National Association for the Advancement of Colored People, the women's Africa committee of the United Mutual Life Insurance Company, and the national health project of Alpha Kappa Alpha sorority.

Osborne received the Mary Mahoney Award in 1946 in recognition of her work in broadening professional opportunities for black nurses. In 1949 New York University named her its nurse of the year. After her retirement on December 30, 1966, she moved to Oakland, California, where she died on December 12, 1981. She was survived by a sister, Mamie McGruder of Los Angeles. In 1982, Nurses' Educational Funds, Inc., established the Estelle Massey Osborne Memorial Scholarship to be given each year to a black nurse seeking a master's degree in nursing.

## PUBLICATIONS BY GENEVA ESTELLE MASSEY RIDDLE OSBORNE

"The Negro Nurse and the War." *Opportunity* 21 (April–June 1943): 44–45, 92.

"The Negro Nurse Student." *American Journal of Nursing* 43 (August 1943): 806–10.

"What Price Quotas?" *Public Health Nursing* 36 (August 1944): 389–93.

With J. Nelson. "The Negro Nurse Looks toward Tomorrow." *American Journal of Nursing* 45 (August 1945): 627–30.

"Community Support and the R.N.: Nurses Must Face Their Social Responsibilities." *Trained Nurse and Hospital Review* 117 (July 1946): 46–48.

"The Nurse Shortage—A Concern for the Negro Public." *Opportunity* 25 (January–March 1947): 22–23.

"Status and Contributions of the Negro Nurse." *Journal of Negro Education* 18 (Summer 1949): 364–369.

With M.E. Carnegie. "Integration in Professional Nursing." *Crisis* 69 (January 1962): 5–9.

## BIBLIOGRAPHY

Carnegie, M.E. *The Path We Tread.* Philadelphia: J.B. Lippincott, 1986.

"Estelle Massey Riddle Osborne." Obituary, *American Journal of Nursing* 82 (February 1982): 322.

"Estelle Massey Riddle Osborne." Obituary. *Newsletter of the National Black Nurse's Association* 9 (January 1982): 1, 2.

"Estelle Massey Riddle Osborne." Obituary. *Nursing Outlook* 30 (February 1982): 78.

Osborne, G.E.M.R. Autobiographical notes. M. Elizabeth Carnegie Nursing Archives. Hampton University School of Nursing, Hampton, Va.

Osborne, G.E.M.R. Interview with author. 21 June 1976. New York, N. Y.

Safier, G. *Contemporary American Leaders in Nursing.* New York: McGraw-Hill, 1978.

Yost, E. *American Women in Nursing.* Philadelphia: J.B. Lippincott, 1947.

Patricia E. Sloan

# Sophia French Palmer

## 1853–1920

Few women have exerted more influence in the development of nursing than Sophia French Palmer, the first editor of the *American Journal of Nursing.* Palmer served as editor during the first 20 years of the journal's infancy, a time that was crucial to its survival. A born crusader, she used her editorials to promote needed changes in nursing. She addressed such issues as the future direction for nursing education, nurse registration, the formulation and administration of nurse practice acts, the organization of active alumnae groups, and the establishment of nursing standards and regulations.

Palmer was born in Milton, Massachusetts, on May 26, 1853. She was the fifth daughter and seventh of the ten children of Simeon and Maria Burdell Spencer Palmer. Palmer was a descendent of the first colonists to settle in New England. Although a physician, her father practiced medicine only when circumstances required, devoting the majority of his time to literary pursuits.

Like much of her personal life, the details of Palmer's early education are not clearly identified. It is only after her admission to nursing school that we can cite specific information. Palmer did not enter nurses' training until 1876, when she was 22. She was admitted to the Boston Training School of Nurses (later the Massachusetts General Hospital School of Nursing), where Linda Richards was superintendent.

After graduating in 1878, Palmer spent approximately 18 months in Philadelphia caring for patients of the famous physician S. Weir Mitchell. She then accompanied a mentally ill patient to California, where she remained for two years.

In 1883 Palmer became superintendent of St. Luke's Hospital in New Bedford, Massachusetts, where she worked to establish a training school. She resigned this position, however, after the hospital reduced its number of nurses for economic reasons, and she returned to Massachusetts General Hospital as charge nurse under Anne Maxwell. Palmer took charge of various wards and did substitute nursing work during vacation periods. In addition, she was able to obtain the postgraduate experience here she had advocated throughout her career.

Palmer next moved to Washington, D.C., and assumed the position of superintendent of nurses at Garfield Memorial Hospital. Against opposition from the city's physicians, she founded and became director of the training school for nurses at Garfield Hospital. She later remarked that this particular experience had given her insight into the conflict between physicians and nurses regarding who should control nursing education.

Palmer's talent for writing came into play in her next position, editor of the *Trained Nurse and Hospital Review*, originally published by the training school of Buffalo General Hospital. Her editorials demonstrated her impatience with blind acceptance of circumstances.

In 1896 Palmer accepted the directorship of Rochester City Hospital (later Rochester General Hospital) in Rochester, New York. For approximately five years, she attempted to incorporate her ideas of nursing education. During her last year at this post, she also assisted with the establishment of the *American Journal of Nursing* and took a three-month leave of absence to study journalism. In the summer of 1900 she was chosen by the Nurses' Associated Alumnae of the United States and Canada to be the editor-in-chief of the journal. She resigned her hospital post in June 1901 to turn her full attention to the fledgling periodical.

At the age of 47, Palmer assumed responsibility as both editor and business manager of the *American Journal of Nursing*. She used her own home as an office for over a decade and remained as editor until her death 20 years later.

As editor, Palmer fought for those causes that would have a direct impact on nursing's progress. Through her outspoken editorials, she made the journal a powerful influence for the establishment of a united nursing profession, reforms in nursing education, the development of protective legislation, effective communication in nursing, and accurate information on social issues. She firmly maintained, however, that the journal should remain neutral on political issues.

Although Palmer's primary goal was the growth and development of the journal, she was an active participant in nursing's crucial endeavors. She was one of the founders of the American Society of Superintendents of Training Schools for Nurses and assisted with the writing of its constitution and bylaws. She was involved with the initial organization of the Nurses' Associated Alumnae of the United States and Canada. She also was the first chair of the Delano Memorial Fund and assisted in drafting the resolution brought before the Red Cross Board that requested rank for nurses.

Palmer was a leader in the movement to secure state registration for nurses. Her initial involvement began in 1899, when she enlisted the aid of the New York State Federation of Women's Clubs to establish legislation for the regulation of nurses' training and practice. She used the *American Journal of Nursing* in an educational campaign to announce meetings, to render favorable statements about registration, and to publish proposed registration bills as examples for nurses in other states. When New York's law passed in 1903, Palmer was one of five nurses appointed to the state board of nurse examiners and was elected its first president. She also is credited with being the first to suggest the appointment of training-school inspectors by state boards.

Palmer was an extremely private individual. Even her adoption of an eight-year-old child, Elizabeth A. Palmer, in 1906, was little known. Elizabeth Palmer died from tuberculosis in her 20th year. Katherine DeWitt, her friend and assistant, respected Palmer's wishes for privacy and did not record any personal information about her. In the event of her own death, Palmer had given specific instructions that a simple outline of her life was all she wished published. In addition, she did not want any memorial dedicated to her. Instead, she wanted the cost of the *American Journal of Nursing* included in alumnae dues. However, this was never achieved.

Palmer died on April 27, 1920, at the age of 66 after suffering a cerebral hemorrhage at her summer cottage in Forest Lawn, New York. Her ashes were buried at Forest Hills cemetery near Boston, where her parents and adopted daughter had been interred. Despite her wish for no memorials, the Sophia F. Palmer Library of the *American Journal of Nursing* (1953) and the Palmer-Davis Library of the Massachusetts General Hospital School of Nursing honor her memory.

## PUBLICATIONS BY
## SOPHIA FRENCH PALMER

"Alumnae Associations." *Trained Nurse and Hospital Review* 14 (April 1895): 201.

"Editorially Speaking." *Trained Nurse and Hospital Review*, June, July, August, September, October, November, December, 1895. All of these columns were written by Palmer and were not titled.

"Editor's Miscellany." *American Journal of Nursing*, 1900–07. These were in addition to the editorial comments and were numerous throughout these years. "Editor's Miscellany" once again appeared in the 1911 and 1912 journals.

"Editorial Comments." *American Journal of Nursing*, 1900–20. The editorials are extremely numerous during these years. They were not titled.

"Present Work and Future Possibilities of the Trained Nurse in the Care of the Sick Poor in Their Homes." *Trained Nurse and Hospital Review* 15 (September 1895): 114.

"Effect of Registration upon the Educational Standards of Training-Schools." *American Journal of Nursing* 4 (July 1904): 773.

"The Essential Features of a Bill for the State Registration of Nurses, and How to Pass It." *American Journal of Nursing* 7 (March 1907): 428.

"Efficiency in Hospital Management, the Need of the Personal Equation in Service versus Public Pride in Equipment." *American Journal of Nursing* 8 (January 1908): 252.

"State Societies, Their Organization and Place in Nursing Education." *American Journal of Nursing* 9 (September 1909): 956.

## BIBLIOGRAPHY

American Journal of Nursing. Files, 1900–20. Nursing Archives, Mugar Memorial Library, Boston University.

American Society of Superintendents of Training Schools for Nursing. Annual reports of conventions.

Christy, T.E. *Cornerstone for Nursing Education: A History of the Division of Nursing Education of Teachers College, Columbia University, 1899–1947*. New York: Teachers College Press, 1969.

"Portrait of a Leader: Sophia F. Palmer." *Nursing Outlook* 23 (December 1975): 746.

DeWitt, K. "Nursing News and Announcements." *American Journal of Nursing* 18 (November 1917): 171.

Fitzpatrick, M.L. *Prologue to Professionalism.* Bowie, Md.: Robert J. Brady, 1983.

James, E.T., et al., eds. *Notable American Women.* Vol. 3. Cambridge, Mass.: Harvard University Press, 1971.

Mary Adelaide Nutting Historical Collection. Teachers College, Columbia University.

National League of Nursing Education. *Twenty-first Annual Report.* New York: National League of Nursing Education, 1915.

Nursing Education Department Archives. Teachers College, Columbia University.

Pennock, M.R., ed. *Makers of Nursing History.* New York: Lakeside Publishing, 1940.

Roberts, M.M. *American Nursing: History and Interpretation.* New York: Macmillan, 1954.

M. Patricia Donahue

# Sara Elizabeth Parsons

## 1864–1949

Sara Elizabeth Parsons organized several schools of nursing, served as superintendent of nurses at Massachusetts General Hospital, and was chief nurse of an army hospital in France during World War I. She wrote the first history of the Massachusetts General Hospital School of Nursing.

Parsons was born April 21, 1864, in Northboro, Massachusetts. During her childhood, she lived in Oxford, Massachusetts, where her mother was a milliner and dressmaker. She attended private schools and high school in that area.

At the age of 20, she entered the training school for nurses at Boston City Hospital. However, after three months she returned home to care for her ill mother. For seven years after the death of her mother, she cared for her two small half-sisters. Finally, in 1891 she returned to her education by enrolling in the Boston Training School for Nurses, forerunner of the Massachusetts General Hospital School of Nursing. She was graduated in 1893.

Following graduation, Parsons served as a head nurse at Massachusetts General Hospital, then took one year's advanced work at the McLean Hospital for the mentally ill in Waverly, Massachusetts. After receiving a diploma in 1895, she remained at McLean for one year as a supervisor. Throughout her career, psychiatric nursing remained a dominant interest.

In 1897 Parsons was appointed superintendent of nurses at Butler Hospital, Providence, Rhode Island, where she organized a school of nursing. Two years later, she resigned to join a group of doctors and nurses who volunteered for service on the hospital ship *Bay State* and made three trips to bring back the sick and wounded from Cuba and Puerto Rico. After the Spanish-American war, Parsons went to the state mental hospital in Northhampton, Massachusetts, hoping to establish a school of nursing, but she was unable to do so. She became ill with typhoid fever and left in 1900 for an eight-month trip abroad.

Returning from Europe, Parsons was appointed superintendent of nurses at Adams Nervine Hospital in Jamaica Plain, Massachusetts, a position she held for three years. This was followed by another year abroad, then one year's study in the hospital economics course at Teacher's College, Columbia University. From 1906 to 1909 she was employed by the Sheppard and Enoch Pratt Hospital in Towson, Maryland, where she organized its school of nursing.

In 1909 Parsons returned to Massachusetts General Hospital to enroll in a newly established six-month course in hospital administration. Her next position was in Derby, Connecticut, where she equipped a new hospital and recommended administration policies.

In 1910 she was appointed Superintendent of Nurses at Massachusetts General Hospital, a position she held until 1920. Responsible for the school of nurs-

ing, she made many changes: the appointment of two full-time instructors when previously there were none, the introduction of a three-month probationary period, the establishment of student government, the raising of educational requirements, the beginning of a library, and the improvement of working conditions for students. Concerned about recreation for students, she helped organize a glee club and instituted classes in folk dancing. She also is credited with introducing the case method of teaching in nursing.

Active in the school's alumnae association, in 1911 Parsons helped establish its periodical, the *Quarterly Record*. She also helped initiate its plan for the school's endowment fund. During her tenure at Massachusetts General Hospital, she served as president of the Massachusetts Nurses' Association, vigorously supporting its legislative efforts. In 1916 she was elected president of the National League of Nursing Education, having previously served as its secretary and vice-president.

Her book, *Nursing Problems and Obligations*, was published in 1916. Throughout her career, she also wrote numerous articles primarily for nursing journals, although a few were published in medical journals.

Parsons had joined the Red Cross in 1911. From 1917 to 1919, she took a leave of absence from her job to serve as chief nurse of base hospital 6 during World War I. The unit included more than 60 nurses, most of whom were graduates of Massachusetts General Hospital's training school. They sailed for France early in 1917 and returned home in February 1919.

Parsons took an active part in the effort to secure military rank for nurses and appeared at a hearing before the Subcommittee on Military Affairs of the U.S. Senate. At the hearing, she spoke of indignities suffered by nurses in areas such as pay, transportation, and military leave. The nurses were successful in their efforts and the bill passed Congress the next year and was signed into law.

After her return from military service in Europe, Parsons resumed her duties at

Massachusetts General Hospital but resigned one year later. She then surveyed schools of nursing in Missouri, Arkansas, and Oklahoma and assisted nurses in those states with nursing legislation.

In 1922 at the invitation of the trustees of the Massachusetts General Hospital, she returned to Boston to write a history of its school of nursing. As a result, she was considered the school's first historian. From 1924 to 1926, she was registrar of the Central Directory of Nurses in Boston, sponsored by the district nurses' association.

Parsons traveled extensively during her retirement years beginning in 1926, living with a sister and niece in France for two years and taking a long boat trip from Montreal, through the Panama Canal, with stops in Mexico, Hawaii, and Alaska. Her various travels were funded in part first by her stepfather and later by one of her half-sisters in gratitude for the time she cared for the family after the death of her mother.

In 1937 Parsons became a resident of Mt. Pleasant Home in Jamaica Plain, Massachusetts, where she lived until her death. She outlived both half-sisters and died on October 25, 1949.

## PUBLICATIONS BY
## SARA ELIZABETH PARSONS

### BOOKS

*Nursing Problems and Obligations.* Boston: Whitcomb and Barrows, 1916.

*History of the Massachusetts General Hospital Training School for Nurses.* Boston: Whitcomb and Barrows, 1922.

### ARTICLES

"Personal Experience in Training School Organization." *American Journal of Nursing* 3 (June 1903): 673–77.

"Nursing of the Insane." *Trained Nurse and Hospital Review* 36 (April 1906): 205–7.

"Practical Results of State Registration for Nurses." *American Journal of Nursing* 7 (March 1907): 465–67.

"The Sliding Scale of Charges for Private Duty Nurses." *American Journal of Nursing* 11 (June 1911): 694–96.

"Concerning Training Schools." *Boston Medical Surgical Journal* 165 (August 1911): 211.

"The Case Method of Teaching." American Journal of Nursing 11 (September 1911): 1009–11.

"Hospital Social Service." In *Annual Report NLNE, 1914, and Proceedings of 20th Convention.* Baltimore, Md.: Williams and Wilkins, 1914.

"Educational Standards for Nurses. State Registration and Training School Inspection." *Boston Medical Surgical Journal* 170 (April 1914): 574–75.

"The Age Limit." *American Journal of Nursing* 14 (October 1914): 21–23.

"Encouraging Signs in Nursing Education." *American Journal of Nursing* 15 (January 1915): 274–76.

"Necessity of a Background." *American Journal of Nursing* 15 (May 1915): 640–42.

"The Effect of American Red Cross Standards on Training Schools, Nursing Organizations, and the Nursing Profession." *American Journal of Nursing* 15 (August 1915): 1008–12.

"Why Private Duty Nurses Should Organize." *American Journal of Nursing* 16 (January 1916): 299–301.

"Ethics Applied to Nursing." *American Journal of Nursing* 16 (May 1916): 693–96.

"The Student Nurse." *American Journal of Nursing* 16 (August 1916): 1094–98.

"Impressions and Conclusions Based on Experiences Abroad by Overseas Nurses." *American Journal of Nursing* 19 (August 1919): 829–34.

### BIBLIOGRAPHY

Johnson, S. "Sara E. Parsons: 1864–1949." Nurses' Alumnae Association files, Massachusetts General Hospital. Mimeo, n.d.

Perkins, S. *A Centennial Review: The Massachusetts General Hospital School of Nursing 1873–1973.* Boston: Massachusetts General Hospital Nurses' Alumnae Association, 1975.

Peterson, A. "The Nurses' Fight for Military Rank." *Trained Nurse and Hospital Review* 109 (August 1942): 98–100.

"Sara Parsons." Obituary. *American Journal of Nursing* 49 (December 1949): 818–19.

"Who's Who in the Nursing World: Sara Parsons." *American Journal of Nursing* 24 (March 1924): 460.

Signe S. Cooper

# Mavis Orisca Pate

## 1925–1972

Mavis Orisca Pate is representative of the long tradition of missionary nurses from various religious groups who were willing to give up their lives while serving as missionaries in some of the world's trouble spots. Pate was killed while working in the Middle East.

Born on December 23, 1925, in Ringgold in the rural parish of Bienville in Louisiana, Pate was the second of two daughters of J.B. and Mattie Bell Green Pate. She attended schools in Ringgold and graduated from Ringgold High School in May 1942.

Following the example of her older sister and sole sibling, Gwendolyn, Pate entered the North Louisiana Sanitarium School of Nursing in Shreveport, from which she graduated in 1945. Almost immediately she began working in the operating room at the sanitarium. To further her education, she took a postgraduate course in operating room technique and management for six months at the Polyclinic Medical School and Hospital in New York City in 1948.

Soon .after her return to Louisiana, Pate entered the school of nursing at Northwestern State College, from which she received a bachelor's degree in nursing. As part of the scholarship award given her in 1951, she agreed to assist with the nursing service, assist with student health, and counsel students. She graduated with the highest average of any woman at the college and received an award, the "Pin of Distinction" from the Natchitoches chapter of the American Association of University Women.

Pate moved to Tyler, Texas, in 1956, where she worked as operating room supervisor at the Medical Center Hospital. While at the hospital, she compiled an operating room manual.

Pate took a one year leave of absence to join with Health Opportunity for People Everywhere (Project HOPE), then being set up by the Eisenhower administration. She was selected operating room supervisor in the first group of 25 nurses who sailed on the hospital ship *HOPE* in 1960,

and she published a diary of the Indonesia and South Vietnam experiences.

Pate applied to the foreign missions board of the Southern Baptist Convention for appointment as missionary following her enrollment at Southwestern Baptist Theological Seminary in Fort Worth, Texas. In July 1964 she was given an assignment in East Pakistan, now Bangladesh, and in Thailand. In January 1970 she was transferred to the Gaza Strip, then part of Israel.

In Gaza, Pate taught operating room techniques in the school of nursing as well as serving as a Sunday school teacher. She was killed on January 16, 1972, when the van, painted white to resemble an ambulance, in which she was carrying some children was fired upon by Arab guerrillas. Permission was obtained from the Israeli government to bury her in Gaza and the lone grave of Mavis Pate lies in the compound behind the school of nursing building at the Baptist Mission there.

## PUBLICATIONS BY MAVIS ORISCA PATE

### BOOKS

*Diary of Hope.* New Jersey: Ethicon, 1962.

*The Prep Manual.* New York: Edward Weck, 1967.

### BIBLIOGRAPHY

Bullough, B., and V. Bullough. "What We Should Know about Nursing's Christian Pioneers." *Journal of Christian Nursing* 4 (1987): 10–14.

Collins, M. and E. Rowe. "Nursing vs. Church Work: The Myth of the Higher Call." *Journal of Christian Nursing* 3 (1986): 40.

Jenni, J. "Life in Gaza Strip Said 'Not Good' Now," *Shreveport Times*, 24 September 1972.

"Magnificent Americans." *America* 104 (1961): 654–55.

"Medical Ship Sails." *New York Times*, 1 July 1960.

"Missionary Nurse Slain in Gaza." *Baptist Message* 87 (January 27, 1972): 1, 3.

Moore, M. "The Death of a Missionary." *Shreveport Journal*, 6 February 1972.

"Project Hope Underway." *American Journal of Nursing* 60 (1960), 1500–02.

"Ship of Hope." *Saturday Review* 18 (March 28, 1964).

Vaillot M. *Commitment to Nursing.* Philadelphia: Lippincott, 1962.

Walsh, W. *HOPE in the East.* New York: E.P. Dutton, 1970.

P.J. Ledbetter

## Blanche Pfefferkorn

### 1884–1961

Blanche Pfefferkorn is recognized for her many contributions to the development of nursing education and the improvement of nursing service. She served for almost 25 years as a member of the professional staff at the headquarters of the National League of Nursing Education.

Pfefferkorn was born in January 1884 in Baltimore, Maryland, the daughter of Leopold and Helen Einstein Pfefferkorn. She was one of five siblings and was a graduate of the Western High School in Baltimore.

She received her nursing diploma from the Johns Hopkins Hospital Nurses' Training School in 1911 and a bachelor of science degree from Columbia University in 1916. Pfefferkorn later was awarded the Isabel Hampton Robb Fellowship for graduate study at Teachers College, Columbia University, New York City, and received her master of arts degree from that institution in 1928.

After her graduation from Johns Hopkins, she worked as an assistant in the operating room at Bellevue Hospital in New York City (1911–12), as supervisor in the operating room at Harlem Hospital (1912–13), and as superintendent of nurses at Harlem Hospital (1913–14). She was instructor and assistant professor of nursing at the University of Cincinnati from 1916 to 1923, departmental secretary at the division of nursing education at Teachers College from 1927 to 1930, and director of special studies at Bellevue Hospital from 1930 to 1932.

For 17 years prior to her retirement in 1949, Pfefferkorn served as director of studies at the National League of Nursing Education, where she contributed much to nursing education and nursing service not only for the league, but also for other organizations in the health field. She published numerous articles on nursing subjects and also coauthored a history of the Johns Hopkins School of Nursing from 1907 to 1949. Pfefferkorn was a pioneer in professional nursing research. Her publications had a wide influence on the development of standards in nursing education and nursing service.

Pfefferkorn occupied local, state, and national positions in the American Red Cross, the Ohio State Association of Graduate Nurses, the Ohio State League of Nursing Education, and the American Nurses' Association. She served as the second executive secretary of the National League of Nursing Education and carried for four years the major responsibility for organizing and developing the league's program and services.

On her retirement in 1949, the league expressed respect and appreciation for the personal and professional contributions of Pfefferkorn. She died suddenly in Los Angeles on June 4, 1961, and was survived by two siblings.

### PUBLICATIONS BY BLANCHE PFEFFERKORN

#### BOOKS

*Clinical Education in Nursing.* New York: Macmillan, 1932.

*An Activity Analysis of Nursing.* New York: s.n., 1934.

*Administrative Cost Analysis for Nursing Service and Nursing Education.* Chicago: American Hospital Association, 1940, 1947.

*The Johns Hopkins Hospital School of Nursing, 1889–1949.* Baltimore: Johns Hopkins Press, 1954.

#### ARTICLES

"On Teachers and Teaching." *American Journal of Nursing* 22 (February 1922): 350–53.

"Adjustment in the Educational Program for Nursing." *American Journal of Nursing* 24 (November 1924): 1126–32.

"Department of Nursing Education. Nursing as an Educational Project." *American Journal of Nursing* 26 (April 1926): 301–05.

"Improvement of the Nurse in Service—an Historical Review." *American Journal of Nursing* 28 (July 1928): 700–10.

"Measuring Nursing Quantitatively and Qualitatively." *American Journal of Nursing* 32 (January 1932): 80–84.

"Nursing and Medical Education." *American Journal of Nursing* 33 (December 1933): 1188–92.

"The League Is Working on Records." *American Journal of Nursing* 35 (June 1935): 563–67.

## BIBLIOGRAPHY

Alan Mason Chesney Medical Archives. Johns Hopkins Medical Institutions, Baltimore.

"Blanche Pfefferkorn." Obituary. *Baltimore Sun,* 14 June 1961.

Munson, H.W. *The Story of the National League of Nursing Education.* Philadelphia: W.B. Saunders, 1934.

Lilli Sentz

## Harriet Newton Phillips

### 1819–1901

Although Linda Richards is generally referred to as the first trained nurse in America, there is evidence that the honor may belong to Harriet Newton Phillips. She was also among the first to receive a nursing certificate, to perform community nursing and missionary service, and to take postgraduate training.

Phillips was born on December 29, 1819, in Pennsylvania. The names of her parents are unknown, but records indicate that they were both born in Pennsylvania and that Phillips had at least one sister, Mary.

There is little information about Phillips until 1862, when she joined the Western Sanitary Commission. From October 1862 until November 1863, she was a nurse at the General Hospital, Jefferson Barracks near St. Louis when she reported for duty as a nurse at the General Hospital, Benton Barracks in St. Louis. She is listed on the February 1864 rolls at General Hospital 19 in Nashville, Tennessee. She was discharged from the army in March 1864.

In October 1863 the Female Medical College of the Woman's Hospital of Phila-

delphia began holding classes. Influenced by the Society of Friends, Florence Nightingale, and Elizabeth Blackwell about the need to educate women in matters concerning their own health and for the medical and nursing professions, Ann Preston delivered a series of lectures on the training of nurses. It is probable that Phillips began her training here shortly after her discharge from the army. The lectures included anatomy and physiology, pharmacology, and chemistry. Phillips was taught the practical arts of nursing by Emeline Cleveland, the resident physician.

Reports indicate that Phillips only attended the school briefly since she left the hospital in 1864 to follow her profession in the community. She returned in 1869, when she was appointed to the position of head nurse and also assisted in the training of nurses. She later became matron at the Woman's Hospital. In 1872 she again left the hospital to engage in missionary work among the American Indians in northwestern Wisconsin, where she remained until 1875.

In June 1875 Phillips began working as matron in San Francisco with the Chinese population. She returned to the Woman's Hospital in Philadelphia for postgraduate training in 1878. Five years later, she moved from Philadelphia to Gladwyne, Pennsylvania. Toward the end of her life, she lived with a niece, Mary Egbert, in Gladwyne. She died on August 29, 1901.

## BIBLIOGRAPHY

Brockett, L.P. *Woman's Work in the Civil War.* Philadelphia: Hubbard, 1888.

"Harriet Newton Phillips." Obituary. *Norristown Daily Herald,* 30 August 1901.

Kalisch, P., and B. Kalisch. *Advancement of American Nursing.* Boston: Little, Brown, 1978.

Large, J.T. "Harriet Newton Phillips, the First Trained Nurse In America." *Image* 8 (1976): 49–51.

Matthews, I. Interview with author.

Robinson, V. *White Caps, the Story of Nursing.* Philadelphia: J.B. Lippincott, 1946.

"Do You Know?" Editorial. *New England Journal of Medicine* 215 (1936): 946.

Lilli Sentz

## Mary Genevieve Phillips

1903–1980

The distinguished military career of Mary Genevieve Phillips included being chief of the Army Nurse Corps from 1947 to 1951. Her assignments also included that of director of nurses, Armed Forces of the Western Pacific during World War II and two other key positions in the Office of the Surgeon General. After her retirement, she entered full-time service in the Sisters of the Visitation of St. Paul.

Phillips was born on December 2, 1903, in Eau Claire, Wisconsin, to Mr. and Mrs. James E. Phillips. She was one of nine children.

She was graduated from Medford High School in 1921 and attended Sauk County Rural Normal School to prepare for teaching. She then attended two summer sessions in 1924 and 1925 at the University of Wisconsin in Madison while she taught in the rural schools of Sauk County, Wisconsin.

In the fall of 1926, Phillips entered the Army School of Nursing at Walter Reed General Hospital in Washington, D. C. An honor student, she was described as intelligent, cooperative, dependable, and deeply interested in nursing.

Upon graduation in 1929, Phillips became a second lieutenant and was assigned to the Army School of Nursing, where she was an instructing supervisor until 1933. In December 1933 while assigned to forts Slocum and Jay, New York, she attended Teachers College, Columbia University, in her free time. She received a B.S. degree in nursing education in 1935.

Her first overseas assignment was as a general-duty nurse in the Philippine Department, first at Fort Stotsenburg, Pampanga, and then at Sternberg General Hospital in Manila during the years 1936–39. This helped prepare her for subsequent key assignments in the Pacific.

In December 1939 Phillips returned to Walter Reed General Hospital, where she practiced nursing until January 1941, when she was promoted to first lieutenant and transferred to the station hospital at Ft. Devens, Massachusetts, as chief nurse. Her promotion to captain came in 1942.

In May 1943 Phillips was promoted to major and appointed deputy superintendent of the Army Nurse Corps, serving under Florence Blanchfield. She was promoted seven months later to the rank of lieutenant colonel, as promotions were accelerated during World War II.

One of her major tasks during her assignment as deputy superintendent was related to military nurses' uniforms. With the rapid expansion of the Army Nurse Corps during the war, it was difficult to supply each nurse with the proper uniform. Nurses in the Pacific theater of operations at the outbreak of the war had been issued little more than the regulation duty uniform. Discomfort and discouragement persisted for the nurses.

During this critical period, Phillips focused on the development of new uniforms. These included special types suitable for the variety of tropical, temperate, and arctic climates where nurses were assigned. Phillips selected and tested materials as well as worked with the civilian manufacturers, who had difficulty securing enough material to meet the demand. For her work during this period of expansion, Phillips was awarded the Legion of Merit.

On July 31, 1945, Phillips became the director of nurses for the Armed Forces of the Western Pacific and was responsible for handling the redeployment and the demobilization of nurses. She also set up the nursing service for the occupation forces in Japan and Korea. Phillips received the Army Commendation Ribbon for her contributions in this assignment.

In the spring of 1947, she returned to the Office of the Surgeon General. The retiring superintendent, Florence Blanchfield, suggested that the regular army nurses (approximately 894 in number) recommend a successor. Phillips had the distinction of being chosen by them. In October 1947 Phillips became the eighth chief of the Army Nurse Corps. She was the first graduate of the Army School of Nursing to serve as chief of the corps.

Phillips's accomplishments during this period were varied. She was concerned with implementing the directive that gave army nurses the status of regularly commissioned officers on a permanent basis. In addition, although the Army Nurse Corps was exempted from the army-wide requirement that all commissioned officers hold or achieve baccalaureate degrees, the corps in 1950 did set the goal for its officers to complete an accredited program leading to an undergraduate degree, preferably in nursing.

Phillips also was involved with organizing the nurse corps section of the Officers' Reserve Corps, which was created by the Army-Navy Nurses' Act of 1947. She developed policies that allowed reserve nurses on extended active duty to participate in the nurse corps graduate education programs. Reserve nurses not on active duty could request assignments for training purposes to reserve units near their homes to maintain proficiency in nursing practice.

Phillips also provided extension courses for army nurses and instituted staff-education programs for nurses at all installations. In addition, she sponsored the establishment at the University of Pittsburgh of two-week nursing workshops. At Phillips's suggestion, the first civilian nursing leaders were appointed as consultants to the surgeon general for matters pertaining to army nursing.

In October 1949 a 48-week pilot course of instruction for enlisted personnel on the practical-nurse level was set up under her direction at the Army Medical Center, Washington, D.C. Phillips's purpose for this course was to release registered nurses for professional nursing. Additional courses were later established as required to meet patient-care needs.

Phillips succeeded in having a nurse permanently assigned to the supply division to advise on procurement, development, and modification of supplies and equipment used by nurses in the care of patients. Also on her recommendation, nurses were assigned to the management research branch to initiate projects in the study and improvement of the administration and operation of army hospital nursing services.

During the end of Phillips's assignment as chief, the United States became involved in the Korean War. The strength of the Army Nurse Corps increased during the conflict from 3,460 in July 1950 to 5,397 in July 1951.

In September 1951 Phillips retired. For the next eight years, she took care of her mother. Following her mother's death, Phillips in 1960 was received into the Sisters of the Visitation of St. Paul and was given the name of Sister Mary Genevieve. She suffered a coronary thrombosis and was professed in the hospital in March 1963; she later returned to the convent and was professed with due ceremony in August 1964. Six months later, she suffered an aneurysm that resulted in paralysis of her lower extremities. For the next 5 years, her condition worsened gradually. She died on January 30, 1980, after suffering a massive stroke and is buried in Resurrection Cemetery, St. Paul, Minnesota, in a plot reserved for the Sisters of the Visitation.

## PUBLICATIONS BY MARY GENEVIEVE PHILLIPS

"The Army Nurse Corps—and the Future." *Red Cross Courier* 28 (January 1949): 20, 30.

## BIBLIOGRAPHY

De Sales, M. Letter to Ruth Anne Vihinen, 20 March 1986.

Kelly, R.B. "History of Nursing Service in the South Pacific." Washington, D.C.: National Archives, 1946. Unpublished manuscript. RG 112.

Mehl, J.M. *A Concise Biography of Colonel Mary Genevieve Phillips, ANC.* Washington, D.C.: Historical Services Division, Center of Military History, 1980.

Phillips, M.G. Official officer records. Washington, D.C.: U.S. Army Center of Military History, 1980.

Shields, E.A. *Highlights in the History of the Army Nurse Corps.* Washington, D.C.: U.S. Army Center of Military History, 1981.

Sisters of the Visitation of St. Paul. Letter to Ruth Anne Vihinen, 1 February 1980.

Ruth Anne Vihinen
Rosemary T. McCarthy

## Drusilla Rageu Poole
### 1921–1981

Drusilla Rageu Poole was a nursing educator and administrator who practiced and taught in China, Korea, and throughout the United States. Her nursing career was devoted to strengthening hospital-based in-service education and to providing basic nursing preparation for army nurse cadets during her tenure as director of the Walter Reed Army Institute of Nursing.

Poole was born March 5, 1921, in Cornersville, Tennessee. Her father, John Poole, was a barber, and her mother was a homemaker. There were two younger daughters in the family, which moved frequently within Tennessee during Poole's childhood.

After graduation from high school, Poole worked her way through two years at Martin Junior College in Pulaski, Tennessee. In the fall of 1940, she was admitted to Scarritt College for Christian Workers in Nashville and graduated in 1942 with an A.B. degree. After commencement, she worked for two years for the Methodist church as club director at the Bethlehem Center in Charlotte, North Carolina.

Poole entered the Yale School of Nursing in New Haven, Connecticut, on September 14, 1944, with financial support from the U.S. Cadet Nurse Corps. She became prepared as an advanced nurse clinician in medical-surgical nursing and was awarded a master's degree in nursing in May 1947. In 1966 she matriculated at the University of Texas at Austin and was granted a Ph.D. in 1969 with a major in education.

In 1947, after graduation from Yale, Poole was accepted as a four-year "permanent appointee" by Yale-in-China, an organization that was under the auspices of Yale University and that sponsored the Yale elementary and middle schools, the Hsaing-Ya premedical and medical schools, and Hsaing-Ya nursing and midwivery schools in Changsha, Hunan Province, China.

While still in New Haven, Poole studied Mandarin Chinese at Yale's institute of Far Eastern Languages. During this time, the political upheaval in China and the civil war between the Nationalist and Communist Chinese threatened to delay her departure to Changsha. She embarked for China on March 12, 1948, and arrived in Hong Kong on April 6, 1948.

Poole developed a deep affection for and strong commitment to the Chinese people and to nursing education during her period in China. She worked long days as superintendent of nurses and clinical supervisor of students at Hsaing-Ya Hospital and as instructor in the nursing school. However, her activities were repeatedly jeopardized during her two years in China. Intrusions included temporary evacuations to the coast, eventual occupation of Changsha and the hospital compound by the Chinese Communists, widespread drafting of students into the armed forces, dwindling medical supplies, intensifying anti-American propaganda, isolation from contact with the West, and, ultimately, house arrest in the spring of 1950.

While under house arrest, Poole sewed on the silks she had purchased in better times. At night, she would sneak outside to visit with a Chinese doctor who was under house arrest in the neighboring building. After repeated interrogations and after all her personal property was taken from her, she decided to flee in May 1950.

Upon her arrival in New York in August 1950, Poole was asked to brief the State Department on the situation in China. She then returned to New Haven, where she assumed positions first as a staff nurse and then as head nurse with a chest surgery unit at Grace-New Haven Hospital.

In 1952 she moved to Fitchburg, Massachsetts, where she became clinical instructor and supervisor in surgical nursing at Burbank Hospital. Soon after she became director of in-service education and assistant director of nursing service at Emory University Hospital in Atlanta, Georgia.

In 1954 Poole joined the U.S. Army Nurse Corps and moved to Fort Sam Houston, Texas. By 1957 she had achieved the rank of captain and was stationed at

Walter Reed Hospital in Washington, D.C. Of deep concern to her at this time was the role of nursing in emergency and disaster services. She headed the National League for Nursing Disaster Nursing Project at the University of Minnesota School of Nursing (1958–59). Poole returned briefly to the Far East in 1963 as chief nurse supervisor for the Army Nurse Corps in Korea.

After completing her doctoral studies at the University of Texas at Austin in 1969, Poole became director of the Walter Reed Army Institute of Nursing (WRAIN). Under her leadership, the WRAIN program provided full tuition and a stipend for baccalaureate nursing education to highly qualified young men and women concurrently enlisted in the army and enrolled in a college or university. Poole's students graduated as first lieutenants in the U.S. Army and became nursing leaders who saw her as a strong and inspiring role model.

On May 21, 1972, Poole delivered the dedication address for the nursing memorial in Arlington National Cemetery. In 1973 she was selected by the surgeon general to receive the Dr. Anita Newcomb McGee Award for outstanding army nursing service, an honor presented by the Daughters of the American Revolution. Poole retired from the military in 1974 and, in the same year, was presented the Distinguished Alumnae Award from the Yale School of Nursing.

Poole died of intestinal cancer on December 11, 1981 at Sam Houston, Texas. She was buried with full military honors in the national cemetery at Fort Sam Houston and was survived by her sister, Geneva Poole Pitt of Nashville, Tennessee, as well as by several nieces and nephews.

## PUBLICATIONS BY DRUSILLA RAGEU POOLE

"Mrs. Chase Goes to China." *American Journal of Nursing*, 48 (December 1948): 797–98.

"In-service Education Reaches a Milestone." *American Journal of Nursing* 53 (December 1953): 1456.

"Searching for Know-How: Toward Progress in Nursing Service Through In-service Educa-

tion." *Military Medicine* 120 (June 1957): 426–29.

Preparing Hospital Nursing Staffs for Disaster Service. *Nursing Outlook* (October 1958): 586 ff.

"Roles and Functions of Staff Development Directors." *Journal of Continuing Education in Nursing* 8 (May–June 1977): 31–41.

## BIBLIOGRAPHY

Barrett, K. Oral history, 1986. Emory University Hospital Nursing Service, Atlanta, GA.

Biehusen, Y.R. Oral history, 1986. Emory University Hospital Nursing Service, Altanta, Ga.

Brown, B. Oral history, 1986. Emory University Hospital Nursing Service, Atlanta, Ga.

Helmann, E. Oral history, 1986. Emory University Hospital Nursing Service, Atlanta, Ga.

Kishpaugh, B. Oral history, 1986. Emory University Hospital Nursing Service, Atlanta, Ga.

Office of Alumnae Affairs. Yale University School of Nursing, New Haven, Conn.

Office of the Registrar. Scarritt College, Nashville, Tenn.

Office of the Registrar. University of Texas, Austin.

Office of the Registrar. Yale University School of Nursing, New Haven, Conn.

Parkhill, S. Oral history, 1986. Emory University Hospital Nursing Service, Atlanta, Ga.

Yale-China Collection. Sterling Archives, Yale University, New Haven, Conn.

Judith C. Hays

## Amy Elizabeth Pope
### 1869–1949

One of nursing's most prolific writers in the early part of the twentieth century, Amy Elizabeth Pope contributed to the education of nurses in the United States and abroad. Many of her books were translated into other languages and had widespread use in the United States, Canada, England, and Australia.

Pope was born June 30, 1869, in Quebec, Canada, to Alexander and Mary Pope. She was educated in private schools in Quebec and then entered the Presbyterian Hospital School of Nursing in New York City. A member of that school's first class, she was graduated in 1894. A dedicated learner, Pope enrolled in a number of postgraduate courses during her career, including courses at St. Bartholomew's Hospital in London, Gardner Gymnasium in New York City, Pratt Institute in Brooklyn, and Teachers College, Columbia University, New York City.

Pope served in a number of positions at Presbyterian Hospital. One year after she was graduated from its school of nursing, she was appointed night superintendent of the hospital. In 1896 she was granted a six-month's leave of absence to gain further experience at St. Bartholomew's Hospital in London.

Pope's visit to England was her first of many travels. She served as a Red Cross nurse in the Spanish-American War at Fortress Monroe in Virginia, in Puerto Rico, and in the Philippines. She returned from Manila in October 1900 and then sailed for Havana, Cuba, where she worked in Los Animos Hospital during a yellow fever epidemic.

In January 1904 after a six-month preliminary course for beginning student nurses was initiated at Presbyterian Hospital's training school for nurses, Pope was appointed instructor in practical nursing, demonstration, and pharmacology. While Pope was serving in this position, Anna Maxwell, superintendent of nurses, received many requests for assistance from superintendents at other schools of nursing. In responding to the requests for information and suggestions for setting up preliminary nursing courses, Pope discovered that her descriptions might provide material for a textbook. Helped by Maxwell, she wrote *Practical Nursing, A Textbook for Nurses*, which first appeared in 1907.

Although Maxwell was listed as the book's senior author, it is likely that Pope wrote the major portion of the text, as Maxwell carried heavy responsibilities. Five editions were published, the last one by Pope and Virna Young. Titled *Art and Principles of Nursing*, it appeared in 1934. The best known of Pope's writing, the book was widely used in the United States.

Pope resigned her position as instructor and was appointed to the nursing staff of the Isthmian Canal Commission. She sailed for Panama in May 1905, and she served as dietician in Ancon (now Gorgas) Hospital.

In 1907 the governor of Puerto Rico appointed Pope to organize the Government Insular Training School in San Juan. After two years, Pope returned to her alma mater as instructor and stayed two years before leaving for California in 1911. She was an instructor at St. Luke's Hospital School of Nursing in San Francisco from 1914 to 1928, then accepted a position as housemother at Bellevue Training School, New York City. She also did private-duty nursing, accompanying patients to Paris and to Bad Nauheim, Germany.

Pope's major contribution to her profession was her publications; she was writing at a time when few other nurses were doing so. Her first published work was *Home Care of the Sick*, published in 1904. Beginning in 1907 and continuing for nearly 20 years, she had a book published almost every year, with two being published some years. In all she wrote over 20 books. Subjects included pharmacology, chemistry, anatomy and physiology, and (with a coauthor) dietetics, all designed as basic texts for nursing students.

Pope died October 28, 1949, at Garden Hospital in San Francisco. She was survived by a brother, Alfred H. Pope, of Portland, Oregon; a sister, Emma M. Pope, of Toronto, Canada, and two nephews. She was buried in Cypress Lawn Cemetery in San Francisco.

### SELECTED PUBLICATIONS BY AMY ELIZABETH POPE

*Home Care of the Sick*. Chicago: American School of Home Economics, 1904.

With A.C. Maxwell. *Practical Nursing, A Textbook for Nurses*. New York: Putnam, 1907.

With M.L. Carpenter. *Essentials of Dietetics*. New York: Putnam, 1908.

With T. Pope. *A Quiz Book of Nursing for Teachers and Students*. New York: Putnam, 1909.

*Textbook of Anatomy and Physiology for Nurses*. New York: Putnam, 1913.

*Physics and Chemistry for Nurses.* New York: Putnam, 1916.

*A Textbook of Simple Nursing Procedures.* New York: Putnam, 1917.

*Pope's Manual of Nursing Procedures.* New York: Putnam, 1919.

*Materia Medica, Pharmacology and Therapeutics for Nurses.* Philadelphia: W.B. Saunders, 1921.

*A Medical Dictionary for Nurses.* New York: Putnam, 1928.

*A Practical Dietary Computer.* New York: Putnam, 1928.

With V.M. Young. *Art and Principles of Nursing.* New York: Putnam, 1934.

### BIBLIOGRAPHY

"Amy Elizabeth Pope." Obituary. *American Journal of Nursing* 50 (February 1950): 134–35.

"Authors in the Nursing Field: Amy Elizabeth Pope." *Trained Nurse and Hospital Review* 77 (July 1926): 19.

Lee, E. *History of the School of Nursing of the Presbyterian Hospital, New York, 1892–1942.* New York: G. P. Putnam's Sons, 1942.

Pennock, M.R. "Amy Elizabeth Pope." In *Makers of Nursing History.* New York: Lakeside Publishing, 1928.

Roberts, M.M. *American Nursing: History and Interpretation.* New York: Macmillan, 1954.

Signe S. Cooper

# Louise Matilda Powell

## 1871–1943

Louise Matilda Powell was the key figure in establishing the baccalaureate nursing program at the University of Minnesota. She also served as dean of the Western Reserve University School of Nursing.

Born in Staunton, Virginia, on March 12, 1871, Powell was the daughter of Hugh Lee and Ella Stribling Powell. She had a brother and a sister. Her early education was in private school in Virginia and at Stuart Hall in Staunton, where she trained to be a teacher.

After working as a grade school teacher, Powell decided that the care of the sick was her vocation and entered nursing school at St. Luke's Hospital in Richmond, Virginia. Regarded as influential in this career shift was her maternal grandfather, Francis T. Stribling, a physician who had served as superintendent of what later came to be known as the Western State Hospital for the Insane in Staunton. Stribling had become known and admired for his introduction of new methods for the humane treatment of patients.

After graduating in 1899, Powell became superintendent of nurses at St. Luke's Hospital, and she remained there until 1904. From 1905 until 1908, she served as infirmary nurse at the Baldwin School in Bryn Mawr, Pennsylvania. In 1908 she entered Teachers' College, Columbia University, in New York City as part of the largest class (16 total) of nurses to enter the college up to that time. Adelaide Nutting, then head of the nursing program, was impressed with her work, and when Richard Olding Beard, the physician-founder of the University of Minnesota School of Nursing, asked Nutting for assistance in finding a superintendent for the school, she recommended Powell.

Powell became the second superintendent of nurses at the University of Minnesota School of Nursing, succeeding Bertha Erdman, who had taken the school through its initial year. It was Powell, working closely with Beard, who organized and developed the school, which pioneered a new type of education for nursing.

Powell's administration (1910–24) saw a variety of innovations. A five-year curriculum, leading to the degree of bachelor of science and graduate in nursing, was established in June 1919. In December 1920 the university approved the Central School of Nursing, admitting as associates of the university three other institutions: the Minneapolis General Hospital, the Charles T. Miller Hospital, and the Northern Pacific Beneficial Association Hospital. In 1921 Beta chapter of Alpha Tau Delta, now a national nursing sorority for baccalaureate students, was installed.

In 1922 Powell's title was changed from superintendent of nurses to director of the University of Minnesota School of

Nursing, a position she held until she resigned in 1924 to become dean of the Western Reserve University School of Nursing. She remained in that position as long as her health permitted.

Throughout her life, Powell continued her education. She did postgraduate clinical work at the Hospital for Sick Children, Mt. Wilson, Maryland, and at the Municipal Hospital for Contagious Diseases, Philadelphia, Pennsylvania. She studied at Teachers College, Columbia University, where she secured a diploma in education and was awarded a bachelor's degree at Smith College, Northampton, Massachusetts; and at the University of Virginia in Charlottesville. Twice during her tenure at Minnesota she took sabbatical leaves for further study.

As a member of the nursing profession, Powell made contributions in several areas. She contributed to professional journals, with articles on such diverse topics as tuberculosis nursing and student government. At various times, she held offices in several professional organizations, including the following: president, Minnesota League of Nursing Education; vice-president and director, National League of Nursing Education; secretary, treasurer, and director, Minnesota Nurses' Association; member of state and national committees, American Red Cross; and honorary president, Minnesota Organization for Public Health Nursing.

The problems with which Powell and her colleagues struggled included attracting students of the caliber that a university school of nursing could accept, establishing a curriculum and broadening facilities of instruction, trying to upgrade inadequate housing for nurses, and countering objections that came, on occasion, even from medical staff members. Tribute was paid her by the University of Minnesota in recognition of her contribution to nursing education when, in celebration of the school's 30th anniversary in 1939, the nurses' residence was renamed Louise M. Powell Hall, the first university building to be named for a living person.

In 1926 Powell, who never married, retired to live in Charlottesville and later in Staunton, Virginia, with her sister Lucy Lee Powell. For several months prior to her death, which occurred unexpectedly on October 6, 1943, at her home in Staunton, she had lived at her brother's home in Lexington, Virginia. He survived her. She is buried in Staunton beside her mother and sister.

### PUBLICATIONS BY LOUISE MATILDE POWELL

"The History of the Development of Nursing at the University of Minnesota." *Alumnae Quarterly* 17 (January 1937): 4–13.

"Education in Tuberculosis for Student Nurses." *American Journal of Nursing* 22 (November 1921): 98–102.

Department of Nursing Education: "Student Self Government in Schools of Nursing." *American Journal of Nursing* 20 (March 1920): 471–8.

"Existing Affiliations between Universities and Training Schools." *National League of Nursing Education, Annual Report* (1915): 106–14, and *Proceedings of the 21st Convention*, Baltimore, Md.: Williams & Wilkins, 1915.

"How the Training School for Nurses Benefits by Relation to a University." *American Society of Superintendents of Training Schools for Nurses, Annual Report* (1911): 150–58, and *Proceedings of the 17th Convention*, Baltimore, Md.: J.H. Furst, 1911.

### BIBLIOGRAPHY

Beard, R.O. "The University School of Nursing." Dedication Program, Nurses' Hall, University of Minnesota, 27 October 1933.

Densford, K.J. "Louise Matilde Powell, R.N., B.S." *Alumnae Quarterly, University of Minnesota School of Nursing* 25 (January 1944): 34.

Gray, J. *Education for Nursing: A History of the University of Minnesota School.* Minneapolis, Minn.: University of Minnesota Press, 1960.

"Minnesota Women." *Alumni News, University of Minnesota*, October 1970, 20–22.

Brenda H. Canedy

# Sister Regina Purtell

1866–1950

A Catholic sister in the Daughters of Charity of St. Vincent de Paul, Sister Regina Purtell is best known for her service as an army nurse with Theodore Roosevelt's Rough Riders in the Spanish-American War. She gained further distinction as a fighter of disease when she nursed victims of influenza in Texas, typhoid in Alabama, and influenza and leprosy in Louisiana.

Born Ellen Purtell on November 14, 1866, in Monches, Wisconsin, she was one of three daughters and two sons of John and Catherine Sullivan Purtell. Little is recorded about her childhood and school days. She entered the Daughters of Charity community from her home town in 1897 and at the age of 32 made her religious vows, taking the name of Sister Regina. Coming from a family that produced eight doctors, two of them her brothers, she was devoted to the art of healing and showed exceptional talent for organizing and directing patient care in hospitals.

Sister Purtell's crusade against disease as a nurse spanned more than 37 years. It began when she answered an appeal from President William McKinley for nurses to serve in the Spanish-American War. As the first volunteer, she was assigned to the Rough Riders division of the army hospital at Montauk Point, Long Island. Appalled by the unsanitary conditions, she made the substandard hygienic conditions her main target. Convinced of the need for reforms, she reorganized the hospital, establishing quality standards of care. She nursed the sick and wounded in the Rough Riders division, and patients praised the care they received.

When a typhoid epidemic broke out in Huntsville, Alabama, during the war, Sister Purtell was called on to help fight it. Her prior army experience proved invaluable in dealing with the disease and helping to prevent its spread.

At the end of the Spanish-American War, Sister Purtell was honored for her service. She returned to the nursing duties she had left at St. Mary's Hospital in Evansville, Indiana. From 1898 to 1919 she was in charge of male wards at St. Vincent's Hospital in Indianapolis.

Bank presidents, lawyers, and prominent businessmen were not only Sister Purtell's patients, but were also grateful friends who praised her nursing care. When President Theodore Roosevelt had to undergo surgery, he chose St. Vincent's Hospital to have the benefit of her excellent nursing care.

During her years at St. Vincent's Hospital, Sister Purtell's expertise as a troubleshooter in controlling disease often was requested. She always was willing to move and assume responsibility for nursing services on short notice. In 1918 she was transferred to an emergency campus at the University of Texas at Austin when an influenza epidemic broke out among the student body. She converted the largest fraternity house into a temporary medical facility and supervised the nursing care given to the stricken students.

In 1919 Sister Purtell was sent to the hospital in Carville, Louisiana. Her services to the patients of the leprosarium and her contributions to the success of the hospital's unique program for lepers were nationally recognized, and she was singled out as the heroine of the smallpox epidemic that ravaged the patients at Carville. She was the first to recognize the symptoms of smallpox and went into quarantine with them to continue their nursing care.

In 1957 the Daughters of Charity at Carville were presented with the Distinguished Service Award, the highest award of the U.S. Department of Health, Education, and Welfare. In his recommendation for this citation, Edgar Johnwick, medical officer in charge of Carville, cited Sister Purtell's dedication during the smallpox epidemic.

Due to failing health, Sister Purtell went into semiretirement at the age of 68 at Providence Infirmary in Mobile, Alabama. The remaining 15 years of her life she waged a different crusade—a missionary one. Mounting a letter-writing campaign requesting aid for the foreign mission, she circled the globe seeking help for missions in China, Japan, India, Africa, and other outposts.

When plans to demolish the Providence Informary became imminent, Sister Purtell was transferred to DePaul Sanitarium in New Orleans, Louisiana. She died on October 24, 1950, at the age of 84 and was buried in St. Vincent's Cemetery in New Orleans after a full military funeral, the first accorded a nun in Louisiana. Sister Purtell was survived by two sisters, her two brothers and four nephews.

## BIBLIOGRAPHY

Archives of the Daughters of Charity. Marillac Provincial House, St. Louis, Mo.

"Famed Crusader Against Disease Dies Here at 84." *New Orleans States*, 24 October 1950.

Hannefin, D. "The Daughters of Charity at Carville: 1896–1981." *Vincentian Heritage* 11 (1981): 76–78.

"Military Rites Held Here for Renowned Nun." *New Orleans States*. 25 October 1950.

"Nurse Who Helped Rough Riders Dies." *New York Times*, 25 October 1950.

Picayne, I. "Nun Who Nursed Wounded is Dead." *New Orleans Times*, 25 October 1950.

"Roosevelt's War Nurse Dies at 84." *New Orleans Times*, 25 October 1950.

"U.S. Health, Welfare Department's Highest Award Given to Nun Who Staffed Leprosarium," *New World*, 12 April 1957.

Kathleen Smyth

# Frances Reiter

## 1904–1977

Frances Reiter is best known for her contributions to nursing education and practice. She coined the term *nurse clinician* in 1943 in a speech and was a strong advocate of advanced preparation for nurse clinicians.

Born in 1904, Reiter was a graduate of the Johns Hopkins Hospital Training School for Nurses. She entered nursing practice in 1931 as head nurse at Johns Hopkins. In 1936 she moved to Pittsburgh, Pennsylvania, to become assistant director of nursing services and nursing education at Montefiore Hospital. During this time, she earned a bachelor of science degree in nursing education and a master of arts degree in teaching biological sciences from Teachers College, Columbia University, New York City.

From 1941 to 1945 Reiter served as instructor at several different schools: Johns Hopkins, Bryn Mawr, Boston University, and Massachusetts General Hospital. In 1945 she became instructor at Teachers College, Columbia University, and over the years was promoted to full professor. In 1960 she became the first dean of the Graduate School of Nursing, New York Medical College, which later became the Lienhard School of Nursing at Pace University. She retired in 1969.

Active in research, Reiter served as project director of the United States Public Health Service's study, "Quality of Nursing Care: A Report of a Field Study to Establish Criteria." She was chair of the American Nurses' Association's committee on education, which in 1965 issued a position paper stating that all persons licensed to practice nursing should be educated in institutions of higher learning. She also believed that the greatest potential for nursing was in the long-term care situation, and it was here that the nurse could find professional fulfillment. This was the role of the nurse clinician as she conceived it.

Reiter was a member of the executive committee of the first editorial board of the journal *Nursing Research*. She received the American Nurses' Association's Honorary Membership Award, the Florence Nightingale Award of the International Red Cross, the Distinguished Service Award from the National League for Nursing, and the Medal of Excellence from the New York Medical College. She was an honorary fellow of the American Academy of Nursing.

Reiter died in Cherry, Illinois, on January 18, 1977, after a long illness.

## PUBLICATIONS BY FRANCES REITER

### BOOKS

With M.E. Kakosh, *Quality of Nursing Care: A Report of a Field Study to Establish Criteria*. New York: Graduate School of Nursing, New York Medical College, 1963.

## ARTICLES

"Preparation of Clinical Instructors," *American Journal of Nursing* 44 (1944): 106.

"Where Is the Head Nurse?" *American Journal of Nursing* 48 (1948): 156–157.

"*Promotion and Staffing*," *American Journal of Nursing* 61 (May 1961): 56 ff.

"Choosing the Better Part," *American Journal of Nursing* 64 (December 1964): 65–68.

"The Nurse Clinician," *American Journal of Nursing* 66 (February 1966): 274–80.

## BIBLIOGRAPHY

"Frances Reiter, Prominent Educator, Dies." *American Journal of Nursing*" 77 (March 1977): 349, 488.

Vern L. Bullough

# Helena Willis Render

## 1896–1970

Helena Willis Render was a pioneer advocate of nursing's need to break away from the image of nurses as overseers responsible for cleanliness and order in hospital wards. Instead, she emphasized the individuality of the patient and the importance of a therapeutic nurse-patient relationship in developing patients' self-esteem and helping them recover from an illness. Render's 1947 prize winning book, *Nurse-Patient Relationships in Psychiatry*, not only became a classic but changed the nature of psychiatric nursing. Render held that the primary objective in teaching psychiatric nursing was to force the student to see the patient as a person. She taught that what the nurse said and did influenced what the patient said and did. She also emphasized the importance of psychosomatic medicine, the interrelationship of body and mind. She believed it was essential that nurses recognize emotions and feeling states in people in order to modify patients' attitudes and moods. In order to acquire this ability, she recommended that nurses study facial expressions, postures, and gestures of figures portrayed in works of art. She also recommended the study of literature, especially the classics, for understanding the dynamics of human behavior.

Render was born June 16, 1896, in St. John's, New Brunswick, Canada. Her father was George Willis; her mother's name is not known. Render attended St. John's High School, after which she was employed as a stenographer. In 1916 she entered the Central Maine General Hospital School of Nursing in Lewiston, Maine, from which she graduated in 1918.

Render moved early in the 1920s to Cleveland, Ohio, where she was the first supervisor and instructor of the neuropsychiatric division of Cleveland City Hospital from 1922 to 1925. She went on to attend the Francis Payne Bolton School of Nursing at Western Reserve University, from which she graduated in 1932. After her graduation, she moved to Iowa to become chief nurse of the Iowa State Psychiatric Hospital. It was while there that she taught her students the method of recording their interactions with the patients. These records were then summarized for a teacher-student conference, where they were interpreted and evaluated. It was these methods which formed her ideas about nurse patient relationships. One of her students was Gwen E. Tudor Will who also was important in psychiatric nursing.

Render married Norman D. Render, M.D., a staff physician at the Psychiatric Hospital on January 1, 1937. After her marriage she left state employment and devoted herself to research and writing. Her influence on modern psychiatric nursing is regarded as extremely important, particularly for the early development of interpersonal nursing.

In 1953 Render suffered a cerebral vascular accident. In 1962, after the death of her husband, she entered the Nebraska P.E.O. (Philanthropic Education Organization) Home in Beatrice, Nebraska, where she lived until her death. In November 1964 she contributed an article to *Nursing Outlook*, reporting how her stroke had affected her life. Render died October 28, 1970, in the Beatrice Lutheran Hospital. She was buried in the cemetery of the private nursing home where she had lived. There were no survivors.

## PUBLICATIONS BY HELENA WILLIS RENDER

### BOOKS

*Nurse Patient Relationships in Psychiatry.* New York: McGraw-Hill, 1947.

### ARTICLES

"Teaching Psychiatric Nursing." *Mental Hygiene* 21 (October 1937): 79–88.

"The Understanding Heart." *American Journal of Nursing* 37 (December 1937): 1356–59.

"Creative Aspects of Psychiatric Nursing." *American Journal of Nursing* 50 (July 1950): 433–36.

"My Old Age." *Nursing Outlook* 12 (November 1964): 31–33.

### BIBLIOGRAPHY

Anderson, V., Coordinator of Development and Alumni Relations, Case Western Reserve University, Cleveland, Ohio. Letter, February 26, 1987.

DeVore, J., Administrator, Nebraska P.E.O. (Philanthropic Education Organization) Home. Letter, February 24, 1987. Telephone conversation, June 27, 1987.

Driskill, S., Personnel Clerk, Cleveland Metropolitan General Hospital, Highland View Hospital, Cleveland, Ohio. Letter, February 26, 1987.

Editor: Iowa State Association of Registered Nurses, Des Moines, Iowa, BULLETIN, January 1937, page 19. (marriage announcement of Mrs. and Dr. Render).

"Historical Development of Psychiatric Nursing." (Prepared for the working conference on Graduate Education in Psychiatric Nursing, held in Williamsburg, Virginia, November 26–30, 1956. National League for Nursing.

Ingersoll, F.E., Director, Central Maine Medical School of Nursing, Lewiston, Me. Letters, November 17, 1980, February 18, 1987. Telephone conversation, May 1986.

Kelso, Dennis, J., Health Services Administrator, The University of Iowa. Letter, February 24, 1987.

Meyers, R.N.M.S., Executive Director, Iowa Nurses' Association, Des Moines, Iowa. Letter, January 31, 1980.

Rasmussen, Etta H., Associate Professor, The University of Iowa, Iowa City. Letter, February 8, 1980. Telephone conversation, March 1980.

Wallace, Helen D., Nebraska P.E.O. (Philanthropic Education Organization) Home. Letter, March 1980.

Weiss, Olga, R.N.M.A., author and former associate editor of "Nursing Outlook." Revised Mrs. Render's book during Render's illness. Correspondence February 22, 1980, March 19, 1980.

Will, Gwen E. Tudor. "A Sociopsychiatric Nursing Approach to Intervention in a Problem of Mutual Withdrawal in a Mental Hospital Ward." *Psychiatry* 15 (May 1952): 193–217.

Will, Gwen Tudor. Director of Community Care, The Berkshire Mental Health Center, Pittsfield, Mass. Letter, February 19, 1980.

Marguerite Lucy Manfreda

# Linda Ann Judson Richards

## 1841–1930

Linda Ann Judson Richards was one of the pathbreakers in nursing. She was night superintendent of Bellevue Training School in New York City, the first of the American training schools patterned after the so-called Nightingale model, and was an early head of the Boston Training School, another of the Nightingale schools, which later became the Massachusetts General Hospital School of Nursing. Though she claimed to be America's first trained nurse, that honor may belong to one of several nurses, including Harriet Newton Phillips. Richards opened the first training school for nurses in Japan based on American models.

Born July 27, 1841, near Potsdam, New York, Richards was the youngest of four daughters of Sanford and Betsy Sinclair Richards. Her family was devoutly Christian, and she was christened Melinda Ann Judson Richards after a well-known missionary, Ann Judson. When Richards was still under five years of age, her family moved to Wisconsin and purchased land on the site of what later was Watertown. Shortly after this, however, her father died, and her mother returned to Vermont with her children.

Richards grew up in the towns of Derby and Lyndon, Vermont, and for a time lived with her maternal grandfather, a deeply religious person who had a great deal of influence on her. She attended the Lyndon common schools and nearby Barton Academy. Her mother died when she was 13, and for a time, she lived in the household of a local physician and assisted him in the care of his patients. This and a religious experience influenced her choice of nursing as a career.

In order to support herself, Richards went to work in the 1860s at the Union Straw Works in Foxboro, Massachusetts. Some of her spare time was spent caring for neighbors who were ill. In 1870 she went to work at Boston City Hospital as an assistant nurse, an experience that she reported as disillusioning. She found her co-workers to be ignorant and heartless and their work limited to what later was done by ward maids. Although she was offered the position of head nurse after only three months, she felt she did not know enough to take the job and did not see that the job would give her any opportunity to learn.

At this time, Richards heard about a nurses' training school being organized at the New England Hospital for Women and Children in Boston. She enrolled as a member of the first of five student classes in September 1872. At the hospital, she worked on the wards under supervision and sat in on lectures by the medical staff of the hospital. One year later, she was given the first diploma issued by this school, hence her claim to being the first trained nurse. There were, however, other schools, although not all of them issued diplomas.

After graduation, Richards accepted a position as night superintendent at the newly established Bellevue Training School in New York City, the first school to be organized on the Nightingale model in the United States as set forth by Nightingale at St. Thomas's Hospital in London.

She returned to Boston a year later to become the superintendent of another Nightingale school, the Boston Training School. The school was under the direction of an independent committee, which had a contractual arrangement with the hospital to open specified wards for training pupils. In the first year of its existence, it had two superintendents, and by the time Richards arrived, there was strong opposition from the hospital's medical staff. Staff members considered the untrained nurses as adequate and saw no reason to continue the training program. Richards quickly disarmed the opposition, developed a program of regular classroom instruction, and manged to open all the wards to pupils. She was soon recognized not only as superintendent of the school, but as superintendent of nurses as well. Her success gave confidence and support to the entire movement for the professional training of nurses.

After three years at the Boston school (later the Massachusetts General Hospital School of Nursing), Richards resigned in order to travel to England to study the Nightingale system. Florence Nightingale, with whom she consulted, arranged for her to be received as a visitor at St. Thomas's Hospital School of Nursing in London. From there she went on to observe nursing at King's College Hospital in London and at the training school at the Edinburg Royal Infirmary.

When she returned to Boston in the fall of 1877, Richards worked with Edward Cowles, superintendent of Boston City Hospital, to develop a training school as an integral part of the hospital. This model was quickly imitated by other hospitals. Eventually, this weakened the independent power of nursing education, since it brought education under the control of the hospital authorities.

Richard's tenure as matron of the hospital and superintendent of the training school lasted less than one year. In August 1879 she took a leave of absence due to illness and did not return until three years later.

Richards resigned in 1885 in order to serve as a missionary in Japan. On her arrival in Japan in January 1896, she entered into an intensive study of Japanese, and by the autumn of that year, she had opened Japan's first training school for nurses, located at the Doshisha Hospital in Kyoto. The school was the first in any of the mission fields to follow the then-emerging American two-year plan, and many of the instructional materials were Japanese translations of American works. Richards spent five years in Japan, supervising the nursing school, teaching Bible classes, and conveying the Christian message. She returned to the United States in March 1891 due to health problems.

She continued to be active in nursing organizations on her return. Richards was the first president of the American Society of Superintendents of Training Schools in 1894, and she purchased the first share of stock in the *American Journal of Nursing* in 1900. She also served as a member of the committee that established the hospital economics program at Teachers College, Columbia University. Although she was honored for her early leadership, she found herself in disagreement with the objectives of the nursing organizations, especially those regarding nursing legislation and registration.

Richards also continued to work as a nurse, but her ill health often led her to serve in each capacity for comparatively short periods. For a six-month period in 1891, she was head of the Philadelphia Visiting Nurse Society. She left this to establish a training school at Philadelphia's Methodist Episcopal Hospital (1892). She then reorganized and strengthened the nursing school in the New England Hospital for Women and Children (1893–94), the Brooklyn Homeopathic Hospital (1894–95), and the Hartford Hospital (1895–97) in Connecticut. this was followed by two years as the superintendent of the training school at the University of Pennsylvania Hospital in Philadelphia.

By the turn of the century, Richards took on another cause, the upgrading of nursing in mental hospitals. She served as director of training schools at the Taunton Insane Hospital (1899–1904) in Massachusetts and followed this with similar positions at the Worcester Hospital for the Insane (1904–5) in Massachusetts and at the Michigan Insane Asylum in Kalamazoo, Michigan (1906–9). She then returned to Taunton before her retirement in 1911 at age 70.

For a time after her retirement, Rich-ards lived on a farm near Lowell, Massachusetts, with a cousin. The last five years of her life were spent as an invalid following a cerebral hemorrhage. She died April 16, 1930, at the New England Hospital in Boston at the age of 88. Her ashes were placed in Forest Hills Cemetery in Boston. The National League for Nursing created the Linda Richards Award in 1962 to be given to a nurse making a unique contribution of a pioneering nature.

## PUBLICATIONS BY
## LINDA ANN JUDSON RICHARDS

### BOOKS

*Reminiscences.* Boston: Whitcomb and Barrows, 1911. Reprint. Philadelphia: J.B. Lippincott, 1949.

### ARTICLES

"Early Days in the First American Training School for Nurses." *American Journal of Nursing* 16 (December 1915): 174–79.

### BIBLIOGRAPHY

Baker, R. *America's First Trained Nurse: Linda Richards.* New York: Julian Messner, 1959.

Collins, D.R. *Linda Richards: First American Trained Nurse.* Champaign, Ill.: Garrard Publishing, 1973.

Richards, L. Biographical questionnaire. In "Memoranda Concerning Missionaries," Vol. 9. United Church Board for World Ministries Library, Boston, Mass.

Richards, L. Letters. Sophia Smith Collection. Smith College, Northampton, Mass.

Richards, L. *Notable American Women; 1607–1950.* Vol. 3, Edited by Edward T. James, Cambridge, Mass., Harvard University Press, 1971.

Sloan, I.W. *America's First Trained Nurse.* Boston: School of Nursing, New England Hospital for Women and Children, 1941.

Vern L. Bullough

# Mary Roberts Rinehart

## 1876–1958

One of the most widely read American authors of the first half of the twentieth century, Mary Roberts Rinehart combined her nurse's training and writing skills to praise and promote the nursing profession at a critical time in its history. In *Kings, Queens and Pawns*, a best seller she wrote as a correspondent in World War I, she interpreted war through the eyes of the wounded and sick and the nurses who cared for them. She also used nurses as heroines in some of the detective novels and stories that make up the bulk of her writing.

Rinehart was born August 12, 1876, in Allegheny, Pennsylvania, a suburb of Pittsburgh. She was the older of two daughters of Thomas Beveridge and Cornelia Grilleland Roberts; her sister, Olive, was four years younger. Both parents were of Seceder Presbyterian ancestry from Northern Ireland and had emigrated to western Pennsylvania. Their strict faith engendered a feeling of danger lurking amid happiness, which became a theme of Rinehart's fiction. Thomas Roberts was a clerk, sewing-machine salesman, and inventor who enjoyed only brief business success. After an especially disheartening failure, he committed suicide in 1895.

Rinehart attended Allegheny High School. She edited and wrote for the school newspaper, was in the debating society, and graduated at age 16 with ambitions to enter medicine. She envied the social status of a woman doctor in the neighborhood and had had some personal nursing experience the previous year when her mother was seriously ill.

Too young for acceptance into any medical school, Rinehart entered the Pittsburgh Training School for Nurses in 1893. Her first tour of the hospital was conducted by Stanley Marshall Rinehart, head of surgery, who later became her husband.

Although beset by health problems, she graduated in 1896, becoming one of only about 500 graduate nurses in the United States at the time. Her marriage took place four days later, and by the time she

was 25, she had borne three sons: Stanley, Jr.; Alan; and Frederick.

Through the early years of her marriage, Rinehart suppressed the urge to write. However, she began writing and selling verses at age 27 at the encouragement of a nurse who was caring for her during a bout of diphtheria. After the verses, she sold a story based on one of her husband's cases, and soon she began to see writing as a solution to family financial difficulties brought on by stockmarket reverses.

Although her writing brought increasing income, her success contrasted uncomfortably with the less brilliant career of her husband. He discouraged her writing, especially during the early years. However, her first mystery novel, *The Circular Staircase* (1908), established her as the founder of a new genre of comic detective fiction. Eventually, she produced more than 60 books.

During January and February 1915, Rinehart toured World War I camps and hospitals as a representative of the secretary of war and as a correspondent for the *Saturday Evening Post*. Although her book *Kings, Queens and Pawns* (1915) contains significant interviews with royalty, it is those interviews with military and civilian wounded from all walks of life that give it its emotional impact.

In 1917 Rinehart took a postgraduate surgical nursing course. She obtained credentials as a Red Cross nurse in June 1918 and requested permission to return to the front. Eventually this was granted, and she arrived in Paris shortly before the signing of the Armistice. However, she stayed on to tour hospitals and carry out assignments for the U.S. War Department.

After the war, Rinehart lived in Washington, D.C., and became a champion of the Blackfoot Indians and the women's suffrage movement. When her husband died in 1932, she moved to New York City. She reported on the coronation of England's King George VI and was an air-raid warden during World War II. Her sons Stanley, Jr., and Frederick had joined John Farrar to form Farrar and Rinehart publishers in 1929, and after that much of her work came into print through her sons' various firms.

One of several fiction works in which Rinehart drew on her nursing experience is *Miss Pinkerton, Adventures of a Nurse Detective*, a collection of four novels and novelettes. In its opening, she described how patients' secrets, traditionally entrusted to doctors and clergymen, were becoming entrusted also to a third party, the trained nurse.

In 1936 Rinehart had surgery for breast cancer, and in 1947 she tried to alert women to its dangers in an article, "I Had Cancer," for the *Ladies' Home Journal*. That year her name also was in the news because her longtime cook tried to murder her. Shortly afterward, her home was one of 70 destroyed in a disastrous fire at Bar Harbor, Maine.

Rinehart died in her sleep of a heart ailment in New York City on September 22, 1958. She was survived by her three sons and six grandchildren. She is buried in Arlington National Cemetery.

During her lifetime, Rinehart was awarded the Mystery Writers of America Special Award in 1954, a medal from Queen Elisabeth of Belgium honoring her war service, honorary membership in the Blackfoot Indian tribe, and an honorary Litt.D. degree from George Washington University.

## PUBLICATIONS BY MARY ROBERTS RINEHART

### BOOKS

*Kings, Queens and Pawns*. New York: George H. Doran Co., 1915.

*My Story*. New York: Rinehart and Company, 1948.

*Miss Pinkerton, Adventures of a Nurse Detective*. New York: Rinehart and Company, 1959.

### ARTICLES

"I Had Cancer." *Ladies Home Journal* 64 (July 1974): 143–48.

### BIBLIOGRAPHY

Cohn, J. *Improbable Fiction, the Life of Mary Roberts Rinehart*. Pittsburgh: University of Pittsburgh Press, 1980.

"Rinehart, Mary Roberts (Mrs.)." *American Women 1935–40*. Detroit: Gale Research,

Welter, B. "Rinehart, Mary Roberts." In *Notable American Women, the Modern Period*. Cambridge, Mass.: Belknap Press of Harvard University Press, 1980.

"Mary Roberts Rinehart Is Dead; Author of Mysteries and Plays." *New York Times*, 23 September 1958.

Alice P. Stein

# Isabel Adams Hampton Robb

## 1860–1910

Isabel Adams Hampton Robb was the first president of the American Nurses' Association, originally called Nurses' Associated Alumnae of the United States and Canada. Robb was one of the few early nursing leaders who was also a wife and mother. Among other things, she was the initiator of the grading policy for nursing studies and practice in training schools for nurses. Her ambitions for uniformity in nursing education and practice nationally and internationally were left to be carried out by her successors after her accidental death at age 50.

Robb was born July 1860 in Welland, Ontario, Canada, the fourth of seven children. Robb's parents, Samuel James and Sarah Mary Lay Hampton, were originally from Cornwall, England.

Robb attended public school in Welland and then Saint Catherines Collegiate Institute in St. Catherines, Ontario, where she received a teacher's certificate. She taught for approximately three years in Merritton, Ontario, before applying for nursing education at Bellevue Hospital Training School for Nurses in New York City.

Robb graduated from the two-year course at Bellevue in 1883 and joined fellow students at St. Paul's House, a small hospital in Rome, Italy. She remained there for 18 months, caring for English and American travelers. She also traveled in France, Italy, and Germany. Upon her return to the United States, Robb was offered a position as superintendent of nurses at the Illinois Training School for Nurses at Cook County Hospital in Chicago.

During her three years at the Illinois school (1886–89), Robb took a leadership role in nursing education. She introduced the first grading policy for nursing studies and practices in the United States. She abolished the practice of having students do private-duty nursing to help support the hospital or school. This gave the student nurses more time to concentrate on their studies. Robb broadened student training by beginning an affiliation with Presbyterian Hospital, which had patients who were different from those of Cook County Hospital. Robb resigned in 1889 from this position to accept a similar one at the Johns Hopkins Hospital in Baltimore, Maryland.

Because the Johns Hopkins school was in its early stages, Robb had stronger control over standards than she had in Chicago. She carefully developed the school of nursing of the first privately endowed school in the United States and continued the graded curriculum she started at the Illinois school. She firmly believed in quality nursing and felt that both experience and the liberal arts were essential in education. She started an affiliation between Johns Hopkins Hospital and the Mt. Wilson Sanatorium for Infants to enable the students to gain experience with infant care. In addition to administering the school and teaching (with Lavinia Dock as assistant), she also wrote her classic text, *Nursing: Its Principles and Practice*, originally published in 1894.

The faculty at Johns Hopkins, the first medical school to be fully integrated into a university, was regarded as the leader in health care, not only in the United States, but in the world. Robb's work and contacts there put her into the mainstream of leadership in nursing. At the World Congress of Charities, Correction, and Philanthropy, which met in conjunction with the World's Fair in Chicago in June 1893, Hampton was chair of the nursing subsection and planned the program. After consultation with Florence Nightingale, she also arranged many of the invitations

for other speakers. She was determined to use the meeting to begin a nursing organization to address the problems of the profession.

After the formal sessions of the congress, Robb invited those interested to discuss a nursing organization. From this came the American Society of Superintendents of Training School, the forerunner of the National League for Nursing. The Nurses' Associated Alumnae of the United States and Canada also evolved from this group and later became the American Nurses' Association.

Robb resigned from her position at Johns Hopkins Hospital in June 1894 to marry Hunter Robb, a physician associate in gynecology at Johns Hopkins. The wedding took place in London, England, on June 11. Robb's decision to marry was not approved by her colleagues, most of whom were worried that her marriage would mean a loss to nursing. Their response demonstrates the extent to which early nursing leadership roles were held by unmarried women.

When the Robbs returned to the United States after their travels, they settled in Cleveland, Ohio, where Hunter Robb became professor of gynecology at Western Reserve University. The couple's first child, Hampton Robb, was born on December 25, 1895.

Typical of the women of her social class, Robb never again worked as a nurse. Instead, she turned to volunteer activities, almost all of which involved nursing. She did some teaching at the Lakeside Hospital Training School for Nurses, served as a member of the board of female managers for the Lakeside Hospital and training school, and was a member of the board of directors for the Cleveland Visiting Nurse Association. Through her connections, she was able to arrange for nursing students to have an affiliating experience with the visiting nurse association. She also continued to be active in the emerging professional nursing organizations that she helped form.

During the annual meeting of the American Society of Superintendents of Training Schools for Nurses in Boston in 1895, Robb presented the ideas of a three-year training course, an eight-hour work day for nurses, and the dissolution of student stipends, with the money used for stipends to be invested in educational materials. Though originally neither proposal was well received, each eventually was incorporated into nurse training programs.

In 1897 Robb was elected president of the newly formed Nurses' Associated Alumnae of the United States and Canada, a position she held until the birth of her second son, Philip. From this organization and the Society of Superintendents, Robb continued to work toward uniformity in nurse education and practice. At the 1898 Society of Superintendents meeting, Robb suggested that the teachers of nurse training programs should have the best knowledge of the principles of nursing and methods of teaching. A committee, with Robb as chair, was formed to establish a course in hospital economics which later became the Department of Nursing Education at Teachers College, Columbia University, New York City.

Robb was one of the founding committee members for the establishment of a publication, the *American Journal of Nursing*, for the Associated Alumnae. She also was a member of the central committee of the American Red Cross Nursing Service. Her second book, *Nursing Ethics*, dealt with her ideals of nurse conduct and was published in 1900. As president of the Associated Alumnae she also initiated the formulation of a code of ethics.

Robb was invited to be a member in the International Council of Women in 1899, and in 1900 she helped to form the International Council of Nurses. She believed there should be uniformity in nursing education and practices not only on a national level, but also on an international level. Thus, at the congress of the International Council of Nurses in London in 1909, Robb proposed the establishment of an international educational standard and was named chair of the committee formed to achieve this. The year before (1908), she had been elected president of the Society of Superintendents.

On her way to meet her son on April 15, 1910, Robb was struck by a streetcar when she jumped onto the tracks out of the path of an automobile. She was survived by her husband and two sons. Services were held in Cleveland, at Johns Hopkins Hospital School of Nursing, and at Illinois Training School. Robb was buried in her husband's home town, Burlington, New Jersey.

Money received after her death was used to establish the Isabel Hampton Robb scholarship fund. This fund continued to be enriched by donations made in tribute at the deaths of other nursing leaders. The Isabel Hampton Robb scholarship fund for nursing education became the basis for Nurses Educational Funds (NEF), a private foundation that contributes scholarships to nurses earning advanced degrees.

## PUBLICATIONS BY ISABEL ADAMS HAMPTON ROBB

*Nursing of the Sick.* Proceedings of the papers and discussions of the International Congress of Charities, Correction and Philanthropy, Chicago, 1893. Reprint. New York: McGraw-Hill, 1949.

*Nursing: Its Principles and Practice.* Philadelphia: W.B. Saunders, 1894.

*Nursing Ethics.* Cleveland: E.C. Koeckert, 1900.

*Educational Standard for Nurses.* Cleveland: E.C. Koeckert, 1907.

## BIBLIOGRAPHY

Christy, T.E. Portrait of a Leader: Isabel Hampton Robb. *Nursing Outlook* 17 (1969): 26–29.

Moody, S. "Isabel Hampton Robb: Her Contribution to Nursing Education." *American Journal of Nursing* 38 (October 1938): 1131–39.

Noel, Nancy. "Isabel Hampton Robb: Architect of American Nursing." Ph.D. diss., Teachers College, Columbia University, 1978.

Rodabauch, M.J. "Isabel Hampton Robb." *Notable American Women,* edited by E.T. James. Cambridge, Mass.: Belknap Press of Harvard University Press, 1971.

Nancy L. Noel

## Mary May Roberts

1877–1959

Throughout her lifetime, Mary May Roberts worked diligently to place the field of nursing on a higher standard. Although her achievements in nursing practice, organizational work, public relations, and hospital and nursing-school administration were notable, it was in the area of nursing journalism that she excelled. As editor of the *American Journal of Nursing* for 28 years, she was a prolific spokesperson for the profession of nursing during a time of nearly perpetual crisis for nursing and nurses. The expert care of the patient was her primary objective; the well-educated nurse was the vehicle to accomplish it.

Roberts was born on January 30, 1877, in Duncan City, Michigan. She was the eldest of the four children of Henry W. and Elizabeth Scott Elliot Roberts, both of English and Scottish ancestry. Duncan City was a company town owned and operated by a sawmill firm, for which her father worked. She enjoyed a happy family life, actively participated in winter sports, and attended the company school. In 1895 she graduated as valedictorian of her four-member class from a high school in nearby Cheboygan.

Despite her father's opposition, Roberts applied to the Jewish Hospital Training School for Nurses in Cincinnati, Ohio. She was an excellent student and graduated in 1899. For the next 18 years, her professional experience occurred in a variety of settings. These included clinic nurse at the Baroness Erlanger Hospital in Chattanooga, Tennessee (1899); superintendent of nurses at the Savannah Hospital in Georgia, where she organized the school of nursing and directed it for three years (1900–1903); assistant superintendent of nurses and acting superintendent for one year at the Jewish Hospital in Cincinnati (1904–06); private-duty nurse and acting supervisor in the obstetric department of the Evanston Hospital in Evanston, Illinois (1906–08); and superintendent of nurses at the Christian R. Holmes Hospital in Cincinnati (1908–17).

With the outbreak of World War I, Roberts resigned her hospital post to work with the American Red Cross. She was appointed director of the bureau of nursing of its lake division, which included Ohio, Indiana, and Kentucky. In that capacity, she worked to recruit hundreds of nurses from the area for service with the armed forces.

On July 22, 1918, Roberts reported for military duty as a reserve nurse at Camp Sherman, Ohio, to direct a unit of the Army School of Nursing. After joining the Army Nurse Corps in October, she was made chief nurse and director of the Army School of Nursing at Camp Sherman. She held these positions until her discharge from the military in September 1919.

At the age of 42, Roberts entered Teachers College, Columbia University, in New York City to study for a college degree. Two years later (1921), she received a bachelor of science degree and a diploma in nursing-school administration. Her appointment as editor of the *American Journal of Nursing* was announced in March 1921. At first she was coeditor with Katharine DeWitt; she became editor in 1923, when DeWitt became managing editor. Roberts was given the title of editor-in-chief in January 1947. During her three-decade tenure as editor, she campaigned for higher professional standards in nursing.

Many personal and professional characteristics contributed to Roberts's success as the editor of the *American Journal of Nursing*—her nursing experience, flexibility, adaptability, clarity of vision, creativity, wit, analytical ability, and unending concern for the welfare of humanity. She also had the business acumen that was necessary to direct such an enterprise. Under her leadership, circulation increased from 20,000 to 100,000, the scope of the magazine's content broadened, and the journal became highly respected.

As editor, Roberts was tuned to the needs of individual nurses who regarded her as a great teacher. Consequently, she traveled extensively in the United States and abroad, surveying nursing, identifying its problems, and attempting to develop solutions. Roberts also used the pages of the journal to create an extensive network among nurses all over the world. Through her example, nurses were encouraged to write and interpret the nursing profession.

Roberts extended her influence on nursing in several ways, In 1932 she sponsored a plan to make the National League of Nursing Education the education department of the American Nurses' Association. She also assisted with the development of a public information program in 1934, the Nursing Information Bureau (NIB). A program was sponsored by the three existing nursing organizations (ANA, NLNE, and National Organization of Public Health Nursing), but was largely supported by the journal. Roberts served as the director of this Nursing Information Bureau and remained so until 1948, when financial difficulties resulted in its dissolution.

Roberts represented nursing on a number of projects and committees involving physicians, hospital administrators, nurses, and social scientists. These activities included the following: member of the Committee on the Costs of Medical Care, organized in 1927 to survey the cost and distribution of health services; nurse representative on the New York Academy of Medicine's Committee on Medicine in the Changing Order; nurse consultant to the Committee on the Grading of Nursing Schools (1928–34); alumnae representative on the board of trustees of Teachers College, Columbia University (1930–32); member of the advisory committee of the Cornell University-New York Hospital School of Nursing (1932–42); consultant to the Procurement and Assignment Service of the War Manpower Commission (1943–45); member of the Joint Commission for the Improvement of the Care of the Patient until her retirement in 1949; member of the Nursing Council on National Defense during World War II; and member of the Committee on the Function of Nursing, which was appointed by the faculty of the division of nursing education of Teachers College.

Roberts was president of her alumnae association and of the Ohio district and state nurses' associations. She was appointed to the examining committee of the Ohio State Medical Board (Ohio Board of Nursing Education and Nurse Registration) after laboring to secure the passage of Ohio's nurse practice act. She served on numerous committees of the American Nurses' Association, the National League of Nursing Education, and the National League for Nursing. From 1923 to 1944 she served on the national committee of the American Red Cross Nursing Service.

Roberts also engaged in many international nursing activities. She was an ardent supporter of the International Council of Nurses and used the pages of the *American Journal of Nursing* to promote its objectives. For two years, she served as the council's vice-president; she also served as chair of its publications committee and as a member of its ethics committee. She was invited by the Rockefeller Foundation to travel through Europe, visiting nursing centers from 1930 to 1931.

Roberts was named editor emeritus upon her retirement from the *American Journal of Nursing* in 1949. She continued to participate actively in the nursing profession and maintain contact with the journal. She put most of her energy, however, into writing the now classic *American Nursing: History and Interpretation* (1954). Another book followed in 1957, *The Army Nurse Corps—Yesterday and Today.* She also continued to write editorials, biographies, and book reviews for both the journal and *Nursing Outlook.* She also became involved as chair of the National League for Nursing's committee on early nursing source materials.

Numerous awards were bestowed upon Roberts during her career in nursing. She received both the International Red Cross Florence Nightingale Medal and the Mary Adelaide Nutting Award for Leadership in Nursing in 1949. Other awards included the Bronze Medal of the Ministry of Social Welfare of France (1933); the Army Certificate of Appreciation, the highest honor the U.S. War Department bestows on a civilian (1949); an honorary life membership in the American Hospital Association (1949); the Mary M. Roberts Award established by the New York State Nurses' Association (1949); and the first citation awarded by Skidmore College's department of nursing (1956). Roberts particularly valued the establishment of the Mary M. Roberts Fellowship in Journalism by the *American Journal of Nursing* in 1950.

At the age of 81, Roberts suffered a stroke while at work on an editorial in the *American Journal of Nursing* offices. She died on January 11, 1959, at the Columbia Presbyterian Medical Center in New York City.

## PUBLICATIONS BY
## MARY MAY ROBERTS

### BOOKS

*American Nursing: History and Interpretation.* New York: Macmillan, 1954.

*The Army Nurse Corps: Yesterday and Today.* Washington, D.C.: U.S. Army Nurse Corps, 1957.

### ARTICLES

*American Journal of Nursing.* Editorials, 1921–49.

"The Story of the Department of Nursing and Health. Teachers College, New York." *American Journal of Nursing* 21 (May 1921): 518.

"Student Life at Teachers College." *American Journal of Nursing* 21 (August 1921): 782.

"Supervision in a Changing Age." *American Journal of Nursing* 22 (January 1922): 290.

"The Spirit of Nursing." *American Journal of Nursing* 25 (September 1925): 734.

"Florence Nightingale as a Nurse Educator." *American Journal of Nursing* 37 (July 1937): 773.

"Current Events and Trends in Nursing." *American Journal of Nursing* 39 (January 1939): 1.

"Those with the Will Should be Helped with the Bill." *Nursing Outlook* 1 (November 1953): 615.

"Private Duty Nurses: Do Research and Studies Affect You and Your Work?" *American Journal of Nursing* 54 (July 1954): 657.

"Lavinia Lloyd Dock—Nurse, Feminist, Internationalist." *American Journal of Nursing* 56 (February 1956): 176.

"We Work for Peace Through Health." *American Journal of Nursing* 56 (December 1956): 1539.

"We Pay Tribute to Charles-Edward Amory Winslow." *Nursing Outlook* 5 (March 1957): 155.

"Nurses' House." *American Journal of Nursing* 57 (September 1957): 1172.

"Nursing Services after Five Years of NLN." *Nursing Outlook* 6 (January 1958): 13.

"A New Look at the History of Nursing." *Nursing Outlook* 6 (February 1958): 79.

"Stella Goostray, Distinguished Administrator, Professional Leader, and Good Neighbor." *American Journal of Nursing* 58 (March 1958): 352.

## BIBLIOGRAPHY

Best, E. "Miss Mary M. Roberts—An Appreciation." *International Nursing Review* 6 (April 1959): 16.

Collection of Biobibliographical Miscellaneous Materials. National Library of Medicine, Bethesda, Md.

Fitzpatrick, M.L. *Prologue to Professionalism.* Bowie, Md.: Robert J. Brady, 1983.

"The Journal's Golden Anniversary." *American Journal of Nursing* 50 (October 1950): 583.

Lewis, E.P. "Mary M. Roberts: Spokesman for Nursing." *American Journal of Nursing* 59 (March 1959): 338.

"Mary M. Roberts." *Canadian Nurse* 55 (March 1959): 240.

"Mary M. Roberts." *Nursing Outlook* 7 (February 1959): 72.

Mary M. Roberts Collection. Nursing Archives. Mugar Memorial Library, Boston University.

"Mary M. Roberts Retires As Editor." *American Journal of Nursing* 49 (May 1949): 261.

Sicherman, B., and C.H. Green, eds. *Notable American Women, The Modern Period.* Cambridge, Mass.: Harvard University Press, 1980.

M. Patricia Donahue

# Margaret Sanger
## 1879–1966

Margaret Sanger was the nurse leader of the American birth-control movement. She worked to establish birth-control clinics and was a founder of the Planned Parenthood Federation of America.

Sanger was born September 14, 1879, in Corning, New York, the sixth of 11 children and third of 4 daughters of Michael Hennessey and Anne Purcell Higgins. Her father, the owner and operator of a stone-monument shop, had run away from a Canadian farm as a teenager to serve as a drummer boy in the Union army. An outspoken free thinker, Higgins was a strong supporter of the atheist Robert Ingersoll and the single-tax advocate Henry George and at times seemed more interested in his causes than his stone-carving business. Her mother, a devout Catholic and an active tubercular at the time of Margaret's birth, was pregnant at least 18 times, 7 of which ended in miscarriages.

Sanger was not baptized until March 23, 1893, and the ceremony took place in secret in order not to antagonize her father. Her baptismal name was Margaret Louise Higgins. Though she was confirmed secretly one year later, she soon left the church. Sanger associated both her mother's tubercular cough and the family's financial insecurity with her parent's high fertility. Also influencing her thinking was the fact that her mother died at age 49, while her father, whom she much admired, lived to be 80, a difference that added to her determination to gain some measure of reproductive autonomy for women. Her two older sisters helped support the family from an early age, and it was due to their efforts that Sanger was able to attend school.

Sanger's childhood was marked by rebellion against authority and a dislike of her home town. She left the Corning schools in the eighth grade after a teacher complained that she was paying more attention to her new gloves than to her lessons. Her two older sisters then paid part of her tuition at Claverack College, a private, low-cost preparatory school near Hudson, New York. Sanger contributed to her tuition by working in the kitchen.

After three years at Claverack, Sanger turned to teaching in the primary school in Little Falls, New Jersey. She soon realized that she was not suited to teaching and left the job to return to Corning to take care of her dying mother. After her mother's death in March 1899, she rebelled against her father's attempt to control her. She left Corning and entered the newly established nursing school at White Plains Hospital near New York City.

While a student, Sanger was found to have tuberculosis, from which she suffered for several years. After completing the two-year training program, she attended the Manhattan Eye and Ear Hospital for postgraduate training. She met architect William Sanger, who knew many of the people esteemed by her father. In spite of her guilt feelings over the possible waste of her sisters' investment in her education, she married him on August 18, 1902.

Within six months, Sanger was pregnant. Her tuberculosis flared up, and most of her pregnancy was spent in a sanitarium in Saranac, New York. Shortly before her delivery she returned to New York City, where her son Stuart was born.

Following the delivery, Sanger returned to the sanitarium, although she apparently suffered from depression as much as from tuberculosis. Shortly after she left the sanitarium for the second time, the Sangers moved to a new home in Hastings-on-the-Hudson in suburban Westchester County. A second son, Grant, was born in 1908, and a daughter, Margaret, in 1910. Sanger grew increasingly restless with her role as mother and wife and turned with her husband to the Socialist party as a channel for her interest.

After moving back to New York City, Sanger began doing home nursing and became an activist in the International Workers of the World (IWW) in an effort to organize textile workers. She made important contributions to the IWW strikes of 1912–13 in Pennsylvania, New Jersey, and Massachusetts and gained national publicity and sympathy through her role in the evacuation of the children of strikers from Lawrence, Massachusetts, to New York.

Sanger testified in Congress about the poor state of the strikers' children. She began to lecture on the condition of women in the labor force, emphasizing problems with family and children. She gradually became convinced that women needed representation as an interest group in the struggle for social justice. She argued that sexual reform was the paramount issue for women, more important even than the struggle for higher wages.

In 1912 Sanger nursed a woman, Sadie Sachs, suffering from septicemia following an abortion. Sachs was not yet 30, had three children, and neither wanted nor could afford more children. Sachs survived, was told not to become pregnant again, and turned to Sanger for advice. Sanger could give no effective help, and Sachs quickly became pregnant again. She died during an abortion with Sanger in attendance.

After this, Sanger began disseminating information about female sexuality. She and her increasingly alienated husband traveled to France, he to study art and she to study the French methods of family planning. After collecting birth control devices and information, she returned with her children to the United States, leaving her husband to continue his studies in Europe.

To disseminate her new-found message, in 1914 Sanger began publishing a militant feminist journal, *The Woman Rebel*, in which she announced she would break the law by publishing contraceptive information. She was indicted for violating the postal code, yet she refused to cooperate with her attorneys. By this time, her husband was back in the United States after being forced to leave France with the outbreak of World War I, and he urged her to continue her struggle. Leaving the children with him and under indictment, she left again for Europe. She left behind a pamphlet, *Family Limitation*, with instructions for him to distribute it.

During her year in Europe, Sanger met such sex reformers as George Drysdale and Havelock Ellis. Through Ellis, she learned about the Mensinga diaphragm, widely used in the Netherlands.

While Sanger was in England, her husband was arrested for distributing a copy of *Family Limitation*. His arrest and the death of her daughter from pneumonia brought her back to the United States in October 1915. Both events aroused public sympathy for her, and with the death of Anthony Comstock, the secretary to the New York Society for the Suppression of Vice and special postal agent, opposition to disseminate contraceptive information

disappeared. Within six months of her return, the government dropped its case against her.

Deeply distressed by her daughter's death, Sanger became even more involved in the contraceptive movement. With her younger sister, Ethel Byrne, also a nurse, she opened a clinic in the Brownsville section of Brooklyn in October 1916. The clinic provided contraceptive advice until police closed it; Sanger was found guilty of violating an 1873 New York law forbidding dissemination of contraceptive information.

However, the judge's decision indicated that it was permissible for a physician to prescribe the use of condoms to prevent venereal disease. Sanger interpreted the decision as a mandate for doctor-staffed birth-control clinics, and although she continued to send revised editions of *Family Limitation* to those requesting it, she increasingly spent time lobbying for the removal of legal prohibitions concerning medical advice about contraceptives. This concession to physicians was opposed by Mary Ware Dennet, Sanger's rival for the leadership of the contraceptive movement in the 1920s.

Increasingly Sanger broke her ties with her old comrades, played down her radical past, and stressed eugenic arguments for contraception. She found financial support from among the wealthy; with this support, she organized the American Birth Control League in 1921 and it became a national lobbying organization. In 1942 this group became the Planned Parenthood Federation of America.

By 1923 Sanger had enough support to open the Birth Control Clinical Research Bureau in New York City, the first doctor-staffed clinic. Under the direction of physician Hannah Stone, a careful clinical record was established, demonstrating the safety and efficacy of contraceptive practice. It served as a model for other clinics, over 300 of which had been established by 1938. Most of them were staffed by female doctors and supported by female volunteers.

The Sangers were divorced in 1920. In 1922 Sanger married J. Noah Slee, a millionaire manufacturer who contributed much to her cause. Their marriage lasted until his death in 1943.

Slee donated funds to found the Holland Ranto Company in 1925 to manufacture the diaphragms that Sanger regularly had been smuggling into the United States. Sanger fought a series of court battles to establish the legality of the birth-control clinics, and in the *United States v. One Package* in 1936, a case brought by Sanger's Committee on Federal Legislation for Birth Control, the 1873 law prohibiting the mailing of contraceptive materials was overturned. This decision was a major factor in the 1937 resolution of the American Medical Association to recognize contraception as a legitimate medical service.

After winning this case, Sanger moved to Tucson, Arizona, where she and Slee had built a retirement home. Her brand of feminism increasingly had been deemed counterproductive by the new leaders of the birth-control movement, who hoped to gain acceptance of their cause from voluntary health organizations. However, in 1952 Sanger played an important role in the founding of the International Planned Parenthood Foundation, and she was instrumental in obtaining the funds that led to the birth-control pill being placed on the market.

Sanger died of congestive heart failure in 1966 after a four-year stay in a Tucson nursing home. She was survived by both her sons and numerous grandchildren, one of whom, Alexander Sanger, wrote his honor's thesis at Princeton University about his grandmother.

## PUBLICATIONS BY MARGARET SANGER

*Women and the New Race.* New York: Brentano, 1920.

*The Pivot of Civilization.* New York: Brentano, 1922.

*Happiness in Marriage.* New York: Brentano, 1926.

*Motherhood in Bondage.* New York: Brentano, 1928.

*My Fight for Birth Control.* New York: Farrar, 1931.

*Margaret Sanger: An Autobiography.* New York: W.W. Norton, 1938.

Sanger edited three journals: *Woman Rebel* (1914); *Birth Control Review* (1910–40); and *Human Fertility* (1940–48).

## BIBLIOGRAPHY

Gray, M. *Margaret Sanger.* New York: Richard Marek, 1979.

Lader, L. *The Margaret Sanger Story and Fight for Birth Control.* Garden City, N. Y.: 1955.

Sanger, M. Papers. American Birth Control League Papers. Harvard University.

Sanger, M. Papers. Library of Congress, Washington, D.C.

Sanger, M. Papers. Sophia Smith Collection, Smith College, Northampton, Mass.

Vern L. Bullough

## Helen Irene Denne Schulte
### 1889–1971

An early collegiate nursing educator, Helen Irene Denne Schulte founded the school of nursing at the University of Wisconsin (now University of Wisconsin-Madison), the first collegiate nursing program in the state and among the first in the country. Her approach to collegiate nursing education laid a foundation for a sound educational approach later emulated by others.

Schulte was born on May 2, 1889, in Peterborough, Ontario, Canada, the daughter of Henry and Elizabeth Denne. Her early schooling was in Peterborough, and she attended Collegiate Institute in Peterborough and Queen's University in Kingston, Ontario, from which she received her B.A. degree in 1911. She completed the nursing program at the Presbyterian Hospital in Chicago, receiving her diploma in 1915.

Schulte served as a nurse with the Canadian forces during World War I and was one of the over 2,500 Candian nurses who served overseas. For her military service, she was presented with the Order of the Royal Red Cross by Queen Mary of England.

After the war ended, she returned to Chicago and worked for several years at Presbyterian Hospital, advancing in position from supervisor to instructor to assistant superintendent. She was then invited by Charles Bardeen, dean of the University of Wisconsin Medical School, to start a school of nursing at the university.

Schulte accepted the position at the university in 1924. She served both as the superintendent of nurses of the new Wisconsin General Hospital (now University of Wisconsin Hospitals) and as director of the school of nursing. Upon her appointment, she was granted faculty status as full professor.

The first students were accepted into the school in 1924. As the first collegiate school of nursing in the United States had been established only 15 years earlier, there were few guidelines for Schulte to follow. Initially, the pattern for these programs did not deviate from the traditional hospital schools of nursing. Two curricula were established in the new school of nursing: a three-year program leading to a certificate of graduate nurse and a five-year program that granted a B.S. degree. Schulte was convinced that the university setting provided the sound academic base needed for either program.

Schulte's efforts were directed toward planning and implementing a curriculum suitable for a university program. She believed that a university school of nursing should be accepted as an intregal part of the university. Schulte's identification of the school's need to stimulate nursing research reflects her understanding of the need for both advanced education and research as essential to nursing practice.

In 1928 Schulte attended a conference on nursing schools connected with colleges. Held at Teachers College, Columbia University, New York City, and co-sponsored by the National League of Nursing Education, the conference indicated that Wisconsin was ahead of many of its contemporaries in the development of the collegiate schools. At the conference, Schulte reported that unlike students at many of the other reporting schools, those at the University of Wisconsin were regularly enrolled students, attended classes

with other university students, had access to the university's libraries and other resources, and participated in campus intellectual and social events.

During her tenure, Schulte encouraged graduate staff nurses to seek additional education and arranged special work schedules that permitted them to enroll in university courses. In the severe economic depression of the 1930s, she developed a work-sharing plan so that more nurses could be employed in the hospital in spite of critical budget cuts.

Schulte promoted a plan for fee remission scholarships for the nursing students during the clinical portion of the program, in recognition of their service to the hospital. Her plan was approved by the board of regents and was in effect for many years. This arrangement enabled university enrollment for many nursing students who otherwise would have been unable to finance their educations during the serious economic depression.

Schulte was an active member of the American Nurses' Association, the National League of Nursing Education, and their state and local affiliates, often serving on various committees. She served on the state committee of nurse examiners. She also organized the University of Wisconsin Alumnae (now Alumni) Association.

Schulte appreciated and understood the importance of education for effective nursing practice. A determined woman, she never compromised her educational principles. In spite of considerable opposition by some university faculty members who viewed nursing education as vocational education and inappropriate for the university, she established a school that grew substantially under her effective leadership and a pattern for other collegiate programs to follow.

She resigned from her position in 1937 to marry Walter Schulte, an executive in a battery-manufacturing firm. As was the practice of the time, she abandoned her professional career after her marriage. Nevertheless, she maintained a lively interest in the school she established. The Schultes lived in Freeport, Illinois; Walter Schulte died in 1957.

Schulte died of a cerebral hemorrhage February 5, 1971, in Freeport, and was buried in the Oakland Cemetery there. The University of Wisconsin-Madison School of Nursing was the recipient of a substantial legacy from her, designated for the education of graduate nurses. The school maintains professorships that bear her name, established in 1972.

## PUBLICATIONS BY
## HELEN IRENE DENNE SCHULTE

"Miss Denne's Greetings." *The University of Wisconsin Nurses' Alumnae Magazine* 1 (November 1934): 3, 7.

## BIBLIOGRAPHY

Clark, P.F. "The School of Nursing and Nursing Services in the University of Wisconsin." In *The University of Wisconsin Medical School. A Chronicle. 1848–1948.* Madison, Wis.: University of Wisconsin Press, 1967.

"Helen Denne Schulte." Obituary. *American Journal of Nursing* 71 (April 1971): 800.

"Helen Denne Schulte." Obituary. *Wisconsin State Journal,* 6 February 1971.

"Memorial Resolution of the Faculty of the University of Wisconsin on the Death of Helen Denne Schulte." Faculty Document 39, 5 April 1971.

*Proceedings of Conference on Nursing Schools Connected with Colleges and Universities.* New York: Teachers College, Columbia University, and the National League of Nursing Education, 1928.

Schulte, H.D. Papers. University of Wisconsin-Madison Archives. University of Wisconsin-Madison.

Watson, S. "Wisconsin University Nursing School Evolves Slowly into Graduate Status." *Trained Nurse and Hospital Review* 122 (June 1949): 261–282, 286.

Signe S. Cooper

# Louisa Lee Schuyler

## 1837–1926

In 1873 Louisa Lee Schuyler founded the first Nightingale type training school for nurses in the United States—that associated with Bellevue Hospital. She devoted much of her philanthrophic work to nursing.

Schuyler was born October 26, 1837, in New York City, daughter of George Lee and Elisa Hamilton Schuyler. She was descended from General Philip Schuyler and was a great-granddaughter of Alexander Hamilton. Raised in luxury, she nevertheless showed a concern for others and volunteered as a teacher in one of the schools run by the Children's Aid Society in New York City.

Schuyler's interest in nursing began in the 1850s at a family Christmas party when Schuyler's grandmother fell and broke her arm. From this interest came her service in the Woman's Central Association of Relief, an auxiliary to United States Sanitary Commission during the Civil War. Through her efforts the Woman's Association became the major relief organization.

After the war, Schuyler went to Europe for six years. When she returned in 1871, she began visiting hospitals and became increasingly concerned with the plight of the sick. In 1872 she formed the New York State Charities Aid Association, whose members pledged to regularly visit a charitable institution. It was considered a model for many philanthropic organizations of the twentieth century.

In 1873 Schuyler attempted to improve nursing care by founding a nursing school in connection with Bellevue Hospital in New York City, based on the teachings and model of Florence Nightingale, the first such school to be established in the United States. The aim was to improve the care of the sick.

In 1908 Schuyler organized the New York State Committee for the prevention of Blindness, which under the direction of Carolyn Van Blarcom and with Schuyler's support, mounted the campaign to bring opthalmia neonatorum under control. She was one of the original trustees of the Russell Sage Foundation, a main supporter of nursing in the first half of the twentieth century. She also led the battle for state aid to mental hospitals.

For her service to the poor and the sick, and her support of services for the blind and for the insane, Columbia University in 1915 conferred the degree of doctor of laws upon her, only the second time a woman had received this degree. In 1923 she received a gold medal from the Roosevelt Memorial Association for her extraordinary service in guiding the way modern philanthropy dealt with social service.

Schuyler died October 10, 1926, in Highland Falls, New York, where she had been spending the summer with her cousin, Mary Schuyler Hamilton. She was buried in Sleepy Hollow Cemetery at Tarrytown, New York.

### BIBLIOGRAPHY

Cross, Robert D. "Louisa L. Schuyler." In *Notable American Women*, edited by E.T. James. Vol. 3. Cambridge, Mass.: Harvard University Press, 1971.

"Louisa L. Schuyler." Obituary. *New York Times*, 11 October 1926.

"Louisa L. Schuyler." Papers. New York Historical Society, New York.

"Louisa L. Schuyler." Papers. New York Public Library, New York.

"Louisa L. Schuyler." Papers. Sophia Smith Collection, Smith College, Northampton, Mass.

"Louisa L. Schuyler." Papers. U.S. Sanitary Commission, New York.

Vern L. Bullough

## Alma Ham Scott

1885–?

Between 1929 and 1946, Alma Ham Scott held every professional position in the headquarters of the American Nurses' Association. She worked to increase membership and improve service of professional nursing organizations.

Scott was born in Frankfort, Indiana, on January 21, 1885, one of three children. She spent part of her early life in California and graduated from the San Bernardino high school. In 1907 she graduated from the Presbyterian Hospital School of Nursing in Chicago. Early in her career, she was married for a brief period, but soon divorced.

Scott began her career as a private-duty nurse. During World War I, she served in France at base hospital 13 in Limoges and evacuation hospital 7 in Coulomiers. She returned to the United States in the spring of 1919.

Scott immediately became night supervisor at the Robert W. Long Hospital of the Indiana University School for Nurses. She worked 12-hour shifts and was responsible for the operating room, where her only assistants were student nurses on call.

Illness and death in the family forced her to return briefly to Frankfort. In 1921–22 she studied at Teachers College, Columbia University, New York City. Because she lacked 15 hours of courses, she never received her bachelor's degree.

In January 1924 Scott became educational director of the Indiana State Board of Examination and Registration for Nurses. In this position, she developed a comprehensive system of records for all Indiana nursing schools and established a uniform method for using procedure books. For the board, she wrote a pamphlet on nursing for high-school girls to help attract high-caliber young women into the profession. The outline she used to evaluate nursing schools was published in the *American Journal of Nursing* in July 1925.

During this same period, Scott served as the first executive secretary of the Indiana State Nurses' Association and in that capacity organized its headquarters offices. During her tenure, the alumnae and district associations became fully organized, and a membership campaign netted a 30 percent gain in members.

Scott also served as executive secretary of the Fourth District Association in Indianapolis. While there, she was elected president of the Indiana League of Nursing Education, assisted with organizing the midwest division of the American Nurses' Association (ANA), and served as its first secretary.

In June 1929 Scott was called to the headquarters of the American Nurses' Association as field secretary. By attending meetings and making contacts with nurses in many states, she created a feeling of closeness with the parent organization for nurses throughout the country.

Scott advanced to the posts of assistant director, associate director, acting director, and, in January 1935, director of the ANA. As director, she achieved special distinction through her efforts to integrate the functions of the *American Journal of Nursing*, the National League of Nursing Education, and the National Organization of Public Health Nurses. She also was chair of several ANA committees for the preparation of constitutions and bylaws for new divisions, and was part of a group within the ANA that forestalled problems for the organization.

From 1937 to 1947 she was a member of the International Council of Nurses and was chair of its committee on constitution and bylaws and of a special study committee that dealt with the relationship between the council and the Florence Nightingale International Foundation. She presented a series of reports and recommendations at the Ninth Quadrennial Congress of Nurses in Atlantic City in 1947.

When Scott retired in 1946, she was elected to the board of directors of the ANA and served until 1950.

## PUBLICATIONS BY ALMA HAM SCOTT

"Routine Inspection of Schools of Nursing." *American Journal of Nursing* 25:7 (July 1925): 556–66.

## BIBLIOGRAPHY

Clarke, E.P. "Alma Ham Scott—Organizer." *American Journal of Nursing* 36 (February 1936): 149–52.

"News Mainly About People." *American Journal of Nursing* 35 (March 1935): 283–84.

"Tribute to Alma H. Scott." *American Journal of Nursing* 50 (December 1950): 789.

Alice P. Stein

## Emma Edmonds Seelye
### 1841–1898

Emma Edmonds Seelye is best known as a nurse and spy of the Civil War period who detailed her exploits in the best-selling book *Nurse and Spy in the Union Army*. Later, under her true identity, she continued to nurse Civil War victims.

Seelye was born Sarah Emma Edmondson in December 1841, in Magaguadavic, New Brunswick, Canada. She was the unwanted fifth daughter of Isaac Edmonson and Elizabeth Leeper. Her father was a farmer, characterized by others as a cold, petty tyrant. Disappointed that he had five daughters and that his only son was epileptic and unfit for helping on the farm, Isaac Edmonson drafted his daughters to hoe, chop wood, milk cows, and look after horses.

Seelye and her sisters and brother attended a one-room log parish school. She was a good student, and after her war service, attended Oberlin College but did not graduate.

Seelye learned to handle horses, ride, hunt, and fish. She also became a good marksman. At age 15, when an older man whom her father approved wanted to marry her, she escaped to a neighboring town, where she worked as a milliner. Later, she began to masquerade as a man while selling Bibles and used the name Franklin Thompson. An outstanding salesperson, she continued her masquerade and her career in sales and moved to Hartford, Connecticut, then Flint, Michigan, all the time accepted as a man.

A patriotic abolitionist, Seelye was disappointed when she was rejected from enlisting in the Union army because she did not meet the height requirement. However, in May 1861 she was accepted and enlisted as Franklin Thompson, a male nurse with the rank of private.

Receiving no preparatory training, Seelye was sent to Washington, D.C., where she visited a temporary hospital that was preparing to receive soldiers. During that time, she cared for men with typhoid fever. Nurses either relied on their own judgment or used the book *Nurses in the Army Hospitals*.

Perhaps because of her horsemanship, Seelye next was assigned to be a mailman. Soon she was drafted to join the newly formed Secret Service of the United States Army. The Secret Service had been organized in 1861 by General George B. McClellan, Commander of the Army of the Potomac, to inform him of the movement of Confederate troops, especially around Richmond. In her first secret mission, she disguised herself as a black boy and was sent to discover the strength of fortifications at Yorktown. Her second and most frequent disguise was as an old Irish female peddler. She also disguised herself as a store clerk and as an escaped slave. Going behind enemy lines 11 times, she risked her life to obtain food and provisions or information on the number and location of enemy troups.

The accounts of Seelye's exploits were detailed in her book *Nurse and Spy in the Union Army.* However, one biographer cites discrepancies between her claims and Civil War records.

Seelye reportedly participated in the battles of Bull Run, Williamsburg, Fair Oaks, Antietam, and Fredricksburg. She was an orderly to Brigadier General O.M. Poe. At Vicksburg she contracted a fever and seemed to suffer a physical and mental collapse. Doctors ordered her to apply for a furlough, which was disapproved. With the denial of furlough, doctors urged her to go to the hospital, but she refused. On April 22, 1863, she was absent without leave from the camp of the Second Michigan Infantry near Lebanon, Kentucky.

The accounts of Seelye's contemporaries reveal what was thought and known about her by other members of the Union army. One wrote that she was the lover of General O.M. Poe; another stated that Seelye had been ascertained to have been a female after she left the regiment. However, her closest associates claimed that they never had doubted that she was a man.

Seelye escaped to Oberlin, Ohio, where she stayed at a boarding house and recuperated as Franklin Thompson. Soon she traveled to Philadelphia before returning to Oberlin as Emma Edmonds. While still convalescing, she wrote *Nurse and Spy in the Union Army,* which was published in 1865.

In 1864 she returned to nursing and worked in a hospital in Harper's Ferry that cared for war wounded. She remained there until the end of the Civil War, nursing the sick and wounded and visiting hospitals from Harper's Ferry to Clarksburg, West Virginia. She is reported to have donated most of the proceeds of *Nurse and Spy* to the wounded soldiers.

In Harper's Ferry, Seelye met Linus H. Seely, a widower from New Brunswick, Canada. They were married in Cleveland, Ohio, on April 27, 1867. After the marriage, Seely changed the spelling of their name to Seelye. The couple had three children—Linus, Homer, and Alice Louise—all of whom died in childhood. They also adopted two sons, George Frederick and Charles Finney.

The Seelyes moved frequently, finally settling in Fort Scott, Kansas, where Linus Seelye worked as a carpenter. While in Fort Scott, Seelye decided to clear her name of the charge of desertion and also to apply to the government for back pay, bounty, and a pension. To do this, she requested testimonies from her former colleagues from the Second Michigan Infantry and also from the A.M. Hurlburt Company, imploring them to support her claims of bona fide service. After some struggle and many testimonies on her behalf, on July 5, 1884, Congress allowed her claims and granted her a pension. In 1887 the secretary of war issued her a certificate for proper discharge, and the charge of deserter was removed from her record. On April 2, 1889, Seelye was granted an honorable discharge and her back pay and bounty.

In later years, Seelye lived quietly. In 1875, she and her husband had managed an orphanage run by the Freeman's Aid Society. Throughout this period, Seelye continued to be interested in veterans' activities. In April 1897 Seelye was mustered into the George B. McClellan Post, Number 9, and became the only woman member of the Grand Army of the Republic, which she considered to be a great honor and achievement. Her health began to fail, and she suffered from malaria and other maladies stemming from her war service.

Seelye died on September 5, 1898, in La Porte, Texas. She was survived by her husband, Linus, her sister, Phoebe Sterling, and her son and daughter-in-law, Fred and Lucy Seelye. She was given a military funeral, and her remains later were moved to the military cemetery in Houston. Her burial stone refers to her as "Emma E. Seelye, Army Nurse," and it was as a nurse that she preferred to be remembered.

## PUBLICATIONS BY EMMA EDMONDS SEELYE

Edmundson, Sarah Emma. *Nurse and Spy in the Union Army.* Hartford, Connecticut: W.S. Williams, 1865.

## BIBLIOGRAPHY

Dannett, S. *She Rode with the Generals: The True and Incredible Story of Sarah Emma Seelye, Alias Franklin Thompson.* New York: Nelson, 1960.

Hoyt, H.R. *Three Thousand Years of Espionage.* Englewood Cliffs, N.J.: Prentice-Hall, 1948.

Kinchen, O.A. *Women Who Spied for the Blue and Gray.* New York: Dorrance, 1973.

Klein, A., ed. *Double Dealers.* Philadelphia: J.B. Lippincott, 1958.

Singer, K.D. *Spies and Traitors.* New York: Allen, 1953.

Dorothy S. Tao

# Mother Elizabeth Ann Bayley Seton

## 1774–1821

Mother Elizabeth Ann Bayley Seton contributed to nursing during the early years of United States history, just after the American Revolution. As a young widow, she rejected the idea of remarriage, refused to live in genteel isolation at the expense of caring relatives, converted to Roman Catholicism, and founded the American Sisters of Charity. This religious order for women played a significant role in the development of parochial education and the growth of quality nursing care in American society. She became the first American-born canonized saint in September 1975.

Mother Seton was born on August 28, 1774, the second child of Richard and Catherine Carlton Bayley, in New York City. Her older sister, Mary Magdeline, has been born one year earlier. When she was two years old, her mother died giving birth to a third daughter, who did not survive early childhood.

In 1778 Richard Bayley, a physician and the first city health officer in New York, married Charlotte Amelia Barclay, and the couple had seven children. Mother Seton's father spent long periods of time away from his family due to his duties during the frequent epidemics that plagued the area. Although education for girls in the revolutionary period was often haphazard, Mother Seton developed skills in reading, penmanship and mathematics.

On January 25, 1794, at the age of 19, she married William Magee Seton, a merchant from an established American family. They settled into a happy married life that produced five children and achieved a comfortable standard of living. Anna Maria was born in 1795, William in 1796, Richard Bailey in 1798, Catherine Joseph in 1800, and Rebecca in 1803.

However, William Seton's business began to fail due to financial changes of the time. The year, 1800, Mother Seton's father succumbed to yellow fever during one of the area's seasonal epidemics. Soon after this loss, William Seton began his final battle against tuberculosis. A voyage to Italy, which the couple had hoped would provide a warmer climate to cure the illness proved fruitless. He died in Italy on December 27, 1803.

Mother Seton received support from her husband's Italian business associates, the Filachi brothers, while waiting for a ship to return her to New York. Through them and her travels in Italy, she learned many new ideas, especially those related to the teachings of the Roman Catholic church.

Politically, most American colonies, and New York in particular, reflected staunch Protestant beliefs, and Roman Catholics either had little power or experienced open discrimination. Mother Seton's family belonged to respected Protestant communities, and her attraction to Roman Catholic doctrine created much inner personal conflict. She returned to New York in 1804 and began a personal search that lasted several months. She studied and counseled with Protestant clergy, her family, and Roman Catholic priests.

On March 14, 1805, she became a Roman Catholic. Her family and friends rejected her for this decision, many withdrawing their assistance to her and her children.

A few years later, Mother Seton received an invitation from Father William Du-Bourg of Baltimore, Maryland to establish a school for girls next to St. Mary's Seminary in Baltimore. Maryland had offered a haven for Roman Catholics and tolerance for Protestants since its founding over a century earlier. Mother Seton accepted and went to Baltimore in 1807.

She soon welcomed two of her husband's sisters, Harriet and Cecilia Seton, to assist in the work. Other young women also offered to assist in the school, which gave many young girls their only opportunity for an education. Soon after the school opened, Bishop John Carroll gave her guidelines for living the life of a religious which she shared with the women serving with her. Though deeply involved in her new career, she continued to provide for the physical and spiritual needs of her own children.

Mother Seton had felt the call to establish a religious order for some time, yet funds remained insufficient. After working one year in Baltimore, she received a gift from a wealthy convert who was preparing to enter the priesthood. It consisted of a grant of land and a sturdy farmhouse in Emmitsburg, Maryland, northwest of Baltimore.

On March 25, 1809, Mother Seton took her formal public vows before Bishop Carroll, and by June she left for Emmitsburg with four candidates for the new order and two students from the school. Life in the rural stone farmhouse challenged the early sisters, as it provided few comforts. The nuns had to walk or slowly ride long distances to obtain supplies or to attend mass.

The primary purpose of the order's activities in its early years was to establish a school. However, rural areas did not escape episodic outbreaks of communicable diseases. Thus, the nuns developed skills as bedside nurses during these periods of community need. The number of nuns increased steadily, and soon the Sisters of Charity obtained a larger home.

During the difficult early years of the order's development, Mother Seton led her nuns as they taught rural children and nursed loved ones as well as strangers. They cared for patients suffering from yellow fever, tuberculosis, brain fever, whooping cough, and even bubonic plague. The reputation of these dedicated women grew throughout the region.

Mother Seton lived to see her order grow and spread throughout the region. She died of tuberculosis in Emmitsburg, Maryland, early in 1821 at age 46. Among the survivors was a grandson, Robert Seton, who became a Roman Catholic archbishop.

By 1823 the Sisters of Charity received an invitation to establish a nursing service in a new proprietary infirmary associated with a medical school. The nuns provided housekeeping and cooking services as well as bedside care for patients. Seven branches of the original order grew to provide nursing service and leadership throughout the early period of nursing development.

Mother Seton was declared venerable by the Roman Catholic church in December 1959. She was beatified in March 1963 and canonized in September 1975.

## PUBLICATIONS BY MOTHER ELIZABETH ANN BAYLEY SETON

*Memoir, Letters and Journals of Elizabeth Seton*, edited by Robert Seton. 2 vols. New York: O'Shea, 1869.

## BIBLIOGRAPHY

Dirvin, J. *Mrs. Seton: Foundress of the American Sisters of Charity.* New York: Farrar, Straus and Giroux, 1975.

Melville, A. *Elizabeth Bayley Seton.* New York: Scribner's, 1951.

Melville, A.M. "Seton, Elizabeth Ann Bayley." In *Notable American Women 1607–1950,* edited by E.T. James. Cambridge, Mass. The Belknap Press of Harvard University Press, 1971.

Sisters of Charity Archives. Sisters of Charity Motherhouse, Emmitsburg, Md.

White, C. *Mother Seton: Mother of Many Daughters.* New York: Doubleday, 1949.

Linda Sabin

## PUBLICATIONS BY
## CLARA S. WEEKS SHAW

### BOOKS

*A Textbook of Nursing.* New York: Appleton, 1885. Reprint. New York: Garland Publishing, 1984; 2nd ed., 1892; 3rd ed., 1902; 3rd ed., revised and enlarged, 1916.

### ARTICLES

"Science in the Sick Room." *Popular Science Monthly* 22 (1883): 479–86.

### BIBLIOGRAPHY

"Clara S. Weeks Shaw." Obituary. *American Journal of Nursing* 40 (1940): 356.

Flaumenhaft, E., and C. Flaumenhaft. "Four Books That Changed Nursing." *Journal of the History of Medicine* 42 (1987): 54–72.

Vern L. Bullough

## Clara S. Weeks Shaw

### 1856–1940

Clara S. Weeks Shaw was the author of the first textbook on nursing to be written by an American nurse. *A Textbook of Nursing* was the third of four general nursing textbooks to be written before 1895.

The first two texts were compilations of several authors, many of them physicians. *A Manual of Nursing Prepared for the Training School for Nurses attached to Bellevue Hospital* (New York: Putnam, 1878) was published the same year as *A Handbook of Nursing* (Philadelphia: Lippincott, 1878) which had been prepared for the students at the Connecticut Training School for Nurses. The fourth text was Isabel A. Hampton (later Robb), *Nursing: Its Principles and Practices for Hospital and Private Use* (Philadelphia: Saunders, 1893).

Shaw, a graduate of the Rhode Island State Normal School, had taught school in Newport, Rhode Island, before entering the New York Hospital Training School, from which she was graduated in 1880. She then organized the nursing school at Patterson General Hospital in Patterson, New Jersey, and served as its superintendent from 1883 to 1888. It was there that she wrote her text since she felt nurses needed a text written by and for them. She married in 1888 and retired from active nursing. She died January 14, 1940, at Mountainview, New York.

## Nancy Cornelius Skenadore

### 1861–1908

Believed to be the first native American trained nurse, the life and work of Nancy Cornelius Skenadore are somewhat lost in obscurity. But as the first American Indian nurse, her contribution to her profession is significant.

The Oneida Indians were moved in 1823 from New York State to a reservation southwest of Green Bay, Wisconsin. Skenadore was born on the reservation on June 13, 1861, to Elijah J. and Elizabeth Jordan Cornelius. Little is known of her early life.

Records indicate that Skenadore was educated at the U.S. Indian school at Carlisle, Pennsylvania. She entered the Hartford Training School for Nurses, Hartford, Connecticut, in October 1888 and graduated two years later in October 1890.

Skenadore practiced her profession in Connecticut and later was superintendent of the Oneida Mission Hospital in Wisconsin. She worked at the mission hospital from September 1899 until her marriage to Daniel Skenadore in 1904.

During much of this time, the hospital was without a resident physician, and as Skenadore was probably the only nurse employed by the hospital, the services she provided were especially important.

Skenadore died of a malignancy on September 2, 1908, and was buried in the Hobart Oneida Indian Cemetery near the village of Oneida. Her photograph, along with that of Lavinia Cornelius, another early Indian nurse, hangs on the wall of the Oneida Community Health Center, Oneida, Wisconsin. Earlier there was a tablet in the Oneida (Episcopal) church identifying her as the first "Indian trained nurse" in the U.S. The church was destroyed by fire in 1920.

### BIBLIOGRAPHY

Bloomfield, J.K. *The Oneidas.* New York: James Stuart, 1909.

"Nursing Echoes." *Trained Nurse and Hospital Review* 10 (October 1893): 174.

Richards, C.E. *The Oneida People.* Phoenix, Ariz.: Indian Tribal Series, 1974.

Robinson, V. *White Caps: The Story of Nursing.* Philadelphia: J.B. Lippincott, 1946.

"Survey of Historical Activities." *Wisconsin Magazine of History* 3 (March 1920): 383.

Signe S. Cooper

## Elizabeth Sterling Soule

### 1884–1972

Elizabeth Sterling Soule made contributions in nursing education, public-health nursing, and organized nursing. Known as the mother of nursing in the Pacific Northwest, Soule founded the University of Washington's nursing department in 1921 and established the first integrated nursing program in any university.

On October 13, 1884, Soule and a twin brother were born to Edwin Sterling and Adaline Bates Sterling in East Douglas, Massachusetts, a mill town near Boston. Soule's twin brother died at birth. She and a younger brother had a happy childhood, spending summers at the farm and seashore. Soule took great interest in helping her father, a physician, in his home office and often accompanied him on his house calls. Her father's encouragement to discuss, evaluate, and propose practical solutions to the medical and social problems they encountered probably influenced Soule's later interest in public health and social welfare. During Soule's childhood, her mother became seriously ill, and a nursing graduate of Boston City Hospital came to care for her. Soule showed eagerness to learn procedures from the nurse.

Soule attended elementary and high school in Everett, Massachusetts. After her father died before her high-school graduation, Soule announced her plans to attend a nurses' training school. Discouraged from admission because she was considered too young at 18 years of age, she took a position at a small private hospital in Boston at the suggestion of a family friend.

After one year in the hospital, Soule was recommended by the superintendent of nurses to the superintendent of the Malden Hospital School for Nurses in Malden, Massachusetts, from which she graduated in April 1907.

After her graduation from nursing school, Soule remained on the staff at Malden Hospital for a short time and then resigned to become a private-duty nurse for two years. Inspired by a talk by physician Richard Cabot on public health, Soule enrolled in a four-month course of supervised field experience sponsored by the Boston Instructive District Nursing Association. In 1909, after her completion of the course, Soule became the first district nurse in the Everett Visiting Nurse Association.

During the two years Soule was in Everett, she and Harry W. Soule, a childhood friend, renewed their friendship. They were married on June 11, 1912. Soule resigned her position to go to Seattle, Washington, with her husband.

In Seattle, Soule soon became a visiting nurse for the Metropolitan Life Insurance Company, which was developing a public-health nursing service. In 1915 she became one of only three county nurses in the state. In 1918 Soule became state supervisor of public-health nurses for the combined staff of the Washington Tuberculosis Association and the Red Cross. Her job was to organize and promote public-health nursing. Soule worked from within the organization, learning about the social and economic conditions as well as the health problems in Washington State. In 1920 Soule was appointed state advisory nurse.

In 1918 the University of Washington offered a three-month graduate nursing summer course in public-health nursing. Barbara Bartlett of the University of Michigan came to teach the course, and Soule was appointed by the university to assist her. When Bartlett resigned after three years, Soule, together with her colleagues, persuaded the university's president, Henry Suzzalo, to continue the course on the condition that they find a teacher and enroll 11 students. Soule became that teacher, and at the end of the year, she received an academic appointment.

In January 1921 Suzzalo gave Soule the charge of developing a university department of nursing from courses offered by other departments in the university's college of science, a task she completed by the fall. She soon expanded the department's public-health nursing program and gained the approval of the National Organization for Public Health Nursing (NOPHN). When NOPHN gave high ratings to Soule's program with the exception of her own academic background, Soule resigned. However, Suzzalo urged her to continue her education, and following his advice, she returned to school, earning a B.A. degree in 1926 and an M.A. degree in 1931 from the University of Washington.

Following the development of the graduate public-health program and the preclinical nursing program, which was meant to precede three years of nurse training school in a hospital, Soule began to formulate plans for a four-year program for the nursing department. This program, revolutionary at the time, was to be conducted in conjunction with a large public hospital then in the planning stages. What was different about Soule's

program was its administrative separation of nursing service and nursing education; for the first time, the university was to be responsible for the clinical nursing education of the nursing students, while the hospital would be responsible for their nursing services.

Soule applied to the Rockefeller Foundation for funding, and she was awarded both the funding and a travel fellowship for studying nursing schools and public-health centers in Europe.

Through Soule's efforts, in 1931 the Harborview Division of the University of Washington School of Nursing at the Harborview King County Hospital began with 30 graduate nurses working toward bachelors' degrees and eight basic students who had completed two years of preclinical university courses. Under Soule's direction, the program later became first the School of Nursing Education and finally, in 1945, the University of Washington School of Nursing, which Soule served as dean until 1950.

Soule encouraged many hospitals to use the university for collegiate education for nursing students while offering their hospital facilities to the university for clinical education. In addition, she developed teaching units in state psychiatric hospitals because she believed that such units would prepare competent psychiatric nurses and aides and hence improve patient care.

Continually active in professional organizations, Soule was among the 20 original founders of the Association of Collegiate Schools of Nursing, later becoming its president. She was a member of its board of directors from 1932 to 1944. She was a member of the American Nurses' Association and NOPHN, and she participated in the beginning study of the unification of five national nursing organizations. She also was an honorary member of the National League of Nursing Education (NLNE) and served on the NLNE Committee on Early Nursing and Source Materials.

During World War II, Soule was a member of the Nursing Council on National Defense, a special consultant to the U.S. Public Health Service, and the western representative of the American Red

Cross advisory council. In Seattle, she was a member of the board of the Seattle Visiting Nurse Service. She was the author with Christine McKenzie of *Community Hygiene*.

As one of the pioneers in nursing, Soule had collegial relations with many of the early outstanding nurses; among them were Lavinia Dock, Lillian Wald, and Adelaide Nutting. But the person Soule recalled as most influential to her was Annie Goodrich, who urged Soule to try her collegiate nursing program.

In 1940 the University of Washington Alumni Association awarded Soule its highest honor. In 1944 Montana State College awarded her the honorary doctor of science degree.

After Soule's retirement in 1950, she became dean emeritus and lived in a small house overlooking Lake Washington. She continued participating in university and nursing affairs. Her husband died in 1950. Soule died February 19, 1972, at the age of 92. Her last home address was the Alderwood Manor. Soule was survived by a brother, Lewis E. Sterling of West Medford, Massachusetts.

On June 14, 1986, Soule was inducted into the American Nurses' Association Nursing Hall of Fame. At the same time, the University of Washington announced plans to create the Elizabeth Sterling Soule Endowed Professorship.

## PUBLICATIONS BY ELIZABETH STERLING SOULE

### BOOKS

With C. McKenzie. *Community Hygiene*. New York: Macmillan, 1940.

### ARTICLES

"Building the University School." *American Journal of Nursing* 38 (May 1938): 580–86.

"Elizabeth Sterling Soule, M.A., R.N." In *Nursing Hall of Fame*. Kansas City, Mo.: American Nurses' Association, 1986.

"Goodbye Messr. Chips." *Time*, 3 July 1950.

### BIBLIOGRAPHY

Leahy, K.M. "Elizabeth Sterling Soule." In *National League of Nursing Education: Biographic Sketches, 1937–1940*. New York: The League, 1940.

Loughran, H.A. "Mrs. Soule of Washington: Part I—Her Early Career in Nursing; Part II—The University of Washington School of Nursing." *Nursing Outlook* 4 (September 1956): 492–96; 4 (October 1956): 567–72.

Soule, E.S. "Development of the University of Washington School of Nursing." Paper presented to University of Washington School of Nursing Class M. 200, 1959.

Soule, E.S. Papers. University of Washington Libraries.

*Who Was Who in America*. Vol 5. Chicago: Marquis Who's Who, 1973.

Dorothy S. Tao

## Adele Grace Stahl
### 1908–1983

Adele Grace Stahl provided leadership in the American Nurses' Association (ANA) Council of State Boards of Nursing for over 30 years. She was recognized throughout the country as an expert on nursing-practice acts and other nursing legislation. She served as administrator and secretary of the Wisconsin State Board of Nursing for most of her nursing career.

Stahl was born December 8, 1908, in Akron, Ohio, the only child of Albert F. and Ethelyn Neff Stahl. After attending public schools, she enrolled in the Frances Payne Bolton School of Nursing, (Case) Western Reserve University, in Cleveland, Ohio. She was awarded her B.S. degree in 1931. She later received a certificate from the Merrill Palmer School of Child Development in Detroit, Michigan (1935). Additional postgraduate work was in public administration at Syracuse University in Syracuse, New York.

Stahl began her nursing career in 1931 as a head nurse in Babies' and Children's Hospital in Cleveland. She then was appointed an instructor in nursing at Western Reserve University from 1932 to 1934. She left Cleveland in 1935 for Syracuse, New York, as an instructor at the Syracuse

Memorial Hospital School of Nursing and two years later became assistant director of nursing education.

Stahl came to Wisconsin in 1938 as assistant director of the state board of health's bureau of nursing. Two years later, she was appointed director and was responsible for the licensure of registered and practical nurses and for the approval of the schools of nursing in the state.

In 1949 major legislative changes created a separate department of nurses in Wisconsin state government. This unit remained autonomous until 1967, when the Wisconsin State Department of Regulation and Licensure was established for all licensing boards. Stahl was the only person to serve as administrator of the state department of nurses; Wisconsin was the only state to have had a separate administrative department for nurses. She was also the first woman department head to serve in the governor's cabinet in Wisconsin state government.

In her work, Stahl devoted her efforts to helping nurses understand the legislative process. She frequently taught sessions in legislative workshops and conferences on legal aspects of nursing.

At the national level, Stahl worked for the American Nurses' Association Council of State Boards of Nursing from 1943 to 1974. She served as the council's chair (1953–56 and 1970–71) and on its executive committee (1953–56 and 1968–71). Nursing has been a leader among licensed groups in the use of national examinations, and Stahl's contributions to this activity extended over three decades. She sought to keep standards responsive to the ongoing changes in the health-care delivery system and in society.

Professionals in related health-care organizations relied on Stahl to provide accurate, unbiased information on nurses, nursing, and health care. She remained firm in her conviction of the need for high standards, and she always documented what she said.

During her tenure, Stahl sought and received legislative approval and funding to conduct two statewide studies on nursing and nursing education. One was completed in 1955, the other in 1973. Both studies had a substantial impact on the improvement of nursing in the state. Stahl frequently counseled groups in other states planning to conduct similar studies.

Stahl was instrumental in initiating support for legislation and legislative rules that provided scholarships for Wisconsin's registered nurses. The scholarship program was launched in 1945 in an effort to alleviate the critical shortage of nurses and continued until 1978. Initially, these scholarships were financed from surplus funds from the department of nurses budget; her careful management assured surplus funds each year. Later, additional scholarships for teachers were secured from general state funds.

A member of the Wisconsin Nurses' Association, Stahl served on its committee on legislation for many years. She served as consultant to a number of voluntary associations and state agencies, including the Wisconsin Nurses' Association, the Wisconsin League for Nursing, the Wisconsin State Board of Vocational and Adult Education, the Wisconsin State Bureau of Personnel, the Wisconsin State Department of Health and Social Services, the Wisconsin State Board of Pharmacy, and the Milwaukee County Civil Service.

Stahl received several honors in recognition of her outstanding contributions to the health and welfare of the citizens of Wisconsin. In 1958 the Milwaukee Board of Vocational and Adult Education presented her its Civic Service Award in recognition of the important contributions she made to the development of professional and practical nurse education in the Milwaukee area. The Wisconsin Hospital Association presented her with its Award of Merit in 1960. The Distinguished Civic Service Award was presented to her by the Wisconsin State University. Oshkosh (now University of Wisconsin-Oshkosh) in 1971. That year, she also was honored with a resolution of the Wisconsin Nurses' Association in recognition of her contributions to nurses, nursing, and health.

In 1974 Stahl was awarded an honorary doctoral degree from Marquette University. The following year, she was awarded the John XXIII Distinguished Service Award from Viterbo College, La Crosse, Wisconsin, an award given to those who, in the service of humanity, have distinguished themselves in the spirit of Pope John XXIII. She also received a Friend of Extension Award from the University of Wisconsin-Extension in 1974.

Stahl retired in 1974 and remained in Madison until her death on September 25, 1983.

## PUBLICATIONS BY ADELE GRACE STAHL

"Prelude to Licensure." *American Journal of Nursing* 59 (September 1959): 1259–60.

## BIBLIOGRAPHY

"Adele G. Stahl." Obituary. *American Journal of Nursing* 84 (April 1984): 550.

"Adele G. Stahl." Obituary. *Capital Times* (Madison, Wisconsin), 27 September 1983.

"Know Your Madisonian: Adele G. Stahl." *Wisconsin State Journal*, 2 April 1963.

Mirr, M. "The Evolution of the Wisconsin Nurse Practice Act." Master's thesis, University of Wisconsin-Madison, 1981.

Partridge, E. "Wisconsin's Scholarship Program for Graduate Nurses." *American Journal of Nursing* 56 (December 1956): 1562–63.

"Stahl, Adele G." In *Who's Who of American Women*, Vol. 4. Chicago: A.N. Marquis, 1961–62.

Stahl, A.G. Interview with M. Mirr, 30 June 1981. Madison, Wis.

Signe S. Cooper

# Mabel Keaton Staupers

1890–

Mabel Keaton Staupers had a leadership role in orchestrating the World War II-era struggle for the integration of black nurses into the armed forces' nurses corps and into the mainstream of professional nursing. The author of numerous articles, her most significant publication is *No Time For Prejudice: A Story of the Integration of Negroes in Nursing in the United States* (1961). She was the first salaried executive secretary of the National Association of Colored Graduate Nurses.

Staupers was born in Barbados, West Indies, on February 27, 1890. In April 1903 she and her parents, Thomas and Pauline Doyle, migrated to the United States, settling in September into the Harlem community of New York City.

Following completion of early primary and secondary education in New York City, Staupers won admittance into the Freedmen's Hospital School of Nursing in Washington, D.C. Entering the school in 1914, she was graduated three years later with class honors. In 1917 she also was married to James Max Keaton of Asheville, North Carolina. The couple's marriage ended in divorce. In 1931 she married Frisby Staupers of New York City.

Like most black graduate nurses of the day, Staupers began her professional career in private-duty nursing, first in New York City and then in Washington, D.C. In 1920 in cooperation with physicians Louis T. Wright and James Wilson, she helped to organize the Booker T. Washington Sanatorium, the first private facility in the Harlem area allowing black doctors to treat patients. She served this institution as administrator and director of nurses.

Receipt of a 1921 working fellowship to the Henry Phipps Institute for Tuberculosis in Philadelphia, Pennsylvania, enticed her away from New York. She later was assigned to the Jefferson Hospital Medical College in Philadelphia, where she observed a demoralizing system of racial segregation and discrimination. This experience toughened her resolve to fight for full and equal opportunity in all health programs and services and within professional nursing organizations.

In 1922 under the auspices of the New York Tuberculosis and Health Association, Staupers conducted a survey of the health needs of the Harlem community, including an evaluation of the services offered for the care of minorities in tuberculosis institutions in New York City and the state. Her emphasizing the problems raised by tuberculosis in the Harlem ghetto led to the organization of the Harlem committee by the New York Tuberculosis and Health Association in order to more effectively channel efforts and resources. She was appointed as its first executive secretary and continued in this capacity for 12 years, serving 9 of them under the direction of Harry Hopkins of Works Projects Administration fame.

In 1934 Staupers accepted an invitation to become the first executive secretary of the National Association of Colored Graduate Nurses (NACGN). The NACGN had been founded in 1908 to champion the interests and to promote the professional development of black women nurses. One impetus was the fact that the leading nursing organizations, the American Nurses' Association (ANA) and the National League of Nursing Education, had refused to accept individual membership from black nurses residing in 17 states. Every southern state association barred black women, thereby making the majority of black women nurses professional outcasts in a large section of the country.

Grants from the General Education Board of the Rockefeller Foundation and the Julius Rosenwald Fund enabled the NACGN not only to employ Staupers, but also to move into permanent headquarters at Rockefeller Center, where all the major national nursing organizations had offices. Staupers assumed her position mindful of the crisis confronting black nurses in the United States. The majority of nurse training schools denied them admission, many visiting nurses' associations and municipal health departments paid them lower wages than their white counterparts, and promotion to high-level administrative positions was virtually impossible to achieve except in segregated black institutions.

An ardent integrationist and feminist, Staupers set as her primary long-range objective the full integration of black female nurses into the mainstream of American nursing. One way to accomplish this was to strengthen NACGN and to develop programs that would best serve the immediate needs of black nurses. Staupers spent the first few years collecting data, organizing state and local nursing associations, advis-

ing and counseling black nurses, and representing them in the larger community. She worked closely with NACGN's biracial national advisory council, which was organized in 1938 as a means of developing greater interest in and support for the association's programs.

The struggle to win professional recognition and integration of black nurses into American nursing acquired new momentum and urgency with the outbreak of World War II. Staupers seized the opportunity created by the war emergency and the increased demand for nurses to project the plight of the black nurse into the national limelight. She encouraged nursing groups, black and white, to write letters and send telegrams protesting the discrimination against black nurses in the army and navy nurse corps.

By the time of the Japanese attack on Pearl Harbor in December 1941, Staupers already had developed a sharp sense of political timing. When the army set a quota of 56 black nurses and the navy refused even to consider admitting black nurses into the nurse corps, Staupers swung NACGN into action. She publicized the quotas. She joined with other black leaders to meet directly with the army generals and high-ranking government officials to protest the imposition of quotas. The pressure did result in some success, although not as much as was desired. In 1943 Staupers received notice that the navy had decided to place the induction of black nurses under consideration. The army raised its quota of black nurses to 160.

In an effort to draw even more attention to the unfairness of quotas, Staupers requested a meeting with Eleanor Roosevelt. However, it was not until November 1944 that Staupers and the first lady met. During the meeting, Staupers described in detail the black nurses' relationship with the armed forces. Roosevelt, apparently moved by the discussion, applied her own subtle pressure to Norman T. Kirk, the surgeon general of the United States Army, Secretary of War Henry Stimson, and the navy's rear admiral, W.J.C. Agnew.

In the face of mounting pressure, Kirk announced in January 1945 that nurses would be accepted into the Army Nurse Corps without regard to race. That same month, Agnew declared that the navy was open to black women. A few weeks later, Phyllis Dailey became the first black woman to break the race barrier and be inducted into the Navy Nurse Corps. In 1946 an exhausted but exhilarated Staupers relinquished her position as executive secretary of NACGN to take a much-needed rest.

Although she no longer occupied a visible position of leadership, Staupers continued to press for the integration of black nurses into the ANA. In 1948 the ANA's house of delegates opened the gates to black membership, appointed a black woman nurse as assistant executive secretary in its national headquarters, and witnessed former NACGN president Estelle Massey Riddle's election to the board of directors. With the removal of this barrier, NACGN at its 1949 convention voted itself out of existence. The following year, Staupers, then president of NACGN, presided over its formal dissolution.

Staupers received many accolades for her leadership. The crowning acknowledgement and recognition of her role and contribution in the quest of civil rights for black nurses came from the Spingarn Award Committee of the National Association for the Advancement of Colored People, which in 1951 chose Staupers to be the 36th recipient of the Spingarn Medal.

## BIBLIOGRAPHY

Carnegie, M.E. *The Path We Tread: Blacks in Nursing, 1854–1984.* Philadelphia: J.B. Lippincott, 1986.

Cobbs, W.M. "Mabel Keaton Staupers, R.N. 1890–." *Journal of the National Medical Association* 61 (March 1969): 198–99.

Hine, D.C., ed. *Black Women in the Nursing Profession: A Documentary History.* New York: Garland Publishing, 1985.

———. "Mabel K. Staupers and the Integration of Black Nurses into the Armed Forces." In *Black Leaders of the Twentieth Century,* edited by J.H. Franklin and A. Meier. Urbana, Ill.: University of Illinois, 1982.

Staupers, M.K. Papers. Spingarn-Moorland Research Center, Howard University, Washington, D.C.

Darlene Clark Hine

# Jessie Lulu Stevenson (West)
## 1891–1976

As a public-health nurse, Jessie Lulu Stevenson became a stimulating force in the improvement of many nursing services throughout the country. She specialized in orthopedic nursing and wrote several books in that field.

Stevenson was born in 1891, the daughter of Henry A. and Lulu M. Davis Stevenson.

Stevenson received a bachelor's degree from the University of South Dakota in 1915 and spent the next three years as instructor of English at Moorhead (Minnesota) High School and at Lead (South Dakota) High School. She attended Harvard Medical School and the University of Chicago and received a physical therapy certificate from Northwestern Medical School in Chicago. In 1921 she graduated from Presbyterian Hospital School of Nursing in Chicago and was the recipient of a Visiting Nurse Association scholarship.

Stevenson began her nursing career in Chicago, where she served as the orthopedic director of the Visiting Nurse Association for 17 years and as supervisor of the widely known orthopedic unit at Northwestern University Medical School. She had previously worked in New York as orthopedic director of the National Organization of Public Health Nursing (NOPHN).

In 1939 NOPHN received a subsidy from the National Foundation for Infantile Paralysis to provide for a consultant in orthopedic nursing, and Stevenson was appointed. Few nurses were trained to work with social workers, physical therapists, and other specialists in the development of effective programs. The service, begun by Stevenson, became a model for the improvement of many nursing services. The Joint Orthopedic Nursing Advisory Service (JONAS), financed by the National Foundation of Infantile Paralysis and administered by NOPHN, was organized in 1941, and a consultant, Carmelita Calderwood, was engaged by the National League of Nursing Education to work in cooperation with Stevenson.

JONAS provided consultant services to individuals, hospitals, schools of nursing, universities, and nursing-service agencies. For several years, it administered scholarship funds provided by the foundation. The service was so successful that it was continued during the postwar period of mounting incidence of polio, and it became the prototype for the Joint Tuberculosis Nursing Advisory Service, established shortly after World War II.

Stevenson's goals for nursing were the prevention of illness and disability and establishing the best nursing care for the sick so that they might recover as quickly as possible.

The author of numerous professional articles, Stevenson also published several books, including *Posture and Nursing* (1942), *Care of Poliomyelitis* (1940), *The Nursing Care of Patients with Infantile Paralysis* (1940), and *Congenital Malformations and Birth Injuries* (1954). She was a member of the American Nurses' Association, the National League for Nursing Education, and the National Organization for Public Health Nursing, and she served one term as president of the American Physiotherapy Association.

The wife of Harry R. West, Stevenson died on May 21, 1976, of cancer at the age of 84 at the Valley Verde Convalescent Home in Santa Barbara, California. She had used the name Stevenson professionally throughout her career.

## PUBLICATIONS BY JESSIE LULU STEVENSON (WEST)

### BOOKS

*Care of Poliomyelitis.* New York: Macmillan, 1940.

*The Nursing Care of Patients with Infantile Paralysis.* New York: National Foundation of Infantile Paralysis, 1940.

*Posture and Nursing.* New York: NOPHN, 1942.

*Orthopedic Conditions at Birth.* New York: Joint Orthopedic Nursing Advisory Service, 1943.

*Congenital Malformations and Birth Injuries.* New York: Association for the Aid of Crippled Children, 1954.

### ARTICLES

"Home Care of Children Who Had Poliomyelitis." *Public Health Nursing* 16 (August 1924): 403–405.

"After-care of Infantile Paralysis." *American Journal of Nursing* 25 (September 1925): 729–733.

"The Infantiles." *Public Health Nursing* 21 (July 1929): 348–352.

"The Kenny Method." *America Journal of Nursing* 42 (August 1942): 904–910.

"Public Health Nursing in the 1943 Polio Epidemic." *Public Health Nursing* 36 (July 1944): 336–339.

"An Orthopedic Service for the Community." *Public Health Nursing* 37 (December 1945): 607–611.

"Looking Toward the Future." *Public Health Nursing* 41 (January 1949): 36–41.

## BIBLIOGRAPHY

Howes, D. *American Women.* Teaneck, N.J.: Zephyrus, 1974.

"Jessie Lulu Stevenson West." Obituary. *New York Times,* 24 May 1976.

Roberts M.M. *American Nursing History and Interpretation.* New York: Macmillan, 1954.

Lilli Sentz

## Isabel Maitland Stewart

### 1878–1963

Throughout her lifetime, Isabel Maitland Stewart filled the roles of scholar, author, historian, researcher, and nursing leader. She is best remembered, however, as American nursing's most influential spokeswoman in the area of education for approximately 45 years. At Teachers College, Columbia University, she developed the first course dealing specifically with the teaching of nursing, a course that eventually was expanded to become an entire program for the preparation of teachers of nursing. Her work on a multitude of national and international nursing committees provided for significant and lasting contributions to the advancement of nursing education.

Stewart was born January 14, 1878, in Fletcher, Ontario. She was the fourth of nine children. Her parents, Francis Beattie and Elizabeth Farquharson Stewart, had emigrated to Canada with their families from Aberdeenshire, Scotland.

The entire Stewart family engaged in reading, writing, politics, and religious affairs. Children in the Stewart household were encouraged and expected to engage in conversations. The parents' strong belief that educational advantages should be provided for all ensured that the girls in the family had the same educational opportunities as the boys.

Stewart's formal education began in an ungraded school. At age 11 she passed an entrance examination and was admitted to a high school in the nearby city of Chatham. After two years in this program, she moved with her family to Morton, Manitoba, Canada. Although Francis Stewart's lack of business sense and utlimate financial failure had necessitated the move, the family entered with zest into the pioneering experience in the new country and shared in the exciting adventures of frontier life. Consequently, Stewart completed her secondary education in Manitoba, where she taught in a small, ungraded country school for a short time. She then attended Manitoba Normal School, where she received her teaching certificate and diploma in 1895. For nearly four years after that, she taught in both ungraded and graded schools in Manitoba, with one year devoted to advanced work at the Winnipeg Collegiate Institute.

Teaching at the elementary level did not prove satisfactory to Stewart. In February 1900 she entered Winnipeg General Hospital Training School, attributing her decision to a desire for a broader experience of life and a more stimulating, engrossing type of work. This was not a popular decision with family members, who felt that she was throwing away a good education.

While a student nurse, Stewart observed many aspects of nursing that would require the adoption of unpopular causes. It was her increasing devotion to the examination and analysis of such issues that ultimately led to her profound interest in the history of nursing and the texts that she wrote on the subject.

The beginning of Stewart's nurses' training marked the beginning of her in-

volvement in a constant struggle to revolutionize the education of nurses and to free women who had been placed in a subservient role. Her ideas coincided with those of nursing leaders of the day, who had begun to organize for the control of their own educational standards and for the improvement of nursing practice. They saw that the united energies of all nurses and all schools would be needed in any serious attempt to attack the chaos in educational standards and ideals.

Following graduation in 1903, Stewart practiced as a private-duty nurse, did district nursing in Winnipeg, and held a position as head nurse in medical nursing in the Winnipeg General Hospital. During this four-year period as a practicing nurse in Canada, she became known for her organizational efforts. She assisted in the establishment of a visiting nurse society in western Canada and in a journal for the alumni association of the Winnipeg General Hospital Training School.

Stewart eagerly began to follow the progress in the transition of nursing education from apprenticeship to professional education. In 1907 she was drawn to an article written by M. Adelaide Nutting that described new educational opportunities available for graduate nurses at Teachers College. She entered the program in 1908 and planned to stay only one term because of inadequate funds. However, she was able to continue with a small scholarship from the American Society of Superintendents of Training Schools for Nurses (ASSTSN).

Stewart obtained a special certificate in hospital economics in 1909, a special diploma in hospital economics in 1910, a B.S. degree in 1911, and the M.A. degree and master's diploma in 1913. She was the first nurse in the department to receive a master's degree. Although she intended to acquire a Ph.D. and continued taking course work, her doctoral work was never finished. Nevertheless, she was awarded three honorary degrees: an L.L.D. degree from Western Reserve University in 1948, an L.H.D. degree from Columbia University in 1954, and an L.L.D. degree from the University of Manitoba in 1956.

Nutting quickly recognized Stewart's

special abilities, and she frequently asked for Stewart's assistance in the endeavors of the department. At the end of her first year in the program, Stewart became an assistant to Nutting. During Stewart's 39 years at Teachers College from 1908 to 1947, she successively held the positions of assistant, instructor, assistant professor, and associate professor and ultimately succeeded Nutting as professor in Nursing Education on the Helen Hartley Foundation and director of the division of nursing education in 1925. A close friendship and working relationship developed between the two nursing leaders and lasted 40 years until Nutting's death in 1948.

Stewart's attention to developments in general education and her utilization of its principles in nursing education ultimately led to recognition of her abilities in education. In 1944 she was elected second vice-president of the American Council on Education. In this capacity, she was able to introduce many general educators to nursing as an educational rather than a training program.

Early in her professional career, Stewart began her contributions to nursing organizations. These organizations provided for her an essential vehicle for improvement of professional training and curriculum in schools of nursing throughout the country. Her contributions to professional organizations include the following: member of the ASSTSN and the Associated Alumni of the United States and Canada; secretary (1915), second vice-president (1920), and member of the board of directors (1925–43) of the National League of Nursing Education (NLNE); editor of the department of nursing education of the *American Journal of Nursing* (1916–21); editor of the *Nursing Education Monographs*; one of the founders of the Association of Collegiate Schools of Nursing (ACSN); and first secretary and president (1937–41) of the board of directors of the ACSN.

Internationally, Stewart also was recognized for her unique contributions. She actively participated in the work of the International Council of Nurses (ICN) and was chairman of the NLNE's committee on international affairs. She was perhaps best known as chair of the ICN's committee on education from 1925 to 1947. During her tenure, she prepared *The Educational Program of the School of Nursing*, a classic document that focused attention on the need for well-organized educational programs in nursing in all countries. Her international involvement also included membership in the Florence Nightingale International Foundation and acting as an advisory member of the Florence Nightingale Memorial Foundation Committee.

During the two world wars, Stewart continued to stress the need for qualified nurses. She wrote many of the nursing publicity and recruitment materials for World War I and chaired the curriculum committee of the Vassar Training Camp. At the onset of World War II, she suggested the formation of a National Nursing Council for National Defense. She was appointed chair of its committee on educational policies and resources and, with the help of committee members, prepared a plan that requested federal funds for nursing education. Funds were obtained, and the United States Cadet Nurse Corps was established with the assistance of Stewart, who served as a member of its advisory committee.

For many years, Stewart worked closely with the curriculum committee (originally the education committee) of the NLNE as secretary (1914–19) and then as chair (1920–37). Three important studies emerged from this committee. The first, published as the *Standard Curriculum for Schools of Nursing* (1917), contained a systematic plan for the education of nurses and included specific courses along with their objectives, content, and methods. The second, published as the *Curriculum for Schools of Nursing* (1927), was a revision and expansion of the first, in which a job analysis technique was used to outline the functions and qualifications of the nurse, constituting the practical objectives of the nursing school curriculum. The word "standard" was dropped to avoid the notion that it was a requirement to be adopted by schools of nursing. In 1935 Stewart urged that another revision be made to meet the cur-

Clara Dutton Noyes

Katherine M. Olmsted

Betty Ann Olsen

Sara Elizabeth Parsons

Mary Genevieve Phillips

Drusilla Rageu Poole

Amy Elizabeth Pope

Louise Matilda Powell

Helen Irene Denne Schulte

Sister Regina Purtell (upper row, center)

Mother Elizabeth Ann Bayley Seton

Nancy Cornelius Skenadore

Adele Grace Stahl

Julia Catherine Stimson

Barbara Anna Thompson (Sharpless)

Dora Elizabeth Thompson

Julia Charlote Thompson

Adah Belle Samels Thoms

**Shirley Carew Titus**

Katherine Tucker

Daisy Dean Urch    Cornelia Van Kooy

rent trends in nursing education necessary to comply with community needs.

The project proved to be one of the most far-reaching and ambitious nursing education efforts undertaken and included the participation of representatives of all the professional organizations, allied professions, and the community. It was a process of sharing in which participating individuals and groups were educated through their involvement. The report, *A Curriculum Guide for Schools of Nursing* (1937), was the product of Stewart's leadership.

Although Stewart's activities and interests in the research area are less widely known, they are nonetheless significant. Intrigued by time and motion studies for improvement of efficiency in industry, she began around 1925 to investigate the potential of this technique for nursing. Her activity analysis of nursing attempted to differentiate between nursing and nonnursing functions. Eventually she published the *Nursing Education Bulletin*, possibly the first research journal in nursing. As a tribute to her impact on nursing research, the Isabel Maitland Stewart Professional Chair in Nursing Research was established at Teachers College in 1961.

Stewart was a prolific writer who interpreted modern trends in both general and nursing education. Her 123 articles, 17 pamphlets, and 2 books (now classics in nursing literature) were extensively utilized around the world and regarded as valuable resource material. *A Short History of Nursing* (1920), written with Lavinia L. Dock, was published in several revised editions. *The Education of Nurses* (1943) not only traced the development of education for nursing from its foundations, but also discussed the philosophy of nursing education.

Throughout her lifetime, Stewart was recognized for her accomplishments. She received an honorary membership in the History of Nursing Society of McGill University (1928), the Adelaide Nutting Award from the National League of Nursing Education (1947), the Pro Benignetate Humana Medal from the government of Finland (1949), the Florence Nightingale Medal from the International Committee of the Red Cross Society (1955), and membership in numerous honorary societies.

Following her retirement from Teachers College in 1947, Stewart continued to live near the university. She devoted her time to writing, working on Nutting's papers, and serving as chair of the National League for Nursing's committee on historical source material. At the age of 85, she died of a heart attack in the home of her nephew, Henry E. Sharpe, in Chatham, New Jersey, on October 5, 1963. Services were held at St. Paul's Chapel, Columbia University, New York City. She was survived by two sisters, Helen Gordon Stewart of Victoria, British Columbia, and Mrs. William C. McKillican of Ottawa, Ontario, Canada.

## PUBLICATIONS BY ISABEL MAITLAND STEWART

### BOOKS

With Lavinia L. Dock. *A Short History of Nursing.* New York: G.P. Putnam's Sons, 1920, 1925, 1931, 1938; 5th ed. with Anne L. Austin, as *A History of Nursing.* New York: G.P. Putnam's Sons, 1962.

*The Education of Nurses, Historical Foundations and Modern Trends.* Macmillan Nursing Education Monograph. New York: Macmillan, 1943.

With Agnes Gelinas. *A Century of Nursing.* New York: G.P. Putnam's Sons, 1950.

### PAMPHLETS

*Developments in Nursing Education since 1918.* Washington: U.S. Office of Education Bulletin No. 20, 1921.

### ARTICLES (SELECTED)

"Problems of Nursing Education." *Teachers College Record* 11 (May 1910): 7–26.

"A Bird's-eye View of Nursing History." *American Journal of Nursing* 17 (June 1917), 958–966. Also in *NLNE Annual Report,* 1917, and *Proceedings of 23rd Convention.* New York: NLNE, 1918.

"The Movement for Shorter Hours in Nurses' Training Schools." *American Journal of Nursing,* 19 (March 1919): 439–443.

"Readjustments in the Training School Curriculum to Meet the New Demands in Public Health Nursing," *American Journal of Nursing,* 20 (November 1919): 102–09.

"Trends in Nursing Education." *American Journal of Nursing* 31 (May 1931): 601.

"Florence Nightingale—Educator." *Teachers College Record* 41 (December 1931): 208–23.

"Mary Adelaide Nutting, 1858–1948." *Teachers College Record* 50 (December 1948): 199–201.

"A Half-Century of Nursing Education." *American Journal of Nursing* 50 (October 1950): 617–21.

With Bess V. Cunningham. "Maude B. Muse—Nurse, Educator, Author, and Creative Thinker." *American Journal of Nursing* 56 (November 1956): 1434–36.

### BIBLIOGRAPHY

Christy, T.E. *Cornerstone for Nursing Education: A History of the Division of Nursing Education of Teachers College, Columbia University, 1899–1947.* New York: Teachers College Press, 1969.

———. "Portrait of a Leader: Isabel Maitland Stewart." *Nursing Outlook* 17 (October 1969): 44.

Donahue, M.P. "Isabel Maitland Stewart's Philosophy of Education." *Nursing Research* 321 (May–June 1983): 140.

———. "Isabel Maitland Stewart's Philosophy of Education." Ph.d. diss., University of Iowa, 1981.

———. Nursing: *The Finest Art. An Illustrated History.* St Louis, Mo.: C.V. Mosby, 1985.

Fitzpatrick, M.L. *Prologue to Professionalism.* Bowie, Md.: Robert J. Brady, 1983.

Goostray, S. "Isabel Maitland Stewart." *American Journal of Nursing* 54 (March 1954): 302–06.

Hart, M.E. "Isabel Maitland Stewart, 1878–1963." *Nurses' Alumnae Journal,* Winnepeg General Hospital (1964): 7–10.

Mary Adelaide Nutting Historical Collection. Teachers College, Columbia University.

McManus, R.L. "Isabel M. Stewart—Foremost Researcher." *Nursing Research* 11 (Winter 1962): 4

Nursing Education Department Archive. Teachers College, Columbia University.

Stewart, I.M. "Reminiscences of Isabel M. Stewart." 1961. Oral History Office, Columbia University.

Taylor, E.J. "Isabel Maitland Stewart—Educator." *American Journal of Nursing* 36 (January 1936): 38.

M. Patricia Donahue

## Julia Catherine Stimson
### 1881–1948

Julia Catherine Stimson pioneered in the fields of voluntary Red Cross service and military nursing during the early years of the twentieth century. Through her efforts and those of her peers, nurses played a significant role in the nursing care of military personnel during war and peace. She also represents the first generation of educated nurses who during World War I served in the military without the benefit of military rank or position. This generation of nurses did such an outstanding job of meeting the nursing needs of war victims that later generations of nurses eventually received the rank and recognition they deserved.

Stimson was born in Worcester, Massachusetts, on May 26, 1881, the second of seven children of the Reverend Henry Albert Stimson and Alice Weaton Bartlett Stimson, both from old New England families. Stimson's maternal grandfather served as president of Dartmouth College, and her father's family had many outstanding community and political leaders active in late nineteenth-century America.

The family believed in higher education and active service to others and encouraged all the children to pursue useful careers. Stimson's father served several Congregational parishes during her younger years, then assumed a position, which he held for 35 years, as secretary of the American Board of Commissioners for Foreign Missions. These changes in his career facilitated educational opportunities for his children. Stimson attended public schools in St. Louis, Missouri, and New York City before preparing for college at the Brearley School in New York City. She graduated from Vassar College in 1901 with a B.A. degree. She then did graduate work at Columbia University in biology and in medical drawing.

After completing her academic work, Stimson considered studying medicine. However, a meeting with one of nursing's most vigorous leaders, Annie Goodrich, then superintendent of the New York Hospital Training School at Cornell, changed her goal to nursing.

Stimson entered the nurses' training program in March 1904 and was graduated in May 1908. Her first position was superintendent of nurses at Harlem Hospital, New York City. This municipal hospital served many poor, underprivileged patients, and Stimson's strong family tradition of service to others stimulated her to find new ways to serve the non-medical needs of the hospital's needy. With Florence Johnson, another nurse, she organized a social-service department to help families cope with problems after discharge.

In 1913 Stimson moved to St. Louis to become superintendent of nurses at Washington University Hospital. While there, she also completed an A.M. degree in sociology, biology, and education at Washington University in St. Louis in 1917.

During this prewar period, Stimson became a Red Cross volunteer reserve nurse, assisting in the organization of Missouri nurses to prepare for disaster relief. She led some of these nurses in assisting victims of the Ohio floods during 1913.

World War I placed heavy demands on many nurses. Stimson enlisted in the Army Nurse Corps to direct Red Cross-sponsored base hospital unit 21, organized through Washington University. One month after the declaration of war, the hospital unit arrived at Rouen, France. During the difficult months that followed, Stimson wrote to her family of her life and the struggles of her nurses at the base hospital. These letters, complied by her family, became a book entitled *Finding Themselves*.

By April 1918 Stimson became the chief of Red Cross nurses in France while maintaining her army commitment. Seven months after her move to the directorship of the Red Cross, she received an army appointment as director of nursing services for the American Expeditionary Forces. This position proved particularly demanding, as she directed the activities of 10,000 army nurses during the final days of the war and through the difficult six months following the war.

Stimson received the Distinguished Service medal as well as other citations for her tireless efforts during the war. She also received the British Royal Red Cross and the French Médaille de la Recon-

naissance Française and the Médaille d'Hygiéne Publique for her services during the recovery period after the war.

In June 1919 Stimson became the dean of the Army School of Nursing, taking over the program from her former mentor, Annie Goodrich. She held that position until the school closed in the early 1920s. By December 1919 the task of superintendent of the Army Nurse Corps became part of her increased responsibilities. Throughout the crucial postwar years, Stimson committed her time and energies to improving the status of nurses in the army. She also worked to improve corps organization and personnel practices. Always an active member in the major professional organizations, she joined their efforts after the war to achieve rank for nurses serving in the military.

The efforts of the nurses and congressional supporters in this area proved only partially successful. Congress granted nurses relative rank, giving them some authority within the realm of hospital units, and entitled them to some benefits, but their salaries and scope of authority did not correspond to those of men of identical rank. As superintendent, Stimson became a commissioned officer with the relative rank of major in 1920. She served the army as major and superintendent until 1937, when she retired.

In 1942 at the age of 62, Stimson was recalled by the army to assist in recruiting nurses for the World War II effort. Her strong, outspoken approach concerning the significance of nursing stimulated many nurses to volunteer for service during her six-month tour. Although she could not actively participate in World War II, she gained the satisfaction of seeing nurses receive full commissioned rank in 1947. She was promoted to the rank of colonel in 1948, just before her death.

Stimson met many professional obligations in addition to her military responsibilities. She remained active in all the major nursing organizations, serving as president of the American Nurses' Association from 1938–44. She strongly advocated nursing as a profession for college-educated women. She wrote a textbook entitled *Nurses' Handbook of Drugs and Solutions* (1910) and numerous articles in nursing journals about women in military nursing. Her many honors included an honorary doctorate from Mt. Holyoke College (1921) and the Florence Nightingale Medal of the International Red Cross (1929).

Stimson retired to a home in Briarcliff, New York, and spent summer vacations in Maine. She died at the age of 67 on September 29, 1948, at St. Francis Hospital, Poughkeepsie, New York. Memorial services were held at the Briarcliff Congregational church in Poughkeepsie.

## PUBLICATIONS BY JULIA CATHERINE STIMSON

### BOOKS

*Finding Themselves.* New York: Macmillan, 1918.

### ARTICLES

"Earliest Known Connection of Nurses with Army Hospitals in the United States. "*American Journal of Nursing* 25 (January 1925): 18.

"The Forerunners of the American Army Nurse." *Military Surgery* 58 (February 1926): 133–41.

"The Army Nurse Corps." *The Medical Department of the U.S. Army in the World War.* Vol. 13, Part 2. Washington, D.C.: U.S. Surgeon General's Office, U.S. Government Printing Office, 1927.

"Women Nurses with the Union Forces during the Civil War." *Military Surgery* (January–February 1928).

"History and Manual of the Army Nurse Corps." *Army Medical Bulletin* 41 (1937).

"Ida F. Butler." National League of Nursing Education. *Biographic Sketches, 1937–1940.* New York: The League, 1940.

## BIBLIOGRAPHY

"Julia Stimson." Obituary. *American Journal of Nursing* 48 (November 1948): 675.

"Julia Stimson." Obituary. *New York Times,* 1 October 1948.

"Stimson, Julia Catherine." *The National Cyclopedia of American Biography.* Vol. B. New York: James T. White & Co., 1927, 67–68.

Nichols, J. *Notable American Women.* Vol. 3. Cambridge, Mass.: Belknap Press of Harvard University Press, 1971.

"Who's Who in the Nursing World." *American Journal of Nursing* 22 (October 1924): 1040.

Linda E. Sabin

# Euphemia Jane Taylor

1874–1970

Euphemia Jane Taylor was involved with nursing on an international level. Though primarily a psychiatric nurse, she contributed to nursing in general and throughout her career emphasized a holistic, humanistic approach. She was the second dean of the Yale University School of Nursing and the first American nurse to be elected president of the International Council of Nurses.

Taylor was born April 8, 1874 in Hamilton, Ontario, Canada, the oldest of a family of nine children. Her father believed his daughters should be as well educated as his sons, and Taylor had the advantage of a liberal education. She was a graduate of the Hamilton (Ontario) Collegiate Institute and had attended the Wesleyan Ladies College in Hamilton for two additional years.

Taylor began her nursing studies at the Johns Hopkins Hospital School of Nursing in Baltimore, Maryland, in 1904, with her interest in nursing due in part to the help nurses had given her during the prolonged and difficult illness and death of her father. She received a B.S. degree from Teachers College at Columbia University, New York City, in 1926.

Taylor identified herself with psychiatric nursing but was reluctant to become too specialized. In 1934 she was appointed the second dean at the Yale University School of Nursing in New Haven, Connecticut, replacing Annie Goodrich, who was retiring from that position. Taylor held the position until 1944. She had joined the Yale faculty in 1923 and was named the first professor of psychiatric nursing in 1926 or 1927.

During her tenure at Yale, Taylor served as president of the National League of Nursing Education in 1932 and from 1937 to 1947 was president of the International Council of Nurses (ICN). It was because she was president that the headquarters of ICN were moved from London to New Haven during the World War II years.

For Taylor, the nurse was an idealized version of Florence Nightingale. A nurse had to be all things to all people, able to take her place whenever and wherever she might be called upon to serve.

However, Taylor was pragmatic in trying to seek greater resources for nursing from the university. She was a strong believer in liberal education. Conscious of the disagreements between physicians and nurses as well as among other health professionals, she felt it was important that nursing education be broadened to include those from other specialized fields who have something to contribute to nursing.

Taylor received an honorary master of arts degree from Yale in 1926 and an honorary doctor of humane letters degree from Keuka College, New York, in 1944. After retiring from Yale in 1944, Taylor returned to Canada. She remained active in American nursing, however, up to the middle of the 1950s. She died on May 20, 1970, in Hamilton, Ontario.

## SELECTED PUBLICATIONS BY EUPHEMIA JANE TAYLOR

"Psychiatry and the Nurse." *American Journal of Nursing* 26 (August 1926): 631–34.

"A Mental Hygiene Concept in Nursing." *American Journal of Nursing* 32 (July 1932): 771–82.

"Of What Is the Nature of Nursing." *American Journal of Nursing* 34 (May 1934): 473–76.

"The Right of the School of Nursing to the Resources of the University." *American Journal of Nursing* 34 (December 1934): 1193.

"Twenty-five Years in Nursing Education, President's Address." *American Journal of Nursing* 35 (July 1935): 653–57.

"The International Council of Nurses; A Force for Unity and Peace." *American Journal of Nursing* 50 (October 1950) 615–16.

## BIBLIOGRAPHY

Buckwalter, K.C., and O.M. Church. "Euphemia Jane Taylor: An Uncommon Psychiatric Nurse." *Perspectives in Psychiatric Care* 17 (July 1979): 125–31.

Stewart, I.M. "Effie Jane Taylor." *American Journal of Nursing* 39 (July 1939): 733–37.

Stewart, I.M. "Some Specialists, Effie J. Taylor." *American Journal of Nursing* 30 (January, 1930).

Olga Maranjian Church

## Frances Charlotte Thielbar
### 1908–1962

Frances Charlotte Thielbar was an early advocate of higher education for nurses, nursing research, and the study of psychiatric nursing. She was associated with the development of university graduate nursing programs during a period when master's degree programs for nurses were just beginning to come into existence.

Thielbar was born in River Forest, Illinois, on July 10, 1908, the daughter of Frederick John and Dorothea Burgess Thielbar.

In 1929 Thielbar was graduated from Wellesley College in Wellesley, Massachusetts, with an A.B. degree. She entered the Yale School of Nursing in New Haven, Connecticut, and was graduated in 1932 with a bachelor of science degree in nursing. The University of Chicago awarded her a master of science degree in nursing education in 1938 and a Ph.D. degree in 1951.

After graduating from Yale, Thielbar was appointed an instructor at Butler Hospital in Providence, Rhode Island, a private psychiatric institution with which she had been affiliated as a student. During her employment at Butler, she was promoted to the position of supervisor of nurses.

She became an instructor at the University of Chicago in 1942 and rose in position to assistant, then associate professor of nursing. From 1952 to 1960 she served as chair of the division of nursing education. After her departure, the school of nursing closed and did not reopen.

Thielbar was then appointed to develop the graduate program leading to a master of science degree in nursing at the University of Pennsylvania. Her interest in nursing research may have led to her appointment as chair of the graduate division.

Thielbar's experience in psychiatric nursing was also a qualification that university schools were giving serious consideration when appointing medical-school and nursing-school deans and department directors. Psychosomatic medicine and the integration of mental-health concepts into the curriculum were emphasized. The emotional aspects of illness, community mental health, and the provision of care in community mental-health facilities were topics attracting increasing interest. The concept prevailed that all persons preparing for careers in the health sector should be knowledgeable about matters related to mental health.

Early in her career, Thielbar expressed the belief that a course in psychiatric nursing would help nurses develop the self-understanding that aided in adjustment to nursing work. She advocated placing psychiatric nursing instruction in the second year of the basic nursing curriculum. Thielbar believed that this placement of the course would enable nursing students to apply psychiatric theory and concepts while caring for patients in the general hospital and other health facilities.

Thielbar disapproved of psychiatric nursing affiliation programs that were conducted in mental hospitals and supported financially by states. She believed that these programs contributed to the diploma school faculty's lack of interest in and knowledge of psychiatric theory and resulted in delaying the integration of psychiatric theory and practice in the basic nursing curriculum. With other nursing leaders, she voiced these opinions. Eventually, federal funds became available to diploma schools to employ their own psychiatric nursing instructors. University-prepared teachers joined the diploma school faculties and accompanied and supervised the clinical practice of students when they went to mental hospitals. Gradually, as more qualified teachers became available, the affiliation programs operated by state hospitals went out of existence.

Thielbar stressed the need for nursing research in all settings to improve patient care. Three areas that she believed in need of research were patient care, nursing service, and nursing curriculum. Research methods suggested by Thielbar included the use of a control group, objective recording of nursing situations, analysis of records, and evaluation of nursing interventions.

Thielbar was a member of the American Association of University Women and was active in professional nursing organizations. She was a member of the board of directors and served as secretary of the Rhode Island League of Nursing and she was a member of the Rhode Island Board of Nursing. Thielbar was a director of the American Journal of Nursing Publishing Company. She helped to found and served on the editorial board of one of its publications, *Nursing Research*, from 1952 to 1959. She was treasurer of the Association of Collegiate Schools of Nursing. She also served as chair of the committee on awards of the National League for Nursing and was elected first vice-president of the league in 1952.

The graduate nursing program that Thielbar had been appointed to develop at the University of Pennsylvania opened in September 1961. Six months later, on March 21, 1962, she died in the university hospital of a massive cerebral vascular accident. At the time of her death, she was 54 years old and a resident of Wynnewood, Pennsylvania. She was survived by her mother and her brother, Henry, who made a memorial gift in his sister's name to the University of Pennsylvania School of Nursing. In addition, a collection of books that was the property of Thielbar was donated to the school of nursing and was known as the Thielbar Collection.

### PUBLICATIONS BY FRANCES CHARLOTTE THIELBAR

#### BOOKS

*Administrative Organization of Collegiate Schools of Nursing.* Unpublished Ph.D. dissertation, University of Chicago, 1951.

#### ARTICLES

"Ward Teaching in a Mental Hospital." *American Journal of Nursing* 34 (July 1934): 710–716.

"Nursing School Catalogs Analyzed." *American Journal of Nursing* 39:4 (April 1939):405–13.

"Research in Psychiatric Nursing." *Mental Hygience* 32 (April 1948): 115–22.

"Administrative Organization of Collegiate Schools of Nursing." *Nursing Research* 2:2(October 1953): 52–53.

#### BIBLIOGRAPHY

Connolly, M. Coordinator Alumni Relations, Yale University School of Nursing, New

Haven, Conn. Correspondence, November 14, 1979.

"Frances Thielbar." Obituary. *New York Times*, 24 March 1962.

"Frances Thielbar." Obituary. *Nursing Research* 11 (Spring 1962): 67.

"Frances Thielbar." Obituary. *American Journal of Nursing* 62 (May 1962): 139.

Gorbin, M., University of Pennsylvania School of Nursing, Philadelphia, Pa. Telephone conversation, April 1986.

Lynaugh, J.E., University of Pennsylvania School of Nursing, Philadelphia, Pa. Telephone conversation, April 1986.

Manfreda, Marguerite. Personal conversation, Chicago, Ill., October 1956.

Manfreda, Marguerite. *The Roots of Interpersonal Nursing.* privately published by the author, Wallingford, Conn.: Author, 1982.

Marguerite L. Manfreda

# Barbara Anna Thompson (Sharpless)

## 1889–1973

Barbara Anna Thompson Sharpless greatly influenced the standards of nursing and nursing education in her various roles as nurse, nurse educator, and nurse administrator on the local, state, and national levels. Although she assumed her husband's surname when she married him in 1951, she was professionally known under her maiden name.

Thompson was born November 1, 1889, in Sault Sainte Marie, Michigan, to William A. and Alice Graham Thompson. Although not much is known about her childhood, at some time prior to her graduating from high school, her family moved to Glenwood, Minnesota. After graduating from Glenwood High School, she taught for two years at country schools in North Dakota. During this time, she met another teacher who was planning on entering nurses' training. Although Thompson had not previously been interested in nursing, she decided to enter the field also.

In 1910 Thompson entered the third nursing class at the University of Minnesota in Minneapolis. The University of Minnesota School of Nurses was unique in that the school was formed as part of the university; thus, nursing students had the same privileges and status as other university students. Because the university program was new, student nurses were faced with inconvenient and crowded classrooms and limited living quarters.

Thompson graduated with a graduate of nursing diploma in 1913. After graduation, she did private-duty nursing and was a supervisor of the operating room at St. Andrew's Hospital and Minneapolis City Hospital. In 1915 she took a postgraduate course at Lakeside Hospital in Cleveland, Ohio. Between 1915 and 1916 she returned to private-duty nursing.

In 1916 Thompson became a head nurse on a women's floor at the University of Minnesota Hospital. As a result of American involvement in World War I, in April 1918 all head nurses at the hospital became part of the University of Minnesota base hospital 26 and departed for France.

Shortly after arriving in France, Thompson was one of ten individuals transferred to evacuation hospital 7, then stationed in Coulommiers, France. The hospital moved with the battle lines, and in December 1918 the unit moved to Prum, Germany, and became part of the army of occupation. Thompson returned to the United States in June 1919 aboard the ship *Prince Frederick Wilhelm*, on which she was acting chief nurse in charge of 50 nurses. For her contributions overseas, Thompson received the victory medal from the United States Government.

After returning from overseas, Thompson supervised two surgical floors and taught nursing arts to beginning nurses at Research Hospital in Kansas City, Missouri. In 1920 she returned to Minnesota and became a nursing arts instructor at the Charles T. Miller Hospital in St. Paul during the early years of that institution's nursing program. During the summer of 1920, Thompson attended the summer session at Teachers College, Columbia University, New York City.

In 1921 Thompson joined the University of Minnesota's school of nursing faculty. As chair of the nursing arts committee, Thompson co-authored a text with Marion L. Vannier, *Nursing Procedures* (1929), that outlined procedures for nursing students so that a consistent technique would be used in the four hospitals with which the students were associated. The textbook was revised several times.

Between 1926 and 1928, Thompson served as an assistant to Marion L. Vannier, director of the University of Minnesota's school of nursing. In 1928 when Vannier took a short sabbatical leave, Thompson became acting director of the school. During her interim as acting director, she added two graduate courses to the curriculum. After leaving the faculty of the University of Minnesota in 1928, Thompson returned to school and was awarded the degree of bachelor of science in nursing education by the University of Minnesota College of Education.

Thompson is credited for designing a combined treatment and assignment sheet for use in hospitals. Previously, large sheets of orders for medicines and treatments were recopied every day by the head nurse or charge nurse. The method designed by Thompson utilized a Kardex in which cards for each patient were placed so that a permanent copy of a patient's treatments could be kept in an easily accessible location. Most hospitals in the United States adopted this method of organizing assignments and treatments of patients.

After serving as director of nurses at Minneapolis General Hospital in 1933, Thompson became the director of the bureau of nursing education and the secretary of the board of examiners for the state of Wisconsin. She served in this position until 1938.

Thompson was a member of the National League of Nursing Education, the American Nurses' Association, the Women's Overseas Service League, the Minnesota State League of Nursing Education, Sigma Theta Tau, and Alpha Tau Delta. Between 1938 and 1940, Thompson was

the assistant secretary for the committee on accrediting for the National League of Nursing Education. Her role as assistant secretary was to help establish the league's accreditation program for schools of nursing. With the assistance of another member of the accrediting committee, she surveyed over 100 nursing schools, collecting data for developing norms for national accreditation of schools.

After the survey was completed, Thompson became the director of nurses and director of the school of nursing of St. Luke's Hospital in Denver, Colorado, from 1943 to 1944. Between 1944 and 1946, she served as a consultant for the U.S. Cadet Nurse Corps in Washington, D.C. In this capacity, she was a consultant for 250 schools of nursing.

Upon completing her job as consultant to the nurse corps, Thompson moved to California. During 1948 to 1954, she held various positions, such as director of nurses at Santa Barbara General Hospital, instructor in the extension division of the University of California at Los Angeles, director of nurses at Cottage Hospital in Santa Barbara, and dean at Knapp College of Nursing. After her tenure at Knapp College of Nursing (1953–54), she retired from an active nursing career.

While living in California, Thompson met Samuel F. Sharpless, an architect. They married in 1951 and made their residence in Woodland Hills, California.

Although retired from active nursing, Thompson returned to Minnesota in 1959 to receive the 50th Year Anniversary Citation from the University of Minnesota School of Nursing for her contributions in establishing a high standard of nursing education at the institution. She also wrote a series of articles about various nursing leaders.

Thompson died September 23, 1973, in Camarillo, California.

## PUBLICATIONS BY BARBARA ANNA THOMPSON (SHARPLESS)

### BOOKS

With M.L. Vannier. *Nursing Procedures*. Minneapolis, Minn.: University of Minnesota Press, 1929.

## ARTICLES

"A Combined Treatment and Assignment Sheet." *American Journal of Nursing* 32 (April 1932): 407–09.

With M.H. Coe and F.E. Marks. "School of Nursing." In *Masters of Medicine*, edited by J.A. Meyers. St. Louis, Mo.: Warren and Green, 1968.

## BIBLIOGRAPHY

"Barbara A. Thompson." *American Journal of Nursing* 38 (February 1938): 220.

"Barbara A. Thompson." *American Women* 3 (1939–40): 903.

"Barbara A. Thompson." Obituary. *Alumni News*, University of Minnesota 75 (October 1975): 15.

Gray, J. *Education for Nursing: A History of the University of Minnesota School.* Minneapolis, Minn.: University of Minnesota Press, 1960.

"Honor New Nursing Chief." *Milwaukee Sentinel*, 5 September 1934.

"Luncheon Arranged for Nursing Director." *Milwaukee Journal*, 2 September 1934.

"Milwaukee Nurses Accord Welcome to New State Director." *Milwaukee Leader*, 5 September 1934.

"Minnesota Women." *Alumni News*, University of Minnesota 72 (October 1972): 20–22.

University of Minnesota. *Yearbook 1913.* University of Minnesota Archives, University of Minnesota, Minneapolis.

Michaelene P. Mirr

# Dora Elizabeth Thompson

## 1876–1954

Dora Elizabeth Thompson was the fourth superintendent of the Army Nurse Corps and served from September 1914 to December 1919. She was the first regular army nurse to hold the position and the first superintendent of the corps during a world war.

Thompson was born November 20, 1876, in the village of Cold Springs, New York. She was the eldest child of Arthur and Dora Thompson. Her Canadian-born father was a carpenter, and her mother was born in New York of English parents. She had at least one brother, W. A. Thompson.

Not much is known of Thompson's early years until she entered her nurse's training at the New York City Training School, Blackwell's Island, New York. Thompson graduated in 1897 and took a postgraduate course in operating room procedures, for which she received a diploma. She was selected as head nurse of the operating room, where she worked from 1897 to 1899, and then spent four years (1899–1902) in private-duty nursing in New York City.

Thompson entered the Army Nurse Corps in April 1902. Her first assignment was at San Francisco General Hospital, where all newly appointed members of the corps were sent for instruction. For several years, she was alternately on duty in San Francisco and on temporary duty on transport ships between the Philippines and San Francisco General Hospital. After completing the written examination required for promotion to the grade of chief nurse, she was appointed chief nurse at San Francisco General Hospital in August 1905.

Thompson distinguished herself by her efficiency and cool-headedness during the 1906 San Francisco earthquake and resultant fire, which destroyed the hospital power plant and water connection. Thompson planned for additional quarters for staff and volunteers while seeing to the care and comfort of patients, nurses, and refugees.

After nearly six years without leave, Thompson was sent to Alaska in 1908. From there she was transferred to the Philippine Islands, where she served at two hospitals and on the transport ship *Sheridan.* She was appointed chief nurse at the Division Hospital in Manila in December 1911. Although she was recommended by Jane Delano to succeed Delano as superintendent of the Army Nurse Corps, Isabel McIsaac was appointed instead.

In 1914 Thompson was reassigned to Washington, D.C., to work briefly under McIsaac. In September 1914 after McIsaac's death, she was appointed the fourth superintendent of the Army Nurse Corps and the first who had served as a regular army nurse. With more than 12 years of experience as a member of the corps, she was especially fitted to the job.

Thompson had little more than general supervisory powers until more responsibilities were thrust upon her as the recognized need for professional nursing services grew. One of her important accomplishments was to reclassify the position of the nurse as directly under the ward surgeon in matters of care of the sick and wounded. She worked unceasingly for nurses to receive increased pay, medical care and insurance, disability and rehabilitation benefits, and uniform allowances but was unsuccessful in securing retirement pay and privileges as well as rank.

Thompson saw the corps increase more than tenfold, first as a result of the Mexican border dispute and then as a result of World War I. In cooperation with the American Red Cross, she was responsible for the recruitment of nurses to fill needs in Europe, Asia, and the United States in military and civilian hospitals, camps, trains, transport ships, government clinics, and training facilities. She worked closely with Jane Delano, head of Red Cross nursing, to maintain standards for entrance to the corps. Before the end of the war, over 21,000 nurses, the largest nurse corps ever attached to an army and composed only of graduate nurses, had been mobilized in active service.

Thompson dealt with the mobilization of nurses, securing their registration, physicals, required certificates of immunization, and holding and shipping orders. She designed and gained approval of an outdoor uniform and made arrangements for uniform allowances or issue by the Red Cross until government contracts could be filled. Special courses were given at St. Mary's Hospital, Rochester, Minnesota, and at selected army hospitals to ensure continuence of needed skills.

In everyday duties, Thompson reported on strengths of the corps, discharges and losses due to illness or disciplinary action, and efficiency. She coordinated with the Red Cross on recruitment, standards of admission, specialized training, and maintenance of those nurses released from active duty by the Red Cross. In addition to updating and closing records of all nurses who had served in the war, the original Red Cross papers on all relieved reserve nurses had to be returned to the Red Cross with a report of active duty activities and ratings. Thompson answered correspondence relating to inquiries about the whereabouts of nurses, disabilities and deaths, and recommendations for job applications. She made monthly reports to the *American Journal of Nursing*. In addition, she was expected to march in parades and represent the Army Nurse Corps at nursing conventions and on education and reorganization committees.

When World War I ended, Thompson began the task of reducing the size of the corps in response to the decreasing need for nursing service. Demobilization stations and reception centers were established, hospitals were reduced in staff or closed, and transportation and lodging was arranged for returning nurses.

After the war, Thompson took a leave of absence in 1919. In November 1919 she was awarded the Distinguished Service Medal for her self-sacrificing devotion of duty during World War I.

On her return to duty, Thompson resigned as superintendent in December 1919. At her request, she was reappointed assistant superintendent with duties in Manila. In July 1920 she was given the relative rank of captain, and in 1924 she returned to Letterman General Hospital in San Francisco to become chief of the nursing service division, where she remained until shortly before her retirement. She retired in August 1932 after more than 30 years of active service.

Thompson lived in San Francisco after her retirement. She spent much time traveling and·made two trips to Europe and several cross-country trips through the United States. She also collaborated with Florence Blanchfield on her unpublished history of the Army Nurse Corps. She never married.

After a long illness, she died at Letterman General Hospital on June 23, 1954, and was buried in the nurses' plot in Arlington National Cemetery in Washington,

D.C. She was survived by nephews W.A. Thompson, Jr., and John S. Thompson and a grand-niece, Zoe Thompson.

On May 12, 1955, the women officers' quarters of Letterman General Hospital in San Francisco, California, was named Thompson Hall. It was dedicated to Thompson with a plaque presented by the San Francisco nurses' American Legion post.

## PUBLICATIONS BY DORA ELIZABETH THOMPSON

"Nursing as It Relates to the War—The Army." *American Journal of Nursing* 18 (August 1918): 1058–60.

"Army Nurse Corps." *American Journal of Nursing* 19 (October 1919): 65–67.

## BIBLIOGRAPHY

Blanchfield, F.A. "Organized Nursing and the Army in Three Wars." Unpublished Manuscript. U.S.A. Center for Military History, Washington, D.C.

Delano, J. "Army Nurse Corps." *American Journal of Nursing* 11(12) (1911): 240.

"Dora E. Thompson." Obituary. *San Francisco Chronicle*, 25 June 1954.

"Dora E. Thompson." Obituary. *San Francisco Examiner*, 25 June 1954.

"Dora E. Thompson." Official biography. Temporary file 201. U.S.A. Center for Military History, Washington, D.C.

Griffith, A. "History of the Army Nurse Corps School of Nursing." Unpublished Manuscript. U.S.A. Center for Military History, Washington, D.C.

*Highlights in the History of the Army Nurse Corps*, edited by E.A. Shields. U.S.A. Center for Military History, Washington, D.C., 1981.

Historical Files of the Army Nurse Corps, 1900–1947. General Correspondence. Surgeon General's Office. Record Group 112, Entry 103.

Kennedy, J.M. Efficiency report, April 30, 1906. Surgeon General's Office. Record Group 112, Entry 108. National Archives, Washington, D.C.

Kennedy, J.M. Letter to Surgeon General's Office, May 1906. Temporary file 201. U.S.A. Center for Military History, Washington, D.C.

Maxwell, P. "History of the Army Nurse Corps, 1775–1948." Unpublished Manuscript. U.S.A. Center for Military History, Washington, D.C.

"News Highlights." *American Journal of Nursing* 55(8) (1955): 913.

Register of Military Service of Members of the Army Nurse Corps 1901–1902. Surgeon General's Office. Record Group 112, Entry 105. National Archives, Washington, D.C.

Roberts, M. *Yesterday and Today.* Washington, D.C.: U.S. Army Nurse Corps, 1957.

Sabine, E. "The Evolution of the Nurse in Government Service." *Trained Nurse and Hospital Review* 80(6) (June 1928): 729–35.

Station Books of Nurses. Surgeon General's Office. Record Group 112, Entry 107. National Archives, Washington, D.C.

Stimson, J. "Army Nurse Corps." *American Journal of Nursing* 20(1) (1920): 68–69.

Thompson, D.E. Letters. Historical Files of the Army Nurse Corps. Surgeon General's Office. Record Group 112, Entry 103. National Archives, Washington, D.C.

U.S. Bureau of the Census. *United States Census, 1880.* Vol. 81. National Archives, Washington, D.C.

Verfuerth, V.P. Office memorandum, 6 July 1954. Surgeon General's Office. RG112. National Archives, Washington, D.C.

"Women You Ought to Know." *Woman's Magazine*, March 1919, 2.

Sarah A. Sandefur
Rosemary T. McCarthy

## Julia Charlotte Thompson

### 1907–1972

Director of the Washington, D.C., office of the American Nurses' Association (ANA) from 1951 to 1972, Julia Charlotte Thompson served as the association's first full-time lobbyist. Her legislative efforts on behalf of nursing set a significant example for her successors.

Thompson was born February 23, 1907, in Marathon County, Wisconsin, the third of eight children of Theodore Adolph and Annie Davis Thompson. Both her parents were born in the United States. She grew up on a farm and attended a one-room school in Fleith (now Rib Mountain) township. After she was graduated from Wausau High School, she enrolled in the Marathon County Normal School in Wausau and completed two summer sessions at Stevens Point Teacher's College (now University of Wisconsin-Stevens Point).

Thompson taught school for a short time before enrolling in the Cook County Hospital School of Nursing in Chicago, receiving her diploma in 1931. After employment as a staff nurse in obstetrics at Cook County Hospital, she was appointed charge nurse in the birth rooms at the hospital in 1932 before serving as head nurse and supervisor in abnormal obstetrics. This was followed by an appointment as night supervisor in the hospital. In 1937–38 she taught obstetric nursing at the Cook County Hospital School of Nursing.

Thompson next served for two years as a staff nurse for the Infant Welfare Society in Chicago. In 1941 she moved to Utah, where she was appointed a staff nurse for rural county nursing by the Utah State Department of Health. In December 1943 she was appointed a supervisor of the Topeka City-Shawanee County Health Department, Topeka, Kansas, and was later named director of its nursing division, where she served until 1951. During part of this time, she attended the University of Michigan and received her B.S. degree in public-health nursing in 1950.

Active in her professional association, Thompson served on the district and state legislative committee in Kansas. She also was a member of the ANA's legislative committee (1949–51).

Thompson joined the ANA staff as assistant executive secretary in 1951 and opened its Washington, D.C., office. She had no nursing precedent to follow, but received a sketchy orientation from Edith Beattie, executive secretary of the District of Columbia Nurses' Association, who had acted as a part-time legislative liaison for the ANA. Thompson attended House and Senate hearings, read the *Congressional Record*, visited congressmen, and conferred with experienced lobbyists. For 20 years she served as ANA lobbyist, concerned not only with nursing, but also with women's rights and with social and health legislation in general.

In 1958 the ANA's house of delegates voted to support the principle of financing

health care for the aged under the Social Security Act. With this directive, Thompson worked for the passage of Medicare legislation, and in 1965 she attended the signing of the Medicare legislation by President Lyndon Johnson. She also worked to improve Social Security for the retired and the disabled.

An example of the range of Thompson's lobbying efforts was her appearance in 1953 at a hearing of the House Ways and Means Committee to grant authority to permit women to deduct child-care expenses from their income taxes. She argued that such a provision would encourage professionally inactive nurses to return to practice and thus relieve the serious nursing shortage the country was then experiencing.

Thompson directed a major effort toward getting federal funding for nursing education, and the legislation for the first federal nursing trainee program was passed in 1956. She also secured passage of the nurse training acts of 1964 and 1971. She was successful in convincing Congress to grant registered nurses in the military the ranks appropriate to their responsibilities.

Thompson not only represented the ANA as its lobbyist, but also helped prepare ANA presidents and others as they represented the association in speaking before congressional hearings. Much of her work was done behind the scenes, but she herself represented the ANA in various ways. For example, she was the association's representative at the 1960 National Conference on Water Pollution. She served on the surgeon general's advisory group on the oral polio vaccine and represented the ANA at the 1961 White House Conference on Aging. During her tenure, the association gained considerable visibility.

Thompson believed that informing nurses of federal activities was essential if they were to respond appropriately. Beginning in 1954, she developed a newsletter, *Legislative News*. In addition, she prepared items about federal legislation and related concerns for each issue of the *American Journal of Nursing*. She did much of this work herself until a public-relations expert was added to the staff in 1959.

Thompson retired in February 1972 and continued to serve the ANA as a consultant while completing her book, *The ANA in Washington*. She died on April 9, 1972. She was survived by two brothers, Marvin and Arthur, and two sisters, Mary Beatty and Anne Fulton.

## PUBLICATIONS BY
## JULIA CHARLOTTE THOMPSON

### BOOKS

*The ANA in Washington*. Kansas City, Mo.: American Nurses' Association, 1972.

### ARTICLES

With Gretchen Gerds and Helen Connors. "Every Nurse a Lobbyist." *American Journal of Nursing* 60 (September 1960): 1242–45.

### BIBLIOGRAPHY

"Julia Thompson." *Nursing Hall of Fame*. Kansas City, Mo.: American Nurses' Association, 1984.

"Julia Thompson." Obituary. *New York Times*, 13 April 1972.

"Julia Thompson Dies." *American Journal of Nursing* 72 (May 1972): 869–70.

Thompson, J. Files. American Nurses' Association, Kansas City, Mo.

Thompson, M. Interview with author.

Signe S. Cooper

# Adah Belle Samuels Thoms

## 1870–1943

Adah Belle Samuels Thoms was a crusader for equal opportunity for black women in nursing, and she had a deep sense of responsibility to improve relationships among persons of all races. As president of the National Association of Colored Graduate Nurses (NACGN), she campaigned for acceptance of black nurses in the American Red Cross and the United States Army Nurse Corps during World War I. She wrote *Pathfinders*, the first book to record the experiences of black nurses, and laid the groundwork that facilitated the merger of the NACGN with the American Nurses' Association (ANA) and the National Organization for Public Health Nursing (NOPHN).

Thoms was born on January 12, circa 1870, in Richmond, Virginia, to Harry and Melvina Samuels. Although little is recorded about her early years, it is known that Thoms had at least one sibling. Her early education was in the elementary public and normal school of Richmond.

Thoms taught school in Richmond before choosing nursing as a career. She was briefly married and carried the surname Thoms throughout her nursing career.

Thoms came to New York City in 1893 and established a residence in Harlem. During the 1890s, she studied elocution and public speaking at the Cooper Union in New York. During the late nineteenth century many women made career changes from teaching, which was an overcrowded profession, to nursing, in which the demand far exceeded the supply. Thoms entered the Woman's Infirmary and School of Therapeutic Massage in New York for a course in nursing, the only black student in a class of 30. She graduated in 1900.

Thoms spent the next three years working as a nurse in New York City and in North Carolina. She worked at St. Agnes Hospital in Raleigh, North Carolina, for one year as a head nurse. Dissatisfied with her basic nursing education, she decided she needed further training.

In 1903 Thoms entered the newly organized school of nursing at Lincoln Hospital and Home in New York City. This hospital was founded in 1893 by a group of white women who met in New York City to consider the destitute condition of the local black population and to devise a plan for relief. In 1898 the nursing school for black women was added and was one of approximately 10 black schools of nursing formed during the 1890s in response to nationwide patterns of racial discrimination and segregation. Lincoln School of Nursing was nationally known and acclaimed for its graduates' quality and performance. The Lincoln Alumnae Association, organized in 1903, was accepted for membership in the New York State Nurses' Association, making Lincoln's graduate nurses eligible for membership in the American Nurses' Association.

In her second year of training, Thoms was appointed head nurse on a surgical ward. She graduated in 1905 and was employed at the hospital as its operating-room nurse and supervisor of the surgical division. In 1906 Thoms was appointed the assistant superintendent of nurses, a position she held until her retirement 18 years later.

During these 18 years and until a director was selected, Thoms served as the acting director of the nursing school from 1906 through 1923. Despite her competence and longevity in the role, it was not the custom to promote a black woman to a major administrative position, even in an institution for black students. Although qualified, Thoms was never appointed director.

In 1913, within her role as acting director, Thoms started a six-month postgraduate course for registered nurses. She recognized early the importance of public-health nursing as a new field in nursing, and in 1917, just five years after the establishment of the National Organization for Public Health Nursing, she added a course in this new field to the school's basic nursing curriculum. Thoms took the first course along with her pupils.

Thoms began working for equal opportunity for black nurses almost immediately after her graduation from Lincoln Hospital. In 1908 she played a key part with Martha Franklin in the organization of the NACGN. As president of the Lincoln Nurses' Alumnae, a position she held for ten years, Thoms invited Franklin to have the first meeting of the NACGN in New York, under the sponsorship of the Lincoln Hospital Alumnae Association. A charter member of this new organization, Thoms was elected its first treasurer. She organized the New York chapter of the NACGN and continued to work closely with Franklin.

Thoms was also a pioneer in the participation of black nurses in international nursing organizations. When the International Council of Nurses met in Cologne,

Germany, in 1912, Thoms was one of the first three black delegates. Always seeking new knowledge, she utilized the trip to travel in Europe and visit several prominent hospitals.

Thoms served as president of the NACGN from 1916 to 1923. During these seven years, she set forth ideas and established policies that in later years were the foundation for advances in education, employment and community alliances for black nurses. In 1916 she began working with the National Urban League and the National Association for the Advancement of Colored People in efforts to change the inadequate conditions of black hospitals and training schools for black nurses. She also was concerned with increasing the NACGN's membership and organizing local and state associations of black graduate nurses. Although the NACGN had a national organizer responsible for organizing state-level black nurses' associations, as president Thoms traveled and addressed state and local nurses' associations.

When Congress declared war on Germany in April 1917, Thoms as president of the NACGN immediately alerted black nurses, urging them to enroll in the American Red Cross nursing service, the only avenue into the U.S. Army Nurse Corps. When black nurses applied to the American Red Cross, they were constantly rejected because of their race. Thoms refused to accept this rejection and organized a campaign to convince the Red Cross to accept black nurses.

By the autumn of 1917, a great deal of correspondence had transpired between Thoms and Jane A. Delano, chair of the American National Red Cross Nursing Service. Delano responded to one of Thoms's letters by stating her willingness to accept black nurses at home and abroad. However, their acceptance and assignment ultimately rested with the surgeon general of the army, who staunchly refused to agree with their enrollment and would not authorize their services. Delano continued to advocate their enrollment and in December 1917 notified Thoms that there would be limited enrollment of black nurses, although there was no immediate hope that they would be assigned to duty.

During the winter of 1917–18, the supply of civilian registered nurses was critically depleted due to the war. Meanwhile, a massive influenza epidemic with a morbidity rate far greater than the war casualties was in progress, resulting in an even more critical shortage. This nurse shortage finally impelled the surgeon general to authorize the use of black nurses. Although the first black nurse enrolled in July 1918, it was not until December 1918, after the war was over, that 18 qualified black nurses were appointed to the Army Nurse Corps with full rank and pay.

Thoms continued her involvement with the American Red Cross after World War I. In April 1921 she attended a conference of the American Red Cross and was assured that the Red Cross wanted all black nurses to enroll so that they would be prepared for duty should the need arise. However, the Red Cross maintained that enrollment did not mean the nurses would be called for duty.

During the 1921 NACGN national convention in Washington, D.C., Thoms was received at the White House by President and Mrs. Warren G. Harding. As she presented a large basket of roses to the president and first lady, Thoms requested that the NACGN be placed on record as an organized body of 2,000 trained women ready when needed for world service.

Thoms also was concerned about ethics in nursing. She asked the older nurses of the NACGN to cultivate the society of younger nurses, using their influence to maintain the ideals of the profession. She believed in the professional identity of nursing and was outspoken against the NACGN merging with the National Medical Association, the black doctors' association. Thoms felt there could be an affiliation without a merger, allowing nurses to retain their identity as a group of nurses. She also argued that the NAGCN could work as a group of nurses toward consolidation with the American Nurses' Association and the National Organization of Public Health Nurses. This position later facilitated the integration of the NACGN in 1951 into the ANA and the NOPHN.

Thoms also furthered her own education. she took continuing education courses at the New School of Philanthropy (later called the N.Y. School of Social Work), Hunter College, and the New School for Social Research, all in New York City. She encouraged black nurses to follow her example and continue their education.

Through her interest in improving the status and acceptance of the black professional nurse, Thoms came to know and work with many American nursing leaders. She worked with Martha Franklin, founder and organizer of the NACGN, and Mary Eliza Mahoney, the first black professional nurse in America. In addition, she had a long-term professional relationship with Lillian Wald of the Henry Street Settlement.

By 1921 Thoms's leadership assumed an additional dimension. That year, she was appointed by the assistant surgeon general of the army to serve on the Woman's Advisory Council of Venereal Diseases of the United States Public Health Service.

Throughout her career, Thoms was an active member of many professional organizations. These included the Harlem branch of the Young Women's Christian Association, the Harlem Committee of New York Tuberculosis and Health Association, the New York Urban League, the National Health Circle for Colored People, St. Mark's Methodist Episcopal Church, the Hope Day Nursery (the only facility at that time offering care to the black children of working mothers), and the Urban League Center of the Henry Street Nursing Committee.

Thoms retired from Lincoln Hospital in 1923. She subsequently married Henry Smith, who died within one year. After her retirement, she continued to be active in the NACGN, the ANA, and the NOPHN. In 1929 she wrote the first history of black nurses. Entitled *Pathfinders*, it is considered a classic historical source of the unique experiences of black nurses.

In 1936 Thoms became the first nurse to receive the NACGN's Mary Mahoney Award. She was admitted to nursing's prestigious Hall of Fame in 1976, after her death.

Thoms resided in Harlem from the time she came to New York until her death. Later in life, her niece, Nannie Samuels, resided with her. She died on February 21, 1943, in Lincoln Hospital, and she was buried in Woodlawn Cemetery in New York under the surname of Smith.

## PUBLICATIONS BY
## ADAH BELLE SAMUELS THOMS

### BOOKS

*Pathfinders.* New York: Kay Printing House, 1929.

### ARTICLES

With C.E. Bullock. "Developments of Facilities for Colored Nurse Education." *Trained Nurse and Hospital Review* 80(1928): 722.

### BIBLIOGRAPHY

"Adah Belle Samuels Thoms." Death certificate. Bureau of Records, New York City Board of Health.

American Nurses' Association. *Nursing Hall of Fame.* New York: American Nurses' Association, publication no. 6[n] 123, 1976.

Danett, S. *Profiles of Negro Womanhood.* Vol. 2. New York: Educational Heritage, 1966.

Davis, A.T. "Architects for Integration and Equality: Early Black American Leaders in Nursing." Ed.M. diss., Teachers College, Columbia University, 1986.

Dolan, J.A. *Goodnow's History of Nursing.* Philadelphia: W.B. Saunders, 1963.

Gripando, G. *Nursing Perspectives and Issues.* 2d ed. New York: Delmar Publishers, 1983.

"The History of the Lincoln Hospital and Home School of Nursing." *American Journal of Nursing.*

Kalisch, P., and B. Kalisch. *The Advance of American Nursing.* Boston: Little, Brown, 1978.

Logan, R.W. "Thoms, Adah B. Samuels." *Dictionary of American Negro Biography,* edited by R.W. Logan and M.R. Winston. New York: W.W. Norton, 1982.

Staupers, M.K. "Thoms, Adah B. Samuels." In *Notable American Women, 1607–1950,* edited by E.T. James. Vol. 3. Cambridge, Mass.: Belknap Press for Harvard University Press, 1971, 455–57.

Roberts, M. *American Nursing: History and Interpretation.* New York: Macmillan, 1954.

Staupers, M. *No Time for Prejudice.* New York: Macmillan, 1961.

Staupers, M.K. Telephone conversation with author, March, July, August 1984, February 1985, April 1986.

Althea T. Davis

## Shirley Carew Titus
### 1892–1967

Shirley Carew Titus was an innovator in nursing education and in securing paid staff nursing in hospitals. She also demonstrated that registered nurses could promote economic security through the use of collective bargaining.

Born in Alameda, California, April 28, 1892, Titus was one of six children of Henry and Sarah Simmons Titus. Much of her early life was spent on a prune ranch in Santa Clara County, California, and she graduated from San Jose High School in California.

Titus received her basic nursing training at St. Luke's Hospital in San Francisco, from which she graduated in 1915. She then went on to obtain a bachelor's degree in 1920 and a diploma in administration of schools of nursing from Teachers College, Columbia University, in New York City. By 1930 she earned a master's degree in philosophy from the University of Michigan and did advanced study at the University of Grenoble in France in 1939.

Titus began one of the first programs to combine nursing with a collegiate degree when she served as director of nursing and principal of the school of nursing at Columbia Hospital in Milwaukee, Wisconsin, during the early 1920s. She had taken this position after working in the rural South for the U.S. Children's Bureau.

In 1925 while serving as director of the nursing service and of the school of nursing at the University of Michigan in Ann Arbor, Titus initiated graduate-nurse staffing, which she justified on the grounds that it would both improve care and free the student for study as opposed to apprentice learning. She argued that costs related to nursing should be itemized and billed to patients, and she predicted that graduate-nurse staffing would mark a new era in hospital economics and provide more ease in curriculum change in nursing schools.

From 1930 to 1938, Titus served as professor of nursing education and dean of the school of nursing at Vanderbilt University in Nashville, Tennessee. She had been appointed to develop the existing nurse education programs into an independent school of university rank in which public health would be integrated into the basic curriculum. The program was supported by the Rockefeller Foundation. Titus began by emphasizing recruitment of students with college preparation, and by 1936 there was a two-year college entrance requirement for the three-year nursing program. By 1939 all those graduating received the baccalaureate degree. The school had its own faculty, dean, and budget. Titus also started the practice of fulltime faculty, which made it possible for the hospital units to use fulltime, prepared nurse supervisors so that both nursing care and education were improved. Also, many registered nurses were prepared for positions in public health, teaching, and supervision through a baccalaureate degree program and various short-term studies.

During her time in Wisconsin, Michigan, and Tennessee, Titus was involved organizationally as well as at the schools in many of the changes taking place in nursing; supply of and demand for nurses were studied; school accreditation was begun; National League of Nursing Education (NLNE) guides for curricula were issued; and recommendations for college level basic and advanced nurse education were made. Titus served on the NLNE board and education committee, on the National Organization of Public Health Nursing education committee, on the Association of Collegiate Schools of Nursing executive and accreditation committees, as president of the Michigan State Nurses Association, and as chairman of the Wisconsin bureau for school and nurse licensing and was a frequent speaker at medical, hospital, and nurses' meetings.

When the war in Europe interrupted her studies in France and forced Titus back to the United States, she became active in nurse organization efforts for procurement and assignment of nurses and civil defense.

Perhaps the capstone of her career was the period from 1942 to 1955, when she served as executive director of the Califor-

nia State Nurses' Association (CSNA). Soon after her appointment federal wage freeze action affected nurses; but by 1943, Titus did win War Labor Board approval of a statewide 15% nurse salary increase. Under her leadership all California hospitals were pressed to further improve salaries and benefits voluntarily. After several years the one voluntary statewide achievement was reducing the workweek to 44 hours in 1946 and to 40 hours in 1947.

Titus asserted that as employed professionals nurses needed the protection of and the legal right to use collective bargaining. In organizing and representing California nurses, Titus faced competition from labor unions and from dissident guild action by some CSNA members. She also faced strong criticism nationwide from many who believed it was unprofessional and unethical for nurses to use collective bargaining.

To carry out her commitment to improve the economics of nursing, Titus served on the American Nurses' Association (ANA) board and committees on finance and ethics, and the board of the *American Journal of Nursing*. From 1946 to 1954 Titus chaired the ANA committee on employment conditions of nurses. To develop the national Economic Security Program first approved in 1944, Titus led this committee in preparing and presenting their report, "Principles of an Economic Security Program," to the 1946 ANA convention. Adopting the report, the delegates approved the previously rejected use of collective bargaining, and ruled against nurses belonging to more than one representation group at the same time.

Titus also led the committee in designing the 1950 "no strike" policy which stated that nurses voluntarily would give up the right to strike and that the employer would recognize and deal with them and their representatives. Unfortunately, employers did not feel obligated to do so.

Titus was the ANA representative on the economic welfare commission of the International Council of Nurses, which in 1953 issued a report on the economic conditions of nurses in 21 countries. She also helped in the fight to overcome the exclusion of nonprofit hospitals from the 1947 Taft-Hartley Act. Under Titus the first professional liability plan for nurses and an illness-disability plan were negotiated. Under her leadership in California, the nurses' association established state and district professional counseling and placement centers, set up a fund for nursing research, and joined with the ANA and the state hospital association in a study of nursing in 40 California hospitals.

Titus also led in upgrading private duty nurse registries, in increasing private duty nurse fees, in developing methods to represent nurses in public employment, and in expanding the legislative program to include endorsement of candidates and lobbying of health measures in addition to those proposed by CSNA.

In her honor, the California State Nurses' Association in 1957 established the Shirley C. Titus Fellowship for educational grants to potential nursing leaders. The ANA in 1976 established the Shirley Titus Award for nurse contributions to its economic and general welfare program. A professorship was named for Titus at the University of Michigan in Ann Arbor.

Titus died March 21, 1967, at the San Francisco home of her sister, Adele Titus. Most of her retirement years had been spent in Mill Valley, California, where she and a Vanderbilt colleague, Mary Dodd Giles, owned a home. She was buried in South San Francisco, California.

## PUBLICATIONS BY SHIRLEY CAREW TITUS

"Health Morale of Student Nurses." *American Journal of Nursing* 22 (1922): 458–62.

With V.M. Brown. "An Experiment in Teaching Nutrition to Student Nurses." *American Journal of Nursing* 23 (1923): 754–57.

"The Nursing Care of Nephritis." *American Journal of Nursing*. 26 (1926): 449–52.

"A Practical Aspect of the Teaching of Dietetics." *American Journal of Nursing*. 27 (1927): 465–73.

"The Place of Extra-Curricular Activities in Schools of Nursing." *American Journal of Nursing* 27 (1927): 958–63

"Meeting the Cost of Nursing Service—an Interesting and Effective Plan in Use at University of Michigan Hospital." *American Journal of Nursing* 27 (March 1927): 165–67.

"Group Nursing." *American Journal of Nursing* 30 (July 1930): 845–50.

"Experiment in General Duty Nursing." *American Journal of Nursing* 31 (February 1931): 197–204.

"The Present Position of Nursing in Hospitals in the United States," *Nosokomeion* 2nd year No. 2, (April 1931): 288–314.

"The New Scutari." *American Journal of Nursing* 33 (September 1933): 877–83.

"Present Trends in Nursing Education." *American Journal of Nursing* 35 (May 1935): 466–73.

"Improvement of Ward Instruction—An 'Analysis of the Obvious.'" *The Pacific Coast Journal of Nursing* 36 (1940): 208–12.

"Economic Security Is Not Too Much to Ask." *Modern Hospital* 61 (September 1943): 71.

"Analysis of Personnel Needs of California State Nurses Association." Report to the CSNA Board of Directors, 1944.

With S. Marrich. "Economic Security for Nurses in Tax Supported Institutions." *American Journal of Nursing* 49 (July 1949): 425–27.

With J. Munier and T. Mermelstein. "Economic Facts of Life for Nurses." *American Journal of Nursing* 52 (September 1952): 1109–15.

"The Head Nurse's Decision." *American Journal of Nursing* 54 (1954): 314–16.

## BIBLIOGRAPHY

Flanagan, L. *One Strong Voice, the Story of the American Nurses' Association.* Kansas City, Mo.: American Nurses' Association, 1976.

Hereford, J. "Roots: A Perspective on the Vanderbilt School of Nursing." Speech presented to Vanderbilt School of Nursing alumni, Nashville, 14 May 1977.

Jamieson, E.M., and M.M. Sewell. *Trends in Nursing History.* 3d ed. Philadelphia and London: W.B. Saunders, 1949.

Losh, W. "CSNA Seeks War Labor Board Pay Raise Dispensation"; *"Statewide Agreement Sought with Hospitals"*; "Support of CSNA Policies on District Level is Vital"; "Example of CIO Nurses Material." *California State Nurses Association News Letter* (complied by Lee and Losh public relations firm, Los Angeles and San Francisco, California) 1 (25 November 1942): 1–4.

Christofferson, E., E. Drake, E. Graham, R. Hanna, M. Quick, J. Robley, J. Squire, and G. Waller. "A Report to Members of California State Nurses Association on Collective Bargaining Representation by CSNA and Correction of Statements Made by the Nurses Guild." Memorandum, 30 August 1946.

*Nursing Practice in California Hospitals.* San Francisco: California State Nurses Association, December 1953.

"Portrait of a Nurse Leader." *Bulletin of the California State Nurses' Association* 52 (April 1956): 102–123.

"Shirley C. Titus." *Bulletin of the California State Nurses Association* 63 (April 1967): 2.

"Shirley Titus, Nurse Leader." Obituary. *San Francisco Examiner*, 22 March 1967.

"Shirley C. Titus Is Dead at 74." *San Francisco Chronicle*, 23 March 1967.

Speckman, M. "Nursing Pioneer." *Independent Journal* (San Rafael, California), 14 May 1960.

A. Lionne Conta

# Sally Tompkins

## 1833–1916

Sally Tompkins was the first woman in the United States appointed as a military officer during wartime. She received an appointment to the rank of captain in the Confederate Calvalry in 1861. She left an outstanding record as a nurse and hospital administrator who stressed cleanliness and good patient care in the midst of the chaos and unsanitary conditions of war-torn Richmond, Virginia, and exemplified many nameless women who performed similar tasks for Confederate soldiers.

Tompkins was born at Poplar Grove, Virginia, in 1833, the third daughter and youngest of four children of Christopher and Maria Booth Patterson Tompkins. Her father worked as a master of merchant vessels and later became a successful cotton agent, justice of the peace, colonel in the militia and representative in the state legislature. He died shortly before the Civil War, and Tompkins moved with her family to Richmond.

After the war broke out, a large house in Richmond was donated for use as a hospital. Tompkins operated this 25-bed hospital, known as the Robertson Hospital, throughout the war and organized women to serve as hospital workers. She succeeded in many of her efforts for the hospital because she had established herself in Richmond as a philanthropist and as a capable bedside nurse. Her reputation for nursing had grown as she cared for several family members, including her well-known father, during severe illnesses.

When the Confederate government moved to close private hospitals in Richmond in an effort to improve organization and reduce malingering, Tompkins appealed to Confederate President Jefferson Davis to leave the Robertson Hospital open. The President responded by appointing Tompkins to an officer's commission in the Confederate Cavalry in September 1861. In lieu of military pay, she received hospital supplies during the war.

Tompkins developed a reputation for strict regulation of sanitary practices. Her clinical practices have been credited with playing an important role in the outstanding record of the Robertson Hospital during the war. Of the 1,333 admissions recorded, only 75 deaths occurred. She also administered the hospital with a rigid discipline based on nineteenth-century evangelical Christianity, temperance and military structure.

In the postwar years, Tompkins slipped back into a quieter lifestyle, working with various charities and occasionally nursing friends and family members. She refused several offers of marriage and remained interested in the affairs of the Confederate veterans. During a visit to Johns Hopkins Hospital in Baltimore, Maryland, many years after the war, she stated that the only treatments she had used for typhoid-fever patients were whiskey and turpentine.

In 1905, as her financial resources began to dwindle, Tompkins accepted an invitation to become a lifetime guest in Richmond's Home for Confederate Women. She died in 1916 as a result of kidney problems and received burial with full military honors at Christ Episcopal Church in Mathews County, Virginia.

### BIBLIOGRAPHY

Bullough, B., and V. Bullough. "The Origins of Modern American Nursing: The Civil War Era." *Nursing Forum* 2 (1963): 13.

Coleman, E. "The Captain Was a Lady." *Virginia Cavalcade,* Summer 1956.

Cunningham, H.H. *Notable American Women.* Vol. 3. Cambridge, Mass.: Belknap Press of Harvard University Press, 1971.

Somerville, M. "Sally Tompkins, Nurse and Confederate Cavalry Captain." *Registered Nurse* 20:10 (October 1957): 75.

Woodward, C.V. *Mary Chestnut's Civil War.* New Haven, Conn.: Yale University Press, 1981.

Linda Sabin

# Ella King Newsom Trader

## 1838–1919

Known as the Florence Nightingale of the Southern army, Ella King Newsom Trader was one of the most respected hospital administrators to serve the Confederacy. Her example influenced the subsequent development of the nursing profession in America.

Trader was born in Brandon, Mississippi, in June 1838 to Thomas S.N. and Julia King. She was the second of seven children. Her father was a Baptist clergyman, and her mother came from an aristocratic Georgia family. The family was financially secure.

In 1849 the family moved to Arkansas, where Trader became an accomplished horsewoman, a training that served her in her subsequent career as a military nurse. She married William Frank Newsom, an educated and wealthy physician on February 6, 1854. He died shortly before the outbreak of the Civil War and left her a substantial fortune.

At the time the war broke out, Trader was residing at Winchester, Tennessee, and was supervising the education of her young sisters at Mary Sharp College. She went to Memphis, Tennessee, in the autumn of 1861 with servants and supplies and began to take instruction in nursing at Memphis City Hospital. There she also trained at the Southern Mothers' Home and subsequently became matron of Overton Hospital.

In December 1861 Trader went to Bowling Green, Kentucky, where the surgeon-in-chief put her in charge of the hospitals in town. After the surrender of forts Donaldson and Henry, she moved to Nashville, Tennessee, and organized the Howard High School into a hospital for the sick and wounded soldiers from those forts. Later, in Marietta, Georgia, she organized hospitals in the buildings surrounding the public square and administered these hospitals for more than one year until the Confederate retreat in 1864 made retention of the hospitals by the Confederacy impossible. After many hardships, she finally reached Atlanta, Georgia.

Throughout the war, Trader exhibited physical and moral courage. Oblivious to personal comfort, she sacrificed her wealth and impaired her health. She exerted considerable power and influence, and many high-ranking Confederate officers became her personal acquaintances.

In 1867, she married William H. Trader, a Confederate officer. He died in 1885 and left Trader and their only surviving child, May, in difficult financial circumstances. Trader's holdings had been lost or expropriated during the war, and she had lost the sight in one eye and was almost completely deaf. An effort to secure a suitable residence for her in Asheville, North Carolina, through popular subscription failed in 1885.

One year later, Trader obtained a government post in Washington, D.C., and until her resignation in 1916 served in various governmental departments. In 1908 her case was brought before the Association of Medical Officers of the Army and Navy of the Confederacy at its annual reunion in Birmingham, Alabama. The members adopted a resolution commending her for her efforts on behalf of the sick, wounded, and dying.

Trader died in 1919 in Washington, D.C., of acute bronchitis and was buried there in Rock Creek Cemetery.

## BIBLIOGRAPHY

Cumming, Kate. *Gleanings from Southland. . . .* Birmingham: Roberts & Son, 1895.

Cumming, Kate. *Kate: The Journal of a Confederate Nurse.* Baton Rouge: Louisiana State University Press, 1959.

Cunningham, H.H. "Trader, Ella King Newsom." In *Notable American Women 1607–1950, A Biographical Dictionary.* Vol. 3. Cambridge, Mass.: Belknap Press of Harvard University Press, 1971.

Richard, J.F. *The Florence Nightingale of the Southern Army. Experiences of Mrs. Ella K. Newsom, Confederate Nurse in the Great War of 1861–65.* New York and Baltimore: Broadway Publishing, 1914.

Lilli Sentz

# Harriet (Araminta) Ross Tubman

## 1820–1913

Though best known for her daring exploits in leading slaves to freedom, Harriet Araminta Ross Tubman had an equally humanitarian career in nursing. She gave distinguished service to the Union army and later to freedmen struggling to adapt to independent living.

Tubman was born about 1820 in Bucktown, Maryland. She was 1 of 10 or 11 children of Benjamin and Harriet Greene Ross, whose parents all had come from Africa as slaves. Early in life, Tubman changed her name from Araminta to Harriet, her mother's name.

As a slave child, Tubman received no education and was severely and frequently punished. When she was 13, an overseer fractured her skull with a heavy weight; for the rest of her life, she suffered frequent spells of somnolence. In 1844 her owner forced her to marry John Tubman, a fellow slave. They never had children.

In 1849 after hearing that she might be sold and moved out of Maryland, Tubman escaped from her owner. Her husband stayed behind and later remarried. Tubman traveled to Philadelphia, Pennsylvania, where she obtained work in a hotel. Later, she lived in St. Catherines, Ontario, where she brought many of the slaves she helped to escape.

In December 1850 Tubman went to Baltimore and guided a sister and her two children to freedom. She joined the work of the underground railroad and carried out 19 rescue missions, which freed approximately 300 slaves. Among them were her parents and several other members of her family.

Tubman's exploits and her public denunciation of slavery gained her national attention, and her friends and admirers came to include Secretary of State William Seward, Ralph Waldo Emerson, John Brown, and many other distinguished citizens. Seward sold her a house he owned in Auburn, New York, at minimal cost, and it became her headquarters for the rest of her life.

In the early days of the Civil War, Tubman was asked by Massachusetts governor John A. Andrew to assist Union soldiers by becoming a hospital nurse. Tubman responded by working as a nurse throughout the war, using her knowledge of roots and herbs to help heal the wounded and sick soldiers. She moved from camp to camp, serving wherever she was needed.

During this time, Tubman was allowed to draw the rations of an officer and soldier but rarely did so. She supported herself by making baked goods to sell in the camps, and she used what extra money she made to help the freedmen. Toward the end of her life, she was granted a small army pension.

During the war, many freedmen lacked shelter and the skills of independent living and sought refuge in the Union army camps. Tubman performed a special service by ministering to them and soliciting the army's cooperation in meeting their needs.

In the spring and summer of 1865, Tubman worked in a freedmen's hospital at Fort Monroe, Virginia. She was instrumental in developing the Port Royal, South Carolina, freedmen's colony, and for some time she worked in its hospital and used it as a base of her operations.

She also served in hospitals in Hilton Head, North Carolina, and Fernandina, Florida.

In 1869 Tubman married Nelson Davis, a Civil War veteran. Settling in Auburn, she ran her home as a shelter for needy black people and continued her nursing activities among them. She died of pneumonia on March 10, 1913, and was given a military funeral. The people of Auburn maintained her home for several years and erected a monument to her in the town.

## BIBLIOGRAPHY

Bontemps, A.A. "Tubman, Harriet." In *The McGraw-Hill Encyclopedia of World Biography*. David I. Eggenberger, editor-in-chief. New York: McGraw-Hill, 1973.

Bradford, S. *Harriet Tubman: The Moses of Her People*. 1886. Reprint. Secaucus, N.J.: Citadel Press, 1974.

Conrad, E. *Harriet Tubman*. New York: Paul S. Eriksson, 1943.

Franklin, J.H. "Tubman, Harriet." In *Notable American Women*. edited by E.T. James. Cambridge, Mass.: Belknap Press of Harvard University Press, 1971.

"Tubman, Harriet." *The Encyclopedia Americana International Edition*. Bernard S. Cayne, editorial director. Danbury, Conn.: Grolier, 1985.

Alice P. Stein

# Katherine Tucker

## 1885–1957

Katherine Tucker was a leader in public-health nursing and nursing education. Her career is remembered as having influenced every aspect of public-health nursing between 1910 and 1949.

A 1907 graduate of Vassar College, Tucker completed her nursing training in 1910 at Newton Hospital in Newton, Massachusetts. After moving to Philadelphia, Pennsylvania, she began her career as a tuberculosis worker in the social service department of the Hospital of the University of Pennsylvania (HUP). In 1912 she became the head worker at the social service department of the New York Dispensary. From 1913 to 1916, she was the social service director of the New York State Committee on Mental Hygiene.

In 1916 Tucker was selected by the Board of Lady Managers of the Visiting Nurse Society (VNS) of Philadelphia to impose order and direction within the organization, which, after 20 years of rapid growth, required professional help.

Tucker proved well qualified for the task. Within ten months, she had fulfilled the expectations of the VNS board for a more efficiently run organization. Her reorganization included a larger staff, a new record-keeping system, better staff supervision, more services for paying patients, and a greater emphasis on the teaching of prevention to patients. By the end of Tucker's first ten years, the VNS was providing two and one-half times more patient care. That year (1926), the society's nurses made over 257,800 visits to over 33,800 patients.

It was as a general director of the VNS that Tucker's lifelong interest in nursing education was initiated. The society's teaching department was one of the first in the country to provide training for students interested in visiting nursing. Through her articles, speeches, and activities within a variety of professional organizations, Tucker actively advocated that public health-nursing should become an important aspect of every training-school curriculum.

During 1916–19, Tucker served as president of the Pennsylvania State Organization for Public Health Nursing. From 1916 to 1918, she was the first vice-president of the National Organization for Public Health Nursing (NOPHN), and she was president from 1919 to 1920. She chaired the NOPHN's educational committee for several years.

In 1919, she left Philadelphia to become the general director of NOPHN. Tucker took over the leadership of the organization as it entered a new and markedly different period. Having recently undergone a period of self-evaluation, the NOPHN looked to Tucker to provide strong guidelines, new direction, and clarity of purpose. That summer Tucker traveled across the country in an effort to meet the members and to discuss the future of their organization. Working with the committee on programs and policies, she developed new goals for the NOPHN.

The Depression, as well as the struggles of many public-health nurses and visiting nurse associations to survive, brought upheaval, crisis, and serious economic losses to NOPHN. Through Tucker's efforts, provisions for voluntary nursing agencies to provide bedside nursing care for the poor were included in the Federal Emergency Relief Act in 1933. She also promoted the inclusion of school, tuberculosis, communicable disease, and maternity nursing into the Civil Works Administration's projects. The outcome was both more nursing care for the poor and more jobs for unemployed public-health nurses.

In 1935 Tucker returned to Philadelphia as professor and director of the department of nursing education at the School of Education of the University of Pennsylvania. The department was founded in 1935 as the result of a proposal from the Pennsylvania Nurses' Association. Its program was designed to prepare students to become teachers, supervisors, and administrators in schools and hospitals, as well as to fill positions in public-health nursing; it was the first program in Pennsylvania to offer college courses to registered nurses.

Tucker remained at the University of Pennsylvania until her retirement in 1949. She died in 1957 at HUP after a lengthy illness. She was survived by a sister, F.A. Saunders, of South Hadley, Massachusetts.

## PUBLICATIONS BY KATHERINE TUCKER

### BOOKS

*Survey of Public Health Nursing.* For the National Organization of Public Health Nursing. New York: Commonwealth Fund, 1934.

### ARTICLES

"Nursing Care of the Insane in the United States." *American Journal of Nursing* 16 (December 1915): 198–202.

"The Training School's Responsibility in Public Health Nursing Education." *Public Health Nurse Quarterly* 8 (July 1916): 99–103.

"Presidential Address to the National Organization for Public Health Nursing." *Public Health Nurse* 12 (June 1920): 457–61.

"The Management of Communicable Disease from the Standpoint of a Public Health Nurse." *American Journal of Nursing* 21 (March 1922): 412–16.

"The Place and Value of Visiting Nursing in Community Health Work." *Public Health Nurse* 14 (October 1922): 499–506.

"Practical Co-operation between Public Health Nurses and Social Workers." *Public Health Nurse* 15 (December 1923): 614–16.

"What is Supervision?" *Public Health Nurse* 16 (July 1924): 327–32.

"Shifts in Emphasis." *Public Health Nurse* 20 (August 1928): 399–404.

"Future Service to Our Members." *Public Health Nurse* 21 (June 1929): 283–87.

"Relation of State Public Health Nursing Services to County and Local Services." *Public Health Nursing* 24 (July 1932): 357–65.

"Biennial Report of NOPHN Activities." *Public Health Nursing* 26 (June 1934): 307–15.

"The Curriculum Study." *Public Health Nurse* 33 (May 1941): 311–14.

"Public Health Nursing in National Defense." *Public Health Nursing* 33 (December 1941): 697–704.

"Curriculum Guide Nears Completion." *Public Health Nursing* 34 (February 1942): 89–90.

## BIBLIOGRAPHY

Buhler-Wilkerson, K. "False Dawn: The Rise and Decline of Public Health Nursing, 1900–1930." Ph.D. diss. University of Pennsylvania, 1984.

Fitzpatrick, M.L. *The National Organization for Public Health Nursing, 1912–1952: Development of A Practice Field.* New York: National League for Nursing, 1975.

"Katherine Tucker." *Public Health Nurse* 21 (January 1929) 1–2.

"Katherine Tucker, Health Expert, 72." *New York Times,* 7 June 1957.

Visiting Nurse Society of Philadelphia. Annual reports, 1916–1929.

Karen Buhler-Wilkerson

# Daisy Dean Urch

1876–1952

Daisy Dean Urch was a leader in nursing education and was often outspoken in her attempts to improve the quality of nursing practice. She called for a better selection of nursing students who were not afraid to speak out, and she believed that nursing students should not be high school or college failures.

Urch was born on a large farm in Clarkston, Michigan, on June 9, 1876, and was the fifth of nine children. The children were taught from an early age about caring for the needs of others in the community, and they discussed family problems together with their parents. When Urch was nine years old, her father died; her mother, a former schoolteacher, continued to give the children a sense of responsibility.

Before she thought of becoming a nurse, Urch received training to become a teacher. She attended the Ferris Institute in Big Rapids, Michigan, then became a kindergarten teacher and school principal in Munising, Michigan.

In 1910 at the age of 34, Urch entered the Illinois Training School in Chicago, Illinois, to begin her nursing education. Originally, she had planned to return to teaching after she completed her nurses' training, but instead she turned to private-duty nursing in Chicago after graduation in 1913. The following year, she became a faculty member at her alma mater, first as head nurse, then supervisor, then assistant to the superintendent of nurses and instructor in nursing technique.

During World War I, Urch served as an American Red Cross nurse overseas from June 1917 to July 1919. She was appointed to the position of temporary chief nurse at base hospital 12 in France. At this time, the nursing profession was not integrated into the military and nurses serving abroad had no rank and could be dismissed from any position by the commanding officer. Urch ran into difficulty in her first assignment abroad and was relieved from duty as temporary chief nurse in December 1917 and reassigned as a nurse in the unit. Due to the lack of any legislation protecting nurses' rights, she had no recourse. The reason for her dismissal was essentially a conflict with the physician in command over nursing care. The evidence of a personal hostility to nurses by the officer—a Major Besley—is indicated by the fact that she went on to serve in other base hospitals and was honorably discharged in July 1919. In addition to her work in American hospital units, she also served as a chief nurse in the British army.

After the war ended, Urch continued her education part time from 1920 to 1927, graduating from Teachers College, Columbia University, in New York City with a B.S. degree and an M.A. degree in administration of schools of nursing. When she was not taking classes during this period, Urch served as an instructor in the Illinois Training School, Chicago, 1921–22; as the director of the San Francisco Hospital School of Nursing, 1923–25; and during 1926 and 1927 as the inspector for schools of nursing in California.

After she obtained her master's degree, Urch was the director of the Highland School of Nursing in Oakland, California, from 1927 to 1933. Many of her publications concerned with the standards of nursing education were written at this time. In a paper on the improvement of nursing practice read before the education committee of the National League of Nursing Education (NLNE), Urch called for a better selection of nursing students. She urged that students who did not do well in high school or college not be recommended to nursing school.

In 1934 Urch moved from California to Winona, Minnesota, and for two years served as educational director for the Minnesota State Board of Examiners of Nurses. She then taught nursing education at the College of Saint Teresa in Winona and was made director of the department. She was considered by her colleagues to be an independent thinker as well as a good executive.

Urch was involved in nursing organization activities and served in the following offices: president, California State League of Nursing Education; president and member of the board of directors, California State Nurses' Association; president, Minnesota League of Nursing Education; member of the board of directors, Minnesota State Organization for Public Health Nursing; and member of the board of directors of the National League of Nursing Education. She also served on the NLNE's committees for accrediting and state board problems.

Urch continued her association with the American Red Cross, serving as an instructor in home-nursing courses during the 1940s until her retirement around 1945. Urch died on June 10, 1952 in Winona.

## PUBLICATIONS BY DAISY DEAN URCH

"Letters to the Editor. Rank for Nurses." *American Journal of Nursing* 20 (December 1919): 247–48.

"Education and Financial Policies in Schools of Nursing." *Pacific Coast Journal of Nursing* 20 (January 1924): 810–12.

"Methods of Securing Intelligent and Interested Co-operation from and through Members of the Nursing Staff." *Pacific Coast Journal of Nursing* 20 (August 1924): 500–04.

"The Value of Affiliated Schools." *Pacific Coast Journal of Nursing* 21 (December 1925): 750.

"The Blooming. What Shall the Fruitage Be?" *Pacific Coast Journal of Nursing* 22 (November 1926): 654–55.

"Rating Scales for Nursing Schools." *Pacific Coast Journal of Nursing* 25 (October 1929): 592–94.

"Creating and Maintaining Good Morale of the Supervisory Nurses in the Hospital." *American Journal of Nursing* 29 (December 1929): 1502–08.

"A Study of the Position and Preparation of Director of Nursing Schools." *National League of Nursing Education: Annual Report 1928, and Proceedings of the 34th Convention.* New York: The League, 1928, pp. 151–64.

"Efficient Nursing Service." *Hospital Progress* 11 (February 1930): 59–60.

"Organization of School of Nursing Committees." *American Journal of Nursing* 31 (March 1931): 337–49.

"What Are We Doing to Improve Nursing Practice?" *American Journal of Nursing* 32 (June 1932): 680–84.

"Student Nurse Education—Discussion of Pre-Nursing Requirements." *Pacific Coast Nursing Journal* 29 (October 1933): 584–86.

"Of Jury Paneling May There Be No End." *American Journal of Nursing* 36 (September 1936): 891–96.

## BIBLIOGRAPHY

American Red Cross Archives. Washington, D.C.

Domitilla, M. "Daisy Dean Urch." In *National League of Nursing Education: Biographic Sketches, 1937–1940.* New York: National League of Nursing Education, 1940.

Theresa Dombrowski

# Margaret Doolin Utinsky

## 1900–?

Margaret Doolin Utinsky is recognized for supplying food rations and medical supplies to American and Filipino prisoners of war in the Philippines during the Japanese occupation of the islands from 1942 to 1945. Her unselfish risk-taking was responsible for saving thousands of lives.

Utinsky was born August 26, 1900, in St. Louis, Missouri, to James Patrick and Lydia Horner Doolin. There are no available records of any siblings. At an early age, she moved with her family to a farm in Canada, where she attended public schools. The date of the family's return to the United States is uncertain.

At age 19, she married John Rowley in Tulsa, Oklahoma, on January 9, 1919. A son, Charles Grant Rowley, was born to the couple that year. The next year, Utinsky's husband died.

As a young widow, Utinsky was responsible for raising and supporting her child. She attended nursing school, graduating in 1924. Specifics of her nursing education are unknown. There are reports of her living or working in Texas and Oklahoma during 1924–27. One report suggests that she worked in a hospital in Galveston, Texas, in 1924.

In 1927 Utinsky planned to vacation in the Philippines with her son for six months. The vacation evolved into permanent residence for 18 years.

Settling in Manila, the Philippines, Utinsky pursued her career as a nurse and performed private nursing duties in various hospitals in the city. It appears that she also performed nursing in Baguio, in northern Luzon province.

She married an American citizen and civil engineer, John Paul Utinsky, in 1924 in the Philippines. The couple maintained their home in Manila after their marriage. Utinsky volunteered as a nurse with the Red Cross and operated a servicemen's canteen at a Manila hospital.

In January 1942 the Japanese invaded the Philippine Islands. To avoid internment by the Japanese, Utinsky obtained forged citizenship papers and assumed a Lithuanian identity. In May 1942 she was granted permission to travel as a nurse with the Philippine Red Cross to Bataan and Tarlac to aid injured civilian Filipinos.

During this initial relief expedition, Utinsky was in contact with two American medical officers. Through them, she learned of the desperate need for food and medical supplies for the American prisoners of war. Knowing that her own husband, captured at Bataan, was among them, Utinsky tried to meet the needs of the imprisoned.

Through the efforts of Utinsky and some Filipinos and Catholic priests, the needed money and supplies were delivered to the soldiers. In turn, prisoners supplied information about prison conditions and captured military personnel to be relayed to the American military intelligence. This system, headed by Utinsky, was known as the "Miss U" organization.

In August 1942 John Paul Utinsky died of malnutrition in Cabanatuan prison camp. After his death, his widow became even more determined to relieve the suffering of as many prisoners as possible. She sold all her personal possessions for cash to buy food and medicine for the Americans and Filipinos. Supplies were bought for prisoners at Camp O'Donnell and Camp 1, and at Cabanatuan, McKinley, Bilibid, and Las Pinias prisons.

Utinsky continued working as a private-duty nurse in Manila to maintain her credibility as a Lithuanian. The Japanese were highly suspicious of her, however, and in September 1943 took her prisoner. She was tortured, beaten, and placed in solitary confinement for 32 days at Fort Santiago, Manila. Utinsky was released in critical medical condition. Subsequently, she spent six weeks in Doctors' Hospital as a patient recuperating from leg wounds, a broken jaw, and malnutrition.

The underground continued until late 1943, when a Japanese hit list was discovered to contain the names of many of the organization's members, including Utinsky herself. She escaped to the mountains on the Bataan peninsula, where she remained with American guerrilla fighters in the remote mountain areas.

Utinsky established a rudimentary hospital for the wounded and ill guerrillas. She managed to secure some basic medical supplies and served as the sole healthcare provider. Because of her service to these men, Utinsky received the honorary commission of second, and then first, brevet lieutenant of the guerrilla army.

When the American forces returned to the Philippines, Utinsky gained access to Manila. She then assisted the military counter-intelligence corps in locating enemy collaborators. Utinsky refused to leave the Philippines until she was assured that known traitors were imprisoned.

In March 1945 Utinsky left the Philippines for the United States. She resided with friends for several months in the Washington, D.C., area. There are no reports of her working as a nurse after her return.

In 1946 Utinsky was officially recognized for her services in the Philippines. In July of that year, the U.S. Congress passed Private Law 79–781, which reimbursed her for the funds she privately donated to buy supplies for the American prisoners. In October 1946 Utinsky was awarded the Presidential Medal of Freedom for her contribution as a civilian to the war effort.

Subseqent information about Utinsky's life is limited. It is unknown whether she sought employment in the United States as a nurse or whether she returned to the Philippines to live and work.

**PUBLICATIONS BY
MARGARET DOOLIN UTINSKY**

*Miss U.* San Antonio, Tex.: Naylor, 1948.

**BIBLIOGRAPHY**

"Bill To Reimburse Nurse." *New York Times*, 3 July 1946.

Brevet Lt. Margaret Utinsky. U.S. Congress, Senate, Congressional Record, 79th Cong., 2nd sess., July 10, 1979. Report No. 1695.

Furnas, H. "Miss U." *Collier's* 117 (January 1946): 34.

"Utinsky, Margaret." *Who's Who of American Women.* 2d ed. Vol. 2. Chicago: A.N. Marquis, 1962.

"Woman Decorated by MacArthur for Aid to Prisoners." *Washington Post*, 17 October 1946.

Claire M. Stackhouse
Rosemary T. McCarthy

# Carolyn Conant Van Blarcom

## 1879–1960

Carolyn Conant Van Blarcom was the first American nurse to become a licensed midwife. She also was the person most responsible for bringing *opthalmia neonatorum*, then the leading cause of preventable blindness, under control in the United States.

Van Blarcom was born June 12, 1879, in Alton, Illinois, the second of two daughters and the fourth of six children of William Dixon and Fanny Conant Van Blarcom. Most of her childhood was spent in Alton, where her father was a financier. He abandoned his family when Van Blarcom was still a small child and left his wife to care for the six growing children. Fanny Conant Van Blarcom, a linguist and a pianist, raised her family in middle-class circumstances despite the absence of her husband.

At age 6, Van Blarcom had rheumatic fever, from which she never fully recovered. As a result, she was educated at home by her mother. Her health was fur-

ther impaired by the early onset of rheumatoid arthritis. Her mother died when Van Blarcom was 14, and she was sent east to live with relatives.

In 1898 Van Blarcom enrolled in the Johns Hopkins Hospital Training School for Nurses. Although sickness kept her out of school for over one year, she graduated in 1901 with such a distinguished record that she was invited to join the faculty. She served as an instructor in obstetrics and as assistant superintendent of nurses at the training school until 1905.

Van Blarcom then went to St. Louis to reorganize a training school for nurses, but the growing severity of her arthritis led to her resignation. Three years later, when her health had improved, she was appointed director of the Maryland Tuberculosis Sanatorium at Sibillisville. From there, she moved to a similar post in New Bedford, Massachusetts, where her success in upgrading the clinic to a well-funded hospital gained wide attention. In 1909 she was appointed secretary of the New York State Committee for the Prevention of Blindness, a position that allowed her to mount educational campaigns in ways to prevent blindness.

Though Carl Siegmund Franz Crede had publicized in 1884 the effectiveness of a 2 percent silver nitrate solution in preventing *opthalmia neonatorum*, Van Blarcom found that many birth attendants, 50 percent of whom were midwives, were unfamiliar with the procedure. Supported by a grant from the Russell Sage Foundation, she then conducted a study of midwifery in the United States, England, and 14 other countries, the results of which she published in *The Midwife in England* (1913). She concluded that the United States was the only "civilized" country that did not protect its mothers and infants by providing for the training and licensing of midwives.

With her book, Van Blarcom emerged as one of the significant figures in the reform of midwifery. As the first American nurse to be a licensed midwife, she wrote for medical journals and popular periodicals, spoke at various conferences, and moved to upgrade midwifery. She helped establish a midwifery school in conjunction with Bellevue Hospital in New York City in 1911, the first such school in the United States.

In 1916 Van Blarcom moved to Illinois as secretary of the Illinois Society for the Prevention of Blindness. During World War I, she served as director of the bureau of nursing service of the Atlantic division of the American Red Cross.

In the decade of the 1920s, Van Blarcom concentrated on the problems of mothers and infants. She served as health editor for the *Delineator*, a popular magazine, and published three books: *Obstetrical Nursing*, a textbook for nurses; *Getting Ready To Be a Mother*, a book for parents; and *Building the Baby*, also a book for lay readers.

Chronic ill health forced Van Blarcom into retirement in the 1930s. She became active again for a brief period in World War II, when she directed a training program for the American Red Cross in Pasadena, California.

Van Blarcom died in Arcadia, California, of bronchopneumonia on March 20, 1960.

### PUBLICATIONS BY
### CAROLYN CONANT VAN BLARCOM

#### BOOKS

*The Midwife in England*. New York: Committee for the Prevention of Blindness, 1913.

*Getting Ready to Be a Mother*. New York: Macmillan, 1922, 2nd ed., 1929; 3rd ed., 1937; 4th ed., 1940; London: Macmillan, 1947.

*Obstetrical Nursing*. New York: Macmillan, 1922, 2nd ed., 1928; 3rd ed., 1933.

*Building the Baby*. New York: Reader's Service Bureau of the News, 1929; Chicago: Public Service Office of the Chicago Tribune, 1929.

#### ARTICLES

"Rat Pie: Among the Black Midwives of the South." *Harper's Monthly Magazine* (February 1930): 322–32.

#### BIBLIOGRAPHY

"Carolyn Conant Van Blarcom." Obituary. *American Journal of Nursing* (June 1960).

"Van Blarcom, Carolyn Conant." In *Makers of Nursing History*, by M.R. Pennock. Privately published 1940.

"Van Blarcom, Carolyn Conant." In *Notable American Women: Modern Period*, cited by Barbara Sicherman and Carol Hurd Green. Vol. 4. Cambridge, Mass: Harvard University Press, 1980, pp. 703–04.

Van Blarcom, C.C. Papers. Alan Mason Chesney Medical Archives. Johns Hopkins Medical Institutions, Baltimore.

Van Blarcom, C.C. Papers. Johns Hopkins Nurses Alumni Association, Baltimore.

Vern L. Bullough

## Cornelia Van Kooy
### 1885–1945

An innovator in the development of public-health nursing, Cornelia Van Kooy is considered the mother of public-health nursing in Wisconsin. Her visionary ideas about the role of the nurse in the prevention of illness had a national impact, and the practice of public-health nursing in Wisconsin served as a model for other states.

Van Kooy was born June 12, 1885, in Utrecht, the Netherlands. Her parents, Mathews and Adrianna Gaasterland Van Kooy, migrated with their family to Milwaukee, Wisconsin, in 1905. She had three brothers, Fred, Siewart, and Jacob, and two sisters, Mona and Adrianna.

Van Kooy was educated in private schools in the Netherlands. In 1907 she entered St. Joseph's Hospital School of Nursing in Milwaukee, and she received her diploma in November 1909.

Employed as a private-duty nurse in Milwaukee for two years following her graduation, Van Kooy then joined the staff of the Milwaukee health department as its first child-welfare nurse. In this position, she helped to organize Wisconsin's first classes for expectant mothers.

In 1914 she joined the staff of the Wisconsin Anti-Tuberculosis Association (WATA—now the Wisconsin Lung Association) as a public-health demonstration nurse. At the time, tuberculosis was the leading cause of death in Wisconsin, and WATA often sent nurses to various counties throughout the state to convince county boards of the nurses' value in the fight against the disease.

During World War I, Van Kooy served with the Milwaukee base hospital 22 as a Red Cross nurse in France. Upon her return to Wisconsin, she was sent by the WATA to the state board of health to organize its bureau of child welfare and public-health nursing, which had been created by the state legislature.

In 1922 Van Kooy returned to WATA to teach a four-month course in public-health nursing offered by the association. This course was designed to prepare public-health nurses, particularly those employed by the counties, for their responsibilities. The course was provided by WATA for several years before public-health nursing was offered in nursing schools.

Five years later, Van Kooy returned to the state board of health to become supervisor of its bureau of public-health nursing, a position she held until her death. In this position, she traveled throughout the state, giving support and counsel to nurses employed by the counties, convincing county boards and state legislators of the value of health and the contributions of the nurses, and taking advantage of all opportunities to teach about health. School visits, especially to one-room rural schools, were an important part of the county nurse's responsibilities, and on occasion, Van Kooy would accompany the nurse on these visits and participate in some of the teaching. She actively promoted health legislation in Wisconsin, often serving on the state nurses' association's legislative committee and as a member of the women's legislative council.

Van Kooy participated in professional organizations at state and national levels. She served on committees of the National Organization of Public Health Nursing and represented that organization on the national Red Cross committee. She also served on state and local Red Cross committees. Van Kooy served twice as president of the Wisconsin (State) Nurses' Association (1924–27, 1929–30). In 1925 she represented the state nurses' association at the eighth quadrennial congress of the International Council of Nurses in Helsinki, Finland.

She also served as a Wisconsin representative to the third White House Conference on Child Health and Protection, called by President Herbert Hoover in 1930, and on its committee on the control of communicable diseases. She was a member of the state committee on nursing education (forerunner of the state board of nursing).

For her contributions to nursing, Van Kooy received several honors. In 1936 Wisconsin nurses awarded her life membership in the National Organization for Public Health Nursing. In 1944 she was awarded honorary life membership in the state organization for public-health nursing. She was elected to Delta Kappa Gamma in 1938.

The Cornelia Van Kooy Trust Fund was established in 1945 by Wisconsin's state organization for public-health nursing and later was administered by the Wisconsin League for Nursing. The fund was designated for furthering public-health education.

Van Kooy was years ahead of her time in her unswerving belief that the public should be partners with the nurse in achieving public-health goals. Under her tutelage, public-health nursing grew from a limited service for those who were sick and poor to broad service for the whole community.

Van Kooy died of a malignancy on September 7, 1945, in Madison, Wisconsin, and was buried in Union Cemetery, Milwaukee. She was survived by her mother, three brothers, and two sisters.

## PUBLICATIONS BY CORNELIA VAN KOOY

"Development of Public Health Nursing in Wisconsin." *Public Health Nurse* 14 (February 1922): 87–89.

"Public Health Nursing Facts for State Boards of Health." *Public Health Nurse* 21 (September 1929): 486.

"Knowing Where Rural Nurses are Going." *Red Cross Courier* 12 (December 1932): 181.

## BIBLIOGRAPHY

Bureau of Public Health Nursing in Wisconsin State Board of Health Records. Archives.

State Historical Society of Wisconsin, Madison.

Cooper, S.S. "Cornelia Van Kooy—Public Health Visionary." In *Wisconsin Nursing Pioneers*. Madison, Wis.: University of Wisconsin-University Extension, 1968.

Cooper, S.S. "Cornelia Van Kooy." In *Famous Wisconsin Women*. Vol. 6. Madison, Wis.: State Historical Society of Wisconsin, 1976.

"Cornelia Van Kooy." In *Dictionary of Wisconsin Biography*. Madison, Wis.: State Historical Society of Wisconsin, 1960.

"Cornelia Van Kooy." Editorial. *Capital Times* (Madison, Wis.), 10 September 1945.

"Cornelia Van Kooy." Obituary. *Trained Nurse and Hospital Review* 115 (October 1945): 280.

"Cornelia Van Kooy." Obituary. *American Journal of Nursing* 45 (October 1945): 871.

"NOPHN Membership to Cornelia Van Kooy." *Bulletin of the Wisconsin State Nurses' Association* 4 (November 1936): 4–5.

Signe S. Cooper

# Ellwyne Mae Vreeland

### 1909–1971

Ellwyne Mae Vreeland served 23 years as an officer in the United States Public Health Service. She developed and ran the first nationwide federal extramural research program for nursing.

Vreeland was born in Stockbridge, Massachusetts, on November 28, 1909, the daughter of William L. and Edith M. Block Vreeland. She trained at the Massachusetts General Hospital School of Nursing between 1929 and 1934. She continued her education by attending classes at the University of Vermont in Burlington in 1935 and 1937, at the University of Rochester in Rochester, New York, in 1938–39, and in 1942 she received a B.S. degree from Teachers College, Columbia University, in New York City. She received an M.A. degree in 1949 from Teachers College.

Vreeland's early career was marked by a series of jobs. She served as a staff nurse and operating-room assistant at General Hospital in Saranac, New York, in 1934–35 and in 1935–36 moved to Stony Wold, in Lake Kushaqua, New York, to a similar position. From 1936 to 1939 she served as staff nurse, night charge nurse, and emergency-division nurse at Strong Memorial Hospital in Rochester, New York. It was during these periods of employment that she attended college in Vermont and in Rochester.

From 1940 to 1942, Vreeland was director of nurses at Schenectady County Tuberculosis Hospital. After receiving her degree from Teachers College, Columbia University, she served as assistant director of nursing and of nurse education at Albany Hospital and Russell Sage College (1943–1945) in Albany, New York.

In 1943 Vreeland also became a consultant to the newly created division of nurse education in the United States Public Health Service. The division oversaw the Cadet Nurse Corps. In 1949 she became chief of the nursing education bureau in the division of nursing resources, and from here she moved on to become chief of the research grants bureau in 1955. Vreeland became chief of the research and resources branches of the newly created division of nursing in 1962.

Awards for nursing research grants under the programs that she directed amounted to more than $8.6 million and funded 132 projects through 1964. Vreeland saw the need for graduate programs for nurses and made available federal funding for that purpose.

During her last four years at the United States Public Health Service, Vreeland served as a senior consultant and head of intramural research. She retired in 1968.

In 1966 she received the United States Public Health Service Meritorious Service Medal for her accomplishments. In 1970 she received the award for distinguished achievement in research and scholarship from the Teachers College Nursing Education Alumni Association. Vreeland wrote numerous articles in nursing journals as well as in other journals. She was a fellow of the American Public Health Association and a member of the Nursing Hall of Fame.

Vreeland died May 12, 1971, in Riviera Beach, Florida.

## PUBLICATIONS BY ELLWYNE MAE VREELAND

### BOOKS

With Leslie W. Knott, and Marjorie Gooch. *Cost Analysis for Collegiate Programs in Nursing*, New York: National League for Nursing, Part 1, 1956; Part 2, 1957.

### ARTICLES

"Some Qualitative and Quantitative Factors in Nurse Education." *Public Health Reports* 63 (December 1948): 1667–91.

"Meeting the Cost of Professional Education." *American Journal of Nursing* 49 (December 1949): 804–06.

"Fifty Years of Nursing in the Federal Government Service." *American Journal of Nursing* 50 (October 1950): 626–31.

"The Nursing Research Grant and Fellowship Program of the Public Health Service." *American Journal of Nursing* 58 (December 1958): 1700–02.

### BIBLIOGRAPHY

"Ellwyne Vreeland." *Who's Who of American Women, 1966–67*. 4th ed. Chicago: A.N. Marquis, 1965, p. 1192.

Vern L. Bullough

## Lillian D. Wald

### 1867–1940

Lillian D. Wald was the originator of public-health nursing and the founder of the Visiting Nurse Service in New York City. She also initiated the first public-school nursing program in the United States and founded the Henry Street Settlement in New York City.

Wald was born on March 10, 1867, in Cincinnati, Ohio, the third of four children and the second daughter of Max D. and Minnie Schwartz Wald. Wald's father moved his family from Cincinnati to Rochester, New York, when Wald was still a young child, hence, she viewed Rochester as her home town. A dealer in optical goods, Max Wald descended from a long line of German-Jewish scholars, rabbis, and merchants. Jewish as well, her mother's ancestors were Polish and German. Wald's grandfather, Gutman Schwartz, lived with the family for several years and had a great deal of influence on her.

Because her father's income was good, Wald was educated in an expensive private school. She learned to speak both French and German. She applied to Vassar College in 1883 but was turned down because she was too young. Instead she traveled for six years and briefly worked as a newspaper correspondent.

In 1889 Wald met a nurse who had been trained at Bellevue Hospital in New York City. This nurse influenced her to enter the nursing profession and she enrolled in the two-year nursing program at New York Hospital in August 1889 at the age of 22. She graduated in March 1891, having had the benefit of guidance by the program's director of nursing, Irene H. Sutliffe.

After graduation from nursing school, Wald entered the Women's Medical College to study for an M.D. degree. She also volunteered her services as a home nurse among the immigrants moving into the lower East Side of New York City. Having been trained in a "hands-on" setting at New York Hospital, Wald felt neither degraded nor diminished by her work among the poor.

Wald determined that the poor on the lower East Side needed immediate help. She left medical school in 1893 and moved into a house on Jefferson Street in order to help the poor within their own community. She began her work with the aid of her friend Mary Brewster, whom she had known at the New York Hospital. Two years later in 1895, Wald and Brewster moved into a nearby house on Henry Street and from there organized services and programs that became the model for similar settlements in the United States, Canada, and Europe.

At the turn of the century and for some time thereafter, over 90 percent of the sick stayed home. Poor people had no money to pay physicians, and hospitals were reserved for extreme cases and generally did little good. Therefore, the Henry Street Settlement was useful not only in that it served Wald and Brewster in bringing nursing services to the poor, but it also served as a means of promoting education, recreation, housing, and relief for the unemployed in the neighborhood. In short, it grew into a multiple-service agency.

Although a few denominational groups had made similar efforts, their work was directed only at members of the denomination offering the service and depended on the occasional efforts of part-time volunteers. Wald and her associates were able to conduct their visiting-nurse activities on a full-time basis because they lived in the neighborhood where the services were needed and because they offered these services without respect to religion or race.

Their efforts attracted others to their cause. Betty Loeb, the wife of one of New York City's financiers, became interested in the activities of Wald and induced her son-in-law, Jacob Schiff, to buy the house on Henry Street for Wald and her visiting nurses.

In 1893 when Wald moved to Henry Street, she had 10 associates, 9 of whom were trained nurses. In 1900 there were 15 nurses, and by 1906 there were 27. During those years, New York City received an average of 20,000 immigrants per day.

The nurses from the settlement received $60 per month, money contributed by the Loeb and Schiff families. Wald was known as a successful fund raiser, and her enterprise continued to grow. By 1913 the Henry Street Settlement had seven houses and two uptown branches. Three years later in 1916, 250 visiting nurses were seeing 1,300 patients per day, and the membership of the visiting nurse service had grown to nearly 4,000. Wald administered a budget of $600,000 per year, all from private contributors. Wald was able to raise large sums in part because she was able to appeal to potential contributors by dealing with individual cases and was able to convey to others a willingness to serve.

The projects and ideas developed by Wald over the years were varied and original. In 1902 she succeeded in persuading the New York City Board of Education to

hire school nurses for the first time. Directly thereafter, she persuaded President Theodore Roosevelt to support the establishment of the Federal Children's Bureau in an effort to protect children from the practices of child labor, which she attacked vigorously in an article in the *American Journal of Nursing* in 1906. The Federal Children's Bureau finally came into existence in 1912 during the administration of William Howard Taft. That same year, Wald founded the Town and Country Nursing Service of the American Red Cross.

Only two years earlier in 1910, Wald had persuaded Columbia University to appoint her friend Mary A. Nutting as the first professor of nursing, thus establishing the first nursing department in any American institution of higher education. She also succeeded in convincing the Metropolitan Life Insurance Company to institute a nursing service for its industrial policyholders. In 1909 she organized the first conference on the prevention of infant mortality at New Haven, Connecticut.

Although Wald considered all of her activities as nursing services and although she objected to being viewed as a social worker, she was nevertheless responsible for several programs beyond the usual scope of nursing. As early as 1900, she agitated for better laws to assure alimony payments for abandoned women. In August 1914 she organized a march against World War I, an event that led the Daughters of the American Revolution to list her as dangerous. She also helped found the Women's Trade Union League in 1903 to protect women from the horrors of the sweat shops of that era.

Wald used the Henry Street Settlement in several different ways. It served as a recreation center for neighborhood families, with swings and other equipment for the use of children. She organized upgraded reading classes for children who needed help, joined Elizabeth Farrell in introducing special school classes for "backward" children, and opened study rooms, where she helped children with homework after school. In 1906 she founded the Vocational Guidance Committee at the Henry Street Settlement.

Wald opened a convalescent home in South Nyack, New York, in 1899, and campaigned in speeches and in writing against the practice of boarding out babies, a practice to which the poor often resorted to alleviate their financial needs. Wald promoted the use of foster homes as a solution. She taught immigrants to save money and supported the cause of organized labor by demanding medical inspection of industry in order to ensure adequate ventilation and other health needs of workers and to prevent the use of child labor. She visited industrial executives and argued for the advantages of ventilation and medical services in factories on the grounds that changes in these areas would save them money.

Wald served on many committees. As early as 1906, she served on the so-called Pushcart Commission in New York City, whose purpose it was to rid the poor neighborhoods of the pushcarts that were not allowed in wealthier areas. She chaired the nurses' emergency council of the Atlantic division of the Red Cross during the influenza epidemic of 1918 and the Red Cross committee on home nursing during World War I. In 1919 she represented the United States at the Committee of Red Cross Societies in Cannes, France. Together with Florence Kelley, she founded the National Labor Committee in 1924.

The influence of Wald was worldwide. In 1924 she visited England, Germany, Italy, and the Soviet Union. Later, she visited Mexico. Wherever she went, she carried the message of public-health nursing. Having refused marriage, Wald had devoted herself entirely to the needs of others. She inspired others to work with her and succeeded in many of her causes because people wanted to do things for her, even if they were not completely convinced of the cause itself. During her lifetime she received the Gold Medal of the National Institute of Social Sciences (1912), the Rotary Club Medal, and the Better Times Medal.

In 1925 Wald began to suffer from heart trouble and anemia. Nevertheless, she continued her rigorous schedule until 1932, when she was forced to reduce her work load because of an operation from which she never fully recovered. In 1933 she gave up her position as head worker at the Henry Street Settlement and moved to Westport, Connecticut. There she wrote her second book, *Windows on Henry Street*, in which she described her career since the publication of *The House on Henry Street* in 1915. In 1937 she gave up her position of president of the board of the Henry Street Settlement.

Wald died at her Connecticut home on September 1, 1940. Her ashes were buried in the family plot in Rochester, New York.

In September 1971 a bronze bust of Wald was placed into the Hall of Fame for Great Americans at New York University.

## PUBLICATIONS BY LILLIAN D. WALD

### BOOKS

*The House on Henry Street.* New York: Henry Holt, 1915.

*Windows on Henry Street.* Boston: Little, Brown, 1933.

### ARTICLES

"Nurses' Social Settlements." *American Journal of Nursing* 1 (June 1901): 682–84.

"The Treatment of Families in Which There Is Sickness." *American Journal of Nursing* 4 (March, April, May 1904): 427–31, 515–19, 602–6.

"Child Labor." *American Journal of Nursing* 6 (March 1906): 366–69.

"Best Helps to the Immigrant Through the Nurse." *American Journal of Nursing* 8 (March 1908): 464–67.

*American Society of Superintendents of Training Schools for Nurses, Annual Report.* Baltimore, Md.: American Society of Superintendents of Training Schools for Nurses, 1910.

"The Doctor and the Nurse in the Industrial Establishment." *American Journal of Nursing* 12 (February 1912): 403–8.

"Forty Years Service." *Pacific Coast Journal of Nursing* 35 (June 1939): 333–35.

### BIBLIOGRAPHY

Brenner, Robert H. "Lillian D. Wald." In *Notable American Women*, edited by E.T. James. Vol. 3. Cambridge, Mass.: Harvard University Press, 1971.

Callahan, Jean. "Lillian D. Wald." *The Women's Book of Records and Achievements*, edited by L.D. O'Neill. New York: Doubleday, 1979.

Christy, T.E. "Portrait of a Leader—Lillian D. Wald." *Nursing Outlook* 18 (March 1970): 50–54.

Duffus, R.L. *Lillian Wald, Neighbor and Crusader.* New York: Macmillan, 1938.

Epstein, B.W. *Lillian Wald, Angel of Henry Street.* New York: J. Messner, 1948.

Hill, R.W. "The Papers of Lillian D. Wald." *Social Service Review* 36 (December 1962): 462–63.

"Lillian D. Wald." Obituary. *New York Times,* 2 September 1940.

"Lillian D. Wald." Obituary. *Public Health Nursing* 32 (October 1940): 639–40.

"Our First Public Health Nurse, Lillian D. Wald." *Nursing Outlook* 19 (December 1962): 659–60.

Schutt, B.G. "A Prophet Honored: Lillian D. Wald." *American Journal of Nursing* 71 (January 1971): 53.

Smith, H. "Lillian Wald." *New Yorker* 5 (14 December 1929): 32.

"Wald, Lillian D." *American Women, 1935–1940,* edited by D. Howe. Vol 2. Detroit: Gale Research, 1981.

Wald, L.D. Papers. Department of Education Archives. Teachers College, Columbia University.

Wald, L.D. Papers. New York City Public Library, New York.

Waters, Y. *Visiting Nursing in the United States.* New York: William F. Fell, 1909.

Woods, R.A. and A.J. Kennedy. *The Settlement Horizon.* New York: Arne Press, 1970.

Yellowite, Irwin. "Lillian D. Wald." *Encyclopedia Judaica,* edited by C. Roth and Geoffrey Wigoder. Vol. 16. Jerusalem, Israel: Keter Publishing, Co., 1970.

Gerhard Falk

# Mary Curtis Wheeler

## 1869–1944

Mary Curtis Wheeler's tenure as the superintendent of the Illinois Training School for Nurses was the longest in the school's history. She also was the first nurse who served as inspector of schools of nursing in Illinois.

Wheeler was born on July 12, 1869, in Brooklyn, New York, to Mr. and Mrs. Norman Willis Wheeler. She spent her early years in Brooklyn until she reached the age of seven, when her mother died. The children were then sent to live with relatives in Wisconsin and later with other relatives. Eventually, her father brought his family together in Buffalo, New York. With his innovative approach to shipbuilding, he was successful enough to move on with his family to Bath, Maine, where he started the Bath Iron Works and established himself in the business.

Wheeler returned to Wisconsin to attend Ripon College in the city of Ripon. After graduation in 1890, she moved on to Chicago, where in September 1891 she enrolled in the Illinois Training School for Nurses. Her descriptions of her student days include 12-hour shifts, dishwashing duties, and rooms with no heat. She graduated in 1893.

From 1893 to 1899, Wheeler was superintendent of the school for nurses at Sherman Hospital in Elgin, Illinois. During this six-year period she also studied at the University of Michigan in Ann Arbor.

In the fall of 1899, Wheeler became the superintendent of Blessing Hospital in Quincy, Illinois, a post she held until 1910. She took a leave of absence in 1903–4 to take the hospital economics course offered by Nutting at Teachers College, Columbia University, in New York City.

After leaving Blessing Hospital, Wheeler spent nearly one year traveling and studying. In 1911 she was elected secretary of the newly established Illinois State Board of Nurse Examiners. This office included the duties of inspector of schools of nursing, and Wheeler was the first nurse to hold this important position. She also was president of the American Society of Superintendents of Training Schools during 1912–13.

In August 1913 Wheeler was invited by her alma mater, the Illinois Training School for Nurses, to fill the position of superintendent. Of the twelve different superintendents during the life of the school (1880–1929), Wheeler served the longest. During her tenure, the school faced political opposition as well as difficult adjustments during and after World War I.

Wheeler resigned in 1924 after giving the school the stability so that it was recognized as a leader of midwest nursing.

Wheeler's popularity among her students was matched by praise from her colleagues and school and hospital administrators. Poems were written about her, yearbooks were dedicated to her, and the graduating class of 1925 honored her by presenting a grandmother clock to the school with a plaque bearing her name.

After her departure from the school, Wheeler became the general secretary of the Michigan State Nurses' Association, a post she held from 1925 through 1930. At some point thereafter, she studied occupational therapy. In 1933 an article in the *American Journal of Nursing* announced the opening of the Goodwill-Cook County School of Occupational Therapy, with Wheeler listed as its principal and as a graduate of the St. Louis School of Occupational Therapy.

Wheeler was a member of the national committee on the Red Cross nursing service during World War I and on the board of the American Nurses' Association (ANA). She was chair of the publications committee of ANA and was considered largely responsible for collecting and compiling data for the first list of accredited schools of nursing.

In her retirement, Wheeler traveled to Florida and made it her home. She died on September 29, 1944, at the age of 75. She was buried in Valparaiso, Florida.

## PUBLICATIONS BY MARY CURTIS WHEELER

### BOOKS

*Nursing Technic.* Philadelphia: J.B. Lippincott, 1918, 2nd ed., 1923; 3rd ed., 1930.

### ARTICLES

"Just As I Am." In *Illinois Training School Annual*, vol. 2. Chicago: Illinois Training School for Nurses, December 1920.

### BIBLIOGRAPHY

Illinois Training School for Nurses, Class of 1925. *The Reflector.* Chicago: Illinois Training School for Nurses, 1924.

"Mary Curtis Wheeler." Obituary. *American Journal of Nursing* 45 (February 1945): 164.

"Reminiscences of Mary Curtis Wheeler." *The Reflector.* Chicago: Illinois Training School for Nurses, 1924, p. 59.

Schryver, G.F. *A History of the Illinois Training School for Nurses, 1880–1929.* Chicago: Illinois Training School for Nurses, 1930.

Olga Maranjian Church

## Walt (Walter) Whitman
### 1819–1892

Though best remembered for a book of poems that became a landmark in American literature, Walt (Walter) Whitman also achieved national recognition in his time as a tireless volunteer nurse of Civil War victims. He recorded his impressions of his Civil War experiences in several of his literary works.

Whitman was born in West Hills, a farming community near Huntington, Long Island, New York, on May 31, 1819. He was the second of nine children of Walter and Louisa Van Velsor Whitman, who were of English, Welsh, and Dutch ancestry. Both parents were poorly educated, and his father worked as a farmer and carpenter. There was much illness among the children; one brother died insane, and the youngest brother was retarded. Another brother died of tuberculosis of the throat, and one sister was neurasthenic. Whitman was devoted to all of them and helped support his retarded brother. One of the children died in infancy.

Whitman attended school in Brooklyn, where the family lived from approximately 1823 to 1833. He dropped out of school at age 12 and worked in Brooklyn as a printer's helper, a journeyman compositor, and an itinerant schoolteacher. He also held several modest journalistic and other posts, including editing the *Long Islander*.

In 1855 Whitman published the first edition of *Leaves of Grass*, his masterwork, at his own expense and began calling himself "Walt." His book of poems was either ignored or criticized by the general public, but Ralph Waldo Emerson read it and called it extraordinary. Whitman continued to revise the book and to publish new editions throughout his life.

In 1862 Whitman went to Virginia to visit his younger brother George, who had been wounded in the Civil War. A man of deep sensitivity, Whitman was so moved by what he saw in the hospital that he went immediately to Washington, D.C., to volunteer his services as a nurse. At its peak, the city had about 40 large army hospitals, and Whitman's favorite soon became Armory Square, near the Smithsonian Institution, where many of the worst cases were brought.

Whitman supported himself by writing and by working a few hours each day in the army paymaster's office. He spent most of his remaining waking hours visiting the wounded in the hospitals, bringing them paper, pencils, tobacco, and food, and helping when needed in surgery or in changing dressings. His friends, including Emerson, and many strangers gave him money to help buy his gifts for the soldiers.

In a letter dated February 1864 to Dr. LeBaron Russell, he wrote: ". . . I have been occupy'g my time nearly altogether among the wounded and sick. . . . I act as an independent visitor and helper among the men, fix'g as before on the cases that most need. I never miss a single day or night, week day or Sunday vist'g some poor, young soul in bodily and mental tribulation" (Gohdes, 71–72).

Whitman recorded his experiences and impressions in two books of poems, *Drum Taps* (1865) and *Sequel to Drum Taps* (1865–66), and in a prose work, *Memoranda during the War* (1875), which later became part of *Specimen Days and Collect* (1882). In *Specimen Days and Collect*, he praised the work of the nurses: "Some of the nurses are excellent. . . . the magnetic touch of hands . . . the expressive features . . . the silent soothing of her presence, her words, her knowledge . . . are precious and final qualifications" (Viking edition, pp. 521, 557).

Whitman estimated that in three years of nursing service, he had ministered to between 80,000 and 100,000 wounded and sick soldiers from both armies. During that time, he experienced some troubling bouts of dizziness, and a paralytic stroke he suffered in 1873 was believed by his doctors to have resulted from an infection incurred while he was working as a nurse. After the stroke he went to live with his brother George in Camden, New Jersey, and later bought his own home there.

Whitman died on March 26, 1892, in Camden. After his death, his home became a memorial to him. He was survived by his brother, George.

## PUBLICATIONS BY WALT (WALTER) WHITMAN

### BOOKS

*Leaves of Grass.* Brooklyn, N.Y.: Privately published, 1855. Many subsequent editions.

*Drum Taps.* New York: n.p., 1865.

*Sequel to Drum Taps.* New York: n.p., 1867.

*Memoranda during the War.* Camden, N.J.: By the author, 1875.

*Specimen Days and Collect.* Philadelphia: R. Welch & Co., 1882.

### ARTICLES

"Army Hospitals and Case, Memoranda at the time, 1863–1866," *The Century.* 36:6 (October): 825–30.

### BIBLIOGRAPHY

Gohdes, C., and R.G. Silver, eds. *Faint Clews and Indirections.* Durham, N.C.: Duke University Press, 1949.

"Walt Whitman's Career." *New York Times,* 27 March 1892.

"Walt Whitman's Funeral." *New York Times,* 28 March 1892.

"Whitman, Walt." *Encyclopedia Britannica.* Vol. 23. Chicago: Encyclopedia Britannica, 1973.

Whitman, W. *The Viking Portable Library Walt Whitman.* New York: Viking Press, 1945.

Alice P. Stein

## Emilie Willms

### 1888–1969

Referred to as the second Florence Nightingale by the people of Greece, Emilie Willms became a leader in the development of nursing and nursing education in Greece. She provided nursing services to Greece for 26 years, including during the difficult World War II era.

Born in Bremen, Germany, on September 1, 1888, Willms came to the United States as a young child. After graduating from the school of nursing of the Homeopathic Hospital of Essex County, Newark, New Jersey, in 1912, Willms held several posts in the United States before her departure for Greece in 1928. From 1918 to 1925, she was head worker in the settlement area of the Silver Lake, New Jersey, welfare association. She became tuberculosis nurse with the New Jersey Tuberculosis League in 1925 and later assistant superintendent and operating-room nurse at the Dover, New Jersey, General Hospital. During those years, she also did graduate work in tuberculosis nursing and at the New York School of Social Work.

Willms's international career began when she arrived in Greece in January 1929 to take the post of superintendent of the American Women's Hospital School of Nursing at Kokkinia. The school had been established in 1923 by Ruth Parmelee. In 1935 Willms was transferred to the Municipal Hospital, Athens, where she organized the nursing service under the sponsorship of the American Women's Hospital in Greece. She was later transferred to Children's Hospital, Athens, for the same purpose.

In 1940 at the time of the German invasion of Greece, Willms was appointed director of nurses at the 7th Military Hospital in Athens. The building, which formerly had accommodated 250 children, was used for more than 700 wounded soldiers, and inadequate staff and lack of surgical supplies compounded the problems. In April 1941 the Nazis took over Athens, and shortly thereafter Willms was offered the position of chief nurse for the entire country. With characteristic courage, she replied to the German commander-in-chief that she had joined the staff of the American Women's Hospital in 1929 to work with the Greeks, not for the Germans.

Willms and Parmelee were among the last group of 30 Americans to leave Greece in July 1941 for the United States. Until her return to Greece 23 months later, Willms worked as supervisor of the medical department and instructor in advanced medical nursing at Jersey City Medical Center. At the end of April 1943, she joined Parmelee at the Central Club for Nurses in New York City, and in September she embarked as part of a six-member technical assistance team under the auspices of the Near Eastern Foundation.

After helping to organize a health-clinic program for refugees in the Sinai desert, Willms sailed aboard the mercy ship *Immera*, taking food, clothing, and medical aid to 24 of the populated Cyclades Islands. Following the war, she helped restore the nursing service at Athens Municipal Hospital and was assigned once more to the Children's Hospital, where she remained until the school came under the direction of an American-trained Greek nurse.

On the point of returning home, Willms was asked to head the Rehabilitation Center for the Civilian Disabled, which had been started by the Near East Foundation and the American Mission of Greece. She accepted. In 1955 her contract with the Near East Foundation expired, and after 26 years of service to Greece, she sailed for home.

Willms received many honors. As early as 1933, she was presented by the Greek Ministry of Hygiene with the Knight of the Order of Phoenix, and in 1940 she received the British Red Cross Medallion. She was decorated by the Greek government with its War Services Medal following the war, and she also received awards for meritorious service in social welfare and in service to the disabled. In May 1956 her alma mater, the East Orange General Hospital, presented a scroll to her citing her outstanding contributions to nursing. She was a member of the Hellenic National Graduate Nurses' Association and chair of the private-duty section for Greece of the International Council of Nurses. She wrote several professional articles on nursing in Greece.

Willms settled in East Orange, New Jersey, and began working on her memoirs. Her health had deteriorated since a coronary attack in Athens, and she suffered from arthritis, failing eyesight, and various minor ailments. She never married.

Willms died in January 1969 at the East Orange General Hospital as a result of two strokes. Her unfinished memoirs were completed by her friend Ethel S. Beer.

## PUBLICATIONS BY EMILIE WILLMS

"A First Graduating Class." *American Journal of Nursing* 30 (October 1930): 1281–83.

## BIBLIOGRAPHY

Beer, E.S. *The Greek Odyssey of an American Nurse.* Mystic, Conn.: Verry, 1972.

Goodnow, M. *Nursing History.* 9th ed. Philadelphia: Saunders, 1953.

"Greek Government Honors Miss Willms." *American Journal of Nursing* 49 (January 1949): 12.

"Miss Willms Honored." *American Journal of Nursing* 56 (June 1956): 702.

"Miss Willms Returns." *American Journal of Nursing* 41 (December 1941): 1459–60.

"Nurses in Greece Honored." *American Journal of Nursing* 38 (April 1938): 480–81.

Lilli Sentz

# Anna Dryden Wolf

## 1890–1985

Anna Dryden Wolf's career began in the World War I era and spanned the challenges and difficulties of the 1930s and 1940s. She held teaching and administrative positions that demanded her devotion and creativity, she endeared herself to generations of nurses through her love for nursing and dedication to those in need.

Wolf was born June 25, 1890, the third of four children to Lutheran missionary parents in Gunthur Madras Presidency, South India. In 1893 she came to the United States with her three siblings and lived with relatives in Pennsylvania and North Carolina for seven years. Her parents returned to the United States in 1900, and the family reunited in Baltimore, Maryland.

Wolf received her basic education in private schools in Maryland, culminating in a B.A. degree from Goucher College in Towson, Maryland. She entered the Johns Hopkins Hospital School of Nursing in 1912. She was awarded two trustee scholarships for 1914 and 1915, graduating with the class of 1915. Immediately after graduation, she continued her education at Teachers College, Columbia University, in New York City. She enjoyed the stimulating experiences created by teachers like Mary Adelaide Nutting and Annie Goodrich, who taught in the program at that time.

Wolf returned to Johns Hopkins as an assistant to Elsie Lawler and to instruct student nurses at the hospital during the years spanning World War I. She prized these years of hectic activities because they helped her see how much society needed educated nurses in times of national crises. Wolf questioned some of the strict discipline and rigid rules of the program, which she felt adversely affected young, impressionable students. She favored a more democratic and professional model based on accountability. This concern was a characteristic that endeared her to many students.

In late 1918, Wolf moved to the Vassar Training Camp for a term as an instructor. During this experience, she taught bright, college-educated women in a special program designed to produce professional nurses for the war effort.

During the postwar period, Wolf traveled to Peking, China, to serve as superintendent of nurses in the Union Medical College. She worked to overcome cultural barriers while directing staff, and she accomplished the task by using a democratic system of administration that included counseling people and sharing responsibilities.

In 1924 Wolf was appointed to the position of dean of the school of nursing, which symbolized the full acceptance in China of nursing as an academic pursuit.

When Wolf returned to the United States in 1925, she received an Isabel Hampton Robb Fellowship and spent another year at Teachers College. She then began five years as associate professor of nursing and director of nursing at the University of Chicago. Some of her accomplishments in this position include the organization of an all-graduate nursing staff supported by auxillary personnel and the development of university courses on nursing administration.

In the midst of the depression, Wolf returned to New York to serve as the director of nursing and of the school of nursing at the New York Hospital. This job challenged her to organize a nursing service that had been consolidated from four institutions. The hospital recently had moved into new facilities and had added outpatient and psychiatric services. Wolf held the job for nine years.

In late 1940, she assumed her last major position by becoming the director of the school of nursing and nursing service at Johns Hopkins Hospital. During Wolf's tenure at Johns Hopkins, she met the intense demands of patient care and nursing education with her consistent, methodical approach to problem solving. These demands increased during World War II, and Wolf guided her nurses through the stresses that the resulting shortages created.

Wolf's peers noted that she was a director who could see clearly the tie between nursing education and nursing service. After the crisis of the war years, she worked to improve nursing education and to achieve progress in clinical nursing, which had lagged during the war.

In addition to her academic honors and scholarships, Wolf received an honorary doctorate from Goucher College in 1955. She committed much of her time throughout her career to numerous professional organizations. Her primary role in most of these activities was to serve on active committees that did much of the work for these organizations. The list of government and special national committees includes the national advisory committee of the Ameri-

can Red Cross, the subcommittee on nursing education, of the war manpower commission, and the National Nursing Council for Defense and War.

Wolf resigned from her position at Johns Hopkins in 1955 and began her retirement. She moved to Florida but never lost her interest in nursing and in the nursing programs at Johns Hopkins, and she took great pleasure in the student award given yearly in her honor.

Wolf died on July 5, 1985, in St. Petersburg, Florida, at the age of 95.

## PUBLICATIONS BY ANNA DRYDEN WOLF

"Evolution in Nursing Service." *Nursing Outlook* 4 (January 1956):47–49.

## BIBLIOGRAPHY

Clappison, G. *Vassar's Rainbow Division.* Lake Mills, Iowa: Graphic Publishing, 1964.

Johns, E., and B. Pfefferkorn. *The Johns Hopkins Hospital School of Nursing, 1889–1949.* Baltimore, Md.: Johns Hopkins Press, 1954.

Wiedenbach, E. "Anna Dryden Wolf." *Nurses' Alumnae Magazine* 89 (October 1940): 83–87.

Linda Sabrin

## George Anna Muirson Woolsey
### 1833–1906

George Anna Muirson Woolsey, also known as Mrs. Francis Bacon, worked as a nurse and hospital organizer during the Civil War. After the war, she was involved in the establishment of the Connecticut Training School for Nurses at New Haven Hospital, one of the first Nightingale schools opened in this country.

Woolsey was born in Brooklyn, New York, on November 5, 1833. She was the fourth child of Charles William and Jane Eliza Newton Woolsey. The family included seven other children, and three of Woolsey's sisters also were involved in nursing during the Civil War.

Woolsey, lived primarily in New York City during her childhood, as the family had moved there after Charles Woolsey died in 1840. Woolsey attended Rutgers Female Institute in New York City and in 1850 was sent to a private boarding school in Philadelphia. In 1862 the family helped found the Presbyterian Church of the Covenant.

Woolsey received her education in nursing at the New York Hospital in May 1861. She went there for an instructional program offered through the Women's Central Association of Relief (WCAR), which eventually became a branch of the U.S. Sanitary Commission. Any additional education that she had in nursing was based on experience.

The Woolseys were a prominent New York family, well educated and active in social causes. When the Civil War broke out, the entire family became involved by making bandages and supplies in their homes. Woolsey's original assignment (July 1861) in Civil War nursing was in the war camps of Washington, D.C., with her sister Eliza. Over the next few months, the sisters called on Dorothea Dix, visited other hospitals, organized and worked in the Patent Office Hospital, received other nurses sent by the WCAR and helped them get started in their work, worked with Louisa Lee Schuyler, and requested and received chaplains for the hospitals.

Between this first assignment and her last assignment in August 1864, Woolsey had a variety of experiences and ample opportunity to contribute to nursing in the Civil War. Her work included visiting jails to deliver personal care items to contraband slaves; outfitting, supervising the care of the wounded, and preparing food on the first hospital transport ship; working on four other hospital ships; assisting the superintendent at the Portsmouth Grove Hospital in Newport, Rhode Island, (the first time female nurses were given such responsibility in general hospitals); nursing the wounded after the battle at Gettysburg; and organizing and supervising four other hospitals. Her experience of caring for the wounded at Gettysburg is recorded in her book, *Three Weeks at Gettysburg* (1863).

In 1866 she married physician Francis Bacon and moved to New Haven, Connect-

icut. Bacon was a Yale Medical School graduate who became a successful surgeon after the Civil War. Woolsey's interests in nursing and children were shared by Bacon, and they worked together on several projects.

Woolsey's major postwar nursing contributions revolved around the Connecticut Training School for Nurses. When the school was established at New Haven Hospital in 1873, Woolsey assisted with its setup and management. She served on the board of managers for 33 years, on the executive committee, as secretary of the board of administration, and as chair of the committee on instruction. Her husband served on the board of managers for 39 years.

From her experience in the war, Woolsey had specific ideas about nursing education. She believed that nurses needed certain characteristics and training in order to be knowledgeable about caring for the sick. Her ideas, along with her organizational abilities, benefited the Connecticut Training School.

At the request of the training school board of managers, Woolsey wrote *A Handbook of Nursing for Family and General Use*. Appearing in 1878 without any author listed, it was the second book of its kind published in the United States and was widely used by other schools. She also contributed an article about the foundation of the Connecticut Training School for Nurses in the *Trained Nurse and Hospital Review*. In the interest of preserving the family history, she collaborated with her sister Eliza Woolsey Howland in writing *Letters of a Family during the War for the Union 1861–1865*.

In addition to her work with the school, Woolsey was active in other social causes. She served ten years (1883–93) as a member of the Connecticut State Board of Charities, which inspected hospitals, prisons, reformatory schools, insane asylums, and almshouses. Child welfare was an interest for both Woolsey and her husband; in 1896 they donated a summer house on Long Island Sound to the Newington Hospital for Crippled Children.

Woolsey died at her home in New Haven, Connecticut, on January 27, 1906.

She was buried in the Bacon family plot at Grove Street Cemetery in New Haven.

## PUBLICATIONS BY GEORGE ANNA MUIRSON WOOLSEY

### BOOKS

*Three Weeks at Gettysburg.* New York: U.S. Sanitary Commission, 1863.

*A Handbook of Nursing for Family and General Use.* Philadelphia: Lippincott, 1878.

With E.W. Howland. *Letters of a Family during the War for the Union 1861–1865.* New York: Privately published, 1899.

### ARTICLES

"Foundation of the Connecticut Training School for Nurses." *Trained Nurse and Hospital Review* (October 1895): 187–93.

### BIBLIOGRAPHY

Austin, A.L. "Abbey Woolsey, George Woolsey, and Jane Woolsey." In *Notable American Women 1607–1950,* edited by E.T. James. Vol. 3. Cambridge, Mass.: Belknap Press of Harvard University Press, 1971.

Austin, A.L. *History of Nursing Source Book.* New York: G.P. Putnam's Sons, 1957.

Austin, A.L. *The Woolsey Sisters of New York 1860–1900.* Philadelphia: American Philosophical Society, 1971.

Connecticut Training School. Papers. Yale Medical Library, Yale University, New Haven.

Glass, L.K. "Abbey H. Woolsey," "George Anna M. Woolsey," and "Jane S. Woolsey." In *Biographical Dictionary of Social Welfare in America,* edited by W.I. Trattner. New York: Greenwood, 1986.

Nutting, M.A., and L.L. Dock. *A History of Nursing.* Vol. 2. New York: G.P. Putnam's Sons, 1907.

Stewart, I.M. *The Education of Nurses.* New York: Macmillan, 1943.

Laurie K. Glass

# Marie Marguerite Dufrost de Lajemmerais d'Youville

## 1701–1771

Marie Marguerite Dufrost de Lajemmerais d'Youville was the first American-born founder of a religious community. The Community of Grey Nuns, the Sisters of Charity of Montreal, is dedicated to helping the poor and abandoned of the world and foremost among its work is dedication to nursing. The nuns founded numerous hospitals, orphanages, old-age facilities and schools of nursing in diverse parts of the world. Though technically a Canadian, she had great influence upon American nursing, both through her grey nuns who were among the early American nurses and through the nursing schools established by the order.

Born October 15, 1701, in Varennes, Canada, d'Youville was a descendant of one of the foremost families in what was then called New France. Her father, Christophe Dufrost de Lajemmerais, had been an officer in the French army and a hero of the French and Indian Wars when he married her mother, Marie-Renée Gaultier. The eldest of six children, d'Youville was seven years old when her father died, leaving the family without income. D'Youville's mother cultivated their land and supplemented the family income with her fine needle work until being granted a small government pension six years after de Lajemmerais's death.

In July 1712 d'Youville was sent to the convent school of the Ursuline Sisters of Quebec. She boarded there for two years and received the only formal education she would ever receive. When d'Youville was 17 and ready to enter into a marriage agreement with one of the sons of a prominent Varennes family, her mother remarried. Her stepfather, Timothy Sullivan, was not considered a socially acceptable match, and the scandal removed all possibility of d'Youville's proposed marriage. Within two years the family left the village of Varennes for Montreal.

In Montreal, d'Youville met François d'Youville, confidential agent of the governor general of New France. François d'Youville had inherited his father's position with the governor general and was also involved in illicit trade of liquor for furs with the Indians. He was supported and protected in this trade by the governor general. The couple was married on August 12, 1722. The marriage proved to be an unhappy one. Nevertheless, d'Youville bore six children, four of whom died in infancy. The two who survived eventually became priests.

In 1730 d'Youville's husband died, leaving her destitute with two children and pregnant with her sixth child. D'Youville opened a portion of her house as a small shop, and with the help of her family, was able to attract merchants who would allow her to sell their goods on consignment. In addition, she sold her own handiwork, candies, and cakes. She was a successful businesswoman; the quick sale of her first consignments encouraged additional merchants to trust her with their goods. Through this venture she was able to provide a living for herself and her children and to pay her husband's debts.

During this time d'Youville became involved in the lay activities of her parish church. Encouraged by her priest she regularly visited the prison, the general hospital, and the sick poor of Montreal. Her charitable work became a regular part of her life.

A turning point in d'Youville's commitment occurred when she welcomed into her home an old blind woman, a stranger to her, whose husband was living in the general hospital. Opening her home to this woman encouraged her to consider inviting other homeless people to share the security of her household. She began to see this as her mission and to realize that she could not do this work alone. She invited other women to join her, and in December 1737 formed a loose society with several of them. The women maintained their own residences and means for livelihood but accepted shared responsibility for the poor who were living with d'Youville. December 31, 1737, is considered the founding of the order; however, it was not until 1753 that the new religious order was formally recognized by the government of New France.

Their work did not go unnoticed, and some considered it inappropriate. D'Youville's family was not happy with her choice of occupation. To the populace of Montreal, d'Youville and her companions were a source of curiosity, ridicule, and slander. A common epithet used against them was "the grey sisters," referring to their habit of dressing in dark grey attire but alluding to the French word for tipsy which is similar to the French word for grey. This play on words eventually became devoid of all harsh meaning and was used by d'Youville to name her community when it was finally established as a formal religious order.

After about one year of informally sharing funds and responsibility, the group of women decided to move to larger quarters to accommodate the poor and themselves. The number of destitute persons who came to live with them very quickly increased to ten. The ladies supported their household through needlework commissions and paying boarders. During the seven years that·they lived in this house, d'Youville's health declined, and she suffered from a malady of the knee that limited her mobility but did not prevent her from maintaining leadership of the small community.

In the winter of 1745, the house was destroyed by fire, and one life was lost. D'Youville had difficulty finding new permanent housing because of the continuing animosity of some government officials. Eventually, in 1746 she was able to rent a large house from a wealthy merchant. After the move to new quarters, her health again failed her. She was seriously ill for several months.

In August 1747 d'Youville was appointed temporary director of the deteriorating, debt-ridden general hospital. Although still too weak to take charge personally of the initial stages of the change in leadership at the hospital, she was able to take certain actions. She ordered a complete inventory of the hospital's contents and an assessment of the structure and needed repairs. She insisted on a thorough cleaning of the entire building. Initial repairs were subsidized by a loan, by income received from boarders, and by contributions from prominent townspeople, relatives, and friends who became sympathetic to d'Youville's cause after she was officially appointed director of the general hospital. In addition to general repair of the building and grounds, d'Youville readied the land for cultivation, as bringing the farms back to a productive level would provide food, as well as revenue, for the inhabitants of the hospital.

By October 1747 many of the most urgent repairs were complete. D'Youville, her companions, the poor in their charge, and the paying boarders moved into the hospital. One of the changes brought about under d'Youville's directorship was the admission of females and children as residents. Another was the establishment of a section of private rooms set aside for Montreal prostitutes, who were brought to the general hospital for care, treatment, and seclusion.

In October 1750 hospital trustees decided to merge the hospital with the general hospital of Quebec. The citizens of Montreal were opposed to the closing of their general hospital. They had come to appreciate the work being done by d'Youville and her companions and realized this action would leave the poor of Montreal without care. After much political maneuvering, the union of the hospitals was revoked in December 1751.

Later the next year, the trustees signed a contract with d'Youville to determine how the general hospital would be administered. Among her stipulations were that her group be allowed to concentrate its energies on assisting the poor and infirm, that inmates not be limited to adult males, and that the group continue to be allowed to take in paying boarders. A clause authorized d'Youville and her companions to present themselves to the bishop for the rules necessary for their establishment as a religious community. The letters patent which recognized the community as a legal entity are dated June 3, 1753. In June 1755 the bishop of Montreal formally approved the rules of the community.

By 1756 the hospital's creditors were paid and the debts settled. D'Youville continued to restore the grounds and the buildings, adding improvements as needed and supporting these efforts through numerous enterprises. The nuns involved themselves in candlemaking, sewing, curing tobacco, selling lime, renting plots of land and carts, and selling produce from the hospital's farms. The boarders and poor who lived in the hospital also contributed their skills and talents to the nuns' efforts.

The 1755 smallpox epidemic established the general hospital as a house for the care of the sick and dying and provided the beginnings of the community's commitment to nursing. During this epidemic, the nuns also visited the homes of the stricken and cared for them there. In 1756 the French and English were at war, and d'Youville provided care for the sick soldiers and prisoners. The government did not honor its agreement to subsidize this care, leaving the hospital to support its growing population of residents. D'Youville continued to find ingenious ways to feed and provide for all hospitalized patients.

The times following the victory of the British were difficult for the conquered French colony. The unstable conditions and the disruption of families caused by the war helped to stimulate a great increase in the number of abandoned babies. D'Youville began to collect these foundlings and bring them to the general hospital. Aware that she was providing a solution to an immense civic problem, General Thomas Gage, the military governor of Montreal, ordered that all fines levied for violations of the city's laws be given to d'Youville's community and used for the care of these infants. D'Youville is credited with the establishment of the first foundling home in North America.

In 1765 the general hospital, along with half of Montreal, was destroyed by a fire that swept through the city. D'Youville immediately began to rebuild and seven months after the fire the residents were able to return to their home. However, the hospital was not completely finished until 1767. She financed this rebuilding through loans, contributions, and the sale of unprofitable land. D'Youville was able to buy Chateaquay, a parcel of largely uncultivated land with many possibilities for the future support of the work of the community. She had land cleared and planted and a water mill and bakehouse built. With Chateaquay, she established a firm financial foundation for the Community of Grey Nuns, the Sisters of Charity of the Hospital General of Montreal, to continue the work she had started in 1737.

On December 23, 1771, d'Youville died after having suffered a series of strokes. She was survived by her sons, François and Charles d'Youville, who had become Catholic priests. She is buried in the vault of the church of the Grey Nunnery in Montreal. She was beatified by the Catholic Church in 1959.

### BIBLIOGRAPHY

Duffin, M. *A Heroine of Charity.* New York: Benzinger Brothers, 1938.

Fitts, M.P. *Hands to the Needy.* Garden City, N.Y.: Doubleday, 1950.

Halpenny, F., ed. *Dictionary of Canadian Biography 1771–1800.* Vol. 4. Toronto: University of Toronto Press, 1979.

McDonald, W.J., ed. *New Catholic Encyclopedia.* Vol. 14. New York: McGraw-Hill, 1967.

Ramsay, D.S. *Life of the Venerable Marie Marguerite DuFrost De Lajemmerais d'Youville.* Montreal: Grey Nunnery, 1895.

Robbins, J.E., and W.K. Lamb, eds. *Encyclopedia Canadiana.* Vol. 10. Toronto: Grolier of Canada, 1968.

Shortt, A., and A.G. Doughty, eds. *Canada and Its Provences.* Vols. 2 and 16. Toronto: Edinburgh University Press, 1914.

Wallace, W.S., ed. *Macmillan Dictionary of Canadian Biography.* Toronto: W.A. Macmillan of Canada, 1978.

Ann Fabiszak

## Louise Zabriskie

1887–1957

Louise Zabriskie was a quadriplegic for much of her career, yet she was a nationally known writer, lecturer, consultant, and administrator in her specialty area. While her professional contributions were substantial in their own right, her remarkable ability and courage in pursuing a career marks her as a special example of nursing courage.

Zabriskie was born in Preston City, Connecticut, in 1887. She attended Northfield Seminary in Massachusetts and Columbia University in New York City. In 1913 she graduated from the New York Hospital School of Nursing and began working as night supervisor at the New York Lying In Hospital. She also worked as a public-health nurse in Nashville, Tennessee, and later as director of field services for the New York Maternity Center Association.

In 1922 she was involved in an automobile accident from which she suffered a broken neck and was left paralyzed from the neck down. Her survival at that time was unusual and her accomplishments even more. She began writing and her *Nurses' Handbook of Obstetrics*, first published in 1929, went through nine editions. She also wrote *Mother and Baby Care in Pictures* which was first published in 1935 and went through four editions. It was published also in Spanish translation.

Despite her physical condition she was able to conduct seminars, classes, and conferences for prospective parents and professionals, much of this growing out of her work with the Maternity Consultation Service, which she established in New York City in 1939 and for which she served as director for 18 years. She believed, taught, and advocated better antepartal care, holding that it directly affected maternal-infant well being. She was appointed a lecturer at the School of Nursing of New York University, a position she held until her retirement. In addition to her lectures she wrote a number of pamphlets and contributed popular articles about mother and baby care to several magazines and journals. She also wrote a regular column for *My Baby Magazine*.

Zabriskie was much sought after as a consultant, and she had great ability to synthesize and use detail in making critical assessments. Determined not to appear handicapped before her classes, she always arrived well in advance of the students and lectured without any evidence of mechanical supports, conveyances, or attendants. She sat tall, immobilized, and propped up behind the desk with a neck brace that reached below the chin. She conveyed the impression of a very dedicated, caring, and adventurous person. She was a superb role model for nurses and a passionate advocate for healthier mothers and babies.

Zabriskie died December 12, 1957, at her home in New York City after a long battle with pernicious anemia. She was survived by a sister, Alice M. Zabriskie, of New York City. A memorial scholarship was established in her name within the New York Hospital Nurses' Scholarship Fund.

## PUBLICATIONS BY LOUISE ZABRISKIE

### BOOKS

*Nurses' Handbook of Obstetrics.* Philadelphia: Lippincott, 1929; 2d ed., 1931; 3d ed., 1933; 4th ed., 1934; 5th ed., 1937; 6th ed., 1940; 7th ed., with Nicholas J. Eastman, 1943; 8th ed., with Eastman, 1948; 9th ed., with Eastman, 1952.

*Mother and Baby Care in Pictures.* Philadelphia: Lippincott, 1935; 2d ed., 1941; 3d ed., 1946; 4th ed., 1953. Translated into Spanish as *El Cuidad de la madre y del niño a través de la illustración.* Bueños Aires: Editorial Guillermo Kraft, 1944.

### ARTICLES

"Baby's First Food." *Parents Magazine* 5 (August 1930): 24.

"Expectant Mothers." *Parents Magazine* 5 (September 1930): 11ff; 5 (October): 80; 5 (November): 78; 5 (December): 30; 6 (January): 52; 6 (February): 70–71; 6 (March): 70; 6 (April): 70; 6 (May): 70–71.

She wrote a column in *My Baby Magazine,* starting in 1946.

### BIBLIOGRAPHY

DeVincenzo, Doris K. Personal reminiscences while attending Zabriskie's classes at N.Y.U.

"Louise Zabriskie." *American Journal of Nursing* 58 (June 1958): 802–03.

"Louise Zabriskie." *New York Times,* 14 December 1957.

Doris K. DeVincenzo

# INDEXES

# DECADES
# OF BIRTH

## BEFORE 1840

Alcott, Barton, Bickerdyke, Blackwell, Cumming, Dix, Mills, H.N. Phillips, Schuyler, Seton, Taylor, Tompkins, Trader, Tubman, Whitman, Woolsey, D'Youville

## 1841–1860

Boardman, Damer, Dempsey, Dewey, Dock, Drown, Fedde, Glenn, Goodnow, Goodrich, Gretter, Hibbard, Kinney, Lathrop, McIsaac, Mahoney, Maxwell, Nutting, Palmer, Richards, Robb, Seelye, Shaw

## 1861–1880

Aikens, Alline, Bailey, Breckinridge, E.C. Burgess, Butler, Cannon, Clayton, Cooke, Crandall, Crowell, Dakin, Delano, De Witt, Draper (?), Dietrich, Eldredge, Fallon, Fitzgerald, Foley, Francis, Franklin, Gabriel, Gardner, Gladwin, Goldman, Goostray, Gowan, Gregg, C.M. Hall, Hansen, Hasson, Hay, Hickey, Hodgins, Jammé, Jean, F.M. Johnson, LaMotte, Lamping, Lent, Livermore, Logan, Maass, Markolf, McGee, McMillan, Mathews, Minnige-rode, Muse, Noyes, Parsons, Pope, Powell, Purtell, Rinehart, Roberts, Sanger, Skenadore, Stewart, Taylor, D.E. Thompson, Thoms, Urch, Van Blarcom, Wald, Wheeler

## 1881–1900

Austin, Beard, Beck, Beeby, Blanchfield, Bolton, Brink, Carr, Davis, Deming, Dolan, Domitilla, Dreves, Fox, Gage, Gault, Geister, Given, Goff, Gowan, Harmer, Haupt, Havey, Hawkins, Hawkinson, Jensen, J.M. Johnson, Kasmeier, Kenny, Kessel, Lee, McIver, Matthews, Pfefferkorn, Olmsted, Render, Schulte, Scott, Soule, Stahl, Staupers, Stevenson, Stimson, B.A. Thompson (Sharpless), Titus, Tucker, Utinsky, Van Kooy, Willms, Wolf, Zabriskie

## 1901–1920

Armiger, Arnstein, Black, Blake, Freeman, L.E. Hall, Ingles, Newton, Osborne, M.G. Phillips, Reiter, Thielbar, J.C. Thompson, Vreeland

## 1921–1940

M.A. Burgess, Christy, Evans, Hornback, Olsen, Pate, Poole

# FIRST NURSING SCHOOL ATTENDED

ALLGEMEINE KRANKENHAUS,
VIENNA, AUSTRIA
 Goldman

ARMY SCHOOL of NURSING,
WALTER REED GENERAL HOSPITAL,
WASHINGTON, D.C.
 M.G. Phillips

BELLEVUE HOSPITAL TRAINING
SCHOOL, NEW YORK, N.Y.
 Dewey, Dock, Draper, Minnigerode,
 Robb

BOLTON SCHOOL OF NURSING,
WESTERN RESERVE UNIVERSITY
 Stahl

BOSTON CITY TRAINING HOSPITAL
 Drown, Gladwin, Hodgins, Maxwell,
 Palmer, Parsons

BUFFALO CHILDREN'S HOSPITAL
 Hansen

BUFFALO GENERAL HOSPITAL
 Gretter

BUFFALO HOMEOPATHIC
(MILLARD FILLMORE)
 Austin

CALIFORNIA WOMAN'S HOSPITAL,
SAN FRANCISCO
 Cooke

CATHOLIC UNIVERSITY,
WASHINGTON, D.C.
 Armiger

CENTRAL MAINE GENERAL HOSPITAL,
LEWISTON, ME.
 Render

CHILDREN'S HOSPITAL,
BOSTON
 Goostray

CITY HOSPITAL #2,
ST. LOUIS, MO.
 Osborne

COLUMBIAN UNIVERSITY
(Now GEORGE WASHINGTON
UNIVERSITY in WASHINGTON, D.C.)
 McGee

COLUMBUS HOSPITAL,
GREAT FALLS, MONT.
 Gabriel

COOK COUNTY HOSPITAL,
CHICAGO, ILL.
 J.C. Thompson

COOPER HOSPITAL, CAMDEN, N.J.
 Fallon

CONNECTICUT TRAINING SCHOOL,
NEW HAVEN, CONN.
 Hassen

351

COTTAGE HOSPITAL,
CRESTON, IOWA
  Given

EVANSTON HOSPITAL, EVANSTON, ILL.
  Newton

FRAMINGHAM HOSPITAL,
FRAMINGHAM, MASS.
  Hawkinson

FREEDMAN'S HOSPITAL,
WASHINGTON, D.C.
  Damer, Davis, Staupers

GEORGETOWN UNIVERSITY,
WASHINGTON, D.C.
  Dolan

HARTFORD HOSPITAL TRAINING
SCHOOL, HARTFORD, CONN.
  Butler, Foley, Skendadore

HOMEOPATHIC HOSPITAL,
BROOKLYN, N.Y.
  Alline

HOMEOPATHIC HOSPITAL,
ESSEX COUNTY, N.J.
  Willms

ILLINOIS TRAINING SCHOOL,
CHICAGO, ILL.
  Delano, De Witt, Glenn, Havey,
  Hawkins, Hay, Lamping, McIsaac,
  McMillan, Urch, Wheeler

JEWISH HOSPITAL,
CINCINNATI, OHIO
  Roberts

JOHNS HOPKINS HOSPITAL,
BALTIMORE, MD.
  Bailey, Carr, Fitzgerald, Fox, Jammé,
  Lamotte, Lent, Noyes, Nutting,
  Olmsted, Pfefferkorn, Reiter, Taylor,
  Van Blarcom, Wolf

KNOWLTON (NOW COLUMBIA)
HOSPITAL TRAINING SCHOOL,
MILWAUKEE, WIS.
  Mathews

LAKESIDE HOSPITAL,
CLEVELAND, OHIO
  Muse

LAS VEGAS HOT SPRINGS
SANITARIUM, N.M.
  Goodnow

LINCOLN HOSPITAL HOMEOPATHIC
SCHOOL, ONTARIO, CANADA
  Thoms

MACK TRAINING SCHOOL OF THE
GENERAL & MARINE HOSPITAL,
ONTARIO, CANADA
  Hibbard

MALDEN HOSPITAL TRAINING
SCHOOL, MALDEN, MASS.
  Soule

MANHATTANVILLE COLLEGE,
PURCHASE, N.Y.
  Christy, Ingles

MEMPHIS CITY HOSPITAL,
MEMPHIS, TENN.
  Trader

MARYLAND HOMEOPATHIC HOSPITAL,
BALTIMORE(?), MD.
  Jean

MASSACHUSETTS GENERAL
HOSPITAL, BOSTON
  Goff, Hall, Kinney, Vreeland

METHODIST HOSPITAL,
BROOKLYN, N.Y.
  Olsen

MICHAEL REESE HOSPITAL,
CHICAGO, ILL.
  Blake

MT. SINAI HOSPITAL,
NEW YORK, N.Y.
  Freeman, Logan

NEWARK (N.J.) GERMAN HOSPITAL,
CHRISTIANA TREFZ SCHOOL
  Maass

NEW ENGLAND HOSPITAL FOR
WOMEN & CHILDREN, BOSTON, MASS.
  Mahoney, Richards

NEWTON HOSPITAL SCHOOL,
NEWTON, MASS.
  Tucker

NEWPORT HOSPITAL, NEWPORT, R.I.
  Gardner

NEW YORK CITY TRAINING SCHOOL,
NEW YORK, N.Y.
  Thompson, D.E.

NEW YORK HOSPITAL SCHOOL OF
NURSING, NEW YORK, N.Y.
  Beard, Dakin, Goodrich, Hall, F.M.
  Johnson, Shaw, Stimson, Wald,
  Woolsey, Zabriskie

NORTHERN LOUISIANA SANITARIUM
SCHOOL, SHREVEPORT, LA.
  Pate

OHIO VALLEY SCHOOL OF NURSING,
STEUBENVILLE, OHIO
  Evans

ONTARIO HOSPITAL, WHITLEY,
ONT., CANADA
  Black

PHILADELPHIA GENERAL HOSPITAL,
PHILADELPHIA, PA.
  Brink, Clayton, Crandall, Gault

PITTSBURGH TRAINING SCHOOL,
PITTSBURGH, PA.
  Rinehart

PRESBYTERIAN HOSPITAL,
CHICAGO, ILL.
  Arnstein, Schulte, Scott, Stevenson
  (West)

PRESBYTERIAN HOSPITAL,
NEW YORK, N.Y.
  Deming, Lee, Pope

READING HOSPITAL,
READING, PA.
  Francis

ROOSEVELT HOSPITAL,
NEW YORK, N.Y.
  Burgess, Gage

ST. ANTHONY'S HOSPITAL,
ST. LOUIS, MO.
  Beck

ST. JOHN'S RIVERSIDE HOSPITAL,
YONKERS, N.Y.
  Dietrich

ST. JOSEPH'S HOSPITAL,
CHICAGO, ILL.
  Crowell

ST. JOSEPH'S HOSPITAL,
MILWAUKEE, WIS.
  Van Kooy

ST. LUKE'S HOSPITAL,
CHICAGO, ILL.
  Beeby, Eldredge

ST. LUKE'S HOSPITAL,
NEW YORK, N.Y.
  Breckenridge

ST. LUKE'S HOSPITAL,
RICHMOND, VA.
  Powell, Thielbar

ST. LUKE'S HOSPITAL,
SAN FRANCISCO
  Titus

ST. MARY'S HOSPITAL,
BROOKLYN, N.Y.
  Hickey

ST. MARY'S HOSPITAL,
DULUTH, MINN.
  Domitilla, Gowan, J.M. Johnson

ST. PAUL CITY & COUNTY HOSPITAL,
ST. PAUL, MINN.
  Cannon

ST. ROSA'S HOSPITAL,
SAN ANTONIO, TEX.
  Kasmeier

ST. URSULA'S COLLEGE,
NEW SOUTH WALES, AUSTRALIA
  Kenny

SHERMAN HOSPITAL,
ELGIN, ILL.
  Geister

SOUTHSIDE HOSPITAL,
PITTSBURGH, PA.
  Blanchfield

SPRINGFIELD TRAINING SCHOOL,
SPRINGFIELD, MASS.
  Matthews

STRATFORD HOSPITAL,
STRATFORD, ONT., CANADA
  Aikens

TORONTO GENERAL HOSPITAL,
TORONTO, ONT., CANADA
  Harmer

UNIVERSITY of CINCINNATI,
CINCINNATI, OHIO
  Dreves

UNIVERSITY OF MINNESOTA,
MINNEAPOLIS, MINN.
  Haupt, McIver, Thompson (Sharpless)

UNIVERSITY OF WISCONSIN,
MADISON, WIS.
  Hornback

WALTHAM TRAINING SCHOOL,
WALTHAM, MASS.
 Gregg, Markholf

WHITE PLAINS HOSPITAL,
WHITE PLAINS, N.Y.
 Sanger

WINNIPEG GENERAL HOSPITAL,
WINNIPEG, ONT., CANADA
 Stewart

WOMEN'S HOSPITAL,
CHICAGO, ILL.
 Kessel

WOMEN'S HOSPITAL,
PHILADELPHIA, PA.
 Franklin, H.N. Phillips

YALE UNIVERSITY SCHOOL of
NURSING, NEW HAVEN, CONN.
 Poole

*DID NOT ATTEND NURSING SCHOOL*
 Alcott, Barton, Bickerdyke, Blackwell,
 Boardman, Bolton, M.A. Burgess,
 Cumming, Dempsey, Dix, Fedde,
 Lathrop, Livermore, Mills, Purtell,
 Schuyler, Seelye, Seton, Tomkins,
 Tubman, Whitman, d'Youville

*UNKNOWN NURSING SCHOOL*
 Utinsky

# AREA OF SPECIAL INTEREST OR ACCOMPLISHMENT

CLINICAL PRACTICE
Blake, Evans, L.E. Hall, Hodgins, Kenny, Kessel, Reiter, Taylor

NURSING EDUCATION
Alline, Armiger, E.C. Burgess, Dakin, Dewey, Domitilla, Dreves, Drown, Gabriel, Gage, Given, Glenn, Goodrich, Goostray, Gowan, Gretter, C.M. Hall, Hawkinson, Hay, Hibbard, Hornback, Ingles, Kasmeier, Lee, Logan, McMillan, Mills, Newton, Nutting, Parsons, Pfefferkorn, Poole, Powell, Richards, Robb, Schulte, Soule, Stewart, Thielbar, B.A. Thompson, Urch, Willms, Wolf, Woolsey

NURSING ORGANIZATION
Beck, Clayton, Damer, Delano, Dietrich, Draper, Eldredge, Francis, Franklin, Hickey, Jammé, McGee, McIsaac, Mathews, Maxwell, Noyes, Osborne, Scott, Stahl, Staupers, Thoms

PUBLIC ACTIVITY
Barton, Boardman, Bolton, Butler, Cannon, Carr, Dix, Dolan, Fallon, Goff, Goldman, McIver, Sanger, Schuyler, J.C. Thompson, d'Youville

ADMINISTRATION
Beard, Dempsey, Fedde, Wheeler

MILITARY
Bickerdyke, Blanchfield, Cumming, Gladwin, Hasson, Kinney, Olsen, M.G. Phillips, Purtell, Seelye, Stimson, D.E. Thompson, Tompkins, Trader, Tubman, Utinsky

PUBLIC HEALTH NURSING AND PUBLIC NURSING
Arnstein, Breckinridge, Brink, Crandall, Crowell, Dock, Fitzgerald, Foley, Fox, Freeman, Gardner, Hansen, Haupt, Havey, Hawkins, F.M. Johnson, J.M. Johnson, Lamping, Lent, Markolf, Matthews, Minnigerode, Olmsted, Seton, Stevenson (West), Tucker, Van Kooy, Wald

WRITING
Aikens, Alcott, Austin, Bailey, Beeby, Black, M.A. Burgess, Christy, Cooke, Deming, DeWitt, Geister, Goodnow, Harmer, Jensen, LaMotte, Livermore, Palmer, Pope, Render, Rinehart, Roberts, Shaw, Van Blarcom, Vreeland, Whitman, Zabriskie

OTHER
Blackwell, Davis, Gault, Lathrop, Maass, Mahoney, Pate, H.N. Phillips, Skenadore, Titus

# STATES AND COUNTRIES OF BIRTH

## COUNTRIES

**AUSTRALIA**
Sister Kenny

**BARBADOS, W.I.**
Staupers

**CANADA**
Aikens, Blackwell, Damer, Draper, Goff, Gretter, Harmer, Hibbard, Hodgins, Logan, McMillan, Nutting, Pope, Render, Robb, Schulte, Seelye, Stewart, Taylor, d'Youville

**ENGLAND**
Black, Gladwin, Hansen

**GERMANY**
Willms

**INDIA**
Beeby, Wolf

**ITALY**
Fitzgerald

**IVORY COAST, WEST AFRICA**
Olsen

**LITHUANIA**
Goldman

**NETHERLANDS**
Van Kooy

**NORTHERN IRELAND**
Jensen

**NORWAY**
Fedde

**SCOTLAND**
Cumming

## UNITED STATES

**ALABAMA**
Kasmeier

**CALIFORNIA**
Cooke, Titus

**CONNECTICUT**
Deming, Foley, Franklin, Zabriskie

**ILLINOIS**
Geister, Glenn, Hay, Mathews, Thielbar, Van Blarcom

**INDIANA**
Dreves, Scott

**IOWA**
Given, McIsaac, Newton, Olmsted

**KENTUCKY**
Hawkins, LaMotte

**LOUISIANA**
Pate

**MAINE**
Alline, E.C. Burgess, Dix

**MARYLAND**
Armiger, Clayton, Hasson, Jean, McGee, Noyes, Pfefferkorn, Tubman

**MASSACHUSETTS**
Barton, M.A. Burgess, Crowell, Freeman, Gardner, Goostray, Hawkinson, Hickey, Lathrop, Lee, Livermore, Mahoney, Markolf, Palmer, Parsons, Soule, Stimson, Tucker (?), Vreeland

**MICHIGAN**
Domitilla, Matthews, Roberts, B.A. Thompson (Sharpless), Urch

**MINNESOTA**
Gowan, Haupt, Kessel, McIver

**MISSISSIPPI**
Trader

**MISSOURI**
Beck, Utinksy

**NEW HAMPSHIRE**
Beard, C.M. Hall

**NEW JERSEY**
Evans, Goodrich, F.M. Johnson, Maass

**NEW YORK**
Arnstein, Austin, Butler, Christy, Crandall, Dakin (?), Delano, Dempsey, Dewey, De Witt, Dietrich, Gage, Goodnow, L. Hall, Kinney, Lent, Maxwell, Mills, Richards, Sanger, Schuyler, Seton, D.E. Thompson, Wheeler, Whitman, Woolsey

**NORTH CAROLINA**
Davis, Dolan

**OHIO**
Bickerdyke, Boardman, Bolton, Carr, Gault, Stahl, Wald

**PENNSYLVANIA**
Alcott, Dock, Francis, Muse, H.N. Phillips, Rinehart

**RHODE ISLAND**
Drown, Gabriel, Shaw (?)

**SOUTH DAKOTA**
Brink, Ingles, Stevenson (West) (?)

**TENNESSEE**
Breckinridge, Poole

**TEXAS**
Osborne

**VIRGINIA**
Minnigerode, Powell, Thoms

**WASHINGTON**
Hornback

**WEST VIRGINIA**
Blanchfield, Evans

**WISCONSIN**
Blake, Cannon, Eldredge, Havey, J.M. Johnson, Lamping, M.G. Phillips, Purtell, Skenadore, J.C. Thompson

**UNKNOWN**
Bailey, Fox, Jammé, Reiter

REFERENCE